Public Relations

Public Relations

A Values-Driven Approach

Second Edition

David W. Guth, APR
The University of Kansas

Charles Marsh, Ph.D.
The University of Kansas

Boston   New York   San Francisco
Mexico City   Montreal   Toronto   London   Madrid   Munich   Paris
Hong Kong   Singapore   Tokyo   Cape Town   Sydney

Series Editor: Molly Taylor
Editorial Assistant: Michael Kish
Marketing Manager: Mandee Eckersley
Editorial-Production Service: Omegatype Typography, Inc.
Composition Buyer: Linda Cox
Electronic Composition: Omegatype Typography, Inc.
Manufacturing Buyer: JoAnne Sweeney
Cover Administrator: Linda Knowles

For related titles and support materials, visit our online catalog at www.ablongman.com

Between the time Website information is gathered and published, some sites may have closed. Also, the transcription of URLs can result in typographical errors. The publisher would appreciate notification where these occur so that they may be corrected in subsequent editions.

Many of the designations used by manufacturers and sellers to distinguish their products are claimed as trademarks. Where those designations appear in this book, and Allyn and Bacon was aware of a trademark claim, the designations have been printed in initial or all caps.

Library of Congress Cataloging-in-Publication Data

Guth, David W.
    Public relations : a values-driven approach / David W. Guth and Charles
Marsh.—2nd ed.
        p.   cm.
    Includes bibliographical references and index.
    ISBN 0-205-35969-8
    1. Public relations.   2. Public relations—Moral and ethical aspects.   I. Marsh,
Charles.   II. Title.
    HM1221.G87   2003
    659.2—dc21

                                                                        2002020542

Printed in the United States of America
10 9 8 7 6 5 4 3 2 1   RRD-VA   07 06 05 04 03 02

Contents

Preface   xvii

About the Authors   xxi

section one

Foundations of Public Relations

This section of the book lays the foundations for the practice of values-driven public relations. As noted within these pages, public relations is important to the conduct and maintenance of free societies. And it is a discipline that is often misunderstood. These six chapters bring the profession, the issues confronting it, and its values into focus.

Chapter 1

What Is Public Relations?   1

Public Relations: Separating Fact from Fiction   2

The Search for a Definition   4

Public Relations Defined   5

QuickBreak 1.1
PRSA'S VIEW OF THE PROFESSION   6

Theory versus Reality   8

The Hunt–Grunig Models of Public Relations   9

Public Relations and Marketing   10

Why a Public Relations Career?   11

A Profile of Practitioners   11

QuickBreak 1.2
A PROFESSION OR A TRADE?   12

Values Statement 1.1
J.C. PENNEY COMPANY   13

The Public Relations Process   14

The Traditional Four-Step Model of the Public Relations Process   14

The Dynamic Model of the Public Relations Process   15

The Role of Values in Public Relations   16

Actions Speak Louder Than Words—Part I   17

Values-Driven Public Relations   17

Actions Speak Louder Than Words—Part II   18

Whose Values Should You Follow?   19

QuickBreak 1.3
HOW ORGANIZATIONS ESTABLISH THEIR VALUES   20

SUMMARY   21

DISCUSSION QUESTIONS   22

Memo from the Field
JOANN E. KILLEEN, KILLEEN
COMMUNICATIONS   22

👍 *Case Study 1.1*
MAKING NEW FRIENDS AT COORS   24

👎 *Case Study 1.2*
THE HARSH LESSONS OF HISTORY   26

It's Your Turn
THE QUESTION   28

KEY TERMS   28

NOTES   29

Memo from the Field
MIKE SWENSON, BARKLEY EVERGREEN
& PARTNERS   48

👍 *Case Study 2.1*
WRESTLING FOR SUCCESS   50

👎 *Case Study 2.2*
A LIST TO AVOID   52

It's Your Turn
CAREER DAY AT HIGH SCHOOL   53

KEY TERMS   54

NOTES   54

Chapter 2

Jobs in Public Relations   31

Where the Jobs Are   32
Corporations   32
Nonprofit Organizations and
Trade Associations   36

Values Statement 2.1
PUBLIC RELATIONS SOCIETY OF AMERICA   37

QuickBreak 2.1
THE VALUES OF SUCCESSFUL EMPLOYERS   38

Governments   38
Public Relations Agencies   39
Independent Public Relations
Consultants   39

QuickBreak 2.2
GETTING THAT FIRST JOB OR INTERNSHIP   41

Public Relations Activities and Duties   42

QuickBreak 2.3
CHARACTERISTICS OF SUCCESSFUL PUBLIC
RELATIONS CAREERS   44

Salaries in Public Relations   45

QuickBreak 2.4
THE PEOPLE IN PUBLIC RELATIONS   46

What's Important in a Job?   46

SUMMARY   47

DISCUSSION QUESTIONS   48

Chapter 3

A Brief History of Public Relations   56

Premodern Public Relations   57
Trends Leading to the Development
of Modern Public Relations   58

QuickBreak 3.1
A REAL EVENT OR A PSEUDOEVENT?   60

Values Statement 3.1
THE UNITED STATES CONSTITUTION   61

Pre–20th-Century America   61

QuickBreak 3.2
THOMAS PAINE: REVOLUTIONARY PRACTITIONER?   62

The Seedbed Years   63
Theodore Roosevelt (1858–1919)   65
Ivy Ledbetter Lee (1877–1934)   66

War and Propaganda   68
Edward L. Bernays (1891–1995)   69

QuickBreak 3.3
THE STRANGE CASE OF THE ZIMMERMAN
TELEGRAM   70

QuickBreak 3.4
THE MOTHER OF PUBLIC RELATIONS   72

Why Bernays and Not Lee?   73

The Postwar Boom   73
Postwar Social Activism   74

QuickBreak 3.5
OTHER NOTABLE FIGURES FROM PUBLIC
RELATIONS' PAST 75

The Downsizing of the United States 76
The Baby Boomers Come of Age 77

"Future History" 77

SUMMARY 78

DISCUSSION QUESTIONS 79

Memo from the Field
MICHAEL DEVLIN, ROCK AND ROLL HALL
OF FAME AND MUSEUM 79

Case Study 3.1
REMEMBERING THE VICTIMS 81

Case Study 3.2
TORCHES OF FREEDOM 84

It's Your Turn
MEGASHOP COMES TO SUNNYVIEW 86

KEY TERMS 87

NOTES 87

Chapter 4
The Publics in Public Relations 90

What Is a Public? 91
Why Do We Need Relationships
with Publics? 92

The Publics in Public Relations 93
Traditional and Nontraditional Publics 94
Latent, Aware, and Active Publics 96

QuickBreak 4.1
YOUR TAX DOLLARS AT WORK 97

Intervening Publics 97
Primary and Secondary Publics 97
Internal and External Publics 98
Domestic and International Publics 98

**What Do We Need to Know about
Each Public? 99**
Coorientation 101

**The Traditional Publics
in Public Relations 102**
Employees 102

QuickBreak 4.2
SABOTAGE IN THE WORKPLACE 106

The News Media 107

Values Statement 4.1
SACRAMENTO POLICE DEPARTMENT 108

Governments 109

QuickBreak 4.3
JAMES BOND SAVES THE WHALES? 111

Investors 112
Consumers/Customers 114

QuickBreak 4.4
THE CUSTOMER IS ALWAYS RIGHT? 117

Multicultural Communities 118
Constituents (Voters) 120
Businesses 122

SUMMARY 124

DISCUSSION QUESTIONS 124

Memo from the Field
GORDON LINDSEY, J.C. PENNEY COMPANY 125

Case Study 4.1
CLOUDY DAYS FOR SUNBEAM 126

Case Study 4.2
PARROTT TALKS; RAND McNALLY LISTENS 128

It's Your Turn
THE TUITION INCREASE 129

KEY TERMS 130

NOTES 130

Chapter 5
**Communication Theory and
Public Opinion 135**

The Power of Public Opinion 136
A Communication Model 138

QuickBreak 5.1
MOKUSATSU 140

Theories of Persuasion 141
The Magic Bullet Theory 141
The Two-Step Theory 142
The N-Step Theory 142
Diffusion Theory 143
The Agenda-Setting Hypothesis 143

QuickBreak 5.2
FRAMING CAMPAIGN 2000 144

Uses and Gratifications Theory 146
A Two-Way Process 146

QuickBreak 5.3
THE THIRD BATTLE OF BULL RUN 147

Motivation 148
Maslow's Hierarchy of Needs 148
Examples of Maslow's Theory at Work 149

QuickBreak 5.4
MONROE'S MOTIVATED SEQUENCE 150

Persuasion and Public Opinion 151
Aristotle, Persuasion, and
Public Relations 152
Public Opinion Defined 153
The Evolution of Public Opinion 153

QuickBreak 5.5
A PUBLIC OPINION CHECKLIST 155

Values Statement 5.1
PROVINCIAL EMERGENCY PROGRAM 156

Persuasion versus Manipulation 156

SUMMARY 157

DISCUSSION QUESTIONS 157

Memo from the Field
RENÉ PELLETIER, BAROMÈTRE INC. 158

Case Study 5.1
USING PUBLIC RELATIONS TO BAN LAND MINES 160

Case Study 5.2
CITIZENS FOR A FREE KUWAIT 162

It's Your Turn
THE ACME WIDGET COMPANY 164

KEY TERMS 165
NOTES 166

Chapter 6
Ethics in Public Relations   167

What Are Ethics? 168
Ethics Codes for Values-Driven
Public Relations 168

QuickBreak 6.1
THE ETHICS CODES OF PRSA AND IABC 169

**Objectivity versus Advocacy: A Misleading
Ethics Debate 171**
Objectivity versus Advocacy:
The Solution 173

QuickBreak 6.2
ARISTOTLE, CONFUCIUS, AND THE
GOLDEN MEAN 174

Challenges to Ethical Behavior 174
Dilemmas 175
Overwork 175
Legal/Ethical Confusion 175
Cross-Cultural Ethics 176
Short-Term Thinking 177
Virtual Organizations 177

The Rewards of Ethical Behavior 177

QuickBreak 6.3
IMMANUEL KANT AND THE CATEGORICAL
IMPERATIVE 179

Achieving Ethical Behavior 179
Ethics Audits 180
Integrating Ethics into the Public
Relations Process 180
The Potter Box 180
The Potter Box at Work 182

Values Statement 6.1
GOODWILL INDUSTRIES OF ORANGE
COUNTY 183

QuickBreak 6.4
JEREMY BENTHAM, JOHN STUART MILL,
AND UTILITARIANISM 185

QuickBreak 6.5
JOHN RAWLS AND SOCIAL JUSTICE 186

SUMMARY 187

DISCUSSION QUESTIONS 187

Memo from the Field
TERRIE WILLIAMS, THE TERRIE
WILLIAMS AGENCY 188

Case Study 6.1
CAPPUCCINO WITH VALUES, PLEASE: STARBUCKS
COFFEE COMPANY 189

Case Study 6.2
UNDISCLOSED INTEREST: GLAXO WELLCOME
AND THE COMMITTEE TO PROTECT MDIs 192

It's Your Turn
TROUBLE BREWING 194

KEY TERMS 194

NOTES 195

section two

The Public Relations Process

Now that the foundations for the practice of public relations have been established, this section of the book focuses upon the discipline's four-step process: research, planning, communication, and evaluation. Although this process is both strategic and tactical, an emphasis on values remains at its core. Successful practitioners rely upon the critical thinking skills introduced in these five chapters.

Chapter 7

Research and Evaluation **197**

The Value of Research and Evaluation 198

QuickBreak 7.1
ISSUES MANAGEMENT AND THE AIDS EPIDEMIC 200

Developing a Research Strategy:
What Do I Want to Know? 202
Client Research 202
Stakeholder Research 202

QuickBreak 7.2
MEASURING RELATIONSHIPS 203

Values Statement 7.1
BUREAU OF LABOR STATISTICS 204

Problem–Opportunity Research 204

Evaluation Research 204

Developing a Research Strategy:
How Will I Gather Information? 205
Secondary (Library) Research 205
Feedback Research 206
The Communication Audit 206
Focus Groups 209

Survey Research 212
The Survey Sample 212

QuickBreak 7.3
THE FLORIDA FOLLIES 213

The Survey Instrument 219

QuickBreak 7.4
FIVE WAYS TO ASK QUESTIONS 220

Analyzing Survey Results 221
Back to City Hospital 223

SUMMARY 224
DISCUSSION QUESTIONS 224

Memo from the Field
WALTER K. LINDENMANN, INDEPENDENT PUBLIC
RELATIONS CONSULTANT   225

Case Study 7.1
SOWING SEEDS OF DISCONTENT   226

Case Study 7.2
FIGHTING BACK WITH FACTS   229

It's Your Turn
TINKER, EVERS & CHANCE   231

KEY TERMS   231

NOTES   232

Chapter 8

Planning: The Strategies of Public Relations   234

The Basics of Values-Driven Planning   236
Different Kinds of Public Relations Plans   237

Ad Hoc Plans   237
Standing Plans   237
Contingency Plans   238

QuickBreak 8.1
PLANNING FOR THE ENTIRE ORGANIZATION   239

Why Do We Plan?   240

To Keep Our Actions in Line
with Our Organization's
Values-Based Mission   240
To Help Us Control Our Destiny   240
To Help Us Better Understand and Focus
Our Research   241
To Help Us Achieve Consensus   241
To Allow Effective Management
of Resources   241

Values Statement 8.1
BOEING COMPANY   242

How Do We Plan?   242

Consensus Building   243
Brainstorming   243

Goals, Objectives, and Tactics:
The Written Plan   245

QuickBreak 8.2
THE PRSA PLANNING GRID   246

QuickBreak 8.3
THE CHALLENGE OF MEASURABILITY   251

Expanding a Plan into a Proposal   251
Qualities of a Good Plan   252

SUMMARY   253

DISCUSSION QUESTIONS   253

Memo from the Field
FRED REPPER, RETIRED PUBLIC
RELATIONS CONSULTANT   254

Case Study 8.1
BOEING, BOEING, GONE   255

Case Study 8.2
MILLENNIUM DOOM   258

It's Your Turn
PLANNING A BLOOD DRIVE   260

KEY TERMS   260

NOTES   260

Chapter 9

Communication: The Tactics of Public Relations   262

Communicating with Specific Publics   263
Tactics as Messages and Channels   264

Special Events   265
Controlled Media   266

QuickBreak 9.1
DON'T FORGET THE NET   267

Uncontrolled Media   268
Controlled versus Uncontrolled Media   268

Values Statement 9.1
JOHNSON & JOHNSON   269

Tactics and Traditional Publics   270

Employees   271

News Media   274

Investors   281

QuickBreak 9.2
BEATING THE ODDS: SUCCESSFUL
NEWS RELEASES   282

QuickBreak 9.3
THE VIAGRA VNR   283

Community Groups   284

Governments   286

Customers   287

QuickBreak 9.4
LOBBIES IN THE U.S.A.: WHO HAS THE CLOUT?   288

Constituents (Voters)   290

Businesses   291

Accomplishing the Tactics   292

SUMMARY   293

DISCUSSION QUESTIONS   294

Memo from the Field
SHIRLEY BARR, SHIRLEYBARR
PUBLIC RELATIONS   294

Case Study 9.1
THE GREAT CANADIAN COVER-UP   296

Case Study 9.2
THE DOG THAT DIDN'T BARK: ABERCROMBIE
& FITCH AND MADD   298

It's Your Turn
THE TUITION INCREASE REVISITED   300

KEY TERMS   301

NOTES   301

Chapter 10
Writing and Presentation Skills   303

The Importance of Writing and
Presentation Skills   304

A Context for Public Relations Writing   305

The Writing Process   305

Credibility: Stage One
of the Writing Process   308

QuickBreak 10.1
WRITING FOR DIVERSE PUBLICS: TIPS
FOR INCLUSIVE LANGUAGE   309

Research: Stage Two
of the Writing Process   310

Organization: Stage Three
of the Writing Process   312

Writing: Stage Four of the Writing
Process   314

QuickBreak 10.2
TEN TIPS FOR WRITING BETTER SENTENCES   316

Revision: Stage Five
of the Writing Process   318

Macroediting: Stage Six
of the Writing Process   319

Microediting: Stage Seven
of the Writing Process   319

Approval: Stage Eight
of the Writing Process   320

Distribution: Stage Nine
of the Writing Process   322

Evaluation: Stage Ten
of the Writing Process   323

Writing for the Ear   324

QuickBreak 10.3
GRAMMAR ON THE WEB   325

The Process of Successful Presentations   327

Researching Your Presentation   327

Values Statement 10.1
KELLOGG COMPANY   328

Planning Your Presentation   328

Making Your Presentation   331

QuickBreak 10.4
CONQUERING THE PRESENTATION JITTERS   332

Evaluating Your Presentation   333

SUMMARY   333

DISCUSSION QUESTIONS   334

Memo from the Field
REGINA LYNCH-HUDSON, THE WRITE PUBLICIST   334

Case Study 10.1
"LETTER FROM BIRMINGHAM JAIL"   336

Case Study 10.2
ONLINE OUTRAGE: EMULEX AND THE FAKE
NEWS RELEASE   338

It's Your Turn
ELAYNE ANDERSON'S SPEECH   341

KEY TERMS   341

NOTES   341

Chapter 11

New Communications Technology   343

New Technology in the Net Generation   344
  Is the Medium the Message?   345
  The Role of Values in Message and
    Medium Selection   347

The Digital Revolution   347
  Convergence and Hypermedia   348
  Convergence Issues   349
  Virtual Public Relations   351

Computer Technology   351

  Values Statement 11.1
  MOTOROLA, INC.   353

The Internet   353

The History of the Internet   354
Individuals as Gatekeepers   357

QuickBreak 11.1
SPINNING THE WEB   358

Individuals as Publishers   359
Other Internet Issues   361

QuickBreak 11.2
THE MILLENNIUM BUG   362

Wireless Communications Technology   364
  Satellite Communications   365

  QuickBreak 11.3
  SATELLITE MEDIA TOURS   366

  QuickBreak 11.4
  HIGH-TECH TOOLS   368

Why New Isn't Always Better   370

SUMMARY   370

DISCUSSION QUESTIONS   371

  Memo from the Field
  CRAIG SETTLES, SUCCESSFUL.COM   371

  Case Study 11.1
  THE MOUNT EVEREST TRAGEDY   373

  Case Study 11.2
  CAUGHT IN THE EYE OF HURRICANE CHAD   375

  It's Your Turn
  HALE & HARDY ALL-NATURAL GRANOLA BARS   379

KEY TERMS   380

NOTES   380

section three

Public Relations Today and Tomorrow

Public relations practitioners operate in a dynamic and intense environment. We live in a time of great changes that test our values. The final section of this book examines the profession's critical issues. Emerging professionals will confront many, if not most, of these challenges in the coming years. These five chapters bring the challenges into focus.

Chapter 12
Crisis Communications   383

A New "Day of Infamy"   384
Putting Crisis Plans in Action   386
Crises Can Happen to Anyone   387
The Anatomy of a Crisis   387
QuickBreak 12.1
THE LESSONS OF DALLAS   388
What Is a Crisis?   390
Crisis Dynamics and the Lessons
of *Challenger*   391
QuickBreak 12.2
FIRE IN THE HOLE   394
Crises Can Bring Opportunity   395
Crisis Communications Planning   397
Step One: Risk Assessment   397
QuickBreak 12.3
THE CRISIS PLOTTING GRID   399
Step Two: Developing the Plan   400
Step Three: Response   406
Step Four: Recovery   407
QuickBreak 12.4
THINGS TO DO *BEFORE* A CRISIS BREAKS   408
Crisis Planning Ethics   408
Values Statement 12.1
PEPSICO   410
SUMMARY   410
DISCUSSION QUESTIONS   411
Memo from the Field
TOM DITT, NORTH CAROLINA DIVISION
OF EMERGENCY MANAGEMENT   411
Case Study 12.1
SSGN KURSK AND *USS GREENEVILLE*   413
Case Study 12.2
CLASSIC CRISES: TYLENOL AND PEPSI   415

It's Your Turn
DEATH OF A SALESMAN   417
KEY TERMS   418
NOTES   418

Chapter 13
Public Relations and Marketing   421

Public Relations and Marketing   422
The Decline of Mass Marketing   422
The Growth of Consumer-Focused
Marketing   423
Public Relations, Advertising, and
Marketing: Working Together   424
The Impact of Consumer-Focused Marketing
on Public Relations   425
The Impact of Public Relations on
Consumer-Focused Marketing   425
QuickBreak 13.1
IMC AND MORE   426
Values Statement 13.1
THE J.M. SMUCKER COMPANY   427
Differences between Public Relations and
Consumer-Focused Marketing   427
A Closer Look at Marketing   428
Marketing Public Relations   429
A Closer Look at IMC   430
Focusing on Individual Consumers   431
Sending One Clear Message   431
QuickBreak 13.2
DIRECT MAIL: ALSO KNOWN AS JUNK MAIL   432
How IMC Works   434
Creating an IMC Campaign   435
Applying IMC   437
QuickBreak 13.3
UNSAFE HARBOR   438
Problems with 21st-Century Marketing   439
SUMMARY   441

DISCUSSION QUESTIONS   442

Memo from the Field
VIN CIPOLLA, HNW INC.   442

Case Study 13.1
REVOLVOLUTION   444

Case Study 13.2
REEBOK AND THE INCUBUS   446

It's Your Turn
MAKING THE PITCH   447

KEY TERMS   448

NOTES   448

Chapter 14
Cross-Cultural Communication   450

Cultures: Realities and Definitions   451
International Public Relations   452

Cultural Attributes   453
Attitudes about Time   453
Attitudes about Formality   454
Attitudes about Individualism   455

Values Statement 14.1
SPECIAL OLYMPICS   456

Attitudes about Rank and Hierarchy   456
Attitudes about Religion   456

QuickBreak 14.1
THE MELTING-POT MYTH   457

Attitudes about Taste and Diet   457
Attitudes about Colors, Numbers,
   and Symbols   458
Attitudes about Assimilation
   and Acculturation   458

**Cross-Cultural Communication:
   Definitions and Dangers   459**
Encoding and Decoding   460
Gestures and Clothing   461
Stereotyping   462

QuickBreak 14.2
LOST IN TRANSLATION: PART ONE   463

**Achieving Successful Cross-Cultural Public
   Relations: A Process   463**
Stage One: Awareness   464
Stage Two: Commitment   464
Stage Three: Research   465

QuickBreak 14.3
LOST IN TRANSLATION: PART TWO   466

Stage Four: Local Partnership   466

QuickBreak 14.4
DOUBLE-WHAMMY CULTURE CLASH   467

Stage Five: Diversity   467
Stage Six: Testing   468
Stage Seven: Evaluation   468
Stage Eight: Advocacy   468
Stage Nine: Continuing Education   468

SUMMARY   470

DISCUSSION QUESTIONS   470

Memo from the Field
BILL IMADA, IMADA WONG
COMMUNICATIONS GROUP   471

Case Study 14.1
PITNEY BOWES SENDS A MESSAGE   472

Case Study 14.2
BORDER WARS FOR WAL-MART   474

It's Your Turn
CULTURES CLOSE TO HOME   476

KEY TERMS   476

NOTES   476

Chapter 15
Public Relations and the Law   479

Public Relations, the Law, and You   480

**Public Relations and the First
   Amendment   481**

Political versus Commercial Speech   482
The Key: Know Your Own Business   483

Federal Agencies That Regulate Speech   484
The Federal Trade Commission   485

QuickBreak 15.1
THE FREEDOM OF INFORMATION ACT   485

The Securities and Exchange
Commission   486

QuickBreak 15.2
SEC RULE 10b-5   490

The Federal Communications
Commission   491

Values Statement 15.1
AGENCY FOR TOXIC SUBSTANCES
AND DISEASE REGISTRY   492

The Food and Drug Administration   493

Libel   494
The Burden of Proof in Libel   494
Actual Malice   495
Common Law Libel   496

QuickBreak 15.3
"FREE SPEECH ROCKS!"   497

Privacy   498
The Four Torts of Privacy   498
Privacy Issues in Public Relations   499

Copyright   500
Copyright Guidelines   501
The Digital Millennium Copyright Act   501

QuickBreak 15.4
R.I.P. LARRY BUD MELMAN?   502

Fair Use   503
Protecting Your Intellectual Property
Rights   504

Litigation Public Relations   505
Public Relations as a Legal Strategy   505
The Use of LPR Tactics   506
Is LPR in Society's Best Interests?   507

SUMMARY   509

DISCUSSION QUESTIONS   509

Memo from the Field
RICHARD S. LEVICK, LEVICK STRATEGIC
COMMUNICATIONS   510

Case Study 15.1
THE COURT OF PUBLIC OPINION   512

Case Study 15.2
THE LION ROARS   513

It's Your Turn
SUPERGAS   515

KEY TERMS   516

NOTES   517

Chapter 16
Your Future in Public Relations   520

A New Century with New Challenges   521
Public Relations' Mixed Legacy   521

Social Forces and Public Relations   522
The Global Spread of Democracy   522

QuickBreak 16.1
PUBLIC RELATIONS IN THE NEW RUSSIA   522

Globalization   524
The Changing Face of the United States   525
The Growth in World Population   526

QuickBreak 16.2
THE GROWING HISPANIC MARKET   528

QuickBreak 16.3
IT'S NOT EASY BEING GREEN   530

Feminization of the Workplace   531

QuickBreak 16.4
SEXUAL HARASSMENT   532

Values Statement 16.1
LEAGUE OF WOMEN VOTERS
OF THE UNITED STATES   535

Where Public Relations Is Headed   535

QuickBreak 16.5
VIRTUAL PUBLIC RELATIONS   538

Your Future in Public Relations **539**

The Future of Values-Driven
Public Relations 541

SUMMARY **543**

DISCUSSION QUESTIONS **543**

Memo from the Field
DIRK MUNSON, 2001–2002 PRSSA NATIONAL
PRESIDENT 544

Case Study 16.1
THE NESTLÉ BOYCOTT 545

Case Study 16.2
PR IN THE FACE OF TERROR 547

It's Your Turn
BATTLING BAMBI 551

KEY TERMS **552**

NOTES **552**

Appendix

**Public Relations Society of America
Member Code of Ethics 2000** **556**

Glossary 563

Index 581

Preface

In the three years since Allyn and Bacon published the first edition of this book, we have been constantly reminded of the power of values and the importance of public relations. In that short time, human experience has covered a spectrum of emotions—from the joy of scientists' decrypting the human genetic code to the horror of history's worse act of terrorism. Our successes and failures often stem from our ability—or inability—to communicate with one another. Those who can communicate and can help conflicting forces find common ground will play an important role in the future of our planet. Public relations is well suited to that role.

The second edition of this book was near completion when a horrific event caused the authors—and most of the world—to pause and reflect on the human condition. The terrorist attacks of September 11, 2001, opened a new and uncertain chapter of history. Although a small concern in the grand scheme of things, the authors nevertheless faced a significant challenge. With publication deadlines rapidly approaching, they attempted to include a first draft of a rapidly evolving history.

Lacking the perspective that comes with the passage of time, the authors have struggled to present a relevant, appropriate focus on the attack and the events that immediately followed. At the moment these words are being written, bombs are falling in Afghanistan and health officials are scrambling to address the threat of anthrax-contaminated letters. The authors cannot know what will have transpired between the time they drafted these comments and when you pick up this book and begin reading. The authors attempted to present the events of September 11, 2001, in an insightful and balanced manner. Only time will tell whether they have succeeded.

It has been more than 100 years since the first public relations agency opened in the United States. During the 20th century, the practice of public relations grew from a vague notion to a powerful force in democratic societies. As we begin a new century, the profession has made impressive gains in respect and access to power. Yet, in a very real sense, public relations has a public relations problem. Although its roots date back to the beginning of recorded history, the fact remains that public relations—both as a profession and as a discipline—remains largely misunderstood.

Public relations is an honorable profession with a glorious past and a brilliant future. Like any other human pursuit, it also has its share of flaws. However, at a time when much of the world is embracing democratic institutions for the first time, public relations is an important catalyst for bringing change and promoting consensus. Through the practice of public relations, organizations and individuals communicate their ideas and advance their goals in the marketplace of ideas. This concept is increasingly understood within the nations of Eastern Europe, where, since the fall of communism, the demand for public relations education has skyrocketed.

Public Relations: A Values-Driven Approach introduces this dynamic profession to the practitioners of the 21st century. Through a realistic blend of theory and practical examples, this book seeks to remove the veil of mystery that has shrouded the profession from its very beginnings. Using the conversational style of writing favored by today's college students, this book takes the reader on a journey of discovery, often through the eyes of leading practitioners and scholars.

Values-Driven Public Relations

As the title suggests, however, these pages contain more than just a recitation of facts and concepts. This book champions what we call *values-driven public relations*: an approach that challenges practitioners to align their efforts with the values of their organization, their profession, their targeted publics, and society itself.

Values-driven public relations is a logical response to a dynamic and diverse society in which complex issues and competing values bring different groups of people into conflict. This approach links communication with an organization's values, mission, and goals. Today, public and private organizations are increasingly held accountable for their actions by a variety of stakeholders. No longer is an organization's behavior measured solely by traditional indicators of success, such as profits, stock dividends, and jobs created. Additional measures of social worth now include an organization's relationships with its employees, its communities, its customers, and its physical environment. Stakeholders expect decisions to be made in an ethical framework. *Public Relations: A Values-Driven Approach* prepares future practitioners and the organizations they represent for a world of increased responsibility, scrutiny, and accountability.

Public Relations in the Social Context

Another notable feature of this book is its discussion of relevant issues within a broader social context. Public relations did not develop, nor is it practiced, in a vacuum. Throughout history the practice of public relations has been shaped by great social forces. Its emergence in the United States was linked to the Industrial Revolution and the related Populist Era reforms. The 20th century's military and social conflicts served as catalysts for the profession's growth. Public relations was also transformed by the economic globalization and technological advances of the 1980s and 1990s. *Public Relations: A Values-Driven Approach* provides this broad social context so that future practitioners can have a clearer understanding of the so-called real world they are about to enter. The book includes full chapters on history, ethics, law, cross-cultural communication, and new technologies. Throughout the book, students are directed to online sources of further information.

Features

A major goal of this book is to strengthen students' problem-solving skills. Every chapter provides two hypothetical but realistic **scenarios:** the opening scenario and It's Your Turn, at the end of each chapter. Each scenario places students in the shoes of a practitioner and challenges them to create an ethical, values-driven, effective solution. Each chapter also includes relevant case studies that expose students to successful as well as unsuccessful public relations approaches. Following each scenario and case study are questions designed to engage students in a meaningful analysis of the issues raised. The book further promotes problem-solving skills by introducing a variety of processes that guide students through the stages of research, planning, communication, evaluation, and ethical decision making.

Public Relations: A Values-Driven Approach also contains pedagogical elements that engage students in the subject matter. Each chapter begins with a list of learning **objectives** that set the stage for the topics that lie ahead. **QuickChecks,** a series of questions focusing on the book's content, are interspersed as learning aids throughout each chapter. **QuickBreaks,** lively and relevant sidebars, bring depth and texture to each chapter. In keeping with the values focus of this text, **Values Statements** from a broad range of organizations are scattered throughout the book. A list of **key terms** appears at the end of each chapter, and a full **glossary** is provided at the end of the book. Each chapter also includes a **Memo from the Field,** a message to students from one of today's leading public relations professionals. These professionals represent a broad range of public and private interests and reflect the diversity of the society upon which they wield so much influence.

Acknowledgments

The authors want to thank the dozens of people, many of whom were unknown to them before the writing of this book, who contributed greatly to this effort. The authors also want to thank Dean James Gentry and the faculty, staff, and students of the William Allen White School of Journalism and Mass Communications at the University of Kansas for their advice, support, and patience during this project. A special acknowledgment goes to student Philippe Stefani, who translated one Memo from the Field from French to English. The authors also extend their gratitude to the dozens of companies, agencies, and individuals who gave their permission for the use of photographs, publications, and other artwork used in the text.

Sixteen men and women gave their valuable time to write memos to the students who will read this book. The value of providing firsthand wisdom to students is immeasurable. The authors would like to acknowledge the contributions of Joann Killeen of Killeen Communications; Mike Swenson of Barkley Evergreen & Partners; Michael Devlin of the Rock and Roll Hall of Fame and Museum; Gordon Lindsey of J. C. Penney Company; René Pelletier of Baromètre Inc.; Terrie Williams of The Terrie Williams Agency; independent public relations consultant Walter Lindenmann;

retired public relations consultant Fred Repper; Shirley Barr of Shirleybarr Public Relations; Regina Lynch-Hudson of The Write Publicist; Craig Settles of Successful.com; Tom Ditt of the North Carolina Division of Emergency Management; Vin Cipolla of HNW Inc.; Bill Imada of Imada Wong Communications Group; Richard S. Levick Esq. of Levick Strategic Communications; and 2001–02 PRSSA National President Dirk Munson.

A group of dedicated educators provided many suggestions for this new edition and, in doing so, helped the authors maintain a focus on the needs of students who read this book: Thomas H. Bivins, University of Oregon; Randy Bobbitt, The University of North Carolina at Wilmington; Anne Stiehm Eastey, Normandale Community College; Bosah Ebo, Rider University; Nickiann Fleener, University of Utah; and Thomas R. Flynn, Slippery Rock University.

Once the text was written and the necessary artwork and permissions secured, the burden of this project shifted to the talented editors, designers, and technicians of Allyn and Bacon: Molly Taylor and Michael Kish, as well as the team at Omega-type Typography, Inc.

Last, and certainly not least, the authors thank their families for their love and unwavering support during this long and challenging process. They are our inspiration and motivation.

This book is dedicated to victims and heroes of September 11, 2001, as well as all those who fight and die for our shared values.

David W. Guth, APR
Charles Marsh, Ph.D.

About the Authors

The authors of this book come from very different backgrounds but share a passion for public relations education. Both are associate professors at the William Allen White School of Journalism and Mass Communications at the University of Kansas. They also share real-world experience in the dynamic profession of public relations.

Before becoming an educator, David W. Guth served as a broadcast journalist in six states and won numerous local, state, regional, and national reporting honors, including the prestigious George Foster Peabody Award. He has also served as a public relations practitioner in the public and private sectors, including holding several positions in North Carolina state government. As an educator, Guth coauthored *Media Guide for Attorneys*, a publication that received regional and national awards. In addition to his teaching and research responsibilities, Guth has served as crisis communications consultant to several government agencies and public utilities. Guth is an accredited member of the Public Relations Society of America. His international experience includes public relations work in Japan, Italy, and Russia.

Charles Marsh has a Ph.D. in English literature and 20 years of business communications experience. He is the former editor of *American Way,* the in-flight magazine of American Airlines, and the former senior editor of corporate publications for J.C. Penney. He is the author of *A Quick and (Not) Dirty Guide to Business Writing* (Prentice-Hall, 1997) and has won national and regional awards for writing and editing. In addition to teaching, Marsh has been a communications consultant to J.C. Penney, Ralston Purina, the USA Film Festival, the United States Information Agency, the American Management Association, and other organizations. His international experience includes public relations work in France, Italy, Spain, Kyrgyzstan, and Costa Rica.

Public Relations

chapter one

What Is Public Relations?

objectives

After studying this chapter, you will be able to

■ explain the definition of public relations

■ understand the different roles public relations practitioners play

■ describe the four-step public relations process

■ appreciate the role of personal, organizational, and societal values in the practice of public relations

The New Job

scenario

You have just been appointed vice president for public relations at a manufacturing company. Your new company is facing a variety of challenges and opportunities. The company has had several layoffs over the past few years because of slumping sales. Industry analysts attribute the company's problems to outdated production equipment and a flood of foreign imports.

In an attempt to make the company more competitive, management wants to secure financing to expand and modernize operations. However, it has run into some major roadblocks. The financial community is concerned about the long-term survival of the company. Several Wall Street analysts believe the company is ripe for a hostile takeover. Employees and their union representatives have expressed concerns about the many changes taking place. Local environmentalists have said they are unhappy with the company's handling of toxic waste.

But it's not all bad news. Your company recently won an award for community involvement and employee volunteerism. And a poll in a local newspaper showed that, despite all the problems, your company is still one of the most respected employers in the region.

You haven't even had time to find out where the water fountain is when you're invited to the company president's office and asked, "What do you think we should do?"

Welcome to the real world. Welcome to public relations.

Public Relations: Separating Fact from Fiction

In the opening scene of the 1956 movie *The Man in the Gray Flannel Suit*, actor Gregory Peck commutes home by train following a hard day's work in New York City. A traveling companion asks if he might be interested in a job in public relations.

"But I don't know anything about public relations," Peck's character says in surprise.

His friend's reply: "Who does? You have a clean shirt. You bathe every day. That's all there is to it."

The term *public relations* and its abbreviation, *PR*, are often used (and abused) by those who have little or no understanding of its meaning. Some treat *public relations* as a synonym for words such as *publicity, propaganda, spin,* and *hype.* Some use the term as a pejorative, something inherently sinister. Others think of it as fluff, lacking in substance. The news media often contribute to the confusion. According to a study of 100 news stories that used the term *public relations*, fewer than 5 percent of them used it correctly. Researcher Julie K. Henderson wrote that 37 percent of the stories used *public relations* in a negative manner, and only 17 percent contained a positive reference.[1]

But look again. All around us is evidence of public relations at work. Who can forget the jockeying for public opinion in the tense 36-day Campaign 2000 stand-off between George W. Bush and Al Gore? In the nation's first postelection presidential campaign since 1876, the two candidates and their surrogates battled one another for the hearts and minds of the American people. In what *New York* magazine called "the biggest publishing event of all time," more than 3 million copies of *Harry Potter and the Goblet of Fire* were sold within the first 48 hours of its release in July 2000. This success came on the heels of an imaginative campaign that

THE DISNEYLAND, RESORT:
A PARTNERSHIP OF HISTORIC PROPORTIONS

Anaheim, California, home to DISNEYLAND® park for over 45 years, once a place where orange groves lined the landscape. As the popularity of the park grew from the day it opened on July 17, 1955, so did the city of Anaheim. In fact, over the course of nearly five decades the city experienced explosive and uncontrolled growth that resulted in a region in serious need of a facelift. Nearly fifty years old, DISNEYLAND too was in need of a facelift. As Walt Disney Imagineering General Manager of the new DISNEYLAND Resort commented, "If DISNEYLAND had started as the only development and the only green, it was now the only green in a sea of asphalt."

In 1990, the city and Disney got together to discuss the future. "Together, during the early part of the decade we worked hard and articulated common goals and objectives around which we could rally," said Galen. "That vision included a master plan for the area that incorporated both a Disney Resort Specific Plan and an Anaheim Resort Plan. The city wanted to increase its tourism revenues through expansion and expand the convention facility to remain competitive, while ensuring the long-term future of DISNEYLAND through expansion — the crown jewel of Disney theme parks." In partnership, Disney proposed both an expansion of DISNEYLAND and the redevelopment of the resort area.

The planning challenges were immense, including the upgrading of existing infrastructure and providing for the efficient use of limited land, balancing overlapping needs and systems for complex visitation patterns to gain consensus. The city had these same challenges with the convention center and area-wide tourism services to the proposed new land uses and how to solve the logistical problems of building in the midst of existing neighborhoods and thousands of people's lives.

LET THE SUN SHINE IN – A 50-foot tall "Sun" made of gold titanium and coated with shattered glass and tile sits atop a perpetual wave fountain for all guests to appreciate at the entrance of DISNEY'S CALIFORNIA ADVENTURE™ park, opening to the public February 8, 2001. Because the structure faces north, away from the real sun, six heliostats...

THE SUN GOES DOWN ON PARADISE! – There will be plenty of nighttime fun in the Paradise Pier land of DISNEY'S CALIFORNIA ADVENTURE™ park in Southern California. Attractions on this lively boardwalk include "California Screamin'" rollercoaster, the giant "Sun Wheel" and the thrilling "Maliboomer" which shoots riders 180-feet up its tower with breathtaking speed. DISNEY'S CALIFORNIA ADVENTURE in Southern California, located next door to DISNEYLAND® park, opens to the public February 8, 2001.

...RNIA POSTCARD – The entrance to DISNEY'S CALIFORNIA ADVENTURE™ park ...I California welcomes guests with stunning, gold-plated 11.5-foot letters, two ...mic tile-mural walls depicting icons from Northern and Southern California, and ...ersion of the Golden Gate Bridge. DISNEY'S CALIFORNIA ADVENTURE park in ...lifornia, located next door to DISNEYLAND® park, opens to the public ...2001.

Disney California Adventure The Disney Company's use of public relations led to the creation of a public–private partnership that resulted in a $4.2 billion redevelopment project with a new amusement park. (Courtesy of The Disneyland Resort)

whipped up a frenzy of anticipation that another publication called "Pottermania."[2] Public relations played a critical role for public school officials coping with the horror of the April 1999 shooting rampage that left one teacher and 14 students dead at Columbine High School in Littleton, Colorado. This was true both during the chaotic hours immediately following the tragedy and in the search for healing and closure in the months and years that followed. On a much happier note, collaboration among local government, local businesses, and the Disney Company led to a $4.2 billion redevelopment project in Anaheim, California, and the successful February 2001 opening of a new amusement park, California Adventure. Without community support generated by a carefully orchestrated public relations campaign, this largest partnership of public and private interests in the state's history would never have become a reality.[3]

Many try to define public relations strictly in terms of these kinds of high-profile images. However, *publicity* and *public relations* are not synonymous. As you will learn in Chapter 9, publicity is just one of many tactics used by public relations practitioners. Perhaps it is best to think of public relations as a tapestry, with many parts intricately woven into one whole cloth.

Public relations helps foster mutually beneficial relationships. When the major employer in Tumbler Ridge, British Columbia, announced it was leaving town, the small mining community faced extinction. Vancouver-based public relations agency Verus Group found itself in a unique position, having been retained by three clients with decidedly different interests. The company wanted the agency to handle media relations. The town wanted the agency to help sell the hundreds of homes put up for sale as mining families departed for greener pastures. After establishing safeguards to avoid what could be considered a conflict of interest, Verus Group brought the town and the company together with a third client, a real estate agency that specialized in marketing towns that had lost their major industry. By bringing the three clients together and helping them find common ground, Verus Group orchestrated an international multimedia campaign that successfully repositioned Tumbler Ridge as a haven for outdoor enthusiasts.[4]

Some of the best public relations activity occurs when it appears as if nothing has happened at all. Few think to attribute high employee morale, increased productivity, or good corporate citizenship to public relations. But they should. When an orchestra sells out a concert or when a growing number of people decide against drinking and driving, it is easy to forget that these successes may well be benefits of sound public relations strategies. Even knowing where to vote, go to school, and shop is often the result of good public relations.

Public relations casts a broad net.

The Search for a Definition

So what is public relations? To borrow a phrase from a popular 1950s television game show, that is the $64,000 question. Unfortunately, there is no definitive answer. The modern practice of public relations first came under serious study in the early 1900s, and educators and practitioners have struggled ever since with its definition. At the beginning of the 21st century, defining public relations remains an issue.

We promise to give you our own definition of public relations; we think it's a good one. But first, we want to ask you a question: What do *you* think public relations is? (Don't worry: This is an ungraded quiz!) We will not be surprised if you say "I don't know" or if your answer is vague. It is a hard question—so hard, in fact, that even people who practice public relations on a daily basis have yet to arrive at a single definition to describe what they do.

This confusion was illustrated in a survey of accountants, attorneys, and public relations practitioners. The three groups were selected because they had something in common—a counselor relationship with their clients. Each group was asked about its profession and its place within organizational structures. Although the accountants and attorneys clearly understood their roles, the public relations practitioners did not. This caused the study's authors to raise a pertinent question: If public relations practitioners are unclear about who they are and what they do, why should they expect anyone else to understand?[5]

There isn't even any consensus on what to call the profession. Because of the supposedly negative connotations carried by the term *public relations,* many organizations opt to use euphemisms such as "public affairs," "public information," "corporate communications," or "community outreach" to describe the function. Burson-Marsteller, one of the world's largest public relations agencies, describes itself in its web site as a "global perception management firm."

Other organizations, especially government agencies, try to hide their public relations practitioners from the eyes of jealous rivals and zealous budget-cutters by giving them seemingly innocuous titles, such as "special assistant" or "information manager." One state agency had its listing removed from the North Carolina state government telephone directory in an effort to avoid detection. Instead of answering the telephone by saying "public information office," the staff was instructed to answer by repeating the office's extension number.[6]

Public Relations Defined

In 1976, in an effort to eliminate some of the confusion, public relations pioneer and scholar Rex Harlow compiled 472 different definitions of public relations. From those, Harlow came up with his own 87-word definition, which stressed public relations' role as a management function that "helps establish and maintain mutual lines of communication, understanding, acceptance, and cooperation between an organization and its publics."[7]

Others have sought to define public relations in fewer words. In *Managing Public Relations,* educators Todd Hunt and James E. Grunig opt for a 10-word definition: "the management of communication between an organization and its publics."

QuickBreak 1.1

PRSA'S VIEW OF THE PROFESSION

The **Public Relations Society of America (PRSA)** is the world's largest organization for public relations practitioners. It has defined the profession in the following manner.

Official Statement on Public Relations[8]

Public relations helps our complex, pluralistic society to reach decisions and function more effectively by contributing to mutual understanding among groups and institutions. It serves to bring the public and public policies into harmony.

Public relations serves a wide variety of institutions in society such as businesses, trade unions, government agencies, voluntary associations, foundations, hospitals, and educational and religious institutions. To achieve their goals, these institutions must develop effective relationships with many different audiences or publics such as employees, members, customers, local communities, shareholders, and other institutions, and with society at large.

The managements of institutions need to understand the attitudes and values of their publics in order to achieve institutional goals. The goals themselves are shaped by the external environment. The public relations practitioner acts as a counselor to management and as a mediator, helping to translate private aims into reasonable, publicly acceptable policy and action.

As a management function, public relations encompasses the following:

- Anticipating, analyzing, and interpreting public opinion, attitudes, and issues which might impact, for good or ill, the operations and plans of the organization.

- Counseling management at all levels in the organization with regard to policy decisions, courses of action, and communications, taking into account their public ramifications and the organization's social or citizenship responsibilities.

- Researching, conducting, and evaluating, on a continuing basis, programs of action and communication to achieve informed public understanding necessary to the success of an organization's aims. These may include marketing, financial, fund-raising, employee, community or government relations, and other programs.

- Planning and implementing the organization's efforts to influence or change public policy.

- Setting objectives, planning, budgeting, recruiting, and training staff, developing facilities—in short, managing the resources needed to perform all of the above.

- Examples of the knowledge that may be required in the professional practice of public relations include communication arts, psychology, social psychology, sociology, political science, economics, and the principles of management and ethics. Technical knowledge and skills are required for opinion research, public issues analysis, media relations, direct mail, institutional advertising, publications, film/video productions, special events, speeches, and presentations.

In helping to define and implement policy, the public relations practitioner utilizes a variety of communication skills and plays an integral role both within the organization and between the organization and the external environment.

One area of agreement among public relations practitioners is the definition of the term **public:** any group of people who share common interests or values in a particular situation—especially interests or values they might be willing to act upon. When a public has a relationship with your organization, the public is called a **stakeholder,** meaning that it has a stake in your organization or in an issue potentially involving your organization.

The fact is that as long as people are people, they will continue to view the world with differing perspectives. That's why it may be best to avoid the debate over the exact wording of a public relations definition and, instead, to concentrate on the various elements of the profession itself. Here is where one finds consensus. Common to any comprehensive definition of public relations are the following elements:

■ *Public relations is a management function.* The relationship between an organization and the publics important to its success must be a top concern of the organization's leadership. The public relations practitioner provides counsel on the timing, manner, and form important communications should take. In other words, practitioners aren't just soldiers who follow orders; they're also generals who help shape policy. And like all managers, they must be able to measure the degree of their success in their various projects.

■ *Public relations involves two-way communication.* Communication is not just telling people about an organization's needs. It also involves listening to those same people speak of their concerns. This willingness to listen is an essential part of the relationship-building process.

■ *Public relations is a planned activity.* Actions taken on behalf of an organization must be carefully planned and consistent with the organization's values and goals. And since the relationship between an organization and the publics important to its success is a top concern, these actions must also be consistent with the publics' values and goals.

■ *Public relations is a research-based social science.* Formal and informal research is conducted to allow an organization to communicate effectively, possessing a full understanding of the environment in which it operates and the issues it confronts. Public relations practitioners and educators also share their knowledge with others in the industry through various professional and academic publications.

■ *Public relations is socially responsible.* A practitioner's responsibilities extend beyond organizational goals. Practitioners and the people they represent are expected to play a constructive role in society.

You may have noticed a common theme running throughout this list: the concept of **relationship management.** Far-sighted, well-managed organizations know they must have good relationships with publics important to their success. A 1992 study that sought to define excellence in public relations noted that having good relationships with these publics can save an organization money by reducing the likelihood of threats such as litigation, regulation, boycotts, or lost revenue that result from falling out of favor with these groups. At the same time, the study said that an organization makes more money by cultivating good relationships with consumers, donors, shareholders, and legislators.[9] Therefore, nurturing these relationships is one of the most important roles public relations practitioners can play.

However one chooses to frame its definition, there is one other important aspect to public relations: It plays a critical role in the free flow of information in democratic societies. When American colonists declared their independence from Great Britain in 1776, they said, "Governments are instituted among men, deriving their just powers from the consent of the governed."[10] The meaning of this phrase is clear: For democratic societies to function in a healthy manner, the government and the people must reach a consensus on matters of importance. Consent cannot occur without the exchange of information and ideas. That, in turn, requires communication. Those who cannot communicate effectively in democratic societies are left at a distinct and sometimes dangerous disadvantage.

Public relations plays a critical role in effective communications. Through public relations, individuals and organizations enter the great marketplace of ideas. And, through the proper application of public relations, practitioners participate in the search for consensus.

Theory versus Reality

The confusion surrounding the definition of public relations stems in part from differences between the theory and the reality of the profession. Nowhere are these differences more evident than in the first definitional element: the concept of public relations as a management function. This is an area in which corporate managers and public relations practitioners are sometimes in conflict. Former Mobil Corporation executive Herb Schmertz, who masterminded his company's "in-your-face" approach to dealing with the news media, encapsulated this conflict when he wrote that "public affairs is far too important to be left to public affairs professionals."[11] Although Schmertz's statement actually calls for a strong management role in public relations, it can easily be misinterpreted to imply that there is no role for practitioners in management.

A study conducted by researchers at Bowling Green State University demonstrates this conflict. More than two-thirds of the practitioners surveyed said their role was to develop "mutual understanding" between management and the public. However, fewer than one-third of the same practitioners said they thought their managers would agree. Most said their bosses viewed public relations as "persuasion, information dissemination, or propaganda."[12]

The Hunt–Grunig Models of Public Relations

The models used in the Bowling Green study were patterned on the research of Professors Todd Hunt and James Grunig, who identified four models that they said public relations practitioners generally follow:

1. In the **press agentry/publicity model,** the focus of public relations efforts is on getting favorable coverage, or publicity, from the media. In this model accuracy and truth, Hunt and Grunig contend, are not seen as essential.[13] A 1989 study showed that this was the most widely practiced model of public relations. The same study showed, however, that it ranked third in order of preference among practitioners.[14]

2. In the **public information model,** the focus is on the dissemination of objective and accurate information. Hunt and Grunig say that people following this model serve as "journalists in residence," acting in much the same manner as news reporters.[15] The aforementioned study showed that this was the second most practiced model of public relations. It ranked last, however, in order of preference among practitioners.[16]

3. The **two-way asymmetrical model** is a more sophisticated approach in which research is used in an effort to influence important publics toward a particular point of view. Hunt and Grunig describe this as a "selfish" model, one that does not lend itself to conflict resolution.[17] The 1989 study showed that this was the least practiced of the four models. It ranked first, however, in order of preference among practitioners.[18]

4. The **two-way symmetrical model** is the model Hunt and Grunig prefer. It focuses on two-way communication as a means of conflict resolution and for the promotion of mutual understanding between an organization and its important publics.[19] However, the 1989 study showed that this was only the third most practiced model of public relations. It ranked second in order of preference.[20]

Which public relations model an organization chooses to follow depends on several factors. In smaller organizations, which often deal with fewer people and have less complex issues to address, the practitioner tends to be more a communications technician than a counselor. Organizations that rely on public relations practitioners with relatively little experience usually limit the practitoners' role to technical tasks, such as news release writing and brochure design. The role a practitioner assumes is also influenced by an organization's history. A University of Kansas study showed that the more experience an organization has in dealing with crises, the greater the likelihood that the public relations role is closely tied to the organization's management.[21]

Each organization has its own distinctive personality. The reality is that an organization's internal environment can dictate the degree of influence public relations has. Sometimes corporate culture can inhibit good public relations practices. One study of organizations identified four barriers that practitioners often face in the corporate culture: a lack of access to top management, an unwillingness of management to pay for or grant authority to gather information, a resistance to timely and accurate disclosure, and differences over how managers and practitioners view the role of public relations. The study concluded that "many public relations practitioners must feel they face an impossible task: They must act effectively and with integrity, and they must accomplish both goals as they labor under the weight of constraints that can make effective, responsible action virtually impossible."[22]

Public Relations and Marketing

Another definitional issue is whether public relations should be considered a separate discipline at all. Some very learned people argue that public relations is a component of a different field encompassing many persuasive communications: **integrated marketing communications (IMC)**. (This topic is discussed in significant detail in Chapter 13.) However, other, equally learned individuals bristle at the thought of public relations being covered by an all-encompassing IMC umbrella.

The authors of this book support the latter view. We see IMC as a customer-focused marriage of three distinct disciplines: advertising, marketing, and some functions of public relations. As you may have noticed, some people think of public relations as "free advertising" and of advertising as marketing. However, each term represents a distinct discipline:

- **Advertising** is the use of controlled media (media in which one pays for the privilege of dictating message content, placement, and frequency) in an attempt to influence the actions of targeted publics.
- **Marketing** is the process of researching, creating, refining, and promoting a product or service and distributing that product or service to targeted consumers.
- **Public relations** is the management of relationships between an organization and its publics.

Not every marketing situation requires the use of all three disciplines. Marketing, the central concept in IMC, focuses on customers. We respectfully suggest that public relations practitioners engage in relationships that go far beyond customer communications. Although this is a debate that may best be conducted in an atmosphere that includes beverages and peanuts, the debate is indicative of the broader struggle public relations practitioners have faced since the dawn of the 20th century—to have public relations accepted as a separate and significant profession.

The confusion over what public relations is demonstrates why any attempt to define the profession is best done in broad strokes. In truth, public relations is part art and part science. It is a dash of inspiration and a lot of perspiration. It is also very hard work that is often at its best when it goes unnoticed. This, in part, explains why public relations was ranked 12th in a list of the 250 most stressful jobs in the United States—ranked as less stressful than being a police officer or an air traffic controller, but more stressful than being a college basketball coach or a member of Congress.[23]

Quick ✔ Check

1. What are the five essential elements in the definition of public relations?
2. How is public relations related to the concept of relationship management?
3. What are the Hunt–Grunig models of public relations, and why are they significant?
4. How do public relations and marketing differ?

Why a Public Relations Career?

You may already be asking, "Why would anyone want a career in a field as misunderstood and demanding as public relations?" Good question. Now, a better answer: because there is no other job quite like it. Public relations skills are transferable across a broad range of career opportunities. Regardless of a person's career interests—such as health care, sports marketing, environmental management, government and politics, business and finance, or public service—there is no organization that cannot benefit from wise public relations counsel. Every organization has a need to maintain healthy relationships with its important publics. That is where the public relations practitioner exerts influence. Public relations is a profession that demands and rewards creativity and integrity. It's a profession in which you can see the results of a job well done. It is a career in which you can make a difference.

A Profile of Practitioners

Because public relations is not licensed in the United States, no one knows exactly how many people practice it. A 1999 survey conducted by the U.S. Bureau of Labor Statistics estimated that 118,280 people worked as "public relations specialists." The BLS listed another 67,210 as "public relations managers." In comparison, the BLS estimated that there were 100,600 "advertising and promotion managers" and 202,710 "marketing managers" in 1999.[24] According to the BLS publication *2000–01 Occupational Outlook Handbook,* "Employment of public relations specialists is expected to increase faster than the average for all occupations through 2008."[25]

In a broad sense, public relations can be practiced within five organizational structures:

- *Public relations agencies:* companies that contract to provide or supplement public relations services for others. These agencies are often affiliated with advertising agencies to provide integrated marketing communications (IMC) services for their clients (see Chapter 13).
- *Corporations:* public relations units within companies. Corporate practitioners are company employees.
- *Government:* public, taxpayer-supported units within government agencies. These units offer counsel on governmental policies and disseminate information vital to the healthy functioning of a democracy. These practitioners are government employees.

A PROFESSION OR A TRADE?

Adding to the confusion about what public relations is and where it fits into an organization's structure is an ongoing debate: Is public relations a profession or is it a trade? One educator commented at a recent national conference that "I find the continuing discussion and emphasis over public relations professionalism interesting, but also damned irritating."[26] However, this is a debate over more than mere semantics and prestige. The salaries practitioners earn, their influence on decision making, and the degree to which they are regulated hang in the balance.

Generally recognized qualities that distinguish professions from other career pursuits are

- the need for a certain level of education as a prerequisite to entering the profession;

- support of the profession by ongoing research published in scholarly journals or in professional association publications;

- the establishment of ethical standards, usually in the form of a code of ethics; and

- some form of licensing or government control.

Doctors and lawyers are professionals who clearly meet these criteria. Each has to receive an advanced academic degree and is expected to remain informed on the latest developments in his or her field. Both professions are supported by significant bodies of research and have established codes of ethics. And one cannot be a doctor or lawyer until a state licensing board gives its stamp of approval.

When it comes to public relations, the dividing line between profession and trade is not as well defined. In one recent nationwide survey, there was little consensus on what constitutes a standard of professional performance. Answers varied significantly, depending on the respondent's age, level of education, race, level of experience, and geographic location.[27]

There also is the question of whether public relations should be licensed. Licensing proponents, including the late Edward L. Bernays, an acknowledged "father" of modern public relations, see licensing as a way of weeding out unqualified practitioners and raising the stature and salaries of those who are licensed. Others see government-sanctioned licensing as burdensome and as an infringement on First Amendment rights to freedom of expression.

Organizations such as PRSA and the **International Association of Business Communicators (IABC)** have sought to promote public relations as a profession through the establishment of voluntary accreditation programs. Practitioners must gain a certain level of experience and demonstrate a certain degree of knowledge before receiving accreditation: **APR,** for **Accredited in Public Relations,** by PRSA and/or **ABC,** for **Accredited Business Communicator,** by IABC. Both organizations also promote professionalism with support of scholarly research and through the enforcement of codes of ethics.

- *Nonprofit organizations or trade associations:* public relations units that serve not-for-profit organizations or specific business/interest groups. These practitioners usually are employees of the organizations they serve.

- *Independent public relations consultants:* self-employed public relations practitioners. These practitioners may contract with clients on a per-job basis or may be placed on a retainer, much like a public relations agency.

Values Statement 1.1

J.C. PENNEY COMPANY

J.C. Penney Company, one of America's largest department store retailers, operates more than 1,230 stores in all 50 states, Puerto Rico, Mexico, and Chile. The company was founded in 1902 in Kemmerer, Wyoming.

The Penney Idea
Adopted in 1913

1. To serve the public, as nearly as we can, to its complete satisfaction.
2. To expect for the service we render a fair remuneration and not all the profit the traffic will bear.
3. To do all in our power to pack the customer's dollar full of value, quality, and satisfaction.
4. To continue to train ourselves and our associates so that the service we give will be more and more intelligently performed.
5. To improve constantly the human factor in our business.
6. To reward men and women in our organization through participation in what the business produces.
7. To test our every policy, method, and act in this wise: "Does it square with what is right and just?"

—From *The Illustrated JCPenney*

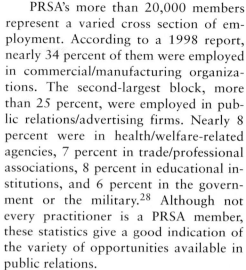

PRSA's more than 20,000 members represent a varied cross section of employment. According to a 1998 report, nearly 34 percent of them were employed in commercial/manufacturing organizations. The second-largest block, more than 25 percent, were employed in public relations/advertising firms. Nearly 8 percent were in health/welfare-related agencies, 7 percent in trade/professional associations, 8 percent in educational institutions, and 6 percent in the government or the military.[28] Although not every practitioner is a PRSA member, these statistics give a good indication of the variety of opportunities available in public relations.

Not only is public relations practiced in a wide range of settings, but its practitioners use a broad spectrum of communications skills. Some of the more traditional public relations tasks include news release writing, brochure design, creation of annual reports, and development of marketing materials. In recent years, however, there has been a revolution in communications technologies, and public relations practitioners have been at the cutting edge of change. Practitioners are now engaged in web site development, satellite teleconferencing, and the creation of interactive CDs. The need to stay up to date on the emerging communications technologies of the 21st century is just part of the challenge and the fascination of public relations.

Quick ✔ Check

1. Is public relations a profession? Why or why not?
2. What are the five organizational structures in which public relations is commonly practiced?
3. Is the number of jobs in public relations growing?

The Public Relations Process

Although the technology used in the practice of public relations is constantly changing, the process that guides public relations is one that stands the test of time. Most public relations experts agree that public relations is conducted within the framework of a four-step process. But would this really be public relations if there were agreement on what to label each of the steps? Remember: This is public relations, the profession of a thousand definitions.

The Traditional Four-Step Model of the Public Relations Process

A variety of names have been used to describe the four steps of the public relations process. Some instructors, in an effort to help students memorize the various steps for the inevitable midterm exam, have favored the use of acronyms such as ROPE (research, objective, planning, and evaluation) and RACE (research, action, communication, and evaluation). In adding our two cents' worth to the debate over what to call each of the four steps, we opt for a more straightforward, if less glamorous, approach (see Figure 1.1): research, planning, communication, and evaluation.

- **Research** is the discovery phase of a problem-solving process: practitioners' use of formal and informal methods of information gathering to learn about an organization, the challenges and opportunities it faces, and the publics important to its success. Remember the scenario that opens this chapter, the one in which you're the new vice president of public relations for an organization facing several challenges? The scenario concludes with the company's president asking, "What do you think we should do?" Part of your answer should be "research."

- **Planning** is the strategy phase of the problem-solving process, in which practitioners use the information gathered during research. From that information, they develop effective and efficient strategies to meet the needs of their clients or organizations.

- **Communication** is the execution phase of the public relations process. This is where practitioners direct messages to specific publics in support of specified goals. But good plans are flexible: Because changes can occur suddenly in

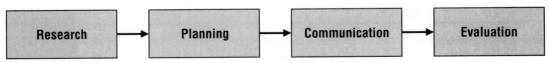

FIGURE 1.1   The Traditional Four-Step Model of the Public Relations Process

the social or business environment, sometimes it's necessary to adjust, overhaul, or abandon the planned strategies. It's worth repeating here that effective communication is two-way, involving listening to publics as well as sending them messages.

■ **Evaluation** is the measurement of how efficiently and effectively a public relations effort met the organization's goals.

The Dynamic Model of the Public Relations Process

Although there is a simple elegance in defining the public relations process in the traditional four-step manner, this model can be strengthened. One possible problem is that this traditional model suggests a linear process: Step two follows step one, step three follows step two, and so forth. Unfortunately, this linear model oversimplifies a very dynamic process. If the linear model were likened to a dance, it would be a conga line.

In reality, public relations is more like a square dance (see Figure 1.2). The implication of the traditional four-step model is that evaluation is the last thing done. However, in this era of downsizing and increasing accountability, evaluation should occur in each phase of the public relations process. Research should identify ways to measure the effects of a public relations program. Those measurements must then be built into any plan that is developed. As the plan is being executed, we should be sensitive to the need to adjust our efforts to account for any miscalculations or changes in the environment. That, in turn, may call for additional research. Finally, evaluation provides critical information about whether the goals of the plan were met and about lessons learned for future public relations efforts.

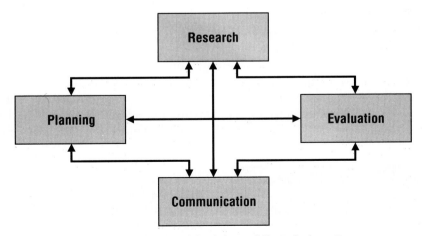

FIGURE 1.2   The Dynamic Model of the Public Relations Process

The Role of Values in Public Relations

Another potential shortcoming of the traditional four-step model is that its simple language does not adequately provide a solid foundation for the entire process. An organization's core values should govern the public relations process from its inception to its conclusion—but the traditional model doesn't indicate that. In many ways, a values-driven public relations process is similar to the process of planning a trip for spring break. As you begin to research where to go, you first identify your values: fun, companionship, safety, price, and so forth. Those core values establish the framework within which you'll gather research, plan your trip, go on your trip, and, finally, evaluate its success.

Let's use a second hypothetical example to illustrate what we mean. If an organization says it values the opinions of its employees, it would not make any sense for that organization to conduct research that doesn't take into account the employees' opinions. And it would make even less sense to launch a plan that, in the pursuit of some other short-term gain, winds up showing that the organization is insensitive to employee concerns. That is why it is necessary to understand an organization's values before engaging in the public relations process. And because good relationships with important publics are critical to any organization's success, it is equally important to understand the values of those publics. Some may argue that this approach limits information gathering and stifles creativity. However, that is exactly what values are supposed to do: establish the boundaries within which we are willing to operate.

This lack of focus on values is perhaps the biggest flaw in the traditional four-step model of public relations. At a time when organizations are being held accountable far beyond the balance sheet, their values-inspired mission and goals must be at the forefront of all their research, planning, communication, and evaluation.

A common complaint against public relations practitioners is that they occasionally act as if the ends justify the means. Some choose to flirt with or even to ignore the boundaries of ethics. Gossip columnist Liz Smith has complained that when she tries to verify tips with celebrity publicists, "they just lie and say it isn't so."[29] Others, failing to pause and consider their organization's core values, sometimes find themselves in the uncomfortable position of trying to place their actions in an ethical framework after the fact. Isn't it much better to snuff out a fire before it causes irreparable damage? Issues of values, ethics, and social responsibility must be addressed throughout the public relations process: The continued growth of public relations as a profession depends on it.

Quick ✔ Check

1. What are the four steps of the traditional public relations process?
2. Why is public relations considered a dynamic process?
3. What role should values play in the public relations process?

Actions Speak Louder Than Words—Part I

Too often, unintended actions speak louder than the lofty words found in an organization's mission statement:

- Bridgestone/Firestone recalled 6.5 million of its tires in August 2000 after the National Highway Traffic Safety Administration began investigating whether tire failures may have led to as many as 174 traffic fatalities. However, the company's CEO remained silent on the subject for more than a month, leaving surrogates to blame others for the tire's flaws. Even more disturbing were reports from the Ford Motor Company and the private advocacy group Public Citizen that the tire maker had known about the problem for some time.

- The Coca-Cola Company came under intense criticism in June 1999 for its failure to respond quickly to reports of more than 1,000 European consumers experiencing nausea after drinking its products. That led to Coca-Cola products being briefly banned in four nations. The company said the problem appeared to have been linked to a production problem at its Antwerp plant. However, it wasn't until two weeks after the first reports of children getting sick from drinking Coca-Cola products that the company apologized to consumers.

- The animal rights group People for the Ethical Treatment of Animals wanted to protest the dairy industry's production methods when it parodied the "Got Milk?" campaign by suggesting that college students should drink beer instead. An official of Mothers Against Drunk Driving said the advertising campaign was irresponsible. PETA's telephones and web site were also inundated by complaints.

Why did these organizations get black eyes? Because their actions—real or perceived—didn't live up to their stated values. Such incidents always leave a stronger impression than the inspirational words of a mission statement.

Values-Driven Public Relations

How can organizations try to ensure that their actions match their words? We advocate an approach we call **values-driven public relations.** Values-driven public relations incorporates a dynamic version of the four-phase process of research, planning, communication, and evaluation into the framework defined by an organization's core values (Figure 1.3). We offer an alternate definition of public relations: *Public relations is the values-driven management of relationships between an organization and the publics that can affect its success.*

Values-driven public relations is the process of uncovering not just where an organization wishes to go but also the principles the organization will observe in getting there. The process begins with the consideration of values during the research phase—those of the organization and the various publics important to its success. Those values,

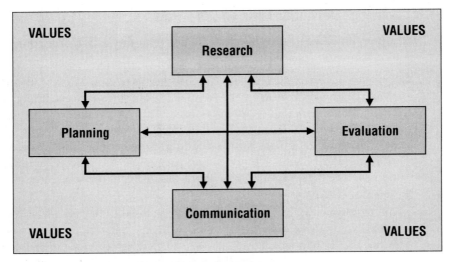

FIGURE 1.3   Values-Driven Public Relations

in turn, are incorporated into planning and communications. Values-driven public relations also means being accountable for adherence to those values when we evaluate our actions.

If that sounds easy, it isn't. We live in an increasingly diverse and complex world. New technology and the forces of globalization bring different interests into greater contact—and often into conflict. This reality was driven home by the violent protests that accompanied the World Trade Organization meeting in Seattle, Washington, in November 1999. Thousands of protesters concerned about the negative effects of globalization took to the streets. They briefly interrupted the WTO meeting by locking arms and blocking access to the meeting site. What followed were curfews, violent clashes with police, and the looting of downtown businesses. If anything, the events in Seattle were the antithesis of values-driven public relations: Everyone was yelling, but no one was listening.

Actions Speak Louder Than Words—Part II

At the same time, a variety of publics are holding public and private organizations more socially accountable. No longer is the bottom line seen as the only thing that matters. Although social responsibility may seem idealistic to some, its applications are very real-world:

■ In 1996, *Business Ethics* magazine cited the St. Paul Companies as one of the nation's 100 most-profitable, public, and socially responsible companies. The

Minneapolis-based insurance company won praise for its support of downtown revitalization. When asked how his company could justify to shareholders a $2.5 million contribution to a new museum, CEO Douglas Leatherdale said, "I have three thousand people whom I ask to come downtown to work every day, and I have a responsibility to provide for them a clean, safe, and thriving environment in which to come to work."[30]

■ Another company on *Business Ethics'* list was the Adolph Coors Company, which had been the target of union and employee rights problems in the 1970s and 1980s. But the editors noted that the company's recent history has been one of employee diversity and social responsibility. "We are a different company today than we used to be," said Peter Coors, the company's vice chairman and CEO, as well as the founder's great-grandson.[31]

■ On September 2, 1998, Swissair Flight 111 crashed off the Nova Scotia coast, killing all 229 people aboard. Within minutes, e-mail messages began to pour in from frantic relatives and friends who thought they had loved ones aboard the flight. Swissair officials strove to respond to each e-mail within three minutes. Swissair received high marks for its sensitivity in dealing with victims' families.[32]

Whose Values Should You Follow?

In the research phase of the public relations process, an organization must, of course, identify and consider its own values—but it must also do more: It must identify the values of involved publics and, perhaps, the values of society itself. Sometimes it can be difficult to decide which values to follow. If there is conflict between organizational and societal values, organizations must make a difficult choice.

This does not imply that one must always adhere to society's values. For example, there was a time in the United States when society condoned slavery, denied women the right to vote, and allowed children to work long hours in unhealthy conditions. An organization may choose to swim against the tide of public opinion. If it chooses to do so, however, it should do so by choice, not chance. Values-driven public relations can be a catalyst for making this crucial decision.

Values-driven public relations is similar to the traditional four-step approach to public relations but it has significant differences. In values-driven public relations the role of organizational, public, and societal values is explicit, rather than implicit. Values-driven public relations also employs a decidedly nonlinear process, in which there are constant checkbacks on values, research, strategies, and execution. Most important, the practice of values-driven public relations answers the most ardent critics of public relations by placing ethical decision making first.

Let's close by returning again to that opening scenario in which you're vice president for public relations at a manufacturing company. Faced with several public relations challenges and opportunities, the president has just asked, "What do you think we should do?"

QuickBreak 1.3

HOW ORGANIZATIONS ESTABLISH THEIR VALUES

J.C. Penney has *The Penney Idea,* a group of seven governing values written in 1913. One of the values is "To test our every policy, method, and act in this wise: Does it square with what is right and just?"

Hallmark Cards has *This Is Hallmark,* a statement of "Beliefs and Values." One of the statement's five "Beliefs" declares, "We believe that distinguished financial performance is a must, not as an end in itself, but as a means to accomplish our broader mission." One of the statement's four "Values" is "ethical and moral conduct at all times and in all our relationships."

Johnson & Johnson is governed by the one-page *Johnson & Johnson Credo,* which begins, "We believe our first responsibility is to the doctors, nurses, and patients, to the mothers and fathers, and all others who use our products and services."

How did these respected, successful organizations—and others like them—develop their written statements of values? Each organization has its own system, but two ingredients seem common to the values identification process. First, it's a job for a dedicated committee, not an individual. Debating with others helps us clarify what we truly believe. Second, a statement of values must be written, must be well known, and must play an active part in an organization's everyday operations. Only in that way can it be tested and improved.

If an organization lacks a written statement of values, its public relations program is a ship without a rudder. An organization can begin to develop a **values statement** by forming a committee or committees to answer these questions:

1. Why are we in business?

2. What does our organization want to be known for—both today and a generation from now?

3. What should our publics expect from us?

4. What are our highest priorities?

5. Where do we want to go, and whom do we want along for the ride?

Part of your answer, as noted above, is "research." And to that one word, you'll add a key request: "And may I please have a copy of the company's values statement?" Welcome to values-driven public relations.

Quick ✔ Check

1. How do you define *values-driven public relations,* and how does it differ from the traditional definition of public relations?
2. In values-driven public relations, whose values should we follow?
3. What are some examples of public relations decisions in which values played a key role?

6. What should our role be in our community and in our industry?

7. Whose organization is this?

8. To whom do we have obligations?

9. Why should someone want to work for this organization?

The answers to these questions should be used to create a short statement of the organization's core values. Stating each value as a principle can help you move from a values statement to a **mission statement;** in other words, stating each value as a principle can help you move from an idea to a proposed action. For example, J.C. Penney values justice in all its actions. In *The Penney Idea,* that value is stated as a principle: "To test our every policy, method, and act in this wise: Does it square with what is right and just?"

Let's look for a moment at the first question: "Why are we in business?" The obvious answer for many organizations might seem to be "to make money." But it's not money that people crave as much as it is what money can provide:

a nice home, food, education, the ability to help others. Hallmark's statement of beliefs and values notes that money is not an end; rather, it's a means toward accomplishing Hallmark's broader mission.

The *Johnson & Johnson Credo* has served that company particularly well. The company won praise from customers, politicians, journalists, and other key publics for its immediate willingness to put the safety of its customers ahead of company profits during two product-tampering incidents in the 1980s. By adhering to its *Credo,* Johnson & Johnson emerged as one of the most respected companies in the world.

Like many strong, values-driven organizations, Johnson & Johnson periodically evaluates its *Credo* in the context of current business situations. In a values-driven organization, a statement of values or a mission statement should be as much a part of the everyday environment as coffee, meetings, and lunch plans.

Summary

Public relations is a very important but often misunderstood profession. Even those who practice it have difficulty in developing a definition for public relations with which everyone can agree. Despite differences in wording, proper definitions of public relations contain five basic elements: Public relations is a management function, involves two-way communication, is a planned activity, is a social science based on research, and is socially responsible. There is also broad agreement that relationship building is at the heart of good public relations. That requires consideration of values—those of both the organization and the publics important to its success.

The manner in which public relations is practiced depends largely on the structure of the organization it serves. Although public relations should be a major concern of management, some organizations relegate its practitioners to the role of technicians. Some view public relations as an element of integrated marketing communications. However, others—including the authors of this book—view it as a separate and distinct discipline.

The traditional view of public relations is that it is performed through a four-step process: research, planning, communication, and evaluation. The problem with that view is that it implies a linear, or sequential, approach. Although the traditional process forms a foundation, public relations is a dynamic process in which any of these four phases can occur at any time. When practitioners conduct this process while closely adhering to values—those of the practitioner, the organization, and the society—the process evolves into what is known as values-driven public relations: the values-driven management of relationships between an organization and the publics that can affect its success.

DISCUSSION QUESTIONS

1. Before you read this chapter, how would you have defined *public relations*?
2. Why, in your opinion, is there so much disagreement over a standard definition of public relations?
3. In your opinion, should some form of licensing be mandatory for public relations practitioners?
4. What role does relationship management play in public relations?
5. How would you describe values-driven public relations to a friend who was curious but knew very little about public relations?

Memo
from the
Field

Joann E. Killeen, APR,
Fellow PRSA,
President, Killeen
Communications,
Los Angeles

Joann E. Killeen, APR, Fellow PRSA, is one of the industry's youngest Fellows, a distinction held by just under 400 public relations practitioners in the Public Relations Society of America. Killeen, president of Killeen Communications in Los Angeles, writes and lectures on strategic planning, technology, investor relations, public relations, issues and crisis management, as well as marketing for small businesses. Elected to serve as the 2002 Chief Executive Officer and Chairman, Board of Directors, of the Public Relations Society of America, Killeen is the first Public Relations Student Society of America member to rise through the volunteer ranks and become chairman. Killeen was a PRSSA member in the early 1970s while earning her degree in journalism from California State University at Northridge. She also holds a master's degree in communications management from Simmons College in Boston.

Thirty years ago when I began to study for my undergraduate degree in journalism, public relations was just a two-course elective. The course work at the time focused primarily on media relations and a few communication theories. Today the world of public relations is rich and robust with numerous colleges and universities offering both undergraduate and graduate degrees in the field. Business leaders today not only understand the value of public relations but also insist that a chief public relations officer sit at the management table. In this relatively short time span the world has become receptive to this important business discipline—the role of public relations.

While the career path I have chosen has been dynamic and personally rewarding, there are tips I have wished someone had shared with me at graduation time that would have made a difference for me earlier in my career.

The Top Ten Things I Wished I Knew When I Graduated from College

1. Learn the language of business.   Business leaders are looking for communicators who know not only the world of words but also the world of numbers. If you can't understand and interpret a company's financial statements for communications purposes, re-enroll in classes and learn. Without this valuable skill set, you'll never be viewed as a key player on the company's executive team.

2. Learn conflict resolution skills and be willing to negotiate.   The majority of public relations practitioners are always ready to say YES before they understand what they are agreeing to do. Most will say yes for fear of not being accepted. Always learn to listen to both sides of an issue and make sure you are confident that you have studied the entire situation before passing judgment or blame.

3. Learn a foreign language.   Learn another language so you can appreciate the beauty of the English language. I studied Spanish for four years and thought I would never have an opportunity to speak it again. Now that I run businesses in Southern California, I find that I use Spanish every day and wish I had kept up with the language while I lived in Boston.

4. Travel outside the United States.   Truly the only way to appreciate the United States for what it is and what it has to offer its citizens and visitors is to travel the world. Learn the differences and learn what makes us all one giant universe of mankind.

5. Learn to write clearly and precisely.   Clear, simple and precise. If you don't like to write and are not willing to take additional course work and constructive criticism, change majors. Someone who has an endless supply of red pens, pencils or markers will eventually edit everything that is written in the English language and sees the light of day. It's a fact of life in the communications business. No one's sentence escapes the wrath of a good copy editor who knows the language.

6. Be willing to try, and be willing to fail.   Rather than hide or say that you can't do something, jump in and do just the opposite of what you wanted to do in the first place. The only way to grow is to move to your fears and conquer them. If you are afraid, then you are facing a challenge. Just do it. You'll find the answer you are looking for soon enough.

7. Learn the value of contacts, and network, network, network. Always make every single interaction with another human being count. For today's struggling new college grad could tomorrow be the man or woman who is running a Fortune 100 company when you need a job. Always take the time to talk to someone whether you are looking for a job or are interested in hiring someone. Remember, no one starts at the top. Be willing to put in your time and learn everything that you can along the way. Mentoring is a lost art.

8. Make the commitment to lifelong learning. Just because you graduated and took your last final, don't think that you are finished with education. Keep the mind busy and challenge yourself with new ideas. Reading a new magazine each month or trying out something new may lead to a whole new way of life for you. Boredom is no excuse for a PR professional. Read, read, and read.

9. Maintain a healthy balance between lives, work, family and personal time. Never let your job become the entire focus of your life. While it is tempting to make that first and right impression by spending excessive time at the office, all work makes one very unhappy and the stress can lead to serious illness.

10. Maintain a sense of humor. Nothing in this life is worth worrying about. Just worry about the things that you can control and let the rest go. Public relations can be a stressful business, but with the careful management of your personal time and energy you can maintain a sense of humor. Remember to laugh a lot every day for it helps rid the body of stress and can make a difference in your life and those who choose to be around you.

Case Study 1.1

Making New Friends at Coors

It is amazing how time—and the use of values-driven public relations—can heal old wounds.

The Coors Brewing Company, a subsidiary of Adolph Coors Company, has become a model for corporate support of diversity. *Fortune, Latina Style,* and *Business Ethics* magazines have cited Coors as one of the nation's best companies for minority employees. The National Association for Advancement of Colored People, the National Association of Women Business Owners, and the Anti-Defamation League have also recognized the Golden, Colorado-based brewer for its efforts to reach out to people of all colors, creeds, and abilities. This is an impressive turnabout for a company that only a few years earlier had been seen as out-of-touch, out-of-step, and in danger of falling victim to legal challenges and declining market share.

The turnaround in Coors' image began in the 1980s as it was forced to address changes in society and the beer industry. The company had been the target of a union-led boycott stemming from charges that the company's employment practices discriminated against Hispanic, black, and female applicants. To remain competitive in a changing beer industry, Coors was also forced to transform its product from a regional label to a nationally distributed brand.

Perhaps the most dramatic change in the corporate culture came about through a restructuring of management. Since its founding a century earlier, the Coors Brewing Company had been strictly a family-run business. And the Coors prominently supported conservative causes—some of which were unpopular among many of the company's targeted consumers. In an effort to lessen the impact of inheritance taxes, the company went public and, in turn, added the voices of outside shareholders to its decision-making processes. And although the company still remained under the control of the Coors family, the reins of power were turned over to a younger generation.[33] The company began to reassess its values, asking (as we state previously in this chapter), "Where do we want to go, and whom do we want along for the ride?"

The first major changes occurred when Coors settled longstanding disputes with important publics. The company entered into economic development agreements in 1984 with Hispanic and black groups, which have resulted in more than $1 billion in investment and employment initiatives. The company took steps to attract and retain female employees, especially in management and nontraditional occupations. Coors also became the first Fortune 500 company to revise its affirmative action policy to include sexual orientation.[34]

From 1995 to 1997, Coors undertook a program to provide diversity training for each of its more than 5,000 employees.[35] But the company has done more than that: Coors has created eight employee diversity councils that, together, constitute its Diversity Advisory Action Group. The councils identify and advise company management on diversity issues and sponsor educational programs not only for company employees but for society as well. The eight diversity councils are the Coors African American Association, the Coors Hispanic Employee Network, the Native North American Indian Council, Lesbian and Gay Employee Resource, Silent Coors (for individuals who are hearing impaired), Women at Coors, Coors Asian Network, and Coors Veterans Group.

An example of Coors' diversity commitment was a national American Indian Powwow in Golden, sponsored by the Native North American Indian Council, in 1998. "Tribal nations from across the United States were represented, along with examples of Native American handcrafted items from various regions," said Jeanne Donovan, chairwoman of the council. The event, Donovan said, "was a wonderful opportunity to learn more about Native American heritage."[36]

Today, members of minority groups work at the highest levels of the nation's third-largest brewer. Hugo Patino, Coors' vice president of research and development, oversees all the company's brewmasters and, ultimately, the taste of its products. Patino was born in Monterrey, Mexico, and became a U.S. citizen in 1998. The son and grandson of brewers in Mexico, Patino has become a fixture in Coors commercials that target Hispanic consumers.

"It was an honor and a joy to do those ads," Patino said. "Innovation and diversity are key business philosophies at Coors. As a Hispanic who understands the culture, and as a brewer who understands beers, it is a distinct cultural and business honor to be the Coors voice to Hispanic consumers."[37]

DISCUSSION QUESTIONS

1. Why did the Coors Brewing Company decide to embrace diversity?
2. Does the fact that increased revenues are linked to diversity efforts undermine the sincerity of those efforts?
3. In working to promote the interests of so many diverse special interest groups, does Coors risk diluting its efforts? Why or why not?
4. Why should companies such as Coors actively support diversity in the workplace? What does a company gain?
5. The first sentence of this case study cites Coors' efforts as an example of values-driven public relations. Do you agree or disagree with this statement? Why?

Case Study 1.2

The Harsh Lessons of History

It is often said that those who fail to learn from history are doomed to repeat it. For evidence to support this statement, look no farther than Bridgestone/Firestone, Inc.

The tire company announced in August 2000 the recall of 6.5 million Firestone-brand ATX, ATXII, and Wilderness tires used on some popular sport utility vehicles. This followed widespread reports of tread separation at high temperatures. The National Highway Traffic Safety Administration reported in February 2001 that 174 fatalities had been linked to these tire failure.[38]

By May 2001, the Ford Motor Company, maker of the popular Explorer, announced it would replace all 13 million Firestone tires on its vehicles in what it called a "precautionary" move. Ford President and Chief Executive Officer Jacques Nasser said, "There are early warning signs about these tires, and we will not ignore them."[39] This move came one day after Bridgestone/Firestone announced it was severing its nearly 100-year business relationship with Ford.

Ford had raised concerns about the safety of the Firestone tires at least two years earlier. The NHTSA had received its first complaints about the tires as early as 1992. In 1999, Ford began voluntarily replacing Firestone tires on thousands of its sport utility vehicles in Saudi Arabia, Venezuela, Thailand, and Malaysia.[40]

From the very beginning of the controversy, Bridgestone/Firestone officials maintained that their tires were safe. They said that no evidence existed to suggest that properly maintained and inflated tires would come apart at high speed in hot weather. The officials blamed consumers, automakers, and even some of their own employees. Not until several national retailers removed the tires from their shelves and Ford had launched its own investigation did Bridgestone/Firestone Executive Vice President Gary Crigger go before reporters to announce the recall and say, "Nothing is more important to us than the safety of our consumers."[41]

Unfortunately, this is not the first time that the Firestone name has been linked to deadly tire-safety issues. In the late 1970s and early 1980s, Firestone endured a similar controversy involving the Firestone 500 tire, which had been one of the most popular brands of its day. But within one year of the start of production, Firestone engineers acknowledged in an internal memorandum that "we are making an inferior quality radial tire, which will be subject to belt-edge separation at high mileage."[42] Instead of dealing with the problem, Firestone engaged in a cover-up by blaming consumers, suing to keep NHTSA from publishing critical research, and even lying to Congress.

Eventually, the company was forced to undertake the largest tire recall in U.S. history, costing $140 million. It also faced more than $2 billion in damage claims from the families of 41 people allegedly killed by the faulty tires. Firestone had to close seven of its North American plants and sell many of its assets to deal with the lawsuits and declining sales. Ironically, Firestone's weakened financial condition helped Bridgestone acquire the company in 1988.

Although we must wait for definitive word on the safety of the tires, the verdict is in on Bridgestone/Firestone's public relations performance. Its public relations agency, Fleishman-Hillard, dropped the $2.5-million-a-month account in September 2000. Critics suggested that this was because of the tire maker's slow response to the crisis and its unwillingness to follow the agency's advice. Although Bridgestone/Firestone has since hired a new agency, some question whether it can salvage the reputation of the company.[43]

Perhaps it is unfair to compare the Firestone 500 turmoil of the late 1970s and the ATX and Wilderness tire controversy of the early 2000s. Those were different times, and it was a different company. However, as long as the new company continues to carry the name of the old company, Bridgestone/Firestone executives have a responsibility to learn from their own corporate history.

DISCUSSION QUESTIONS

1. Is it fair to criticize Bridgestone/Firestone's public relations actions even while the safety of its tires is still under investigation?
2. What might you have done differently in response to the reports of tire failures?
3. What should you do if officials at another company blame your company for product or service failures?
4. Is it fair for the authors to link this problem to one that happened nearly a quarter-century earlier?
5. Bridgestone/Firestone's public relations agency dropped the account at the height of the controversy over the company's tires. Later, the tire maker ended its business relations with Ford. What do you think are appropriate reasons for severing a relationship with a client or customer?

It's Your Turn

The Question

"What am I going to do after I graduate from college?" It's an important question that you (and every other college student) must ponder. And it is a decision in which a lot of people have taken interest: your parents, your friends, your spouse (if you are married), your significant other (if you are not), and even the loan officer at the bank that may have lent you the money to pay for your education.

The fact that you are reading this textbook means that you may be considering a career in public relations. Sure, this course may only be an elective, and your parents may have a billion dollars set aside in a trust fund for you. But, just for argument's sake, let's pretend you are thinking about a career in public relations. Regardless of whether you are a traditional college student, right out of high school, or a nontraditional student who has come back to the classroom after an absence, someone is going to ask you The Question: "So, what are you going to do after you graduate?"

"I am going to be a public relations practitioner," you say proudly.

"I can't believe my ears," says your puzzled questioner. "You want to be a spin doctor? A mouthpiece? A flack? Why on earth would you want to do that?"

Try responding to your hypothetical questioner by

- explaining what, exactly, public relations is;
- discussing why public relations practitioners can be something other than just spin doctors, mouthpieces, and flacks;
- telling of the variety of workplaces in which public relations is practiced; and
- describing the importance of public relations to the healthy functioning of democratic societies.

KEY TERMS

Accredited Business Communicator (ABC),
    p. 12
advertising, p. 10
Accredited in Public Relations (APR), p. 12
communication, p. 14
evaluation, p. 15
International Association of Business
    Communicators (IABC), p. 12
integrated marketing communications
    (IMC), p. 10
marketing, p. 10
mission statement, p. 21
planning, p. 14

press agentry/publicity model, p. 9
public, p. 7
public information model, p. 9
public relations, p. 10
Public Relations Society of America
    (PRSA), p. 6
relationship management, p. 7
research, p. 14
stakeholder, p. 7
two-way asymmetrical model, p. 9
two-way symmetrical model, p. 9
values-driven public relations, p. 17
values statement, p. 20

NOTES

1. Julie K. Henderson, "Negative Connotations in the Use of the Term 'Public Relations' in the Print Media," *Public Relations Review* (spring 1998): 45–54.

2. Alison Stateman, Jeff Reese and John Elsasser, "The Top PR Stories of 2000," *Public Relations Tactics* (January 2001): 19.

3. Dennis John Gaschen, "California Adventure Dreamin'," *Public Relations Tactics* (February 2001): 10.

4. Chris Cobb, "Heartbreak 'Ridge': How Public Relations Helped Save a Mining Town," *Public Relations Tactics* (February 2001): 11.

5. Eric Denig, ed., *A Geography of Public Relations Trends: Selected Proceedings of the 10th Public Relations World Congress* (Dordrecht, the Netherlands: Martinus Nijhoff, 1985), 244–249.

6. David W. Guth, "Crises and the Practitioner: Organizational Crisis Experience As It Relates to the Placement of the Public Relations Function" (master's thesis, University of North Carolina–Chapel Hill, 1990).

7. Rex F. Harlow, "Building a Public Relations Definition," *Public Relations Review* (winter 1976): 36.

8. "Official Statement on Public Relations" adopted by the Public Relations Society of America Assembly, 6 November 1982.

9. James E. Grunig, ed., *Excellence in Public Relations and Communication Management* (Hillsdale, N.J.: Lawrence Erlbaum, 1992), 1–30.

10. *Declaration of Independence* (Washington, D.C.: Commission on the Bicentennial of the United States Constitution).

11. Herb Schmertz with William Novak, *Good-Bye to the Low Profile: The Art of Creative Confrontation* (Boston: Little, Brown, 1986), 5.

12. "Survey Confirms Practitioner/Management Goal Conflicts," *Public Relations Journal* (February 1989): 9.

13. Todd Hunt and James E. Grunig, *Public Relations Techniques* (Fort Worth, Texas: Harcourt Brace College, 1994), 8–9.

14. James Grunig and Larissa Grunig, "Models of Public Relations and Communications," in *Excellence in Public Relations and Communication Management*, ed. James F. Grunig. (Hillsdale, N.J.: Lawrence Erlbaum, 1992), 304.

15. Hunt and Grunig.

16. Grunig and Grunig.

17. Hunt and Grunig.

18. Grunig and Grunig.

19. Hunt and Grunig.

20. Grunig and Grunig.

21. David W. Guth, "The Relationship between Organizational Crisis Experience and Public Relations Roles," *Public Relations Review* (summer 1995): 123–136.

22. Michael Ryan, "Organizational Constraints on Corporate Public Relations Practitioners," *Journalism Quarterly* (summer–autumn 1987): 473–482.

23. Les Krantz, *1995 Jobs Rated Almanac,* as cited by *USA Weekend,* 2–4 February 1996, 5.

24. 1999 National Occupational Employment and Wage Estimates, U.S. Bureau of Labor Statistics, online, http://stats.bls.gov.

25. *2000–01 Occupational Outlook Handbook,* U.S. Department of Labor, Bureau of Labor Statistics, online, http://stats.bls.gov.

26. Richard Alan Nelson, "The Professional Dilemma," *PR Update* (November 1994): 1.

27. Glen T. Cameron, Lynne M. Sallot, and Ruth Ann Weaver Lariscy, "Developing Standards of Professional Performance in Public Relations," *Public Relations Review* (spring 1996): 43–61.

28. "PRSA Statistical Information," Public Relations Society of America, online, May 1998, www.prsa.org.

29. "Gossip Columnists Trash Celeb PR Pros as Useless," *O'Dwyer's PR Services Report,* 25 October 2000, 1.

30. "The Best Corporate Citizens: Is Your Company on Our List of the Nation's 100 Most Profitable, Public and Socially Responsible Companies?" *Business Ethics* (May/June 1996), online, www.depaul.edu/ethics/biz15.html.

31. "The Best Corporate Citizens"

32. Sharon Machlis, "Web Aids Swissair Response," online, CNN, 15 September 1998, www.cnn.com.

33. Allen H. Center and Patrick Jackson, *Public Relations Practices: Managerial Case Studies and Problems,* 4th ed. (Englewood Cliffs, N.J.: Prentice Hall, 1990), 138–149.

34. Coors Brewing Company, online, www.coors.com.

35. Robert Schwab, "Some Firms Stick with Diversity," *Denver Post,* 31 August 1997, online, Lexis-Nexis.

36. "Native North American Indian Council to Hold Powwow," PR Newswire, 29 July 1998, online, Lexis-Nexis.

37. "Coors Introduces Hispanic Ad Campaign," PR Newswire, 21 March 1997, online, Lexis-Nexis.

38. National Highway Traffic Safety Administration Statement, online, 6 February 2001, www.nhtsa.dot.gov/hot/Firestone/Update.html.

39. "Ford Motor Company to Replace All 13 Million Firestone Wilderness AT Tires on Its Vehicles," online, news release issued by Ford Motor Company, 22 May 2001, http://media.ford.com/newsroom.

40. Ed Meyer, "Tire Concerns Are Years Old," *Akron Beacon Journal,* 22 August 2000, online, www.ohio.com/bj/news/2000/August/22/doc/024221.htm.

41. "Bridgestone Recalls Tires," online, CNN, 9 August 2000, www.cnn.com.

42. Dennis L. Wilcox, Phillip H. Ault and Warren K. Agee, *Public Relations: Strategies and Tactics* (New York: Harper and Row, 1986), 324.

43. Stateman, Reese and Elsasser, 16.

chapter two

Jobs in Public Relations

objectives

After studying this chapter, you will be able to

- name the basic areas of employment in public relations

- discuss specific jobs and related duties within public relations

- explain the differences between public relations managers and public relations technicians

- describe salaries and levels of job satisfaction within public relations

The Commute from New York

scenario

Let's again hop aboard that commuter train from The Man in the Gray Flannel Suit, *which we described at the beginning of Chapter 1. The executive portrayed by actor Gregory Peck has just confessed that he doesn't know anything about public relations. Imagine that you are sitting across the aisle from him. You now have the knowledge to tell him a lot about this mysterious profession.*

You could define it for him: Public relations is the values-driven management of relationships between an organization and the publics that can affect its success.

You could tell him that public relations ideally is a function of management and that it's a socially responsible activity based on research, planning, and two-way communication.

You could even tell him about the public relations process: research, planning, communication, and evaluation.

But what if he looks you in the eye and asks, "What are the jobs in that broad field? What would my duties be? How much money would I make?"

Let's reroll the film and help you prepare to answer his—and, perhaps, your own—questions.

Where the Jobs Are

In the above scenario, as you explained the profession of public relations to your fellow commuter, you might also remember to tell him something else you learned in Chapter 1: Broadly speaking, jobs in public relations exist in five different employment settings:

- corporations;
- nonprofit organizations and trade associations;
- governments;
- public relations agencies; and
- independent public relations consulting.

Each of these five areas contains a variety of sometimes startlingly different public relations jobs. Ideally, however, each job helps an organization fulfill its values-driven mission and goals. To help you answer the question about jobs and job duties, let's start by examining the different jobs within these five categories.

Corporations

You could tell your fellow commuter that not only do corporations offer most of the jobs in public relations, but they also offer the greatest variety of jobs. Corporations are organizations that produce goods or services for a profit. They include manufacturers such as Ben & Jerry's ice cream, for-profit health-care providers such as Humana, retailers such as The Gap, sports organizations such as the World Wrestling Federation, and a host of other for-profit organizations.

In most corporations, public relations jobs focus on specific publics. Corporate public relations practitioners often specialize in one of the following: employee relations, media relations, government relations, community relations, or consumer relations (or marketing communications). If the corporation is publicly owned—that is, if it sells stock—some practitioners specialize in investor relations. In each of these areas, ideally,

Press Box   An important tactic in sports public relations is operating a press box for visiting media, such as those attending this Major League Soccer match. (Courtesy of David Guth)

practitioners conduct research; advise the organization's top management; and plan, execute, and evaluate relationship-management programs. Although we certainly don't want to downplay the importance of research and counseling, the reality is that most young practitioners begin their careers by creating communications such as newsletter stories and web sites. Therefore, let's look at some of the traditional entry-level tasks.

■ **Employee relations:** Communication tasks in employee relations can include production of newsletters and magazines, video programs, web sites, and special events.

■ **Media relations:** Communication tasks can include production of news releases and media kits (see Chapter 9) and presentation of news conferences. More advanced communication tasks can include speechwriting and preparing scripts for video news releases. Media-related counseling duties can include preparing executives for interviews.

■ **Government relations** (sometimes known as *public affairs*): Communication tasks can include producing brochures, reports, and videos for lobbies and political action committees (see Chapter 9). Advanced duties can include testifying before government fact-finding commissions, monitoring the activities of government units at all levels, and preparing reports.

■ **Community relations:** Communication tasks can include maintaining contact with local special-interest groups such as environmental organizations. New practitioners also often help coordinate special events such as tours of their organization's facilities. Upper-level duties can include overseeing a corporation's charitable contributions, organizing employee volunteer efforts, and lending support to special events such as blood drives and United Way fund-raising campaigns.

■ **Consumer relations,** also known as *marketing communications:* Communication tasks usually focus on product publicity. Such duties can include preparing news releases and media kits, implementing direct-mail campaigns, organizing special

---

Central Intelligence Agency   contact us   notices   search   site map   index

Director of Central Intelligence   CIA Home Page

PRESS RELEASES AND STATEMENTS

FOR IMMEDIATE RELEASE
19 September 2001

CIA *World Factbook 2001* Now Available

The World Factbook 2001 is now available on the Central Intelligence Agency Web site (http://www.cia.gov). *The World Factbook* remains the CIA's most popular and most widely disseminated product. In addition, thousands of commercial, academic, and other Web sites link to or replicate the Web version of the Factbook.

This reference work provides a snapshot, as of January 1, 2001, of wide-ranging, hard-to-locate information about geography, people, governments, economies, communications, and armed forces for countries from Afghanistan to Zimbabwe. The nine primary information categories and 100 subcategories for most entities include geographic coordinates, Gross Domestic Product, number of telephones, natural resources, legal systems, political parties, illicit drugs, mortality rates, and more. Included among the 267 geographic listings is one for the "World," which incorporates data and other information summarized where possible from the other 266 listings.

News Release An important part of public relations involves delivering stories to the news media through news releases. Many organizations, including the Central Intelligence Agency, post their news releases on their web sites. (Courtesy of the Central Intelligence Agency)

"A new light on business communications."

advise   instruct
educate
enlighten
awareness   knowledge
guide
teach
lead
inform
nurture
cultivate

IN THIS ISSUE ...

Houseclean your brand

Leaders cultivate leaders

CowParade

Reputation and relationship

Is it time to "de-focus" your customers?

During the past two decades, focus groups have become a mainstay in the marketing and advertising research mix. And with current market trends swinging toward Customer Relationship Management (CRM), focus groups seem like the perfect vehicle to find out what customers really want.

Not so, according to B. Joseph Pine II and James H. Gilmore in a recent issue of *Context* magazine. "Guidance from a focus group can be downright dangerous ... simply confirming to companies that what they are doing is right and discouraging them from striking off in a new direction," say the authors. But as any good marketer knows, customer research is imperative to gaining mindshare and marketshare. So here are three suggestions from Pine and Gilmore to get more bang out of customer opinion:

Search for Uniqueness: *"Design your offerings to eliminate the sacrifice each customer encounters."* The major premise of using focus groups is to find the commonality between customers. But Pine and Gilmore suggest creating a "de-focus" group to find what individual preferences your

> **Because innovation is more important than ever in today's economy, "guidance from a focus group can be downright dangerous."**

customers sacrifice when they use your products. Then create products and services that are truly customer intimate.

Observe Your Customer in Action: *"It is the using of the goods or service that defines the customer experience."* Focus groups concentrate on talking about products or services. But to get a real understanding of your customers' opinions, observe how they interact with your product or service and how they use it in their business or personal life.

Research Every Day: *"Engage individual customers every day in live, continuous, point-of-interaction research."* Ask your customers' preferences as they are using and/or buying your products and/or services and then create an innovative way to track and implement those suggestions.

Abandoning focus groups completely might be a drastic move, but personalized customer comments may become far more valuable to CRM-driven corporations. By listening to individual voices rather than group-thinking, your company will stay ahead of the solution economy trend.

Luminary is published by Morningstar Communications Company, providing marketing and brand-building counsel to help leading companies grow. Comments and questions are always welcome at counsel@morningstarcomm.com. If you would like a digital version, please contact us or sign up on our Web site.

Morningstar Communications would like your opinion ...
Are you implementing personalized customer research? What do you think of the concept of "de-focus" groups? Log on to our Web site and let us know–www.morningstarcomm.com.

Summer 2001

MORNINGSTAR
COMMUNICATIONS COMPANY

Newsletters Morningstar Communications of Kansas City uses *Luminary* newsletter to educate current customers and attract new ones. (Courtesy of Morningstar Communications Company)

promotional events, enlisting and training celebrity spokespeople, and coordinating communication efforts with advertising campaigns.

■ **Investor relations:** Communication activities that target investors and investment analysts can include producing newsletters and other forms of correspondence directed at stockholders, producing an annual financial report to stockholders, planning and conducting an annual meeting for stockholders, maintaining a flow of information to investment analysts, and other activities designed to inform investors about a corporation's financial health and business goals. Investor relations practitioners often oversee the legally required disclosure of financial information to stockholders and to the government.

Other key publics can be the basis for additional corporate public relations jobs and activities. Such publics can include

■ vendors, which are the organizations that supply your corporation with needed materials;

■ professional organizations and trade associations; and

■ retired employees.

Nonprofit Organizations and Trade Associations

Let's now tell your fellow commuter about public relations jobs in nonprofit organizations and trade associations. And, once again, let's focus primarily on entry-level communication tasks rather than on research and counseling. Nonprofit organizations can include universities, hospitals, churches, foundations, and other groups that provide a service without the expectation of earning a profit. Some nonprofit organizations, of course, are local. Others, such as the United Way, are nationally known. Still others, such as the Red Cross and Amnesty International, have international duties and reputations.

Public relations duties within a nonprofit organization often are similar to public relations duties within a corporation. Well-run nonprofit organizations have practitioners in employee relations, media relations, government relations, community relations, and sometimes marketing communications. However, because nonprofit organizations have no stockholders, they don't engage in investor relations activities. Instead, they have donor relations; fund-raising; and, if appropriate, member relations.

Communication tasks in donor relations, fund-raising, and member relations can include producing newsletters, videos, and web sites; writing direct-mail solicitations; and organizing special events.

Trade associations are often grouped with nonprofit organizations because, like those organizations, they offer services without the primary motive of earning a profit. Trade associations include such groups as the American Library Association and the International Guild of Professional Butlers. Trade associations offer their members benefits that can include insurance programs, continuing education, networking, and

Values Statement 2.1

PUBLIC RELATIONS SOCIETY OF AMERICA

PRSA is the world's largest organization for public relations professionals. Its nearly 20,000 members, organized worldwide in more than 100 chapters, represent business and industry, technology, counseling firms, government, associations, hospitals, schools, professional services firms, and nonprofit organizations.

PRSA Member Statement of Professional Values

This statement presents the core values of PRSA members and, more broadly, of the public relations profession. These values provide the foundation for the *Member Code of Ethics* and set the industry standard for the professional practice of public relations. These values are the fundamental beliefs that guide our behaviors and decision-making process. We believe our professional values are vital to the integrity of the profession as a whole.

Advocacy

- We serve the public interest by acting as responsible advocates for those we represent.
- We provide a voice in the marketplace of ideas, facts, and viewpoints to aid informed public debate.

Honesty

- We adhere to the highest standards of accuracy and truth in advancing the interests of those we represent and in communicating with the public.

Expertise

- We acquire and responsibly use specialized knowledge and experience.

- We advance the profession through continued professional development, research, and education.
- We build mutual understanding, credibility, and relationships among a wide array of institutions and audiences.

Independence

- We provide objective counsel to those we represent.
- We are accountable for our actions.

Loyalty

- We are faithful to those we represent, while honoring our obligation to serve the public interest.

Fairness

- We deal fairly with clients, employers, competitors, peers, vendors, the media, and the general public.
- We respect all opinions and support the right of free expression.

—From "PRSA Member Code of Ethics 2000," PRSA web site

a unified voice in efforts to influence legislative processes. Public relations jobs in trade associations include employee relations, media relations, government relations, and marketing communications. Communication tasks in member relations are often designed to educate and update members through newsletters and other publications, web sites, videos, and special events such as annual conventions. The American

QuickBreak 2.1

THE VALUES OF SUCCESSFUL EMPLOYERS

What do enduring, successful companies have in common? In the book *Built to Last: Successful Habits of Visionary Companies,* authors James Collins and Jerry Porras examine the workings of companies that have thrived despite occasional adversity and changing environments.[1] One foundation of such companies, the authors say, is a set of clear, strongly held, companywide core values:

> Core values [are] the organization's essential and enduring tenets—a small set of general guiding principles; not to be confused with specific cultural or operating practices; not to be compromised for financial gain or short-term expediency. . . .
>
> The crucial variable is not the content of a company's ideology, but how deeply it believes its ideology and how consistently it lives, breathes and expresses it in all that it does. Visionary companies do not ask, "What should we value?" They ask, "What do we actually value deep down to our toes?"

Built to Last examines the long-term success of 20 companies, including IBM, Johnson & Johnson, Motorola, Procter & Gamble, and Walt Disney. "Yes, they seek profits," say the authors, "but they're equally guided by a core ideology—core values and a sense of purpose beyond just making money."

As you consider a career in public relations and as you evaluate the different kinds of employers and job duties, be sure to study the values of those employers. Many organizations now list their values statements on their web sites. What, if anything, do those organizations say they value? Do their actions match their beliefs? Are their values so clear that they can guide public relations policies and actions? In the words of James Collins and Jerry Porras, will you select an employer that's built to last?

Medical Association, for example, offers its members the prestigious *Journal of the American Medical Association.* Another task in member relations involves recruiting new members through such actions as direct-mail campaigns.

Governments

Maybe your fellow commuter would be more interested in conducting public relations for the government. Tell him not to limit his search to the federal or central government of a nation: Jobs in public relations can also be found within state and local governments. Political parties and independent agencies created by the government, such as the U.S. Postal Service, also employ public relations practitioners.

Public relations jobs within government bodies generally focus on three key publics: voters, the news media, and employees.

Government public relations practitioners operate under a variety of job titles, including **press secretary, public information officer, public affairs officer,** and **communications specialist.** Entry-level communication duties can include writing news releases, responding to constituent concerns, and writing position papers that help politicians articulate their beliefs. Upper-level duties can include speaking with reporters, writing speeches for politicians, and briefing officials on public opinion.

At the federal level in the United States, the term *public relations,* with its connotation of persuasive communication, is rarely used. Public relations practitioners within the federal government prefer euphemisms such as *public information.* One reason for their skittishness is the Gillett amendment, passed by the United States Congress in 1913, which flatly declares, "Appropriated funds may not be used to pay a publicity expert unless specifically appropriated for that purpose." Similar restrictions can exist at state and local levels.

Voters in most countries clearly don't want their tax dollars used for campaigns to persuade them of the wisdom of governmental actions and policies. However, voters also insist that government officials communicate with citizens and respond to their needs and concerns. So public relations *does* exist at all levels of government—but rarely, if ever, is it called by that name.

Public Relations Agencies

Maybe a **public relations agency** is the place for your fellow commuter. Public relations agencies assist with the public relations activities of other organizations. Corporations, nonprofit organizations, trade associations, governments, and even individuals hire public relations agencies to help manage and execute various public relations functions. A corporation, for example, may have its own in-house public relations staff—but for its annual report to stockholders or for a complicated overseas venture, it may hire a public relations agency for research, planning, communication, and evaluation. As we'll discuss in Chapter 13, in the 1990s many public relations agencies merged with advertising agencies to provide a wide range of integrated, consumer-focused communications.

Practitioners in public relations agencies often are assigned to accounts. An account includes all the public relations activities planned and executed for one particular client. Individual accounts are managed by an **account executive** and, often, one or more assistant account executives. Also working on each account are writers, who often are called communications specialists; designers; production supervisors; researchers; and, increasingly, online specialists for web site design and maintenance. Workers within an account sometimes wear more than one hat; for example, a writer may also be a researcher. Additionally, practitioners often are assigned to more than one account.

Public relations agencies can range from small shops with only a handful of employees to divisions within advertising agencies to huge international operations such as Hill & Knowlton, Burson–Marsteller, Fleishman–Hillard, and Edelman Public Relations Worldwide.

Independent Public Relations Consultants

Maybe your fellow commuter would prefer to work for himself. An **independent public relations consultant** is, essentially, a one-person public relations agency.

When Interstate Brands Corporation—the baker of Hostess Twinkies snack cakes—learned that Lewis Browning had eaten a Twinkie a day since 1941 (20,000-plus Twinkies!), it turned his story into a news release that gained national attention and won a top award in a regional public relations competition. (Courtesy of Interstate Brands Corporation/Hostess Twinkies)

Organizations or individuals hire the consultant to assist with particular public relations functions. Generally, however, a public relations consultant offers a smaller range of services than an agency. Many consultants, in fact, specialize in a particular area of public relations, such as crisis communications, speechwriting, web site design, or training others in the basics of good public relations.

Some independent consultants, however, thrive as generalists. In the book *Real People Working in Communications,* author Jan Goldberg writes:

> Those who work as generalists in the field must be able to perform a wide array of duties at the same time. On any given week they may write press releases for one client, design a brochure for another, approach an editor for a third, meet with a talk show host for a fourth, implement a promotion for a fifth, set up a press conference for a sixth, put together a press kit for a seventh, work out the beginnings of a client contract for an eighth, and field media questions for a ninth![2]

Note that eighth duty well. Like public relations agencies, independent consultants often must seek new clients even as they conduct business for current clients. The major appeal of independent consulting is also its biggest burden: The consultant alone bears the responsibility for success or failure.

QuickBreak 2.2

GETTING THAT FIRST JOB OR INTERNSHIP

You may be reading this chapter and thinking, "Great. I'm beginning to understand where and what the jobs are. But how do I get one?" We'll examine your future in public relations more thoroughly in Chapter 16. But let's preview a few dos and don'ts about communicating with potential employers.

Do

- thoroughly research a potential employer before applying.

- send an error-free application letter and a flawless résumé. Three-quarters of personnel/human resources departments say they disregard job-application letters with grammatical errors or typos. Thirty-four percent say they prefer to receive e-mail applications.[3]

- prepare for a job interview by reviewing your research on the potential employer and preparing knowledgeable questions to ask.

Don't

- send a form letter asking for a job. Instead, include specific, organization-related information that shows why you want this particular job.

- ask about salary and benefits. Let the potential employer introduce that subject.

- forget to send a brief, typed thank-you letter after each interview.

Unpolished résumés and inadequate application letters can crush the dreams of eager job seekers. Managers at Robert Half International, a recruiting and job-placement company, collect and share real-world job-application blunders.[4] Among their favorites:

- "Very experienced with out-house computers."

- "If you hire me away from this nightmare, you'll save me thousands in therapy."

- "References: None. I've left a path of destruction behind me."

Your application letter and résumé should persuade an organization to interview you. Recently, the *Wall Street Journal* asked employers to list the worst job-interview fiascoes they had ever encountered.[5] Among the notable don'ts in this hall of shame were

- the candidate who assumed that a female manager was a secretary. He put his feet on her desk and said, "Get me a Coke"—which is no way to treat a secretary or anyone else.

- the candidate who, during a lunch interview, reached into his soup bowl and began pulling apart long strands of cheese.

Sometimes bad examples are the best examples. Before applying for a job in public relations, painstakingly proofread your application letter and résumé. Have others proofread them. Then proofread them again. And again. And stay away from those out-house computers.

![Quick Check]

1. What are the five broad areas of employment within public relations?
2. Which of those five areas offers the most jobs?
3. What is the Gillett amendment? How does it affect public relations within the U.S. federal government?

Public Relations Activities and Duties

You've conveyed all this information to your fellow commuter, and you've done a great job. But your success generates even more questions: Now he wants to know specifically what kinds of tasks he'll be performing at least five days a week for at least eight hours a day. You *could* sneak off the train at the next stop—but instead, let's humor him. As a public relations practitioner, how *would* he spend his days?

Since approximately 1970, public relations researchers have devoted a great deal of time to answering that question. Professor David Dozier, who has extensively studied the daily duties and tasks of public relations practitioners, groups public relations practitioners into two broad categories:

- **Public relations managers:** They solve problems, advise other managers, make policy decisions, and take responsibility for the success or failure of public relations programs. Public relations managers are most often found in organizations that operate in rapidly changing environments and in organizations that encourage employee input.

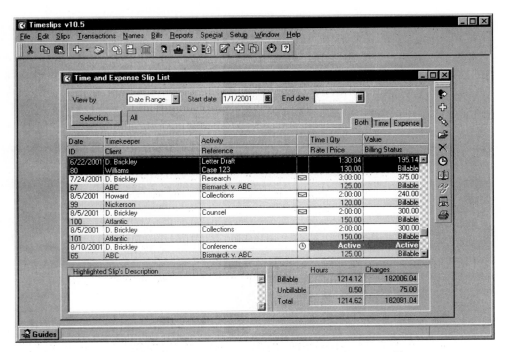

Time Sheet For billing purposes, public relations practitioners often record how they spend each working day. (Courtesy of Timeslips)

■ **Public relations technicians:** They rarely make key strategic decisions, and they rarely advise others within the organization. Instead, their primary role is to prepare communications that help execute the public relations policies created by others. They are more likely to be found in organizations in which the environment is stable and predictable.[6]

Based on a national survey of PRSA members, Table 2.1 shows that public relations managers and public relations technicians do indeed spend their working hours in different ways. The most time-consuming task for managers is planning public relations programs, which ranks 10th for public relations technicians. The most time-consuming task for public relations technicians is disseminating (or sending) messages, which ranks 13th for public relations managers. Table 2.1 also suggests that gender may affect how public relations practitioners spend their days.

TABLE 2.1 How Public Relations Practitioners Spend Their Time[7]

TASK	RANK FOR FEMALE TECHNICIANS	RANK FOR MALE TECHNICIANS	RANK FOR FEMALE MANAGERS	RANK FOR MALE MANAGERS
Disseminating messages	1	1	13	13
Writing, editing, producing messages	2	2	15	15
Implementing decisions made by others	3	6	17	17
Making media contacts	4	3	6	11
Implementing new programs	5	7	3	5
Correspondence/telephone calls	6	4	12	14
Implementing event planning/logistics	7	5	9	7
Managing public relations programs	8	8	2	2
Meeting with peers	9	11	16	16
Planning public relations programs	10	10	1	1
Making communication policy decisions	11	12	4	3
Evaluating program results	12	13	8	8
Conducting or analyzing research	13	15	14	12
Meeting with clients/executives	14	14	7	10
Planning and managing budgets	15	9	5	6
Counseling management	16	17	10	4
Supervising the work of others	17	16	11	9

As you might expect, oftentimes it's not a matter of being always a manager and never a technician, or vice versa. Several studies show that public relations practitioners can have jobs that combine both managerial and technical duties.[8]

Let's mention a final public relations task that's rarely mentioned in surveys of working professionals: recording how you spend your time. Public relations agencies generally bill clients by the hour, and in an agency your supervisors will want to know how you spend each 15-minute block of time. Many corporations, odd as it may seem, also chart time in this manner. For example, a corporation's public relations department may bill the corporation's college recruiting department for the preparation of brochures and videos. An important part of ensuring the financial success of your organization or your department may well be your scrupulously detailed record of how you've spent your working days.

QuickBreak 2.3

CHARACTERISTICS OF SUCCESSFUL PUBLIC RELATIONS CAREERS

A recent study by journalism professors Lynne Sallot, Glen Cameron, and Ruth Ann Weaver Lariscy surveyed public relations professionals throughout the United States to identify widely accepted standards for professional performance. The researchers' conclusion? Public relations professionals do agree on the characteristics of success—but they don't realize they agree. Professionals incorrectly believe that their colleagues don't share their vision of the qualities that constitute successful public relations.

Several characteristics did emerge as identifiers of success in public relations. In order of importance, those characteristics are

1. A public relations practitioner should help an organization respond to its constituents (e.g., employees and other publics).

2. A practitioner should have direct contact with the company president or CEO.

3. A practitioner should analyze a situation and its possible solutions when making a decision.

4. A public relations department/unit should strategically set goals and objectives before implementing a campaign (see Chapter 8).

5. A public relations practitioner has a responsibility to serve as a liaison between an organization and its publics.

That final characteristic suggests that public relations practitioners should understand and appreciate all sides of a relationship between their organization and a particular public. Practitioners call this function a **boundary role** because they operate on the boundary of their organization—the point where their organization comes into contact with important publics. In a boundary role, practitioners act for the good of the relationship because that relationship is vital to the success of the practitioner's organization. Fulfilling a boundary role sometimes means that practitioners must ask their own organization to change to benefit an important relationship.

Despite the encouraging conclusions of the survey just described, the researchers reported that the profession cannot yet clearly define the qualities of successful public relations: "Practitioners in the field seldom accurately perceive how their peers view professional standards."[9]

1. What specific job duties consume the most time in public relations?
2. How do the job duties of a public relations manager differ from those of a public relations technician?
3. Why do public relations practitioners record how they spend their working hours?

Salaries in Public Relations

Now that you can exhaustively tell your fellow commuter about how public relations professionals spend their days, you may want to anticipate his next question: "How much money will I earn?"

According to a University of Georgia study, the median starting public relations salary in 2000 for graduates of U.S. journalism and mass communications programs was $28,964. New public relations practitioners in the Northeast and West earned the highest starting salaries, and those in the South earned the lowest. Slightly more than 80 percent of those new practitioners received medical insurance as part of their salary and benefits package.[10]

In 2000, PRSA and IABC teamed up to administer one of the most extensive surveys of the public relations profession ever conducted. Among the survey's salary findings were:

- The average annual salary for practitioners worldwide is $69,000 in U.S. dollars. In the United States, the average annual salary is $72,000. In Canada, it is $46,000 in U.S. dollars. In other countries, annual salary averages $66,000 in U.S. dollars.

- The median starting salary for entry-level practitioners is $29,000. For low-level managers, it is $43,000; for mid-level managers, $60,000; and for senior managers, $85,000.

- The highest-paid practitioners are consultants, earning an average $160,000 a year. The next highest paid are public relations vice presidents, senior or executive vice presidents, or presidents/executive directors/CEOs, averaging between $130,000 and $160,000 a year.

- Corporations pay the highest annual salaries (median $70,000), followed by public relations agencies (median $52,000) and nonprofit organizations (median $40,000). The study announced no median salary for government practitioners.

- Annual salaries differ by gender, with men earning a median $65,000 and women earning a median $50,000. (Practitioners' length of service may affect this disparity, but gender discrimination remains a reality in many professions.)[11]

QuickBreak 2.4

THE PEOPLE IN PUBLIC RELATIONS

The PRSA/IABC year 2000 worldwide survey of practitioners offers a detailed description of the profession of public relations—including a snapshot of the average practitioner: "The typical respondent to the PRSA/IABC survey is female, 39, responsible for both internal and external communication programs; has been in the profession for 13 years; earns $69,000 annually plus a bonus of $10,000."

Highlights of the survey include the following:[12]

Employment

- On average, public relations practitioners have been with their organization for 6 years and in their current position for 3.5 years. The average practitioner has worked in public relations for 13.5 years.

On the Job

- Fifty-one percent of respondents have direct access to senior management at least once a day.

- Almost 40 percent of respondents agree that groups or teams make their organization's communications-program decisions.

- The most-reported change in working conditions is the increasing use of computer technology.

Gender

- Forty-eight percent of respondents agreed with the statement "Men still maintain the top job positions over women in the public relations/corporate communications profession."

Accreditation and Education

- Almost 25 percent of respondents are accredited through PRSA or IABC.

- Sixty-six percent of respondents have an undergraduate university degree. Twenty-five percent have a master's degree.

Although the PRSA/IABC salary survey provides an extensive review of practitioner salaries, its findings may distort reality a bit. At best, the two organizations represent only a fraction of all public relations practitioners. The people surveyed include many of the profession's best and brightest—meaning that the salary figures could be skewed higher than reality. However, as we'll see in the next section, public relations practitioners enjoy their jobs so much that salary is not their top consideration in job satisfaction.

What's Important in a Job?

Finally, you may want to turn the tables and ask your fellow commuter a question: What does he want in a job? His answer may surprise you.

Since the early 1990s, the Families and Work Institute of New York has conducted one of the most comprehensive ongoing studies of what the U.S. workforce wants in a job. In its most recent study, the institute concluded that salary, though important, ranks below many other job attributes that motivate employees: "The quality of workers' jobs and the supportiveness of their workplaces are the most powerful predictors of . . . job satisfaction, commitment to their employers, and retention. Job and workplace characteristics are far more important predictors than pay and benefits."[13]

That is especially true for public relations. In the PRSA/IABC survey, salary was at best seventh on the list of important job-satisfaction attributes.[14] Some 95.5 percent of respondents said that salary was important to job satisfaction—but that high percentage was exceeded by the 99.4 percent who said creative opportunity was important, the 99.2 percent who said access to technology was important, the 97.7 percent who said professional development opportunities were important, and the 96.2 percent who said recognition by colleagues was important.[15]

Public relations practitioners may wish that their salaries were higher, but they've discovered something more important than money: In 1999, 80 percent agreed with the statement "If I had it to do over again, I would choose a career in public relations/corporate communications"—an increase from the 65 percent who agreed in 1996.[16]

That might be a good final answer for your fellow commuter before you both exit the train. As you fold your newspaper and grab your briefcase, you can look your inquisitive acquaintance in the eye and state with confidence that public relations practitioners find their careers satisfying and rewarding.

Quick ✔ Check

1. What is the average annual starting salary for entry-level jobs in public relations?
2. Who are the highest paid public relations practitioners? Do women practitioners earn as much as men practitioners?
3. Is salary the most important aspect of a job to workers in the United States?

Summary

For all their differences, public relations jobs have one thing in common: Ideally, each public relations job has the mission of helping an organization build productive relationships with the publics necessary to its success. Most of the jobs in public relations can be found in five broad settings: corporations, nonprofit organizations and trade associations, government, public relations agencies, and independent public relations consulting.

Within those five broad areas, jobs and job duties vary widely. Public relations practitioners function as managers who counsel other managers and design public relations programs or as technicians who prepare communications. Oftentimes, a practitioner fulfills both roles, depending on the task at hand.

Salaries vary within the profession, with independent consultants earning the highest average salaries. Studies of the U.S. workforce, however, show that salary is not the most important factor in job satisfaction. Such qualities as open communication rank higher than salary in many surveys. Studies of public relations practitioners show that most enjoy their work and believe that they are meeting their personal career goals.

DISCUSSION QUESTIONS

1. Why do corporations have so many different areas of employment for public relations practitioners?
2. Why, in your opinion, have web sites become a standard communication medium in public relations?
3. What are the attractive elements of a public relations manager's job? What are the attractive elements of a public relations technician's job?
4. What do you consider to be the most important element of job satisfaction? How does your answer compare with the findings of national studies?
5. Now that you've read this chapter, what is your opinion of the public relations profession? Does it seem to be an attractive career? Why or why not?

Memo
from the
Field

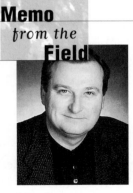

Mike Swenson,
President, Public
Relations, Barkley
Evergreen & Partners,
Kansas City

Before joining Barkley Evergreen & Partners in 1987, Mike Swenson worked as a news reporter, director, and producer for the NBC affiliate in Topeka, Kansas. He also served as press secretary to former Kansas Governor John Carlin. At Barkley Evergreen & Partners, Swenson developed CrisisTRAK, the agency's crisis communications planning and 24-hour preparedness program. Swenson is a certified consultant with The Institute for Crisis Management.

In 1993 Swenson was named PR Professional of the Year by Kansas City's PRSA chapter. In 1997 he received the Arthur E. Lowell Award for excellence in organizational communication, Kansas City/IABC's highest honor for professional achievement and civic involvement. To date, Swenson is the only Kansas City professional to receive both awards.

When you strip away everything else about the business of public relations, the foundation left standing is that this is a business about relationships.

At the root of every strategy and tactic that we develop and implement lies the desire to establish, grow, or improve a relationship between individuals, groups, or organizations. It's what makes this field so interesting and rewarding.

Regardless of which avenue you eventually choose to take (agency, corporate, nonprofit, etc.), there are some absolute truths that hold if you intend to be successful in public relations.

This is a business that requires passion. Webster's defines a passionate person as someone with an intense emotional drive and enthusiasm that results in a compelling effect. That's not a bad definition of a successful public relations pro. It will be your job as a public relations professional to summon your enthusiasm day in and day out to foster good relationships for your client or organization. We have to believe in what we are doing if we expect others to be influenced by our programs. Passion is important because passionate people tend to be more creative. Creativity is a key component to successful public relations.

Public relations professionals must be persevering. Ours is not a business where results will come easily. Influencing public opinion doesn't happen overnight. There is nothing more rewarding, however, than developing the right strategies, taking the time and effort to implement them properly, and then seeing the results you set out to achieve.

Public relations requires discipline and patience. We are constantly counseling our clients about the importance of communicating a consistent message. Successful professionals in public relations listen to their own counsel and remain disciplined in managing their programs.

Perhaps the most important quality I look for when interviewing potential associates at Barkley Evergreen & Partners is their sense of urgency. Deadlines drive our business. People with a high sense of urgency are people who are dependable. They do what they say they are going to do. They don't make excuses or blame others. These are people who want to succeed; they will take responsibility for making sure they are taking advantage of every opportunity that comes their way and then will dig a little deeper to find the opportunities that didn't.

A sense of urgency means you do the little things too. You return phone calls right away; you remember client birthdays; you thank your colleagues for their help in making your project a success; and so on. It means understanding that when it comes to successful public relations, it's not OK to wait until tomorrow. If you do not take care of your business today, it may not be there to take care of tomorrow.

The wonderful thing about our business is that you can see and feel the difference you make. There is both art and science involved in a successful public relations campaign. If you are someone with passion, perseverance, creativity, and, most of all, a high sense of urgency, then you have found the perfect career to pursue.

Case Study 2.1

Wrestling for Success

In 1986, Syracuse University All-America wrestler Wayne Catan took the mat against world champion Yury Voroboiev. Catan came in second.

A month earlier, he had wrestled in his weight-class finals at the National Collegiate Athletic Association championships. He came in second.

Catan graduated and entered public relations. In 2000, he was nominated for *PRWeek* magazine's Solo Practitioner of the Year award. He came in second.

Then one of Catan's biggest clients, Pets.com, famous for its mascot, a sock-puppet dog, went out of business—a loss of almost $250,000 a year in revenues. In 2001, Catan was again nominated for Solo Practitioner of the Year. He won.

Wayne Catan is a winner.

As the president, writer, researcher, secretary, coffee maker (and only employee) of Catan Communications in New Jersey, Catan doesn't believe in accepting defeat. "Every day when I wake up, whether I'm sick, tired, or cranky, I've got to hit the pavement," he says. In naming Catan Solo Practitioner of the Year, *PRWeek* noted that Catan "grapples with the mundane tasks that large agencies usually pay other people to do—filing, answering phones, compiling media lists, writing his own press releases, and making all of his own pitch calls."[17]

Catan also must constantly prospect for new clients. One fertile field has been guest-speaking opportunities at area wrestling events and school parent–teacher meetings. "You would be surprised how many high school kids' parents are executives and require PR," he says.[18]

Does Catan's never-ending search for new business mean that he must occasionally compromise his values? Not even close. In 1998, Catan resigned as the public relations consultant for a well-known boxing promoter whose fighter had just lost to heavyweight champion Evander Holyfield. Catan quit after refusing to issue a statement accusing Holyfield of illegal punches. When the promoter disregarded Catan's advice and publicly condemned Holyfield, Catan became his own client, issuing the following statement: "[The fighter] lost, and I want every sports writer and client to know that [I] did not release the protest statement."[19] Catan's accountant might have winced at the financial loss, but public relations practitioners applauded his integrity. "Sports Publicist KO's Boxing Promoter" read the headline in a prominent public relations newsletter.[20]

Catan doesn't fire all his clients. He's enjoyed national successes with

- Sammy Sosa, the home run–hitting superstar of the Chicago Cubs. Catan helped with the "Sammy Claus Tour," which took Sosa to five cities, where he gave gifts to underprivileged children.

- Pet Sitters International, an organization of professional "babysitters" for pets. Catan helps with the annual "Take Your Dog to Work Day." He became a media favorite when he was asked to explain the exclusion of cats: "There are still cat box issues to deal with."[21]

■ Sabol Sports, creator of the Puffer, a golf putter whose shaft holds up to four cigars. Catan helped win mentions in news media including *Sports Illustrated, Parade, USA Today,* AP, CNN, and CNBC.[22]

Journalists and public relations practitioners still wonder whether one of Catan's most notable consulting efforts was a real lawsuit or a publicity tactic. The media attention began when Pets.com, a Catan client, sued comedian Robert Smigel for reportedly saying that the company stole the idea for its sock-puppet dog from Smigel's Triumph, the Insult Comic Dog. Triumph was a popular puppet on NBC's "Late Night with Conan O'Brien."

"We didn't make this up," said Catan, defending the lawsuit. "They started it."[23]

Whether the legal battle was a true grudge match or an inspired promotional idea, the news media noticed. "Sock Puppet Suit Gets Pets.com Good Press" declared one headline.[24] Predictable pun-filled headlines followed:

TV Dog Puppets Engage in Hand-to-Hand Combat

Puppy Puppet Socks It to Foe in Dog-Eat-Dog Case

Did He Have a Hand in Pets.com Puppet?

Pets.com Poop$ on Conan's 'Pup' Pet[25]

Catan and his client steadfastly upheld the legitimacy of the lawsuit, which they eventually settled out of court.

The high-profile dogfight lost energy when Catan's client went out of business—just months before he won the *PRWeek* Solo Practitioner of the Year award.

As a former collegiate athlete, Catan probably dreads sports clichés, but he might agree that success isn't a destination; it's a journey. Decades ago, after his heartbreakingly close loss to world champion Yury Voroboiev, Catan said, "I hate when I lose—but I thought I did pretty well. I've been improving every match. It's only a matter of time before the tables are turned. Things are getting closer."[26]

That attitude, more than any gold medal, makes Wayne Catan a winner.

DISCUSSION QUESTIONS

1. What qualities does Wayne Catan have that make him a successful public relations practitioner?
2. What are the advantages and the disadvantages of being an independent public relations consultant?
3. If you had been asked to issue the statement condemning Evander Holyfield, would you have resigned? Why or why not? Does Values Statement 2.1 (p. 37) affect your decision?
4. Would you have advised Pets.com to sue Robert Smigel? Why or why not?

Case Study 2.2

A List to Avoid

One of the highlights (or lowlights, if it shines on you) of the year for public relations practitioners is the release of an irreverent list of the worst public relations disasters of the past 12 months. Compiled since 1995 by Fineman Associates Public Relations of San Francisco, the list balances an utter lack of mercy with a wicked sense of humor. It offers a wealth of case studies on how *not* to conduct successful public relations.

Among the winners of this dubious distinction:[27]

■ *The District of Columbia's Department of Public Assisted Housing:* "Hungry for positive publicity, the [department] sent out a press release . . . announcing a large drug bust taking place at a public housing complex in the city. The only trouble was that they sent the release out the day before the bust, the story ran over the radio, the drug dealers were warned and the raid called off."

■ *Structural Dynamics Research Corporation of Cincinnati:* "It was . . . National Take Our Daughters to Work Day, so [an SDR employee] took his eight-year-old daughter to the office with him. It so happened that SDR decided to fire [him] that day and unceremoniously escorted him and his daughter from the building. The story ran nationwide, giving the company an image of cold-heartedness and bringing attention to its own financial problems."

■ *America West Airlines:* "An America West flight was in the air when it turned back to pick up the California Angels baseball team, whose charter flight had been grounded. At first, passengers were excited at the prospect of sharing the plane with baseball stars. That was until the passengers were dumped to give the team the plane to itself. The outraged passengers had to wait for other flights. 'I don't think it's a public relations disaster,' an America West spokesperson told the Associated Press. Yeah, it is."

■ *R.J. Reynolds Chairman Charles Harper:* "At RJR's annual meeting in Winston-Salem (N.C.), the chairman was asked about children and secondhand smoke. He said that if children don't like to be in a smoky room, they'll leave. Told that infants can't leave, he said, 'At some point, they will learn to crawl.' The remark was covered nationally, brought more outrage from the public interest groups, and overshadowed other news about the meeting."

■ *American Society of Composers, Authors and Publishers (ASCAP):* "It was reported in the press that ASCAP sent out a letter to summer camps—including the Girl Scouts and Boy Scouts—informing them that a fee was required to use any of its members' copyrighted songs. As a result, several Girl Scout camps, which wouldn't pay the fees, stopped singing around the campfire. The national media warmed to this story. ASCAP had to take out full-page newspaper ads denying that it had ever intended to strong-arm the scouts and prevent campfire singing."

■ *WPYX-FM, Latham, New York:* "As a promotion, the radio station holds what it calls 'Ugliest Bride' contests. From newspaper wedding announcements, the radio hosts pick the bride they deem the ugliest. Callers win by guessing which photograph was chosen. [Once], in a departure from usual practices, the station aired the bride's full name and place of employment. Hello, $300,000 lawsuit, an AP story, and a mean-spirited image."

There you have it: how not to conduct successful public relations. If you decide to pursue a career in this wonderful, challenging profession, we hope you'll set many lofty goals for yourself. One of them should be never to appear on the annual Fineman list.

DISCUSSION QUESTIONS

1. Which of the above public relations blunders is, in your opinion, the worst? Why?
2. Many of the above gaffes were committed by people not in public relations. How could public relations practitioners within the organizations have prevented those errors?
3. Should the organizations cited respond to their presence on the annual Fineman list? Or should they ignore it?
4. Suppose that you're head of public relations for each of the above organizations. The terrible event has just happened. Now the reporters are at your door. What do you tell them?
5. Do you think Fineman Associates Public Relations runs a risk by associating itself with bad public relations?

It's Your Turn

Career Day at High School

Imagine that word of your growing knowledge of public relations has spread throughout your community. A local high school invites you to its annual career day and asks you to speak on where the jobs are in public relations. In addition, you learn that the students would like to hear a little about the advantages and disadvantages of each job area.

From reading this chapter, you know the five broad areas of employment in public relations—but what are the advantages and disadvantages of each? For example, one of those five areas encompasses public relations agencies. In your opinion, what are the advantages of working for a public relations agency? What might be the disadvantages? You may wish to consult some working professionals to answer these questions, but don't discount the role of common sense.

You might even wish to expand your presentation into discussing the manager and technician roles in public relations: What might be the advantages and disadvantages of those roles?

Good luck. Your high school audience eagerly awaits your presentation.

KEY TERMS

account executive, p. 39

boundary role, p. 44

communications specialist, p. 38

community relations, p. 34

consumer relations, p. 34

employee relations, p. 33

government relations, p. 33

independent public relations consultant,
  p. 39

investor relations, p. 36

media relations, p. 33

press secretary, p. 38

public affairs officer, p. 38

public information officer, p. 38

public relations agency, p. 39

public relations managers, p. 42

public relations technicians, p. 43

NOTES

1. James Collins and Jerry Porras, *Built to Last: Successful Habits of Visionary Companies* (New York: HarperBusiness, 1994), 8, 73, 88.

2. Jan Goldberg, *Real People Working in Public Relations* (Lincolnwood, Ill.: VGM Career Horizons, 1997), 88.

3. "E-Mail Is the Preferred Way to Receive Résumés," *HRFocus,* July 2000, online, Lexis-Nexis.

4. Robert Half International's annual collections of résumé and application bloopers are released through PR Newswire and can be accessed via Lexis-Nexis.

5. "Doomed Days: The Worst Mistakes Recruiters Have Ever Seen," *Wall Street Journal,* 27 February 1995, R4.

6. David Dozier, "The Organizational Roles of Communications and Public Relations Practitioners," in *Excellence in Public Relations and Communication Management,* ed. James E. Grunig (Hillsdale, N.J.: Lawrence Erlbaum, 1992), 341–352.

7. Elizabeth Toth, Shirley Serini, Donald Wright, and Arthur Emig, "Trends in Public Relations Roles: 1990–1995," *Public Relations Review* (summer 1998), 145–163.

8. Greg Leichty and Jeff Springston, "Elaborating Public Relations Roles," *Journalism and Mass Communications Quarterly* (summer 1996): 467–468; Toth, Serini, Wright, and Emig.

9. Lynne Sallot, Glen Cameron, and Ruth Ann Weaver Lariscy, "Pluralistic Ignorance and Professional Standards: Underestimating Professionalism of Our Peers in Public Relations," Public Relations Review (spring 1998), 1–20.

10. "Starting Salaries for PR Grads Rose in 2000," *O'Dwyer's PR Daily,* 7 August 2001, online, www.odwyerpr.com.

11. "Profile 2000: A Survey of the Profession, Part I," *Communication World* (June/July 2000), A1–A32; "PRSA/IABC Salary Survey 2000," online, www.prsa.org/ppc.

12. "Profile 2000: A Survey of the Profession, Part I." "PRSA/IABC Salary Survey 2000."

13. "1997 Study of the Changing Workforce: Executive Summary," online, www.familiesandwork.org.

14. "PRSA/IABC Salary Survey 2000."

15. "Profile 2000: A Survey of the Profession, Part I."

16. "PRSA/IABC Salary Survey 2000."

17. "Solo Practitioner of the Year 2001," *PR Week,* online, www.prweekus.com/us/events/awards2001/solo.htm.

18. Jack O'Dwyer, "Pets.com, San Francisco, Names Catan Communications, Min Hill, N.J., as Its First PR Firm," *Jack O'Dwyer's Newsletter,* 24 November 1999, online, Lexis-Nexis.

19. Jack O'Dwyer, "Sports Publicist KO's Boxing Promoter," *Jack O'Dwyer's Newsletter,* 14 October 1998, online, Lexis-Nexis.

20. O'Dwyer, "Sports Publicist KO's Boxing Promoter."

21. Jeffry Scott, "Take Your Dog to Work Day," *Atlanta Journal and Constitution,* 10 April 2001, online, Lexis-Nexis.

22. "Profiles of Sports PR Firms," *O'Dwyer's PR Services Report* (December 1998), online, Lexis-Nexis.

23. Chris Clancy, "Sock Puppet Suit Gets Pets.com Good Press," *O'Dwyer's PR Services Report* (June 2000), online, Lexis-Nexis.

24. Clancy.

25. Michael Precker, "TV Dog Puppets Engage in Hand-to-Hand Combat," *Dallas Morning News,* 29 April 2000, online, Lexis-Nexis; Jennifer Harper, "Puppy Puppet Socks It to Foe in Dog-Eat-Dog Case," *Washington Times,* 1 May 2000, online, Lexis-Nexis; Eric Mink, "Did He Have a Hand in Pets.com Puppet?" *Daily News,* 16 March 2000, online, Lexis-Nexis; Bill Hoffman, "Pets.com Poop$ on Conan's 'Pup' Pet," *New York Post,* 26 April 2000, online, Lexis-Nexis.

26. Rich Cimini, "A Moral Victory for U.S.," *The Record,* 1 April 1986, online, Lexis-Nexis.

27. Fineman Associates Public Relations' annual list is released through PR Newswire and can be accessed online via Lexis-Nexis.

chapter three

A Brief History of Public Relations

objectives

After studying this chapter, you will be able to

- discuss how public relations evolved before it was formally recognized and given a name

- identify the forces that have shaped the modern profession's development

- recognize the major figures and events that influenced the growth of public relations

- explain the issues and trends that are shaping the future of public relations

Foreign Affairs

scenario   *You are an account executive for a large public relations agency in Washington, D.C. Recently, you were approached by the representative of a group of industrialists from a foreign nation that has formal, but sometimes unfriendly, relations with the United States. The U.S. government doesn't like the way that nation treats female citizens and members of ethnic minority groups. The government also sees the nation as a potential military adversary. The representative has said his group would like to hire your agency in an effort to "get the true story" about his country and its policies to the people of the United States. The U.S. State Department believes that these industrialists are closely linked to their nation's ruling regime. The industrialists are willing to pay a substantial fee, and they stress that they will not ask you to do anything that is either unethical or illegal.*

What are the benefits and risks in taking on this group as a client? What factors do you consider most important in making your decision? Would you represent this group?

Premodern Public Relations

In the century since the first public relations agency opened its doors for business, public relations has had a tremendous impact—both good and bad—upon U.S. society. And as we enter the 21st century, the practice of public relations continues to evolve. If we are to have a sense of where the profession is headed, it is useful for us first to take a backward glance at its roots.

Although the phrase "public relations" did not attain its current meaning until the 20th century, the practice of public relations has been evident since the dawn of recorded history. One example of public relations, in which primitive agricultural extension agents gave advice on how to grow better crops, dates back to 1800 B.C. in what is now Iraq.

Some historians believe that the development of public relations is a direct result of Western civilization's first true democracy: the city–state of Athens led by Pericles from 461 to 429 B.C. The dictatorships of the past had been overthrown, and suddenly the male citizens of Athens were free to debate, create, and implement public policy. In that environment, citizens began to study public opinion and the methods of influencing it. That study, known as **rhetoric,** is often seen as the beginning of public relations as a social science based on research, planning, and two-way communication. The practice of rhetoric fell into disuse with the demise of democratic Athens but flourished again in the freedoms of the final century of the Roman republic (100 B.C.), when a philosophy of *vox populi,* the voice of the people, was embraced.

The spread of Christianity during the Middle Ages could, in a modern context, be linked to the application of public relations techniques. Before the development of mass communication technologies, the faith was passed along by missionaries using word of mouth. Among the most notable of these missionaries was Francis of Assisi, who was born a child of comfort and means around 1181. When he was 24 years old, Francis renounced his father's wealth. In the years that followed, Francis spread his teachings of self-imposed poverty and service to the poor across Europe and the Middle East. He died in 1226, but his religious order, the Franciscans, survives to this day. Johannes Gutenberg's Bible, printed in 1456 by means of a revolutionary movable type process, heralded the use of mass communication technologies. The Catholic Church's outreach efforts became more formalized in the 1600s when it established the *Congregatio de Propaganda Fide,* or Congregation for the Propagation of the Faith, to spread church doctrine.

Trends Leading to the Development of Modern Public Relations

The growth of modern public relations was not limited to just one nation. Aspects of what we now know as public relations emerged independently in several societies. For example, organized government public relations efforts in the United Kingdom preceded those in the United States by more than a decade. The National Association of Local Government Officers began in 1905, in part to educate the public about the role of local government in British society.[1] However, the earliest development of the profession appears to have emerged in the United States, where privately owned business and industry embraced public relations in the 1880s. In comparison, private sector public relations was not prominent in Britain until after the Second World War.[2]

The march toward modern public relations began in earnest in the United States after the Civil War. To a large degree, this development paralleled the country's transition from an agricultural to an industrial society. The **Industrial Revolution** brought with it growing pains, which, in turn, redefined the relationships among government, business, and the people. Historians often refer to this period of reforms as

A great wave of immigrants *(shown here receiving health inspections on arrival at Ellis Island)* changed U.S. society and helped set the stage for the development of the new profession of public relations. (Courtesy of The Statue of Liberty–Ellis Island Foundation Inc.)

the **Progressive Era,** which ran from the 1890s to the United States' entrance into World War I in 1917. It was a period in which democracy as well as social and governmental institutions matured. Public opinion grew more important; the nation re-examined and, to a certain extent, redefined itself.

Let's look more closely at how the development of modern public relations is linked to five social trends that had their beginnings in the Progressive Era.

THE GROWTH OF INSTITUTIONS.   The Industrial Revolution spawned the growth of big companies. The resulting concentration of wealth among early 20th-century industrialists such as J. P. Morgan, Andrew Carnegie, and John D. Rockefeller, ran against the traditional American inclination toward decentralized power—as evidenced in the checks and balances established in the Constitution. This, in turn, led to increased regulation of these businesses and consequent growth in the size of government. Led by the University of Michigan in 1897, U.S. colleges and universities began to promote themselves by creating publicity offices.[3] By the 1930s, labor unions began to have clout. As business, government, and labor organizations grew larger, the need for effective communication increased. All three sectors experienced a second growth spurt in the economic boom that followed the end of World War II.

THE EXPANSION OF DEMOCRACY.   Progressive Era reforms such as giving women the right to vote and the direct election of U.S. senators brought more people into the political process and increased the need for public discussion of policy issues. That expansion continued into the mid- to late 20th century. As a result of the civil rights movement, black citizens and other minority groups gained greater access to the political process. Following the Vietnam War, 18-year-olds were also given the right to vote. With the fall of communist governments in Europe and Asia near the end of the 20th century, there has been a growing need for effective communication in emerging democratic societies. Because of the increasing importance of persuasion and consensus, public relations has become an integral part of the democratic process.

TECHNOLOGICAL IMPROVEMENTS IN COMMUNICATIONS.   Each new communication medium presents both challenges and opportunities for reaching large audiences. In the early 1900s the growth of national news services such as the Associated Press and the birth of national magazines such as the *Ladies' Home Journal* gave muckraking reporters a wider audience. The introduction of commercial radio in 1920 and commercial television in 1947 launched the era of instantaneous electronic communication. Developments in satellite and computer technology in the second half of the 20th century further revolutionized communications. With the dramatic expansion of the Internet in the 1990s, the power to communicate with mass publics began shifting away from media companies and toward individuals.

THE GROWTH OF ADVOCACY.   In the late 1800s, a wave of immigrants who brought Old World political ideas to the New World—and, to some extent, the reaction of

QuickBreak 3.1

A REAL EVENT OR A PSEUDOEVENT?

A term increasingly used in some quarters of public relations scholarship is **pseudoevent,** a name applied by historian Daniel Boorstin to activities created for the sole purpose of generating publicity. Some have suggested that the Boston Tea Party was one of the earliest examples of a pseudoevent in U.S. history. They also suggest that events such as pro- and anti–abortion rights marches fall into this category.[4]

This raises two interesting questions: When should something be considered a "real" event versus a pseudoevent, and does it really matter?

As to the first question, the purpose of the activity could be the determining factor between the true and the false. Many are loath to lump together the Boston Tea Party and the Miss America contest, which was created to generate publicity for an extended tourist season in Atlantic City.[5] A beauty pageant just doesn't seem to be in the same league as social or political protest.

However, we live in a democratic society where journalists, virtually free of government restraints, choose what news their readers, listeners, and viewers receive. And although the definition of what constitutes news is broad and subjective, the fact that an independent authority makes that judgment is significant. Not all news is of earth-shattering importance—something for which we should be grateful. Just because someone makes a conscious decision to do something that generates news should not lessen the fact that it is still, in the eyes of someone, news.

That takes us to the second question: Does it really matter whether a public relations tactic is called a pseudoevent? Of course it does. Credibility is at the heart of good public relations practice. Those willing to use the pseudoevent label point out that it doesn't necessarily imply unethical conduct; however, the prefix *pseudo* comes from the Greek word *pseudes,* meaning false. Carried to a logical but extreme conclusion, any effort to generate news coverage could be termed a pseudoevent. The use of such language in describing public relations tactics can undermine the profession and the important role it plays in a free society.

native-born citizens to this human wave from abroad—gave birth to increased political activism. Newspapers evolved from the organs of partisan "yellow journalism" of the 19th century into instruments of social advocacy in the early 20th century. The period after World War II also witnessed the growth of significant social advocacy, including movements for civil rights, women's rights, environmentalism, consumerism, antiwar ideals, children's rights, multinationalism, rights for persons with disabilities, and gay rights. Both those who advocated change and the institutions forced to deal with it found an increasing need for public relations.

THE SEARCH FOR CONSENSUS.   U.S. society is built upon consensus. The nation at one time believed itself to be a melting pot in which various cultures and philosophies would combine into something distinctly American. In recent decades, however, that concept has been largely discredited. It is now accepted that people can *both* be American and

Values Statement 3.1

THE UNITED STATES CONSTITUTION

Delegates from the 13 original states met in Philadelphia from May to September 1787 to draft a constitution for the new nation. Following its ratification by 11 states (North Carolina and Rhode Island ratified it later), the Constitution took effect on March 4, 1789.

We, the people of the United States, in order to form a more perfect union, establish justice, insure domestic tranquillity, provide for the common defence, promote the general welfare, and secure the blessings of liberty to ourselves and our posterity, do ordain and establish this Constitution for the United States of America.

—Preamble, U.S. Constitution

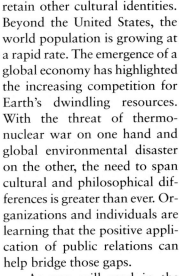

retain other cultural identities. Beyond the United States, the world population is growing at a rapid rate. The emergence of a global economy has highlighted the increasing competition for Earth's dwindling resources. With the threat of thermonuclear war on one hand and global environmental disaster on the other, the need to span cultural and philosophical differences is greater than ever. Organizations and individuals are learning that the positive application of public relations can help bridge those gaps.

As you will read in the coming pages, the development of public relations closely mirrors the growth of the United States. Although the profession evolved in other societies as well, it was in the United States—the great experiment in democracy—that public relations flourished.

Pre–20th-Century America

Although it would be more than a century before the discipline had a name, the use of public relations tactics was evident in pre–Revolutionary America. Perhaps the most famous example is the Boston Tea Party, a publicity event designed to focus attention on British taxation without representation. After the Revolution, public relations tactics were used to change the course of history. In what some have described as history's finest public relations effort, the **Federalist letters** appeared in newspapers between October 1787 and April 1788. Written by Alexander Hamilton, James Madison, and John Jay under the single nom de plume Publius, these letters helped lead the reluctant former colonies to ratify the Constitution of the United States.

The ratification of the Constitution and the Bill of Rights in 1789 remains the most important event in the development of public relations in the United States. The 45 words of the **First Amendment** define the liberties that allow the free practice of this vital profession:

Congress shall make no law respecting an establishment of religion, or prohibiting the free exercise thereof; or abridging the freedom of speech, or of the press; or the right of the people peaceably to assemble, and to petition the Government for a redress of grievances.

QuickBreak 3.2

THOMAS PAINE: REVOLUTIONARY PRACTITIONER?

Before and during the American Revolution, colonial separatists made an intense effort to gain popular support for independence from Great Britain. This 18th-century effort to sway public opinion resembles in many ways the public relations efforts of today. Although they had no radio, television, or Internet to carry their messages, the champions of independence for the colonies made excellent use of the communications channels of their day.

One of those champions was Thomas Paine (1737–1809), who had come to America from England in 1774 after failed attempts at being a schoolteacher, a sailor, a corset maker, and a tax collector. With a passion for liberty and a flair for self-expression, Paine quickly embroiled himself in colonial politics. In January 1776 he represented the views of the so-called radicals in a 79-page pamphlet, *Common Sense*. In it, Paine laid out the rationale for a permanent separation from the crown. He wrote, "The sun never shone on a cause of greater worth . . . now is the seed-time of continental union, faith and honor."[6] More than 100,000 copies of *Common Sense* were sold within three months of its publication. George Washington credited its "sound doctrine and unanswerable reasoning" with convincing reluctant colonists of the need to break from England.[7]

While serving with the Continental Army during the war, Paine published a series of 13 pamphlets, *The American Crisis,* in which he urged colonists to continue their struggle for independence. From this series came one of the most memorable pieces of rhetoric in American literary history. Legend has it that the passage was written on a drumhead by campfire light during one of the darkest periods of the conflict. "These are the times that try men's souls," Paine wrote. "The summer soldier and the sunshine patriot will, in this crisis, shrink from the service of their country; but he that stands *now,* deserves the love and thanks of man and woman."[8] In the final installment of the series, Paine victoriously wrote, "The times that tried men's souls are over—and the greatest and completest revolution the world ever knew, gloriously and happily accomplished."[9]

After the war, Paine sought to spread the fires of democratic revolution to Europe. This endeavor caused him to run afoul of the authorities there and on several occasions almost cost him his life. By the time he returned to the United States in 1802, Paine was vilified for his controversial writings, especially for his criticisms of President Washington. When Paine died in 1809, his body was refused burial in the nation his words helped to create. His bones were sent to England, sold at auction, and lost.[10]

This guarantee of free expression, however, is not absolute. It is constantly being interpreted and refined by the U.S. Supreme Court. There have been times, during war or civil unrest for example, when freedom of expression has been severely tested. But more than two centuries after ratification, the First Amendment still stands as the singular liberty that distinguishes U.S. democracy and, as a consequence, the practice of public relations in the United States.

In the 1800s democracy in the United States continued to mature. Public education was introduced, which resulted in a more literate and well-informed society. As the right to vote was extended to men who did not own property, vigorous public debate emerged. The influence of that debate on the government was clear when President Andrew Jackson appointed Amos Kendall to his so-called kitchen cabinet. Kendall was the first presidential press secretary, serving as Jackson's pollster, counselor, speechwriter, and publicist.

Two other figures in the premodern period of public relations are worth noting. During the Civil War, Jay Cooke headed the United States' first fund-raising drive: Through an appeal to patriotism, Cooke sold government bonds to finance the Union's war effort. Better known, but less fondly remembered by practitioners, is Phineas T. Barnum, who created his circus in 1871 and later proclaimed it to be "The Greatest Show on Earth." Barnum was the father of press-agentry in this country. A master showman, Barnum generated extensive newspaper coverage of his often bizarre enterprises through exaggeration, distortion, and outright lies. To the shame of the profession, some wanna-be publicists still practice Barnum's "publicity for publicity's sake" approach today.

Quick ✔ Check

1. What are some of the earliest examples of public relations—even before the profession was known as public relations?
2. What are the major social trends that have influenced the development of public relations?
3. What remains the most important event in the development of public relations in the United States?

The Seedbed Years

The late public relations historian Scott Cutlip called the initial period in the growth of modern public relations, from the dawn of the industrial age to the outbreak of World War I, "the **Seedbed Years**."[11] It was during this period of growth in U.S. society that organizations first felt the need for formalizing their communications. For example, in 1888 the Mutual Life Insurance Company created a "literary bureau" to publicize its services. One year later George Westinghouse hired a newspaper reporter to help him earn public favor in his battle with Thomas Edison over competing electricity distribution systems. Presidential candidate William Jennings Bryan inaugurated the practice of whistle-stop campaigning during 1896, in large part out of the need for publicity to counter William McKinley's well-financed campaign.

The nation's first public relations agency, the **Publicity Bureau** in Boston, was created in 1900 in recognition of the fact that corporations needed to voice their concerns amid a rising tide of critics. The Publicity Bureau came to epitomize the practice—and the challenges—of modern public relations in its infancy. The Publicity Bureau's clients, which included American Telephone & Telegraph and the nation's railroads, hoped that this new craft known as publicity might stem the increasing demand for government regulation.[12]

Other pioneering practitioners would soon follow. William Wolf Smith opened the national capital's first "publicity business" in 1902. The Parker and Lee agency, the nation's third, opened in New York City in 1904. However, it folded after only four years. That was a common fate of these early agencies.

There were several reasons why early publicity shops met with limited success. First, they were breaking new ground. Although public relations had been practiced in various forms for centuries, the concept of formalized publicity was relatively new. As with advertising on the web today, making public relations profitable in the early days of the 20th century was extremely difficult.

Credibility was also a problem. These early public relations efforts followed a one-way model: Publicity agents were zealous to put forward the view of their clients and often let accuracy fall by the wayside. Sources of information were often hidden, creating a public that was increasingly suspicious of anything carrying a "publicity" label. Real two-way communication did not occur. The ethical divisions between the roles of journalists and practitioners were also not well defined: It was common practice for a journalist to write under his byline (journalists were almost exclusively men in those days) for a newspaper in the mornings and to write anonymous publicity releases in the afternoons.

Early public relations practitioners also faced stiff resistance from newspaper publishers. Although some of this stonewalling was motivated by a desire to protect journalistic integrity, most of the opposition stemmed from economic concerns. The publishers saw publicity releases as "free advertising"—a common misconception still held by many today. To these publishers, free advertising meant lost revenues. The American Newspaper Publishers Association conducted an antipublicity campaign, sending to its membership periodic bulletins that identified publicity agents and the interests they represented.

This was the start of an ongoing tension between practitioners and journalists that still exists. Although journalists treasure their independence and their freedom to judge the performance of others, many of them don't like it when the shoe is on the other foot. When U.S. Department of Energy Secretary Hazel O'Leary hired a public relations consultant in 1995 to evaluate the quality of news coverage her agency received, reporters accused her of using taxpayer dollars to develop an enemies list. The journalists couldn't understand that evaluation was an appropriate activity for a public agency charged with informing the public of matters involving its mission. In his analysis of the flap over the Department of Energy's media monitoring, one public relations consultant wrote that the media monitoring effort was "about as dangerous a threat to the media as Barney and Baby Bop."[13]

Theodore Roosevelt (1858–1919)

Early publicity efforts—especially those targeted at halting the increasing influence of government regulation—achieved only limited success for yet another reason: Theodore Roosevelt. The youngest person to date to serve as president, Roosevelt dramatically transformed the relationships among the White House, big business, and the electorate. Before Roosevelt's succession to the presidency upon the assassination of William McKinley in 1901, the attitude widely held by Washington officials was, in essence, "What is good for big business is good for America." But Roosevelt saw big business' increasing concentration of power—an estimated 10 percent of the population at that time owned 90 percent of the wealth—as a threat to democracy. Roosevelt's administration proceeded to sue 44 major corporations in an attempt to break up monopolies and increase business competition.

Roosevelt also understood—probably better than any other person of his time—the power of harnessing public opinion. He transformed the presidency into what he called his "bully pulpit." Traditional power brokers were opposed to the reforms of Roosevelt's Square Deal, but the president understood the mood of the people and courted their favor through the muckraking press. As researcher Blaire Atherton French has written,

> Theodore Roosevelt was the first to initiate close and continuous ties with reporters, and may be accurately called the founder of presidential press conferences. He brought the press into the White House literally as well as figuratively. The tale goes that he looked out his window one rainy day and saw a group of reporters manning their usual post by the White House gate. Their purpose was to question those coming and going from the White House and in that way to gather news or leads. When T. R. saw them miserable, wet, and

Theodore Roosevelt, the nation's youngest president, is best remembered for using the White House as a "bully pulpit," from which he could rally public opinion in favor of his reform policies. (Courtesy of the Library of Congress)

cold, he ordered that there be a room in the White House set aside just for them. In doing so, T. R. granted them a status they had never previously enjoyed and would subsequently never lose.[14]

Although many of his proposed reforms were thwarted by a stubborn Congress, much of Theodore Roosevelt's success and widespread popularity was a result of his skillful application of public relations. As another researcher has written, Roosevelt "figured out how a president can use the news media to guide public opinion. He did not just hand out information and leave matters in the hands of reporters. He created news."[15]

Ivy Ledbetter Lee (1877–1934)

A man who deserves more credit for the growth of public relations than he has received is Ivy Ledbetter Lee. His was a career that began in triumph and ended in a controversy that outlived him.

The son of a Methodist minister in Georgia, Lee studied at Princeton and worked as a newspaper reporter and stringer. After a brief foray into politics, Lee joined George E. Parker, once President Grover Cleveland's publicity manager, to form a publicity bureau in 1904. The new agency boasted of "Accuracy, Authenticity, and Interest."[16]

This philosophy evolved in 1906 into Lee's "Declaration of Principles," the first articulation of the concept that public relations practitioners (although the term "public relations" had not yet been coined) have a public responsibility that extends beyond obligations to a client. "This is not a secret press bureau," Lee wrote. "All of our work is done in the open."

Lee's "Declaration of Principles" also declared, "In brief, our plan is, frankly and openly, on behalf of business concerns and public institutions, to supply the press and public of the United States prompt and accurate information concerning subjects which it is of value and interest to the public to know about."[17]

Lee's statement, issued at a time when he was representing management's side in a coal strike, changed the direction of the evolving field of public relations. He established ethical standards by which others could judge his work. In doing so, he also brought credibility and professionalism to the field.

Of course, actions speak louder than words, and Lee did not always live up to his own words. Perhaps a kinder interpretation is that he often defined accuracy in very narrow terms. For Lee, accuracy meant correctly reflecting the views of the client—but it did not mean checking to see whether the client's statements were truthful. Because of that questionable logic, during his controversial career Lee often supplied misleading or false information to reporters. The resulting mistrust of Lee and his motives would eventually be his undoing.

Lee had an impressive list of clients. It was Lee who, along with pioneer practitioner Harry Bruno, helped to promote public acceptance of the new field of aviation. Lee was crucial in gaining the needed financial support for a nationwide publicity tour by aviator Charles A. Lindbergh. Lee is also credited for his work with what would

Although his reputation was damaged because of his association with the German Dye Trust, Ivy Lee is more fondly remembered on this historical marker in Rockmart, Georgia, as the "Founder of Modern Public Relations." (Courtesy of Ed Jackson, Carl Vinson Institute of Government, University of Georgia)

eventually become General Mills and the creation of three of its most enduring symbols: Betty Crocker; Gold Medal Flour; and Wheaties, the Breakfast of Champions.[18]

You are judged by the company you keep. The appropriateness of representing controversial clients is an age-old problem for public relations practitioners—see, for example, the Foreign Affairs scenario that opens this chapter. Many of Lee's clients were controversial at the time they retained his services. They included the Anthracite Coal Operators, the Pennsylvania Railroad, and John D. Rockefeller.

However, it would be Lee's worldview and extensive travels that would cause the most damage to his reputation. In many ways Lee was a man ahead of his times. He supported recognition of Soviet Russia at a time when most of his compatriots were fearful of the recent communist revolution in that country. Lee was scorned for his desire for cooperation between the two nations. In less than a decade, however, cooperation between the United States and the Soviet Union would lead to an Allied victory in World War II.

The sharpest criticism was leveled at Lee's work in 1934 on behalf of I.G. Farben, the German Dye Trust. This episode occurred at a time shortly after Adolf Hitler assumed power in Germany. Lee's services were retained by industrialists to help counter a growing anti-German sentiment in the United States. Lee accepted a $25,000 fee with the stipulation that he only provide counsel and not disseminate information for the Germans within the United States. Lee, often referred to by his detractors as "Poison Ivy," was accused of being a Nazi sympathizer. Making matters worse, Lee ignored the advice he had often given others and refused to answer reporters' questions about his German business interests. In what now appears to be a very naive notion, Lee thought he could positively influence the behavior of the government of the Third Reich. In fairness, Lee was not the only person to underestimate the evil embodied in Adolf Hitler. However, this association would stain his name long after his death in 1934.

War and Propaganda

America's entrance into World War I in 1917 had a profound effect on both society and the growth of public relations. The war thrust the United States onto the world stage—a place where many U.S. citizens were reluctant to be. Isolationism grew out of a desire to separate the New World from the problems of Europe. In an earlier time, that had been quite possible. However, with the Industrial Revolution came the growth of U.S. economic power and ties to other nations that were an unavoidable consequence of a growing global economy.

World War I also focused public attention on the use of the mass media as tools of persuasion. People were becoming more familiar with the concept of **propaganda,** which is the attempt to have a viewpoint accepted at the exclusion of all others. The word's etymology stems from the Roman Catholic Church's efforts to propagate the faith during the 17th century. *Propaganda,* as a term, did not carry the negative connotations at the beginning of World War I that it does today. However, its abuse by its most evil practitioner, Nazi Propaganda Minister Joseph Goebbels, discredited propaganda both as a word and as a practice.

To rally the nation behind the war, President Woodrow Wilson established the **Committee for Public Information (CPI).** It became better known as the Creel Committee, after its chairman, former journalist George Creel. Creel was a longtime Wilson friend who had tried to persuade him to run for president as early as 1905, while Wilson was still president of Princeton University. Wilson had been reelected to the White House in 1916 on a promise that he would keep the United States out of the bloody conflict that had been raging across Europe since 1914. With involvement in the war now on the horizon, Wilson leaned toward the advice of his military experts that the press should be strictly censored. Creel, however, as military historian Thomas Flemming has noted, "convinced Wilson that the country needed not suppression but the expression of a coherent pro-war policy."[19]

During the two years that the United States was at war, the CPI churned out more than 75 million pamphlets and books with titles ranging from "Why We Are

Fighting" to "What Our Enemy Really Is." Through what may have been the largest speakers' bureau ever created, the **Four-Minute Men,** 75,000 speakers gave 755,190 talks to drum up home front morale.[20] (The name "Four-Minute Men" came from the length of time volunteers spoke between reel changes at cinemas, which were the most important form of mass entertainment at the time.) CPI filmmakers also produced features such as *Pershing's Crusaders* and *Under Four Flags.* These films not only fanned patriotic fires but also raised $852,744.30—not bad for the days when the price of a movie ticket was only a nickel.[21]

Quick ✔ Check

1. Why did most of the early publicity agencies fail?
2. What contributions did Ivy Ledbetter Lee make to the development of public relations?
3. In what ways did the outbreak of World War I influence the growth of public relations?

Edward L. Bernays (1891–1995)

World War I and the propaganda surrounding it sparked interest in the study and manipulation of public opinion. There was a growing demand for publicity agents to represent the interests of private companies and public agencies. The Creel Committee proved to be a training ground for many of these practitioners. Notable among them was Edward L. Bernays, an acknowledged "father" of public relations. Although Bernays had served as a press agent in several capacities before joining the Creel Committee in 1917, it was after the war that he made his indelible mark.

The Austrian-born Bernays was a nephew of Sigmund Freud, and he played a major role in having Freud's theories on psychoanalysis introduced to America. Before joining the CPI, Bernays served as a newspaper reporter and a theatrical press agent. For the most part, Bernays received high marks for his work with the Creel Committee. However, Bernays' lifelong propensity for self-promotion eventually led to the dismantling of the CPI. At the war's end, Bernays traveled with President Wilson to Paris for the Versailles Peace Conference to provide the president with technical assistance in dealing with reporters. Bernays issued a news release upon his departure announcing that he and 15 other employees of CPI were traveling to France as "The United States Official Press Mission to the Peace Conference." In the release Bernays wrote that "the announced object of the expedition is 'to interpret the work of the Peace Conference by keeping up a worldwide propaganda to disseminate American accomplishments and ideals.'"[22] Creel was angry that Bernays had overstated the CPI's role. Wilson's detractors in Congress began to look upon the CPI as the president's personal publicity machine and pulled its plug.

QuickBreak 3.3

THE STRANGE CASE OF THE ZIMMERMAN TELEGRAM

One of the legacies of World War I was public awareness of the use of propaganda by one nation to influence the actions of another. Despite its negative connotations, propaganda isn't necessarily false information. Often the truth is stranger—and more effective—than fiction. Certainly this was the case during the days leading up to the United States' entrance into World War I.

Despite a series of provocative acts, including the Germans' sinking of the passenger ship

Uncle Sam Recruiting Poster World War I and World War II were catalysts for the growth of government public relations and thus helped create training grounds for new generations of practitioners. (Courtesy of the Library of Congress)

Lusitania in May 1915 at the cost of 1,198 lives, the people of the United States were strongly against intervention into World War I. President Woodrow Wilson had narrowly won reelection in 1916 by running on the slogan "He Kept Us Out of War." Although there was some pro-war sentiment along the East Coast, the area most vulnerable to German submarine attacks, the rest of the country was cool to the idea.

British military intelligence had broken the German diplomatic code and intercepted two "confidential" communications it knew would thrust the United States into the war on the side of the Allies. The first message was confirmation that the Germans had decided to resume submarine attacks on neutral shipping in the Atlantic. The decision to resume unrestricted submarine warfare on February 1, 1917, meant that the Germans were breaking a promise that they had made after the *Lusitania* sinking not to attack U.S. ships in international waters. The British knew that if passions were properly aroused, the United States would go to war.

It was the second message, known as the Zimmerman telegram, that gave the British

The inevitable finger-pointing ensued. Creel blamed Bernays for undercutting the mission of the CPI in a search for personal glory. For his part, Bernays cast blame on Creel for helping to lose the peace. "Lack of effective public relations between President Wilson and the people of the United States, historians confirm, was one of the reasons for the rejection of the League of Nations by the United States," Bernays wrote. "The final breakdown of the League in the early Thirties was due in large part to the same lack of good public relations."[23]

It was Bernays who, in his 1923 book *Crystallizing Public Opinion*, popularized the phrase *public relations counsel*. He said he used the phrase because of the negative connotations attached to terms such as *propagandist*, *publicist*, and *press agent*:

> I wanted something broader than publicity or press-agentry. I called what I did "publicity direction," by which I meant directing the actions of a client to result in the desired publicity. A year later Doris [Bernays' wife] and I coined the phrase "counsel on public relations,"

hope that the Americans would soon join the Allies. In a January 16, 1917, telegram from German Foreign Minister Arthur Zimmerman to his country's ambassador in Mexico, Zimmerman made this startling offer:

> We intend to begin on the first of February unrestricted submarine warfare. We shall endeavor in spite of this to keep the United States of America neutral. In the event this is not succeeding, we make Mexico a proposal of alliance on the following basis: make war together, generous financial support and an understanding on our part that Mexico is to reconquer the lost territory of Texas, New Mexico and Arizona. You will inform the President [of Mexico] of the above most secretly as soon as possible as the outbreak of war with the United States of America is certain.[24]

The telegram went on to suggest that the Mexican government encourage Japan's involvement against the United States as well.

The British waited for an opportune moment to share this news with the U.S. public.

That moment came nearly three weeks later, just as President Wilson was asking Congress for the right to arm merchant ships. In a stroke of luck—from the British point of view—the release of the Zimmerman telegram was followed two days later by the Germans sinking the passenger ship *Laconia*. These factors, along with the fall of the czar in Russia, deeply worried Americans—especially those living in the Southwest and West, who had earlier been against intervention. The resulting firestorm of public opinion eventually led to a declaration of war—only a few months after the nation had voted for peace.

The British propaganda strategy worked in the short term. But after World War I ended in an unsatisfying peace, the propaganda effort also led to a widely held belief that the United States had been tricked into going to war. This fueled a deep-rooted isolation movement, which lasted until the Japanese attack on Pearl Harbor led the nation into a second and even bloodier world war.

which we thought described our activity better—giving professional advice to our clients on their public relationships, regardless of whether such an activity resulted in publicity.[25]

Bernays was not the first ever to use the phrase *public relations*. President Thomas Jefferson used it in an address to Congress in 1807. Attorney Dorman Eaton also used the term in an 1882 talk before the Yale Law School graduating class.[26] However, Bernays was the first to use it to describe the discipline that bears its name.

In his book, Bernays was also the first to articulate the two-way communication concept of public relations. In the same year that *Crystallizing Public Opinion* was published, Bernays taught the first public relations course, at New York University.

Through the years Bernays promoted the interests of a wide variety of clients, including the American Tobacco Company, Lithuanians seeking independence from the Soviet Union, and Procter & Gamble. Bernays took credit for pushing CBS Radio to develop news programming to build up its image. He also acknowledged his role

QuickBreak 3.4

THE MOTHER OF PUBLIC RELATIONS

If Edward L. Bernays is most often credited with being the father of public relations, it is both logical and just that his wife, Doris E. Fleischman, be recognized as the profession's mother. Fleischman was more than Bernays' life partner. She was an equal—yet often invisible—business partner in one of history's most important and successful public relations agencies.

The original power couple of public relations met as children at a beach resort on Long Island, where their families had summer cottages.[27] Fleischman, whose father was a prominent attorney, became a women's page writer for the *New York Tribune* in 1914 and a freelance writer in 1916. She went to work for Bernays in the summer of 1919 at $50 a week as a staff writer. (He paid his male staff writers $75 a week.) At that time Bernays was engaged in what he called "publicity direction" for clients such as opera legend Enrico Caruso and the Russian Ballet.[28]

Bernays and Fleischman married on September 16, 1922. In an act that would come to symbolize this partnership, Fleischman—with her new husband's encouragement—registered at the Waldorf-Astoria for their wedding night using her maiden name. "I had an inner fear that marriage (though I wanted it fiercely with Doris) would take away some of my liberties as an individual if there were always a Mrs. added to my name," Bernays wrote in his memoirs. "I wanted both the ties and the freedom."[29] During their 58 years of marriage, Fleischman and Bernays were truly a team. "My relationship

with Doris was at two levels," Bernays wrote. "At the office we were fairly businesslike and professional, but after working hours our relationship became highly personal."[30] Bernays gives credit to his wife for helping him coin the phrase "public relations counsel." Bernays told one interviewer that his wife "played an equally important role with mine, except that her insight and judgment are better than mine."[31]

Although they may have been equal partners, they certainly haven't received equal recognition: Fleischman remains a shadow lingering in the background of Bernays' career. That is largely because of the way this unique partnership operated. Although the couple closely collaborated on all projects, Bernays made all the client contacts and speeches—and not just because of his propensity for self-promotion. It was a time when women were a rarity in the business world. Many companies were uncomfortable and unwilling to embrace women's ideas. Though this reality was a bitter pill to swallow, the couple played the game by the rules of the day and, by all measures, won.

Even though Doris Fleischman has not received the acclaim achieved by her husband, Bernays was his wife's greatest champion. "These are difficult times, being alone after 58 years of happy twenty-four-hour-a-day companionship," Bernays wrote after Fleischman's death in 1980. "She was a rare woman."[32]

in encouraging women to smoke cigarettes—something he said he regretted much later in life.

Public relations historian Scott Cutlip wrote that Bernays believed in self-promotion to the point that he lost the respect of many of his contemporaries. In one instance, Bernays was fired from an account he had with General Motors because he had gotten more credit for GM's Depression-era relief efforts than had the company.[33]

Nevertheless, in recognition of his role in the advancement of public relations, *Life* magazine named Bernays to its list of the 100 most influential Americans of the 20th century.

Bernays remained a leading advocate for professional public relations until his death at the age of 103 in 1995. Late in his life, Bernays favored the licensing of public relations professionals. "Any dumbbell, nitwit or crook can call himself a public relations practitioner," Bernays told an interviewer. "The only way to protect yourself from dumbbells and crooks is to install intellectual and social values that are meaningful and keep out people who only hand out circulars in Harvard Square."[34]

Why Bernays and Not Lee?

Why isn't Ivy Ledbetter Lee, whose "Declaration of Principles" preceded Edward L. Bernays' *Crystallizing Public Opinion* by 17 years, considered the real founder of modern public relations? It appears that timing and circumstances favored Bernays.

That both men deserve recognition is without question. At a time when what was to become known as public relations was in its infancy, Lee gave the profession credibility and ethical standards. Later, Bernays gave the emerging profession a name and direction.

However, it is also true that both men were not saints. Lee proclaimed the value of truth and accuracy, but he didn't always apply those standards to his own work. As for Bernays, his penchant for self-promotion cost him numerous contracts, caused him to be despised by many of his competitors, and may even have helped to dash hopes for a lasting world peace after World War I.

Both men faced a similar fork in the road during their careers. Their choices helped to seal their reputations. With what may have been good intentions, Lee worked for the Nazis. Bernays declined the same opportunity.

Lee's death in 1934 stilled his voice and ended any chance he might have had to salvage his tarnished reputation. Bernays, however, outlived his contemporary critics. In his writings and in his promotional literature, Bernays actively portrayed himself as the "father of public relations," and he was embraced by an industry that had itself sought recognition and acceptance for so long. Now that they are gone, perhaps history will treat both men as the flawed but notable figures they really were.

The Postwar Boom

Government public relations efforts expanded at the start of U.S. involvement in World War II, when a 1942 presidential order created the **Office of War Information (OWI)**. Headed by veteran newspaper and radio commentator Elmer Davis, OWI had a twofold mission: to coordinate and control the flow of information from the battlefield to the home front, and to engage in experiments in psychological warfare against the enemy. The OWI was the forerunner of the United States Information Agency, which had more than 7,300 employees and an annual budget of approximately $1 billion prior to being absorbed by the U.S. State Department in 1999.

Like its predecessor, the Committee for Public Information, OWI became a breeding ground for a new generation of public relations practitioners. During World War II approximately 100,000 people were trained as public information officers.[35] Once the war was over, many of these "battle-hardened" practitioners turned their wartime activities into careers.

The postwar period witnessed a rapid growth in public relations education. It was during this period, in 1948, that the Public Relations Society of America was formed by the merger of the National Association of Public Relations Counsel and the American Council on Public Relations. The International Association of Business Communicators began in 1970 following the merger of the American Association of Industrial Editors and the International Council of Industrial Editors.

Postwar Social Activism

The period following World War II in many ways resembled the period of the Industrial Revolution: It was a time of significant growth in the size of government, businesses, industries, organizations, and population. The United States was the only economic power to emerge from World War II with its industrial base virtually untouched by the destruction of war. A consumer economy that had been slowed by the Great Depression and put on hold by the war was finally unleashed. Great advances were made in telecommunications, including the introduction of the most important mass communication medium of the 20th century, television.

The postwar decades also saw great social reform and upheaval, including the civil rights movement, consumerism, environmentalism, the antiwar movement, women's rights, gay rights, and multinationalism. Looming over all of this was the Cold War and the constant threat of thermonuclear war. Never had there been a time when the need for effective communication among nations, organizations, and individuals was greater.

Consumer advocate Ralph Nader provided one example of how public relations tactics could be used to make big business change the way it operated. Nader burst on the scene in 1965 with his landmark book *Unsafe at Any Speed,* in which he documented safety problems associated with automobiles, especially General Motors' Corvair. Unhappy with the negative publicity, GM sought to discredit Nader, prompting the consumer advocate to sue the company for investigating his private life. General Motors settled out of court and paid Nader $425,000—which he used to create a watchdog group, the Project on Corporate Responsibility. Nader then became a GM shareholder, which gave him access to the company's annual meetings. Although GM management defeated several PCR resolutions placed before shareholders, Nader was successful in coaxing GM to change its operations in several areas, including concessions on minority representation on the board of directors, environmental awareness, and consumer safety.[36]

Ironically, during the Industrial Revolution, many advocates of social change saw public relations as an attempt by big business to maintain the status quo. During the social upheavals of the second half of the 20th century, that view changed.

OTHER NOTABLE FIGURES FROM PUBLIC RELATIONS' PAST

Leone Baxter—with her husband and partner, *Clem Whitaker,* formed the first agency specializing in political campaigns in 1933.

Carl Byoir—a Creel Committee veteran; formed one of the earliest public relations firms, Carl Byoir & Associates, which is still prominent today.

Harwood Childs—a Princeton University political scientist who expanded upon Bernays' theories and stressed that practitioners should be students of "social effects and corporate conduct."

Pendleton Dudley—an influential figure in early public relations whose firm evolved through the years to DAY, which was aquired by Ogilvy & Mather.

Rex Harlow—a practitioner and educator; founded the American Council on Public Relations, which evolved into the Public Relations Society of America in 1948.

E.H. Heinrichs—a former Pittsburgh newspaper reporter hired by Westinghouse in 1889 to run the nation's first corporate public relations department.

John W. Hill—with partner *Don Knowlton* created Hill & Knowlton, one of the world's largest public relations firms, in Cleveland in 1927.

George V.S. Michaelis—a leading force behind the creation of the Publicity Bureau, the nation's first public relations agency.

Arthur W. Page—a vice president with American Telephone & Telegraph in 1927 who set the standard for corporate public relations, particularly employee relations.

Theodore Vail—organized the first public relations program for AT&T, based upon the then revolutionary concept that public utilities had to please their customers through good service and fair rates.

Hamilton Wright—a vigorous promoter of the growing state of Florida and a pioneer in the promotion of land development and in representing foreign nations in the United States.

Grassroots organizations adopted public relations tactics to influence the actions of business and government. In many ways, the flow of public relations had reversed.

In the spirit of "if you can't beat 'em, join 'em," well-managed companies came to realize the importance of cultivating important publics through public relations. As Edward Grefe and Martin Linsky note in their book *The New Corporate Activism,*

> A new breed of public affairs professionals began emerging who recognized that to build grassroots constituent support, it was necessary to present potential coalition allies with a positive program they could support. Following the example of grassroots organizers, these professionals fostered strategies that would not be simply against something but equally *for* something.[37]

As has been discussed in earlier chapters of this book, late 20th-century public relations practitioners became increasingly important in a wide variety of areas, including crisis communications, community relations, employee relations, and investor relations. Practitioners also play a part in strategic planning, although the scope of their role varies widely throughout the industry. "Within the public relations profession, the ability to influence strategic planning varies widely," wrote Robert W. Kinkead and Dena Winokur in *Public Relations Journal*. "Some practitioners get involved in developing game plans at the highest corporate level, while others simply implement communications moves once a strategy is set by others."[38]

Quick ✔ Check

1. Why is Edward L. Bernays most often credited as being the "father" of modern public relations?
2. How did the end of World War II influence the growth of public relations?
3. In what ways have social movements such as civil rights, women's rights, and consumerism affected the development of public relations?

The Downsizing of the United States

Changes in the world's economic climate brought dramatic consequences starting in the 1970s. The United States had an aging industrial infrastructure that made it difficult for U.S. businesses to compete with more modern facilities in other nations. Former adversaries Germany and Japan, having risen from the ashes of war, began to compete successfully against U.S. companies both in this country and abroad. Those nations had also adopted many management practices that had been pioneered in the United States but seemingly forgotten here. As a result, business and industry began a sometimes painful process of modernizing and **downsizing**. They trimmed layers of middle management, sold unprofitable divisions, and focused on core enterprises. Jobs that had once seemed certain to last forever suddenly disappeared.

This process was hastened in the 1980s when President Ronald Reagan's New Federalism initiative began the process of downsizing the federal government and shifting many of its responsibilities to the states and to the private sector. In part because of tax cuts, deregulation, and reduced payrolls, the 1980s were a period of sustained economic growth. But they were also a time in which the gap between rich and poor widened in the United States.

The downsizing trend had a major impact on public relations. Many in-house public relations departments were either reduced or eliminated entirely. This, in turn, created opportunities for agencies and private consultants to fill the gaps. The irony, of course, is that this downsizing occurred at a time when organizations needed public relations practitioners more than ever—especially when it came to explaining why people were being laid off while their employers reported record revenues and rising executive salaries. A positive development has been a greater awareness of the need for corporate responsibility and volunteerism—areas in which public relations play a major role.

The Baby Boomers Come of Age

At the same time these economic changes were occurring, a technological revolution was taking place. With the invention of silicon microprocessing chips, computers became more powerful, smaller, and more affordable. Desktop publishing came into existence, along with fax machines, e-mail, and teleconferencing. Information became the nation's top commodity. Workers, especially public relations practitioners, became more productive, and a record number of new jobs were created. Unfortunately, these new information-based jobs often paid lower salaries than the old ones they replaced.

Another important change came in the demographic makeup of the workforce. Women entered the job market in record numbers. Civil rights legislation also created opportunities for African Americans and other minority workers. The face of immigration also changed. A century earlier, the majority of immigrants coming to the United States had been from Europe. The nearly 20 million foreign-born residents counted by the U.S. Census in 1990 presented a different picture. Of that number, 44 percent had been added in the 1980s; and of the new arrivals, almost half came from Latin America and nearly one-third from Asia.

Public relations practitioners began to take on a much higher and sometimes negative profile during the 1970s and 1980s, especially in the area of government and politics. This trend actually had begun in the 1960s, when a large percentage of citizens felt that the Johnson administration was not telling the truth about its conduct of the Vietnam War—creating what commentators often referred to as a "credibility gap." In the 1970s, public relations also was criticized for its role during the Watergate scandal. In reality, many of that scandal's principal figures had advertising, not public relations, backgrounds. Had Richard Nixon followed good public relations principles, he might have been able to avoid the ignominy of becoming the first person to resign the presidency.

Following Bill Clinton's use of rapid-response public relations tactics to defeat incumbent George Bush in the 1992 presidential election, public awareness of political counselors—so-called spin doctors—increased dramatically. Some of these counselors, such as James Carville and George Stephanopoulos, later became network political pundits, a role once exclusively held by reporters. Political public relations took center stage in the presidential election stalemate of 2000. Both George W. Bush and Al Gore, trying to appear presidential and above the fray, relied heavily on surrogate spokespersons during the 36-day deadlock.

"Future History"

At the start of the new millennium, there are new challenges for public relations. The world is no longer defined by the Cold War struggle between capitalism and communism. The struggle now is for survival in a world growing increasingly interdependent. The growth of democracy in the former Soviet Union, the ups and downs of Asian economies, and the burning of rain forests in Brazil have become just as important to us as who wins the next Super Bowl. Many of the things that used to bring U.S. society together—such as reliance on families, belief in the notion of a melting pot, and tolerance for different religious beliefs—sometimes seem to pull us apart. Although the ability to communicate is rapidly improving through technological innovation, our capacity to process data in this Information Age is being outpaced by clutter in the communications channels.

At the start of the 20th century, the growth of public relations was linked to great societal changes. At the start of the 21st century, there is no reason to think that that aspect of public relations will change. As modern public relations enters its second century, the challenges facing practitioners are great. But so are the opportunities. Public relations education is spreading throughout the world's emerging democracies, making ours a truly global profession. Practitioners have shown a readiness to master new communications technologies, as they did throughout the 20th century with the introduction of national print media, radio, television, and the Internet. In all likelihood, public relations professionals will be among the first to embrace the new digital communications technologies of the 21st century—including those that we can't even begin to imagine at this time.

Quick ✔ Check

1. How has corporate downsizing affected public relations practitioners?
2. In addition to downsizing, what other social forces influenced the development of public relations near the end of the 20th century?
3. At the start of the 21st century, what are some of the challenges facing the practice of public relations?

Summary

Although public relations did not acquire its name until the 20th century, it has been practiced in some form since the beginnings of recorded time. At the time the United States was formed, public relations tactics were used to rally colonists to the cause of independence and later to support the adoption of the new nation's Constitution.

Modern public relations was born during the Industrial Revolution and began to take root during the period known as the Progressive Era. Its development throughout the past century has been nurtured by great social trends—the growth of institutions, the expansion of democracy, technological improvements in communications, the growth of advocacy, and the search for consensus. The profession's development has also been advanced by historical figures such as Theodore Roosevelt, Ivy Ledbetter Lee, and Edward L. Bernays.

By the end of the 20th century, public relations had begun to take a more central role in social discourse in the United States. Practitioners began to acquire more public visibility—even on some occasions when they would have preferred otherwise. As organizations downsized in an effort to become more efficient and effective in a global economy, public relations practitioners played a pivotal role. And in the dawn of the 21st century, the profession is constantly being challenged to embrace rapidly changing communications technology.

DISCUSSION QUESTIONS

1. Whom do you consider the "father of public relations," Ivy Ledbetter Lee or Edward L. Bernays? Why did you choose one man over the other?
2. In addition to Lee and Bernays, who are some of the other major figures that contributed to the development of modern public relations?
3. What major forces have shaped the development of public relations in the 20th century?
4. What is propaganda, and why has its use been largely discredited?
5. What role, if any, do you see public relations playing in the 21st century?
6. Given your knowledge of the history of public relations, would you accept the client described in the scenario at the beginning of this chapter? Why or why not?

Memo
from the
Field

Michael Devlin,
Senior Director of
Communications,
Rock and Roll Hall of
Fame and Museum,
Cleveland, Ohio

Michael Devlin is the senior director of communications at the Rock and Roll Hall of Fame and Museum. He is responsible for the effective communication of the Rock Hall's mission to each of the museum's primary constituencies. In this capacity, he runs the media relations department and oversees all of the museum's publications and its web site, www.rockhall.com. Before joining the Rock and Roll Hall of Fame and Museum, Devlin was director of healthcare professional marketing at Invacare Corporation for seven years. He ran Invacare's educational programs for physicians, therapists, and healthcare equipment retailers, and was responsible for the production of numerous publications and the educational components of Invacare's web site. Devlin has also held marketing positions at IMG, a sports marketing company, and General Electric.

Born and raised in Belfast, Ireland, Devlin received his undergraduate degree in English from the University of Edinburgh, Scotland, and his masters degree in business from Case Western Reserve University in Cleveland. He has lived in the United States since 1986.

The Rock and Roll Hall of Fame and Museum's mission statement reads as follows:

> The not-for-profit Rock and Roll Hall of Fame and Museum exists to educate the world about the history and significance of rock and roll music. The Museum carries out this mission through its efforts to collect, preserve, exhibit and interpret this art form.

The primary role of the communications department within the museum is to "effectively communicate the Museum's mission to all audiences in a consistent and timely manner." Sounds pretty straightforward. Tuck the mission statement under your arm and go forth, right?

I think that's the approach taken by many of us in the public relations/communications world. We treat the organizations we represent as rather static entities with a clearly defined message that we need to share with our primary audience(s). I would suggest that life is a little more complicated than that.

Not only do the organizations we represent evolve over time, but the primary themes and messages that we need to communicate change frequently and unpredictably. For instance, when I began working at the Rock and Roll Hall of Fame and Museum, the public perception was that the institution was not particularly successful, neither from an attendance nor a financial perspective. The truth was that we were in the middle of a great attendance year and that financially everything was in good shape, as it has been since the museum opened in 1995.

So everything we did in the communications department was designed to challenge this erroneous perspective. I put together a lunch for the local and regional media, I wrote three speeches for our CEO, and I used our own communications vehicles (quarterly magazine, etc.) to reinforce the point that all is well. Within a few months, we enjoyed positive editorials, positive news coverage, and renewed interest in the museum's membership program. With this mission accomplished, it was time to figure out the next theme or message that we wanted to communicate. How does a communications professional make this determination? Who makes this decision?

This is the part of our job that is often overlooked or at least given insufficient attention. You can be the best in the business at communicating to your primary audiences. You can have figured out exactly how to capture and hold the attention of your constituents. But if the message you are communicating is not the one that's most appropriate for your organization, then your efforts are wasted at best, possibly even damaging.

All of this explains why the really successful public relations professionals spend a tremendous amount of time with their attention focused inward, attempting to determine what their organization's message should be in any given day, quarter, or year. How much time does this process require? It probably differs by organization, but, for me, 50 percent feels about right.

That's 50 percent of my time spent listening, probing, exploring, researching, meeting, suggesting, and, of course, just plain walking around. I'll walk into department meetings and sit for a few minutes listening to what's being discussed. I'm continually asking the vice presidents what they're working on. I read minutes of as many meetings as possible. In general, I'm an information junkie. I see my role as teasing information out of people and articulating it, often before they have. Once articulated, I try to build consensus around those points, finally publishing them for the key managers to absorb. Only then do we turn our attention outside the organization and begin to communicate those key points to our audiences.

As it turned out, it was clear that the next "theme" we had to communicate was about our not-for-profit status and the many education programs we run, neither of which was well understood outside the organization. I was able to take this message public with a great deal of confidence because I had done the internal research as well as I could. I knew that I had the support of the museum's senior staff in this message, because I knew it was a message that was important to them.

As a public relations professional, you are paid to communicate on behalf of your organization. Keep taking your organization's pulse to make sure that the meat of your message is as relevant, timely, and significant as it can be.

Case Study 3.1

Remembering the Victims

Reading about history can be educational. Living that history can be hell. And remembering the lives changed and lost on a dark day in history is the job of Kari Watkins.

Watkins is the executive director of the Oklahoma City National Memorial, located on the site of what was at the time the largest mass murder in U.S. history. It was built on the grounds where the Alfred P. Murrah Federal Building once stood. The building was destroyed and 168 innocent people, guilty of no more than being in the wrong place at the wrong time, were killed in an act of terrorism on April 19, 1995.

"There is a reason a lot of memorials have waited 50 years to be built," Watkins said.[39] Different constituencies have different agendas, she noted. And it was the job of those seeking a fitting tribute to the heroes of Oklahoma City to listen to all of them.

In the aftermath of the bombing, Oklahoma City Mayor Ron Norick appointed a 350-member Memorial Task Force. One member of that group was Jeanette Gamba, president and CEO of Jordan Associates, an integrated marketing communications company headquartered in Oklahoma City. But her involvement actually began on the day of the disaster, when she placed telephone calls in a frantic effort to discover whether any of her colleagues or family members were among the dead and injured.[40] Gamba would later head up the memorial's communications subcommittee.

Gamba said that from the very beginning, planning for the memorial was driven by a mission statement developed by people representing a variety of community interests—especially family members of those killed in the bombing, survivors, and rescue workers so deeply touched by the experience:

> We come here to remember those who were killed, those who survived and those changed forever. May all who leave here know the impact of violence. May this memorial offer comfort, strength, peace, hope and serenity.[41]

The Oklahoma City National Memorial was established to remember the 168 people killed in an act of domestic terrorism on April 19, 1995. (Courtesy of Oklahoma City National Memorial)

"In everything we do and in everything we've done from a public relations standpoint, we try to use the mission statement as our foundation," Gamba said. "Doing the right thing to us means going back and checking to see that it is consistent with the mission statement."

Watkins refers to the mission statement as her "memorial bible" and said it drives all the Oklahoma City Memorial's communications. "We want to communicate that it is a place of remembrance and a place of education," she said. "It is not a place to memorialize the perpetrator of the crime."

That mission statement was put to the test during the weeks and months leading up to the June 11, 2001, execution of Timothy McVeigh, the man convicted of building and exploding the truck bomb that destroyed the Murrah building. It was the first federal execution in nearly four decades. Although McVeigh died by lethal injection at the Federal Penitentiary in Terra Haute, Indiana, much of the world's—and media's—attention focused several hundred miles away in Oklahoma City at the scene of the crime.

"The execution was not our story," Watkins said. "We didn't even want to be a part of it."

However, the reality was that Oklahoma City, once again, could not avoid the limelight. Watkins estimates that she received 2,400 requests for some media presence on the memorial grounds. The best that she could hope for was to manage the onslaught.

To that end, approximately 70 media representatives met with state, local, and memorial officials on April 20, just a few weeks before the execution had originally been scheduled. Its purpose was to discuss common concerns and establish ground rules. Although the media were allowed to use the memorial as a backdrop for their coverage, memorial staff and officials treated June 11 as if it were any other day.

"That was our commitment to the survivors and the families," Watkins said.

More important to the people of Oklahoma City, much of the media's focus shifted from McVeigh to the victims of his terrible deed. At the hour of the execution, several television networks ran moving tributes to those who had died in the blast. "Very little happened by accident," Gamba said. "It was all part of the ongoing relationship we had built with the media."

Successful media relations is just one example of a philosophy that has driven memorial organizers since the days immediately following the bombing. They realized that to honor history, they would have to learn from it.

Members of the Memorial Task Force had extensive conversations with the people who engineered the Vietnam Veterans Memorial in Washington, D.C. Just like the war it commemorates, the Vietnam memorial was a source of intense controversy at the time of its dedication in 1982.

"We met with Jan Skruggs, the head of the Vietnam Memorial Committee early on and asked what mistakes had been made," Watkins said. "One of them was that they didn't involve their constituents as much as they should have.

"We knew we couldn't build this memorial without our neighbors on our side," she added.

In the case of the Oklahoma City memorial, a wide range of constituencies exists. They include family members of the deceased, survivors, rescue workers, government officials, the Oklahoma City community, donors, and the news media. Memorial organizers committed themselves to achieving "buy-in" from each group. "There was never a committee that didn't have one of the co-chairs be either a family member or survivor," Gamba said. "It really gave us a channel of input on everything."

In addition to involving key stakeholders, the Memorial Task Force conducted public and private meetings and gathered thousands of written and Internet survey responses. Once an agreement on the mission statement was reached in March 1996, the focus turned to delivering a message that was both clear and consistent. "Our board has made the commitment that we will say one thing and say it united," Watkins said.

President Bill Clinton helped dedicate the $29.1 million memorial on the fifth anniversary of the bombing. Ten months later, President George W. Bush spoke at the dedication of a museum and interactive media center in what had been the gutted shell of a newspaper office across the street from the Murrah building. "Your loss was great, and your pain was deep," Bush said. "Far greater and deeper was your care for one another."[42]

What was once a scene of unbelievable horror had become a place of "comfort, strength, peace, hope, and serenity."

DISCUSSION QUESTIONS

1. How important was the development of a mission statement in reaching the ultimate goal of building a memorial to the victims of the Oklahoma City bombing?
2. Who were the different constituencies that the Memorial Task Force needed to address and how might each public's point of view differ from the others'?
3. Why did Kari Watkins say that the execution of Timothy McVeigh "was not our (the memorial's) story"? Do you agree or disagree with her statement? Why?
4. What role did research play in this case study, and how was that research conducted?
5. What do you think Kari Watkins meant when she said, "There is a reason a lot of memorials have waited 50 years to be built"?

Case Study 3.2

Torches of Freedom

It's called "Big Tobacco," and with good reason. For much of U.S. history, the tobacco industry had unparalleled clout where it matters most, on Capitol Hill. Unfortunately for the people who brought you Joe Camel, that has dramatically changed.

In recent years, Big Tobacco has been reeling from a tidal wave of resentment and scorn. Big Tobacco finally admitted in 1997 what had already been accepted by most people as common knowledge: Cigarettes are addictive and harmful to health. With the help of public relations practitioners, the tobacco industry had vigorously denied the obvious to protect its multibillion dollar empire, even though the link between cancer and cigarettes had been established for more than 60 years.

The early promotion of cigarettes centered on their supposed health benefits. On behalf of the makers of Lucky Strike, Edward Bernays created the Tobacco Society for Voice Culture in 1927. Its letterhead included the slogan "So to improve the cords of the throat through cigarette smoking that the public will be able to express itself in songs of praise or more easily swallow anything."[43] The public wasn't swallowing this—the Tobacco Society for Voice Culture became a source of great amusement and derision. However, American Tobacco Company President George W. Hill, in pursuit of a potentially lucrative and untapped female market, came up with the "Reach for a Lucky instead of a sweet" campaign. Despite the protest from doctors, many women saw Lucky Strikes as a key to weight loss.

One of Bernays' most outlandish—and successful—efforts at tapping into the female market came in 1929, when he had 10 debutantes walk down New York's Fifth Avenue carrying lighted cigarettes aloft. "In the interests of equality of the sexes and to fight another sex taboo, I and other young women will light another torch of freedom by smoking cigarettes while strolling on Easter Sunday," Bernays' secretary telegraphed reporters. "We are doing this to combat the silly prejudice that the cigarette is suitable for the home, the restaurant, the taxicab, the theater lobby, but never the sidewalk."[44]

The Torches of Freedom march created a nationwide stir—exactly what Bernays wanted. Later, he would write, "a beginning had been made, one I regret today."[45]

In fairness to Bernays and other early practitioners, the harmful effects of cigarettes were not fully known in those days. It wasn't until 1930 that scientists in Germany first suggested the link between smoking and cancer. However, even in the early 1900s, a significant amount of scientific literature pointed an accusing finger at smoking.

A 1952 *Reader's Digest* article, "Cancer by the Carton," dramatically brought home the danger of smoking to Americans. That report, and the ensuing publicity, prompted the tobacco industry to hire John Hill, founder of Hill & Knowlton, to rescue lagging sales. Hill's brainchild was the Tobacco Institute Research Committee. In a full-page advertisement in more than 400 newspapers, readers were told that the TIRC would sponsor research into health issues raised by smoking. Sixty-five percent of the public responded favorably to the advertisements. The TIRC would eventually evolve into the Tobacco Institute, which at its height employed more than 120 public relations practitioners and spent more than $20 million annually promoting tobacco.[46]

Under the threat of hundreds of billions of dollars in personal injury lawsuits, the tobacco industry agreed in 1997 to a historic legal settlement with 39 state attorneys general. Under the settlement, the industry said it was willing to submit to nicotine regulation by the Food and Drug Administration for the first time and agreed to pay $368.5 billion in punitive and compensatory damages. That settlement fell through when Congress and the White House tried to change the deal. A second, more modest settlement was reached with 42 states a year later. The new agreement did not require Washington's approval, restricted tobacco industry marketing tactics, and earmarked $206 billion for state health and antismoking education programs. Four states went on to make their own deals totaling $40 billion.[47]

Big Tobacco still faces numerous legal challenges. The U.S. Justice Department filed federal racketeering and fraud charges against four companies in 1999 in an effort to regulate tobacco sales and to impose higher excise taxes on cigarettes. Those companies entered into settlement talks with the government in June 2001.[48] In July 2000, a jury ordered five of the nation's largest cigarette makers to pay a record-setting $145 billion in damages in a class-action lawsuit brought on behalf of 300,000–700,000 sick Florida smokers or their families. At the time this book went to press, the matter was on appeal.[49]

These and other continuing challenges are based in part on internal documents that suggest Big Tobacco executives ignored their own research showing smoking was harmful. Those documents have also raised doubts about industry claims that it doesn't encourage smoking among minors. A report released by the U.S. Surgeon General in March 2001 noted a rise in smoking among teenage girls and blamed tobacco industry marketing practices. Industry officials denied the allegation, citing their efforts to discourage teenage smoking.[50]

It may be unfair to second-guess the motives of public relations practitioners who have worked through the years for Big Tobacco. Only the individuals involved can say how much they knew about the industry's questionable practices and when they knew it. But as evidence of public health dangers and ethical lapses mounted, they would have been well served to have remembered that where there is smoke, there is fire.

DISCUSSION QUESTIONS

1. If you were offered a high-paying public relations job with a major tobacco company, would you take it? What are your reasons? How would past Big Tobacco actions influence your decision?

2. To what degree do you think public relations practitioners should be held accountable for promoting legal products that have potentially dangerous side effects?

3. In addition to tobacco, name other controversial products or services that a public relations practitioner may have difficulty promoting.

4. What role should corporate and personal values play in the promotion of legal products with negative side effects?

5. Does the fact that tobacco companies are paying millions of dollars to promote anti-smoking campaigns improve their image? Does it make any difference whether such expenditures are voluntary or part of a legal settlement?

It's Your Turn

MegaShop Comes to Sunnyview

Your hometown, Sunnyview, has a vibrant downtown commercial district. Many of your neighbors want to keep it that way.

However, change is in the air. Once seen as a small and isolated town, Sunnyview has nearly doubled its size in the past 30 years. And because of a new interstate highway that connects it to a major metropolitan area just 40 miles away, Sunnyview is now viewed as a "bedroom community" for the big city.

This growth has resulted in commercial prosperity. That, in turn, has caught the attention of a major out-of-state retailer, MegaShop Ltd. The company has petitioned the Sunnyview Zoning Board for permission to build a major shopping mall just off of the interstate. MegaShop officials say they are willing to pay for the necessary street and utility improvements. All they need is approval of their request to rezone the mall property from residential to commercial use.

Downtown merchants fear that the new mall will draw both customers and merchants from the downtown commercial district. Such movement, they claim, will eventually lead to the demise of the area. They point to several examples of places where MegaShop malls have dramatically changed the character of the communities in which they have been built.

Because you are well known throughout Sunnyview for your public relations skills, you have been asked to spearhead efforts to block construction of the new shopping mall. MegaShop officials have also called; they too want to retain your services. Several questions immediately come to mind:

- The company is not asking the city for any special favors, so why should I care? Should I even get involved?
- If I decided to oppose the mall project, how would I proceed?
- If I were to represent the interests of MegaShop Ltd., how would I proceed?
- Is this a yes-or-no situation, or are there alternatives?

The decisions are yours. Your would-be clients are waiting. How will you proceed?

KEY TERMS

Committee for Public Information (CPI), p. 68
downsizing, p. 76
Federalist letters, p. 61
First Amendment, p. 61
Four-Minute Men, p. 69
Industrial Revolution, p. 58
Office of War Information (OWI), p. 73

Progressive Era, p. 59
propaganda, p. 68
pseudoevent, p. 60
Publicity Bureau, p. 64
rhetoric, p. 57
Seedbed Years, p. 63
vox populi, p. 57

NOTES

1. Jacque L'Etang, "State Propaganda and Bureaucratic Intelligence: The Creation of Public Relations in 20th Century Britain," *Public Relations Review* (winter 1998): 413.
2. L'Etang.
3. Gary A. Warner, "The Development of Public Relations Offices at American Colleges and Universities," *Public Relations Quarterly* (summer 1996): 36.
4. Dennis Wilcox, Phillip H. Ault, and Warren K. Agee, *Public Relations: Strategies and Tactics*, 5th ed. (New York: Longman, 1998), 247.
5. Wilcox, Ault, and Agee.
6. Norman Foerster, Norman S. Grabo, Russel B. Nye, E. Fred Carlisle, and Robert Falk, eds., *American Poetry and Prose*, 5th ed., pt. 1 (New York: Houghton Mifflin, 1970), 139.
7. Foerster et al., 139.
8. Foerster et al., 146 (emphasis in the original).
9. Foerster et al., 145.
10. Foerster et al., 138.
11. Scott M. Cutlip, *The Unseen Power: Public Relations: A History* (Hillsdale, N.J.: Lawrence Erlbaum, 1994), 1.
12. Cutlip, 10–25.

13. Paul Mccabee, "Ranting over Rating: Hazel O'Leary Meets the Press," *Public Relations Tactics* (January 1996): 13.

14. Blaire Atherton French, *The Presidential Press Conference: Its History and Role in the American Political System* (Lanham, Md.: University Press of America, 1982), 3.

15. Carolyn Smith, *Presidential Press Conferences: A Critical Approach.* (New York: Praeger, 1990), 22.

16. Cutlip, 37–45.

17. Cutlip, 45.

18. Cutlip, 139.

19. Thomas Flemming, "When the United States Entered World War I, Propagandist George Creel Set Out to Stifle Anti-War Sentiment," *Military History,* online, The History Net, www.thehistorynet.com.

20. Charles A. Lubbers, "George Creel and the Four-Minute Men: A Milestone in Public Relations History," *Business Research Yearbook: Global Business Perspectives,* vol. III (New York: International Academy of Business Disciplines, 1996), 719.

21. Flemming.

22. Edward L. Bernays, *Biography of an Idea: Memoirs of Public Relations Counsel Edward L. Bernays* (New York: Simon & Schuster, 1965), 161.

23. Bernays, 177–178.

24. Samuel R. Spencer Jr., *Decision for War, 1917* (Peterborough, N.H.: Noone House, 1953).

25. Bernays, 288.

26. Kathleen O'Neill, "U.S. Public Relations Evolves to Meet Society's Needs," *Public Relations Journal* (November 1991): 28.

27. Bernays, 218.

28. Susan Henry, "Anonymous in Her Own Name: Public Relations Pioneer Doris Fleischman," *Journalism History* 23, no. 2 (summer 1997): 52.

29. Bernays, 217.

30. Bernays, 216.

31. Cutlip, 169–170.

32. Cutlip, 170.

33. Cutlip, 159–225.

34. Alvin M. Hattal, "The Father of Public Relations: Edward L. Bernays," *Communication World* (January 1992): 15.

35. Cutlip, 528.

36. Patrick Jackson and Allen H. Center, *Public Relations Practices: Managerial Case Studies and Problems,* 5th ed. (Englewood Cliffs, N.J.: Prentice Hall, 1995), 167–178.

37. Edward A. Grefe and Martin Linsky, *The New Corporate Activism* (New York: McGraw-Hill, 1995), 3 (emphasis in original).

38. Robert W. Kinkead and Dena Winokur, "How Public Relations Professionals Help CEOs Make the Right Moves," *Public Relations Journal* (October 1992): 18–23.

39. Interview, 16 July 2001.

40. Interview, 16 July 2001.

41. Mission Statement, Oklahoma City National Memorial web site, www.oklahomacitynationalmemorial.org.

42. "Bush Praises Oklahoma City as He Dedicates Bombing Museum," online, CNN Interactive, 19 February 2001, www.cnn.com.
43. Bernays, 374.
44. Bernays, 387.
45. Bernays, 387.
46. John Stauber and Sheldon Rampton, "How the American Tobacco Industry Employs PR Scum to Continue Its Murderous Assault on Human Lives," *Tucson Weekly,* 22 November 1995.
47. "States' Attorneys Are Weighing Whether to Sign Deal," the Associated Press, as reported in the *Kansas City Star,* 18 November 1998, A4.
48. Major Garrett, "Justice Department, Tobacco Companies to Discuss Settlement." online, CNN Interactive, 22 June 2001, www.cnn.com.
49. "Judge Upholds $145 Billion Verdict against U.S. Cigarette Makers," online, CNN Interactive, 6 November 2000, www.cnn.com.
50. Christy Feig, "More Teen Girls Smoking in U.S.," online, CNN Interactive, 27 March 2001, www.cnn.com.

4

The Publics
in Public Relations

After studying this chapter, you will be able to

- define the term *public* as it is used in public relations

- name and describe the different kinds of publics

- list the kinds of information that practitioners should gather about each public

- identify and describe the traditional publics in public relations

Pop Goes Your Wednesday

scenario   *Wednesday starts peacefully at the Kablooie Microwave Popcorn Company, where you are director of public relations. You are planning to spend the morning getting ready for next week's annual meeting of stockholders. Kablooie is a new company, and you are eager to tell stockholders about its recently completed Statement of Values, which begins with these words: "Kablooie Microwave Popcorn Company exists to provide value at a fair price to its customers; to provide a competitive return on investment to its stockholders; and to provide a humane work-place and fair salaries and benefits to its employees."*

Then:

- *Your assistant tells you his 13-year-old daughter just telephoned. In chat rooms all over the Internet, she says, kids are suddenly saying that Kablooie Microwave Popcorn is blowing the doors off microwave ovens and injuring teens. One report says that a popular rock star has been hospitalized in critical condition after being injured by a Kablooie explosion. From coast to coast, kids are telling one another to boycott your product.*

- *Your assistant is still talking when a reporter from your local newspaper calls to ask about the rumor that Kablooie Microwave Popcorn is exploding in microwave ovens and injuring people. You emphatically deny the rumor and promise to call back in 15 minutes.*

- *A beep from your computer tells you that a new e-mail message has arrived. It's from a nationally known investment analyst, asking whether there are any new issues you're expecting to deal with at next week's annual meeting for stockholders. Evidently, she hasn't yet heard about the Internet rumors.*

- *Your secretary brings you a letter from a local Boy Scout troop. In two days the troop will begin selling your product door to door as a fund-raising project. The letter is thanking you for the early delivery of 10,000 packages of Kablooie Microwave Popcorn.*

You immediately decide to implement your company's crisis communications plan (see Chapter 12). Like all good public relations plans, it asks you to identify the most important publics with whom you must communicate.

In this scenario, who are your publics? Which are the most important? Can the new Statement of Values help?

What Is a Public?

Public relations. That's what we call this challenging, rewarding business.

Take a good look at that first word: **public.** That's where we start. Publics are literally the first word in our profession.

So what is a public? As you may recall from Chapter 1, a public is any group whose members have a common interest or common values in a particular situation. A political party can be a public. Upper-level managers in a corporation can be a public. Fans of a popular music group can be a public.

The word *stakeholder* often substitutes for the word *public*, but the two words aren't interchangeable. Some publics may have no connection with the organization that a public relations practitioner represents. But as we note in Chapter 1, a

stakeholder, or stakeholder group, has a stake, or an interest, in an organization or issue that potentially involves the organization. For any given organization, then, all stakeholder groups are publics—but not all publics are stakeholders.

Counting all the publics even in just the United States would be like trying to count the stars—an impossible task. So which publics matter in public relations? With which publics do we build and manage values-driven relationships? Certain publics become important to an organization as its values and values-based goals interact with the environment. Those publics become stakeholders. For example, to fulfill its values-driven goal of healing people, a nonprofit hospital must have a good relationship with the community's physicians. The hospital's values somehow must fit comfortably with the values of the physicians if this vital relationship is to work.

Another example: To fulfill its goal of being a clean, attractive facility, that same hospital must have a good relationship with its custodians. The hospital needs to understand the values of the custodians—such as fair wages—to make that relationship work. As an organization's values interact with the values of different publics, relationships—good or bad—are born. In fact, if we know the specific values-driven goals of an organization and we know the environment in which it operates, we can predict with some accuracy the essential relationships that can help the organization attain its goals.

Sometimes, however, a relationship surprises an organization. A public in the organization's environment can discover a relationship before the organization does. Often, a clash of values triggers that unexpected relationship. For example, a Midwestern county government trying to build a highway around a growing metropolitan area was surprised when Native Americans strongly opposed the proposed route. The highway passed too near, they said, to an area they used for worship. A values-driven goal of the county government—easing traffic congestion within the metropolitan area—had clashed with a religious value of Native Americans in the area. As one values system met another, a relationship was born.

Why Do We Need Relationships with Publics?

Now, what about that second word in public relations: *relations*? Why do organizations build and maintain values-driven relationships with a variety of publics? (We're glad that they do: The relationship-management process provides interesting, rewarding jobs for thousands of public relations practitioners.) But, again, it's worth asking: Why do organizations need relationships with different publics? An excellent answer to this question comes from **resource dependency theory,**[1] which consists of three simple beliefs:

1. To fulfill their values, organizations need resources, such as raw materials and people to work for the organization.
2. Some of those key resources are *not* controlled by the organization.
3. To acquire those key resources, organizations must build productive relationships with the publics that control the resources.

Resource dependency theory tells us that, first and foremost, public relations practitioners must build relationships with publics that possess resources organizations need to fulfill their values-driven goals.

Resource dependency theory can even help us determine which publics will receive most of our relationship-management efforts. Clearly, our most important publics are those that possess the resources our organization needs the most. For example, Pitney Bowes, an international message-management company, focuses on resource dependency theory in the first sentence of its values statement: "Pitney Bowes' relationships with our four constituent groups—customers, employees, stockholders, and the communities—are critical to our success and reputation."[2] In public relations, we build relationships with publics to secure the resources our organizations need to survive and fulfill their values.

Resource dependency theory, therefore, helps explain values-driven public relations. As we describe in Chapter 1, values-driven public relations brings the entire public relations process—research, planning, communication, and evaluation—into a framework defined by an organization's core values. In the planning phase, practitioners establish values-driven public relations goals. To reach those goals, practitioners often must acquire resources held by other publics; this is where resource dependency theory meets values-driven public relations. If our goals are values-driven, the resources we acquire from targeted publics bring our organization closer to fulfilling its values.

Resource dependency theory also helps explain the two-way symmetrical model, the most successful of the four models of public relations (see Chapter 1). Two-way symmetrical public relations works best when there is an exchange of resources. If an organization wants to acquire the resources it needs, it must be willing to give the resource holders something they need. For example, news media have resources most organizations need, including fair and accurate coverage. In return, those organizations have resources news media need, including a willingness to respond to journalists' questions promptly and honestly. In a two-way symmetrical relationship, an organization agrees to exchange resources to fulfill its values-driven goals.

The Publics in Public Relations

Publics may be as impossible to count as the stars, but, like the stars, they can be grouped into categories, including

- traditional and nontraditional publics
- latent, aware, and active publics
- intervening publics
- primary and secondary publics
- internal and external publics
- domestic and international publics

Why bother to group publics into categories? Because knowing which category or categories a public belongs to can provide insight into how to build a productive relationship with it. The thoughtful process of deciding which category or categories a public belongs to can help us learn from our own experiences as well as those of others. So let's examine these categories.

Traditional and Nontraditional Publics

Traditional publics are groups with which organizations have ongoing, long-term relationships. As shown in Figure 4.1, traditional publics include employees, news media, governments, investors, customers, multicultural community groups, and constituents (voters). The fact that these publics are traditional, however, doesn't mean that public relations practitioners can take them for granted. Organizations that

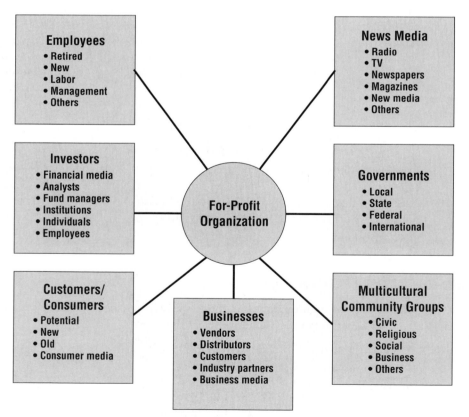

FIGURE 4.1   Traditional Publics in Public Relations A for-profit organization can have dozens of primary publics. Not pictured in this diagram is the most important public for government public relations practitioners: constituents and voters.

ignore the values of employees or of the news media, for example, quickly learn to their sorrow how powerful those publics can be. In Pop Goes Your Wednesday, the scenario that opens this chapter, the investment analyst who e-mails you with a request for information represents a traditional public.

Nontraditional publics are groups that usually are unfamiliar to an organization. For example, in Pop Goes Your Wednesday, the high-tech teenagers in those Internet chat rooms constitute a nontraditional public—a group with which Kablooie hasn't had an ongoing, long-term relationship. Nontraditional publics can be hard to study and may lead you to try some innovative relationship-building strategies. Nontraditional publics are often sparked by changes in a society—such as the growth of Internet chat rooms.

Nontraditional publics can be new and challenging, but it's possible that one day they'll become traditional publics. For example, after the fall of communism in Russia—a definite change in society—independent news media in that country were a nontraditional public for Russian organizations: The organizations had rarely dealt

Congresswoman Kay Granger of Texas addresses the Log Cabin Republicans, the nation's largest organization of gay and lesbian Republicans. LCR Director of Public Affairs Kevin Ivers *(background)* is helping his organization make the transition from nontraditional to traditional public. (Courtesy of Log Cabin Republicans)

with news media that weren't controlled by the government. As time passes, however, Russian public relations practitioners learn more about the values of independent journalists, and vice versa. Though they often face government resistance, Russian news media are well on their way to being considered a traditional public.

Closer to home, gay and lesbian groups might be considered a nontraditional public that, for some organizations, is becoming a traditional public. Whether an organization desires a relationship with these minority groups, the voices of their members often will be heard. Laura Schlessinger, host of the radio advice show "Dr. Laura," definitely heard the voices of gay and lesbian citizens when she blamed them for dooming her move into television. Before launching a television talk show in 2000, Schlessinger reportedly had called homosexuality "deviant" and a "biological error" that needed "reparative therapy."[3] As Schlessinger and Paramount Pictures Television Group prepared to launch the show, they were blasted by a Stop Dr. Laura campaign spearheaded by the Gay and Lesbian Alliance Against Defamation (GLAAD). GLAAD's campaign eventually helped persuade more than 90 sponsors to discontinue ads on the TV show,[4] leading to its cancellation in its first season.

"I'm very proud of the product we had," Schlessinger said. "Unfortunately, it never even had a chance for the audience to decide . . . because the advertisers were intimidated and threatened by GLAAD and their constituency."[5]

Said GLAAD Executive Director Joan Garry, "The gay community has sent a very strong message that we're no longer an easy mark."[6]

Although some organizations view homosexuals as a nontraditional public and reject any relationship building (the president of the nation of Namibia recently ordered police there to "arrest, deport, and imprison" homosexuals[7]), gay and lesbian citizens are in the process of becoming a traditional public for other organizations. United Airlines, Saturn automobiles, and the San Diego Padres baseball team, for example, openly market to gay and lesbian customers. Meanwhile, other organizations, such as the Walt Disney Company, have extended insurance benefits to the lifetime partners of gay and lesbian employees.[8] But the resultant boycott of Disney products by the Southern Baptist Convention, the largest Protestant denomination in the United States, shows that the terms *traditional* and *nontraditional* are relative. One organization's traditional public can be nontraditional to another organization.

Latent, Aware, and Active Publics

Public relations scholars often categorize publics as *latent, aware,* or *active.*[9] A **latent public** is a group whose values have come into contact with the values of your organization, but whose members haven't yet realized it; the members of that public are not yet aware of the relationship. An **aware public** is a group whose members are aware of the intersection of their values with those of your organization but haven't organized any kind of response to the relationship. An **active public,** however, not only recognizes the relationship between itself and your organization but is also working to manage that relationship on its own terms. In Pop Goes Your Wednesday,

YOUR TAX DOLLARS AT WORK

As you're reading this sentence, the federal government of the United States is collecting information about you, your friends, your family—and millions of other Americans.

Sounds scary, right? But that storehouse of information can be incredibly useful to public relations practitioners. Even better, much of the information is online and can be easily accessed at FedStats (www.fedstats.gov).

Need the ethnic makeup of your county? Try the Bureau of the Census. You can reach it through FedStats.

Need employment projections for the coming decades? Try the Bureau of Labor Statistics. You can reach it through FedStats.

Need data on farmers? Try the National Agricultural Statistics Service. On older Americans? Try the Administration on Aging. On prisoners? Try the Federal Bureau of Prisons.

FedStats can connect you to dozens of federal agencies that gather information on the publics that make up public relations. As a taxpayer, you're footing the bill for all those studies, so get your money's worth: Bookmark FedStats for your web browser.

the teenagers in the chat rooms are more than just a nontraditional public; they're also an active public.

Intervening Publics

Let's say that in our Kablooie Microwave Popcorn scenario, you wisely keep your promise to the local newspaper reporter who telephoned. You call her back in 15 minutes and report that you've checked with the top five manufacturers of microwave ovens, and none are reporting problems with Kablooie popcorn. In fact, they've said that such a defect in their ovens is impossible. You give the reporter the names of the public relations officials for those manufacturers, and you fax her a statement from Kablooie's chief executive officer in which he denies the rumors. You even invite her to come tour your factory's quality-control department.

Why spend so much time with one reporter? You know the answer to that: because she has thousands of local readers to whom you want to send the message that Kablooie popcorn is safe. In public relations, any public that helps you send a message to another public is called an **intervening public**. In the Kablooie scenario, one of your most important publics consists of the people of Kablooie Microwave Popcorn's hometown; they're a high-priority public that you're targeting with a specific message to maintain the good relationship between Kablooie and its hometown. If the local newspaper can help you send that message, it is an intervening public.

Primary and Secondary Publics

Publics can also be divided into primary publics and secondary publics. If a public can directly affect your organization's pursuit of its values-driven goals, that public is definitely a **primary public**—a public of great importance. **Secondary publics** are also important. You want to have a good relationship with them—but their ability to affect your organization's pursuit of its goals is minimal. Because resources such as time and money are scarce, public relations practitioners spend most of their time building and managing relationships with primary publics. If resources permit, they also build and manage relationships with secondary publics.

In Pop Goes Your Wednesday, your company's investors are a primary public; your Statement of Values emphasizes that fact. A bad relationship with investors and the people who advise them could immediately and seriously harm the financial security of Kablooie. In this scenario, a secondary public would be local stores that sell microwave ovens. Because they might have to field a few questions, you might telephone them—if time permits. But you wisely decide first to devote your attention to the primary publics that can influence the success of Kablooie Microwave Popcorn.

Internal and External Publics

Publics are either **internal publics** or **external publics;** that is, either they're inside your organization or outside it. Kablooie's employees are an internal public—as well as a primary public. You'd be smart to inform them of the rumors so that they're not surprised by reports in the news media or by inquisitive friends and neighbors. External publics would include investment analysts, news media, the Boy Scouts, and teenagers using chat rooms.

Sometimes, however, the line between internal and external isn't clearly drawn. For example, the alumni of your college or university technically are an external public; they're no longer enrolled, and most have probably moved away. But many of them don't *feel* external—to their dying day, they will be Jayhawks or Tarheels or Longhorns or Horned Toads or whatever mascot brings a tear of pride to their eyes. Smart public relations practitioners identify such feelings and, when appropriate, treat such a public as a member of the organization's family. Although the Kablooie Microwave Popcorn Company is a new organization, imagine it 30 years from now. Will its loyal retired employees feel like an internal or an external public?

Domestic and International Publics

Last but not least, publics are either domestic publics or international publics. **Domestic publics** are those within your own country. But proximity doesn't necessarily mean familiarity. As we saw previously, some domestic publics can be nontraditional publics, requiring effective cross-cultural communication efforts.

International publics are those beyond your country's borders. Increasingly, public relations practitioners are dealing with international publics. For example, suppose that the factory that supplies the packages for Kablooie popcorn is in Mexico. A variety of cross-cultural considerations now confront you. Do you speak Spanish? Does the factory manager there speak English? If your crisis has occurred on May 5 or September 16, will the factory manager answer a telephone call to his or her office? Probably not: Those days are national holidays in Mexico.

What Do We Need to Know about Each Public?

No two publics are the same. And yet the kinds of information we need to gather about each public are remarkably similar. To manage a productive, values-driven relationship with a public, we must be able to answer seven questions about it:

1. *How much can the public influence our organization's ability to achieve our goals?* In other words, is the public a primary public or a secondary public? As much as public relations practitioners would like to have positive, well-maintained relationships with every public, that ideal is simply too impractical; it would stretch their resources too thin. Public relations practitioners must focus most of their attention and efforts on the relationships that spell the difference between success and failure for their organizations.

2. *What is the public's stake, or value, in its relationship with our organization?* As we noted earlier, a relationship between a public and an organization is born when values intersect. What values does the public hold that have brought it into contact with your organization? For example, investors value steady increases in the price of the stock they own. Customers value getting their money's worth. Employees value, among other things, interesting work and good salaries.

Identifying the value or values a public seeks to realize in its relationship with your organization is one of the most important things you can do in public relations. It allows you to explore the possibility of a relationship in which both sides win: The public's values can be recognized and honored, and your organization can achieve its goal for the relationship. That's the heart of values-driven public relations.

3. *Who are the opinion leaders and decision makers for the public?* Members of a public turn to **opinion leaders** for advice and leadership. Stockholders, for example, often turn to successful investment analysts for advice. Employees may turn to union leaders or trusted supervisors. If we can identify the opinion leaders of a public, perhaps we can build a relationship with them that will strengthen our relationship with the entire public.

Not every public has well-defined, easily identifiable opinion leaders, however. For example, in the scenario that opens this chapter, who are the opinion leaders for the millions of teenagers using Internet chat rooms? That particular public is so large that we might be wise to divide it into smaller publics—based on geography or on the particular chat rooms the teenagers frequent—and look for opinion leaders of those smaller groups.

Decision makers are people who have the authority to dictate actions and establish policies for publics. Some publics have easily identifiable decision makers. For example, decision makers for news media are the editors, publishers, directors, and producers who oversee the content of newspapers, magazines, radio programs, television programs, or web sites. The decision maker of a local environmental group probably would be the group's president or board of directors—though any important decision might involve a vote among members. Decision makers can be determined by the goal your organization is trying to achieve. For example, when a company wants to build a new factory, one set of decision makers from which it needs approval may be a local zoning board.

Some publics, however, don't have easily identifiable decision makers. Latent publics or aware publics (as opposed to active publics) may be only loosely organized at best. For example, suppose your organization wants to improve its relationship with local alternative rock musicians. Who are the decision makers for that diverse group—or for the teenagers in the chat rooms? Perhaps the best we can do is to point to opinion leaders for our targeted public.

Even within a single, well-defined public, opinion leaders and decision makers can vary, depending on the issue. For example, a local taxpayers group may have one opinion leader for issues involving sales taxes but a different opinion leader for property tax issues. And on simple matters such as scheduling meetings, the president of the group may be the decision maker. But on more important decisions, such as organizing a protest at City Hall, the board of directors may have to call for a vote among members.

Despite the difficulties, public relations practitioners seek to identify and to build relationships with decision makers and opinion leaders because they often have influence over publics that may be essential to an organization's success.

4. *What is the demographic profile of the public?* **Demographic information** is data about who a public is. For example, besides telling us how many members a public has, a demographic profile of a public might include information about age, gender, income, education, and number of children per family. For each of these characteristics, we would probably want medians and ranges. For example, we probably would like to know the median age of an important public (the age that represents a halfway point, with half the public younger and half the public older than the median age). The range of ages would specify the age of the youngest member of the public as well as the age of its oldest member. Demographic information can help us understand who a public is, how important that public might be to our organization, and what its values might be.

In our Kablooie Microwave Popcorn scenario, we might consider grocery-store chains that carry our product to be a public. Although demographic characteristics such as age and gender might not influence our communications with that large public, we certainly might rank the members of that public by how much Kablooie Microwave Popcorn each company purchases for resale. That information could help us subdivide our grocery-store chain public into smaller publics and provide direction on which chains we might choose to contact first.

5. *What is the psychographic profile of the public?* **Psychographic information** is data about what members of a public think, believe, and feel. For example, are they politically liberal, moderate, or conservative? Are they religious? Agnostic? Atheistic? Do they like sophisticated technology or fear it—or, perhaps, are they indifferent to it? Psychographic information can be harder to collect and measure than demographic information, but it's no less important. Like demographic information, a psychographic profile can help us understand who a public is and what its values might be.

6. *What is the public's opinion of our organization?* Any television sitcom about high school students eventually has a scene in which one student wants to date another and is desperately trying to find out that person's opinion of him or her. It's the same in public relations, though perhaps a little less stressful. A public's opinion of our organization is one of the foundations of our relationship. That opinion tells us whether we approach the relationship as friends, unknowns, or enemies. It would be an embarrassing waste of resources, for example, to create a communications program for a public that we think is hostile—only to discover that that public has a favorable impression of us and is puzzled by our actions.

7. *What is the public's opinion (if any) of the issue in question?* As we've noted before, sometimes a particular issue creates a relationship between an organization and a public. For example, the false stories about Kablooie Microwave Popcorn have suddenly created a relationship between Kablooie and the teenagers using Internet chat rooms. We need to learn what the public thinks about the issue; in particular, we need to know which of the public's values are supported or threatened by the issue.

Coorientation

Coorientation is a public relations research process that can help us discover where our organization agrees and disagrees with an important public on a particular issue. Coorientation can eliminate damaging misperceptions about what each side believes. (As you'll see, coorientation can get a little like the comedy routine in which one actor says, "I think that you think that I think. . . .") In part, coorientation involves asking these four questions:

1. What is our organization's view of this issue?
2. What is the particular public's view of this issue?
3. What does our organization *think* the public's view is? (Does this agree with reality?)
4. What does the particular public *think* our organization's view is? (Does this agree with reality?)

Organizations that use coorientation in public relations are occasionally surprised to discover that they actually agree with a public that they had mistakenly identified as hostile (or, unfortunately, vice versa). Coorientation helps public relations practitioners avoid misperceptions that could damage their relationship-management efforts.

As we said in Chapter 1, the public relations process begins with research. Answering, to the best of our ability, the seven questions just listed is one of the most important parts of public relations research.

Quick ✓ Check

1. In public relations, what is the definition of the word *public*? Of *stakeholder*?
2. What differences separate latent, aware, and active publics?
3. What are the differences between demographic information and psychographic information?
4. What is resource dependency theory?
5. What is coorientation?

The Traditional Publics in Public Relations

Earlier in this chapter we introduced the term *traditional publics*—that is, publics with which organizations have long-term, ongoing relationships. As we noted, *traditional* can be a misleading word. A group that is a traditional public for one organization might be a nontraditional public for another. Many organizations, however, do have long-term relationships with well-established traditional publics, including employees, the news media, governments, investors, consumers, multicultural community groups, constituents (voters), and businesses. In the next several pages, we'll offer brief descriptions of those publics—and, because they change every day, we'll also offer sources you can consult to update your knowledge of these important publics in public relations.

Employees

As the old joke goes, we have good news and bad news. The good news is that two recent surveys show that organization managers consider employee relations to be a top, enduring priority.[10] So what's the bad news? It's symbolized by a year 2000 study that revealed that Canadian corporate chief financial officers believed that poor communications with employees is the biggest challenge their organizations face.[11]

Employees often are the most important publics in public relations. Think about it: If your organization's employees aren't on your side, it doesn't matter how good your relationships with other publics are. So it's good news that organizations are focusing on this key public. But the challenge of building good relationships with employees has never been greater. Employee publics are changing so rapidly that traditional forms of communication are inadequate—and around the world, employee discontent is on the rise.

What changes are reshaping the employee public? Management consultant Robert Barner identifies five:[12]

■ *A distributed workforce:* Employees are scattering. Some work at home and communicate with the office through e-mail and other electronic means. Others

Employee Meeting Poster Employees traditionally value open communication in the workplace. Good Fulton & Farrell, a Dallas-based architectural firm, addresses that value by scheduling biweekly design maintenance meetings to discuss current projects. (Courtesy of Good Fulton & Farrell)

work at sites around the world as organizations continue to expand internationally. For generations, studies have shown that employees prefer to get important information about their organizations through face-to-face meetings with their supervisors.[13] Satisfying that face-to-face preference will become more and more difficult.

Ironically, several important workplace innovations can undermine face-to-face communication. Flexibility in employee schedules—so-called flex time, which allows employees to work shifts of different lengths at nonstandard times—is praised by 67 percent of U.S. and Canadian employees as essential to job success.[14] But those nonstandard hours can mean less "face time" with supervisors. Electronic messages also can reduce the crucial personal element in successful employee communication. "The pervasiveness of e-mail and voice mail makes it more important than ever to make time for face-to-face communication in order to maintain morale," says Donald Ness, of RHI Management Resources in Canada.[15]

■ *The increasing use of "temps":* The use of temporary workers—from secretaries to executives such as chief financial officers—has increased 240 percent over the past 20 years. Today, more than 12 million U.S. employees are temps—about 10 percent of the workforce.[16] In Tokyo, the number of temps skyrocketed 26 percent, to more than 1 million workers, from 2000 to 2001.[17] How will organizations build productive relationships with a workforce that increasingly consists of "here today, gone tomorrow" employees?

■ *The growth of information managers:* A generation ago, most workers built products. Today, a rapidly growing percentage of employees manage information—and they need sophisticated technology to do so. As that technology changes literally from day to day, employees will need continuing education throughout their careers. Two recent studies suggest that these workers will become increasingly unhappy: An international survey revealed that more than 80 percent of employees say that training is "a key component of what they are really looking for in their jobs."[18] Unfortunately, another survey revealed that only 43 percent of U.S. workers are receiving the skills training they need to fulfill their organization's goals.[19]

EMPLOYEE PUBLICS: FAQS

1. *What resources do employees have that their organizations need?*
Primarily commitment. Organizations with committed employees have greater innovation, reduced absenteeism, and significantly greater profits.

2. *What are the greatest challenges to building successful relationships with employees?*
Worldwide, employee discontent is increasing. Employee publics are more diverse than ever. New communications technologies are replacing face-to-face communication.

3. *Where can I find more information on employee publics?*

- *Communication World* magazine, published by the International Association of Business Communicators
- U.S. Bureau of Labor Statistics, online at www.bls.gov
- *Monthly Labor Review,* online at www.bls.gov/opub/mlr/mlrhome/htm

■ *The growth of diversity:* The U.S. Department of Labor estimates that 85 percent of people now entering the workforce for the first time are women or members of minority groups. And that's just in the United States. As organizations expand internationally, the cultural diversity of the workforce will continue to increase. For example, a 3Com Corporation factory in Illinois has 1,200 workers, most of them immigrants, who speak 20 different languages.[20] A 2001 survey of U.S. and Canadian employees concluded that "today's workforce is more diverse than ever. Employees come from different countries and from various ethnic and social backgrounds, each with its own unique mindset and values that impact how they view work."[21]

■ *The aging of the baby boomers:* In the early 21st century, the median age of the U.S. workforce will be 45. As fewer workers seek early-retirement options, organizations will need new strategies for motivating and training an aging workforce.

The authors of this book would add one more significant change that is shaping the new workforce: the impact of the members of so-called Generation X (born 1966–1980), the children of the baby boomers (born 1947–1965). More than half of today's corporate communications executives say that Gen X'ers are different from previous generations.[22] Studies show that, compared with their elders, Gen X'ers are more motivated by money and owning things. Compared with their elders, more Gen X'ers demand an interesting job. Almost half of them view their jobs not as a goal but, instead, as a way of supporting their leisure-time activities. Yet 77 percent say they hope to find one company where they will stay for most of their career.[23] According to one study, members of Generation X have a higher level of job satisfaction than do baby boomers, 55.6 percent to 46.5 percent respectively. However, job satisfaction levels for both groups have declined over the past five years.[24]

As for Generation Y (born after 1980), which includes many readers of this book, research is only beginning. Preliminary results show that 70 percent of Gen Y'ers say that being friends with coworkers is essential to job satisfaction, and 90 percent define success as being trusted to get the job done.[25]

Job satisfaction is fragile. For example, from the 1950s through the mid-1990s, Japanese workers generally were very satisfied with their jobs. Japan's economy was booming, and workers usually stayed with one employer for their entire career. Layoffs were virtually unknown. But in the mid-1990s Japan's economy suffered a significant downturn, characterized by business failures and unemployment. Five years of trouble undermined 50 years of satisfaction. At the end of the 20th century, only 44 percent of Japan's workers were satisfied with their jobs.[26]

Overall, barely half—51 percent—of U.S. employees described themselves as being happy in the workplace in 2000, down from 59 percent in 1995.[27] Surveys differ as to what the U.S. workforce wants: more recognition, more opportunity for advancement, more training—the answers surely differ for every organization.[28] The only consistency seems to be the growing dissatisfaction.

QuickBreak 4.2

SABOTAGE IN THE WORKPLACE

Sabotage in the American Workplace: That's the name of a book that caught the public's eye in 1992 with its amazing tales of the destruction committed by bored, unhappy, uninformed employees.[34]

Take Ron, for example, who worked at a well-known chain of toy stores. The job was boring, he said, but he found ways to liven things up for himself and his coworkers:

> One Christmas the store had a Barbie doll house on display. Every night I would create a different scene by dressing the dolls up in strange outfits and setting them in unusual situations. One time I dressed the Ken doll in a clown outfit, tied Barbie against a balcony, and set Ken up so he was whipping her.

And let's not forget Reggie, who worked in the mailroom of a well-known, politically conservative think tank. Reggie was hired without any kind of orientation program, and when he discovered that the think tank's politics were at odds with his own, he—well, let him tell the story:

> People would mail in checks. . . . So I started randomly taking envelopes, opening them, and throwing the checks in the shredder. I started doing it more and more. I could tell if it was a check by holding it up to the light. If it was, I'd toss it or shred it.

Ron and Reggie make a powerful case that values-driven public relations begins with good employee relations. No organization can maintain productive, long-term relationships with important publics if it is crumbling from within. An informed, committed, and respected workforce provides a solid base for all the relationships that an organization must build.

Another probable source of employee discontent is bad communication. In 1993 one of the most comprehensive studies of the U.S. workforce ever conducted showed that a desire for "open communication in the workplace" was the number one reason why employees left one job to take another.[29] Simply put, employees sought new jobs because they valued two-way communication.

Unfortunately, employees still may not be getting the communication they want and need. One 1999 measurement showed that 57 percent of organizations lack a formal employee-communications strategy.[30] A year 2000 study ranked "skills in communication and interpersonal relationships" as the top qualities employees seek in a boss.[31] But in a recent, exhaustive survey of U.S. and Canadian workers, a majority reported that their supervisors and companies

- did not have good supervisor-to-employee communications;
- did not have good employee-to-supervisor communications;
- did not listen to or implement employee suggestions; and
- did not recognize or reward employees who made worthwhile suggestions.[32]

This gloomy picture is repeated in many nations around the world. Although 61 percent of Danish workers describe themselves as "very satisfied" with their jobs, that number plunges to 16 percent in Japan, 11 percent in China, 10 percent in the Ukraine, and 9 percent in Hungary. The highest figures in Latin America were 44 percent in urban Mexico and 36 percent in Argentina.[33]

Good news and bad news. More than ever before, public relations practitioners recognize the importance of their employee publics. But the challenges of building productive relationships with employees have never been greater.

The News Media

The numbers are impressive. In the early 21st century, the United States has[35]

- more than 10,500 newspapers
- 388 weekly magazines and other periodicals
- 3,447 monthly magazines and other periodicals
- 3,429 quarterly magazines and other periodicals
- 3,751 AM radio stations
- 5,183 FM radio stations
- 1,334 TV stations
- 1,345 cable TV systems

No reliable figures exist for the number of news-related web sites. However, the Pew Research Center reports that more than one-third of U.S. citizens go online for news at least once a week—almost double the number that did in 1998.[36]

Some very important members of those news media are the so-called **gatekeepers**: editors or producers who decide which stories to include and which stories to reject. Without the consent of the gatekeepers, public relations practitioners cannot use the news media as intervening publics. Gatekeepers value news that serves the interests of their audiences. If public relations practitioners can supply that kind of audience-focused news, they should have productive relationships with the gatekeepers of the news media.

Because of the First Amendment and its guarantee of freedom of the press, news media in the United States can, with few limitations, report whatever they perceive to be news. But in emerging democracies around the world, freedom of the press is, so to speak, a hotly contested front-page issue. As new freedoms give rise to modern

---

NEWS MEDIA PUBLICS: FAQS

1. *What resources do news media have that organizations need?*
Fair coverage and the willingness to consider news stories offered by public relations practitioners. The relative objectivity and credibility of the news media can provide what is called an **independent endorsement** or **third-party endorsement** of an organization's news.

2. *What is the greatest challenge to building successful relationships with news media?*
A mutual lack of knowledge. A recent study shows that journalists and public relations practitioners alike value accuracy and fairness—but neither party believes the other holds those values.[37]

3. *Where can I find more information on news media publics?*

- American Society of Newspaper Editors, online at www.asne.org
- Poynter Institute for Media Studies, online at www.poynter.org
- *Gale Directory of Publications and Broadcast Media,* published annually by Gale

Values Statement 4.1

SACRAMENTO POLICE DEPARTMENT

The Sacramento Police Department protects the 370,000 residents of Sacramento, California's capital.

As members of the Sacramento Police Department we accept responsibility for contributing to the quality of life in our community. We believe the character of our Department is best reflected in the quality of service provided by each of our members. We will meet the challenge to provide quality through our shared values and commitment to:

Serve in an impartial, courteous, responsive, and effective manner.

Maintain an attitude which respects the dignity and rights of those we serve.

Facilitate open communications with the public.

Take responsibility for our actions and be willing to admit our mistakes.

Professionalism which is the result of a clear sense of perspective and direction, strengthened by teamwork and innovation.

Remain enthusiastic and put empathy first and foremost in public and employee relations.

Promote community involvement and cooperation.

Be ever mindful that we are members of the public we serve.

All that we do will reflect a "commitment" which ensures we merit the support and trust of our community.

—Sacramento Police Department web site

news media, government officials and journalists around the world are debating the limits of freedom.

In the United States, a continuing problem for the news media is the disproportionately small number of minority journalists. In the wake of violent race riots during the struggle for civil rights, the report of the Kerner Commission in 1968 blasted the U.S. news media for their lack of minority journalists. However, in 1998 the American Society of Newspaper Editors conceded that it would not reach its year 2000 goal of having the minority population of newsrooms reflect the actual minority percentages of the U.S. population.[38] At the beginning of the 21st century, diversity in the U.S. news media looks something like this:

- Almost 12 percent of newspaper journalists are members of minority groups. Slightly more than 5 percent are black, 3.7 percent are Hispanic, 2.3 percent are Asian American, and approximately half of 1 percent are Native American.[39]

- Twenty-one percent of television journalists are members of minority groups. Eleven percent are black, 7 percent are Hispanic, 3 percent are Asian American, and fewer than 1 percent are Native American.[40]

- Only 10 percent of radio journalists are members of minority groups. Five percent are black, 3 percent are Hispanic, 1 percent are Asian American, and 1 percent are Native American.[41]

Any discussion of 21st-century news media must include the concept of **convergence of media**—that is, a blending of media made possible by digital technology (for more on convergence and digital technology, please see Chapter 11). Simply put, digital technology allows journalists to move words, sounds, and images back and forth among radio, TV, newspapers, magazines, and web sites. As a consequence, members of the news media can offer their news in more than one format. The *Chicago Tribune* newspaper, for example, now works closely with affiliated radio and television stations (broadcast and cable) to offer an online edition of the news gathered by all those media. Radio Margaritaville, a station launched by musician Jimmy Buffett, whose fans are affectionately known as Parrot Heads, exists only online (www. radiomargaritaville.com). The station's digital existence allows it to offer a newsletter, merchandise for sale, play lists, and concert schedules, all of which can be examined online while Parrot Heads listen to their favorite music. Public relations practitioners who can offer journalists stories in digital formats suited to several media will thrive in the new world of convergence.

Senator John McCain of Arizona uses news media as an intervening public to reach a primary public: voters. (Courtesy of Senator John McCain)

No matter what background journalists may have, no matter what news medium they represent, they value one thing that public relations practitioners can supply: information—relevant, accurate, complete, timely information.

Governments

You've probably heard that the nine most feared words in the English language are "I'm from the government, and I'm here to help." Government workers actually *can* help public relations practitioners by providing information and interpreting legislation. But they can also harm a practitioner's organization by adopting unfavorable legislation or regulations. As we note elsewhere in this book, too, a continuing issue in public relations is government licensing of public relations practitioners. That hasn't happened yet, but the debate isn't over.

Who are the members of this influential public? They range from the local chief of police to the president of the United States. Government officials exist at the city/county level, the state level, and the federal level.

GOVERNMENT PUBLICS: FAQS

1. *What resources do governments have that organizations need?*

Fair, nonrestrictive regulations, protection from unfair competition in the marketplace, and interpretations or explanations of existing laws.

2. *What is the greatest challenge to building successful relationships with government publics?*

The downsizing of the U.S. federal government is increasing the workload of federal employees and transferring new and sometimes unfamiliar tasks to state and local government employees.

3. *Where can I find more information on government publics?*

- *The Almanac of American Politics,* published by the U.S. government

- *Governing: The Magazine of States and Localities,* published by Congressional Quarterly, Inc.; online at www.governing. com

- FedStats, online at www.fedstats.gov

THE FEDERAL GOVERNMENT. At the federal level, there were 2.79 million nonmilitary employees at the beginning of the 21st century.[42] The U.S. Bureau of Labor Statistics expects that number to decline by almost 10 percent by 2008 as several governmental responsibilities shift from the federal to state and local governments.[43] Federal employees range from the 535 members of Congress to the 876,495 who work for the postal service and the 4,354 who work in federal libraries.[44] A year 2000 survey of federal workers revealed that 60 percent were satisfied with their jobs and 27 percent were dissatisfied, primarily because of supervisor–employee tensions.[45] The federal workforce is increasingly diverse: 22 percent of senior managers are women, up from 10 percent in 1990, and 13 percent of senior managers are members of minority groups, up from 7 percent in 1990.[46]

Most visible among these employees, of course, are the members of Congress, each of whom has his or her own values and agendas. An excellent source for studying each member of Congress as well as the top issues among each member's constituency is *The Almanac of American Politics,* which offers a state-by-state and district-by-district analysis of senators, representatives, voters, and issues.

Lobbyists who work with federal employees, particularly with elected officials, have at least one bit of advice for public relations practitioners: Be well prepared and work fast.[47] Federal employees are busy. In fact, federal employees say that their top job-related need is time away from work to spend with their families.[48]

STATE AND LOCAL GOVERNMENTS. At last measurement, there were 4.8 million state government employees and 10.7 million local government employees in the United States—a total of 15.5 million employees.[49] The U.S. Census Bureau expects that number to increase to 18.48 million by the year 2006.[50] It's important for public relations practitioners to appreciate two opposite trends: As the number of federal workers is decreasing, the number of workers in state and local governments is increasing. Those opposite trends reflect an increasing shift of power as the federal government spins off more programs to state and local governments.

Though members of minority groups represent approximately 26 percent of the nation's population, they fill only 13.4 percent of upper-level, policy-making posi-

QuickBreak 4.3

JAMES BOND SAVES THE WHALES?

It's a whale of a tale: James Bond (actually Pierce Brosnan, one of the many actors to play Agent 007) and an international group of environmentalists face off against a national president and a powerful multinational corporation. And at the center of it all is resource dependency theory.

The conflict began in the mid-1990s when Japan's Mitsubishi Corporation and Mexico's national government announced plans to build a salt factory in Mexico's Baja California region. The factory would mean steady jobs for residents of the economically depressed area, but local fisherman opposed it, and the coastline in question was one of the last remaining breeding grounds of the Pacific gray whale, an endangered species. The project involved building a mile-long pier and turning dozens of square miles of the coast into holding ponds and dikes.

As president of Mexico from 1994 to 2000, Ernesto Zedillo held the ultimate resource: the power to grant or withhold permission to build.

In nurturing its relationship with Zedillo's government, Mitsubishi pledged an improved economy in return for permission to build the factory. Led by actor Brosnan, the environmentalists urged the Mexican government to honor its earlier commitment to protect the area as a national biosphere reserve. Brosnan also helped organize a boycott against Mitsubishi products—a withholding of resources that Mitsubishi desired.

The first James Bond movie was titled *Dr. No*, which may have been Mitsubishi's nickname for President Zedillo when, in March 2000, he declared, "I have taken the decision to instruct the Mexican government . . . to propose the definitive cancellation of the project."

Mitsubishi was gracious in defeat, offering to help find other economic development opportunities for the region. Brosnan was honored by the International Fund for Animal Welfare. And resource dependency remained an important explanation for why groups form relationships with one another.[51]

tions in state governments. Twenty-six percent of those policy makers are women. In fact, in every racial or ethnic category of state policy makers, men outnumbered women: among blacks, 53 percent to 47 percent; whites, 65/35; Hispanic Americans, 67/33; Asian Americans, 67/33; and Native Americans, 75/25.[52]

Studies of local governments also show that members of minority groups are underrepresented. In Colorado, for example, only 7.2 percent of local government employees are members of minority groups. Forty-five percent of local government workers in Colorado are women.[53]

At least one survey shows that local government employees are happier than their state government counterparts. They find that their jobs are more interesting than they expected—but they also find that they have less power than they expected.[54]

Elected officials at all levels of government want to serve their constituents well and be reelected. Public relations practitioners who can help government officials pursue those values will find them to be willing partners in building productive relationships.

Quick ✔ Check

1. Are employees around the world satisfied with their jobs?
2. In media relations, what is an independent endorsement?
3. What does the decreasing number of U.S. federal employees mean for public relations practitioners?
4. For public relations practitioners, what essential resources do employee, media, and government publics possess?

Investors

Companies that sell stock have relationships with investors. The investor public encompasses individual stockholders—and much more:

INVESTOR PUBLICS: FAQS

1. *What resources do investor publics have that organizations need?*

   Investors purchase stocks. Financial analysts, mutual fund managers, and journalists evaluate stocks and make recommendations to investors.

2. *What are the greatest challenges to building successful relationships with investor publics?*

   Investor publics need information and reassurance as stock markets become increasingly volatile. The growing diversity of investors means that old ways of communicating may not be effective.

3. *Where can I find more information on investor publics?*

   - Securities and Exchange Commission, online at www.sec.gov
   - New York Stock Exchange, online at www.nyse.com
   - International Federation of Stock Exchanges, online at www.fibv.com
   - The *Wall Street Journal,* published Monday through Friday by Dow Jones and Company, Inc.

- Financial analysts study the stock markets to advise investors.
- Financial news media include the *Wall Street Journal, Business Week* magazine, the *Wall Street Week* television show, and web sites such as Value Line, at www.valueline.com.
- **Mutual fund managers** supervise what might be called investment clubs. For a fee, mutual fund managers invest a member's contributions (usually monthly payments) into a diverse collection of stocks and bonds. The popularity of mutual funds has soared in the past 20 years.
- So-called **institutional investors** are large companies or institutions that generally buy huge amounts of stock. The California Public Employees Retirement System, for example, is the largest public pension plan in the United States. It represents more than 1 million state and local government employees in California and has assets of approximately $150 billion.
- Employee investors are employees of companies, such as Microsoft, that reward employees with stock in the companies they work for.

Around the world the ownership of stock is booming. In the United States the number of people who own stock quadrupled from 1965 to 1997—but half of that growth came in just seven years, from 1990 to 1997. Forty-three percent of U.S. adults now own stock.[55] NASDAQ, which is the second-largest stock exchange in the United States (behind the New York Stock Exchange) gets 10 to 12 million hits a day on its web site.[56] If current growth trends continue, within one generation two-thirds of U.S. households will own stock.[57]

And the boom isn't just in the United States. At the end of the 20th century,[58]

- The International Federation of Stock Exchanges had 55 members around the world.
- Russia, which had virtually no investors in the mid-1990s, had approximately 500,000 stockholders.
- China, which didn't open its first stock market until 1993, had an estimated 1 million stockholders.
- Stock ownership in older democracies increased, though less dramatically. In Norway, 17 percent of adults owned stock; in Canada, 37 percent; in Great Britain, 26 percent; in France, 15 percent.

What's fueling the worldwide increase in stock ownership? The *Christian Science Monitor* cites six trends:[59]

1. The decline of communism and the growth of capitalist democracies around the world
2. The privatization of companies and industries formerly owned by governments
3. The long-term performance of stocks, which, over a long span, tend to give investors a higher return than do bonds or other investments
4. Baby boomers moving retirement funds into the stock market
5. Declining inflation, which leads to lower interest rates—which, in turn, leads to available money
6. The increased marketing of stocks, as mutual funds (companies that buy and manage portfolios of stock for their customers) promote their services

U.S. investors remain confident about the long-term profitability of their stocks. In 1997, 54 percent said they would make "no major changes" in stock ownership even if the market declined. And 31 percent said they would buy more stock in a declining market "to take advantage of lower prices."[60] In the winter of 2000–2001, those brave words were put to the test when the price of stocks plummeted, dismaying some analysts, but not investors. They did indeed hold their stocks: Only 9 percent actually took money out of the stock market. Another 33 percent said that falling prices encouraged them to buy even more stock.[61] Stockholder confidence held steady even in the wake of the World Trade Center and Pentagon bombings in 2001. The stock market dropped sharply in the days after the bombings, then gradually climbed back to previous levels.

Another factor that may be inspiring confidence in stock ownership in the United States is a lack of confidence in the Social Security system. According to a recent poll, almost half of U.S. workers doubt that Social Security will provide much money for their retirement years.[62] Stock ownership, for many U.S. citizens, is a retirement plan.

Who are these confident U.S. investors? Not, perhaps, who you might think. Table 4.1 lists some data on the investing public.[63]

A growing trend in investing is online trading. Online traders are investors who buy and sell stock through their accounts on sponsoring web sites. Aggressive and high-risk online trading is known as day trading, a practice in which stock owners buy and sell shares throughout the day, seeking quick profits. Currently, only 5 percent of U.S. investors participate in day trading.[64] Although 15 million U.S. citizens do go online frequently to monitor their investments and to look for investing information, less than a third, only 4.5 million, have done any online buying or selling. However, the age bracket that has the highest percentage of online traders is the 35 and younger group.[65] That suggests that as younger generations who have grown up with the Internet grow older and acquire more income, the volume of online trading will increase.

As confident as U.S. investors may be, they're not always content with the management practices of companies whose shares they own. At the end of the 20th century, for example, the number one subject of resolutions that stockholders introduced at companies' annual meetings dealt with regulating the salaries and benefits of top executives.[66]

TABLE 4.1 **U.S. Investors: Who They Are**

- 51 percent are women.
- 45 percent are younger than 50; 12 percent are ages 18 to 29.
- 51 percent are not college graduates.
- 82 percent are white; 10 percent are black; 5 percent are Hispanic; and 1 percent are Asian American.
- 48 percent have incomes of less than $50,000.
- 59 percent invest through mutual funds; 41 percent buy individual stocks.
- 70 percent consider themselves to be active in their communities, compared with 54 percent who do not own stock.

Consumers/Customers

The people of the United States are consumers—big-time consumers. Weekly spending in the United States could purchase the entire annual goods and services output of Ireland or New Zealand.[67]

Consumer spending is the most powerful force in the U.S. economy, totaling more than government, business, and foreign expenditures in this economy combined.[68] Two-thirds of all spending in the U.S. economy is consumer spending.[69]

Annual Report Herman Miller, Inc., an office-furniture design, manufacturing, and maintenance company, has earned praise for targeting investor publics with innovative, visually arresting annual reports. (Courtesy of Herman Miller, Inc.)

CONSUMER/CUSTOMER PUBLICS: FAQS

1. *What resources do consumer/customer publics have that organizations need?*
Loyalty: a willingness to purchase and repurchase an organization's products. Consumers also possess the resource of publicity: Word-of-mouth cheers or jeers are a powerful force in the marketplace.

2. *What are the greatest challenges to building successful relationships with consumer/customer publics?*
Forty-seven percent of U.S. consumers say that customer service is fair or poor. Only 8 percent rate it excellent.[75] The diversity of consumers is increasing. Also, public relations must learn to coordinate its tactics with the tactics of marketing, and vice versa (see Chapter 13).

3. *Where can I find more information on consumer/customer publics?*

- *American Demographics* magazine, published monthly by Dow Jones and Company, Inc.
- U.S. Department of Commerce, online at www.doc.gov
- U.S. Bureau of Labor Statistics, online at www.bls.gov

Who are these big spenders, and what are they spending all that money on? Some facts:

- The average U.S. household has a before-tax income of $43,951. Its annual expenditures total $36,995. Where does the money go? Table 4.2 gives a partial breakdown.[70]

- The biggest spenders are people aged 45 to 54. Households in which the main earner falls into that age bracket spend $46,511 a year. By way of comparison, households in which the main earner is under 25 spend only $21,704 a year. For age 65 and older, the total is $29,864 a year.[71]

- The annual spending power of blacks, Hispanics, and Asian Americans is booming, surging from $600 billion a year in the mid-1990s to more than $1 trillion today.[72]

- Women account for approximately 80 percent of all consumer spending.[73]

- Dating remains big business among U.S. consumers, with spending preferences being dinner (top choice of 43 percent) and a movie or concert (23 percent). Going to a bar was the top choice of only 4 percent.[74]

TABLE 4.2	**How U.S. Households Spend Their After-Tax Income**
Food	$5,031
Housing	$12,057
Apparel and services	$1,743
Transportation	$7,011
Health care	$1,959
Entertainment	$1,891
Personal-care products and services	$408
Alcoholic beverages	$318
Tobacco products and smoking supplies	$300

QuickBreak 4.4

THE CUSTOMER IS ALWAYS RIGHT?

Customer relations (or consumer relations) is the part of public relations that targets the customer public—not only potential customers, but current customers as well. In fact, one recent study reported that most businesses could increase their profits by anywhere from 25 to 100 percent simply by retaining only 5 percent more of their current customers every year.[76]

That impressive statistic may explain why some companies bend over backward to satisfy customer questions and requests—no matter how bizarre the requests may be. The master of bizarre customer inquiries is comedian Don Novello, who, posing as a customer named Lazlo Toth, bedevils corporate America with inane letters, which invariably draw painfully serious responses.

To wit: Novello/Toth wrote McDonald's, pointing out that one of its billboards pictured a small container of jelly next to an Egg McMuffin. Jelly tastes awful on eggs, he as-serted, and suggested that McDonald's change the advertisement.

McDonald's wrote back, politely explaining that some customers like to remove the top muffin of their Egg McMuffin and smear jelly on it. The company even enclosed a coupon for a free Egg McMuffin.

Novello/Toth wrote back: He had tried the jelly and liked it so much that he requested some with a Big Mac hamburger—but the staff at his local McDonald's refused to supply any. Wasn't that a double standard? Wasn't what was good for the Egg McMuffin also good for the Big Mac?

McDonald's wrote back, of course, and politely explained—but you get the picture.

Then Novello/Toth wrote to a bubble-bath company. . . .

The latest collection of Don Novello's adventures in customer relations is *Citizen Lazlo!: The Lazlo Letters, Volume 2* (Workman Press, 1992).

The hottest trend among today's consumers may be online shopping, also known as e-commerce (for electronic commerce). Almost half (48.2 percent) of U.S. citizens older than 18 had made online purchases by 2001, and that impressive number is expected to increase. Amazon.com, selling primarily books and CDs, and eBay, an online auction site, together accounted for almost one-third of those purchases.[77] Households with college-educated people shop online more than do other households, and households with no children use e-commerce more than households with children.[78] Experienced computer users may not shop online till they drop, but 75 percent of experienced web surfers purchase online. For black computer users those numbers fall to 43 percent and for Hispanic computer users, to 42 percent.[79]

Unfortunately, web site design has not kept pace with the boom in online shopping. One new study shows that 65 percent of online shoppers click away from various web sites because they're frustrated or confused by online shopping and purchasing procedures. Even worse, 30 percent of online shoppers say that they'll never return to difficult web sites, and 10 percent have found the process so irritating that they say they will never shop online again.[80]

Regardless of where and how customers do their shopping, what do they value? Any survey gives you the same answer: quality at a fair price. Customers want to get what they paid for—and more.

Multicultural Communities

Public relations professionals must know the so-called movers and shakers in every community in which their organizations do business. Failing to learn who wields power in a community can have catastrophic results, as the developer of a proposed landfill site once discovered:

> One private developer announced a project that soon drew surprisingly intense environmental opposition from local residents. Only months after announcing the planned facility did the developer learn that the town was home to [consumer activist] Ralph Nader.[81]

Besides Ralph Nader, who are the influential publics within our diverse communities? Professor Jerry Hendrix of American University offers a useful breakdown, which appears in Table 4.3.[82] Among these influential groups, which is the most powerful? The answer, of course, depends on the community and the issues involved; but in the 1970s a landmark study of community groups in Louisville, Kentucky, identified the mass media—television, radio, and newspapers—as by far the most influential groups in that city.[83]

However, some of the worst, most expensive public relations fiascoes in recent memory have involved companies perceived as being insensitive to racial or ethnic groups. In the mid-1990s, Denny's, the restaurant chain, faced repeated charges of refusing to seat or serve black customers. In fact, the company paid almost $55 million to settle two class-action lawsuits backed by thousands of reportedly mistreated black customers. Denny's had become "synonymous with discrimination" according to national news media. "It was a hard time for the company," said Dora

---

MULTICULTURAL COMMUNITY PUBLICS: FAQS

1. *What resources do multicultural community publics have that organizations need?*
The willingness to accept an organization as a community member—to be its employees, supporters, customers, and friends.

2. *What is the greatest challenge to building successful relationships with multicultural community publics?*
The sheer number of such groups. Organizations' resources are limited, and they usually cannot build relationships with every public within a community. Organizations must determine which relationships in a community are most essential to the fulfillment of their values.

3. *Where can I find more information on multicultural community publics?*

- U.S. Bureau of the Census, online at www.census.gov

- U.S. Immigration and Naturalization Service, online at www.ins.usdoj.gov

- *American Demographics* magazine, published monthly by Dow Jones and Company, Inc.

- The *Chronicle of Philanthropy,* published weekly; online at www.philanthropy.com

TABLE 4.3	Influential Community Publics

COMMUNITY MEDIA	**COMMUNITY ORGANIZATIONS**
mass media (such as newspapers and television stations)	civic
	business
specialized media (such as entertainment tabloids)	service
	social
COMMUNITY LEADERS	cultural
public officials	religious
educators	youth
religious leaders	political
professionals (such as doctors and lawyers)	special interest groups
executives	other groups
bankers	
union leaders	
ethnic leaders	
neighborhood leaders	

Taylor, Denny's new director of diversity affairs. "Morale was so low. Something had to be done."

Something was done. In one of the most dramatic rebounds in the history of values-driven public relations, Denny's changed leadership and committed to diversity in the workforce and in clientele. Today, Denny's restaurant managers earn their salaries in part by showing specifically how they honor the value of diversity in their restaurants. In 2000, *Fortune* magazine ranked Denny's number one on its list of the nation's top companies for minority employees.[84]

More than ever before, public relations practitioners must foster positive relationships with racial and ethnic publics within their organizations' communities. Otherwise, organizations not only may separate themselves from community goodwill, but they also risk separating themselves from potential employees, customers, investors, donors, and other publics that they depend on to survive. Although the racial/ethnic makeup of every community is different, Table 4.4 shows the U.S. Census Bureau's projections for U.S. population totals and percentages for the year 2008.[85]

As noted in Chapter 16, immigration is also changing communities in the United States. The foreign-born percentage of the U.S. population recently reached its highest level since 1930: Of today's residents, 10.4 percent were born as citizens of other nations. Almost 40 percent reside in the western United States, followed by 23 percent in the Northeast.[86] But even in small communities in southwestern Kansas, the meatpacking industry attracts immigrants from Vietnam and Somalia.

According to the U.S. Census Bureau, 51 percent of today's immigrants to the United States came from Latin America, 25.5 percent came from Asia, and 15.3

TABLE 4.4	Projected U.S. Population Totals and Percentages for the Year 2008	
TOTAL POPULATION	295 million Median age: 37.2 Female: 151 million Male: 144 million	
WHITE POPULATION	201 million (68.1 percent) Median age: 40.7 Age 18 & older: 157 million	
AFRICAN AMERICAN POPULATION	37 million (12.5 percent) Median age: 32.2 Age 18 & older: 26 million	
HISPANIC AMERICAN POPULATION	42 million (14.2 percent) Median age: 27.3 Age 18 & older: 27 million	
ASIAN AMERICAN AND PACIFIC ISLANDER POPULATION	14 million (4.7 percent) Median age: 34 Age 18 & older: 10 million	
AMERICAN INDIAN, ESKIMO, AND ALEUT AMERICAN POPULATION	2 million (0.7 percent) Median age: 29.5 Age 18 & older: 1.5 million	

percent came from Europe. Almost 80 percent fall into the 18 to 64 age bracket. Though 66 percent have at least a high school education, immigrants are more likely than nonimmigrants to be unemployed and living in poverty.[87]

In short, community groups are a diverse lot—and diversity within each group is probably increasing.

Constituents (Voters)

Not every organization considers voters to be a traditional public, though many organizations try to influence the legislative process by building relationships with eligible voters. But for public relations practitioners employed by democratically elected governments, voters are the most important public of all.

In a sense, this group includes every citizen of a nation who is of voting age—a huge and diverse public. In countries where voting is compulsory, such as Costa Rica, a description of this public literally would be a description of the country's adult population. In the United States, however, a description of voters is somewhat easier, because not every eligible citizen votes. In the presidential election of 2000, a meager 50.7 percent divided their votes among George W. Bush, Al Gore, and Ralph Nader. In terms of voter turnout, U.S. voters rank 139th among the world's 163 democracies.[88]

News Release McDonald's Corporation has long recognized the value of reaching out to different ethnic groups in the communities it serves. For a Spanish-language version of this news release, see page 465. (Courtesy of Valencia, Pérez & Echeveste Public Relations)

What do we know about adults in the United States who *do* vote? A landmark 1990s national survey by the League of Women Voters revealed these facts:[89]

■ Voters are an odd mixture of cynicism and optimism: A full 72 percent of voters said they trusted the federal government to do the right thing only part of the time or never at all, and 69 percent said that government is run by "a few big interests" rather than for "the benefit of the people."

■ Voters are committed to their communities, with 68 percent involved in two or more community organizations such as churches or school groups.

■ Though they often believe that they don't have enough information on the candidates and the issues, voters discuss politics with family members and friends and are encouraged by those people to vote.

CONSTITUENT/VOTER PUBLICS: FAQS

1. *What resources do constituent/voter publics have that organizations need?*
Votes and word-of-mouth endorsements. Constituents who approve of their elected representatives can influence the opinions of other constituents.

2. *What is the greatest challenge to building successful relationships with constituent/voter publics?*
Voter apathy, which is particularly high among voters aged 18 to 29.

3. *Where can I find more information on constituent/voter publics?*

- The League of Women Voters, online at www.lwv.org
- *The Almanac of American Politics,* published by the U.S. government
- *Governing: The Magazine of States and Localities,* published by Congressional Quarterly, Inc.; online at www. governing.com

Other studies show that the single greatest indicator of regular voting in the United States is age: The percentage of U.S. citizens age 65 and older who vote tends to be higher than percentages from other age groups.[90]

Even though the civil rights movement in the United States has increased the opportunities for minority citizens to vote, a higher percentage of white adults continues to register and vote compared with percentages of minority group voters. In 1998, 70 percent of white adults were registered to vote. Among black adults, 61 percent were registered; among Hispanic adults, 34 percent; and among Asian and Pacific Islanders, 29 percent.[91] In the 2000 presidential election, 82 percent of all voters were white, 10 percent were black, 4 percent were Hispanic, and 2 percent were Asian American.[92]

In 2000, the U.S. Census Bureau released the following findings about the voting-age population in the United States:

- Whites, women, older people, and those who are married are more likely to vote.

- People with more education, higher incomes, and employment are more likely to vote.

- Homeowners and longtime residents are more likely to vote.

- People living in the West are the least likely to register, but those who do are the most likely to vote.

- Race is not as powerful a determining factor in voting activity as are age, education, and income.[93]

Businesses

Organizations have relationships with a variety of businesses. Why? Because those businesses have resources that the organizations need if they are to fulfill their values-driven goals. Such relationships involve business-to-business communications, often called B2B communications. For example, an organization may have relationships with vendor businesses that supply materials to the organization; distributor businesses that help move the organization's products to consumers; customer businesses that purchase the organization's products; and industry partners, which are in the

BUSINESS PUBLICS: FAQS

1. *What resources do business publics have that organizations need?*
Vendor businesses have supplies and loyalty. Customer businesses have the willingness to purchase and repurchase an organization's products. Direct competitors have the resource of competing fairly.

2. *What are the greatest challenges to building successful relationships with business publics?*
One surprising challenge may be the reputation of B2B communications. *Marketing* magazine reports that B2B is thought to be "the least glamorous part" of public relations.[97] Also, the sheer number of business relationships that an organization has poses a challenge to relationship building.

3. *Where can I find more information on business publics?*
- The United States Chamber of Commerce, online at www.uschamber.org
- Yahoo! Business to Business Marketplace, online at www.b2b.yahoo.com
- *Business Week* magazine, published weekly by the McGraw-Hill Companies; online at www.businessweek.com

same type of business and work with the organization to help influence legislative and regulation processes at different levels of government. That same organization has sometimes-uneasy relationships with direct competitors. Public relations practitioners communicate with a variety of different businesses to build productive relationships.

B2B communications is big business, and it's growing. In 1999, U.S. businesses spent $23 billion on B2B communications, excluding spending on B2B advertising and promotions. Industry analysts expect that U.S. spending on B2B communications will increase to $32 billion in 2004.[94] According to one estimate, 45 percent of all public relations work in England is now B2B communications.[95] Seven of England's 10 most profitable public relations agencies earn more than half their revenues from B2B communications, and Camargue, one of those agencies, specializes exclusively in B2B communications. According to Managing Director Andrew Litchfield, the agency doesn't intend to expand beyond B2B because it enjoys working with clients that understand the value and effectiveness of public relations. "It feels like a more mature market," he says. "We're not exhausting ourselves telling people why PR costs what it does."[96]

Quick ✔ Check

1. What is the demographic profile of people in the United States who invest in the stock markets?
2. What age group in the United States spends the most money on consumer goods and services?
3. In a study of influential publics in Louisville, Kentucky, which group was identified as the most influential?
4. For public relations practitioners, what important resources are possessed by investor, consumer, community, constituent, and business publics?

Summary

A public is a group of people who share a common value or values in a particular situation. In other words, publics unite around their values. For employees, the core value may be job security. For an environmental group, maybe it's clean air and water. An organization forms relationships with publics that have the resources it needs to fulfill its values-driven goals. However, when the values of a public intersect with the values of an organization, a relationship—whether the organization wants it or not—is born.

Traditional publics may vary among different organizations. For many organizations, however, long-established traditional publics include employees, the news media, governments, investors, consumers, multicultural community groups, constituents (voters), and businesses.

Publics can and do change constantly, but the questions a practitioner must answer about each public remain the same. Whether a public is latent, aware, or active, if it has the power to influence an organization, a practitioner must answer these questions:

- How much can the public influence our organization's ability to achieve our goals?
- What is the public's stake, or value, in its relationship with our organization?
- Who are the opinion leaders and decision makers for the public?
- What is the demographic profile of the public?
- What is the psychographic profile of the public?
- What is the public's opinion of our organization?
- What is the public's opinion (if any) of the issue in question?

Not until those questions are answered can public relations practitioners strive to build the relationships that will help an organization achieve its values-driven goals.

DISCUSSION QUESTIONS

1. Your authors state that the most important publics in public relations are employee publics. Do you agree? Why or why not?
2. Can you think of examples of nontraditional publics that have become—or are becoming—traditional publics?
3. Why do public relations practitioners try to identify opinion leaders and decision makers for each public?
4. Why is it important to identify a public's stake in an issue of importance to a practitioner's organization?
5. In our opening scenario, how would you classify the local Boy Scout troops? Are they a primary or a secondary public?

Memo *from the* Field

Gordon Lindsey,
Associate Information
Manager, J.C. Penney
Company, Dallas

Gordon Lindsey has worked for J.C. Penney for 19 years. He currently oversees the company's employee news communication functions (which include a daily news service on the company's intranet) and the company's archives and museum. He also writes speeches for the company's executives. Before joining J.C. Penney, he worked for eight years in both a nonprofit organization and in an agency.

The authors of this book write in Chapter 4 that "No organization can maintain productive, long-term relationships with important publics if it is crumbling from within." I agree.

Today, most companies recognize that employees are one of their more important publics, often the most essential to success.

I work in retailing. And in my company we know that most customers' opinions of our company will not be formed by executive speeches, news releases, and appearances, but by the experience customers have with the sales help in our stores. For our customers, that sales person *is* the company.

This means we in management must care about the attitudes and behavior of those people on the front line. The experiences customers have with these employees often determine whether a customer will shop with us again. And the most profitable shoppers for a retail company are its repeat customers.

Critical though employee relations may be, it is not easy for many companies to do it well, for a number of reasons. For one, employee publics can be diverse. The interests of hourly workers are not the same as middle management's, even though they all work for the same company. And intensified competition, which is now increasingly global, means companies must become more efficient and flexible. One frequent way to do that is to acquire or merge with another company. Another frequent way is to restructure operations.

These actions often lead to layoffs. Layoffs in turn lead to a deep distrust among employees for a company's executive leadership. Once the trust has been broken, it can be hard to repair. But distrust cannot be ignored, if a company's management expects employees to support the company's goals and strategies.

Employees, too, make employee relations complicated. Employees are changing, particularly the younger generation. They do not fit easily into the old command structure on which most companies have been traditionally built. Today's workers want more collaboration. This can be hard for older executives to accept.

And, at least in the prosperous economy at the turn of the century, many workers have more employment options than ever. In retailing, competition for labor is very intense, as other businesses recruit from our traditional employee base.

So what can companies do to improve employee relations? Let me mention three actions that I think are essential to good employee relations:

1. *Be sure employees hear important company news, especially news that affects them, from the company first.* Nothing depresses, indeed enrages, employees more than to hear first about a plant closing or a restructuring from their local newspaper or TV station. They expect to hear it from the company first.

Securities and Exchange Commission rules sometimes make this hard to accomplish. The rules require publicly owned companies to release information that can affect a company's stock price to the news media and investment community simultaneously with other publics. But companies with good employee relations find ways to make sure that employees get the news at the same time as other publics.

2. *Keep executive actions and words consistent.* What executives do usually carries more weight with employees than what they say. So if executives are to enjoy credibility, they must be sure their actions and words are saying the same thing.

As a corollary, I would also say that executives are wise never to promise more than they can deliver. Nothing erodes trust like the acids of hypocrisy and broken promises.

3. *Finally, cultivate the personal touch.* Surveys show that employees like best to hear news face-to-face from their supervisors. Good supervisors, therefore, cultivate that form of communication and recognize the power of the personal touch.

Case Study 4.1

Cloudy Days for Sunbeam

In the mid-1990s the Sunbeam Corporation, maker of home appliances, was a favorite of financial analysts, who advise investors on which stocks to buy and which to sell. The company had hired Albert Dunlap, a tough CEO with a reputation for turning around faltering companies. And the analysts applauded in February 1998 when Sunbeam released information on its plans to acquire three other consumer-products companies. Sunbeam's future looked bright.

But then the storm clouds rolled in.

Scarcely a month after announcing the acquisitions, Sunbeam shocked investors and investment analysts with word that it expected to lose money in the first quarter of the new fiscal year and had fired its executive vice president for consumer products.

"To analysts who have praised Sunbeam . . . the most alarming aspect of [the] announcements was how little warning the company had given to investors," declared the *Wall Street Journal*.[98]

And those analysts weren't happy.

"There really is a credibility issue," said one.

"The investment community has been blindsided," said another.[99]

Investment analysts possess a resource that stockholder-owned companies covet: the power to persuade investors to buy or hold stocks in particular companies. With its surprise announcement, Sunbeam damaged its ability to acquire that resource.

Matters soon got worse. After a meeting that Sunbeam organized to reassure investment analysts, Dunlap confronted an analyst who had recommended that his clients sell their Sunbeam stock. According to the analyst, Dunlap "grabbed me by my left shoulder, put his hand over his mouth and near my left ear and said: 'You son of a bitch. If you come after me, I'll come after you twice as hard.'"[100]

But it was *Barron's*, a weekly investment newspaper, that did the heavy hitting. Less than a month after Dunlap's reassurances to analysts, *Barron's* charged that Sunbeam had misled investors and analysts by using "artificial profit boosters" to sweeten the previous year's impressive profits. The devastating story concluded, "[Dunlap's] enemies, including disenchanted shareholders, angry security analysts, and bitter former employees, are growing in number. . . ."[101]

Finally, distrust of the financial picture painted by Dunlap's team spread to Sunbeam's board of directors. *Business Week* magazine reported that board members felt "betrayed" and "misled about the company's financial condition."[102] The board fired Dunlap, disavowed his financial projections, and issued the remarkable statement that Sunbeam's official financial report from the previous year "should not be relied upon."[103]

The moral of Sunbeam's story? Like most other publics, investment analysts, investors, and members of boards of directors don't like to be left in the dark.

DISCUSSION QUESTIONS

1. Shouldn't public relations practitioners keep quiet when there's bad news that could affect the performance of their company's stock? Why not let investment analysts discover the news on their own?
2. Why, in your opinion, did Sunbeam's board of directors issue the remarkable statement that the company's financial report from the previous year might be unreliable?
3. If you were an investment analyst, what would be your response to a company executive who swore at you and threatened you?
4. Are the financial analysts who monitored Sunbeam partly to blame for being deceived? After all, in its scathing report about Sunbeam's finances, *Barron's* used information that anyone can acquire by visiting the web site of the Securities and Exchange Commission (www.sec.gov).

Case Study 4.2

Parrott Talks; Rand McNally Listens

The 1990s were a wild decade for mapmakers: the disintegration of the Soviet Union; the reunification of Germany; land transfers in the Middle East; the status of Parrott, Virginia; China's reacquisition of Hong Kong; border disputes in South America. . . .

Wait a minute: Parrott, Virginia?

That's right. Thanks to a 10-year-old boy and a values-driven company that realized how one small public can connect with others, Parrott—population 800—is now on the map.

Chris Muncy, a fourth-grader from Mishawaka, Indiana, was a mapmaker's dream. By kindergarten he knew all his state capitals, and every summer, before visiting his grandparents in Parrott, he'd get out his family's *Rand McNally Road Atlas* to trace each bend in the road of the upcoming journey.

But Chris had a problem: Parrott wasn't on the map.

"For years people groused about not being in the atlas," confessed one resident of Parrott. "You kind of assume they didn't want you to be on their map. And what could we do?"[104]

Chris knew what to do: He sent a letter to Rand McNally, publisher of the best-selling *Rand McNally Road Atlas*. "I'm going to get a road atlas every year for the rest of my life," he wrote. "I want you to put the town where my grandpa, great-grandma, grandma and uncle live in. It's called Parrott, Virginia."[105]

A letter from a 10-year-old boy about his grandparents' hometown could easily be ignored. But Rand McNally's response was consistent with its clearly stated values:

> Our products bring the world to its people. They lend insight and understanding to global geopolitical events, unlock the power of a child's imagination, help travelers manage journeys more efficiently, deliver new vistas that lead to incisive learning, and drive the commerce of nations.[106]

Instead of replying with a regretful form letter, Rand McNally studied Parrott, Virginia. Though the town was small, it did qualify for inclusion in the *Road Atlas*. In fact, there was just enough room between the towns of McCoy and Belspring to include a small black dot labeled "Parrott." And so Rand McNally helped "unlock the power of a child's imagination." It put Parrott on the map.

But the story doesn't stop there. In satisfying the desires of one tiny public, Rand McNally attracted the attention of a few larger publics: The story of Chris Muncy, Parrott, and Rand McNally received two full minutes of coverage on *ABC World News Tonight*. It received a spread, with photos, in *People* magazine. United Press International put the story on its newswire, and news media throughout the nation informed their audiences about a boy, a town, and a company that listens and responds. That's a lot of publicity for satisfying the needs of one seemingly uninfluential public. (Yes, Rand McNally did issue a news release telling the story of how Parrott came to be on the map.)

The residents of Parrott held the first parade in the town's two-century history, and the grand marshal, waving proudly from a fire engine, was Chris Muncy. An official of Rand McNally attended and presented Chris with a new *Road Atlas* containing a new dot labeled Parrott. There to record it all were journalists from major news media throughout the United States.

At the end of the parade in Parrott, Chris surveyed his success and pronounced it "Pretty neat!"[107]

The public relations staff at Rand McNally probably agreed.

DISCUSSION QUESTIONS

1. Can a public have only one member?
2. Should Rand McNally have issued a news release? Doesn't that seem like bragging?
3. Why was Chris Muncy's story so appealing to national news media?
4. How do you suppose Rand McNally's public relations team learned about Chris' letter?
5. Rand McNally is a privately held company; it doesn't have stockholders. Why, then, does it value positive national publicity?

It's Your Turn

The Tuition Increase

The top administrators of your college or university have just summoned you to their conference room. They want your expertise in public relations because they're about to announce a 15 percent increase in tuition, scheduled to begin next academic year. The increase, they say, will fund four crucial programs:

- A small day-care center will be started for the children of nontraditional students.
- A 3 percent increase above the already scheduled salary increase for professors will bring their salaries to the level of their peers at other universities. Staff members such as librarians, however, won't receive a comparable raise.
- There will be 25 new annual scholarships for women athletes.
- Students from Latin America, a group that is underrepresented on campus, will also receive 25 new annual scholarships.

The administrators confess that they're deeply concerned that a powerful outcry might force them to cancel the increase, which they believe is the only way to fund the four crucial needs. Thus, they have several questions for you. Given your current state of knowledge of your actual college or university,

1. What internal publics could influence the success of the proposed tuition increase?
2. What external publics, if any, could influence the fate of the proposed tuition increase?

3. Which of those publics could exert the most influence? Which would exert the least?
4. What, probably, is the core value of each individual public? Are all the core values the same?
5. What would be the opinion of each public about the proposed tuition increase?
6. Who are the opinion leaders for each public? Who are the decision makers for each?
7. How could you collect demographic and psychographic information on each public?
8. Are there any intervening publics that administrators might attempt to use to reach other publics?

Finally, what questions might you have for the administrators? Would it help you to see your college or university's values statement or mission statement? What specific questions, if any, do you think each public might address to the administrators?

The administrators would like to give you more time, but they want some quick information right now. What are your answers to the above questions?

KEY TERMS

active public, p. 96
aware public, p. 96
convergence of media, p. 108
coorientation, p. 101
decision maker, p. 99
demographic information, p. 100
domestic public, p. 98
external public, p. 98
gatekeeper, p. 107
independent endorsement, p. 107
institutional investor, p. 112
internal public, p. 98
international public, p. 98

intervening public, p. 97
latent public, p. 96
mutual fund managers, p. 112
nontraditional public, p. 95
opinion leader, p. 99
primary public, p. 97
psychographic information, p. 100
public, p. 91
resource dependency theory, p. 92
secondary public, p. 97
stakeholder, p. 92
third-party endorsement, p. 107
traditional public, p. 94

NOTES

1. Larissa Grunig, James Grunig, and William Ehling, "What Is an Effective Organization?" in *Excellence in Public Relations and Communication Management* (Hillsdale, N.J.: Lawrence Erlbaum, 1992), 77, 80.
2. "Pitney Bowes Statement of Value," online, www.pitneybowes.com.
3. Lisa de Moraes, "Discharge Orders for Dr. Laura," *Washington Post*, 31 March 2001, online, Lexis-Nexis.
4. De Moraes.
5. Adam Buckman, "Gays Killed My Show: Dr. Laura," *New York Post*, 4 April 2001, online, Lexis-Nexis.

6. De Moraes.
7. "Another African Epidemic: Scapegoating Is Africa's Worst Scourge," *Wall Street Journal Europe,* 3 March 2001, 10.
8. Cherie Jacobs, "More Companies Extend Benefits to Same-Sex Partners," *Tampa Tribune,* 12 August 2001, online, Lexis-Nexis.
9. James E. Grunig and Fred C. Repper, "Strategic Management, Publics, and Issues," in *Excellence in Public Relations and Communication Management,* ed. James E. Grunig (Hillsdale, N.J.: Lawrence Erlbaum, 1992), 125.
10. "Annual Defined-Contribution Survey, 2000," *Pension Benefits* (May 2001), online, Expanded Academic Index; "Hill & Knowlton-Yankelovich Study Reveals America's Corporations Focused on Employee Communications as Morale Sags," a news release issued by Hill & Knowlton, 20 October 1997, online, Lexis-Nexis.
11. Joan Milne, "We Need to Talk," *Canadian Manager* (spring 2000), online, Lexis-Nexis.
12. Robert Barner, "The New Millennium Workplace: Seven Changes That Will Challenge Managers—and Workers," *The Futurist* (March–April 1996), 14–19.
13. Gloria Gordon, "Senior Executives and Corporate Communicators, Wake Up!" *Communication World* (August–September 1997): 42–43.
14. "It's Not All about a Paycheck: Findings from the 2001 Randstad North American Employee Review," online, www.us.randstad.com.
15. Milne.
16. Max Jarman, "Paradox of Temp Jobs," *Arizona Republic,* 9 May 2001, online, Lexis-Nexis.
17. "Temp Agencies Enjoying Balmy Days," *Nikkei Weekly,* 23 April 2001, online, Lexis-Nexis.
18. "It's Not All about a Paycheck."
19. David Freeland, "Communication: So What's New?" *Communication World* (December 1997–January 1998): 15.
20. Timothy Aeppel, "Babel at Work: A 3Com Factory Hires a Lot of Immigrants, Gets Mix of Languages," *Wall Street Journal,* 30 March 1998, A1.
21. "Effective Managers Must Evolve Their Generational Stereotypes: Findings from the 2001 Randstad North American Employee Review," online, www.us.randstad.com.
22. "INS Survey Identifies Key Factors Influencing Network Professionals' Job Satisfaction," news release issued by International Network Services, 3 March 1998, online, Lexis-Nexis.
23. "Effective Managers Must Evolve Their Generational Stereotypes."
24. "More Americans Dissatisfied with Their Jobs: A Conference Board Report," online, www.conference-board.org.
25. "Effective Managers Must Evolve Their Generational Stereotypes."
26. Linda Grant, "Unhappy in Japan: International Morale Watch," *Fortune,* 13 January 1997, online, Lexis-Nexis.
27. Sharon Linstedt, "Friendship Is Top Reason for Happiness on the Job Site," *Buffalo News,* 14 May 2001, online, Lexis-Nexis.
28. "Top Employees Motivated More by Maintaining Reputation Than by Pay," a news release issued by Watson Wyatt Worldwide, 4 April 2000, online, www.watsonwyatt.com/homepage/index.html; "It's Not All About a Paycheck." Linstedt.
29. Sue Shellenberger, "Some Workers Find Bosses Don't Share Their Family Values," *Wall Street Journal,* 12 July 1995, B1.
30. "1999 Communications Study," Watson Wyatt Worldwide and the International Association of Business Communicators, 4.
31. "What Makes a Good Boss," *HR Focus* (March 2000), online, Lexis-Nexis.

32. "Richard Miller and Joseph Cangemi, "North American Employee Attitudes in the 1990's: Changing Attitudes for Changing Times," *Education* (spring 2000), online, Expanded Academic Index.

33. "Majority of Americans, Western Europeans, Latin Americans Are Satisfied with Jobs; Eastern Europeans and Asians Give Less Glowing Endorsement of Their Job Life," a news release issued by Ipsos-Reid, online, 8 January 2001, www.ipsos-reid.com/media.

34. Martin Sprouse, ed., *Sabotage in the American Workplace* (San Francisco: Pressure Drop Press, 1992).

35. *Gale Directory of Publications and Broadcast Media*, 134th ed. (Detroit: Gale, 2000), xxiii.

36. "Internet Sapping Broadcast News Audience," a news release issued by the Pew Research Center, online, 11 June 2000, www.people-press.org/media.

37. Lynne Sallot, Thomas Steinfatt, and Michael Salwen, "Journalists' and Public Relations Practitioners' News Values: Perceptions and Cross-Perceptions," *Journalism and Mass Communication Quarterly* (summer 1998): 369–370.

38. Felicity Barringer, "Editors Debate Realism vs. Retreat in Newsroom Diversity," *New York Times,* 6 April 1998, online, Lexis-Nexis.

39. "ASNE Census Finds Newsrooms Less Diverse," a news release issued by the American Society of Newspaper Editors, online, 3 April 2001, www.asne.org/kiosk/diversity/2001Survey/2001CensusReport.htm.

40. "RTNDA Foundation Research: 2000 Women and Minorities Survey," online, www.rtnda.org/research/womin.html.

41. "RTNDA Foundation Research: 2000 Women and Minorities Survey."

42. "Federal Government Civilian Employment by Function," U.S. Bureau of the Census, online, www.census.gov.

43. "Federal Government, Excluding the Postal Service," U.S. Bureau of Labor Statistics, online, www.bls.gov/oco/cg/cgs041.htm.

44. "Federal Government Civilian Employment by Function."

45. "OPM Finds Workers Generally Satisfied, But Rewards, Labor, Other Concerns High," *Government Employee Relations Report,* 11 April 2000, online, Lexis-Nexis.

46. "OPM Finds Workers Generally Satisfied, but Rewards, Labor, Other Concerns High."

47. James D. McKevitt, "Making Friends on the Hill," *Association Management* (October 1996), online, Lexis-Nexis.

48. Marcella Kogan, "All Worked Up: The Demand for Family-Friendly Workplaces Is Growing," *Government Executive* (November 1996), online, Lexis-Nexis.

49. "1999 Public Employment Data: Local Governments," U.S. Bureau of the Census, online, www.census.gov; "State Government Employment Data," U.S. Bureau of the Census, online, www.census.gov.

50. "Employment by Major Industry Division," U.S. Bureau of the Census, online, www.census.gov.

51. Diana Marcum, "The Footprint of a Whale," *Los Angeles Times Magazine,* 29 April 2001, online, Lexis-Nexis; "IFAW Honors Pierce Brosnan for Efforts to Protect Wildlife," PR Newswire, 15 November 2000, online, Lexis-Nexis; "After Five-Year Battle, Mitsubishi Ends Baja Mexico Salt Plant Project," PR Newswire, 2 March 2000, online, Lexis-Nexis.

52. Linda De Leon and Walied Taher, "Expectations and Job Satisfaction for Local-Government Professionals," *American Review of Public Administration* (December 1996), online, Lexis-Nexis.

53. De Leon and Taher.

54. De Leon and Taher.

55. Richard Nadler, "Stocks Populi," *National Review,* 9 March 1998, online, Lexis-Nexis.

56. David R. Francis, "Stock Markets Win the Masses," *Christian Science Monitor,* 25 March 1998, online, Lexis-Nexis.

57. Nadler.

58. International Federation of Stock Exchanges, online, www.fibv.com; David R. Francis, "Stock Markets Win the Masses," *Christian Science Monitor,* 25 March 1998, online, Lexis-Nexis.

59. Francis.

60. Richard Nadler, "Stocks Populi," *National Review,* 9 March 1998, online, Lexis-Nexis.

61. John Dillin, "Few Investors Ran from the Market Bear," *Christian Science Monitor,* 23 April 2001, online, Lexis-Nexis.

62. Hank Ezell, "Counting on Social Security Not Wise," *Atlanta Journal and Constitution,* 25 March 2001, online, Lexis-Nexis.

63. "Investors Think, Act, and Vote Differently Than Non-investors," a news release issued by Zogby International, online, 23 October 2000, www.zogby.com/news.

64. "Investors Think, Act, and Vote Differently Than Non-investors."

65. "Datadog," *American Demographics* (March 2001), online, Lexis-Nexis.

66. "The Pay's the Thing," *Wall Street Journal,* 10 April 1997, A1.

67. Peter K. Francese, "Big Spenders," *American Demographics* (August 1997): 52.

68. Elia Kacapyr, "Disposable Dollars Determine Spending," *American Demographics* (June 1997): 18.

69. Kacapyr.

70. "Consumer Expenditures in 1999, Table 6," U.S. Bureau of Labor Statistics, online, www.bls.gov.

71. "Consumer Expenditures in 1999, Table 3," U.S. Bureau of Labor Statistics, online, www.bls.gov.

72. Gerry Khermouch, "An Almost-Invisible $1 Trillion Market," *Business Week,* 11 June 2001, online, Lexis-Nexis; Gerry Myers, "Consider the Customer: Mutual Respect," *American Demographics* (April 1997): 20.

73. Sharon Goldman Edry, "No Longer Just Fun and Games," *American Demographics* (May 2001), online, Lexis-Nexis.

74. Rebecca Gardyn, "Toplines," *American Demographics* (April 2001): 11.

75. "What Consumers Want from Businesses," *Sales & Marketing Management* (August 2000): 78.

76. Frederick F. Reichheld, *The Loyalty Effect* (Boston: Harvard Business School Press, 1996), 33.

77. "Nearly Half of All Americans Buy Online," Business Wire, 24 April 2001, online, Lexis-Nexis.

78. *Newsbytes PM,* 4 November 1998, online, Lexis-Nexis.

79. Gardyn, 16.

80. Joan Raymond, "No More Shoppus Interruptus," *American Demographics* (May 2001), online, Lexis-Nexis.

81. David McDermitt and Tony Shelton, "The 10 Commandments of Community Relations," *World Wastes* (September 1993), online, Lexis-Nexis.

82. Jerry A. Hendrix, *Public Relations Cases,* 4th ed. (Belmont, Calif.: Wadsworth, 1998), 18–19.

83. Kim A. Smith, "Perceived Influence of Media on What Goes On in a Community," *Journalism Quarterly* 61, no. 2 (1984): 263.

84. Tannette Johnson-Elie, "Denny's Turnabout Means Fair Play for Minority Employees," *Milwaukee Journal Sentinel,* 31 October 2000, online, Lexis-Nexis.

85. "Resident Population of the United States," U.S. Bureau of the Census, online, www.census.gov.

86. Lisa Lollock, "The Foreign Born Population: March 2000," U.S. Bureau of the Census, online, www.census.gov.

87. Lollock.

88. Tim Donnelly, "Statistics Show How America Voted," University Wire, online, 17 November 2000, Lexis-Nexis.

89. "Alienation Not a Factor in Nonvoting," news release issued by The League of Women Voters, 26 August 1996, online, www.lwv.org/mellsumm.html.

90. Jennifer Day, "Voting-Age Population Projected to Pass 200 Million Mark, Census Bureau Says," news release issued by the U.S. Bureau of the Census, 13 May 1998, online, www.census.gov.

91. Jennifer C. Day and Avalaura L. Gaitheriujj, "Voter Registration in the Election of November 1998," U.S. Bureau of the Census, online, www.census.gov

92. Roger Clegg, "Racial Divide," *Legal Times,* 20 November 2000, online, Lexis-Nexis.

93. Day and Gaitheriujj.

94. Rebecca Gardyn, "Moving Targets," *American Demographics* (October 2000), online, Lexis-Nexis.

95. "PR League Tables: Top 50 Business-to-Business," *Marketing,* 21 May 1998, online, Lexis-Nexis.

96. "PR League Tables: Why Trade PRs Are Hooked on the Net," *Marketing,* 25 May 2000, online, Lexis-Nexis.

97. "PR League Tables: Why Trade PRs Are Hooked on the Net."

98. Douglas A. Blackmon, "Sunbeam Shares Dive As Investors Doubt Dunlap," *Wall Street Journal,* 6 April 1998, A16.

99. Blackmon.

100. John A. Byrne, "How Al Dunlap Self-Destructed," *Business Week,* 6 July 1998, 60.

101. Jonathan R. Laing, "Dangerous Games: Did 'Chainsaw Al' Dunlap Manufacture Sunbeam's Earnings Last Year?" *Barron's,* 8 June 1998, 19.

102. Byrne, 64.

103. "Sunbeam Audit Committee to Conduct Review of Company's 1997 Financial Statements," news release issued by Sunbeam, 30 June 1998.

104. "Thanks to Chris Muncy, the Tiny Town of Parrott, Va., Now Rates a Spot on the Map," *People,* 15 October 1990, online, Lexis-Nexis.

105. "Thanks to Chris Muncy."

106. Rand McNally web site, www.randmcnally.com.

107. Janet Sutter, "Kid Gets Credit for Geographic Breakthrough," *San Diego Union-Tribune,* 3 October 1990, online, Lexis-Nexis.

chapter five

Communication Theory and Public Opinion

objectives

After studying this chapter, you will be able to

■ understand the process of communication and some of the theories of how people react to what they encounter in the mass media

■ identify the forces that motivate people

■ describe the power of public opinion and the process under which it develops

■ recognize the differences between the use of persuasion and manipulation in public relations

The Village Historical Association

You own a public relations agency in a small community that has a long and proud history. Several Revolutionary War skirmishes took place in the fields surrounding the village. Many of the homes in your town were built during the colonial period. It is a quiet place, and an organization your agency represents, the Village Historical Association, wants to keep it that way.

That is why you are surprised when you pick up the morning newspaper from your doorstep and read the front-page headline "Plans for Battlefield Shopping Mall Announced." As you read further, you note that the out-of-state corporation that is planning to develop the site says the mall will generate hundreds of jobs and pump millions of dollars into the local economy.

As expected, the president of the Village Historical Association telephones to tell you that the organization plans to oppose the mall vigorously. However, the president of the local chamber of commerce believes the development will bring life to an economically stagnant community.

Permission to build rests with the local zoning board. How should you proceed?

The Power of Public Opinion

Anyone with even a passing knowledge of history knows of the Holocaust and the unspeakable horror that confronted Jews living in Europe. The German Führer Adolf Hitler and his Nazi henchmen committed history's worst crimes against humanity in a twisted effort to purge the world of Jews.

Lesser known, however, is the role that *German* public opinion had in sparing the lives of 2,000 Jewish prisoners in March 1943. These prisoners, mostly men, had non-Jewish German spouses. The prisoners had been scheduled for transport to Auschwitz, the most notorious of the Nazis' death camps. However, the power of public opinion—something you might not expect to be a concern of a totalitarian regime—forced the Nazis to halt the shipment and release the prisoners, most of whom survived the war.

Hundreds of women staged protest rallies outside the Berlin jail in which the prisoners were held—right in the very heart of the capital of the Third Reich. The women gathered every night for a week shouting, "Give us our husbands back!" Guards fired gunshots on several occasions in an attempt to disperse the crowd. However, the protests continued until the authorities gave in and released the prisoners. With the tide of the war turning against the Nazis, Gestapo Chief Heinrich Himmler did not want to risk German public support for the nation's war effort.[1]

If public opinion could force the Nazis to change their policies, think of its power in a peaceful democracy. The very essence of a democratic society is that public policies are created as a result of words, not weapons. Effective communication is a key to success. So is the ability to persuade others to accept or at least respect your point of view. Both are at the heart of the practice of public relations.

As we've said before and will say again, good public relations involves two-way communication between an organization and the publics important to its success. Responding to the concerns and needs of others is a big part of public relations. Ultimately, you want to create a mutually beneficial environment in which both an organization and its publics can flourish. That environment is achieved through the give-and-take that characterizes two-way communication. It is not enough for an organization to be a good listener. It also must be a good communicator. Successful companies and individuals excel in letting others know their values and preferences. And in today's results-oriented environment, success is often measured by one's ability to persuade others to come around to a certain way of thinking.

In this chapter's opening scenario, an out-of-state developer wants to build a shopping mall near a historic site. Although the thought of a shopping mall near a Revolutionary War battlefield offends the sensibilities of some, there is another side to the story. The development is expected to breathe life into a depressed local economy. The issue has the potential for sparking a heated debate that could divide the community. However, your client has certain values it does not want to compromise.

Listening to and persuading others—that is the major balancing act faced by today's public relations practitioners. It is also the focus of this chapter, in which the theories and practices of persuasive communication are discussed.

Even Ronald Reagan, considered one of the best communicators to live in the White House, faced the challenge of overcoming noise in the environment when promoting his administration's policies. (Photo by David Guth)

A Communication Model

Before we discuss how public opinion is formed, let's look at the process of communication. After all, it is the essential core of the profession of public relations. Social scientists have made numerous attempts to develop what are known as "communication models": graphic representations that are useful in helping us understand the dynamics of the communication process. Some of the models that have been developed by communication theorists are simple in their design and others are elaborate. All have their merits. For the purposes of this discussion, we have selected a model that has a relatively uncomplicated design but which takes into account some complex forces (Figure 5.1). The six ingredients of that model are noise, the source, the message, the channel, the receiver, and feedback.

NOISE.   Sometimes referred to as static, **noise** envelops communication and often inhibits it. Noise can take both physical and intangible forms. It can have a physical quality, such as that experienced when a person is trying to talk with someone in a large crowd. The crowd noise can make it difficult to understand everything being said. However, noise does not have to be audible to inhibit communication. A person's state of mind can also block effective communication. An example is the mental "static" experienced by a person who is reeling from an emotional event and is not really listening to what is said. There are also times when for a variety of reasons—cultural, religious, and generational among them—we erect barriers to communication. In these instances, we often generate "noise" because we don't like either the message or the messenger.

SOURCE.   The **source** is where a communication originates. The source is also the first part of the coorientation model mentioned in Chapter 4. How a source views its

FIGURE 5.1
A Communication Model

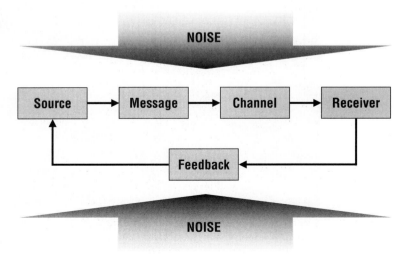

audience—and is viewed by an audience—can help or hinder communication. Source credibility can be influenced by a variety of factors, including reputation, context, and communication ability. For example, a particular elected official was once seen as a leading advocate for strong family values. His subsequent arrest on a morals charge, however, undermined his credibility and ultimately ended his political career.

MESSAGE.   The **message** is the content of the communication. To a large degree, successful formation of the message relies on knowledge of both the purpose of the message and its intended receiver. If the message is not relevant or is not in language understood by that receiver, it will probably be misunderstood or ignored. It wouldn't make sense for your professor to speak to the class in French—unless, of course, it was a French class.

CHANNEL.   The **channel** is the medium used to transmit the message to the intended receiver. The selection of the most appropriate channel or channels is a key strategic decision. Like the source, the channel must be relevant and credible to the intended receiver. And much like a broadcast channel on an old-time radio, the channel can be susceptible to static. In this case, static is defined as physical and psychological forces that can make it difficult for the receiver to acquire the message. For example, many public relations practitioners have had their well-planned efforts at obtaining publicity foiled by breaking news stories that have caused reporters to focus their attentions elsewhere. One of your authors had three painstakingly planned news conferences derailed by attempted political assassinations in the same year.

RECEIVER.   The **receiver** is the person or persons for whom the message is intended. The receiver is also the second part of the coorientation model mentioned in Chapter 4. How the receiver views the source—and is viewed by the source—can help or hinder communication. The most effective communications are those that specifically target the intended receiver. For reasons already stated, the communicator must select the source, message, and channel with the needs of the receiver in mind. That, in turn, requires a thorough knowledge of the receiver, including its needs, values, predispositions, and communication ability. After all, what good does it do to communicate if the intended audience is not listening?

FEEDBACK.   **Feedback** is the receiver's reaction—as interpreted by the source—to the message. Without this final step, true communication does not occur. Feedback lets you know whether the message got through and how it was interpreted. Think of a stand-up comedian: If the audience laughs, the joke was funny. If there is silence, the joke failed. Good communicators, especially public relations practitioners, actively seek feedback. Feedback, often in the form of telephone calls and letters, can be spontaneous. However, that isn't always the case. Sometimes special mechanisms are established to generate feedback, such as toll-free telephone numbers and public opinion polls.

As stated before, social scientists have developed a variety of communication models. However, the models all have something in common: Communication is a lot like an electrical circuit—if a short or break occurs anywhere along the wire, nothing happens. No communication takes place if the source is not seen as credible, the message is not relevant, the channel is filled with static, the receiver is not listening, or feedback is lacking.

A breakdown in the communication process was evident in May 1970, when President Richard Nixon attempted to reach out to anti–Vietnam War protesters. The president made a predawn visit to the Lincoln Memorial, where antiwar activists, mostly college students, were camped out awaiting the start of a major protest

QuickBreak 5.1

MOKUSATSU

Communication fails when a source sends a message that cannot be understood or is misinterpreted by the receiver. Never has that fact had more tragic consequences than at the end of World War II, when the decision to use atomic bombs may have hinged on a misunderstanding over the meaning of a single Japanese word.

The decision to use the recently developed bomb against Japanese targets was not an easy one for President Harry Truman. On the one hand, the bomb might shock the Japanese military into surrendering, thus avoiding the bloody consequences of a full-scale military invasion of the island nation. On the other hand, Truman also knew that many civilians would be killed in an atomic attack. However, the signs coming out of Tokyo were not good. Although the Japanese military had been crushed as a result of three years of terrifying and unrelenting warfare, its leaders said Japan would never surrender.

Truman decided to give the Japanese one last chance before unleashing the bomb. In what has become known as the Potsdam Declaration, Truman told the Japanese that they had to surrender unconditionally or face unspecified consequences. Japanese Prime Minister Kantaro Suzuki, an aging civilian aristocrat, wanted to negotiate peace quickly with the Americans. But Suzuki also knew that the military, which dominated the government, would not let him.

When asked by the military press for his response to the Potsdam Declaration, the prime minister said, "We *mokusatsu* it." Suzuki thought he had been clever. *Mokusatsu* is a Japanese word that has a variety of interpretations, largely dependent on who is perceived as its source. In saying "We *mokusatsu* it," Suzuki was speaking for himself and asking the Americans to keep negotiations open and make another peace offer. However, Truman believed the prime minister was speaking on behalf of the military. In that context, *mokusatsu* was interpreted as meaning "hold in silent contempt."

Believing that the Japanese had rejected the United States' last olive branch, Truman authorized the use of atomic bombs. Hiroshima was attacked on August 6, 1945. An estimated 92,000 people were killed and an unknown number suffered long-term effects from radiation. Another 40,000 people died three days later in the atomic bombing of Nagasaki. One week later, the Japanese surrendered.

rally. The meeting didn't go well. Nixon said he spoke to the students about his and their mutual desire to end the war—but he said they didn't really listen. The students told reporters that the president talked about sports and surfing and "wasn't really concerned about why we were here." Whichever version of the event you accept, the outcome was undeniable: a communication breakdown that reinforced the mistrust that Nixon and the students had of one another.[2] For true communication to take place, it must be a two-way process.

Quick ✓ Check

1. What are the six elements of the communication model used in this text?
2. What are some of the things that can block communication?
3. Why is listening essential to good communication and effective public relations?

Theories of Persuasion

Having looked at the process of communication, let's next look at how mass communications affect public opinion. Theories on how this interaction occurs have been evolving since the mass communications technology explosion began in the early 20th century.

The Magic Bullet Theory

World events had a great influence on early theories of mass communications. As you may remember from the history chapter of this book, research interest in persuasion and public opinion heated up in the wake of the use of propaganda techniques during World War I. The growth of fascism in Europe and Asia during the 1930s largely paralleled the growth of the first electronic mass medium, radio. Out of these developments came the first mass communications theory, the **magic bullet theory** of mass communications. This theory, illustrated in Figure 5.2, is grounded in a belief that the mass media wield great power over their audiences. It was thought that if a sender developed just the right message, the so-called magic bullet, people could be influenced to do almost anything. The problem with this approach to mass communications is that it supposes that people are weak-willed robots unable to resist finely sculptured appeals.

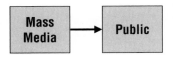

FIGURE 5.2   The Magic Bullet Theory of Mass Communications

The Two-Step Theory

By the end of World War II, the magic bullet theory had been largely discredited. Social scientists began to understand better the role of intervening publics in influencing public opinion. From this realization evolved the **two-step theory** of mass communications, the foundation of which is the belief that the mass media influence society's key opinion leaders, who in turn influence the opinions and actions of society itself (Figure 5.3). These key opinion leaders were said to include elected public officials, powerful business executives, and religious figures. Although the opinion leaders were seen as powerful, this theory remained based on the belief that the mass media were powerful forces in molding public opinion.

FIGURE 5.3 Two-Step Flow of Mass Communications

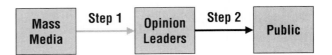

The N-Step Theory

Recognizing that different people may be credible in different contexts, communication researcher Wilbur Schramm developed the **n-step theory** of mass communications (Figure 5.4). It was similar to the two-step theory in that it stressed the role of opinion leaders. However, under the n-step theory, key opinion leaders may vary from issue to issue. For example, you may view NBA legend Michael Jordan as an expert on basketball,

FIGURE 5.4 N-Step Flow of Mass Communications

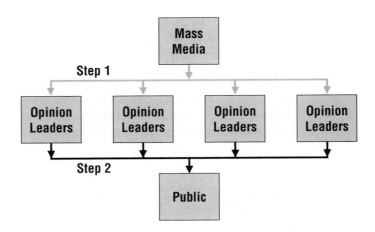

but you would probably find retired Westinghouse/CBS executive Michael Jordan a more credible source for information about communications technology.

Diffusion Theory

Unlike its predecessors, the **diffusion theory** of mass communications was based on a belief that the power of the mass media is not as much to motivate people as it is to inform them (Figure 5.5). Under this theoretical view of mass communications, people have the power to influence members of their own peer groups. Agricultural extension agents have followed this approach for decades. The agents provide farmers with information on how they can improve their crop yields. If a farmer adopts an approach that works, he or she spreads the word of this success to other farmers. In other words, the idea is passed along through a diffusion process. In a sense, everyone can become an opinion leader.

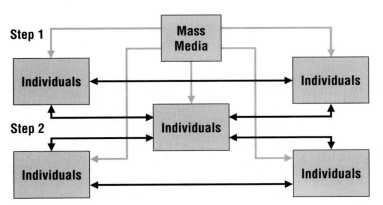

FIGURE 5.5   Diffusion Theory

The Agenda-Setting Hypothesis

The most significant and widely accepted view of how the mass media interact with society is currently the **agenda-setting hypothesis.** It is based on the simple principle that the mass media tell people not what to think, but what to think about. In other words, the media set the public agenda (Figure 5.6).

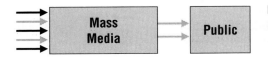

FIGURE 5.6   The Agenda-Setting Hypothesis

FRAMING CAMPAIGN 2000

George W. Bush said it was all but over. Al Gore said it had only just begun. And President Bill Clinton joked, "The American people have spoken, but it is going to take a little time to determine exactly what they said."

Social scientists who study public opinion and the role the mass media play in its formation often do so using what is known as **framing theory.** Researcher Robert Entman has defined framing as communicating an idea in such a way that an audience is influenced, either intentionally or unintentionally, by the way it is expressed.[3] The application of framing theory was obvious—and important—during the 36-day stalemate that followed the 2000 presidential election.

More than 100 million U.S. voters cast ballots for president on November 7. Vice President Al Gore carried the nation by approximately a half-million votes. But for the first time since the election of 1888, the winner of the popular vote had lost the only count that really mattered, the Electoral College. Texas Governor George W. Bush won 271 electoral votes to

Gore's 267 to become the 43rd president of the United States. However, Gore did not concede the election until December 13, five weeks and one day after the last ballot was cast. The vice president later joked privately that it had been "a long election night."

The reason for the delayed decision was a dispute over Florida's 25 electoral votes. Out of the nearly 6 million votes cast in the Sunshine State, Bush led the election night count by a mere 1,784 votes. Following a mandatory recount, his lead dwindled to 327 votes. The Democrats went to court seeking further recounts, claiming that thousands of Gore votes had not been tabulated because of faulty punch-card ballots. In turn, the Republicans went to court to stop further recounts that they said were selective and lacking clear standards.

Paralleling the legal battle was a battle for public opinion. The stakes were high, and both sides needed public support to continue their fight for the presidency. This is where framing theory came into play. Gore tried to frame the

---

We see examples of the agenda-setting hypothesis at work in every morning's newspaper. Have you ever noticed how one issue can dominate the newspapers—and public debate—for several weeks, only to be replaced by another? One such example is the long-running public debate over the safety of nuclear power. The issues surrounding this subject are largely the same today as they were 30 years ago. However, it is only when there is a dramatic incident, such as the accidents at Three Mile Island in 1979 or at Chernobyl in 1986, that the issue moves to the top of the public agenda. Even then, the focus on nuclear power safety lasts only until another hot issue emerges to replace it on the front pages and in the nightly newscasts.

If you take the agenda-setting hypothesis to its next logical step, it raises an important question: If the media tell us not what to think but what to think about, who tells the media what to think about? Media in democratic societies have the independence to report on any topic they choose, so who sets the media's agenda?

debate to show that he was not a poor loser and that he would accept the voters' verdict once all the ballots in question had been counted. For his part, Bush tried to frame the debate to show that he had won the election and that a recount would amount to changing the rules in the middle of the game. Had either man lost the backing of key supporters, sustaining their legal efforts would have been politically and financially difficult.

Both Bush and Gore tried to frame their comments by "looking presidential" during this period. That meant appearing to be above the fray, calmly taking in the many twists and turns of the postelection period. To that end, both campaigns enlisted former U.S. secretaries of state as their key spokespersons in Florida. With them was an army of lawyers, politicians, and media consultants. While both candidates stayed in the background, their surrogates slugged it out for the hearts and minds of the electorate.

Part of the effort to look presidential involved one the nation's most powerful symbols, the Stars and Stripes. When Bush spoke to the nation for the first time after the election, two U.S. flags flanked his lectern. When Gore appeared, he had four flags. The Battle of the Flags had been joined. Every time a candidate or his running mate subsequently appeared, more flags showed up in the background. Amused by this spectacle, David Letterman placed dozens of flags on the set of his late-night talk show in what he called an effort "to calm the American people."

Letterman had nothing to worry about. Throughout the 36-day electoral stalemate, the American people were, for the most part, patient. Although many overseas media portrayed the United States as a country in chaos, several nationwide surveys indicated that Americans were willing to wait until all the issues were resolved. When the U.S. Supreme Court resolved the electoral dispute in Bush's favor, other surveys showed an electorate willing to accept the decision.

The answer is equally important: Organizations and individuals are free to use public relations techniques to influence the media and thereby to put their imprint on the public agenda. And many organizations and individuals do just that. Historically, presidents of the United States have been particularly good at setting the media's agenda. Because of the power and prestige of the White House, almost anything a president does or says is news. Every president from Washington on has tried to influence news coverage in an attempt to control the public agenda. However, because presidents are not alone in understanding these dynamics, each has enjoyed only mixed success.

The experiences of recent presidents has been typical. Bill Clinton succeeded in convincing the majority of the public that the Republican-controlled Congress was responsible for a January 1996 shutdown of the federal government, even though his veto of the budget precipitated it. On the other hand, Clinton was unsuccessful in his effort to win public support for a comprehensive health-care package, largely because his opponents successfully framed the issue as government intrusion on personal liberties. This pattern of mixed results in controlling the agenda continues with Clinton's successor. Despite razor-thin majorities in both houses of Congress, George W. Bush won widespread public approval of major tax-cut legislation early in his term. However, that support declined when an economic slowdown helped fuel charges from the president's opponents that the tax cuts had been ill advised.

Uses and Gratifications Theory

This brings us to yet another evolution in communications theory. In recent years, theorists have noted that the agenda-setting hypothesis is based on a model in which the receiver is seen as a passive participant in the communication process. If this model is correct, theorists point out, then the source has the ultimate power of persuasion over the receiver. However, this concept of a passive receiver is being challenged by what is known as the **uses and gratifications theory.** The technological advances of recent years have resulted in an explosion of available mass communications channels. Researchers say that the real power now rests in the ability of receivers to pick and choose their channels of information. Although many communicators may seek to persuade the audience to take a particular course of action, the audience serves as a gatekeeper—in effect, deciding to whom it will grant influence (Figure 5.7).[4]

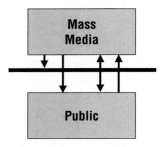

FIGURE 5.7   Uses and Gratifications Theory

A Two-Way Process

Mass communications theory appears to have undergone a complete reversal. It has evolved from a belief that people are powerless to resist the mass media to an acknowledgment of the public's supremacy over media. This new view suggests that persuasion, like communication, is a two-way street. According to *Excellence in Public Relations and Communication Management,* a publication of the IABC Research Foundation, "The concept of negotiation, rather than domination or persuasion, is the key to understanding the effects of communication and public relations programs."[5]

Let's go back to the opening scenario of this chapter. Each side of the battlefield mall debate has its merits. The people who want to build the mall say it will bring important economic benefits to the community. Those who oppose the plan fear it will desecrate a historically significant site where people died fighting for independence. If each side enters this debate unwilling to listen to the other, sparks will no doubt fly. Eventually, one side will win and the other side will lose. But the controversy will not end there. The lingering effects of the ill will created by such a controversy could have

THE THIRD BATTLE OF BULL RUN

If the scenario at the beginning of this chapter has a familiar ring to it, that's because something like it really happened. The real-life showdown was between the Walt Disney Company and a coalition of historians and environmentalists. The controversy became, figuratively and literally, the Third Battle of Bull Run.

In November 1993 Disney announced plans to build a 3,000-acre historical theme park, Disney's America, near Haymarket, Virginia. Peter Rummell, president of Disney Design and Development Company, said the theme park would "allow guests to celebrate the diversity of the nation, the plurality and conflicts that have defined the American character." Among the planned attractions were a Civil War–era village; a section about Native Americans (with an accompanying white-water raft ride); a high-speed thrill attraction called the Industrial Revolution; and a tribute to the nation's immigrants, incorporating music, food, and a multimedia presentation.[6]

The location selected was only 35 miles west of Washington and a few miles from the Manassas National Battlefield, site of two Civil War battles, the first and second battles of Bull Run. State officials enthusiastically supported the Disney plan, largely because of the projected 3,000 jobs and $1.5 billion in tax revenues the development was supposed to create during its first 30 years.

Opposition to the park focused on two points of contention: the park's content and its environmental impact. Award-winning documentary producer Ken Burns summed up the attitudes of both historians and environmentalists when he wrote, "This project has the possibility of not only sanitizing and making 'enjoyable' a hugely tragic moment of our past, but of physically destroying, through subsequent development, the exquisite landscape where the ghosts of our collective past still have the power to mesmerize us with the palpable fact of our often sad history."[7]

Significantly, Confederate forces won both battles of Bull Run. This time, too, the defending army would carry the day. Just as the Union forces had appeared unbeatable at the start of both encounters, so did Disney. However, just like the rebels before them, the theme park opponents had the superior battle plan. Within five days of the initial announcement, the leaders of the local Piedmont Environmental Council developed a winning strategy: Generate enough criticism nationwide to force image-conscious Disney to back away.

And that's exactly what happened. Disney officials pulled the plug on the project on September 28, 1994. In making the announcement, Disney's Rummell said, "We recognize that there are those who have been concerned about the possible impact of our park on historic sites in this unique area, and we have always tried to be sensitive to the issue."[8]

political, social, and economic ramifications for years. If the two sides enter the discussion willing to listen to each other's concerns, however, a compromise is possible. Historic preservation and economic stability are not necessarily mutually exclusive concepts. The key to keeping the peace is two-way communication.

Motivation

Having discussed the communication process and the various theories on how mass communications influence people, we now focus on the individual. What motivates a given individual to do something? What forces are in play when we try to influence someone's behavior? What kind of appeals can spark action? These are questions psychologists and sociologists have pondered for centuries.

Although many theories explain why people do the things they do, one simple explanation is best: People usually act in their own self-interests. This may not seem, on the surface, to be a very earth-shattering revelation. However, this simple truth is at the heart of molding public opinion. But how do people determine their self-interests? You can look to your own parents for the answer.

As strange as it may seem, your parents were once teenagers. If they grew up in the late 1960s and early 1970s, it is very possible that they owned bell-bottom jeans, wore long hair, and spoke of a desire for a peaceful world governed by a loose-knit philosophy known as "flower power." At the center of this popular culture was the most successful rock band the world had ever known, the Beatles. John, Paul, George, and Ringo had a generation believing that if you sought peace and tranquillity, "all you need is love."

If only it were that simple. Unfortunately, the Beatles were wrong.

Maslow's Hierarchy of Needs

Long before the Fab Four sang that love is the central force behind everything, psychologist Abraham Maslow developed a theory to explain how people determine their self-interests: **Maslow's Hierarchy of Needs** (Figure 5.8). The basis of the theory is that some needs are more basic than others and, therefore, must be fulfilled first.[9] On Maslow's list, love comes in only third.

According to Maslow, the lowest (most basic) order of needs is our *physiological* needs. These are the biological demands our bodies make for food, water, rest, and exercise. He included sex among our most basic needs, but only as it related to the continuation of our species. Love and romance had nothing to do with it. By Maslow's way of thinking, if humans do not fulfill their physiological needs, little else matters.

According to Maslow, *safety* is the next order of need. By "safety needs" he means things such as personal security, comfort, and orderly surroundings. To understand Maslow's ranking, assume for a minute that you are in shelter in the middle of a war zone. Bombs and bullets are flying all around you. The shooting is expected to last for weeks. As long as you stay in that shelter, you are safe. However, suppose that shelter has no food or water. Maslow believed that, eventually, you will leave that shelter and forgo personal safety to fulfill your physiological needs. Otherwise, you will die anyway.

The third order of need is *acceptance,* or what Maslow referred to as love and belongingness. This is where the Beatles come in. At this level, we seek out love, a sense

FIGURE 5.8   Maslow's Hierarchy of Needs

of belonging, an affiliation with others through group memberships. Still, this is only third on the list. Pretend that you have entered our imaginary bomb shelter only to find that it is filled with people you do not like and vice versa. Under Maslow's hierarchy, you are willing to endure any annoyance and indignity that may occur from these uncomfortable arrangements because of the safety the shelter provides.

Next on Maslow's hierarchy is *self-esteem* needs, for which we strive to earn recognition and view ourselves as being successful. Everyone wants to be seen as a winner. However, people are often willing to let their self-esteem suffer if doing so provides some measure of acceptance. That is why some people choose to remain in abusive, unhealthy relationships. It isn't until the victim understands that this isn't true acceptance or that physiological or safety needs are threatened that the abusive relationship ends.

The highest order is *self-actualization* needs. With apologies to the U.S. Army's marketing slogan, this is how we try to "be all that we can be." We reach self-actualization when we achieve a goal just for the sake of achieving that goal. Climbing a mountain "because it is there" is an expression of self-actualization. Some people never achieve self-actualization because they haven't fulfilled the requirements imposed by lower order needs. In some ways, self-actualization is like the Great American Novel that many people say they will write but never do—because their attention is constantly focused on more pressing needs.

Examples of Maslow's Theory at Work

Just a guess: You are not reading about Maslow's Hierarchy of Needs as an expression of self-actualization. Your motivation is probably a result of a need to fulfill your

QuickBreak 5.4

MONROE'S MOTIVATED SEQUENCE

In an era in which change is the only constant, it is refreshing to see an idea that has stood the test of time. In the mid-1920s, Purdue University Professor Alan H. Monroe developed an organizational pattern for persuasive messages that has come to be known as **Monroe's Motivated Sequence.**[10] Nearly 80 years later, it remains a standard for persuasive communication.

Building persuasive messages using Monroe's Motivated Sequence involves a five-step process. Let's look at that process using a real-world example: a company executive trying to motivate employees to improve quality by reducing workplace errors:

- **Attention**. Get the attention of the audience through a dramatic story, quote, or statistic. Tell the audience why the topic is important to it.

    "One of our competitors has been forced to cut back production and lay off some of its employees. Its sales have dropped because of consumer complaints of shoddy products. We can't afford to have that happen here."

- **Need**. Show that a significant problem exists and that it won't go away by itself. Document the need with relevant examples.

    "There is a great deal of competition in today's global economy. Consumers are demanding quality. If they don't get it from us, they have plenty of other options."

- **Satisfaction**. Now that a need has been shown, offer solutions. They should be reasonable solutions that adequately address the need.

    "By working together, the management and employees of this company can de-

velop reasonable training programs to improve the quality of our products and reduce production-line errors."

- **Visualization**. Tell what will happen if nothing is done to solve the problem. Explicitly tell the audience the consequences of its choices.

    "In recent weeks, our research department has noticed an increasing number of consumer complaints. We are headed down the same road as our competition. If we don't make changes, it is likely that some of us will lose our jobs."

- **Action**. Tell the audience members what they, personally, can do to solve the problem. It is important that the actions requested are explicitly stated.

    "I am asking you to make a personal commitment to quality. Don't be afraid to share your ideas for improving our products. Volunteer to serve on the various committees we are establishing to examine this issue. Help make this company's mission statement—'providing quality products and services'—a reality."

It is not a coincidence that the example cited here is closely linked to the company's mission statement. Values should serve as the foundation of all persuasive communication.

In today's world of the six-second soundbite, the art of persuasive speaking may seem irrelevant. But it is just as important today as it was in Monroe's time. Monroe's Motivated Sequence is a tried-and-true method of making one's points in a logical and persuasive manner.

safety needs: Failure to read the material assigned by your professor could well put your grade at risk! However, there is more to this stuff than just passing your next test. Maslow's theory figures prominently in the practice of public relations.

Almost every election year, political pundits remind us that "bread-and-butter" issues are more important to voters than such things as national security. Bill Clinton defeated incumbent George Bush in the 1992 presidential election largely because of his campaign staff's adherence to one guiding principle written on a poster in campaign headquarters: "It's the economy, stupid!" The 2000 presidential election campaign was practically devoid of any discussion of international issues. Despite continuing violence in the Middle East and political upheaval in the Balkans, the two major candidates focused almost exclusively on the economy, the environment, education, and Social Security.

From Maslow's point of view, so-called bread-and-butter issues are those that have an impact on our physiological needs, the most basic order of needs we have. For many years, national security issues also focused on our most basic physiological need—the need to survive. But with the end of the Cold War and the lessening of the danger of nuclear war, the threat to survival has eased, as has the importance of foreign policy issues.

We can see the practical use of Maslow's theory in other ways. When environmental groups such as Greenpeace seek public support, their messages focus on physiological needs—specifically, the survival of the planet. When social service organizations seek additional funding, they realize that an appeal to the public's unfulfilled safety needs will be more effective than one based in either acceptance or self-actualization. By the same token, an appeal to personal self-esteem will have a greater chance of success among affluent audiences, whose physiological and safety requirements have been met, than among lower-income audiences struggling to fulfill basic needs.

Do people stop and think, "What would Maslow have me do under these circumstances?" Of course not. However, we instinctively follow Maslow's model. Self-interest is at the heart of motivation. Understanding the needs of the public being targeted is the key to successful communication and persuasion.

Persuasion and Public Opinion

Since the beginning of recorded history, people have pondered the question of how to persuade others to take a desired course of action. And it is a very important question. The persuasion of others and the molding of public opinion are central to our concept of a society, the manner in which people choose to organize themselves.

In democratic societies, we organize ourselves around a core belief in fulfilling the will of the people. However, history has shown us that democratic societies operate best when there is a willingness to seek consensus on matters of importance to all. That, in turn, requires a willingness among the members of these societies to engage in public debate. It is during this debate that we either persuade others to come over to our point of view or are persuaded to accept the opinion of someone else. A measure of these ongoing discussions is what we commonly refer to as public opinion.

Persuasion and public opinion are vital elements in the practice of public relations. As has been stressed in many places throughout this textbook, public relations is a two-way process of both communicating and listening. Sometimes the need to convince others about the advisability of a certain course of action arises. In that situation, we try to persuade others to adopt our point of view. However, we must also be sensitive to public opinion and the concerns of others. At its best, public relations is not about winning or losing. Instead, it is about building and maintaining mutually beneficial relationships. That is why understanding the dynamics of persuasion and public opinion is so critical to successful public relations.

Aristotle, Persuasion, and Public Relations

Aristotle said that **persuasion** takes three forms: **logos,** or an appeal to reason; **pathos,** or an appeal to emotions; and **ethos,** or an appeal based on personality or character. He said that a persuasive argument may use one of these forms exclusively or in any combination with the others.

Aristotle believed the decision to choose one form of persuasion over another depended on several factors: the circumstances in which the appeal is made, the specific nature of what is being argued, and the makeup of the audience being addressed.[11] To state this concept in simpler terms: The selection of an appropriate persuasive appeal depends on determining what you are saying, where and when you are saying it, and to whom you are saying it. This concept should sound familiar to you. It is pivotal to the practice of public relations.

Aristotle did believe that ethos, the persuasive value of a communicator's character, is the most powerful of the three modes of persuasion. In his classic book *Rhetoric,* he says that a communicator's character "may almost be called the most effective means of persuasion he possesses."[12] That's one reason why practitioners should strive to practice ethical, values-driven public relations: Their well-earned good name can help build the relationships that are essential to their organization's success.

Aristotle's analysis of persuasion raises an important question that is currently being debated within professional and academic circles: Is persuasion an appropriate activity for public relations practitioners? Some people believe that the goal of persuasion is inconsistent with the two-way communication requirement for effective public relations. Two-way communication, by definition, implies a willingness to listen to the needs and concerns of the targeted public and act accordingly. Persuasion linked to one-way communication tends to ignore a central tenet of motivation, that people act in their own self-interests. Any effort at persuasion that does not first take into account the public's point of view is poor public relations—and probably won't work. However, when practiced at its highest levels, public relations identifies common interests and promotes actions that are mutually beneficial. Therefore, in that context, persuasion is a **compliance-gaining tactic** appropriate for public relations practitioners.[13]

Public Opinion Defined

In much the same way that an atom is the basic building block of matter, **belief** is the basic building block of public opinion. A belief is one's commitment to a particular idea or concept based on either personal experience or some credible external authority. For example, many people who have traveled to and experienced Paris believe that it is the most beautiful city in the world. However, others who have never been to France may feel the same way because they have heard it from sources they consider credible, such as friends, travel guides, and popular culture.

When a belief starts affecting the way we behave, it creates an **attitude**. To put it another way, an attitude is a behavioral inclination. For example, if a belief that Paris is a beautiful city causes you to start reading about Paris, encourages you to enjoy French cuisine, or just encourages you to look positively upon all things Parisian, you have developed an attitude.

If that attitude is strong and inspires you to share it with others, you have developed an **opinion**. By definition, an opinion is an expressed behavioral inclination. That opinion can be expressed verbally, by telling others how much you admire Paris, or non-verbally, by adopting French fashion as your own preferred style.

That takes us to **public opinion,** the average expressed behavioral inclination. Public opinion takes into account a wide range of positions that people may have on the same issue. For example, a majority of people may feel that Paris is a beautiful city. A small minority may disagree. Yet another group may have no opinion at all. Together, those three groups constitute public opinion on the issue of the beauty of Paris.

As noted in Chapter 4, the publics of public relations can be divided into what are known as latent, aware, and active publics. Which one of these defines a particular public depends on the degree to which the public realizes and cares about the intersection of its values with an issue. The same can be said for public opinion. **Latent public opinion** is the result of people having varying degrees of interest in a topic or issue but being unaware of the interests of others. **Aware public opinion** occurs when people grow aware of an emerging interest. **Active public opinion** occurs when people act—formally or informally, and often not in unison—to influence the opinions and actions of others.

We can see this at work in a case study at the end of this chapter. At the time of the Persian Gulf War, U.S. public opinion opposing human rights violations and atrocities committed during war was latent. Not until alleged atrocities committed by Iraq were publicized did public opinion become aware. It was when those atrocities were give a human face and voice—which may not have expressed the truth—that public opinion became active in support of U.S. intervention into the conflict.

The Evolution of Public Opinion

Although persuading one person to adopt a particular point of view can be difficult, the true challenge is to persuade large numbers of people. That is the essence of decision making in a democratic society—a public debate that leads to a public consensus and, eventually, to public policy. The evolution of public opinion can be outlined as follows:[14]

1. Public opinion starts with *an already present mass sentiment*, a consensus that developed as a result of earlier public debates.
2. Public opinion begins to evolve when *an issue* is interjected into that consensus. For something to be considered an issue, it has to affect a variety of groups and be seen as evolving.
3. Like-minded individuals coalesce into *a public*. Often these publics can be characterized as being either pro or con. However, many issues are complex and have more than two sides.
4. The various publics engage in *public and private debate* over the issue. This debate can take many forms. It is at this stage that the practice of public relations has its greatest influence among publics that have not yet formed a strong opinion.
5. There is an unspecified period of *time* during which the debate occurs and people make up their minds. The amount of time needed for this to happen varies from issue to issue. With some issues, such as gun control and abortion, the debate seems never to end.
6. Eventually the debate leads to a consensus, which is known as *public opinion*.
7. In turn, that public opinion precipitates some form of *social action*, such as a policy change, an election, or the passing of a new law.
8. At this point the issue evolves into a *social value;* this, in turn, becomes a part of the already present mass sentiment, and the public opinion process begins anew.

Let's use an issue as old as the earth itself to illustrate the public opinion process in action. When the Kansas State Board of Education voted in August 1999 to remove the teaching of evolution from state science standards, it awakened a debate that many had thought had been settled (an already present mass sentiment).

The board had not banned the teaching of Charles Darwin. Nor did it require the teaching of creationism. But this action (an issue) had the effect of inciting the champions of opposing views (like-minded individuals coalescing in publics). The National Science Teachers Association called the school board's decision "a disservice to the students of Kansas."[15] Charles Colson, founder of the Prison Fellowship Ministries, defended the board's action as "a protest against placing any scientific theory beyond the reach of criticism"[16] (public and private debate).

The evolution debate had raged almost one year (time passes) when Kansas voters ousted three anti-evolution school board candidates—two of whom were incumbents—in an August 2000 primary election (consensus results in formation of public opinion). With the new mandate from voters and a shift in the balance of power, the board reinstated the original teaching standards in February 2001 (social action). At that point, the debate was resolved (social value), and evolution was welcomed once again in Kansas schools (an already present mass sentiment). Anti-evolution groups, however, vowed to re-open the debate (the public opinion process begins anew).

A PUBLIC OPINION CHECKLIST

Volumes have been written about how to influence public opinion, but here are 10 key guidelines you should remember:

1. *You may not be the best judge of public opinion.* Don't trust hunches or gut reactions. They could be wrong. Base your decisions on solid research and analysis.

2. *People resist change.* Change is often viewed as a threat. For that reason, do not assume that a targeted public understands the benefits of a proposal. Spell them out.

3. *"WIIFM" (What's In It For Me?).* Social psychologist Hadley Cantril wrote, "Once self-interest is involved, opinions are not easily changed."[17] Don't tell targeted publics why something is good for you. Instead, describe how the desired action benefits them.

4. *People believe what they want to believe.* When people have their minds made up on an issue, they tend to seek out information that reinforces their position. They also tend to avoid or block out what social scientists call **cognitive dissonance**—the mental disturbance resulting from encountering information that runs contrary to their beliefs.

5. *Plant seeds in fertile ground.* It is easier to provide information than it is to shape an opinion. It is also easier to shape an opinion than it is to change an opinion. You can't afford to waste limited time and resources on those who have already decided against you. You can achieve greater success by directing public relations efforts to those who are already on your side and those still willing to listen.

6. *"KISS" (Keep It Simple and Straight).* In the clutter that makes up mass communications, it is the simplest of messages that are most likely to get through and register with a public. Symbolism is often more effective than a complex explanation of concepts.

7. *Demonstrate knowledge of the issue.* When public opinion is undecided or running against you, presenting all sides of the issue tends to be the most effective approach. It also provides an opportunity to demonstrate the comparative strength of your position.

8. *When among friends, preach to the choir.* When public opinion is on your side, stick to your message. In this case usually no need arises to discuss the other side of the issue. Your job isn't so much to change public opinion as to solidify it into action.

9. *Actions speak louder than words.* People are impressed when you actually do what you say you are going to do. Empty promises breed mistrust; keeping your word builds credibility.

10. *Get in the last word.* When there is little to choose from between opposing views, a determining factor tends to be the argument heard last.

The dynamics of the public opinion process point out the need for companies and organizations to conduct ongoing programs of public relations. Because public opinion is always evolving, one-shot efforts at influencing it are rarely effective. Sometimes public opinion crystallizes very quickly, as it did after the outbreak of the Persian Gulf War in January 1991. Public opinion is also very fluid and can evolve over time, as

Values Statement 5.1

PROVINCIAL EMERGENCY PROGRAM

The Provincial Emergency Program (PEP) is charged with maintaining effective response and recovery programs to reduce the human and financial costs of emergencies and disasters. A division of the British Columbia Ministry of the Attorney General, PEP is headquartered in Victoria, British Columbia, in Canada.

The Provincial Emergency Program, in its relationship with the public, partners and employees, adheres to the principles of:

   openness, honesty, fairness and mutual respect;

and strives to be:

   proactive, progressive and innovative;

   dependable, effective and accessible;

   cooperative and consultative.

— PEP web site

with the dramatic change in public attitudes toward civil rights since the early 1960s. Public relations practitioners need to keep their fingers constantly on the pulse of public opinion. Only then are they properly prepared to guide their organizations through potentially stormy seas.

Persuasion versus Manipulation

Understanding the dynamics of public opinion is essential to the practice of public relations. However, as is true with most things in life, it is possible to get too much of a good thing. Although it is often desirable to win people over to a particular point of view, there is a great temptation to try to manipulate public opinion to achieve one's goals. The 1997 movie *Wag the Dog* gave us a glimpse of that behavior. In the film presidential spin doctors, eager to avoid political fallout from an embarrassing scandal, manufactured a fake war to divert public opinion. The ruse worked—but only for a brief period of time. By the end of the movie, the moviegoer was left with the impression that the web of lies was beginning to unravel.

Of course, that was just a movie—for which we should be grateful. But *Wag the Dog* does, nevertheless, illustrate two valuable lessons for public relations practitioners. First, it suggests the need to draw the line between influencing and manipulating public opinion. **Manipulation,** by its very nature, suggests something underhanded. It is true that one may reap short-term gains by telling half-truths or by putting narrow interests ahead of broader ones, but it is also true that those gains are short lived. Manipulation, whether real or perceived, comes with a cost: credibility. No one likes to feel as if he or she has been used. Manipulation also runs contrary to the ideal of public relations as a problem-solving discipline whose practitioners seek alternatives that are mutually beneficial to all parties concerned.

A second valuable lesson is that those who seek to master public opinion often become a slave to it. This results in a lack of leadership. A common complaint we hear these days about politicians and corporate executives is that they are too often driven by public opinion polls. Instead of acting on what they believe, they seek to do what is popular. Although public opinion is important in democratic societies, so are values. It is often necessary to forgo what is popular for what is right. Think how different human history would be if certain special individuals had not, at critical moments, put their values ahead of public sentiment. Public relations is a values-driven discipline. Those values are determined by what we believe, not necessarily by what is popular.

Quick ✔ Check

1. What are the three kinds of persuasive appeals identified by Aristotle?
2. How does public opinion develop?
3. What is the difference between manipulation and persuasion?

Summary

History has shown us that communication is a fragile process. It can fail in a variety of ways, including a lack of source credibility, an irrelevant message, an inappropriate channel, an inattentive receiver, the absence of feedback, or the presence of physical or psychological noise.

With the growth of communications technology in the 20th century, people initially feared that mass media could dominate public opinion. This fear led to the development of what came to be known as the magic bullet theory. However, as the technology of mass communications evolved, so did our understanding of mass media. Now we realize that mass media do not tell us what to think, but rather influence what we think about. That concept is known as the agenda-setting hypothesis. However, even that theory is evolving. According to uses and gratifications theory, the *real* power to persuade resides with individuals, who can pick and choose from thousands of information sources and are driven by their own self-interests—especially their need to survive.

The evolution of public opinion is a dynamic process that never ceases; for this reason, organizations need to stay attuned to changes in public attitudes and conduct ongoing programs of public relations.

Although efforts to win people over to a point of view are legitimate, manipulation of public opinion by underhanded means is counterproductive. Those who engage in manipulation lose credibility and may become slaves to the public mood.

DISCUSSION QUESTIONS

1. Can and should public relations practitioners try to influence public opinion? Does our ability to persuade have any limits?
2. Describe the process of communication. What are some factors that can cause communication to break down?
3. Does an explanation exist for why some things serve as stronger motivations to action than others?

4. To what degree do you think mass media influence you? How does your personal experience relate to the various theories of mass communications?

5. What would be a good example of an issue that has undergone a rigorous public debate and emerged as a social value? Describe the process by which this happened.

Memo *from the* Field

René Pelletier, President, Baromètre Inc., Montreal

René Pelletier has worked in the research field for nearly 30 years. He has held senior executive positions with firms such as CROP Inc., Sorécom (of which he was president for 15 years), and Gallup before founding his own company, René Pelletier Groupe-Conseil Inc., in 1990, and assuming the leadership of Baromètre Inc. in 1996. He has conducted more than 700 research studies on behalf of different levels of government, as well as for a wide variety of clients in fields such as public services, private service industries, consumer goods, food products, communications, and public affairs.

Pelletier has a masters degree in sociology, with a specialization in applied communications research. A former president of the Professional Association of Marketing Researchers, he is also a founding vice president of CAMRO (Canadian Association of Marketing Research Organizations), a group that establishes strict standards for the industry.

For public relations practitioners, the main role of surveys is to enable them to make decisions based upon facts—as accurately as possible. Those facts concern their publics' beliefs and behaviors about the situation they are dealing with or the company for which they manage public relations.

When should we conduct a survey? Unless an unexpected crisis happens, most successful practitioners conduct public opinion surveys before, during, and after their communication work. I intentionally exclude crisis management surveys in order to concentrate on the most productive and intelligent use of surveys in normal situations.

Before Communicating

Most observers, including public relations practitioners, usually have an inaccurate picture of public opinion. In more than 30 years of professional experience, I have witnessed most of my clients either underestimating or overestimating public support for their projects; I have seen them emphasizing wrong arguments, thinking they would have an immediate and important influence upon public opinion. I have also seen clients neglecting the most powerful lever because they underestimated its influence upon public opinion. Every public relations practitioner concerned about managing a client's image or a project, and who hopes for success, should work with an exhaustive and accurate picture of public opinion before taking any action. This picture will ideally include such information as

1. Who knows or doesn't know your client or product?
2. What are the perceived strengths or weaknesses of the client or product?
3. How credible is your spokesperson (or spokespeople)?
4. Among the arguments you intend to use to influence public opinion, which is or which are the most powerful arguments, the most powerful levers able to influence opinion?
5. What is the profile (both demographic and psychographic) of your primary intervening public—that is the public most likely to have an influence on your targeted public?
6. How big is the gap between reality and your goal? For instance, if only 3 percent of your client's targeted public knows about your client, you won't use the same strategy you would use if your client is known by 60 percent or 70 percent. In the same way, if 70 percent of your client's targeted public has a negative opinion, your challenge will be very different than if that opinion were favorable.
7. What are the losses and damages your client's targeted publics fear most? Why? Can your client counterbalance those possible losses? Are those feared losses real? Are they accurately assessed or overevaluated by the public?*

The more accurate and exhaustive the portrait, the better the choice of messages, targeted publics, and communication channels; the final results, too, will be better. Planning a campaign without such a picture of public opinion is like hunting blindfolded and without any knowledge of what prey to search for!

During Communication

Most professional communicators don't measure public opinion during the communication process. Why should we do so? To check the basics: Is the public reached the same one we targeted? Is our message understood and interpreted as planned? Do the people exposed to our message have a more favorable perception of our client or product? Overall, are we on the way to reaching our objectives, or do we have to make some adjustments?

After Communication

Unless you work with a client or brand image on a long-term basis, you will have to conduct your actions within a timeframe, with goals that have to be attained by precise deadlines.

Having a precise deadline will enable you to understand better than anyone else the dynamic of public opinion, how much it changed (or didn't change) since the

---

*It is probably the most important information to survey when organizing a lobby about a specific project (mall in a residential area, possible closing of a factory, building of a possible pollutant factory in a region, use of green areas for industrial means, etc.).

beginning of the communication process, and how you could most efficiently communicate with your publics during the next months or years.

Clients too often consider a final measurement as being of little use, whereas public relations practitioners often dread it, as it will be seen, in part, as an evaluation of their work. However, I know that the best communication agencies propose that final measurement. It becomes an important tool in understanding the way public opinion changes.

In Finishing . . .

—Never believe that you know what people think before asking them.

—Never believe that public opinion is logical. It often contains paradoxes, and that's normal.

—If people don't understand your message, it is easier to change the message than to change people!

—Simplicity and conciseness of the message are the hardest elements to create, but they are the most effective in the end. The most common mistake among communicators without experience is failing to speak in the language of the public. Successful politicians know the power of short, image-laden sentences or one liners.

—Today's crisis is often the result of yesterday's negligence.

The three elements a public relations practitioner should take into account before making decisions concerning a client are public opinion, public opinion, and public opinion.

Case Study 5.1

Using Public Relations to Ban Land Mines

When representatives of 121 nations gathered in Ottawa, Canada, in 1997 to sign a treaty banning the use of land mines, the ceremony signaled the success of grassroots public relations in marshaling worldwide public opinion.

Antipersonnel land mines, buried just below the ground's surface and triggered when someone steps on them, continue the horrors of war long after the last battles are fought. Some land mines are abandoned and others are forgotten or lost. Regardless of the reason they are left behind, the mines take a terrible toll. At the time of the Ottawa treaty signing, it was estimated that up to 100 million land mines in 69 countries killed or maimed more than 25,000 people a year—an average of one person every 22 minutes.[18]

The International Campaign to Ban Landmines (ICBL) started in 1991 as a three-person effort in a Vermont farmhouse and ultimately grew into a worldwide network of more than 1,000 organizations. Thanks to the efforts of ICBL, the nations of the world not only banned land mines but pledged $500 million to aid in their removal. And ICBL and its coordinator, Jody Williams, won the 1997 Nobel Peace Prize.

At first, the organizers of the campaign relied heavily on fax machines and telephones to get their message to like-minded organizations, elected officials, the news media, and other opinion leaders. However, Mary Wareham, coordinator of the U.S. Campaign to Ban Landmines, an ICBL member organization, said e-mail soon played an increasingly important role. "It's fast, convenient, easy to use, and it's cheap," Wareham said.[19]

Robert Muller, president of the Vietnam Veterans of America Foundation, whose organization was an early supporter of the land-mine ban, told the *New York Times* that the Internet was another key to the ICBL campaign's success. "The fact that we can move information around at immediate speed and low cost is the key to moving any massive group of organizations and people."[20]

By May 1996, the ICBL had grown to a coalition of 500 nongovernmental organizations in 30 countries. Within eight months, those numbers would double. "We created the momentum for this political process," Wareham said.[21]

A major boost to the ICBL's campaign came in February 1997, when Britain's Princess Diana traveled to Angola and later to Bosnia to observe the clearing of land mines and to meet with their victims. Reporters and photographers who had chronicled every aspect of her failed marriage to Prince Charles followed her to the minefields and, in turn, brought the issue of land mines to the world's attention.

Shortly after Diana's death in a Paris car crash, the leader of a British ICBL affiliate said, "Probably her greatest legacy has been the massive increase in interest she has generated in this subject."[22] Ironically, the princess died just as an 89-nation conference convened in Oslo, Norway, to draft the treaty. After three weeks of intense negotiations and lobbying, the conferees agreed to a document that called for a complete ban of the use of land mines within a decade.

Even with this success, some work remained unfinished. Several major military powers, including the United States and China, refused to sign the treaty for a variety of reasons. For example, the United States claimed the limited use of land mines to protect U.S. military outposts in Cuba and along the Demilitarized Zone between North and South Korea is justified. The ICBL continued to lobby the nonsigning nations after the December 1997 treaty-signing ceremony in Ottawa.

The Norwegian Nobel committee recognized the campaign to rid the world of land mines by awarding it the Nobel Peace Prize in 1997. The committee decided that the ICBL and Williams should equally divide the $1 million award that goes with the prize. Moments after the award was announced, Williams told reporters she was "a little stunned."[23]

In making the announcement, the Nobel committee said, "The ICBL and Jody Williams started a process which in the space of a few years changed a ban on antipersonnel mines from a vision to a feasible reality."[24]

DISCUSSION QUESTIONS

1. The Internet, including e-mail, is credited with much of the success of the ICBL's campaign against land mines. Do you feel the group could have been as successful without these communications tools? How could the campaign have been carried out without the Internet?

2. Why is it or why is it not appropriate to call this campaign successful in light of the refusal of the United States and other major military powers to sign the anti–land mine treaty?

3. How pivotal was Princess Diana's role in the development of the treaty? Do you think the timing of her death had any effect on the outcome?

4. What is your opinion of the use of celebrities and special events to call attention to worthy causes that might otherwise go unnoticed?

5. Can the United States offer a values-based defense of its refusal to sign the treaty? What might that defense be?

Case Study 5.2

Citizens for a Free Kuwait

For some, the 1991 Persian Gulf War has become an example of effective public relations. For others, it has become a case study for its abuse. You be the judge.

This much is not in dispute: Within hours of Iraq's August 2, 1990, occupation of Kuwait, a campaign was under way to convince the people of the United States of the need to use military force against the invaders. An organization calling itself Citizens for a Free Kuwait hired public relations giant Hill & Knowlton to marshal public support for war. Over the next five months, an effective—and ultimately successful—campaign was waged. A coalition of Western and Arab nations, led by the United States, launched a war to liberate Kuwait on January 17, 1991. The military intervention lasted only six weeks and ended with Iraq's withdrawal from Kuwait.

In many ways the Hill & Knowlton campaign was fairly traditional. It included special observances on 20 college campuses, a day of prayer observed in churches nationwide, the delivery of media kits to reporters, and the distribution of thousands of "Free Kuwait" T-shirts and bumper stickers. Hill & Knowlton also hired a public opinion research firm, the Wirthlin Group, to take the public pulse and to learn what might sway people to support military intervention. Although public opinion was decidedly against going to war to protect the supply of oil, the research uncovered sentiment that suggested war might be more acceptable if it were aimed at ending atrocities.

This brings us to the most controversial aspect of the Hill & Knowlton campaign. On October 10, 1990, a 15-year-old Kuwaiti girl, identified only as Nayirah, tearfully testified before a body called the Congressional Human Rights Caucus about Iraqi atrocities she said she had seen at a Kuwait City hospital. Her family name was concealed, ostensibly to protect relatives still living in occupied Kuwait. In her statement Nayirah said, "I saw the Iraqi soldiers come into the hospital with guns, and go into the room where fifteen babies were in incubators. They took the babies out of the incubators, took the incubators, and left the babies on the cold floor to die."

What was known as the "incubator incident" became a rallying cry for war. President George Bush mentioned the incident several times during public debate. The incident was cited in United Nations debates. Seven U.S. senators mentioned Nayirah's account before voting in favor of a resolution that gave the president legal authority to use force against Iraq. That resolution passed the Senate by only five votes.

Although the evidence of Iraqi atrocities against civilians during its occupation of Kuwait is substantial, no tangible evidence exists that documents whether the incubator incident ever happened. Independent human rights organizations have been unable to verify Nayirah's account. An ABC News crew that entered Kuwait as the country was being liberated found the incubators right where they were supposed to be. The story's credibility was further undermined when it was learned that the only person claiming direct knowledge of the incident, Nayirah, was actually the daughter of Saud al-Sabah, Kuwait's ambassador to the United States.

There are other disturbing aspects. The PRSA *Code of Professional Standards for the Practice of Public Relations* at that time stated that "a member shall be prepared to identify publicly the name of the client or employer on whose behalf any public communication is made." Hill & Knowlton was accurate in noting that Citizens for a Free Kuwait had a broad-based membership representing people both in and outside of Kuwait's government. However, of the nearly $12 million raised by the committee for the pro-war public relations campaign, $11.8 million came from Kuwait's ruling family.

The PRSA code also stated that "a member shall not engage in any practice which has the purpose of corrupting the integrity of the channels of communication or the processes of government." Although nothing in the arrangement was illegal, it was not widely known that the Congressional Human Rights Caucus—the group that sponsored Nayirah's testimony—maintained free office space in Hill & Knowlton's Washington offices. In addition, the Congressional Human Rights Caucus is a private foundation and not an official committee of Congress. Witnesses can tell the Caucus anything they want under oath without any threat of prosecution.

The PRSA code further stated that "a member shall not knowingly disseminate false or misleading information and shall act promptly to correct erroneous communications for which he or she is responsible." A Kuwaiti dentist, who claimed to be a surgeon, repeated the incubator story in testimony before the United Nations Security Council on November 27, 1990. He claimed to have supervised the burial of 120 newborn babies who had died as a result of the alleged atrocity. Confronted with his testimony after the war, however, the dentist admitted that he had no direct knowledge of the incubator incident. Although the dentist was not a PRSA member, and therefore not covered by the organization's ethical standards, he was coached by public relations practitioners who were.

"The first casualty when war comes is truth," said Senator Hiram Johnson when the United States entered World War I in 1917. But truth can be elusive. The incubator incident may have happened exactly the way Nayirah described it. However, we may never know that with certainty. What is known is that sufficient circumstantial evidence exists to lead a reasonable person to doubt the veracity of Nayirah's claims.

It is not likely that the incubator story, in and of itself, made the difference between peace and war. Other political, social, economic, and military issues were involved in the decision. Nor does Hill & Knowlton bear sole responsibility for the controversy. That responsibility is shared by the Congressional Human Rights Caucus and by all those who so readily embraced the story without independent verification. However, one thing is certain: Once again, the ethical standards of public relations practitioners became the focus of international debate.

DISCUSSION QUESTIONS

1. Was the decision to hide Nayirah's identity appropriate? Do you think the concealment made any difference in the debate over whether the United States should go to war against Iraq?
2. Citizens for a Free Kuwait listed dozens of members from all walks of life. However, the overwhelming majority of its funding came from the Kuwaiti royal family. Is it appropriate to characterize this group as a "grassroots" organization?
3. Suppose, for a moment, that the incubator story were false. Would public relations practitioners have been justified in using it even so, to achieve what they saw as a moral purpose—the liberation of Kuwait?
4. If you had been hired to represent Kuwait, what tactics would you have used to sway public opinion in favor of U.S. intervention?
5. The Persian Gulf War ended very quickly with the liberation of Kuwait back in 1991. In light of the fact that the war is now history, do any of the issues raised in the case study have relevance today?

It's Your Turn

The Acme Widget Company

You are vice president for public relations at the Acme Widget Company. It doesn't matter what widgets are. What does matter, however, is that you have a problem.

Acme Widgets has been a major employer in the local community for 40 years. Over the past 2 years, however, foreign competition using prison labor has cut severely into Acme's profits. That has forced Acme to lay off nearly one-third of its original workforce. Acme is not the only widget maker facing this problem. However, no widget maker has taken the lead in seeking help from the federal government in terms of special tax breaks, regulatory relief, or special tariffs on foreign widgets.

Employee morale is low. The Amalgamated Widget Workers of America, the union representing rank-and-file employees at Acme, is threatening a work slow-down to protest the layoffs.

Meanwhile, Acme officials believe that an upgrade of water and sewer services to their plant is key to economic revitalization, but local government officials are balking at such a move. They say the upgrade is too expensive a proposition for the city to undertake; and besides, they are upset with the manner in which Acme has handled the layoffs. Several leaders of area religious organizations and neighborhood groups have said they agree with the local officials.

To address this situation, you realize you must answer several questions:

1. Who are the publics that Acme needs to influence?
2. What would be some potential goals of a public relations program you might propose?
3. What kind of persuasive appeal would have the greatest chance of success with each of the publics you have identified? That is, for each public, which kind of appeal do you think would be the most effective, and why do you think so?
4. What are some compliance-gaining tactics you might use to advance your goals?

The survival of Acme depends on your answers. Can effective public relations save the company?

KEY TERMS

active public opinion, p. 153
agenda-setting hypothesis, p. 143
attitude, p. 153
aware public opinion, p. 153
belief, p. 153
channel, p. 139
cognitive dissonance, p. 155
compliance-gaining tactic, p. 152
diffusion theory, p. 143
ethos, p. 152
feedback, p. 139
framing theory, p. 144
latent public opinion, p. 153
logos, p. 152
magic bullet theory, p. 141

manipulation, p. 156
Maslow's Hierarchy of Needs, p. 148
message, p. 139
Monroe's Motivated Sequence, p. 150
noise, p. 138
n-step theory, p. 142
opinion, p. 153
pathos, p. 152
persuasion, p. 152
public opinion, p. 153
receiver, p. 139
source, p. 138
two-step theory, p. 142
uses and gratifications theory, p. 146

NOTES

1. Nathan Stoltzfus, "Dissent in Nazi Germany," *The Atlantic Monthly* (September 1992): 87–94.

2. Richard M. Nixon, *RN: The Memoirs of Richard Nixon* (New York: Grosset & Dunlap, 1978), 460–466.

3. Robert Entman, "Framing: Toward Clarification of a Fractured Paradigm," *Journal of Communication* 43, no. 4: 51–58.

4. James E. Grunig et al., eds., *Excellence in Public Relations and Communication Management* (Hillsdale, N.J.: Lawrence Erlbaum, 1992), 165.

5. Grunig.

6. "Plans Unveiled for 'Disney's America' Near Washington, D.C.," Walt Disney Company news release, 11 November 1993.

7. Ken Burns, "TV Documentarian's Advice to Disney: Scrap Your Theme Park," *Potomac News,* 24 May 1994, A11.

8. Nick Kotz and Rudy Abramson, "The Battle to Stop Disney's America," online, Cosmos Club Internet site, www.his.com/~cosmos/1997/disney.html.

9. Abraham Maslow, *Motivation and Personality* (New York: Harper & Row, 1954), 9.

10. Raymie E. McKerron, Bruce E. Gronbeck, Douglas Ehninger, and Alan H. Monroe, *Principles and Types of Speech Communication,* 14th ed. (Boston: Allyn & Bacon, 2000), 153–164.

11. Edward P. J. Corbett, *Classical Rhetoric for the Modern Student* (New York: Oxford University Press, 1971), 50.

12. Aristotle, *Rhetoric,* trans. W. Rhys Roberts (New York: Modern Library, 1954), 25.

13. Grunig, 331.

14. Based on Lang and Lang's *Collective Dynamics,* cited in *PRSA Accreditation Study Guide* (New York: Public Relations Society of America, 1993), 38.

15. "Statement of the National Science Teachers Association in Response to the Kansas State Board of Education's Actions to Remove Evolution from State Standards," 13 August 1999, online, www.nsta.org.

16. Charles Colson, "Is the Sky Falling?: The Kansas Evolution Vote," Prison Fellowship Ministries web site, www.neighborswhocare.org.

17. Hadley Cantril, *Gauging Public Opinion* (Princeton, N.J.: Princeton University Press, 1972), 226–230.

18. "121 Nations Sign Historic Landmine Treaty," online, CNN Interactive, 4 December 1997, www.cnn.com.

19. K. C. Wildmoon, "Peace through E-Mail," online, CNN Interactive, undated, www.cnn.com.

20. Wildmoon.

21. Wildmoon.

22. "Princess Diana's Anti-Mine Legacy," online, CNN Interactive, 10 September 1997, www.cnn.com.

23. "Anti–Land Mine Activists Win Nobel Peace Prize," online, CNN Interactive, 10 October 1997, www.cnn.com.

24. "The Nobel Peace Prize for 1997," online, Norwegian Nobel Institute web site, www.nobel.se/announcement-97/peace-97.

chapter six

Ethics in Public Relations

objectives

After studying this chapter, you will be able to

- define what is meant by the word *ethics*
- specify categories of ethics codes
- understand the most common ethical challenges
- describe the ethics codes of important philosophers from Aristotle to John Rawls
- use the Potter Box to analyze ethical dilemmas

Choose and Lose

scenario

You are an upper-level public relations practitioner for an international manu-facturing company. Your primary duty is internal (employee) public relations. Three days ago, the CEO of your company told the news media that a much-publicized though minor environmental hazard in your company's production pro-cess had been eliminated. The person responsible for eliminating the hazard is one of your best friends. And right now, she really needs your friendship: Because of a death in her family, she's going through a rough time.

As your concern for her grows, you learn, by accident, that she hasn't eliminated the environmental hazard; it still exists. In her distraught condition, she doesn't even realize that she hasn't corrected it. You're afraid that telling her will damage your friendship, one of the few positive things in her life right now. But if the CEO discovers the oversight, he may fire her—which, you fear, would deepen her depression. And, of course, you're concerned that the news media will find out that they were given, albeit unintentionally, false information.

What do you do?

What Are Ethics?

"It is clear," wrote 20th-century philosopher Ludwig Wittgenstein, "that ethics cannot be put into words."[1]

END OF CHAPTER.

OK, we're kidding. But Wittgenstein has a point. Defining ethics can be tough—almost as tough as behaving ethically.

Look at the history of the word itself. The word *ethics* traces its origins to *ethos*, the Greek word for character. That makes sense: Good ethics build character and reputation. Bad ethics destroy them.

But if we push the word's history further back to its ancient Indo-European roots, we find that *ethics* shares the same linguistic ancestor with such words as *sober, solitary,* and even *suicide.* Living an ethical life—personally and professionally—is a constant challenge. The history of the word *ethics* reinforces that sobering truth for us.

Ethics are beliefs about right and wrong that guide the way we think and act. The late John Ginn, a journalism professor at the University of Kansas, often told his students, "Ethics are not something that we *have.* They're something that we *do.*" Ideally, once we decide what our values are, we embrace guidelines for behavior that will help us reach those values. Those guidelines become our ethics code. Our ethics code governs what we're willing to do—and what we're unwilling to do. Ethics aren't something we occasionally think about and then toss into a dark closet. Instead, we use them every day to help us honor and attain our values. In other words, ethical behavior isn't a distant goal. Rather, it's a part of daily life.

Ethics Codes for Values-Driven Public Relations

Public relations professionals live their lives under the guidance of several ethics codes: international codes, societal codes, professional codes, organizational codes, and personal codes. Let's look at examples of each.

INTERNATIONAL CODES.   As more organizations build relationships with publics in other nations, international codes of business ethics are emerging. One of the best known is the Caux Principles of Business, created by the Caux Round Table, a group of international business leaders that meets annually in Caux, Switzerland. Drafted

QuickBreak 6.1

THE ETHICS CODES OF PRSA AND IABC

Members of the Public Relations Society of America pledge to abide by the *Member Code of Ethics 2000*. Based on the values of advocacy, honesty, expertise, independence, loyalty, and fairness (see p. 37), the PRSA ethics code specifies six "Core Principles," including the following two:

- "Free flow of information: Protecting and advancing the free flow of accurate and truthful information is essential to serving the public interest and contributing to informed decision making in a democratic society."
- "Safeguarding confidences: Client trust requires appropriate protection of confidential and private information."

Each core principle includes guidelines that define in greater detail the principle's intent. For example, the following list reproduces the guidelines for the "free flow of information" principle.

A member shall:

- Preserve the integrity of the process of communication.
- Be honest and accurate in all communications.
- Act promptly to correct erroneous communications for which the practitioner is responsible.

- Preserve the free flow of unprejudiced information when giving or receiving gifts by ensuring that gifts are nominal, legal, and infrequent.

Members of the International Association of Business Communicators are governed by the *Code of Ethics for Professional Communicators*. Like PRSA's code, the IABC code specifies guidelines for ethical conduct. Its values echo those of PRSA in many areas, especially in the realms of truth and accuracy. According to the IABC code, "Professional communicators uphold the credibility and dignity of their profession by practicing honest, candid, and timely communication and by fostering the free flow of essential information in accord with the public interest." IABC also maintains an Ethics Committee to "offer advice and assistance to individual communicators regarding specific ethical situations." Both organizations can enforce sanctions against members who do not adhere to their ethical standards.

The complete text of the PRSA ethics code can be found in the appendix of this book.

in 1994, the Caux Principles begin by emphasizing values-driven actions: "We seek to begin a process that identifies shared values, reconciles differing values, and thereby develops a shared perspective on business behavior acceptable to and honored by all."[2] The Caux Principles are online, at www.cauxroundtable.org.

SOCIETAL CODES. The Ten Commandments, a foundation of Judeo-Christian culture, are an example of a societal ethics code that influences the lives of millions of people throughout the world. Other religions, of course, have codes to help their believers achieve obedience to divine will. Eighteenth-century historian Edward Gibbon said of the Koran, the holy book of Islam, "From the Atlantic to the Ganges, the Koran is acknowledged as the fundamental code, not only of theology, but of civil and criminal jurisprudence; the laws which regulate the actions and property of mankind are guarded by the infallible and immutable sanction of the will of God."[3]

PROFESSIONAL CODES.   Unlike members of some professions, public relations practitioners have no central, binding code of ethics. We're not licensed by a central organization, as are doctors and lawyers. Many public relations practitioners, however, voluntarily join organizations that do have binding ethics codes. The two largest such organizations in the world are the Public Relations Society of America (PRSA) and the International Association of Business Communicators (IABC). Unfortunately, not everyone is familiar with public relations ethics codes. The managing editor of one of the best-known business magazines in the United States recently told the publisher of *Jack O'Dwyer's Newsletter,* a public relations industry publication, that he was "not aware that PR people had a code of ethics."[4] Ouch.

Aaron Feuerstein, owner of Malden Mills Industries, followed his personal ethics code and kept his employees on the payroll after his fabric factory was destroyed by fire in 1995. (Courtesy of Malden Mills Industries, Inc.)

ORGANIZATIONAL CODES.   Many organizations have written ethics codes that employees are asked to read, sign, and follow. Often, members of an organization's public relations staff are asked to help draft, evaluate, and revise these codes. One example of a corporate code of ethics can be found at J.C. Penney. The company's *Statement of Business Ethics* covers three areas of ethical behavior: compliance with law, conflicts of interest, and preservation of company assets. But its most valuable section may be its introduction, which says, "It isn't possible to describe the infinite variety of situations to which our policies apply. . . . No set of principles can eliminate the need for human judgment."

PERSONAL CODES.   In December 1995, when a fire destroyed his Malden Mills fabric factory in Lawrence, Massachusetts, Aaron Feuerstein won national acclaim for enforcing his personal code of ethics: He kept his workers on the payroll for 90 days as he reestablished the business and began rebuilding the factory. The praises he won embarrassed him, Feuerstein said, because all he had done was live up to a personal commitment he made long ago to care for his employees. " 'You should not oppress the worker,'" he explained, quoting from the Torah, or Jewish law. " 'He is poor and needy, whether he be thy brethren or a stranger.' "[5]

Objectivity versus Advocacy: A Misleading Ethics Debate

As the practice of public relations moves into the 21st century, we still face an ethical debate as old as communication itself. At the heart of the debate lies this question: Are public relations practitioners ethically obligated to communicate the *full* truth of a matter? In all our different relationship-building activities, do we strive to present an unbiased view of the complete truth as we know it? Or do we strive to present only the information that benefits our organization—in other words, do we deliver only selective truth? To oversimplify, are public relations practitioners objective communicators, like journalists, or are we advocates, like lawyers?

Some practitioners charge that total objectivity would lead us to tell the truth but ignore the consequences of what we say. Imagine, for a moment, the consequences of telling every public everything you know about the organization you represent. Surely, not every public has a right to know everything. Legally, some information, such as employee health records, must be confidential. And surely you wouldn't betray strategic secrets that help your organization stay competitive. Advocacy, with its focus on the consequences of communicating, can seem more suitable than objectivity for public relations.

If, however, we choose to operate solely as advocates, we soon encounter the sticky issue of selective truth. In attempting to build relationships with publics, are we allowed to withhold damaging information that certain publics have a right to know? Sometimes we can withhold such information legally—but can we do so ethically? Some practitioners say yes. They maintain that our society has become adversarial, like a courtroom. Public relations practitioners engaged in a debate, they say, need present only the facts that help them, trusting that opponents will present other facts and that a judge—the public—will decide the truth of the matter. In fact, two scholars of public relations ethics wrote:

> An adversarial society assumes that spokespersons with alternative views will emerge to balance the [public relations] advocate. If that doesn't work, some will argue the journalist or some other consumer advocate, motivated by an objectivity and stewardship ethic, will assure some balance in the public messages.
>
> The reality is that there is no guarantee in the court of public opinion that adversaries will square off. Yet, just as a lawyer has no obligation to be considerate of the weaknesses of his opponents in court, so the public relations person can clearly claim it is another's obligation to provide countering messages. . . .
>
> In an adversary society, truth is not so important as the obligation of opposing counsel to create scenarios that conflict with those of their opponents.[6]

But as soon as we decide that we're advocates willing to avoid telling damaging truths, we encounter several problems that could seriously damage our effectiveness as relationship builders:

- *Problem 1:* Public relations practitioners often serve their organizations as counselors on ethics and social responsibility.[7] If we're known to be purveyors of selective truths, we can't function effectively in this role. Who would believe us?

- *Problem 2:* Not all publics are external. Why would employees believe a fellow employee in the public relations department who was known to frequently withhold facts from outside publics such as news media?

- *Problem 3:* Speaking of internal publics, should they be treated as adversaries? Should we, as practitioners, communicate selective truths to employees and expect them to counter with their own selective truths—all in the hope that the real truth will somehow emerge? Surely not.

- *Problem 4:* Delivering selective truths according to an adversarial model runs counter to the two-way symmetrical concept of public relations, which, as we noted in Chapter 1, is the ideal for many organizations. The two-way symmetrical model involves treating others as we would wish to be treated.

- *Problem 5:* Is being an organization's advocate the true mission of a public relations practitioner? In Chapter 1 we suggested a broader mission: to be a manager of relationships with publics that are essential to your organization's success. Sometimes that role indeed involves being your organization's advocate to other publics. Sometimes, however, it may involve a reversal: It may involve being an external public's advocate within your own organization. That is, you may need to urge your organization to change its behavior in response to the needs of an important external public. Public relations professionals are more than just advocates; they are managers of relationships.

Finally, delivering selective truths to our publics may well violate the ethics codes of both PRSA and IABC, which urge communication that is honest, accurate, candid, and in the public interest. In fact, if we withhold certain truths, we may well violate the values of our own organization. In short, a policy of delivering adversarial, selective truths is counterproductive. Such behavior works against a public relations practitioner who hopes to manage relationships successfully.

But where does that leave us? At their extremes, both objectivity and advocacy seem counterproductive. Let's return for a moment to the scenario that opens this chapter. Remember the unresolved environmental hazard and the CEO who inadvertently misinformed the news media? If your choices are simply absolute objectivity versus advocacy based on selective truth, the alternatives seem clear: If you were absolutely objective, with no concern for consequences, you would immediately tell the CEO that he misinformed the news media and that they must be told; you wouldn't care about the impact on your friend. If you were an advocate delivering selective truths, perhaps you would still tell the CEO—but you wouldn't advise informing the news media. You wouldn't see that you have a responsibility to correct their misperception.

Is that all there is? Are you stuck with a stomach-churning choice between damn-the-consequences objectivity and selective truth? Fortunately, many practitioners believe that a point of ethical balance—a golden mean—exists between these two unsettling extremes.

Objectivity versus Advocacy: The Solution

In recent years, public relations practitioners have worked hard to develop an ethical solution to the objectivity–advocacy debate. That solution, as we discussed in Chapter 1, is the growing role of public relations as a management function.

How does being a manager—instead of being someone who simply carries out orders—help solve the ethical nightmare of 100 percent truth versus selective truth? Increasingly, public relations practitioners are helping to create their organizations' policies before those policies are implemented. According to a 2000 survey of public relations practitioners conducted by PRSA and IABC, 81 percent of practitioners in the United States and Canada meet with their organization's top management at least once a week.[8] Public relations professionals can advise other leaders within their organization about the impact policies may have on various publics. They can vigorously discourage unethical proposals by noting the impact such proposals could have on key publics—such as news media.

Finally, the entire objectivity-versus-advocacy debate seems to be based on a misleading question: Are public relations practitioners objective communicators or are they advocates? What if the answer is "none of the above"? Many practitioners respond to the debate by saying that public relations practitioners are, first and foremost, relationship managers. Their priority is building honorable, ethical relationships between an organization and the publics that are essential to its success. Sometimes relationship management calls for delivering unpopular truths, either to a public or to the organization itself. And sometimes relationship management involves being an advocate—even if that means advocating the viewpoint of an important public within your own organization. In all their actions, however, public relations practitioners are acting for the good of the relationships that sustain an organization.

QuickBreak 6.2

ARISTOTLE, CONFUCIUS, AND THE GOLDEN MEAN

Is it all right to tell a lie? If we answer quickly, most of us will probably answer no. Telling a lie, we will say, is wrong. It's unethical.

As we've said before, if only life were that simple. Let's complicate the situation. Is it unethical to tell a lie to save someone's life? Here's a classic ethical question: If you were hiding an innocent victim of political persecution in your attic and representatives of the corrupt regime asked whether you were hiding that individual, would you lie? Or would you tell the truth and betray an innocent person?

Moral absolutes can be troublesome. We can almost always think of exceptions to the moral guidelines we generally follow. Those exceptions can help us understand the concept of the **golden mean,** developed by the Greek philosopher Aristotle (384–322 B.C.).

Aristotle believed that ethical conduct existed at a point of balance and harmony between the two extremes of excess and deficiency. That point

of balance is the golden mean. For example, Aristotle would contend that it's unethical *never* to lie (one extreme), just as it's unethical *always* to lie (the opposite extreme). The challenge of the golden mean lies in answering the crucial question *when:* When is it all right to lie? In what specific circumstances could lying be considered an ethical course of action?

A century before the birth of Aristotle, the Chinese philosopher Confucius (551–479 B.C.) established much the same principle with his *Doctrine of the Mean.* "The superior man cultivates a friendly harmony without being weak," Confucius wrote. "He stands erect in the middle, without inclining to either side."[9]

Finding the golden mean isn't easy. But as we seek to discover the ethical course between absolutist extremes, we learn more about the values that govern and will govern our lives.

Quick ✔ Check

1. What does the word *ethics* mean?
2. In our society, who establishes ethics standards?
3. What problems are associated with an advocacy/selective truth philosophy of public relations?
4. What is a golden mean? How does that concept apply to ethics?

Challenges to Ethical Behavior

Having a corporate code of ethics is one thing; making it work is another. Many kinds of challenges stand in the way of ethical behavior. For one thing, some ethical questions aren't easy. They can keep you lying awake at night, staring at the ceiling and trying to select the right course of action amid four or five unappealing options. Also, overwork sometimes conceals ethical obligations while the damage has already begun. Still another challenge is being aware of the mistaken assumption that something legal is always ethical. Or perhaps the business practices of an international client lead you into unfamiliar cross-cultural ethical territory. Or perhaps the challenge lies in the dangers of short-term thinking, or of working in a so-called virtual organization in which values clash. Let's discuss each of these challenges.

Dilemmas

Some ethical challenges are called *dilemmas*—meaning difficult quandaries in which every potential solution will cause pain. A dilemma isn't simply a problem; it's a problem that lacks a good, painless solution. The Choose and Lose scenario that opens this chapter is an example of a dilemma. No matter which course of action you select, you seem to hurt or betray someone who trusts you: your CEO, your friend, the news media, or the publics that might suffer from the environmental hazard.

In real life, the London office of Hill & Knowlton, one of the world's largest public relations agencies, encountered a dilemma in 2001 when officials of the Iranian Embassy asked to meet with the agency. According to *PRWeek* magazine, the Iranian officials wanted to improve their relationship with the British government. Because the government in Iran was divided between pro- and anti-Western factions, however, Hill & Knowlton was stumped: It wanted to collect fees and help the pro-Western voices in Iran but couldn't guarantee that it wouldn't inadvertently aid Iranian voices hostile to the United Kingdom, the United States, and other Western nations. When discussions broke down, Hill & Knowlton officials seemed relieved.[10]

Overwork

Is it possible to work too hard? Yes, if doing so clouds your judgment. You, and your organization, have an ethical obligation regarding workload: You should shoulder only the work that you can efficiently handle in a typical 40- to 50-hour workweek. Hard work is probably a value within your organization—but so are quality and accuracy. You have an ethical obligation to control the quality of your work. Overwork can also rob you of time you ideally would devote to self-analysis—that is, to thinking about your organization's values and your own values and checking to see whether all your actions are working toward those values.

Legal/Ethical Confusion

What is legal isn't always ethical—and, to a lesser degree, what is ethical may not always be legal. For example, does any law prevent you from remaining silent when you're mistakenly praised for someone else's work? Your silence wouldn't be illegal—but, by most standards, it would be unethical. Or perhaps your supervisor asks you whether a particular project is done. You're a little behind, but you're certain you can finish it this afternoon; because you know she won't ask for it until tomorrow, you say it's done. The small lie isn't illegal, but is it a breach of your personal ethics code? Probably. Simply following the law isn't enough to guarantee ethical behavior.

When Tylenol capsules laced with cyanide killed seven people in the Chicago area in 1982, executives at Johnson & Johnson had no legal obligation to launch a nationwide recall of the product. Company lawyers may even have feared that such an action would be an admission of liability. However, Johnson & Johnson recalled the product out of what company officials felt was a moral obligation to their customers. Despite substantial short-term financial damage, the economic impact of the recall was temporary. In the long run, Johnson & Johnson was praised for its business ethics and was able to save its position as the maker of this country's premier over-the-counter pain reliever.

Can something illegal be ethical? Can doing the right thing involve breaking the law? You may have seen the 1999 movie *The Insider,* based on the true story of Jeffrey Wigand, a tobacco company employee who discovered that his company was increasing the addictive power of cigarettes. But Wigand had signed a confidentiality agreement pledging not to reveal corporate secrets. As he later explained, he had to choose: He could honor his legal commitment to his employer, or he could honor his personal ethics code. He chose the latter and exposed company secrets on the news program *60 Minutes.* His former employer sued him for violating his confidentiality agreement, but his testimony helped lead to the tobacco industry's multibillion-dollar settlement to help pay for smoking-related medical expenses. As a condition of that settlement, the lawsuit against Wigand was dismissed.[11]

Cross-Cultural Ethics

Let's say you're doing business overseas and you're given an expensive vase by one of the many companies seeking to establish a partnership with your organization. Giving gifts to new acquaintances is standard in the culture you're visiting. Can you ethically accept the gift? Or do you reject it as a bribe?

Professor Thomas Donaldson of the Wharton School of Business notes two extremes in the range of your possible responses to the gift: cultural relativism and ethical imperialism. Both, he says, are wrong. Cultural relativism is the belief that no set of ethics is superior to any other set. With cultural relativism, you could accept the gift, saying, "It may violate my sense of ethics, but I'm just honoring the ethics of my host nation." Ethical imperialism is the belief that your system of ethics has no flexibility and no room for improvement; your system overrules every other system. With ethical imperialism, you would quickly reject the gift, saying, "Sorry, but this looks like a bribe to me."

Donaldson suggests a middle ground:

When it comes to shaping ethical behavior, companies should be guided by three principles:

■ Respect for core human values, which determine the absolute moral threshold for all business activities.

■ Respect for local traditions.

■ The belief that context matters when deciding what is right and what is wrong.[12]

In other words, be clear on your own beliefs but willing to explore the beliefs of others. Is that lavish gift a bribe—or is it a genuine gift of friendship, an important part of the culture you're visiting? If it's clearly a bribe, you politely but firmly explain that you can't accept it. If it's a genuine gift, perhaps your organization's policy allows you to accept it on behalf of the company. Maybe you can donate it to charity when you return home.

Short-Term Thinking

The classic example of someone engaged in short-term thinking is the person who plugs a leaking dam with a lit stick of dynamite. The short-term problem is solved, but at too high a cost. A public relations practitioner who deceives members of any public, from reporters to employees, is guilty of short-term thinking. Eventually, the deception may be revealed, damaging the long-term relationship between the practitioner and the public.

Virtual Organizations

An emerging threat to ethical behavior comes from virtual organizations, which are temporary organizations formed by smaller units to complete a specific job. For example, an independent public relations consultant might team up with an architectural agency and a developer to try to persuade a community that it needs a new shopping center. These different units would consider themselves part of one organization for the duration of the project; when the project ends, so does the organization.

Dramatic improvements in communications technology have spurred the growth of virtual organizations, allowing them to include partners from different locations throughout the world. But unfamiliar partners or a lack of internal communication can lead to clashing values and ethics. In *Marketing Ethics: An International Perspective,* Professor Bodo Schlegelmilch writes, "How such organizations can create a sense of shared values and ethics, and how such organizations can be controlled by any external bodies, will constitute one of the key challenges in business ethics in the future."[13]

The Rewards of Ethical Behavior

Let's ask a blunt question: What's the payoff for ethical behavior? What's in it for you?

Payoffs for ethical behavior, of course, are many, but among the most important is simply the deep satisfaction of doing the right thing. This chapter is based on the assumption that you want to be an ethical person who works for an ethical organization. Virtue, you've heard, is its own reward.

However, ethical behavior has other bonuses—compensation, perhaps, for the sheer difficulty of behaving ethically. There's growing evidence that ethical behavior can

Wearing denim to the office could be the most productive thing you've done all year.

When you wear denim to the office on Friday, October 9, you'll be helping find a cure for breast cancer. All you need to do is donate $5 for breast cancer research and wear denim to work that day. It's that easy to help eradicate the disease that takes a woman's life every 12 minutes. Nothing could be more productive. Please see your Lee National Denim Day Event Coordinator to sign up.

Lee **National Denim Day**
O C T O B E R   9 ,   1 9 9 8

All contributions benefit the Susan G. Komen Breast Cancer Foundation.

©1998 Lee Company, a division of VF Jeanswear, Inc.

Paycheck Stuffer   Since 1996 the Lee Apparel Company, maker of Lee Jeans, has raised more than $35 million for breast cancer research by sponsoring Lee National Denim Day. Many public relations practitioners believe that organizations can "do well by doing good." (Courtesy of the Lee Apparel Company)

lead to promotion within your organization. A Harvard University study of successful leaders concluded that a powerful correlation exists between leadership and "strong personal ethics."[14] Many public relations practitioners believe that good ethics positively affect an organization's financial success. In recent years, in fact, more than 30 studies have shown a direct link between good ethics and good profits. However, the 2000 National Business Ethics Survey of U.S. companies concluded that a code of ethics alone has no effect on profits. Instead, values-based ethics must truly be a part of an organization's culture.[15]

Not everyone is persuaded by the many studies that tie an organization's profits to its good ethics. "There is not one scintilla of evidence to demonstrate that having a good ethics policy increases profits," a professional ethics consultant recently told the *Wall Street Journal*. But, he added, "there are some modicums of evidence to show that a lack of one is extraordinarily costly."[16]

At the very least, we can say that good ethics are probably good for business—and that bad ethics are probably bad for business. The odds favor doing the right thing.

Quick✓Check

1. How is a dilemma different from a problem?
2. Is legal behavior always ethical? Is illegal behavior always unethical?
3. In the business world, is ethical behavior financially profitable?

IMMANUEL KANT AND THE CATEGORICAL IMPERATIVE

The German philosopher Immanuel Kant (1724–1804) contributed the concept of the "categorical imperative" to the study of ethics. Despite the fancy name, the concept is fairly simple. Let's say that you're experiencing an ethical crisis that has several different possible solutions. Kant would tell you to imagine that a universal maxim—a clear principle designed to apply to everyone in the world—will be the outcome of whichever course of action you choose. For example, one course of action might be for you to make a promise that you know you can't keep. Kant would ask you to imagine such an action becoming standard behavior for everyone. Clearly, the consequences would be disastrous.

In *Fundamental Principles of the Metaphysic of Morals,* Kant writes, "Act only on that maxim whereby thou canst at the same time will that it should become a universal law."[17] When you discover a course of action that could and probably should be a universal law, that is a **categorical imperative.** And a categorical imperative, says Kant, is a course of action that you must follow.

How would you apply Kant's theory of categorical imperatives to the scenario that opens this chapter? You would imagine that each possible course of action created a maxim that everyone in the world would follow. You would then reject any course of action that created a maxim that could lead to undesirable behavior if it were truly adopted by everyone. For example, one such maxim might be "It's all right to deceive the news media to protect our employees." Would that be a categorical imperative you'd want the world to follow every day?

Achieving Ethical Behavior

Ethical behavior in an organization must start with top management. Public relations practitioners can monitor and counsel on ethical matters, but ultimately an organization's top managers must lead by example. Leadership carries with it a special ethical burden. Today's business climate doesn't tolerate executives who have a "do as I say, not as I do" attitude. When it comes to accountability, executives do well to remember the sign on President Harry Truman's White House desk: The Buck Stops Here.

Executives, with the assistance of public relations counsel, should create an environment that helps the organization to focus constantly on the importance of ethical behavior in its relationships with others. Creating this environment involves

- conducting periodic ethics audits to help you assess the current state of affairs in your organization;

- integrating a constant awareness of values and ethics into the four-step public relations process (described in Chapter 1); and

- using a system such as the Potter Box (see below) for analyzing ethical challenges when they do occur.

Ethics Audits

An audit is a process of examination, evaluation, and recommendations. Most of us, probably, have heard of financial audits, in which a professional auditor examines an organization's income and expenditures and makes recommendations for improvement. In an **ethics audit,** we should ask and answer six basic questions:

1. What is our organization's ethics code?
2. How do we communicate that code to ourselves and others?
3. What do key publics—including employees—know about our ethics code?
4. What successes in ethics have we recently had, and why?
5. What setbacks in ethics have we recently had, and why?
6. What can we do to bolster strengths and reduce weaknesses in our ethics?

Periodically answering these questions and correcting any seeming deficiencies can help your organization build the necessary foundation for ethical behavior.

Integrating Ethics into the Public Relations Process

As we'll discuss in Chapter 12, the best time to solve a problem is before it starts. That's certainly true of challenges to ethical relationships: The best time to solve them is before they become problems. How can you attempt to do that? By ensuring that a focus on values is at the heart of your four-step public relations process.

In the *research* phase, as you scan the horizon searching for issues that may affect your organization, you should be well aware of your organization's written values. When you begin to research a particular issue, you should both remind yourself of those values and gather information on the values of the involved publics. Any clashes among those sets of values should alert you to a potential ethics problem.

In the *planning* phase, you should test every proposed action against your organization's values and against the values of important publics.

In the *communication* phase, you should implement every action with a clear understanding of how it reflects the values of your organization and the involved publics.

In the *evaluation* phase, you should study whether your completed actions were indeed in accordance with your organization's values. You should also consider the impact of the actions on the values of the involved publics. Any lapses or clashes should initiate a study to see whether problems stemmed from the actions or from your organization's values.[18]

Table 6.1 summarizes the key questions at each stage of the process.

The Potter Box

With your periodic ethics audits and your values-driven public relations process, you've established a foundation. But let's be realistic: Some challenges, like the hypothetical case study that begins this chapter, appear out of the blue. We can't prevent them. All we can do is try to react effectively and ethically. A helpful tool in such

TABLE 6.1	**Incorporating Values into the Public Relations Process**

Incorporating values into each step of the public relations process can help an organization achieve ethical behavior.

I. RESEARCH

- In this problem or opportunity, which of our organization's values are affirmed or challenged?
- In this problem or opportunity, what are the relevant values of the key publics involved?

II. PLANNING

- Are the goals, objectives, and tactics under consideration consistent with our organization's values?
- Are the goals, objectives, and tactics under consideration consistent with the values of our targeted publics? If not, could effective alternative courses of action honor our targeted publics' values?

III. COMMUNICATION

- As we enact our plan, are our actions consistent with our organization's values?
- As we enact our plan, are our actions consistent with the values of our targeted publics? If not, could effective alternative courses of action honor our targeted publics' values?

IV. EVALUATION

- Are the methods of evaluation we propose consistent with our organization's values?
- Are the methods of evaluation we propose consistent with the values of our targeted publics? If not, could other effective methods of evaluation honor our targeted publics' values?
- Were all our actions in addressing this problem or opportunity consistent with our organization's values? If not, why not? Were inconsistencies avoidable?
- Did any of our actions in addressing this problem or opportunity violate the values of our targeted publics? If so, why? Was the violation avoidable?

situations is the **Potter Box.** Designed by Ralph Potter, a professor of divinity at Harvard University, the Potter Box helps people analyze individual ethical crises.[19] It derives its name from its boxlike format (see Figure 6.1).

To analyze an ethical problem with the aid of the Potter Box, you follow an eight-step process:

1. Define the situation as objectively as possible (Definition box).
2. State the different values that you see involved in the situation and compare the merits of the differing values (Values box).
3. State a principle that each identified value honors. That is, imagine each value as the basis for a categorical imperative, as described in QuickBreak 6.3 (Principles box).

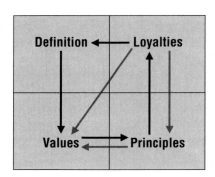

FIGURE 6.1   **The Potter Box**

4. Consider examining other, standard ethical principles that might apply (see the QuickBreaks throughout this chapter). Do those principles suggest any new values that might apply to this situation? Compare the merits of all the relevant principles.

5. For each principle, answer this question: If I base my actions in this situation on this principle, to whom am I being loyal? (Loyalties box).

6. Ask yourself if you feel loyalty—or believe you should feel loyalty—to any other individuals or groups in this situation. If you identify new loyalties, do they suggest new principles and values that you haven't considered? Are there individuals or groups noted in the definition toward which you feel no loyalty? If so, why?

7. Select a course of action that embraces the most compelling values, principles, and loyalties. Examine it in the light of your definition. If it still seems to be the best choice, implement it. Again, this is not easy. But in each possible course of action, you can now see which values, principles, and loyalties you're honoring.

8. Evaluate the impact of your decision.

This eight-step process won't automatically tell you what the most ethical course of action is. But it can help you dissect the situation so that you can examine choices and consequences, justify your decision to yourself and others, and learn from the experience of implementing the decision. The Potter Box can help you practice values-driven public relations.

The Potter Box at Work

Let's apply the Potter Box to Choose and Lose, the scenario that opens this chapter:

1. *Definition box:* Three days ago, the CEO of my company told the news media that a much-publicized environmental hazard in our company's production process had been eliminated. The person responsible for eliminating the hazard is one of my best friends. Right now, she really needs me because she's going through a rough time dealing with the death of her oldest child. Yesterday I learned that she hadn't eliminated the environmental hazard; it still exists. In her condition, she doesn't even realize that she

Values Statement 6.1

GOODWILL INDUSTRIES OF ORANGE COUNTY

Goodwill Industries of Orange County, California, helps people with disabilities find rewarding employment that benefits employers and employees alike. Founded in 1924, Goodwill Industries of Orange County is accredited by Goodwill Industries of America, Inc.

Mission

The mission of Goodwill Industries of Orange County is to provide people with disabilities the opportunity to achieve their highest levels of personal and economic independence.

Vision

We envision a world where all individuals with disabilities and other barriers to employment will have opportunities to enjoy the full benefits of competitive employment. Goodwill will focus on being the leader in providing quality education, training, and employment services. The core of Goodwill programs will empower individuals to be productive and independent, based on their abilities and interests.

Values

We believe in the inherent value of work; work has a greater value than charity.

We trust and respect the dignity and creative potential of every person.

We strive for superior quality in our programs and services.

—Goodwill Industries of Orange County web site

hasn't corrected it. I'm afraid that telling her will damage our friendship, which is one of the few positive things in her life right now. But if our CEO discovers the oversight, he may fire her—which, I'm afraid, could deepen her depression to a dangerous level.

2. *Values box:*

A. Friendship
B. Duty to CEO and company
C. Duty to environment
D. Honesty with news media

3 and 4. *Principles box:* Note how these correspond to the above values.

A. Honor friendships. Never damage a friendship.
B. Support the integrity of the CEO and the company in all your actions. Do nothing to undermine the integrity of the CEO and the company.
C. Take every possible action to protect the environment. Do nothing that hurts the environment.
D. Be absolutely truthful with the news media. Never lie to them. Correct every factual error.

Now you ask whether other, standard ethical principles apply. Aristotle's golden mean (QuickBreak 6.2)? Mill's principle of the greatest good for the greatest number (QuickBreak 6.4)? John Rawls' demand for unbiased social justice for all, with special consideration for society's least powerful (QuickBreak 6.5)?

Mill and Rawls help you to realize that you've left out a key value: the health and welfare of people who may be affected by the uncorrected environmental hazard. You now add this as value E, and you add a corresponding principle to the Principles box.

Ethics Helpline Poster   Mired in an ethical dilemma? If you're an employee of Sprint Corporation, help—or at least understanding—may be just a phone call away. (Courtesy of Sprint Corporation)

At this point, you may decide that the strongest principles are A, B, D, and E: support of your friend, your CEO/company, the news media, and people at risk from the environmental hazard, respectively. You can think of minor exceptions to C—such as damaging the environment slightly by building a new home. As you think more, you begin to wonder about A: Never damage a friendship. Don't you sometimes have to tell a true friend something she doesn't want to hear? Are some values more important than the very important value of friendship? You reluctantly begin to think yes, some are.

Regarding value E, you can think of companies whose processes create environmental hazards, but this doesn't excuse your company's processes because you've pledged to eliminate the hazard in question. You believe you must honor principle E, which might be phrased as *Do not initiate or continue manufacturing processes that injure the health and welfare of others.*

5 and 6. *Loyalties box:* Note how these correspond to the above principles.

A. To my friend
B. To the CEO and the company
C. To a clean environment
D. To the news media and their audiences
E. To people affected by the environmental hazard

As you seek to determine the most ethical action in this situation, you begin to see that if you remain loyal only to your friend and say nothing, you're damaging the environment, hurting your company's important relationship with the news media, and hurting those affected by the hazard. You realize that such damage will affect your organization's ability to reach its goals. Failure to

QuickBreak 6.4

JEREMY BENTHAM, JOHN STUART MILL, AND UTILITARIANISM

The English philosophers Jeremy Bentham (1748–1832) and John Stuart Mill (1806–1873) helped develop the philosophy of utilitarianism. **Utilitarianism** holds that all our actions should be directed at producing the greatest good for the greatest number of people.

The obvious question here is What is the greatest good? According to utilitarianism, the greatest good is the action that produces the greatest happiness. "Actions are right in proportion as they tend to promote happiness, wrong as they tend to produce the reverse of happiness," writes Mill in *Utilitarianism*.[20] Bentham and Mill don't mean cheap, momentary, sensual happiness. They mean profound, lasting happiness, the kind produced by justice and love.

Utilitarianism asks us to consider courses of action that may not benefit us. "As between [a person's] own happiness and that of others," writes Mill, "utilitarianism requires him to be as strictly impartial as a disinterested and benevolent spectator."[21]

You might consider utilitarianism when you face a dilemma—that is, when you face an ethical problem in which every option has a downside. Utilitarianism would suggest that you select the solution that creates the greatest happiness—or perhaps the least unhappiness—for the greatest number of people.

How might you apply utilitarianism to the Choose and Lose scenario that opens this chapter? Simply put (though hard to do), you would examine which course of action creates the greatest good for the greatest number of people.

reach those goals will affect your coworkers' ability to send children to college, to plan for retirement, to assist elderly parents, and other important concerns.

Utilitarianism's philosophy of the greatest good for the greatest number of people urges you to act out of loyalty to the environment and three large groups: your company, the news media, and people affected by the hazard. But you still wonder: Now that the choices and consequences are clearer, must you be disloyal to your friend?

7. *Decision and action:* You decide that the greatest good in this ethical dilemma demands that the CEO be told, the problem be corrected, and the news media be informed. You approach an official in the company's human resources department with the following plan:

—You will gently inform your friend of the problem and help her correct it.

—The human resources official will inform the CEO of the death in your friend's family and the consequent depression your friend is experiencing. The official will inform the CEO that your friend needs to meet with him on an important matter—but the official will not reveal the failure to correct the environmental hazard. Your friend will do that.

—Along with the official from the human resources department, you will accompany your friend to the CEO's office, and she will tell him of the omission and of her corrective actions.

—You will help prepare a news release to be sent to all appropriate news media. In that release, the company will announce the error and state what it is doing to ensure that such temporary inaccuracies never happen again. Your strategy is to explain that the uncorrected problem was the result of an inadvertent human error and that steps are being taken to correct the possibility of a recurrence.

—You will increase your efforts to support your friend and, with the official from human resources, will explore what company policies and programs are available to help her.

8. *Evaluation:* Most publics—including the news media—are impressed by honesty and will forgive unintended errors. But you'll still evaluate the reaction of important publics such as employees and journalists. You'll also evaluate your friend's progress in dealing with her grief. Your evaluation of this episode will also, no doubt, lead you to establish procedures to verify information before it is distributed throughout your company and to the news media.

QuickBreak 6.5

JOHN RAWLS AND SOCIAL JUSTICE

What do we owe to those less fortunate than we are? In decision-making processes, who speaks for the powerless who may be affected by the decisions? These questions concern advocates of social justice such as John Rawls.

In his book *A Theory of Justice,* Rawls urges decision makers to recognize and consider the values of all affected publics, not just those having the power to influence decisions. Rawls recommends two particular techniques for an ethical decision-making process:[22]

- Rawls suggests that before a decision is made, decision makers figuratively don a **"veil of ignorance"** that strips away their rank, power, and status. The veil of ignorance strategy asks decision makers to examine the situation objectively from all points of view. In particular, it asks them to imagine lifting the veil of ignorance only to discover that they are now a member of one of the affected publics instead of the decision maker.

- Rawls suggests that to redress social injustice, the most disadvantaged publics in a situation should receive the most advantages—with the exception of freedom. Freedom, he says, is an advantage that must be shared equally. All other resources, however, should flow to those who have the least. Power should flow to the powerless, and wealth should flow to the poor.

Rawls' theory of social justice may sound extreme, but it shares some similarities with values-driven public relations. It asks us to identify, respect, and build relationships with the publics whose values come into contact with the values of our organizations.

Quick ✓ Check

1. What is a categorical imperative?
2. In the four stages of the public relations process, where should we consider values?
3. What is an ethics audit? What questions should we ask in the course of an ethics audit?
4. What ethical principle is the foundation of utilitarianism?
5. In order, what are the four stages of the Potter Box?
6. What is meant by the veil of ignorance? How can it assist ethical decision making?

Summary

No thinking person will ever say that living an ethical life is easy. But the rewards of ethical behavior are substantial. We can attain those rewards by constantly examining our ethics codes and how well our actions live up to our high standards. Sometimes our only reward is the satisfaction of knowing that we analyzed a tough situation and followed the most ethical course of action. Hardly a day goes by, on the other hand, that we read our morning paper without finding evidence of unethical behavior in the business world. The penalties for unethical behavior can be substantial, leading to lost profits and, often, lost jobs. And for public relations practitioners, unethical behavior can mean the loss of credibility, which is one of our most valuable possessions.

The ethics that affect public relations come from five general sources: international codes, societal codes, professional codes, organizational codes, and personal codes. Practitioners must know these codes and should be familiar with ethical decision-making processes such as the Potter Box if they hope to tackle successfully traditional ethical challenges that arise from dilemmas, overwork, legal/ethical confusion, values of other cultures, short-term thinking, and virtual organizations. Examining your organization's values, as well as those of important publics, at every stage of the public relations process can help you achieve ethical, values-driven behavior.

It's hard to write about ethics and not sound preachy. That's not our purpose in this chapter. But ethical behavior is indispensable in values-driven public relations. For our society, for our organizations, for our important publics, and for ourselves, we should strive for nothing less.

DISCUSSION QUESTIONS

1. Where do you stand in public relations' objectivity–advocacy ethics debate? Should practitioners always tell 100 percent of what they know? Or is selective truth telling acceptable? If so, when?
2. What organizations have news media recently featured for ethical behavior? For unethical behavior?

3. From what you know of Johnson & Johnson's Tylenol crisis, how might that company have applied the utilitarian philosophy? How might it have applied categorical imperatives? How might it have applied the Potter Box?

4. Are John Rawls' theories of social justice unrealistic for for-profit businesses? Why should for-profit businesses care about powerless, disadvantaged publics?

5. Can you think of an instance in which you would *not* select an action that meant the greatest good for the greatest number? In that case, what would your alternative selection tell you about your values?

Memo
from the
Field

Terrie Williams, President, The Terrie Williams Agency, New York (Photo by Dwight Carter)

Terrie Williams is founder of The Terrie Williams Agency, which specializes in "public relations with a cause," community outreach programs, deal brokering, and executive coaching. Past and present clients include Eddie Murphy and Miles Davis (the agency's first clients), Janet Jackson, Johnnie Cochran, Sean "Puffy" Combs, Rev. Hezekiah Walker, and Sally Jessy Raphael.

Williams' third book, *A Plentiful Harvest: Creating Balance and Harmony Using 7 Living Virtues,* was published by Warner Books in October 2002. She graduated cum laude in 1975 from Brandeis University with degrees in psychology and sociology, and earned a master of science degree in social welfare from Columbia University.

As you've read in this chapter, ethics and values play an important role in the success of your personal and professional lives. There are several ethics codes that we should live by, and there are organizations to join (PRSA and IABC) that have binding ethics codes.

Unfortunately, our profession is still perceived as one that does not adhere to a strict set of laws regarding values. Consider the nicknames for PR pros: "hacks," "spinmeisters," "yes people." All denote behavior that is a bit unethical. Makes it seem like we'll do anything to get a placement or a boldface mention.

I might have a way we can change those negative attitudes. A couple years ago I found I was becoming a bit disenchanted—11 nonstop years of running your own business will do that. Not that I was going to close up shop: I just thought we could do a little something extra with our clients and our projects. The world of public relations can be so much more than placements and media impressions. I have enjoyed success, and I have been blessed. And I know that the best way to say thank you to all those who have done so much for me is to give something back and pass it on to those who will follow us.

So I decided to take on projects that excited me, and I refocused the mission of the agency. I wanted to work on projects that would have a positive impact on the community. I began to advise clients that they needed to get involved with community outreach programs.

Amazingly, I discovered that what excited me also excited my clients, and soon I was serving them even more effectively because of my renewed energy and enthusiasm.

I'll give you one example of how my agency helped a client enhance its brand name, increase its consumer base, *and* help a lot of folks in the process. For our client, Moet & Chandon Champagne, we conceived and implemented a program we called Network of Success. The program consisted of a series of events held around the country that brought together business leaders and young professionals for an evening of networking, a panel discussion, and fine food and champagne. The program—which ran for three years—was a tremendous success! Not only did Moet reap the benefits of increased sales, but we also provided thousands of young professionals with important career information, guidance, contacts, and opportunities.

As successful businesspeople and entrepreneurs, we have plenty of opportunities to give back and help someone else. It may be through the programs you develop at work, or you can do it on your own. There are a zillion organizations out there that would benefit from a helping hand. In fact, volunteerism is a way of life for many businesspeople today, despite their frenzied schedules at work and at home. Many folks are finding that their lives are lacking somehow (as I did a few years ago) and discovering that helping to make someone else's life better nourishes the soul and makes for a more productive life.

Who knows? If more and more PR people lean this way—and adhere to the professional ethics of our business—we could work the greatest "spin" of all: changing the negative impressions of our industry.

Case Study 6.1

Cappuccino with Values, Please: Starbucks Coffee Company

Every now and then, Starbucks Coffee Company probably makes a bad cup of coffee. And every now and then, like every organization, it makes a bad decision. What separates Starbucks from many other organizations, however, is its values-driven willingness to publicly evaluate its decisions.

In the frenzied first hours after the September 2001 terrorist attack on the World Trade Center, a Starbucks employee in New York City sold bottled water to a paramedic. Starbucks had intended to donate the water, but, in the chaos, a company employee made a mistake.

When Starbucks President Orin Smith learned of the error, he phoned the ambulance company to apologize and to reimburse the paramedic. He instructed his public relations team to issue a news release, apologizing for the action. He then did his best to ensure that his employees were donating water, coffee, and other Starbucks products to rescue workers and to the injured.[23]

Ironically, he was communicating with employees who could have chosen to stay home: After the terrorist attacks on New York and Washington, D.C., Starbucks temporarily closed its North American stores to allow employees to be with their families. But Starbucks stores in New York City chose to remain open. One of them supplied free coffee and other products to the emergency room staff at St. Vincent's Hospital, just blocks from the collapsed World Trade Center.[24] A week later, Smith received a thank-you letter from a St. Vincent's nurse:

> I wasn't scheduled to work, but I needed to go to the ER and help. . . . Hours passed and the staff was getting tired. I told my co-worker Jay, "I would love to have a cup of Starbucks right now." We didn't want to leave the ER, not knowing what would come through the doors. An hour later, I noticed my co-worker Karen with a cup of Starbucks! She informed me that the Starbucks on Greenwich Avenue brought fresh coffee and water for the ER staff. Mr. Smith, I cannot tell you how much that cup of coffee meant to me. . . . I want to thank you personally for your generosity and support.[25]

"I have never been more proud of Starbucks [employees] than I am right now," Smith responded, via a news release—but he could not forget Starbucks' one departure from its values: "The decision [to charge the paramedic] is not defensible and is totally inconsistent with what we stand for."[26] Days later, Starbucks donated $1 million to relief efforts in New York and Washington, D.C.[27]

Earlier in 2001, when protestors tried to disrupt Starbucks' annual meeting for stockholders, the company again demonstrated its willingness to test its actions against its values. A Starbucks executive offered to meet with the protestors to discuss Starbucks' policies on food additives, which was one of the issues in question. Unfortunately, the protesters were not as accommodating. "We won't meet with them until they agree to meet our demands," said their spokesperson.[28]

Starbucks' commitment to its values helped place it on *Business Ethics* magazine's 2001 list of "America's most profitable and socially responsible companies."[29] Since 1996, the company has won more than a dozen national and regional awards for ethical behavior.

"How does [Starbucks] inspire ethics in its employees?" asked one journalist recently. "By promoting its values. The company starts with a mission statement, which includes six guiding principles."[30] Starbucks' mission statement reads as follows.

Starbucks Mission Statement: Establish Starbucks as the premier purveyor of the finest coffee in the world while maintaining our uncompromising principles while we grow.

The following six guiding principles will help us measure the appropriateness of our decisions:

- Provide a great work environment and treat each other with respect and dignity.
- Embrace diversity as an essential component in the way we do business.

- Apply the highest standards of excellence to the purchasing, roasting, and fresh delivery of our coffee.
- Develop enthusiastically satisfied customers all of the time.
- Contribute positively to our communities and our environment.
- Recognize that profitability is essential to our future success.

Starbucks' mission statement and principles almost guarantee conflict. Striving for profits while also striving for quality and striving to be a good corporate citizen can pull a company in at least three different directions. Such was the case in 2000 when protestors targeted Starbucks for reportedly paying poverty-level prices to coffee growers in developing nations. At the company's annual meeting, the protestors demanded that Starbucks purchase Fair Trade coffee beans. Fair Trade means that individual farmers in developing nations grow the beans and earn a fair price for them. Competing beans grown by conglomerates are cheaper but often leave the farmers impoverished.

Starbucks' response illustrated the creative tensions that characterize its mission statement and principles. Company officials said they had studied Fair Trade beans but had not found any that matched Starbucks' standards—a direct reference to the company's mission of supplying "the finest coffee in the world." However, the officials also pledged to look harder—a direct reference to the company's principles of excellence in purchasing and building better communities. Within days, Starbucks had purchased 75,000 pounds of Fair Trade beans, and it pledged to buy more if it could find additional beans that met company standards. Within seven months, Starbucks had placed Fair Trade products in its stores throughout the world.[31]

Starbucks' continual willingness to measure its actions against its values earns admiration even from potential detractors. "The company is often grudgingly considered by many social activists to be a 'socially responsible' company," said one analyst.[32] The student newspaper at Brown University put a similar sentiment in slightly different words: "Even though Starbucks exemplifies corporate ickiness, the giant coffee company [has begun] selling Fair Trade Certified Coffee."[33]

Aristotle wrote that true virtue lies in finding the point of ethical balance and harmony among extremes. Starbucks' values-driven willingness to seek an ethical balance among its obligations to many publics—including employees, stockholders, customers, and coffee bean farmers—provides an example of ethical public relations in a world that lacks easy answers.

DISCUSSION QUESTIONS

1. What is your opinion of Starbucks' mission statement and guiding principles?
2. After the terrorist bombing of the World Trade Center, the news media reported that Starbucks sold, instead of donated, water to a paramedic. How might Starbucks have responded? What is your opinion of Starbucks' actual response?
3. Starbucks presumably could have purchased Fair Trade beans earlier than it did. Does its failure to do so make it an unethical company?

4. What advice do you think John Rawls would have offered Starbucks as it considered its decision whether to buy Free Trade beans?

5. What advice do you think Immanuel Kant would have offered Starbucks as it considered its decision whether to buy Free Trade beans?

Case Study 6.2

Undisclosed Interest: Glaxo Wellcome and the Committee to Protect MDIs

The letters began in 1996 and continued into 1997—9,000 of them, all asking the U.S. Food and Drug Administration to preserve a particular kind of asthma inhaler known as an MDI. What prompted the deluge?

Many of the letters referred to information received from an organization called the Committee to Protect MDIs.[34] And in August 1997, as the FDA continued to open its mail, the Associated Press reported that the letter writers were in fact "unwitting lobbyists" for Glaxo Wellcome, a British-based pharmaceutical company that "quietly backed" the Committee to Protect MDIs.[35]

Glaxo Wellcome produced an MDI that used ozone-depleting chlorofluorocarbons, or CFCs. The FDA was considering a ban on the devices. At stake was leadership in the $761 billion inhaler market. Pharmaceutical companies in the United States and Europe were scrambling to produce inhalers that didn't use CFCs—and, according to the Associated Press report, Glaxo Wellcome had fallen behind in the race.[36] An early crackdown on inhaler CFCs by the FDA could have been disastrous for the company's U.S. market share.

Many of Glaxo Wellcome's tactics in lobbying the government were beyond reproach. A company representative spoke with news media and discussed problems with alternatives to CFCs. Glaxo Wellcome also openly financed a survey by Allergy and Asthma Network/Mothers of Asthmatics Inc. that showed that asthma sufferers opposed a quick crackdown on CFCs in their inhalers.[37]

But the Committee to Protect MDIs was another matter. The Associated Press included it in an exposé of "groups with high-minded names that often obscure the financial interests of those behind them." Such groups, the AP charged, "provide avenues for businesses to influence policy-makers . . . while leaving few fingerprints."[38] An earlier AP story noted that "doctors, patient advocates and federal regulators" disagreed with the committee's claims. The president of the Allergy and Asthma Network/Mothers of Asthmatics Inc. declared, "They are being too frightening about it. . . . To me, it's a scam."[39]

Such indirect lobbying isn't necessarily illegal in the United States. But is it ethical? The Public Relations Society of America had a clear stand on the issue. Its *Code of Professional Standards for the Practice of Public Relations* at that time stated in part that

A member shall not use any individual or organization professing to serve or represent an announced cause, or professing to be independent or unbiased, but actually serving another or undisclosed interest.

Did Glaxo Wellcome attempt to hide its involvement with the Committee to Protect MDIs? The public relations consultant who oversaw the committee told the AP that she couldn't remember how her involvement began. She wouldn't answer AP's questions about the committee's membership or finances.[40]

Ironically, much earlier in the CFC debate, the *Pharmaceutical Business News* reported that Glaxo Wellcome denied it was lobbying to delay a ban on CFCs. That same story, however, noted the "aggressive lobbying" of a group called the Committee to Protect MDIs. The story closed with a long quotation from the head of the committee—the same consultant who later wouldn't discuss membership or financing.[41]

To its credit, Glaxo Wellcome didn't stonewall the Associated Press when asked about its connection to the committee. "Glaxo said it underwrote the committee's efforts as part of a broader lobbying campaign aimed at making sure a full range of drugs remain available to people with breathing problems," the AP reported.[42]

The fallout from AP's exposé was brief. Glaxo Wellcome endured a few negative news stories, but the Committee to Protect MDIs vanished from headlines almost as quickly as its own web site went dark.

In a sense, the Committee to Protect MDIs was a success. The FDA did not implement an immediate ban on inhalers with CFCs. Glaxo Wellcome won time to continue its development of environmentally friendly alternatives to its popular CFC-based MDIs. Investment analysts liked the company's prospects, and its 1997 revenues topped $13 billion.[43] In 2000, the company merged with SmithKline Beecham to form GlaxoSmithKline. The public relations practitioner who supervised the Committee to Protect MDIs now represents a different multinational pharmaceutical company and is frequently quoted in news media.

No one, apparently, has asked the thousands who wrote to the FDA if they feel used.

DISCUSSION QUESTIONS

1. Did Glaxo Wellcome's support for the Committee to Protect MDIs represent a quest for "the greatest good for the greatest number"?
2. What potential categorical imperative based on Glaxo Wellcome's support for the Committee to Protect MDIs can you articulate?
3. Does the Potter Box defend Glaxo Wellcome's support for the Committee to Protect MDIs?
4. Are John Rawls' theories of the veil of ignorance and power to the powerless useful for an analysis of the ethics of Glaxo Wellcome's actions?
5. Was Glaxo Wellcome's financing of the Committee to Protect MDIs unethical? If so, why? If not, why not?

It's Your Turn

Trouble Brewing

You're the director of investor relations for a nationwide chain of coffeehouses. Business is good, but competition in the marketplace is fierce. For the past three weeks, your company has been secretly negotiating a merger with its closest competitor. The goal? To create a larger, more competitive company, a move that would definitely please the two companies' stockholders.

As director of investor relations, you've participated in the secret negotiations from the beginning. The CEO of your company has wanted your fact-based opinions on stockholder reaction to different plans as well as your advice on how best to communicate the final decision. You're excited to be operating in hush-hush meetings at such high levels, and you're pleased that your company understands the value of bringing public relations personnel into the decision-making process. You even think that the merger would be good idea, though it would have a serious downside: Several management-level employees from both companies would lose their jobs. The merged company wouldn't need two directors of human resources, for example.

Today, your excitement over the negotiations diminished considerably when one of your best friends, the company's director of administrative services, e-mailed you with some tough questions. She wants to know whether the merger rumors are true. She tells you that she and her husband are about to buy a house, and they're getting ready to send their oldest son to college. She's also concerned that her husband may be about to lose his health insurance because of a continuing medical problem. Losing her job through a merger would be devastating for her and for her family. In fact, she tells you, it would destroy them. She pleads for any information you have—and she reminds you that she and her husband actually moved you into their house when you were so ill with the flu that you couldn't care for yourself.

What should you do? She's a true friend, and it's clear that she's almost sick with anxiety. On the other hand, your CEO has pledged you to secrecy. You're torn between conflicting values and loyalties, but you need to write her back. What will you say? Does the Potter Box offer any assistance?

KEY TERMS

categorical imperative, p. 179

ethics, p. 168

ethics audit, p. 180

golden mean, p. 174

Potter Box, p. 181

utilitarianism, p. 185

veil of ignorance, p. 186

NOTES

1. Ludwig Wittgenstein, *Tractacus Logico-Philosophicus,* trans. D. F. Pears and B. F. McGuinness (London: Routledge & Kegan Paul, 1996), 147.
2. "Caux Round Table Principles for Business," online, www.cauxroundtable.org/ENGLISH.HTM.
3. *New Standard Encyclopedia,* vol. 5 (Chicago: Standard Education Society, 1947).
4. Jack O'Dwyer, "Double Identity of PR Exec Is Unmasked," *Jack O'Dwyer's Newsletter* 29, no. 3 (1996), online, Lexis-Nexis.
5. Kenneth Campbell, "Malden Mills Owner Applies Religious Ethics to Business," Massachusetts Institute of Technology news release, 16 April 1997, online, web.mit.edu/newsoffice/tt/1997/apr16/43530.html.
6. Ralph D. Barney and Jay Black, "Ethics and Professional Persuasive Communication," *Public Relations Review* 20, no. 3 (fall 1994): 189.
7. Larry R. Judd, "An Approach to Ethics in the Information Age," *Public Relations Review* (spring 1995): 35.
8. "Profile 2000: A Survey of the Profession," *Communication World* (June/July 2000): A10.
9. Confucius, *The Doctrine of the Mean,* online, http://classics.mit.edu/Confucius/doctmean.html.
10. Ed Shelton, "Aberrant Regimes Pose a PR Dilemma," *PRWeek,* 1 June 2001, online, Lexis-Nexis.
11. David Enrich, "The Insider Who Blew Smoke at Big Tobacco," *U.S. News and World Report,* 20 August 2001, online, Lexis-Nexis.
12. Thomas Donaldson, "Values in Tension: Ethics Away from Home," *Harvard Business Review* (September–October 1996), online, Lexis-Nexis.
13. Bodo Schlegelmilch, *Marketing Ethics: An International Perspective* (London: International Thomson Business Press, 1998), 11.
14. Shlegelmilch, 145.
15. Thomas Donaldson, "Adding Corporate Ethics to the Bottom Line," *Financial Times,* 13 November 2000, online, Lexis-Nexis.
16. Clay Chandler, "Ambivalent about Business," *Wall Street Journal,* 12 May 1996, B1.
17. Immanuel Kant, *Fundamental Principles of the Metaphysic of Morals,* in *Harvard Classics,* vol. 32 (New York: P.F. Collier and Son, 1910), 352.
18. For more information on integrating ethics into the public relations process, see Thomas Bivins, "A Systems Model for Ethical Decision Making in Public Relations," *Public Relations Review* (winter 1992), 365–384.
19. See Clifford Christians, Mark Fackler, Kim Rotzoll, and Kathy Brittain McKee, *Media Ethics: Cases and Moral Reasoning,* 5th ed. (New York: Longman, 1998).
20. John Stuart Mill, *Utilitarianism,* searchable text online, www.library.adelaide.edu/etext/m/m645u/.
21. Mill, online.
22. John Rawls, *A Theory of Justice* (Cambridge, Mass.: Harvard University Press, 1971).

23. "Starbucks President and CEO Orin Smith Addresses Starbucks Customers," a news release issued by Starbucks Coffee Company, 27 September 2001, online, www. starbucks.com.

24. "Starbucks President and CEO Orin Smith Addresses Starbucks Customers."

25. "New Yorker Shows Support for Starbucks," a news release issued by Starbucks Coffee Company, 18 September 2001, online, www.starbucks.com.

26. "Starbucks President and CEO Orin Smith Addresses Starbucks Customers."

27. "Starbucks Cares," online, www.starbucks.com.

28. Kathy Mulady, "Starbucks: Applause and Protest," *Seattle Post-Intelligencer,* 21 March 2001, online, Lexis-Nexis.

29. "Building an Effective Philanthropic Partnership," *PRNews,* 4 June 2001, online, Lexis-Nexis.

30. Meredith Alexander, "Do You Need an Ethics Office?" *The Industry Standard,* 10 July 2000, online, Lexis-Nexis.

31. Robert T. Nelson, "Groups Plan to Protest Starbucks over Nonuse of Coffee That Pays Growers More," *Seattle Times,* 25 March 2000, online, Lexis-Nexis; "Starbucks Coffee Brings Fair Trade Certified Coffee to Retail Stores," a news release issued by Business Wire, 25 September 2000, online, Lexis-Nexis.

32. T. K. Maloy, "Thanks a Latte: Starbucks Turns 30," United Press International, 6 September 2001, online, Lexis-Nexis.

33. "100% Fair Trade Coffee," University Wire, 17 October 2000, online, Lexis-Nexis.

34. Jim Drinkard, "Group Backed by Drug Companies Got Asthma Patients to Lobby for It," Associated Press, 21 August 1997, online, http://health.phillynews.com/wires/ DRUG.html.

35. Drinkard, "Group Backed."

36. Drinkard, "Group Backed."

37. PR Newswire news release from Allergy and Asthma Network/Mothers of Asthmatics Inc., 24 April 1997, online, Lexis-Nexis.

38. Jim Drinkard, "Secretly Funded Groups Gain Popularity with Lobbyists," Associated Press, *Kansas City Star,* 18 December 1997, A5.

39. Drinkard, "Group Backed."

40. Drinkard, "Group Backed."

41. "Glaxo Denies Lobbying against CFC Inhaler Ban," *Pharmaceutical Business News,* 27 September 1996, online, Lexis-Nexis.

42. Drinkard, "Group Backed."

43. "Investors Impressed with Glaxo Wellcome Pipeline," *Marketletter,* 12 May 1997, online, Lexis-Nexis.

chapter seven

Research and Evaluation

objectives

After studying this chapter, you will be able to

- describe the value of research and evaluation in the public relations process

- recognize the differences between formal and informal research

- develop a strategy for conducting research

- explain the basics of conducting the five most common forms of public relations research

- glean valuable information through effective analysis of survey results

City Hospital Faces Competition

City Hospital has served the people of your community for more than 100 years. It is a public institution run by a board of directors appointed by the city council. The people have come to depend on its inpatient, outpatient, and emergency care facilities. For most of its existence, the hospital has had no direct competition.

However, things have changed. Two years ago a nationwide health-care corporation opened a same-day surgical clinic in your community. City Hospital officials decided that the best strategy was to ignore the newcomer. "The people in our community know us," said the hospital administrator. "They don't want their health in the hands of strangers." Although City Hospital has remained the community's predominant health-care provider, the number of same-day surgical procedures performed has steadily declined. Some of City Hospital's best doctors, nurses, and medical technicians have been hired away by the competition.

The nationwide health-care corporation has now announced it will seek government permission to build a modern full-service hospital in the community. "Competition is a good thing," says the mayor. City Hospital's management doesn't see it that way. It fears a substantial loss of income that could force City Hospital either to close its doors or to merge with some other hospital—possibly even with the competition. That is why the board of directors has hired you as a public relations consultant.

What is the first thing you are going to do?

The Value of Research and Evaluation

The first step in the public relations process is research. The fourth, or last, step is evaluation. Nothing could be more important than those two assumptions. Or more wrong.

Some are tempted to view these two steps as necessary "evils" that allow practitioners to get to the "really important" parts of the public relations process— planning (where strategy and tactics are developed) and communication (where plans are executed). Sometimes, we bypass research and evaluation out of a sense of presumed knowledge: We think we already know everything we need to know to act and that we will know whether we have been successful. Other popular excuses for bypassing the research and evaluation steps are lack of time, lack of personnel, lack of money, and lack of how-to knowledge.

At face value, these may seem like logical excuses. But that's all they are: excuses. **Research** and **evaluation** are cornerstones of good public relations practice. They lead us to explore two areas essential to success in any public relations effort:

- *what we think we know:* Do our assumptions hold up under closer examination? If nothing else, research and evaluation can remove lingering doubts by validating the accuracy of information.
- *what we don't know:* Are pieces missing from the puzzle? By exploring *terra incognita*—unknown territory—we can open doors of opportunity that may otherwise remain closed.

Why not have separate chapters on research and evaluation? We link those parts of the public relations process in this chapter for two reasons. First, as we noted in Chapter 1, public relations is a dynamic, nonlinear process. The traditional four-step process implies a straight-line approach: research, followed by planning, followed by communication, followed by evaluation. However, public relations does not work that way. The four steps are intertwined. Research and evaluation occur at every phase of the public relations process. It's not unusual for practitioners, in the midst of planning, to decide they need more information. Nor is it unusual for public relations professionals to adjust strategy in the midst of its execution based on either feedback or new information.

The second reason we combine the two steps here is that the processes of research and evaluation are closely related. Both involve using similar methods to gather information. It could be said that research is gathering information before the fact and evaluation is gathering information after the fact. That notion has an element of truth, but it's an oversimplification. Instead, we constantly gather information, evaluate it, and seek new information to test a developing hypothesis. Remember your first school dance? You probably picked a dance partner based on an ongoing process of research and evaluation. At first glance across a dimly lit gymnasium, you may have been interested in dancing with a particular person. However, on closer inspection, appearance and behavior may have changed your mind. You may then have sought new information on someone else. Several cycles of research and evaluation may have occurred before you took that big step and ventured onto the dance floor. Public relations is no different—although it is often less traumatic.

Research enabled a public relations firm to gauge the success of the Miller Genuine Draft "reunion ride" celebrating Harley-Davidson's 90th anniversary. (Courtesy of Harley-Davidson Motor Company)

QuickBreak 7.1

ISSUES MANAGEMENT AND THE AIDS EPIDEMIC

An increasingly significant form of problem–opportunity research (see p. 204) is known as **issues management.** Instead of trying to determine the nature of the *present* environment, practitioners engage in issues management as a means of predicting and managing *future* issues and concerns. Issues management often begins with **scanning,** which is short for "scanning the horizon." In the days before satellites and radar, scanning the horizon was the only way to determine whether any potential threats were approaching. This is the concept behind issues management: Through a process of analyzing emerging trends and issues, practitioners can prepare their organizations to respond in a timely and appropriate manner.

For example, many organizations failed to take note of news reports in the late 1970s about a mysterious and fatal disease that claimed its victims by destroying their ability to ward off infections. Even when the disease, AIDS (Acquired Immune Deficiency Syndrome), was finally identified, many felt that its impact was limited to those persons identified as being most at risk. By the mid-1980s, the AIDS epidemic was at the center of a public policy debate in the United States. It had—and continues to have—a dramatic impact on a wide variety of social issues, ranging from health care to public education. Inevitably, the organizations quickest to identify AIDS as an emerging issue were the best prepared to address it.

The Florida Dental Association was one such organization. When it was reported that a Stuart, Florida, woman had died from an HIV infection passed to her during a routine procedure by her dentist, both patients and doctors reacted with alarm. Some state legislators proposed sweeping changes in the law, including mandatory AIDS testing of all health-care providers. Although the Florida Dental Association favored some changes in regulations, it was also concerned that a shadow had been cast upon the entire profession by one isolated incident.

To its credit, the association had already researched the AIDS epidemic. It knew that procedures were already in place to halt the spread of HIV. In news releases and letters to Florida public officials, the association reminded a nervous public that Florida's dentists were responsible professionals who always put the health and safety of their patients first. Through effective issues management, the association was able to defuse volatile public opinion and allow public policy to be made in a calm and reasoned environment.

Issues management involves both scanning and **monitoring.** Scanning, as we said before, means actively looking for issues that could eventually affect your organization. This requires a keen eye and an open mind. Scanning can involve everything from reading local and national newspapers to holding periodic meetings with traditional stakeholder groups. The goal is to scan for all issues and trends with potential for having an impact—whether positive or negative—on your organization. Once an issue is identified, active monitoring should begin. Keep track of the latest developments. When you have gathered sufficient information, your organization can develop a response that is consistent with its values. And this is where the *real* value of issues management is demonstrated: Issues management gives an organization time to act in a manner that allows it to dictate its own course rather than having its course dictated by events.

No one, certainly not the authors of this book, expects you to become an expert researcher based on the information you find in this chapter. Later in your career, it may be that you rarely do in-depth research—it may be someone else's job to do it for you. Nevertheless, it is important that you know enough to be a good consumer of research. *Public Relations Journal* noted that as organizations get leaner, more executives are expecting results that measurably affect organizational goals. But you can't measure success without research and evaluation. Tighter marketing budgets also are dictating that we do more with less. Before million-dollar investments are made in promotional and marketing campaigns, we need to have a sense of whether they will actually work.[1]

Public Relations Journal also cited six ways in which public relations practitioners can effectively use research at every step of the public relations process:[2]

- *To formulate strategy.* By conducting a "gap study" (also known as coorientation research) to determine how perceptions among key audiences differed, New Hampshire paper industry executives learned that the public was generally satisfied with the industry's efforts to curb pollution. This prevented them from launching an unnecessarily defensive public relations campaign.

- *To gauge success.* To boost brand awareness, Miller Genuine Draft Beer sponsored a "reunion ride" in conjunction with the 90th anniversary of the Harley-Davidson Motor Company. Through a series of interviews and a review of sales data from cities along the reunion ride route, both companies saw the event as a success and repeated it five years later.

- *To test messages.* After several pre-Christmas muggings in a downtown shopping center, the management of a shopping mall wanted to know how to reassure shoppers that they would be safe. By testing a series of different messages through focus group research, the mall management avoided overreacting and unnecessarily alarming the public.

- *To size up competition.* In assessing its competitive strengths and weaknesses, a New England bank hired a research firm to conduct comprehensive telephone interviews with a cross section of residents living in the bank's service area. In response to data showing it was not popular among 35 to 45-year-olds, the bank launched a program that resulted in a 10 percent rise in deposits from that group.

- *To get publicity.* New York Telephone commissioned a survey that showed that many New Yorkers didn't know very much about their home state. The results were widely reported, as was the company's sponsorship of a torch run from Manhattan to Buffalo in connection with the World University Games.

- *To sway opinion.* An Ohio ballot initiative would have required cancer warnings on thousands of products from plywood to peanut butter. Through research, opponents learned that the more voters knew about the proposal's impact on their daily lives, the less they liked it. Following an extensive public information campaign, 78 percent of the voters rejected the measure.

Are research and evaluation commonplace in the practice of public relations? They are probably not at the level they should be, but the trend appears to be in the right direction. For example, only 30 percent of the research conducted at Ketchum Public Relations between 1987 and 1991 was designed to measure the effectiveness of public relations efforts. However, in 1992, nearly half the studies included program-evaluation measures. "This is in sharp contrast to previous years, when the largest proportion of research projects by far . . . were carried out principally for PR planning or to support promotional and publicity efforts," said Walter K. Lindenmann, Ketchum's former senior vice president and director of research.[3]

Developing a Research Strategy: What Do I Want to Know?

Getting started in almost any endeavor can be difficult. Research is no different. Before setting out on any journey, it is important to know the destination. A journey into research is no different. That is why the first step when you embark on a research project is to develop a **research strategy.** That involves asking yourself two important questions:

1. What do I want to know?
2. How will I gather that information?

By answering these questions, you develop a research strategy. Your research strategy, in turn, begins to lay the foundation for a successful public relations program. Let's take a closer look at how we might answer the first question.

What we need to know in public relations research falls into one of four categories: client research, stakeholder research, problem–opportunity research, and evaluation research. Quite often research findings can fit into more than one category. However, the information itself is far more important than how it is categorized.

Client Research

Client research focuses on the individual client, company, or other organization on whose behalf the practitioner is working. Efforts are geared toward discovering an organization's size; the nature of the products or services it offers; and its history, staffing requirements, markets and customers, budget, legal environment, reputation, and beliefs about the issue in question. It is also essential to understand a client organization's mission and consequent goals. As noted in Chapter 1, an organization's mission statement is based on the organization's core values. Goals are general statements indicating the direction the organization wants to take and are consistent with an organization's values and mission statement.

Stakeholder Research

Stakeholder research focuses on identifying the specific publics important to the success of the client. These various constituencies are known as stakeholders, for each has a different stake in how the organization responds to various issues. The people

MEASURING RELATIONSHIPS

We bet that you have heard at least one of your professors say something like this: "Your grade is not based on the amount of work you do. It is based on the quality of the work you submit." That's another way of saying that you will be judged by results.

Judging results is a very real-world approach to evaluating success. And it focuses on the most important—and difficult—aspect of evaluation: deciding what constitutes an appropriate measure of success.

For example, how does one measure the success of a news release? Sometimes we measure **outputs,** such as the number of news releases we send to the media. Other times, we measure **outcomes.** Although this could mean the amount of media coverage our news release generates, it is important to remember that we are using the news media as an intervening public. For that reason, a more meaningful measure would be the response of the primary public, the people we are trying to reach through the media. In this case, we may want to measure the number of people who called a toll-free number mentioned in the news release.

Although both approaches provide practitioners with valuable information, they also have their limitations. At best, they measure our public relations activities and the consequent short-term changes in the public relations environment. They also tend to focus only on the target audience's response to a specific program or event. Missing is an understanding of the long-term effects a public relations program has on relationships with key publics.

To address this broader issue, the Institute of Public Relations, based at the University of Florida, established a panel of educators and professionals to search for more meaningful ways to measure the effectiveness of public relations. One of its reports, released in 1999, recommends a process through which practitioners measure the quality of important relationships.

Linda Childers Hon of the University of Florida and James E. Grunig of the University of Maryland wrote that the evaluation of long-term relationships rests on examining six key **components of relationships:**[4]

- **Control mutuality.** The degree to which parties agree on who has the power to influence the actions of the other. In an ideal relationship, the parties share a degree of control.

- **Trust.** The willingness of one party to open itself to the other. This depends upon perceptions of each party's integrity, dependability, and competence.

- **Satisfaction.** The degree to which the benefits of the relationship outweigh its costs.

- **Commitment.** The extent to which each party feels the relationship is worth the time, cost, and effort.

- **Exchange relationship.** The giving of benefits to one party in return for past benefits received or for the expectation of future benefits.

- **Communal relationship.** The provision of benefits to each other out of concern and without expectation of anything in return.

Hon and Grunig believe that by administering a questionnaire that includes agree/disagree statements focusing on these six aspects of a relationship, practitioners will have a more meaningful measure of the effectiveness of public relations programs. In turn, they also believe this approach provides a more accurate measure of the value of public relations to an organization.

Hon and Grunig's report, "Guidelines for Measuring Relationships in Public Relations," is available online, at www.instituteforpr.com.

Values Statement 7.1

BUREAU OF LABOR STATISTICS

The Bureau of Labor Statistics is an independent federal agency charged with collecting and analyzing labor and economic statistics for use by local, state, and federal governments.

Vision

> With the strongest commitment to integrity and objectivity, the Bureau of Labor Statistics will be premier among statistical agencies, producing impartial, timely, and accurate data relevant to the needs of our users and to the social and economic conditions of our nation, its workers, and their families.

—Excerpt from *BLS Strategic Plan,*
FY 1999–FY 2004

important to your organization are not a homogeneous mass. They are a wide range of constituencies, each having its own values, attitudes, concerns, needs, and predispositions. How these stakeholders relate to an organization can change from issue to issue. For example, a teachers' union may oppose proposed tax increases for new roads but favor higher taxes for educational programs. Also, people are often members of more than one stakeholder group. Building on the prior example, a member of the teachers' union may favor new road taxes if the funds are earmarked for the area in which that member lives. Stakeholder research helps you better target the message and the media for that message to the needs of each constituency.

Problem–Opportunity Research

Put in the simplest terms, **problem–opportunity research** is research designed to answer two critical questions: What is at issue, and what stake, if any, does our organization have in this issue? Problem–opportunity research develops background information on a particular topic or issue. It also identifies related trends that may have developed. Ultimately, problem–opportunity research answers a key question: Why is it necessary— or unnecessary—for our organization to act? Sometimes organizations are reactive, responding to events that could shape their destiny. Other times they are proactive, launching those destiny-shaping events. There are even times when doing nothing is the best course of action. Problem–opportunity research helps the organization decide whether and how to act.

Evaluation Research

Although evaluation is listed last among the four steps in the traditional public relations process, today's climate demands attention to **evaluation research**—procedures for determining the success of a public relations plan—from the very beginning. With practitioners facing greater demands for accountability, every public relations plan must achieve an impact that is measurable.

Research shows that evaluation is closely tied to public relations planning. More than half of practitioners questioned in a joint PRSA–IABC survey said they measure program performance against specified objectives. Nearly 9 out of 10 also said that their public relations objectives are tied to overall business objectives. The survey also showed that organizational executives understand that the value of public relations cannot be measured by merely looking at a profit–loss statement. Only 1 percent of those surveyed said the effectiveness of their communications program was measured by sales results.[5]

Evaluation research cannot be an afterthought; practitioners are expected to articulate at the outset of any campaign how success is defined. A clear understanding of the environment before and after the campaign must be achieved. It is not always possible to recreate the original conditions once a campaign has begun. For that reason, determining ways to evaluate success must always be among the first things good public relations research addresses.

Quick ✓ Check

1. Why do public relations practitioners conduct research?
2. When developing a research strategy, what two questions should you ask yourself?
3. What are the four major categories of public relations research?

Developing a Research Strategy: How Will I Gather Information?

First we asked the initial question, "What do I want to know?" Having done that, our next major strategy decision has to do with the methods we will use to gather information. To a large degree, the answer to the question "How will I gather that information?" depends upon the time and resources at our disposal. Those factors, in turn, determine whether the research we are planning to conduct will present a reasonably accurate picture of reality or just a snapshot of some smaller aspect of it.

Using the vocabulary of researchers, this is the essential difference between **formal research** and **informal research.** Formal (also known as quantitative or scientific) research presents an accurate picture. That is because it uses scientific methods designed to create a representative picture of reality. In public relations, formal research generally is used to create an accurate portrayal of a stakeholder group. On the other hand, informal (also known as nonquantitative or nonscientific) research describes some aspect of reality but doesn't necessarily develop an accurate picture of the larger reality as a whole. In public relations, informal research is very useful—but it should not lead us to conclusions about an entire stakeholder group.

Now, back to the question at hand: How will I gather the information I need? Public relations practitioners commonly employ five research methods, some of which are already familiar to you: secondary (library) research, feedback research, communication audits, focus groups, and survey research.

Secondary (Library) Research

Secondary research is probably a research method you know well. It utilizes materials generated by others—sometimes for purposes entirely different from your own.

The alternative to secondary research is **primary research,** which is new research you generate from scratch. Sources used in secondary research include

- Published materials, such as newspaper and magazine articles, library references, various directories, and trade association data. This also includes information available through online databases and services such as Lexis-Nexis, Dow Jones News Service, and various sites on the web.

- Organizational records, such as annual reports, statistics, financial reports, and other disclosures that organizations with publicly held stock are required by law to release. For example, check out the disclosure documents that have been filed with the Securities and Exchange Commission and are available online through the EDGAR search engine, at www.sec.gov.

- Public records generated by governments. With few exceptions, government agencies in the United States are required to operate in the open. These agencies often generate a wealth of useful information, such as the U.S. Census and monthly reports on the nation's economy. Much of this information is available through federal and state depository libraries located in communities and on college campuses around the country. Now that the Internet has gone from being a private tool of researchers to an everyday information source for all, an increasing amount of this information is also available online. For example, check out the FedStats database, at www.fedstats.gov.

Secondary research is especially valuable in providing information you might never have the means to gather on your own.

Feedback Research

Feedback research enables an organization to receive tangible evidence—often unsolicited—of stakeholder groups' responses to its actions. This evidence can manifest itself in many forms, most commonly through letters and telephone calls to the organization. For example, every time the president of the United States speaks on television, White House operators keep a running tally of the number of calls expressing support for or disapproval of what was said. Newspaper clipping services and their radio and television equivalents provide useful ways of discovering what others are saying about you. And a growing number of organizations are soliciting feedback in the form of e-mail through their web sites. Although feedback research is not a formal research method, it can give very strong indications of the public relations environment.

The Communication Audit

Communication audits are research procedures used to determine whether an organization's communications are consistent with its values-driven mission and goals. In completing a communication audit, we review an organization's communications

Bacon's Clipping Bureau Brochure Clipping services, such as Bacon's Clipping Bureau, can help organizations keep track of what is being said about them in the news media. (Courtesy of Bacon's Information Inc., Chicago, Illinois)

and records, and we conduct interviews with key officials. Conducting a communication audit might have prevented embarrassment for former U.S. Vice President Al Gore in 1994. Gore led a commission charged with cutting wasteful government spending. Printing costs for the commission's lavish report, however, exceeded the allowed budget for most federal publications. Although the vice president's goal may have been to highlight the Clinton administration's efforts to curb government waste, the resulting expensive commission publication was not in keeping with that mission. A communication audit should answer five questions:

1. What are the organization's stated goals in relation to its stakeholder groups?
2. What communication activities has the organization used to fulfill those goals?
3. Which communication activities are working well and are consistent with those goals?

4. Which communication activities are not working well toward the achievement of those goals?

5. Given the findings of this audit, what revisions in goals or communication activities are recommended?

THE COMMUNICATIONS GRID.   One illustrative method of conducting a communication audit is a **communications grid.** The various media used by an organization are listed on one axis. Stakeholders important to the organization are listed on the other. An X is placed everywhere a particular stakeholder is reached by a particular medium. This exercise graphically illustrates where efforts have been directed and which stakeholders may have been overlooked.

Figure 7.1 shows a simplified version of a communications grid using the City Hospital scenario that opened this chapter. Each mark on the grid represents communication between the hospital and a key stakeholding public. We know from the scenario that City Hospital officials are concerned about the threat of increased competition. Six of the hospital's many stakeholder publics are its employees, the city officials who appoint the hospital board, the news media, the patients, the doctors who practice at the hospital, and a local health advocacy group. For the purposes of this example, let's assume that the only channels the hospital uses for communication are a weekly newsletter, an annual report, advertising, media kits, e-mail, and the hospital's web site.

The grid illustrates that all publics represented here have access to the hospital's web site. But this is a passive form of communication—the only people who see the web site are those who seek it out. All these publics are exposed to the hospital's

MEDIA USED BY CITY HOSPITAL

CITY HOSPITAL'S STAKEHOLDERS	weekly newsletter	annual report	broadcast and print ads	media kits	e-mail	Internet web site
employees	X		X		X	X
city officials		X	X			X
news media			X	X		X
patients			X			X
doctors		X	X			X
health advocates			X			X

FIGURE 7.1   City Hospital's Communication Channels

advertising. However, the advertising messages may not be well targeted to each of these audiences. Advertising also lacks the credibility that comes with independent third-party endorsement.

The grid also shows us that most of the hospital's communication channels are very selective and may be underutilized. For example, perhaps the hospital should use e-mail in communicating with the news media—reporters often prefer it. The hospital also may want to consider placing its media kits on its web site, making the kits available to reporters whenever they may be needed. If the hospital values keeping its workers informed about current issues affecting their jobs, it may want to share the annual report with employees.

The grid also shows a serious communication gap with two of the hospital's stakeholder publics. First, if one goal is to encourage doctors to refer their patients to City Hospital, sending them just an annual report is probably not enough. And second, the local health advocacy group—which may be very influential with some of the hospital's other stakeholders—is receiving no direct communication. Do you see other similar communication gaps in the grid?

In short, a communications grid is a good way to audit visually whether an organization is reaching all the publics important to its success. However, there is one significant drawback: A grid does not address the messages contained in the various media. Those can be determined only through an analysis of their content.

Focus Groups

Focus groups are an informal research method in which interviewers meet with groups of selected individuals to ascertain their opinions. Although focus group results should not be seen as representative of any particular public, they can indicate a public's knowledge, opinions, predispositions, and behavior.

Focus groups are a popular research method because, compared with survey research (that is, formal questionnaires), they are relatively inexpensive. They also have the advantage of giving the researcher immediate feedback. Focus groups are often used in advance of survey research. The interaction among focus group participants often raises issues that merit further study. Focus groups can even test the clarity and fairness of survey questions.

Focus group research was at the core of an award-winning campaign developed by Ketchum Public Relations for the Appalachian Regional Commission. The ARC knew that the Appalachian region had great potential for attracting tourists, but it wasn't sure how to overcome the region's negative image. Ketchum conducted several focus groups of different publics: people living in the region, people living just outside the region, and people connected to the travel industry. Ketchum determined not only that many people were unaware of the close-to-home recreational opportunities in the region, but also that many did not know they lived in Appalachia. These findings helped Ketchum create a successful campaign focusing on the region's culture, heritage, and scenic beauty.[6]

Focus groups are small, informal gatherings where the participants are encouraged to discuss their concerns, attitudes, and predispositions about the subject at hand. (Courtesy of Consumer Research Associates/Dallas, San Francisco)

HOW TO CONDUCT A FOCUS GROUP.   When preparing to conduct focus group research, we suggest you follow this 10-step process:

   1. *Develop a list of general questions based on information needs.* The questions usually should be open ended, avoiding simple yes/no answers.

   2. *Select as a moderator someone skilled in interviewing techniques.* The moderator must be strong enough to keep the discussion on track.

   3. *Recruit 8 to 12 participants.* Because of the problem of no-shows (people who promise to participate in the focus group but fail to show up), it is necessary to invite a larger number than you need. You can dismiss any extras with a small reward. As to who should be invited to attend, decide on a selection strategy. From what kind of people do you want to hear opinions? Sometimes a screening questionnaire will narrow the field. Participants are often compensated (with money, a free meal,

etc.) for their time. An important rule: Avoid inviting people who have sharply divergent points of view. You are interested in gathering information; you are not interest in conducting a debate. Too much clash can stifle participants who may speak up in a friendlier environment. Even if it means conducting additional focus groups, it is best to keep people with sharply different opinions separated.

4. *Record the session on audiotape or videotape (or both).* Make certain participants know that the session is being recorded. It may be necessary to reassure them that the tape provides a record of what was said and will not be used for any other purposes.

5. *Observe the session.* In addition to the moderator, others should watch the focus group. They should record their impressions in notes. They do not participate in the session. Some facilities allow these observers to watch the proceedings from behind two-way mirrors. In many cases, however, observers sit quietly along the wall of the room in which the session is being held.

6. *Limit the discussion to 60–90 minutes.* When the conversation starts repeating itself, that is a sign to wrap it up.

7. *Discuss opinions, problems, and needs—not solutions.* It is very likely that participants are not qualified to discuss solutions.

8. *Transcribe the tape of the session.* This makes it much easier to analyze participant comments.

9. *Prepare a written report on the session.* Identify participants by name, age, occupation, hometown, and any other pertinent information. Where possible, use direct quotations.

10. *Remember that focus groups are informal research.* Opinions stated in a focus group do not necessarily represent everyone else's view. At best, they serve as indicators of public opinion. However, they can be considered even stronger indicators if multiple focus groups yield the same comments.

Although these are the recommended steps for conducting focus group research, we also realize that sometimes it is necessary to bend the rules. For example, time and distance may make it difficult to get everyone together in the same room at the same time. Under those circumstances, the use of teleconferencing technology may provide a viable alternative. How one gathers information isn't really the issue. What matters is whether the information gathered is useful and reliable.

Quick ✔ Check

1. What is secondary research?
2. What is the purpose of a communication audit?
3. What are some of the reasons a researcher may choose to conduct a focus group rather than a survey?

Survey Research

When you are unable to gather the information you need through secondary research or informal research methods, conducting a formal survey may be your best choice. Although **survey research** can be both expensive and time consuming, it can also be a highly accurate way to gauge public opinion. Through the use of specifically worded questionnaires and a carefully selected list of people, researchers are able to make judgments about a much larger population. In essence, surveys provide a snapshot of what people are thinking on a particular subject at a moment in time.

With the practice of public relations becoming more results driven and cost conscious today than ever before, surveys are a very useful tool in targeting communications and measuring results. Through computer analysis, survey research makes it easier to select the right target, use the appropriate message, communicate through the most effective channels, and measure the results.

Of course, some surveys are better than others. When the local newspaper asks its readers to vote on a "question of the day," is that a valid survey? When the local television station conducts "person-on-the-street" interviews, do those interviews necessarily reflect the opinions of the larger community? The answer to both questions is no. But if you change the question and ask whether any useful information can be gleaned from those two approaches, the answer is yes.

It is also true that some surveys are more accurate than others. We are often faced with conflicting results. For example, a television network call-in poll once asked, "Should the United Nations continue to be based in the United States?" Two-thirds of the 185,000 callers said no. However, when a second survey conducted by the same network asked the same question but used a more scientific method, only 28 percent answered in the negative.[7] How do we know which result to believe?

The degree to which survey results can be seen as an accurate reflection of a larger population depends on two key factors: the composition of the people we are surveying and the structure of the survey instrument.

The Survey Sample

A sample is a portion of a public that we select for the purpose of making observations and drawing conclusions about the public as a whole. In other words, when we question members of a large stakeholder group, we generally don't question every member. Instead, we question a portion, or sample, of that public. A sample is said to be a **representative sample** of a targeted population when it is of sufficient size and when every member of the targeted population has an equal chance of being selected for the sample. Although surveying a representative sample provides a more accurate picture, it is not always practical because of time, cost, and personnel considerations.

For example, which would give you a better picture of U.S. public opinion regarding gun control: an informal poll of your classmates or a formal nationwide survey? Clearly, the latter would provide the more accurate picture. However, the informal poll would at least have its advantages in terms of time, money, and effort.

THE FLORIDA FOLLIES

Although U.S. citizens will remember Election Night 2000 for a long time, many in the television industry would just as soon forget it.

All the major broadcast and cable networks initially projected at 7:50 P.M. (Eastern Time) that Vice President Al Gore had won the pivotal state of Florida. They recanted around 10 P.M., saying the race was too close to call. By midnight, it became apparent that whoever won Florida would become the next president of the United States. Armed with new numbers, the networks declared shortly after 2 A.M. that Texas Governor George W. Bush had won. However, a little more than one hour later, the networks pulled Florida back into the undecided column for a second time. There it would stay until the U.S. Supreme Court settled the dispute five weeks later.

NBC News anchor Tom Brokaw said, "Not only do we have egg on our face, we have the whole omelet." At CBS, Dan Rather was telling his viewers, "To err is human, but to really foul up requires a computer." CNN anchor Bernard Shaw looked around the studio in amazement and asked his colleagues, "Do you like your crow well done?"[8]

In hindsight, it is easy to see where the seeds of the debacle were planted. The five networks and the Associated Press had all relied on the same data. In a cost-cutting move, they created the Voter News Service in 1990. The idea was simple: VNS would collect the raw data samples and project election winners. The system had worked well over the years, although it had resulted in at least two incorrect projections in races for the U.S. Senate.[9]

Unfortunately, an internal audit conducted after the election showed that VNS operated with bad data. The number of absentee ballots was twice as high as had been anticipated. Sampling errors in 45 precincts inflated Gore's numbers. VNS also used a flawed model, basing its projections on Florida's 1998 gubernatorial election instead of the 1996 presidential election. By basing its projections on flawed exit poll data rather than on real numbers, VNS inflated Gore's lead by 16 percentage points.[10]

The journalists who lived through the embarrassment of the Florida Follies can take comfort in the fact that they were not the first to blow the big story based on faulty survey data. A *Literary Digest* survey predicted in 1936 that Kansas Governor Alf Landon would beat incumbent President Franklin D. Roosevelt by a margin of 57 to 43 percent. Roosevelt won reelection in a landslide. Twelve years later, an even more memorable blunder occurred. Most of the nation's pollsters boldly predicted that New York Governor Thomas E. Dewey would easily defeat President Harry Truman in the 1948 election. However, Truman won by more than 2 million votes. Out-of-date samples were to blame in both survey disasters. The pollsters failed to take into account major shifts in the make-up of the population.

The lesson of these and other Novembers is that a survey is only as good as the sample on which it is based. Just ask the networks.

And informal results aren't necessarily worthless. To the contrary, they provide an indication of what public attitudes may be—within the limitations of the sample. In this case, those limitations are the size of your sample and the fact that not everyone in the nation has an equal opportunity of being chosen for questioning. You would not be able to say that your classroom poll was an accurate reflection of national opinion. However, if everyone in your class had the same opportunity to express his or her opinion, those results would be representative of the class' views on gun control.

How big should the sample be? No one answer is correct. Nor does a simple explanation exist. At issue here are what statisticians call **confidence levels,** the statistical degree to which we can reasonably assume the outcome is an accurate reflection of the entire population. As a general rule, the larger the sample, the more accurate the outcome is. However, we do come to a point where additional numbers do not significantly improve accuracy. Statistical accuracy within two or three percentage points is usually the best one can hope for. That is why most nationwide surveys are limited to around two thousand respondents. The people who administer those surveys have found that the heightened accuracy obtained by adding more to the sample does not justify the additional cost.

DEVELOPING A SAMPLING STRATEGY.   Developing a sampling strategy is a step critical to the administration of an accurate survey. Sampling can be as much an act of creativity as writing the survey instrument itself. However, as mentioned earlier, it is not always possible or practical to administer a formal survey. Issues such as cost, time, and staffing often come into play. Before we discuss some of the more common sampling strategies, a few definitions are in order:

- **sample:** the segment of a population or public a researcher studies to draw conclusions about the public as a whole.

- **sampling frame:** the actual list from which the sample, or some stage of the sample, is drawn. The sampling frame is important because the accuracy of your list will affect the accuracy of the survey. For example, using the local telephone book as a sampling frame excludes people who have unlisted telephone numbers and people who cannot afford telephone service. As a result, the survey may underrepresent the attitudes of either the very rich or the very poor. Survey results should always be reported in the context of the limitations of their sampling frame.

- **units of analysis:** what or whom you are studying to create a summary description of all such units. It is important to be clear about units of analysis because you don't want to make a common error in analyzing results—comparing apples to oranges. The results of a survey of attitudes of students in your classroom should not be used to describe the attitudes of all students because the units of analysis in your sample were students in your classroom, not all students. The views of students in your classroom may not be representative of those of all students.

- **probability sampling:** the process of selecting a sample that is representative of the population or public being studied. The sample is considered to be representative when it is large enough and when all members of that population or public have an equal chance of being selected for the sample. Usually within a few percentage points, known as the sampling error, the results of a survey of a representative sample are considered an accurate reflection of the sampling frame.

- **nonprobability sampling:** the process of selecting a sizable sample without regard to whether everyone in the public has an equal chance of being selected. This sampling technique is often chosen because of time, cost, or personnel considerations. This does not mean that the results are without value. To the contrary, nonprobability sampling results can give researchers an indication of public opinion. However, those results cannot be said to be an accurate reflection of the attitudes of any particular public.

It is important for you to understand these concepts because they are central to your selection of a sampling strategy. The challenge of survey research is to use a sampling technique that serves two masters: a desire for accuracy and a need to achieve it in a logistically realistic and cost-effective manner. Using some techniques, it is possible to be both accurate *and* cost effective.

NONPROBABILITY SAMPLING.   In the real world of public relations, practitioners are often challenged to conduct survey research with little time, money, or staffing at their disposal. This often leads to using a form of nonprobability sampling known as **convenience sampling**—the administration of an informal survey based on the availability of subjects. As the name suggests, this approach has the advantage of being easy to do. However, it also sacrifices accuracy.

The so-called person-on-the-street interviews seen in newspapers and on television are examples of convenience sampling. Reporters often ask a "question of the day" to passersby in an attempt to gauge the mood of their community on a particular topic. But instead of getting an accurate picture of community attitudes, these reporters are only measuring the opinions of the people who happen to be walking by that spot at that time. A reporter standing on an inner-city sidewalk may get answers to questions about the state of the economy that differ greatly from answers obtained in a suburban shopping mall. Even the time of day can make a difference. Women who work at home and do their shopping during the day may have attitudes that differ from those of women who work outside the home and shop at night.

Does this mean that data obtained from an informal survey are useless? No, it doesn't. Data obtained from such a survey can provide an *indication* of public opinion. The more indicators you have pointing in the same direction, the greater the chance that your data are accurate. For example, if the aforementioned reporter gets the same answers in both inner-city and suburban locations, it is more likely that these answers accurately reflect the community's attitudes toward the state of the economy.

In the same breath, however, we'd like to repeat that all informal surveys should be taken with a grain of salt. In and of itself, an informal survey should not be considered an accurate picture of reality. At best, it is just one interpretation of the world, an interpretation that may or may not be correct. The only way our mythical on-the-street reporter can gauge the community's attitudes toward the economy is to conduct formal survey research using a sample representative of the entire community.

PROBABILITY SAMPLING.   When planning to conduct formal probability sampling, you have a choice of several techniques. All of them have one important element in common: *Every person within the sampling frame has an equal chance of being selected for the sample.* In other words, surveys based on these sampling techniques have a high probability of being an accurate reflection of public opinion. These are some of the most common probability sampling strategies used by public relations practitioners:

■ **Simple random sampling** (Figure 7.2) is the most basic form of probability sampling. But often it is not practical. Simple random sampling involves assigning a number to every person within the sampling frame. By making a random selection of numbers, as in drawing numbers out of a hat, you develop a representative sample. However, think how tedious it would be to assign a number to every name in the local telephone book. Because simple random sampling can be a cumbersome process, especially with large sampling frames, this technique is seldom used in practice.

■ **Systematic sampling** (Figure 7.3) is a more practical approach to probability sampling. Through a standardized selection process, it is possible to create a sample that is both representative and easy to develop. At its most basic level, systematic sampling involves the selection of every Kth member of a sampling frame. For example, let us assume that your college or university has 25,000 students. The sampling frame for your survey is a computer printout of enrolled students. If you are seeking a sample

FIGURE 7.2   Simple Random Sampling
In this example, every individual is assigned a number—in this case, a number from 1 to 100. To achieve a sample of 20 individuals, 20 numbers are selected at random.

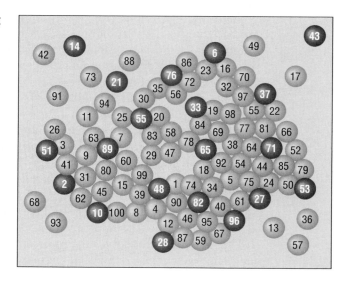

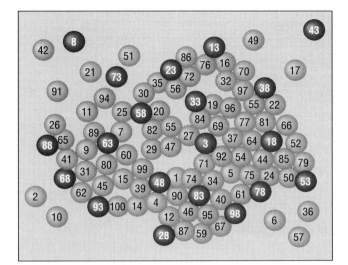

FIGURE 7.3   Systematic Sampling In this example, we want to achieve a sample size of 20. There are 100 individuals in the sampling frame. The value of K is 100/20, or 5. Therefore, we pick every fifth individual for our sample.

of 250 names from a sampling frame of 25,000, then K = 25,000/250, or 100. In this scenario, you would select every 100th name from the enrollment printout for the sample. Compare this with the work involved in simple random sampling, and it is easy to see why many researchers choose to go this route.

■ It is often hard to identify a perfect sampling frame. Although a city telephone directory gives you the names of most city residents, it excludes those who do not have a telephone, who tend to be poor, and those with unlisted numbers, who tend to have higher incomes. In this case, the extremely rich and extremely poor may be underrepresented. One way to overcome a flaw in a sampling frame is by using what is known as **cluster sampling** (Figure 7.4). This technique involves breaking the population into homogeneous clusters and then selecting the sample from individual clusters. For example, pretend that you are interested in conducting research on how men and women differ in their attitudes toward binge drinking. For the sake of this argument, let us also pretend that your sampling frame is students enrolled in public relations courses. If your school is typical of the national trend, there is a strong probability that women will easily outnumber men. To achieve a sample that is half men and half women, you group the students' names into different gender pools and select an equal number of names from each pool. Cluster sampling is generally not as accurate as simple random sampling or systematic sampling. Under certain conditions, however, it can be the most practical.

■ One way to ensure that a sample is an accurate reflection of a specific population is to survey *everyone*. That is what is known as taking a **census** (Figure 7.5)—that is, surveying every member of the sampling frame. A well-known census is the decennial

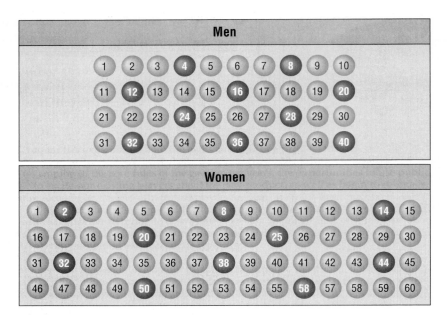

FIGURE 7.4   Cluster Sampling In an attempt to correct an imbalance in the sampling frame, individuals with similar characteristics are clustered. In this example, systematic sampling is used within each cluster to develop a sample containing 10 from each group.

FIGURE 7.5   Census In a census, everyone in the sampling frame is selected.

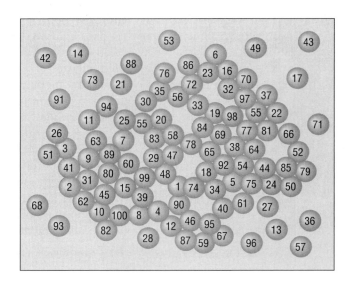

U.S. Census, in which an attempt is made to count and analyze every person living in the United States. Although a properly done census has the advantage of accuracy, this technique comes up short when it comes to practicality. It may be easy to administer a questionnaire to everyone in your class, but how easy would it be for you to survey everyone in your college or university? A major complaint with the U.S. Census is that it is virtually impossible to survey each of the more than 250 million people living in this country. Critics say it is the economically disadvantaged who are most often missing from the final count. That alleged shortcoming is important because the distribution of federal assistance and other services, most often needed by this population, is largely dependent on census data.

Quick ✔ Check

1. What two elements are critical to the administration of an accurate survey?
2. How does a sample differ from a sampling frame?
3. What is the major difference between probability and nonprobability sampling?

The Survey Instrument

Creating a good survey instrument is just as important as having a good survey sample. Even if you identify a sample that is representative of the population you want to study, a faulty questionnaire can render your results meaningless. It is not just *whom* you ask the questions, but also *how* you ask them that matters.

There are many considerations you need to keep in mind when developing survey questions. The questionnaire should use language that is appropriate for and readily understood by the public for whom the survey is intended. Researchers wouldn't ask elementary school students, homeowners, and nuclear scientists the same questions about nuclear power. Each group has a different level of understanding of the issue; therefore, the questions need to be tailored to the knowledge level of each group. In certain situations it may be necessary to provide background information before asking a question.

Questions asked on surveys cannot be vague if they are to have any real meaning. Questions have to be explicit, not indirect. Ask exactly what you want to know. If respondents are guessing at what a question means, their answers cannot serve as an accurate measure of anything (except, of course, of someone's inability to write clear questions).

Use words that have clear and specific meanings. For example, let's consider a question about presidential job performance. Suppose respondents are given the choice of answering the question using these options: gnarly, groovy, super, cool, and awesome. Can these survey results have any real meaning? The problem is that what

QuickBreak 7.4

FIVE WAYS TO ASK QUESTIONS

1. **Contingency questions:** Whether a respondent is expected to answer a specific question is often contingent upon the answer to an earlier question. For example, if a respondent indicates that he or she doesn't like ice cream, it would make no sense to ask that person in the next question to identify his or her favorite flavor of ice cream. Therefore, the second question is a contingency question. Respondents who answer yes about liking ice cream will answer the next question. Those who answer no will be instructed to skip it.

2. **Dichotomous questions:** These are either/or questions such as true/false, yes/no, and positive/negative. They are sometimes used to set up contingency questions. In the previously cited example, a no answer would make it unnecessary for the respondent to answer the next question about favorite flavor. The respondent would be instructed to skip that question.

3. **Rating scale questions:** These questions measure the range, degree, or intensity of attitudes, something a dichotomous question cannot do. An example of a rating scale question is one that news and polling organizations often ask about the president's job performance. Respondents are asked to respond to the statement "I think the presi-

dent is doing a good job." Their options are to strongly agree with the statement, agree, disagree, strongly disagree, or express no opinion. These kinds of questions can give researchers a more detailed read on public opinion than dichotomous questions can provide.

4. **Open-ended questions:** These questions don't define a range of possible answers (called a response set). In other words, the respondent is left to fill in the blank. Answers to these questions can provide detailed information. However, they are the most difficult to analyze because they can't be tabulated as quickly as answers to questions in which the response set is specifically defined.

5. **Closed-ended questions:** These are questions in which the response set is specifically defined. To put it another way, respondents are required to select their answer from a predetermined menu of options. The risk with these questions is that researchers may leave out certain options or may overemphasize other options. Another problem to watch for is answers that overlap slightly. However, these questions are significantly easier to analyze than open-ended questions.

may be gnarly to one person could be groovy to another. For the survey results to have real meaning, the words used in the survey must have precise definitions. A good survey instrument also keeps the questionnaire reasonably short. The longer the survey, the more likely that people will decline to participate because they "don't have the time."

Avoid bias in the wording or ordering of questions. The manner in which a question is worded can influence the response. Even the placement of the question can influence responses to questions that follow. For example, suppose you are answering a survey that poses a series of questions about high taxes, then asks, "What is the most important issue facing government today?" Because of the earlier questions, you may be primed to answer, "High taxes, of course!"

Don't ask objectionable questions. Even the most sensitive information can be obtained if questions are worded tactfully. Also, save the toughest questions for last. Asking the toughest questions first could abruptly end the process or bias subsequent responses. Demographic questions regarding matters such as age, income, and political affiliation can also be sensitive. Often, researchers place demographic questions at the end of the questionnaire in the belief that members of the sample won't skip them because they've already invested time in filling out the rest of the survey.

A way to avoid problems is to pretest the questionnaire. If the survey instrument has any bugs, it is best to find them before distributing surveys on a large scale. Run a small test first to make sure that the questions are understandable, all biases corrected, and objectionable questions removed.

When it comes time to administer the survey, logistics must be considered as well. Can the personnel requirements be met? Can the survey be administered within the desired time frame? Does the survey plan fit into the budget? The people who administer the survey, the data collectors, must be trained. Without training, data collectors could inadvertently influence the outcome of the survey. They should be trained to administer the survey the same way every time. Collectors should also know how to answer respondent questions about the survey. One wrong answer could blow the whole thing! Will they use the telephone, or meet with members of the sample face to face? Or, as is common, will you simply mail out the survey and dispense with data collectors?

Analyzing Survey Results

Once all the data are collected, the time has come to analyze and report the results. This is a public relations text, not a statistics text, so any attempt at this point to offer a detailed explanation of statistical analysis would not do the subject justice. However, we do not want to ignore the subject entirely. Raw data without structure or purpose are meaningless. Analysis gives data context so that their meaning can be understood.

The truth is that the overwhelming majority of practitioners never conduct survey research. Instead, they pay someone else to do it for them. That's OK. But how do you know whether the research you are buying is good? That's why this discussion of sampling and questionnaire development is important. If you plan to make a career in public relations, you need to be a good consumer of this and all kinds of research.

For the purposes of this discussion, let us start with two basic definitions:

- **attributes:** characteristics or qualities that describe an object. In the case of an individual, attributes can be gender, age, weight, height, political affiliation, church affiliation, and so on.
- **variables:** a logical grouping of qualities that describe a particular attribute. Variables must be exhaustive (incorporating all possible qualities) and mutually exclusive. For example, the variables associated with the attribute of gender are female and male.

The purpose of analysis is to get a clearer picture from the data. The deeper the analysis, the clearer the picture. The most basic form of analysis is **univariate analysis.** As the name suggests, it is the examination of only one variable. An example of a univariate analysis would be the examination of responses to the question Do you like ice cream? By counting the responses to that question, we would know the total number of people who said yes and the total number who said no. But that is all that we would know.

If we were to examine the same question using two variables, however, the results would become more meaningful. This is what is known as **bivariate analysis.** A bivariate analysis of the question Do you like ice cream? could look at two variables: whether respondents like ice cream and the respondents' gender. We might find that men answer the question differently from women. That, in turn, could affect a variety of marketing decisions.

If we turn to **multivariate analysis,** the examination of three or more variables, our survey results would have even greater depth. Carrying our example to its logical conclusion, let's add the variable of age to our analysis of the ice cream question. Such an analysis could find that younger men and older women like ice cream more than their counterparts in other age groups. If our goal is to promote the sale of ice cream, these results suggest that we need to work harder to attract younger women and older men to the frozen delight. That information is far more valuable to us than only knowing the raw numbers.

Although this sounds like pretty complicated stuff, it really isn't. You use statistical analysis all the time. When you take pride in the knowledge that your college basketball team has lost only one game all year on its home court, you have done a bivariate analysis—comparing the variables of victories and game locations. And when you note that your team hasn't lost a conference game at home this season, you have added a third variable, conference membership. That is a multivariate analysis. (It makes you look at ESPN basketball analyst Dick Vitale in a much different light, doesn't it?)

Again, we acknowledge that this is an elementary approach to a very complex subject. If you are interested in numbers-crunching, more power to you. Take some research and statistics courses. However, if you don't see yourself in that role, please remember that this information is offered as a reminder that survey analysis is conducted on many levels and can yield a lot of valuable information.

Back to City Hospital

Let's close by returning to the City Hospital scenario that opened this chapter. What would be your first steps in addressing the public relations problems and opportunities before you? We hope you'd begin determining your research strategy by asking those two all-important questions:

1. What do I want to know?
2. How will I gather that information?

You'd soon decide, perhaps, that you want to know what the values of the hospital are as articulated in its mission statement. You'd want to know who the key stakeholder groups are and what they think of both City Hospital and its new competition. You'd also want to learn as much as you could about City Hospital. And you'd want to learn as much as possible about the hospital's new competition. Finally, you'd want to learn what the desired outcome of this situation is—so you can measure your ultimate success.

Where will you find the answers to those questions? Both primary and secondary research would be useful in this scenario. You'd start with secondary research—but, if resources allow, you'd certainly do primary research as well. An initial survey of the opinions of important stakeholder groups seems appropriate. And how might you use focus groups?

After your public relations plan has been executed, you may want to survey the important stakeholder groups again to see whether you have changed any opinions or strengthened any relationships. And that suggestion brings us full circle in this chapter. With that second survey, you'd be using research to conduct evaluation—and that evaluation may well prompt new research that launches a new public relations campaign on a newly discovered issue. As we noted earlier, research and evaluation are intertwined in values-driven public relations.

Quick ✔ Check

1. When writing a survey questionnaire, what should you consider in wording questions?
2. What are some of the logistical considerations you should take into account before administering a survey?
3. What are the differences among a univariate analysis, a bivariate analysis, and a multivariate analysis? Why would you want to do any of them?

Summary

As organizations become more results-oriented, public relations practitioners are increasingly expected to defend their decisions and measure the effectiveness of the actions they propose. That is why research is critical to the practice of public relations. Research enables a practitioner to understand a client, the problems/opportunities facing the client, and the stakeholders important to the client's success. Evaluation research enables a practitioner to determine the success of communication strategies and the strength of relationships.

Not all research is created equal. Formal research has the advantage of providing a more accurate picture of reality. However, conducting informal research may be necessary because of time, cost, or staffing considerations. Although not as accurate a reflection of reality, informal research results still can help you piece together a picture of the world. Before embarking on research, it is important to have a clear understanding of what kinds of information you are seeking and what is the best way for you to gather it. That is known as developing your research strategy.

The five most common forms of public relations research are secondary (library) research, feedback research, communication audits, focus groups, and surveys. Secondary research is making use of material generated by someone else, sometimes for a purpose other than that for which it was originally intended. Feedback research involves analyzing both solicited and unsolicited communications an organization receives from its stakeholders. Communication audits indicate whether an organization's communications are consistent with its values-driven mission and goals. Focus groups are an informal research method in which a small group of people are brought together to discuss their values, concerns, needs, attitudes, and predispositions. The successful use of survey research depends on both a good sample and a good survey instrument or questionnaire. The value of survey research is that, when properly conducted and analyzed, it provides a reasonably accurate snapshot of reality. That, in turn, provides a solid foundation for a public relations plan.

DISCUSSION QUESTIONS

1. How might evaluation research be used to launch a new public relations campaign?
2. Which research should you ordinarily conduct first: primary research or secondary research? Why?
3. How is issues management a part of problem–opportunity research?
4. Why aren't focus groups necessarily representative of a larger public?
5. What is the difference between probability sampling and nonprobability sampling? What is the advantage of probability sampling? Is nonprobability sampling without value?
6. Using the City Hospital scenario at the beginning of this chapter, what research technique(s) would you use to discover the attitudes and opinions of one of the key stakeholders? Which stakeholder would you select and why? What kinds of information would you seek?

Memo *from the* **Field**

Dr. Walter K. Lindenmann, Independent Consultant and Former Director of Research, Ketchum Public Relations Worldwide

Independent public relations consultant Walter K. Lindenmann created the Communications Research and Measurement Department for Ketchum, an international public relations agency. When he retired in 2000 after 12 years with Ketchum, *PRNews* wrote, "His efforts for the past couple decades have helped make measurement the priority it is throughout the PR community." To honor Lindenmann's service, Ketchum renamed its SMART Award scholarship, for graduate students in public relations, the Walter Lindenmann Award.

During his career Walter Lindenmann has supervised more than 1,200 research projects in public relations, marketing, and advertising, most of them for large corporations, financial service organizations, trade associations, government agencies, utilities, charitable organizations, and education and health groups. He also has extensive experience in designing and executing research projects aimed at measuring the effectiveness of public relations programs and activities. In 1999 he was named chairman of the newly formed Commission on PR Measurement and Evaluation of the Institute for Public Relations.

A sociologist with a Ph.D. from Columbia University, Lindenmann has lectured and conducted seminars throughout the world.

Experienced public relations practitioners—no matter where they work, whether in the corporate sector, not-for-profit groups, trade and professional associations, the health-care industry, government, counseling firms, or schools or academic institutions—have come to recognize that public relations cannot ever be carried out effectively without some type of research being conducted.

Research is essential for public relations planning, program development, tracking, monitoring, and evaluation. It also is quite crucial when an organization needs to obtain information quickly in order to deal with a crisis. If public relations activities are carried out without any research at all, then the public relations practitioner ends up operating in the dark, without any insights and without necessary background information.

For most public relations practitioners, research usually takes one of two forms—secondary or primary. As the name implies, secondary research examines studies that have been done by others in the past. More specifically, secondary analysis is a technique for extracting from previously conducted opinion studies new knowledge on topics other than those that were the focus of the original studies. Secondary analysis does this through a systematic reanalysis of a vast array of already existing research data.

There are literally hundreds of sources that public relations practitioners can turn to for secondary data. In addition to examining newsletters, reference books, trade association materials, and library files, practitioners can extract an extensive amount of already existing data from the Internet and from such government sources as the U.S. Census Bureau and the U.S. Bureau of Labor Statistics.

Primary research involves conducting original studies. Data collection techniques that public relations practitioners rely on when carrying out original research include conducting a census, doing computer-assisted self-interviewing, carrying out focus groups and face-to-face interviews, conducting mail surveys, conducting Internet polling, and much, much more.

In recent years an increasing number of public relations practitioners have been using research as a means of measuring the effectiveness of their public relations programs and activities. Sometimes cynics question whether one can really measure the impact of public relations.

In my professional judgment, public relations effectiveness can most definitely be measured, if one sets clear and precise targeted goals and objectives in advance of a public relations project or activity. It is impossible to assess the success or failure of anything unless you have something specific to measure that failure or success against.

If a public relations practitioner sets a vague goal of hoping to have people somehow become better informed about his or her organization, the success or failure of the consequent public relations efforts will be very hard to measure. However, if the practitioner knows through research that perhaps only 40 percent of a given audience segment is well informed about something related to his or her organization, and if the practitioner wants to improve that well-informed portion to, say, 50 percent, then it is possible to measure success or failure in reaching that specific objective.

It is not at all difficult to measure individual components of public relations, such as the success or failure of a publicity campaign, the effectiveness of a community relations program, or the impact of an investor relations event or speakers' program. If goals and objectives are well defined in advance and are spelled out as precisely as possible, then measurement of results is possible.

Case Study 7.1

Sowing Seeds of Discontent

It is known as the "Terminator" and has nothing to do with Arnold Schwarzenegger's classic sci-fi movie. But to many farmers and environmentalists around the world, it is just as scary.

We are not talking about killer robots. This Terminator is a genetically engineered seed designed to render the seeds of its offspring sterile. Doing so blocks farmers from saving the seeds and ensures that agribusiness companies have a steady source of income.

To companies such as Monsanto, the world's second-largest seed company, Terminator technology seemed to make good business sense. By developing seeds resistant to its own herbicides, Monsanto was creating markets for both products. But developing the technology costs millions of dollars. The Terminator—officially known as Technology Protection System—was designed to protect that investment.

However, some have not shared Monsanto's enthusiasm. "The small farmers in the developing world who still rely extensively on their ability to hold back their seeds . . . who can get wiped out by one bad season, would suddenly find themselves with no seeds for the next year and no money to buy new seeds," said Ismael Serageldin of the World Bank.[11]

To others, the environmental risks of this technology are even greater. Some environmentalists fear that cross pollination of genetically altered crops with those in neighboring fields could result in widespread crop damage. An even broader concern is that the spread of Terminator technology could result in a lack of biodiversity, which, in turn, could result in crop failures and famine.

During the late 1990s, Monsanto and the Terminator became the target of a broad coalition of scientists, farmers, and environmentalists. The catalyst of this opposition was Monsanto's decision to purchase a Mississippi company that, along with the U.S. Department of Agriculture, had developed the Terminator. Monsanto, which was already under fire for its aggressive efforts to keep farmers from saving seeds, appeared to be cornering the seed market. For the opponents of Terminator technology, those factors, as well as the company's close ties to regulators in Washington, cast Monsanto in the role of a villain.

For many, the controversy over Terminator technology became symbolic of a much broader debate over the use of genetically modified (GM) food. As one of the leaders in research and development of GM food, Monsanto found itself in the center of a political firestorm. "In Europe and developing countries, genetic engineering is viewed not just as scientific advancement but as a social force that controls people and what they grow," the *St. Louis Post-Dispatch* reported. "For those who think that way, the Terminator has become a powerful symbol."[12]

In October 1998, scientists and farm economists at the World Bank in Washington voted to ban the use of the Terminator in their projects. The USDA received more than 2,000 letters and e-mails from 55 nations opposing its use.[13]

Another issue that dogged Monsanto was consumer safety. Research on the long-term effects of GM food was inconclusive. Undaunted, the company proclaimed the safety of its products in public statements and advertising. But those tactics came under attack. The United Kingdom Advertising Standards Authority (ASA) accused Monsanto of misleading the public about the safety of GM products. The

ASA upheld 81 complaints about misleading newspaper advertisements. It was particularly critical of the company's claims that its GM tomatoes were proven to be safe, even though the tomato had not been approved in 20 countries and was not available in the United Kingdom.[14]

Monsanto was publicly embarrassed when an environmental group disclosed that the caterers at the company's British headquarters had banned some GM foods from the employee canteen. "In response to concern raised by our customers, we have taken the decision to remove, as far as it is practicable, GM soya and maize from all food products in our restaurant," the food service announced in a written statement.[15]

"Of course this is amusing," said Friends of the Earth spokesman Neil Verlander. "But there is a serious point: the extent to which there has been an outcry against GM foods in this country."[16]

Time also awarded Monsanto the dubious distinction of having the year's worst public relations, saying "the firm acted more like a chemical company than a food giant and failed to convince consumers of the benefits of GM products."[17]

On October 6, 1999, Monsanto Chairman Robert Shapiro announced that the company would not pursue commercial development of Terminator technology. Shapiro also accepted personal blame for his company's poor public relations performance. As if to give special emphasis to his *mea culpa*, Shapiro made his remarks at a Greenpeace business conference in London.

"We started with the conviction that biotechnology was useful," Shapiro said. "We have tended to see it as our task to convince people that we were right and that people with different points of view were wrong. We have irritated and antagonized more people than we persuaded. Too often we forgot to listen."[18]

As part of its attempt at public outreach, the company introduced "The New Monsanto Pledge," which included a commitment to "dialogue, transparency, respect, sharing, and delivering benefits."[19] The company also created a series of advisory panels so it could open a dialogue with a variety of stakeholders.

"Monsanto's decision is at least a recognition that it has heard the public outcry and that the public has a role in how the technology develops," said Dr. Jane Rissler of the Union of Concerned Scientists. "The biotech industry up to now has been ignoring public opinion."[20]

DISCUSSION QUESTIONS

1. Could Monsanto have avoided public controversy over the Terminator without undermining its own business interests and values?
2. Is it wrong for companies such as Monsanto to aggressively protect their business interests in the face of a consumer backlash?
3. What methods of research would you have conducted if you were in charge of the company's public relations?
4. Did Monsanto cave in to public pressure at the expense of its belief in production of genetically modified food products?
5. What do you think the Monsanto pledge means by "transparency"?

Case Study 7.2

Fighting Back with Facts

Do you know anybody who drinks to get drunk? If you don't, your experience may soon change. Recent research suggests that your chances of knowing a binge drinker are improving.

Research at more than 100 U.S. colleges found that frequent binge drinking among students increased during the 1990s. For the purposes of the study, conducted by the Harvard School of Public Health, *binge drinking* is defined as five drinks in a row for males and four drinks in a row for females. A *drink* was defined as 12 ounces of beer or wine cooler, 4 ounces of wine or a 1.25-ounce shot of liquor. During the 1999 study, more than 42 percent said they had been binge drinking within two weeks of the survey. Twenty-three percent said they went on a binge at least *three* times in the two weeks prior to the survey.[21]

The problem of binge drinking on college campuses is not about a traditional rite of passage into adulthood. It's about young people dying. A 1997 incident at Louisiana State University brought the problem into focus for many. A 20-year-old fraternity pledge started drinking before a football game. And he drank at the frat house after the game, despite a university ban on alcohol. The celebration then moved to a local bar. Shortly after returning to the fraternity house, he died. His blood-alcohol level was .588 percent, nearly six times higher than the minimum required for proof of intoxication.[22]

An isolated incident? Hardly. Every year brings new tragedies. A student at the University of Illinois was found dead by roommates, presumably of alcohol poisoning. An intoxicated Cornell University student fell down a gorge and died. At Michigan State University, a student died after downing two dozen shots at a birthday celebration. At Pennsylvania State University, a woman was found clinging to life on her 21st birthday, her blood-alcohol level nearly seven times the legal limit. And all this happened during the first month of the fall 1999 semester.[23]

The good news is that the truth can save lives. At Hobart and Williams College in Geneva, New York, researchers have discovered that college students drink less when they learn their classmates drink less. That message is the basis of a model program that resulted in a 21 percent reduction in drinking on the Hobart and Williams campus over a two-year period.

"No matter how much alcohol is being consumed, students almost uniformly across campuses exaggerate what they think is typical of their peers," said Professor Wesley Perkins of Hobart and Williams.[24]

To change this misconception, Hobart and Williams officials incorporate alcohol research findings into "campus factoids" displayed on campus computer screen savers. They use an electronic media campaign and incorporate alcohol-abuse awareness issues into the classroom. They have also received federal funds to expand the program to other schools.

Professor Terry L. Rentner, head of the public relations sequence at Bowling Green State University (Ohio), decided to use Perkins' research to tackle the problem of binge drinking on her campus. But she chose to go about it in a nontraditional manner.

"Most universities have developed educational programs which address alcohol related issues," Rentner said. "Those programs convey information about the physical and psychological effects of alcohol, and they are designed for a mass audience."

"They usually are not effective."[25]

The Bowling Green approach, which has been judged by the U.S. Department of Education as one of the top six in the country, attacks the problem on a smaller, more targeted scale. The program focuses on small groups of students considered at high risk for binge drinking. Those groups have included freshmen, athletes, and members of fraternities and sororities. In small groups, students are asked to complete a survey on how much alcohol they consume and how much they think their peers consume. After the surveys are tabulated, a second meeting is held to discuss the results.

"Without fail, students think their peers are drinking more than they actually are," Rentner said. She said that once the truth is exposed, students feel less pressure to drink to "fit in."[26]

The program appears to be working. During a two-year period in which binge drinking rose by 4 percent nationwide, the rate dropped by 2.5 percent on the BGSU campus. Rentner does not take full credit for the improvement, noting that the program is part of a comprehensive community–campus effort to curb binge drinking.

The battle is also being waged on other fronts. At Dartmouth College, students returned to campus to find advertisements describing a campus survey conclusion: 58 percent of students don't think alcohol is important to have at a party. The University of Arizona has been spreading the word that most students don't drink heavily. Approximately 1,600 resident assistants at the 15 state universities in Michigan have been trained in alcohol intervention. The University of Delaware, as well as other schools, contacts parents when students violate alcohol policies.[27]

To their credit, many student organizations have chosen to tackle the problem, as well. One example can be found at Michigan State, which has established a vigorous anti-alcohol campaign. Following a binge-drinking death and an alcohol-fueled riot, many in MSU's Greek community sobered up. The taps have been turned off.

"Our overall living conditions improved," said Lambda Chi fraternity member Ben Glime. "Our overall academic [grade point average] went up."[28]

DISCUSSION QUESTIONS

1. Why do you think the authors of this book placed this case study at the end of the chapter on research and evaluation?

2. What makes the alcohol-abuse program at Bowling Green State University different from traditional programs? What prevents more colleges and universities from taking this approach?

3. What are some of the research methods cited in this case?
4. Is binge drinking a problem on your campus? How do you know? How can you find out? Are any programs addressing the issue; if so, how effective are they?

It's Your Turn

Tinker, Evers & Chance

Your public relations agency has been retained by the noted accounting firm Tinker, Evers & Chance. It is the community's largest accounting firm and has been for nearly 20 years. In recent years, however, Tinker, Evers & Chance's billings have grown only 2 percent annually, a rate far below the industry average.

Two weeks ago one of the firm's major clients switched its account to a nationwide accounting company that just opened a local branch office. That same company has also lured away several of Tinker, Evers & Chance's most promising junior partners.

Hiring your public relations agency was the idea of Pat Tinker, one of three senior partners. Tinker owns 50 percent of the firm, so the others agreed to go along— reluctantly. Today is the first time you have met with all three senior partners.

"People just don't know who we are anymore," Tinker said. "What we need is a new image."

"Tinker, Evers & Chance has a great image in this community," senior partner Paula Evers counters. "I doubt that any slick public relations gimmicks will do us any good."

The third senior partner, Frank Chance, takes his opposition a step further. "Good accountants don't need an image," Chance argues. "Good accountants get all the business they need by word of mouth."

After this testy exchange, all eyes in the room are on you. Tinker looks you square in the eye and says, "What's your first move?"

■ What *is* your first move?

■ What do you need to know about the firm?

■ Who are the major stakeholders, and what kind of information do you want from them?

■ How can you show the reluctant partners whether public relations can make a difference?

KEY TERMS

attributes, p. 222
bivariate analysis, p. 222
census, p. 217

client research, p. 202
closed-ended questions, p. 220
cluster sampling, p. 217

commitment, p. 203

communal relationship, p. 203

communication audits, p. 206

communications grid, p. 208

components of relationships, p. 203

confidence levels, p. 214

contingency questions, p. 220

control mutuality, p. 203

convenience sampling, p. 215

dichotomous questions, p. 220

evaluation, p. 198

evaluation research, p. 204

exchange relationship, p. 203

feedback research, p. 206

focus groups, p. 209

formal research, p. 205

informal research, p. 205

issues management, p. 200

monitoring, p. 200

multivariate analysis, p. 222

nonprobability sampling, p. 215

open-ended questions, p. 220

outcomes, p. 203

outputs, p. 203

primary research, p. 206

probability sampling, p. 214

problem–opportunity research, p. 204

rating scale questions, p. 220

representative sample, p. 212

research, p. 198

research strategy, p. 202

sample, p. 214

sampling frame, p. 214

satisfaction, p. 203

scanning, p. 200

secondary research, p. 205

simple random sampling, p. 216

stakeholder research, p. 202

survey research, p. 212

systematic sampling, p. 216

trust, p. 203

units of analysis, p. 214

univariate analysis, p. 222

variables, p. 222

NOTES

1. Betsy Wiesendanger, "A Research Roundup," *Public Relations Journal* (May 1994): 23.

2. "Six Ways to Use Research," *Public Relations Journal* (May 1994): 26–27.

3. Walter K. Lindenmann, "Public Relations Research: A Look at What's Happening on the Commercial Side of the Fence" (paper presented at the 1993 AEJMC conference).

4. Linda Childers Hon and James E. Grunig, "Guidelines for Measuring Relationships in Public Relations," Institute of Public Relations, 1999, online, www.instituteforpr.com.

5. "Profile 2000—A Survey of the Profession," *Communication World* (June–July 2000): A15–A17.

6. "Bronze Anvil Winners 1995: Research Category," *Public Relations Tactics* (July 1995): 18.

7. Brad Edmondson, "How to Spot a Bogus Poll," *American Demographics* (October 1996): 10–15.

8. Rich Noyes, "How Election Night Became a Sit-Com," Human Events Online, 17 November 2000, www.humaneventsonline.com/articles/11-17-00/noyes.html.

9. Noyes.

10. "Polling Service Errors Distorted Florida Election Night Projections, VNS Report Says," online, CNN Interactive, 22 December 2000, www.cnn.com.

11. Erin Hayes, "Seeds of Controversy," ABC News, 2 August 1999, online, www.abcnews.com.

12. Bill Lambrecht, "Critics Vilify New Seed Technology That Monsanto May Soon Control," *St. Louis Post-Dispatch,* 1 November 1998, online, http://home. post-dispatch.com.

13. Lambrecht.

14. "U.K. Slams Monsanto Publicity," *Chemical Week,* 12 April 2000, online, www. findarticles.com.

15. Lyndsay Griffiths, "Double Standard? Monsanto's British HQ Caterer Bans Genetically Modified Food," Reuters, 22 December 1999, online, www.abcnews.com.

16. Griffiths.

17. "The Best (and Worst) of 1999," *Time,* 20 December 1999, online, www.time.com.

18. John Vidal, "We Forgot to Listen, Says Monsanto," *The Guardian,* 7 October 1999, online, www.guardian.co.uk.

19. "The New Monsanto Pledge," Monsanto web site, www.monsanto.com.

20. " 'Terminator' Victory a Small Step in a Long War," online, Environmental News Network, 7 October 1999, www.enn.com (as posted on CNN Interactive).

21. "Frequent Binge Drinking Rises among U.S. College Students, but Abstaining Also Increases," online, CNN Interactive, 14 March 2000, www.cnn.com.

22. "Fraternity Closed, Bar Cited after LSU Drinking Death," online, CNN Interactive, 12 September 1997, www.cnn.com.

23. "College Binge Drinking Kills," About: The Human Internet, 22 September 1999, http://alcoholism.about.com.library/weekly/aa990922.htm.

24. "Frequent Binge Drinking Rises among U.S. College Students, but Abstaining Also Increases."

25. "BGSU Program to Curb Binge Drinking to Serve as National Model," Bowling Green State University News Service, 2 November 1999, online, www.bgsu.edu/offices/pr/ news/1999/binge.html.

26. "BGSU Program to Curb Binge Drinking to Serve as National Model."

27. "College Binge Drinking Kills."

28. "College Town Takes Sober Look at Drinking Problem," online, CNN Interactive, 8 March 1999, www.cnn.com.

chapter eight

Planning: The Strategies of Public Relations

objectives

After studying this chapter, you will be able to

- describe the different kinds of public relations plans

- discuss why public relations practitioners create plans

- explain the process of creating a public relations plan

- summarize the qualities of a good plan

- explain where and how values enter into the planning process

The Art of Planning

scenario

You're the director of public relations for an art museum in a city in the south-western United States. Your museum is renowned for its collection of contemporary Native American art, but the museum also has other, diverse artwork and a growing national reputation.

Like many successful public relations operations, your three-person staff has a well-organized issues-management process. You're constantly scanning the environment for potential problems and opportunities. When you spot a potential issue, you monitor it to see whether action is desirable. Last week, you discovered a possible issue: One of your assistants attended a luncheon sponsored by the Hispanic American Leadership Conference. During dessert, a participant asked her why the museum didn't promote Hispanic artists. Another participant overheard the question and agreed that the museum tended to overlook Hispanic artists.

At your weekly issues-management meeting, you and your team discuss that possible perception within your city's Hispanic community. You agree to monitor the situation. Two days later, another staff member shows you an advertisement that a local corporation placed in Hispanic Plus, *a national magazine that targets graduating seniors. The ad boasts of the exciting Hispanic influence on your city's cultural attractions. Your museum is not mentioned in the ad's list of cultural highlights.*

You're puzzled, because the museum recently hosted a very successful exhibition on mid-20th-century Mexican artists Frida Kahlo and her husband, Diego Rivera. But you're also concerned: Almost one-third of your city's residents are of Hispanic origin. If influential members of that broad public believe that your museum is not serving their interests, consequences for future attendance as well as future budgets could be disastrous. Almost 40 percent of your museum's budget comes from city tax revenues.

You assemble a focus group, and a clearer picture of the potential problem emerges. Members of the focus group loved the Kahlo–Rivera exhibition, but they were unanimous in believing that your museum does nothing to promote Hispanic artists now living and working in your city. Additional in-depth interviews with opinion leaders in the Hispanic public echo that belief. One of the opinion leaders says, "Please don't limit yourself to modern Hispanic art—but don't ignore it, either."

More research turns up some startling misperceptions. You learn that almost 65 percent of your museum's small cash grants to up-and-coming artists went to city residents of Hispanic origin—but that you haven't publicized that fact. And you discover another misperception: The head curator of the museum—herself of Hispanic origin—says to you, "No one can say there's a problem here. We're doing more than enough to support Hispanic-influenced art."

On the wall in your office is a poster that contains the museum's statement of values and its mission statement. One of the values is "Diversity." Below that, part of the mission statement says, "This museum will diligently nurture the artistic interests of the residents of our city."

Given your values-based mission and the damaging misperceptions that your research has revealed, you decide that you must address this emerging problem.

What do you do?

The Basics of Values-Driven Planning

Film critics agree that one of the worst movies ever made is *Plan 9 from Outer Space* (1956), a hilariously inept attempt at a science fiction thriller. The weird plot almost defies description: Space aliens attempt to defeat humanity by raising an army of corpses. Among the goof-ups that draw guffaws from critics and audiences alike are flying saucers that suspiciously resemble spray-painted pie plates (even the strings from which they dangle are visible) and the replacement, in the middle of the film, of the well-known actor Bela Lugosi. Lugosi died after filming began and was replaced by the director's chiropractor, who bore no resemblance to the dead star. Though he hid his face with a cape in most scenes, the chiropractor couldn't disguise the fact that he was almost a foot taller than Lugosi.

Public relations practitioners, however, might offer a different critique of *Plan 9 from Outer Space.* Most would probably agree that the movie is a laughable waste of film—but they might also note that the space aliens' Plan 9 actually had four admirable qualities:

- Plan 9 was *values-driven* (the aliens opposed Earth's development of nuclear weapons).
- Plan 9 was *based on a goal* (although unfortunately the goal was the extermination of the human race).
- Plan 9's desired outcome was *measurable* (the extermination of the human race should be *complete*).
- Plan 9 had a *deadline* (immediately).

What doomed the infamous Plan 9? The aliens underestimated the resourcefulness of the human race. In other words, the planners didn't do their research. And because the previous eight plans from outer space also apparently failed, we can conclude that the aliens did a lousy job of evaluative research as well.

The failure of Plan 9 may have made an enjoyably bad movie, but it does provide a memorable lesson in planning: *A good plan begins with good research.* Let's be even more specific. As we discussed in Chapter 7, the entire public relations process—planning included—begins with (1) client research, (2) stakeholder research, and (3) problem–opportunity research.

We've already seen a version of the research process in The Art of Planning, the scenario that opens this chapter. Scanning and monitoring, which are *problem–opportunity research* techniques, have revealed the Hispanic community's belief that the museum isn't supporting local Hispanic artists. *Client research* has shown that the museum is doing a good job of supporting local Hispanic artists—but that the museum isn't publicizing that success. Last but certainly not least, *stakeholder research* has identified disturbing differences in what key publics think of the situation: Leaders of the Hispanic community think there's a problem; the curator of the museum doesn't.

By this point, you (the public relations director) have studied the issue. You know what the important publics think about it. So you're ready to begin planning, right? Wrong. You still need to answer one more question before you begin planning: *What values-based outcome do you seek?* You're about to take action, so what results do you seek? And will those results be consistent with your organization's values, mission, and goals? In the scenario, the outcome you seek is an improved relationship between your museum and the Hispanic residents of your city. Is that outcome consistent with the museum's values? Indeed it is. One of your organization's stated values is "Diversity." Furthermore, the values-based mission statement poster in your office includes these words: "This museum will diligently nurture the artistic interests of the residents of our community." The improved relationship you seek definitely would help your organization fulfill its mission.

Now you're finally ready for some values-driven planning.

Different Kinds of Public Relations Plans

To attain their organizations' public relations goals, public relations practitioners devise different types of plans. These fall into three basic categories: ad hoc plans, standing plans, and contingency plans.

Ad Hoc Plans

The plan you will create to end the misperceptions surrounding your museum will target a temporary (we hope) situation; therefore it's called an **ad hoc plan.** *Ad hoc* is a Latin phrase that means "for this purpose only." When you and your friends make plans for a party, for example, that's an ad hoc plan. Your plan is important, but it's temporary. It's not something you're going to live with for years (unless your party is truly legendary).

Standing Plans

Because many important relationships are ongoing and long-term, wise organizations have ongoing and long-term plans to nurture those relationships. A plan of this type is often called a **standing plan.** Your museum, for example, probably would devise a standing plan to maintain a positive relationship with Hispanic residents once your ad hoc plan had succeeded.

A weekly newsletter that a multinational corporation publishes for its upper-level managers is part of a standing plan. The newsletter helps the organization fulfill its values-based goal of maintaining a good relationship with some very important employees. Ideally, another part of that standing plan would be frequent opportunities for those upper-level managers to express their concerns to the corporation's top leadership. Remember: Successful public relations is built upon two-way communication and upon an organization's willingness to change when necessary.

One danger of standing plans is that they sometimes stand too long. The plan becomes tradition, and we continue carrying out its directives because, we are told, "That's what we've always done." A plan that stands too long can become divorced from its original values-based goal. For example, we may be publishing a great weekly newsletter for those upper-level managers, but perhaps it's no longer effective because they now need daily, not weekly, updates.

Conducting evaluation research can reduce the danger of obsolete standing plans. As we noted in Chapter 7, evaluation research can help us see whether our plan is meeting its goals. A communication audit, for example, is a form of evaluation research that would examine our organization's communications goals and then check to see how well our communications actions are reaching those goals. An effective communication audit would be the death of an obsolete standing plan.

Contingency Plans

A third kind of public relations plan is called a **contingency plan.** Such plans are used for "what if" scenarios. Through good scanning and monitoring, organizations often spot issues that may require action if they suddenly gather strength. If any such issue has the potential to become powerful, a smart organization prepares a contingency plan. One of the best-known examples of a contingency plan is a crisis communications plan, which is discussed in Chapter 12. Many (though not enough) organizations have a basic crisis communications plan that they practice and can quickly adapt to meet the needs of an emerging crisis.

For example, an animal-feeds manufacturer in Canada recently faced an impending strike by its factory workers. Had the workers walked out, the company's public relations team was prepared to present the company's position immediately to a variety of publics: to the news media (and, through the media, to customers); to non-striking employees; to veterinarians, who often recommend the manufacturer's products; to suppliers; to retailers; to large agricultural customers; and to other key publics. News releases and personal letters were ready to be delivered, a news conference was ready to go, and many other tactics simply awaited the announcement of a strike. The company had taken its standard crisis communications contingency plan and adapted it to the specific circumstance of a factory-worker strike. Fortunately, a last-minute settlement averted the strike. So were all the preparations wasted? No: Planning for possibilities that don't materialize sharpens an organization's readiness for the possibilities that *do* happen.

Despite the different natures of these three kinds of plans—ad hoc, standing, and contingency—they share many characteristics, which we'll discuss next. But one shared characteristic is so important that we'll emphasize it now as well as later: *All public relations plans should be values-driven.* Any public relations plan that you propose should strive to fulfill some area of your organization's values-based mission statement. A good way to win the enthusiastic support of your organization's top managers is to show them exactly how your plan helps to achieve an important business goal. It's not enough to say, "This plan is great! It's going to help us build better relationships with important publics." Instead, show the top managers how those improved relationships help fulfill the organization's values-based mission.

QuickBreak 8.1

PLANNING FOR THE ENTIRE ORGANIZATION

Besides creating ad hoc, standing, and contingency plans, public relations practitioners ideally help create plans at an even higher level: They help determine their organization's values, mission, and specific business goals. Unfortunately, a recent study revealed that 61 percent of public relations practitioners say that top management views them as "implementers" rather than as "strategic planners." However, the same study showed that organizations that *do* view public relations practitioners as strategic planners outperform those that don't.[1]

Public relations practitioners should contribute to organizational planning for two important reasons:

- Realistic values, missions, and business goals depend on a clear understanding of relationships with employees, partners, competitors, and other powerful groups. No organization can achieve its goals without cooperation from its publics. And no one has a better understanding of those essential groups than public relations practitioners.

- A good public relations plan contributes to the fulfillment of an organization's highest aspirations: its values, mission, and business

goals. An organization's public relations team, therefore, must thoroughly understand and eagerly accept those aspirations. The best way for public relations practitioners to achieve understanding and acceptance is to help the organization establish those same values, mission, and business goals. Put this in terms of your own life: You're a lot more likely to support a spring break trip if you get to help plan it.

In a well-run organization, public relations practitioners have frequent and easy access to the organization's top management. That access is particularly important when an organization is creating its values, mission, and business goals. During the 2000 U.S. presidential campaign, *Newsweek* magazine said of Karen Hughes, George W. Bush's press secretary, "She is much more than a press secretary who stays on message. Hughes *believes* the message because she helps to shape it."[2]

The well-informed voice of the public relations team must be heard when an organization is planning its future.

Quick ✔ Check

1. How do an organization's values relate to the public relations planning process?
2. What kinds of research should precede the creation of a public relations plan?
3. What are the three kinds of public relations plans? How do they differ?
4. Why should public relations practitioners help an organization establish its values, mission, and related business goals?

Why Do We Plan?

Effective public relations practitioners spend a great deal of their time making ad hoc, standing, and contingency plans. So it's logical to ask *why?* Why is planning so indispensable to successful public relations? We can think of five good reasons, which we'll detail below.

To Keep Our Actions in Line with Our Organization's Values-Based Mission

As we'll discuss shortly, a good plan is a series of proposed actions designed to produce a specific result. That specific result should advance our organization toward the fulfillment of its values-based mission. Planning prevents random, pointless actions that don't promote our values or our mission. Planning helps us ensure that all our actions are ethical and productive.

Let's put this same philosophy in terms of your own life. Why are you attending college? Chances are, your presence on campus isn't a random action. Instead, your collegiate studies are part of a plan that's consistent with several values in your life: a good education, a good career, and so on. You wouldn't dream of investing so much time and money in something that took you nowhere. It's the same in public relations. We plan in order to avoid waste as we energetically pursue our broader mission.

To Help Us Control Our Destiny

You have surely heard the sports cliché "We control our own destiny." Athletes say it when their team can make it to the playoffs simply by winning—that is, when they don't need the assistance of losses by other teams in other games. Planning helps an organization control its destiny by proactively managing issues rather than just reacting to them. Planning can help an organization ensure that its relationships with key publics are a source of strength, not of weakness.

To appreciate the link between planning and positive relationships, simply apply the link once again to your own life. Imagine that you'd like to spend more time with a particular someone. Are you going to call that person and, with no warning, ask him or her to go out immediately to who knows where because you haven't yet decided?

Or are you going to ask a few days in advance with a specific social agenda? Spontaneity can be fun, but a little planning is indispensable in most good relationships.

Public relations departments that create and implement ad hoc, standing, and contingency plans increase their organization's options in a constantly changing environment. In doing so, they increase their value to the organization.

To Help Us Better Understand and Focus Our Research

Planning puts our research to the test. A detailed plan quickly shows us what we know—and what we don't know. For example, before we plan a specific relationship-building action with an important public, we must know several things:

- Does the relationship really require an adjustment?
- Does our organization want to make the adjustment?
- How will the public probably react to our proposed action?
- Do we have adequate resources to implement the action successfully?

You can probably think of other questions, but note what these have in common: They force us to look closely at our research. Planning helps us ascertain what we truly know, and it identifies areas that require more research.

To Help Us Achieve Consensus

As public relations practitioners transform research into a plan, they seek feedback. Many people, especially an organization's managers, provide input as the plan takes shape. When the planners are satisfied, the plan often goes to the client or top management for formal approval. Thus, when the final plan is drafted, there's a sense of joint ownership and consensus. The organization's decision makers and its public relations team also share a commitment to the success of the plan. Consensus and commitment help an organization avoid misunderstandings regarding relationship-building activities.

To Allow Effective Management of Resources

Resources are finite. (Think of your own entertainment budget, for example.) Public relations managers rarely have enough time, money, equipment, and staff to pursue every public relations issue affecting their organizations. Therefore, any waste of resources is painful. Public relations practitioners create plans because they want every fraction of every resource to move the organization toward its values-driven goals.

It may seem odd to you that the five reasons for planning we've just outlined don't include the notion that we plan in order to change other people's behavior. In reality, much of public relations planning *does* seek to change the behavior of particular publics. A plan designed to motivate a public to do something that it's predisposed to do may well be successful—but recent research suggests that plans

Values Statement 8.1

BOEING COMPANY

Boeing, based in Chicago, develops and produces aircraft, space systems, and missile systems for commercial and national defense purposes.

In all our relationships we will demonstrate our steadfast commitment to:

- Leadership
- Integrity
- Quality
- Customer Satisfaction
- People Working Together
- A Diverse and Involved Team
- Good Corporate Citizenship
- Enhancing Shareholder Value

—Excerpt from "Vision,"
Boeing web site

that seek dramatic or rapid behavioral changes rarely succeed. In the mid-1990s, the Research Foundation of the International Association of Business Communicators completed a comprehensive study of effective public relations and came to what may be a disappointing conclusion: "[C]ommunication programs seldom change behavior in the short term, although they may do so over a longer period."[3]

Behavior or even opinions *may* change, then, but it's a long process. So what do public relations practitioners do? Through research and planning, we build relationships to gain resources (resource dependency theory). After all, this profession is called public *relations*. Good relationships, built on trust, cooperation, and two-way communication, can gradually produce the kinds of behavior that an organization desires from its important publics. Those good relationships can even cause our organization to change its own behavior. The IABC study confirmed that when we seek partnerships with particular publics—partnerships in which both sides win—we stand the best chance of gaining those publics' cooperation as we pursue our business goals. As noted in Chapter 1, this win–win philosophy is called two-way symmetrical public relations.

Public relations practitioners may understand the wisdom of this "partnership" approach to planning, but there's no guarantee that the top leaders of an organization will share that understanding. They may still expect practitioners to design and implement plans aimed at producing immediate behavioral changes. When such changes are possible and ethical, we should try to bring them about. But we also need to educate—diplomatically—our organizations' top leaders. We should seek opportunities to inform them about the wisdom and legitimacy of two-way symmetrical public relations.

How Do We Plan?

Public relations planning usually begins after an organization establishes its mission-related business goals. In an ideal setting, public relations managers help establish those business goals. Once those goals are clear, however, the focus of the public relations team shifts to the development of relationship-management plans that help the organization reach its business goals.

A public relations goal is a general statement of the outcome we want a public relations plan to achieve. The goal of our museum scenario, for example, might be *To improve our museum's relationship with Hispanic residents of this city.*

The sections below describe the phases of the planning process, from consensus building to brainstorming to the creation of a written plan.

Consensus Building

Agreement on the need for action must be reached before planning can proceed. In the museum scenario, do museum managers agree with the above goal? Your research has revealed that the head curator doesn't think there's a problem in the museum's relationship with Hispanic residents. Thus, before you can plan for an improved relationship, you need to persuade her, and perhaps other museum officials, that the museum indeed has a problem. Otherwise, you lack agreement on your goal.

Fortunately, you have solid research you can use to show the curator that a growing problem does exist. Is that enough to win agreement on the goal? Perhaps not. You also need to show her that fulfilling this public relations goal will help the museum fulfill its broader goal. When the curator understands that vital connection, you will probably win her enthusiastic endorsement of your goal. Again, public relations practitioners must clearly link their public relations plans to the broader goals of their organizations.

Brainstorming

Once we've achieved consensus on a goal, we move to a speculative phase in which we explore our options for action: **brainstorming.** We ask tough questions about the quality of our research. We ponder what conclusions we can draw. We discuss what specific actions would be the best relationship builders. A good brainstorming session might even prompt us to revise our goal. In short, we have a wide-ranging, no-holds-barred session in which we frequently ask, "Do we know that for sure?" and "What if we tried this?" One Dallas-based agency tries to ensure creative brainstorming sessions by holding them on a basketball court, mixing planning and playing as practitioners work for some slam-dunk ideas.

To guide a brainstorming session, we recommend—in addition to a basketball court—a system based on a planning grid (see QuickBreak 8.2). A planning grid is a tool that public relations practitioners use to develop communication strategies. It's a systematic approach to the planning process. As a prelude to a formal, written plan, a brainstorming grid highlights four areas for discussion:

- *Publics:* Which publics are or must be involved in the issue? For each public, who are the opinion leaders and decision makers?

- *Values:* What are each public's interests, stakes, or involved values? In other words, why does each public care about this situation?

- *Message:* What message should we send to each public? A successful message addresses a public's values and attempts to get a specified response that would help your organization achieve a particular public relations goal.

- *Media:* Note that the word *media* is plural. You're not limited to just one channel of communication when you send a message to a targeted public.

As a brainstorming session starts to generate ideas, you can write them in a grid. The beginnings of a brainstorming grid for our museum scenario would look something like this:

GOAL: *To improve our museum's relationship with Hispanic residents of this city.*

PUBLIC	VALUE(S)	MESSAGE	MEDIA
Opinion leaders in the Hispanic community.	They want more support for local Hispanic artists.	The museum *is* actively supporting those artists—and it's willing to do more.	Address Hispanic Chamber of Commerce.

In our museum scenario, one *public* we could identify would be opinion leaders within the Hispanic community. We might decide that from the museum's standpoint, the key *value* held by that group is a strong interest in seeing more support for local Hispanic artists. Our *message* could focus on the little-publicized fact that the museum actively supports local Hispanic artists. Finally, we might discuss using face-to-face meetings and a special event as *media* to send that message.

As you brainstorm and begin to formulate a specific plan, be sure to test all the options against your organization's values-based mission statement and goals. As we've noted before, actions that become divorced from values are counterproductive and a waste of resources.

The wonderful thing about brainstorming is that you're not yet making firm commitments. Instead, you're just thinking on paper, or on a chalkboard or a flip chart. However, the brainstorming grid does provide the basic information we need for the next step: the written plan, consisting of goal(s), objectives, and tactics.

Quick ✔ Check

1. Should public relations plans focus on quickly changing the behavior of a public or publics? Why or why not?
2. What strategies should public relations practitioners use to win top management's support for a public relations plan?
3. What is brainstorming? Why is it useful in planning?
4. How does understanding a particular public's values help public relations practitioners create a message for that public?

Goals, Objectives, and Tactics: The Written Plan

A written public relations plan consists of three main elements, as shown in Figure 8.1.

- a goal or goals,
- objectives, and
- tactics, or recommended actions.

The order of the three is important. Not until you've clearly established the goal and shown that it's consistent with your organization's values can you move to objectives. And not until you've specified the objectives and shown that they, too, are consistent

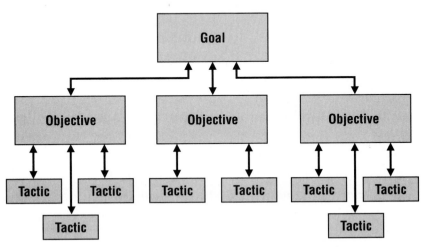

FIGURE 8.1   Goal(s), Objectives, and Tactics
In a public relations plan, a goal determines the necessary objectives, which, in turn, determine the necessary tactics. In executing the plan, a public relations practitioner first executes the tactics; this leads to the fulfillment of the objectives, which, in turn, leads to the fulfillment of the goal.

THE PRSA PLANNING GRID

Ready for a healthy dose of alphabet soup? The Accreditation Board of the Public Relations Society of America recommends that you use PIPP, POST, and TASC grids as part of a three-step planning process.[4]

PIPP, POST, and TASC are memory aids to help you complete three fill-in-the-blank planning grids. The PIPP acronym stands for a process that helps you identify and define the publics your plan may target. It stands for **P**ublic, **I**mportant Segments, **P**rofile, and **P**riority. A PIPP grid looks like this:

Public	Important Segments	Profile	Priority

For each public that you identify, you note the important segments of that public, such as

influential members and decision makers, that may require special attention. You then profile each public: You describe its "unique issues, needs, concerns, special demographics, . . . etc."[5] Profile information helps you determine what communication tactics you'll recommend for that specific group. Finally, you assign each public a priority: Which of the identified publics is the most important to your organization? Which is least?

After PIPP comes POST, which helps you develop specific communication actions. The acronym stands for **P**ublic/Segment, **O**bjectives, **S**trategies, and **T**actics. A POST grid looks like this:

Public/ Segment	Objectives	Strategies	Tactics

with organizational values can you move to tactics, or recommended actions—which, again, must be consistent with organizational values. Let's look at these three elements in more detail.

GOALS.   Your starting point, the **goal,** is a generalized statement of the outcome you hope your plan achieves. For example, in our museum scenario, you've diplomatically persuaded the management team that the goal is

To improve our museum's relationship with Hispanic residents of this city.

Goals often begin with infinitives, such as *to improve* or *to increase.* By beginning your plan with a verb, you place an immediate focus on action.

OBJECTIVES.   Once you have agreement on a well-written goal, you move to the next part of a written plan: the **objectives.** Whereas goals are general statements, objectives define particular ambitions. Objectives, in the words of the PRSA Accreditation Board, are "specific milestones that measure progress toward achievement of a

You begin by naming the identified publics and their important segments. For each public, you then specify objectives, strategies, and tactics. Objectives, which we describe in detail in the text under the heading Goals, Objectives, and Tactics, are measurable results that you hope to achieve with each public. Strategies are general descriptions of the actions you'll take to reach each objective. For example, a strategy in our museum scenario might be "Seek face-to-face opportunities to demonstrate to local Hispanic opinion leaders how our museum is supporting local Hispanic artists." Finally, tactics are specific actions that help you fulfill your strategies.

Having worked through PIPP and POST, you're ready to move to the final step of the three-phase process: outlining the logistics of each tactic. The third acronym, TASC, stands for **T**actic, **A**mount, **S**chedule, and **C**oordinator. A TASC grid looks like this:

Tactic	Amount	Schedule	Coordinator

For each tactic, you list the amount it will cost, when it is scheduled to occur, and who will coordinate its implementation.

From the identification of key publics to the naming of a coordinator for a specific action, the three-part PRSA planning grid can help you assemble the information you need for an effective public relations plan.

goal."[6] For example, we earlier mentioned an ad hoc plan for a party that you and your friends might throw. Your goal, of course, would be to throw a great party. Your objectives would include activities such as identifying and inviting guests; creating a fun, social atmosphere; and so on. You'd have to meet each of these objectives in order to meet your goal.

According to the Institute for Public Relations, good objectives have five qualities. They must

- specify a desired outcome (increase awareness, improve relationships, build preference, adopt an attitude, generate sales leads, etc.)
- directly specify one or several target audiences
- be measurable, both conceptually and practically
- refer to "ends," not "means"
- include a time frame in which the objective is to be achieved, for example, by July 1[7]

In a public relations plan, objectives often focus on the targeted publics. If your plan involves six publics, the plan may well have at least six objectives—because you're seeking to build six different relationships to achieve your goal. However, it is also true that some objectives can serve more than one public. Unfortunately, no magic formula exists that can help you determine the right number of objectives for a goal. The only true test of whether your objectives are sufficient is this question: If I fulfill each objective and manage my resources wisely, will I reach the goal? If the answer is yes, you have the right number of objectives.

In our museum scenario, your objectives might look something like this:

Objective 1: To improve the museum's outreach program to Hispanic residents by November 1.

Objective 2: To increase the Hispanic community's knowledge of the museum's programs by December 1.

Objective 3: To establish a continuing program, by January 1, that informs museum personnel of the museum-related values of this city's Hispanic residents.

If you can fulfill these objectives, you'll surely meet your goal. One of your challenges, however, may be measurability. In particular, you have to decide exactly what you mean by "To improve" and "To increase the Hispanic community's knowledge. . . ." As we stated in Chapter 7, evaluation must be considered and conducted at every step of the public relations process.

The specificity of your objectives will, in all likelihood, be familiar to top managers within your organization. Many organizations practice a philosophy called management by objectives, or MBO for short. MBO involves having managers commit to specific performance objectives for their particular departments. MBO is also used in performance evaluations for employees. Working with their managers, employees agree to specific objectives for the quality and quantity of their work in the coming year. The employees are then judged by how close they came to meeting those objectives. Public relations plans that focus on goals, objectives, and specific tactics are clearly part of the MBO philosophy favored by many of today's organizations.

TACTICS.   When you're satisfied with your goal(s) and objectives, it's time to suggest specific tactics. **Tactics,** or recommended actions, make up the third and final part of a written plan. To fulfill each objective, you need to take specific actions. Thus, you can list recommended actions under each objective. That placement is important. You don't gather your tactics and place them at the end of the plan. Instead, you put one or more recommended actions under each objective to show how you plan to achieve that specific ambition.

Unlike goals and objectives, tactics don't begin with infinitives. They begin with active verbs; they're commands. Thus, in the museum scenario, your first tactic under your second objective might be something like this:

Objective 2: To increase the Hispanic community's knowledge of the museum's programs by December 1.

Tactic 1: Address the November meeting of the city's Hispanic Chamber of Commerce.

That tactic is a good command, but it's not very complete. Who should address the Hispanic Chamber of Commerce? When is the meeting? How can you get on the meeting's agenda? What presentation materials will the speaker use? Besides being expressed as a brief command, each tactic should provide enough specific details to enable someone to implement it. It's common under each tactic to give the following information:

- *brief description* (specifying only what is essential for the action to be executed)
- *deadline*
- *budget*
- *special requirements* (specifying anything out of the ordinary, such as a need for unusual technology)
- *supervisor* (name of the person in charge of seeing that the action is executed)

Our tactic might now look something like this:

Tactic 1: Address the November meeting of the city's Hispanic Chamber of Commerce.

- *Brief description:* Request permission for curator to give a 10-minute presentation on the museum's support for local Hispanic artists. Permission is generally granted if we provide two-weeks' advance notice. Use handouts and computer-generated slides to show the scope of the museum's support for local Hispanic artists. To demonstrate our willingness to change and to be accommodating, the curator should begin her presentation in Spanish (which she does speak) before switching to English. Handouts and slides should be in Spanish and English.
- *Deadline:* Contact Hispanic Chamber of Commerce by November 1. November meeting date is November 21.
- *Budget:* $300 for preparation of handouts and computer graphics.
- *Special requirements:* Take grant-application forms to meeting so that Hispanic Chamber of Commerce members can help distribute them to local Hispanic artists. Ensure that forms are written in Spanish and English.
- *Supervisor:* Public relations director.

Having supplied this much detail, you're ready to move on to your next tactic under Objective 2.

Fleshing out each tactic helps give us the road map we need to reach our goal. When we're finished, we have a highly detailed, realistic, workable plan—in writing.

Public Relations Plan-Y2K
Role-playing Games

Prepared by Jenny Bendel, Public Relations Manager

December 1999
Version 1.0
Situation Overview

Overview

Dungeons & Dragons has experienced both the highs and lows of a product that has been around for 25 years. Incredible popularity, a dedicated fanbase, controversy, and the falling in and out of fashion. With the first revamping of the core rules of the game in ten years, the opportunities to use public relations efforts to excite our existing players about the new product, as well as begin to re-image the brand, re-acquire former players and attract new players are considerable. The high brand recognition factor gives us a head start when developing PR efforts. However, the negative stigma attached to the brand will pose a challenge when trying to convey messages of "newness" and "excitement" about the game to the media. Additionally, the lack of understanding by the media about what a roleplaying game is lends itself to misrepresentation and inaccurate reporting.

As we head into the year 2000 and develop our campaign to stimulate the public, both core and general, about the release of Third Edition, we hope to use the media, grassroots, special event and online PR activities to excite existing players to convert to Third Edition and bring new players into the game. Additionally, we hope to educate the media, parents, educators and other "inf   " in the lives of roleplaying game players about the benefits of roleplaying games.

Objectives/Strategies

☺ **Build anticipation of 3rd Edit**
   among core D&D players.

   ♦ Use targeted core media ou
     Edition product releases an
   ▪ Launch Third Edition in a m
     release.

☺ **Re-image Dungeons & Dragor**

   ♦ Target identified media outlet
     about what a roleplaying gam
   ⇨ Educate media and general pu
   ⇨ Educate teachers, parents and
     Dungeons & Dragons and role
   • Use iconic character to represe
     look as well as character flexibi
   ♦ Create PR campaign to allign D
   ♦ Create PR opportunities with PF
   ♦ Be aware of potential for crisis w

☺ **Re-acquire lapsed players.**

Public Relations Plan Wizards of the Coast Inc., a developer and publisher of game-based entertainment products, and Glodow Nead Communications won a 2001 national Silver Anvil Award from the Public Relations Society of America for their work on launching the third edition of the Dungeons & Dragons® game. PRSA judges praised the campaign's detailed plan, page 1 of which appears above. (Courtesy of Wizards of the Coast Inc.)

THE CHALLENGE OF MEASURABILITY

In *Using Research in Public Relations,* Professors Glen Broom and David Dozier write, "The most frequently asked question in our classes and workshops is 'How much change do you know how to call for in an objective?' The simple response is 'By researching the situation to learn what is possible.'"[8]

Easy to say; hard to do. Objectives must be measurable; otherwise, we can't say for certain when we've reached them. But how do we know what target to specify? When we say "increase" or "improve," exactly what do we mean? Aim too low, and we look cowardly. Aim too high, and we guarantee failure. What's a public relations practitioner to do?

Broom and Dozier begin with excellent advice: Research the situation and decide what's possible. To that solid beginning, we offer these additional pointers:

• Remember that changing a public's behavior, if it can be done at all, is a long-term process. If the top management of your organization agrees, state your objectives in terms of building relationships—objectives that may be easier to achieve and easier to measure than specified behavioral changes.

• When appropriate, consider targeting opinion leaders and decision makers with your objectives. It may be easier to measure the response of this smaller, essential segment of a larger public. This is particularly true if you're seeking to measure the development of a relationship rather than behavioral change.

• If you must establish a clear measurement for behavioral change (such as "Increase by 20 percent the number of employees who . . ."), select a number to which you are guided by research, experience, judgment, and the client's expectations. Then, as you implement the plan and monitor your progress, communicate with the client so that there are no surprises.

Creating measurable objectives is rarely easy. The only comfort we can offer is this: With experience, it does get easier.

Expanding a Plan into a Proposal

Even with your written plan completed, your writing may be unfinished. Some plans exist alone as plans. Sometimes, however, you need to "sell" your plan to a client or a supervisor who may want a greater amount of background information. Often, therefore, a plan is inserted into a larger document called a **proposal**. Agencies often prepare proposals for their clients, and even within corporations public relations practitioners often prepare proposals for top management. A public relations proposal generally contains, in order, these sections:

- a title page
- an **executive summary** that briefly, in one page, describes the problem or opportunity, identifies the targeted publics, lists the specific tactics for addressing the situation, and includes a budget summary

- a **situation analysis** that accurately and fairly describes the current situation in such a way that action seems advisable
- a **statement of purpose** announcing that the proposal presents a plan to address the described situation
- a list and description of publics that the plan targets
- a plan that specifies your goal(s), objectives, and tactics
- other sections as appropriate, such as
  —campaign theme and key messages
  —line-item budget
  —timetable
  —evaluative measures
  —supporting documents (usually in the appendices)

A proposal, as you can see, can be an extensive document. But at its heart is a clear plan consisting of a goal or goals, objectives, and tactics.

Quick ✓ Check

1. How is a goal different from an objective?
2. What are the qualities of a well-written objective?
3. What are tactics? What is their relationship to objectives?
4. How is a plan different from a proposal?

Qualities of a Good Plan

We've covered why we plan and how we plan, and we've seen how a plan can be incorporated in a proposal. Let's turn now to the qualities of a good plan. We've already mentioned some: A good plan seeks measurable results, and it has specific deadlines. What other qualities should a good plan have?

■ *A good plan supports a specific goal of your organization.* As we've said before, don't take for granted that your organization's leaders automatically recognize the value of good public relations. Show them how your plan can help the organization reach a specific business goal.

■ *A good plan stays goal-oriented.* Remember the problem with some standing plans? They stand for so long that we forget why we're following them; instead, we just execute the actions, such as an employee newsletter, because we've always done them. That won't happen if we stay goal-oriented, finding ways to remind ourselves of why we're executing these particular actions.

■ *A good plan is realistic.* Don't promise more than you can achieve. It's OK to dream an impossible dream, but you should plan for an achievable reality. Unrealistic goals and objectives often involve quickly changing a public's behavior. That's not necessarily always impossible, but public relations is much better at building the open and honest relationships that foster gradual changes. Unrealistic tactics include those that require more resources or expertise than your organization can supply.

■ *A good plan is flexible.* Things change. Sometimes important elements of a situation change just as you're launching a plan. If you constantly evaluate the situation, as you should do, you may need to adjust your plan to fit the new circumstances.

■ *A good plan is a win–win proposition.* Whenever possible, the success of your plan should benefit the target publics just as much as it benefits your organization. Forcing a public to change against its will is rarely possible and is almost always bad public relations. A good plan tries to honor each important public's values. When that's not possible, a good plan seeks to minimize damage to important relationships.

■ *Finally, and most importantly, a good plan is values-driven.* As we've noted more than once, if your plan isn't helping your organization achieve its values, it's pointless. It's wasting resources. A good plan resonates with the well-known values of your organization.

Summary

Plans usually fit into one of three categories: ad hoc, standing, or contingency. Successful public relations plans have many qualities, but they share one in particular: They must be clearly tied to an organization's goals. In other words, public relations practitioners must show an organization's top managers how a proposed relationship-building plan aligns with the organization's values and mission. If that connection is not established, the plan will probably die for lack of consensus and approval.

Good public relations plans consist of a general goal or goals; measurable objectives; and specific tactics, or recommended actions. Often, a written plan becomes part of a larger document called a proposal, which practitioners use to present a plan to a client or to their organization's top management.

Good, creative planning is an art—but it's an art based on science. A good plan is goal-directed and research-based. It is realistic and flexible, and it aims for a win–win outcome. Above all, it is values-driven. Finally, a good plan is based on solid, extensive research. Any shortcuts in research can place you in the undesirable company of space aliens, zombies, and the other weird perpetrators of the space aliens' Plan 9. In your own planning efforts, get it right with Plan 1.

DISCUSSION QUESTIONS

1. At what specific points do values enter the public relations planning process?
2. What unique characteristics differentiate ad hoc plans, standing plans, and contingency plans from one another?
3. Can you think of examples—in public relations or otherwise—of standing plans that have stood too long?

4. Why should you go to the effort of producing a written plan if you've already completed a planning grid? If you have a written plan, when should you consider expanding it into a proposal?

5. Why are measurable objectives important to the evaluation phase of the public relations process? What are the advantages of measurable objectives? What are the disadvantages?

Memo
from the
Field

Fred Repper, Retired Public Relations Consultant, Ingram, Texas

Fred Repper is a retired vice president of Public Relations (Public Affairs) for two Texas-based electric utility companies: Central Power and Light Company (1952–1978) and Gulf States Utilities (1978–1985). A public relations consultant from 1985 to 1992, Repper served as a member of the Research Team for the Excellence in Public Relations and Communication Management project, sponsored by the International Association of Business Communicators. He graduated from Texas A&M University (1950) in agricultural engineering and did postgraduate work in irrigation engineering at Colorado State University (1950–1952). A native of Fort Worth, Texas, he now resides in the beautiful Hill Country of southwest Texas. He is married and has four children and 10 delightful grandchildren.

First, I should tell you that I am retired, and at 73 years of age, I don't get too excited about anything unless it's my grandchildren, golf, or an occasional shot of premium bourbon whiskey. But when I read this chapter on strategic planning, I couldn't help but reflect that it would have been great if someone had laid it out so well and so clearly for me when I was starting my career some 50 years ago. It would have saved me a lot of grief and wasted time and money. But no one did. PR and communications were in their infancy. We were just beginning to learn what it was all about—mostly by trial and error.

Strategic planning to me means "Don't get the cart before the horse." Think it through before you jump into the ring. Strategic planning is a guaranteed recipe for success—whether you are CEO of a major corporation, a college professor, a professional golfer, a PR communications director, or a college student. Have a game plan! That's what I liked about this chapter. Your authors lay it out nicely with easy-to-read matrices and acronyms—a complete do-it-yourself guide to successful planning.

In this chapter and elsewhere, your authors refer to two-way symmetrical communications. The words *two-way symmetrical* have been around for only about a decade, and only a few college professors and PR practitioners are beginning to understand them. One-way asymmetrical communication is what everyone used years ago, although we didn't call it that then. It was what we knew best. We simply told our public "how the cow ate the cabbage." Then we sat back and were stunned and mystified when the "telling" didn't change the public's behavior one iota. If we really want to affect the public's attitude and behavior toward an organization, there has to be a better way. And that's where two-way symmetrical communication comes in.

I have never been entirely pleased with the title *two-way symmetrical communication*. It sounds too academic and sterile to me. Perhaps a gentler, kinder, and more descriptive title might be *sympathetic communication*. *Sympathetic*, according to Webster, means having "the ability to understand the needs and feelings of others and to alter or adjust your actions to meet those needs and feelings."

So, sympathetic communication is about *change*. If you expect the members of a public to change the way they act toward your organization—then the organization must also change the way it thinks and acts toward the public.

Sympathetic communication is very subtle communication. Sometimes it is more easily observed than it is read or heard.

However, caution! Change scares an organization the same way it scares an individual. Change can be risky. So make sure that you have thoroughly done your research and devised a strategic plan *before* you recommend change to the big boss. Even then, it will probably be a hard sell. But it will be worth it in every way, because *sympathetic communication gives you more than a dollar's return for a dollar spent. It's where the action is today. It's the new PR.*

Well, you've heard enough from this old geezer. I'm beginning to sound like a professor.

Now, back to my grandchildren, golf, and bourbon.

Case Study 8.1

Boeing, Boeing, Gone

Good public relations planning usually is invisible: The plan unfolds, relationships begin or improve, and organizations move closer to reaching their goals. Only rarely does the world stand back and say, "Wow, what a great public relations plan." But that's what happened in 2001 when Boeing Company's public relations team helped plan the company's move from Seattle to . . . well, to *where?* The *where* is half the story.

"Boeing approached the process with engineers' precision, considering a range of options and eliminating the weaker choices. [It] brought a flair for public-relations drama . . . which has received global news coverage," reported the *Dallas Morning News*.[9] That assessment joined a chorus of praise from journalists, public relations practitioners, business leaders, and politicians.

The decision to leave Seattle became the first remarkable event in Boeing's relocation. In the corporate world, Boeing and Seattle were almost synonymous. William Boeing, a lumber millionaire, founded the company in 1916 in Seattle as the Pacific Aero Company. Within a year, he had changed the name to Boeing Airplane Company. By the end of the 20th century, Boeing's Seattle-based commercial airplane manufacturing unit employed almost 80,000 workers. In 2000, its annual revenues topped $50 billion for the third consecutive year. In 2001, Boeing had customers in 145 countries and employees in more than 60 countries.

Because of the local, national, and international implications of Boeing's impending move, its public relations officials were among the first to learn of the closely guarded secret. To support the move, the public relations team created a plan to secure resources held by four key publics:

■ Employees, who held the resources of continued commitment to the company and a willingness to move to a new city, if asked. Some employees would be moving, some would be staying, and some might even lose their jobs. In all, however, only about 500 top-level jobs would move with the headquarters. Virtually all the manufacturing jobs would remain in Seattle.

Employee relations tactics included asking employees to refer all media questions to Boeing's public relations team; scheduling the move for late summer so that employees' children would be able to begin the school year in the new city; ensuring that employees would be the first to learn of the new location; and offering severance pay to employees who would lose their jobs.[10]

■ Nonprofit groups in Seattle, which had benefited from Boeing's philanthropy. Boeing donated almost $70 million to charitable causes in 2000, most of it in the Seattle area.[11] The recipients of that generosity would soon be in the national media spotlight; thus, they held the resource of helping to preserve Boeing's good name.

Local community relations tactics included a prominent assurance that Boeing's Seattle philanthropy would continue. "The impact [of the move] will be zero," said Boeing's senior executive in charge of corporate philanthropy. "We have a values statement that says we support communities where our people live and work."[12]

■ Publics in the cities Boeing was considering for a new home. These stakeholders included community groups, local governments, businesses, and the news media. These groups held the resource of accepting Boeing as a community member.

Tactics for these publics included news conferences and ensuring that members of Boeing's public relations team were accessible. Boeing appointed top managers to visit each city to meet with community groups and to negotiate for tax breaks and office space.

■ The national and international news media, which, like local media, held the resource of fair, balanced coverage of the move.

Tactics for the news media included news conferences, news releases, the accessibility of the public relations team, and, most important of all, an attention-grabbing way of announcing Boeing's final decision.

When Boeing officials narrowed their clandestine search to three cities—Chicago, Dallas, and Denver—the public relations plan called for removing the veil of secrecy. As the media clamored to learn the winner of the three-way race, Boeing public relations practitioners made it clear that they were following a well-ordered plan. "We have a plan and a process in place, and we're going to stick to that," Boeing spokesman Ken Mercer told reporters.[13]

Public relations practitioners quickly recognized the depth and quality of Boeing's plan. "I'm sure they played out all the scenarios like a war game and were able to guess what people would start checking on next," said a Dallas-based practitioner. "It's a good model."[14]

PRNews magazine noted that the entire relocation plan proceeded smoothly because Boeing's top public relations officials had joined the planning process from the beginning: "The company's three highest communications executives . . . all had seats at the executive table from the beginning planning stages, and it shows."[15]

The most attention-grabbing aspect of Boeing's plan was the tactic for announcing the winning city. CEO Philip Condit would board a private jet in Seattle after filing flight plans to all three cities. Once in the air, he would announce his destination city, which would become Boeing's new home.

"You talk about an old-fashioned stunt," said one admiring public relations professional. "You send your chairman up in a plane with three different flight plans and announce that you'll call the governor [of the winning state] from the air. That's straight out of P. T. Barnum. It's like the corporate version of the 'Survivor' finale. . . ."[16]

Even politicians and business leaders in the contending cities praised the plan. "What Boeing has done is nothing short of brilliant," said a spokesman for Denver's mayor. A representative of Dallas' Chamber of Commerce added, "The Boeing Company is keeping the suspense up."[17]

When CEO Condit finally picked up that phone in his jet, whom did he call? Governor George Ryan of Illinois. Boeing would move to Chicago.

Boeing's search had ended, but praise for its public relations expertise continued. "Boeing's relocation strategy elevates PR to new heights," proclaimed a headline in *PRNews*. A headline in the *San Diego Union-Tribune* stated, "Boeing's way of moving earns high PR marks."[18]

But the most accurate praise came from Dallas-based public relations professional Teresa Henderson. "I think you will find the Boeing case will go into . . . public relations textbooks," she said.[19]

She was right.

DISCUSSION QUESTIONS

1. Boeing officials tried to ensure that company employees were the first public to learn about new developments related to the move. Why?
2. In this case study, where do you find evidence of Boeing employees following the company's clearly defined values?
3. Public relations practitioners and journalists praised Boeing's public relations planners for anticipating problems. What negative issues might have arisen during Boeing's relocation process?
4. Of the three kinds of planning—ad hoc, standing, and contingency—which do you find in this case study?
5. How does Boeing's relocation planning illustrate resource dependency theory, discussed in Chapter 4?

Case Study 8.2

Millennium Doom

The appearance of certain phrases in the news media can make public relations practitioners want to dig a deep hole and pull the dirt in after them. Those devastating
phrases include "public relations disaster," "bad planning," "public relations gaffe,"
"public relations fiasco," and, last but certainly not least, "the handling of the media has been a disaster."[20] In the first weeks of the new millennium, the British news
media launched those criticisms and more at the media relations efforts of the United
Kingdom's Millennium Dome.

The Millennium Dome began with great expectations in 1994 when the British
government established a commission to plan special events for year 2000 celebrations.
By 1996, the commission had decided to build an enormous domed exhibition hall in
Greenwich, east of London. By 1997, construction was underway, and, by December
31, 1999, the Millennium Dome was ready for its first visitors—or so it seemed.

As a government project, the Millennium Dome could not justify a hefty budget
for advertising. Officials chose, instead, to promote the Dome primarily through public relations, particularly media relations. Thus, on opening night—the magical last
night of the old millennium—Dome officials invited the United Kingdom's best-known
journalists to the festivities. At least, that was the plan. Instead, Dome officials chose
to route the journalists through the crowded London subway system, where, with
their families, they were stranded for three hours. They missed most of the Dome celebration and spent most of that memorable night in an underground station.

In retrospect, journalists reported, they should have anticipated the most frustrating evening of their lives. Said one reporter, "[The Dome's] public relations team
habitually treated the most innocent inquiry with a combination of paranoia and de-
fensiveness that caused relations with the press to sour long before virtually every
national newspaper editor and TV chief was trapped in Stratford station on New
Year's Eve."[21] Even the normally reserved *Times* of London newspaper confessed
that the Dome's top media relations officer had earlier said to one of its reporters,
"I am fed up with you and your [obscenity deleted] attitude and your [obscenity
deleted] stories."[22]

With that kind of a relationship, the news media's reactions to the Dome's open-
ing-night transportation woes were predictable:

- "The organizers could not have planned a worse public relations disaster if they
  had tried."[23]

- "The opening of the Millennium Dome has been a public relations disaster, and
  the spin doctors have no one to blame but themselves."[24]

- "One also marvels at the Dome's public relations, which must have broken the
  first lesson on day one at PR school: make sure the opinion formers get their tickets on time and get good seats."[25]

As the first disastrous stories about the stranded journalists emerged, Dome officials reportedly tried to deny the facts. The *Times* newspaper, however, offered a humorous counterattack: "The reporters had the most reliable witnesses possible. Their editors were in the [traffic jam]."[26]

The relentlessly negative news coverage did little to promote attendance: Dome officials planned on 12 million visitors in 2000. The final total was closer to 5 million.

Because the Dome consumed substantially more government funding than anticipated, the United Kingdom's National Audit Office investigated Dome finances. The auditors' report took an unusual detour into public relations practices, gently but clearly blaming poor media-relations planning for a portion of the Dome's failure. In a section titled "Contingency Planning," the National Audit Office concluded:

- On any major project, managers need as much flexibility as possible to respond if things do not go to plan.
- Managers may find it difficult to respond to major unforeseen events unless they have already developed crisis plans. This is not planning for failure. It is planning to make the best of a bad situation.

Near the end of its report, the National Audit Office analyzed the impact of the poor media-relations planning:

> The [Dome] Company considered that negative media coverage of the Dome . . . had a significant depressing effect on visitor numbers. . . . The Company estimates that each time the Dome received "bad press," sales inquiries dropped by 30 percent to 50 percent in the following week.[27]

The saddest conclusion of all, however, may have come from a Dome media-relations official as he led a group of politicians and journalists through the exhibits. "There hasn't been a dull moment at the Dome," he said, "but I think I'll be getting out of public relations after this."[28]

DISCUSSION QUESTIONS

1. Millennium Dome officials hoped that good public relations would make the Dome a worldwide tourist attraction. Were you aware of the Dome before reading this case study?
2. The Millennium Dome relied mostly on public relations to promote itself. Does its failure mean that promotional public relations alone can't succeed without the help of advertising and other marketing techniques?
3. What resource did the English news media have that the Millennium Dome needed? Did Dome public relations officials secure that resource?
4. After the news media were trapped in the underground railway station, Dome officials reportedly denied the incident. What would you have done?
5. One journalist called Dome public relations officials "spin doctors." Have you heard that term before? What does it mean?

It's Your Turn

Planning a Blood Drive

The local chapter of the American Red Cross has approached your class for help with its annual blood drive. The chapter is determined to make this year's drive the most successful ever. It knows that it needs to do a better job of communicating with possible donors—but it's not sure how to do so. The chapter is eager to let you use your growing familiarity with public relations to help it meet its goals.

Rather than target random individuals, your class decides to target groups within your community—and you wisely decide to start with a brainstorming grid (page 244). Thus, you'll need to answer several questions:

- What community groups might urge their members to donate blood?
- What values does each group have that might be recognized, honored, and reinforced by messages about donating blood?
- What values-oriented message could you send to each individual group?
- For each group, what would be the best ways to send that message?
- And, finally, has your brainstorming identified any areas that need additional research?

Remember that this is the brainstorming stage. You're not yet committing to specific ideas, so at this point no idea is too big, too small, too expensive, or too outrageous. What publics, values, messages, and media can you suggest?

If you have time, move on to the PIPP, POST, and TASC planning grids designed by the Public Relations Society of America (QuickBreak 8.2). What information from your brainstorming session would you carry into those actual planning grids?

KEY TERMS

ad hoc plan, p. 237
brainstorming, p. 243
contingency plan, p. 238
executive summary, p. 251
goal, p. 246
objectives, p. 246

proposal, p. 251
situation analysis, p. 252
standing plan, p. 237
statement of purpose, p. 252
tactics, p. 248

NOTES

1. "1999 Communications Study: Linking Communications with Strategy to Achieve Business Goals," a report by Watson Wyatt Worldwide and the International Association of Business Communicators, 1999.
2. "Karen Hughes," *Newsweek*, 25 December 2000, 41.

3. James E. Grunig, "Communication, Public Relations, and Effective Organizations: An Overview of This Book," in *Excellence in Public Relations and Communication Management,* ed. James E. Grunig (Hillsdale, N.J.: Lawrence Erlbaum, 1992), 14.

4. *Accreditation Study Guide, 1993* (New York: Public Relations Society of America, 1993), 89.

5. *Accreditation Study Guide, 1993,* 90.

6. *Accreditation Study Guide, 1993,* 81.

7. "Guidelines for Setting Measurable Public Relations Objectives," Institute for Public Relations Commission on PR Measurement and Evaluation, 1999, online, www.instituteforpr.com/printables/objectives.htm.

8. Glen M. Broom and David M. Dozier, *Using Research in Public Relations: Applications to Program Management* (Englewood Cliffs, N.J.: Prentice Hall, 1990), 40.

9. Alan Goldstein, "Boeing Move to Chicago Began with CEO's Chat with His Wife," *Dallas Morning News,* 11 May 2001, online, Lexis-Nexis.

10. Michael Mecham, "A New Headquarters: Boeing Says, 'Chicago's It,'" *Aviation Week & Space Technology,* 14 May 2001, online, Lexis-Nexis; Kyung Song, "Boeing Deftly Builds Suspense over Move," *Seattle Times,* 10 May 2001, online, Lexis-Nexis.

11. Marsha King and Sheila Farr, "Generous Giant Vows It Will Keep on Giving," *Seattle Times,* 22 March 2001, online, Lexis-Nexis.

12. King and Farr.

13. Angela Shah and Alan Goldstein, "Rumors Put Boeing's New Headquarters in Chicago," *Dallas Morning News,* 10 May 2001, online, Lexis-Nexis.

14. Crayton Harrison, "Dallas–Fort Worth Still Buzzing about Boeing's Decision," *Dallas Morning News,* 11 May 2001, online, Lexis-Nexis.

15. "Boeing's Relocation Strategy Elevates PR to New Heights," *PRNews,* 21 May 2001, online, Lexis-Nexis.

16. "Boeing's Relocation Strategy Elevates PR to New Heights."

17. Shah and Goldstein; Song.

18. "Boeing's Relocation Strategy Elevates PR to New Heights"; Victor Godinez, "Boeing's Way of Moving Earns High PR Marks," *San Diego Union-Tribune,* 25 June 2001, online, Lexis-Nexis.

19. Godinez.

20. Patrick Wintour and Anthony Browne, "The Dome: Triumph or Disaster?" *Observer,* 9 January 2000, online, Lexis-Nexis; Mark Fox, "We Need a Moan-Free Zone for the Dome," *Sunday Express,* 9 January 2000, online, Lexis-Nexis; Dominic Kennedy, "Now for a Few Dome Truths," *Times,* 7 January 2000, online, Lexis-Nexis.

21. John Rees, "Doomed Saucer Crashes to Earth," *Sunday Business,* 10 September 2000, online, Lexis-Nexis.

22. Kennedy.

23. Wintour and Browne.

24. Kennedy.

25. David Lister, "Media: The Editors and the Queuing Zone," *Independent,* 11 January 2000, online, Lexis-Nexis.

26. Kennedy.

27. "National Audit Office: The Millennium Dome," 9 November 2000, online, www.nao.gov.uk.

28. John Chapman, "Tory Julie Roams the Dome," *Express,* 25 May 2000, online, Lexis-Nexis.

Communication: The Tactics of Public Relations

After studying this chapter, you will be able to

- understand what makes a tactic effective
- discuss the traditional tactics in public relations
- select tactics that seem particularly appropriate for specific publics
- describe how to carry out tactics efficiently and effectively

scenario

You are assistant director of public relations for a small but profitable international manufacturing firm based in California. Your company is publicly held; that is, it sells shares of ownership to stockholders throughout the world. Today you helped other members of the management team make a decision that's good news for some of your publics and bad news for others: To save money, your company is going to move a factory from Toronto, Canada, to San José, Costa Rica.

During the decision-making process, you advised the company's leaders about the move's impact on different publics. You suggested specific public relations tactics to be deployed if the company did vote to move the factory to Costa Rica. You even pointed out that some publics would be bitterly disappointed no matter what kinds of relationship-building tactics your company undertook. The best your company could do in those situations, you said, would be to minimize the unavoidable damage to these relationships.

After voting to move the factory, the leaders praised your assistance in helping them understand the wide-ranging impacts of such a decision. Now they've asked you to draw up a plan that recommends specific relationship-building tactics for each affected public. And they've asked you to hurry. The move will be announced next week.

Time to get started. Who are the relevant publics, and what relationship-building tactics do you suggest for each one?

Communicating with Specific Publics

A public relations plan is launched for one of two reasons: either to maintain or to change a relationship with an important public or publics. In Chapter 4 we examined the traditional publics in public relations, such as employees and the news media. In this chapter we examine specific **tactics** you can undertake to influence relationships with those publics. Accomplishing the tactics—often called communication—is the third phase of the public relations process, coming after research and planning. A tactic, once again, is a public relations action designed to have a particular effect on an organization's relationship with a particular public. In this chapter we also examine *how* you can accomplish tactics in a way that helps ensure their efficiency and effectiveness. This chapter also has a crucial link to the previous chapter, on planning: It describes specific tactics you could include as part of your plan. As you'll recall, a plan consists of

- a goal or goals;
- objectives that focus on particular publics; and
- recommended tactics.

This chapter examines traditional (and sometimes not-so-traditional) public relations tactics and offers a strategy for executing them.

Tactics as Messages and Channels

In Chapter 5, as you'll recall, we presented a basic communication model, which looks like this:

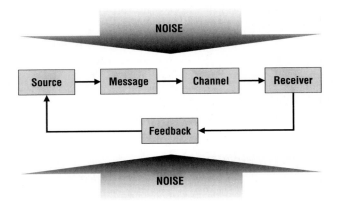

Public relations tactics enter this model as messages and channels. Messages have tactical value because they can influence a relationship. In our Canada to Costa Rica scenario, for example, management (source) could refuse to help (message) the unhappy workers in Toronto (receivers). That message certainly would influence the relationship. On the other hand, management could send a message that it will help the workers find new jobs. That message probably would have a different, more beneficial impact on the relationship. Because public relations tactics are designed to influence relationships, messages definitely are tactics.

More commonly, however, tactics are thought of as channels. A presentation from your company's top official in Toronto to the unhappy workers would be a channel—a tactic—designed to deliver a message and influence the relationship. A brochure that specifies exactly what the company will do for the Toronto workers could be another channel. Sometimes channels and messages are so intertwined that the channel becomes the message. For example, let's say your message to the unhappy workers in Toronto is *We'll help you find new jobs.* One channel for that message could be the creation of a training and placement center to help the employees polish their résumés and brush up on new job skills. In this case, the channel (the training and placement center) is so intertwined with the message (*We'll help you find new jobs*) that the two are indistinguishable. Sometimes, as 20th-century philosopher Marshall McLuhan said, "the medium is the message."[1]

If this seems overly complicated, let's remember our definition of a tactic: a public relations action designed to have a particular effect on an organization's relationship with a particular public. The messages we create can affect relationships; so can the channels that we use to send messages. Thus, both messages and channels can be tactics.

Successful messages and channels must respect the receiver's needs and preferences. An effective message, as we noted in Chapter 8, clearly addresses the receiver's values and interests. Likewise, an effective channel is one that appeals to the receiver. We can't rely exclusively on the channels that are cheapest or easiest, though that may be very tempting. Instead, our messages must flow through channels that our targeted receivers prefer.

So what are the available channels for our messages? A message can be sent through a special event, such as an open house or sponsorship of a particular charity's festival, or it can be sent through controlled or uncontrolled media. Let's take a closer look at these channels.

Special Events

You've certainly heard the cliché that actions speak louder than words. That cliché describes the message-sending power of a **special event.** For example, in our opening

Special events, such as an appearance by the RayWatch "safe-sun" models (see Case Study 9.1, p. 296), can appeal to a variety of publics, including news media. (Courtesy of Canadian Dermatology Association and GCI Group)

scenario, you could simply *tell* the upset employees in Toronto that your company cares about them and that the company will help them. But actions speak louder than words—so what "wordless" actions could *prove* that you'll help? You could offer a generous pay package that includes an extra three months of salary after the employees have been let go. And you could establish that training and placement center to help the workers prepare for new jobs with other employers. Those special events would clearly demonstrate that you're not abandoning your former employees. Instead, your special events would send the message that you value those individuals and that you'll help them through this difficult transition. Special events often weave together the message and the channel.

Special events are designed for the participants, of course, but in many cases they're also designed for observers. Your training and placement center in Toronto, for example, is clearly meant for the workers there—but it also sends a powerful message to workers in your other factories throughout the world: Your company takes care of its employees. That reassuring message should help strengthen relationships with the people who are best able to increase your company's productivity.

Another example of a special event that could target both participants and observers would be a student group's sponsorship of a Halloween party for underprivileged children. The party may send a message to the children, though that seems doubtful; they probably will be enjoying themselves too much to find any kind of message in their fun. But with a little help from the news media, the Halloween party definitely can send a message to important observers: potential members of the student group; university officials; and, perhaps most important, community members who may not have realized the contributions that college students can make to the community. One special event can help build relationships with many different important publics.

When public relations practitioners create a special event designed only to attract the attention of the news media, some practitioners call it a **pseudoevent**. However, as we discuss in Chapter 3, that term may be misleading. Public relations practitioners do not have the final say in what is news. Journalists who cover special events determine what is pseudo and what is not—and what is news and what is not.

Controlled Media

Media channels send words and images to the receiver. Some of those channels, such as newspapers and television news programs, are beyond the direct control of public relations practitioners; we can only give their editors information and hope that they use it. But with other media channels, such as various forms of advertising, employee newsletters, speeches, brochures, and web sites, we control the message. Such media are called **controlled media**. In controlled media, not only do we control the words and images; we also control when the message is sent and how often it's repeated.

Special events often use controlled media to emphasize their main point. For example, you might inaugurate your Toronto training and placement center with a

DON'T FORGET THE NET

Most media relations tactics target radio and television stations, newspapers, and magazines—but don't forget the Net. A Pew Research Center study of online news consumption during the 2000 presidential election concluded that "Campaign 2000 firmly established the Internet as a major source of election news and information." In the 2000 presidential election, 18 percent of U.S. adults went online for election news—a dramatic increase from the 4 percent who did so in 1996.[2]

The most popular online sites for year 2000 election information were, in order, CNN.com, Yahoo and MSN, MSNBC.com, and the web sites of the broadcast television networks. Those seeking information preferred national media to local media, such as hometown newspaper web sites, by a four-to-one margin.

Who went online for news during the 2000 presidential election? The Pew Research Center study identified the following demographics:

- Twenty-eight percent of voters sought online election news.

- Adults age 18 to 29 were more than twice as likely to seek online information as were adults age 50 and older.

- College-educated adults were more than three times as likely to go online for election news as adults who did not attend college.

- Thirty percent of adults from households earning $50,000 or more a year sought election news online. Only 10 percent of adults from households earning under $30,000 went online for election news.

- Twenty-one percent of men went online for election news whereas 15 percent of women sought election news online.

How can you get your organization's news onto the Internet? Target newspapers, magazines, radio stations, and television networks or stations that have web sites. Target web sites that specialize in news about the kinds of goods or services your organization produces. If you distribute news releases through organizations such as PR Newswire and BusinessWire, instruct those organizations to store and index your news releases on their web sites. And just as important, post your news releases on your organization's web site. Someone surfing the Net with a key-word search engine could be pulled right to your organization's online headquarters.

speech from your company's district manager. In that speech, he or she would directly deliver the message to the factory employees: *We appreciate all you've done for us, and we'll help you find new jobs.* You might also produce and distribute a brochure that describes the extended-salary policy as well as the features of the new training and placement center.

You could also use controlled media to manage your relationships with several other affected publics. You could send letters from the chief executive officer to all your stockholders, explaining how they'll benefit from the move. You could place articles in employee newsletters in your other factories around the world, telling employees there that their jobs are not in danger. You could place advertisements in the news media in San José, Costa Rica, notifying residents of the move and seeking employment applications. Such nonproduct advertising is often considered to be part of public relations. You could even include a message from the CEO on your web site. That message could help you manage relationships with publics that initiate contact with you, rather than vice versa.

Uncontrolled Media

Not all media, of course, are controlled. We can't tell television and radio stations which news stories to broadcast. We can't tell web sites such as Yahoo! which news headlines to feature on their homepages. Yet those media can be valuable channels in our quest to send messages to our targeted publics. By **uncontrolled media**, we often mean the news media: newspapers, radio and television stations, magazines, and online news providers. Each of those news providers employs individuals who act as gatekeepers— that is, editors who decide which stories to include and which stories to reject. Even if the gatekeepers decide to publish or broadcast our story, we can't control exactly what information they'll use or what other sources of information they'll seek out. Nor can we control when or how often they will publish or broadcast our story.

Furthermore, uncontrolled media can initiate a story against your wishes. For example, perhaps a television station in Toronto has learned about your factory's planned move to Costa Rica before you're ready to announce it. The station sends a camera crew to your California headquarters with a request to interview the CEO. Should the CEO tell the reporters about the move? Ideally, you've planned for this possibility, and you have a tactic ready. For example, the CEO might simply say, "We'll be making an announcement about that in a few days." That won't satisfy reporters, but at least you haven't allowed a definite message to reach your publics ahead of schedule; just as important, you haven't violated your values by lying. Because the reporters will keep digging, you'd be wise to speed up your timetable to make the announcements as soon as possible.

Not every form of media is easily classified as controlled or uncontrolled. Sometimes a channel can be both. For example, suppose that your organization's director of investor relations initiates a telephone conference call to several investment analysts at the same time. She could begin with a prepared statement about the move to Costa Rica, using the conference call as a controlled medium. But after the statement she might invite the analysts to ask questions. Although she can control the wording of her answers, she can't control the questions. The conference call now becomes, at least partially, an uncontrolled medium.

Controlled versus Uncontrolled Media

So which are better: controlled or uncontrolled media? Neither. Each has its own advantages and disadvantages. The advantages of controlled media include your ability to select the exact words and images that get sent. A possible disadvantage is a lack

Values Statement 9.1

JOHNSON & JOHNSON

Johnson & Johnson is a manufacturer and provider of health-care products and services. The company was founded in 1886 and is headquartered in New Brunswick, New Jersey.

Our Credo:

We believe our first responsibility is to the doctors, nurses and patients, to the mothers and fathers and all others who use our products and services. In meeting their needs everything we do must be of high quality. We must constantly strive to reduce our costs in order to maintain reasonable prices. Customers' orders must be serviced promptly and accurately. Our suppliers and distributors must have an opportunity to make a fair profit.

We are responsible to our employees, the men and women who work with us throughout the world. Everyone must be considered as an individual. We must respect their dignity and recognize their merit. They must have a sense of security in their jobs. Compensation must be fair and adequate, and working conditions clean, orderly and safe.

We must be mindful of ways to help our employees fulfill their family responsibilities.

We are responsible to the communities in which we live and work and to the world community as well. We must be good citizens—support good works and charities and bear our fair share of taxes. We must encourage civic improvements and better health and education. We must maintain in good order the property we are privileged to use, protecting the environment and natural resources.

Our final responsibility is to our stockholders. Business must make a sound profit. We must experiment with new ideas. Research must be carried on, innovative programs developed and mistakes paid for. New equipment must be purchased, new facilities provided and new products launched. Reserves must be created to provide for adverse times. When we operate according to these principles, the stockholders should realize a fair return.

—"Our Credo,"
Johnson & Johnson web site

of credibility. Receivers know that you're controlling the message, and they may wonder whether you're telling the whole truth. Another disadvantage of controlled media is cost: Generally, you pay for control, especially when using advertising to send a message. Unlike public relations, advertising purchases space or time in the news media; and, within legal limits, advertising controls the content of what it purchases.

Credibility and costs are lesser problems with *un*controlled media. Receivers know that you're not controlling the message; that key fact tends to give the message more credibility. As we've noted before, one reason media relations is such an important part of public relations is that the news media can provide a **third-party endorsement** or **independent endorsement** of a news story. That is, in public relations, news media are third parties—neither the sender nor the receiver—that can implicitly offer independent verification of a story's newsworthiness.

Sending messages through uncontrolled media usually costs less than doing so through controlled media. Using uncontrolled media may call for a written news release or a time-consuming meeting with a reporter, so it's not fair to say that uncontrolled media are free—but they generally are significantly less expensive than controlled media.

The disadvantage of uncontrolled media is clearly stated in their name: *uncontrolled*. Public relations practitioners can do their best to ethically influence the messages sent through uncontrolled media, but ultimate control of the message rests with others.

Public relations campaigns generally use both controlled and uncontrolled media. The trade-off is that controlled media ensure precise messages, whereas uncontrolled media are less expensive and offer stronger credibility.

Tactics and Traditional Publics

Public relations tactics range from low-tech, such as face-to-face meetings, to high-tech, such as online interactive videos. However, successful public relations tactics have several qualities in common:

- Successful tactics are part of a written, approved public relations plan that is tied to an organization's values-based mission.

- Successful tactics target publics one at a time. What works for one public may be completely inappropriate for another. However, if a tactic would be effective with more than one primary public, using it for all the appropriate publics could save time and money. A newsworthy special event, for example, could target event participants while also targeting other publics through the intervening public of the news media.

- Successful tactics are based on research about the targeted public's values, interests, and preferred channels of communication.

- Successful tactics send a clear message that targets a public's values and interests even as it strives to achieve an organization's objective. In other words, successful tactics try to create win–win situations in which both the sender and the receiver benefit.

- Successful tactics are evaluated as they're performed and after they're executed.

It would be impossible—and unwise—to create a list of standard public relations tactics to fit every situation. Every public relations challenge is different and requires special, even sometimes unique, tactics. But there are traditional tactics that every practitioner should know. Because successful tactics are directed toward specific publics, let's organize a discussion of traditional tactics around the publics that they might target. Table 9.1 presents a capsule summary of the discussion that follows.

TABLE 9.1	Traditional Tactics for Traditional Publics

Employees	Investors	Customers
face-to-face meetings	newsletters	product-oriented news releases
newsletters	magazines	product-oriented media kits
magazines	letters	special events
videos	annual meetings	open houses and tours
bulletin boards	annual reports	responses to customer contacts
speeches	web sites	bill inserts
intranets	facility tours	
e-mail	conference calls	**Constituents (Voters)**
instant messaging	news releases to financial news	letters
special events	media	newsletters
	media advisories to financial	news releases
News Media	news media	media advisories
news releases		news conferences
media kits	**Community Groups**	speeches
fact sheets	volunteering	face-to-face meetings
backgrounders	donations	web sites
photo opportunity sheets	sponsorships	responses to constituent
media advisories	cause marketing	contacts
pitch letters	speeches	
video news releases	open houses and tours	**Businesses**
actualities	face-to-face meetings	stories in trade magazines
news conferences		extranets
public service announcements	**Governments**	
guest editorials and	lobbies	
commentaries	grassroots lobbying	
letters to the editor	political action committees	
interviews	soft money	
satellite media tours	disclosure documents	
stories for trade or association		
magazines		

Employees

We'll start with employees, which usually constitute every organization's most important publics. If employees aren't well informed and motivated, the quality of an organization's relationships with other publics may not matter; the organization is in danger of collapse.

FACE-TO-FACE MEETINGS.   Virtually every study of internal communications shows that employees' favorite channel for receiving information about their organizations is face-to-face meetings with their immediate supervisors. To use this channel, you may need to work with your organization's human resources or personnel department to create communication training programs for supervisors. Perhaps your organization could use the approach known as MBWA (Management by Walking Around). Managers who aren't "chained" to their desks can initiate spontaneous face-to-face meetings with employees. However, as more organizations allow employees to work at home and "telecommute" by computer, organizing face-to-face meetings with immediate supervisors is becoming more difficult.

NEWSLETTERS.   Newsletters are generally inexpensive, and they have the virtue of putting a message in writing so that employees can review it. Newsletters should be frequent; if they appear infrequently, they run the risk of delivering old news—which means, of course, that they won't be read. Newsletters needn't be limited to paper. If everyone in your organization has easy access to a computer, a newsletter can be online and can include videos, sound clips, links to other sites, and an archive of former issues.

MAGAZINES.   Because they're more difficult than newsletters to produce, magazines usually aren't used to communicate breaking news stories to employees. Instead, magazines contain less time-sensitive stories, such as broad overviews of the organization's values and goals, stories about key employees, and updates on continuing issues. Some organizations mail their magazines to employees' homes, often in hopes that other family members will read them and feel goodwill toward the organization. Like newsletters, magazines can also exist online.

VIDEOS.   A message-bearing video can be used in several ways. Special videos or video newsletters might be shown on monitors in employee cafeterias and break rooms. Or, though this is more expensive, a video containing a particularly important message might be mailed to employees' homes or individually distributed at work. New video production technology makes downloading videos onto web sites fairly easy.

BULLETIN BOARDS.   Low-tech doesn't mean ineffective. Some organizations use controlled-access bulletin boards—often with the messages under a locked glass cover—to deliver daily news to employees. Some large organizations place the cafeteria's daily lunch menu on the bulletin board. Employees checking out the daily desserts just may stop and read other important announcements. Bulletin boards can help organizations meet legal requirements to post information regarding new labor laws or changes in employee benefits.

SPEECHES.   Employees generally like to see and be seen by the big boss. If an organization's leader is a good speaker, a face-to-face speech containing an important message can be highly effective as well as complimentary to an organization's employees. Such a speech means that the leader cares enough to look employees in the eye and tell them about the future of their organization. Copies of speeches can be distributed to specific employees; short speeches and excerpts of longer speeches can also be reprinted in employee newsletters.

INTRANETS.   We all know about the Internet, but what's an *intra*net? It's an organization's controlled-access internal computer network. A well-designed intranet not only provides e-mail processing; it includes an internal web site with department descriptions, links to other web sites, and an area for the latest news. As noted above, it also can contain newsletters, magazines, and videos.

E-MAIL.   According to a recent study, **e-mail** usage has soared to become organizations' most-used employee communications tactic. However, employees consider e-mail to be an organization's least effective official method.[3] Employees report feeling overwhelmed by the volume of e-mail—and they know that it allows supervisors to relay bad news without the awkwardness of a face-to-face meeting. E-mail's convenience can also be its danger: Misunderstandings—or worse—can arise if one doesn't think before posting a message.

INSTANT MESSAGING.   *Forbes* magazine reports that **instant messaging** is one of the hot new employee communications tools within organizations.[4] As most teenagers and young adults know, instant messaging is a network-based computer system that allows several individuals to instantly exchange typed messages with one another. For example, five employees in different locations could conduct an instant messaging meeting on an important project. All five employees could see and respond to messages from one another. As with e-mail, users of instant messaging should not sacrifice clarity and diplomacy for speed and convenience.

SPECIAL EVENTS.   Special events for employees can range from company picnics to special nights at sporting events to more complex tactics, such as your hypothetical training and placement center for your former employees in Toronto. Remember: controlled media such as brochures can often emphasize the message sent by a special event. For example, a groundbreaking ceremony for your new factory in Costa Rica would be a special event for government officials and the news media. A short speech—ideally in Spanish—by your CEO could be a controlled medium within that special event to help ensure that participants and observers receive the message that your company pledges to be a good corporate citizen.

Quick ✔ Check

1. What is a public relations tactic? In what stage of the public relations process do tactics play a role?
2. What's the difference between a message and a channel? When are they the same? When are they different?
3. What are the differences between controlled media and uncontrolled media?
4. What is an intranet?

News Media

Public relations practitioners generally target the news media as an intervening public—that is, as a go-between public that helps carry a message to a primary public. To place a message in the news media, practitioners use a variety of tactics to appeal to the media's so-called gatekeepers: the editors and producers who decide which stories to report and which to reject.

NEWS RELEASES.   The **news release** is one of the most important yet misused documents in all of public relations. A news release, ideally, is an objective, straightforward, unbiased news story that a public relations practitioner writes and distributes to appropriate news media. For example, in our Canada to Costa Rica scenario, you would issue news releases to news media in Costa Rica, in Toronto, in your hometown in California, and in any other cities where your organization has operations. In addition, because you have stockholders, you would issue news releases to the major financial news media around the world. News-release distribution services such as PR Newswire and BusinessWire could help circulate the news releases, and you could post the stories on your organization's web site as well.

Why do we say that news releases are among the most misused documents in public relations? Studies show that gatekeepers throw away more than 90 percent of the news releases they receive. Why? Many news releases commit one or both of two deadly sins: They have no local interest—that is, no appeal to a particular gatekeeper's audience—and/or they're too promotional; they lack the strict objectivity that characterizes good news reporting. An effective news release uses its headline and first paragraph to show a gatekeeper that it contains local interest. For example, your news release to the Toronto news media would be slightly different from your California news release. And far from being promotional, an effective news release sounds as if it were written by an objective reporter, not a public relations practitioner.

Though news releases go to print, broadcast, and online news media, most are written in newspaper style. Nonprint news media take such news releases and, if they use them, rewrite them in their own formats (see Chapter 10). The news media rarely publish or broadcast news releases word for word. If they use a news release, they generally rewrite it, often shortening it or including additional sources.

News releases reach the news media in a variety of ways. They can be mailed, faxed, e-mailed, or distributed through services such as PR Newswire. Occasionally, an organization's news releases are in such demand that it need only post them on its web site. That's the approach used by the Kansas City Chiefs of the National Football League.

MEDIA KITS.   Public relations practitioners use media kits to publicize complex stories that have many newsworthy elements. For example, television networks use media kits to publicize their upcoming programming seasons. A **media kit** packages at least one news release with other supporting documents. Two of the most common types of supporting documents are called *fact sheets* and *backgrounders*. A **fact sheet** is usually a what–who–when–where–why–how breakdown of the news release. Unlike the news release, however, the fact sheet is not written as a story; instead, it's just a well-organized list of the facts. Why include a fact sheet when the media kit already has a news release? Some journalists don't want to see your version of the story; they think you're biased. They want just the facts, and the fact sheet delivers those.

A **backgrounder** is a supplement to the news release. It contains useful background information on, for example, a person or organization mentioned in the news release. Like news releases, backgrounders usually are written as stories. Unlike news releases, however, backgrounders aren't news stories. Some feature testimonials from satisfied customers. Many others read like biographies. For example, you might choose to send media kits to Costa Rican news media so that they can learn more about your company. Your backgrounders might include a short history of the company that expands the brief description contained in your news release. Another backgrounder might be a biography of the CEO that, again, expands the briefer biography contained in your news release.

Media kits can have other documents. If the media kit is publicizing a visually attractive event, such as a groundbreaking ceremony for your new factory in Costa Rica, you might include a **photo opportunity sheet**. Photo opportunity sheets aren't meant for publication, so they can include a little bit of fact-based promotional writing designed to spark a gatekeeper's interest. Photo opportunity sheets tell what, who, when, and where. They can include special instructions for photographers as well as maps showing the location of the event.

Media kits can also include brochures, product samples, and any other document or item that can help gatekeepers make well-informed decisions about the newsworthiness of the story.

VIAGRA FACT SHEET

Viagra™ (sildenafil citrate), now approved by the U.S. Food and [Drug] Administration, is a breakthrough treatment for erectile dysfunction, more commonly known as "impotence."

- Viagra is a tablet that works regardless of the underlying caus[e...] was shown to be effective in men with ED associated with a [variety] of medical conditions, including diabetes, a variety of [...] neurogenic conditions, and depression.

- Viagra is not an aphrodisiac: It enables a man to respond naturally to sexual stimula[tion.]

- Viagra is remarkably effective: The drug improved erections in approximately four o[ut of...] it in clinical trials. Viagra is taken orally in 25-, 50[-...] about 1 hour before anticipated sexual activity.

- Viagra has been extensively tested: In trials worldwide more than 3000 men took [...] attempts resulted in successful sexual interco[urse...]

- Viagra works by increasing the blood fl[ow...] establishing and maintaining an erection; [...] The drug accomplishes this by sel[...] phosphodiesterase type 5, which h[...] monophosphate (cGMP), a necessary [...] flow into the penis. Viagra helps res[...] in response to sexual stimulation.

- Viagra provides men with a marked [...] ED: Previous treatments invol[...] penis, the use of urethral supp[...] surgery, or the use of a vacuum [...] While other therapies prod[...] Viagra enables a man to res[...]

  - The combination of Viag[...] blood pressure. Therefo[...] nitrates in any form.

Pfizer

Pfizer Inc
235 East 42nd Street
New York, NY 10017

www.pfizer.com

News

For immediate release
March 27, 1998

Contacts:
Andy McCormick 212-573-1226
Mariann Caprino 212-733-5686

FDA APPROVES PFIZER MEDICINE VIAGRA FOR ERECTILE DYSFUNCTION

NEW YORK, New York -- The U.S. Food and Drug Administration has approved the breakthrough oral therapy Viagra (sildenafil citrate) for the treatment of erectile dysfunction, Pfizer Inc announced today.

Taken about an hour before anticipated sexual activity, Viagra is a tablet that works naturally with sexual stimulation. Viagra is effective in most men with erectile dysfunction (ED), the medical term for impotence, which is associated with a broad range of physical or psychological medical conditions.

Discovered and [developed by Pfizer,] Viagra is the first in a new class of medica[tions...] that improve bl[ood...] inhibitors has been demons[trated...] patients.

"Viagra is a m[edicine that...] treats a medi[cal...] quality of li[fe...] Steere, Jr., [...] innovative t[herapy...] underscores [...]

ERECTILE DYSFUNCTION PERSPECT[IVE]

The following selections are from letters that Pfizer has received o[ver the] past three years.

- "It may be difficult for someone who has not suffered with impoten[ce to] fully comprehend the effect of this condition on a person's life, but the w[ord] 'devastating' comes close to capturing the feeling..."

- "I suffer from impotence, erectile dysfunction or whatever other nam[e] you may call it...I'm desperate...I want to walk with my head high again...feel like a whole man, not half of one..."

- "...I would very much like to know if [Viagra] would help a rectal cancer patient now in remission eight years with a sigmoid colostomy. This type of surgery rendered me impotent..."

- "Before I took part in the [Viagra] study I was heavily depressed...The feeling of being inadequate, even inferior, let alone impotent, was unbearable..."

- "My boyfriend is a 45-year-old healthy male with an undiagnosable impotence problem...We are desperately trying to find out if this new product is going to be the answer to our prayers, or, if not, he must resign himself to the fact that he will never be able to have his manhood back..."

- "...I am a healthy 50-year-old female involved for the past year with a healthy 44-year-old male who suffers from impotence. We have been to 11 doctors...We have had every kind of test imaginable done, and suffered through many types of corrective action, none of which have worked without great pain to one or both of us..."

- "...I've enjoyed a very active sex life until the past two years. I now feel like less than half of a man, embarrassed so many times, actually getting out of bed to hide in the bathroom and cry...."

# # #

References available upon request.

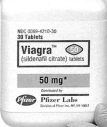

NDC 0069-4210-30
30 Tablets
Viagra™ 50
(sildenafil citrate) tablets
50 mg*
Distributed by
Pfizer Labs
Division of Pfizer Inc, NY, NY 10017

Media Kit Among the many news items in the first media kit for the anti-impotence drug Viagra were a news release, a fact sheet, and a backgrounder that contained endorsements from satisfied consumers. (Courtesy of Pfizer, Inc.)

Media kits ordinarily are mailed to the news media. Increasingly, entire media kits—including news releases, backgrounders, fact sheets, videos, and photographs—are placed on CDs and distributed to the news media (see Chapter 11).

MEDIA ADVISORIES.   Some newsworthy stories take shape so quickly that there's not time to write and distribute a news release. In such situations, public relations practitioners often issue a **media advisory.** Media advisories are also issued to remind the news media about events they may want to cover. Like a fact sheet, a media advisory isn't written as a story; instead, it simply lists the necessary information about what, who, when, where, why, and how. Media advisories are generally faxed or e-mailed to the news media.

PITCH LETTERS.   A **pitch letter** is, in certain circumstances, a replacement for a news release. A pitch letter is a letter to a journalist, a gatekeeper, that "pitches" a story that may not be important but still is interesting. Pitch letters often are used for softer human-interest stories that don't merit the "hard news" approach of a news release yet are newsworthy and would generate favorable publicity for an organization. Unlike news releases, which are sent to several news media at the same time, pitch letters usually are sent to only one news medium at a time. In other words, they offer an exclusive to the news medium.

VIDEO NEWS RELEASES.   Video news releases, commonly called **VNRs,** are distributed to television stations. As online news media become more sophisticated, however, we may see public relations practitioners arranging the online transfer of videos to news media. Video news releases are designed to look like television news stories. Like news releases, VNRs ideally are finished products; they're ready to broadcast. However, most VNRs include a section called **b-roll,** which contains unedited video footage of the news story. Many television stations prefer to create their own version of the story, using b-roll instead of the finished VNR. B-roll, they believe, gives them more control over the presentation of the story.

VNRs are distributed by videocassette, by floppy disk, by CD, and by satellite. A VNR can be beamed to a satellite at a particular time and downloaded by interested television stations, which have been notified, often by media advisories, about the timing and the correct satellite coordinates. Unlike print news releases, VNRs are expensive to produce and distribute. They should be used only for highly visual, highly newsworthy stories.

ACTUALITIES.   **Actualities** are sound bites for radio stations. They're quotable quotes and sometimes accompany written news releases. Actualities usually are placed on cassette tapes and mailed to radio stations, but they also can be distributed through telephone menu systems and through an organization's web site.

NEWS CONFERENCES.   News conferences are like dynamite. They should be used only when necessary—and even then with caution. A **news conference** is a scheduled meeting between an organization's representative(s) and the news media. Your organization should consider scheduling a news conference when—and *only* when—three conditions exist:

- You have a highly newsworthy breaking story. A breaking story is very timely; it can't wait on a news release, media kit, or VNR.
- It is advantageous to meet with reporters as a group, instead of individually.
- You know that journalists will be glad they came; the story is that good.

If your story meets the above three criteria, no problem; your news conference is a productive media relations tactic. But if your story *doesn't* meet those criteria, get ready for trouble: Either journalists will be angry that you didn't use a different communication tactic that shows more respect for their time—or they simply won't come, damaging your reputation as a public relations practitioner. If journalists can get the same information in another form—such as a VNR or a media kit—without being disappointed, use that other form instead of a news conference.

News conferences should be used with caution because they are the ultimate experience in uncontrolled media. You can try to set the agenda with an opening statement,

President George W. Bush uses news conferences as a communications tactic to build relationships with voters, political leaders, and other important publics. (Courtesy of the White House)

but following that, reporters generally get to ask questions—and there is no guarantee that they'll ask questions that you want to answer or are prepared to answer.

When a news conference definitely is the media relations tactic to use, however, consider these guidelines:

- Invite news media to the news conference with media advisories and follow-up telephone calls.

- Schedule the news conference strategically. By this we mean that you should balance your organization's interests against those of the news media. The news media generally prefer a mid-morning schedule. That's the best time for TV journalists who want to broadcast the story on the evening news, and it also benefits newspaper journalists with late-afternoon deadlines for the next morning's paper. A mid-*afternoon* news conference, on the other hand, limits immediate media coverage of the story to your organization's message; it reduces journalists' time for investigation. In scheduling a news conference, you must balance the needs of your organization against the value of a good relationship with the news media.

- Rehearse your presenters. Ask them the toughest questions that reporters may pose, and help them develop honest, credible answers.

- Have very few presenters—ideally, just one. Don't muddle the news conference with several speakers.

- Hold the news conference in a location that's easily accessible and has plenty of parking spaces.

- Hold the news conference in a room that has plenty of electrical outlets for television crews and photographers.

- Begin with a prepared statement. After that, accept questions from journalists. Avoid answering with "No comment." If you can't or won't answer a question, explain why.

- Don't let the news conference run more than one hour.

- Distribute media kits that reinforce and supplement the news story.

- Film and record the conference to provide video- and audiotapes to TV and radio stations that couldn't attend. These recordings also allow you to keep a record of exactly what was said.

PUBLIC SERVICE ANNOUNCEMENTS. Public service announcements, often called **PSAs,** are advertisements created by nonprofit organizations to publicize their services. The news media do not charge for PSAs as they do for commercial announcements. PSAs for the broadcast news media exist in a variety of formats. A broadcast PSA might be simply a short script for a radio announcer to read, or it might be produced like a commercial and distributed on audio- or videocassettes or compact discs. Radio and television stations broadcast PSAs to meet legal public service requirements. Just as with news releases, however, there's no guarantee that the media will use your PSA.

PSAs also target the print media, where they're sometimes called *public service advertisements* or *public service messages*. In newspapers and magazines, PSAs are similar to print advertisements. Organizations provide them in standard advertising sizes and "camera ready," which means ready to be photographed with the rest of the magazine page to make a plate for a printing press. Or, for pages designed on computer screens, print PSAs are distributed on disk and online for easy transfer to a computer file.

PSAs also exist for web sites. In the United States, the Ad Council, a group of corporations and other organizations that creates and distributes PSAs, offers thin horizontal online advertisements called "banners" that promote Smokey Bear, seat-belt safety, education, and other social needs. Organizations wanting to support those causes can, with permission, download a banner from the Ad Council's web site and place it on their own web site.

GUEST EDITORIALS/COMMENTARIES.   Most news media, especially newspapers, are willing to consider guest editorials or commentaries on issues important to the medium's audience. In our Canada to Costa Rica scenario, for example, you might want to consider having your chief executive officer prepare an editorial for a Toronto newspaper. The editorial could defend the move, describing the actions your company took to try to stay in Toronto and explaining why those efforts failed. In reality, the CEO might ask you to write the editorial. He or she might then make a few changes, and the editorial would be sent to the newspaper under the CEO's name.

Unlike news releases, guest editorials or commentaries aren't sent to several different news media at once. Instead, news media are approached one at a time and asked whether they would be interested in such an editorial. Editorials are offered as exclusives. Editors and producers can be contacted by a business letter that's quickly followed up with a phone call.

A related tactic involves meeting with a news medium's editorial board. That board doesn't exist to do favors for your organization, but it should be interested in fairness and fact-based opinions. Some news media have community editorial boards in which selected nonjournalists help a news medium formulate the editorials it publishes or broadcasts. Members of such boards occasionally write the editorials themselves.

LETTERS TO THE EDITOR.   Like a guest editorial or commentary, a letter to the editor allows a member of your organization to express an opinion on an important issue. Unlike an editorial, however, a letter to the editor doesn't require you to contact the news medium first. You simply mail a well-written letter and hope for the best. Though most of us think of sending letters to print media such as newspapers and magazines, radio stations and television stations also sometimes read, on air, letters from members of their audiences. For example, the show *All Things Considered,* on National Public Radio, reads letters from its listeners every Thursday afternoon.

INTERVIEWS.   Yet another way for your organization to publicize its point of view is to offer a high-ranking official to different news media for interviews. Occasionally, interviews for television stations can involve a tactic called a **satellite media tour (SMT)**. During a satellite media "tour," your organization's official actually never leaves a local television studio. Instead, he or she links one at a time, via satellite, with television stations around the world for live or recorded interviews. In the Canada to Costa Rica scenario, for example, your organization's CEO could offer individual interviews to the major television stations in Costa Rica without ever leaving California. Satellite media tours often are publicized by means of media advisories or phone calls to specific television stations.

STORIES FOR TRADE OR ASSOCIATION MAGAZINES.   If your organization is known for its expertise in a particular area, trade or association magazines may well be interested in publishing a story written by one of your experts. **Trade magazines** target members of particular trades and professions: construction companies, farmers, veterinarians, and so on. **Association magazines** are similar, being a benefit of belonging to an organization such as the American Library Association. If your organization offers a product or service that might benefit members of a trade, profession, or association, you can contact these magazines' editors with story ideas. You can also offer your experts should the magazine editors have story ideas for which they're seeking writers. Unlike news releases, such stories are not distributed to several magazines at once. Instead, the story is an arrangement between your organization and one particular magazine.

Investors

Investors are an important traditional public in public relations. By purchasing stock, they represent a source of capitalization for an organization—and because they own stock, they technically are the organization's owners. As we note in Chapter 4, investors include individual stockholders; institutional investors, such as the huge California Public Employees Retirement System; investment analysts; mutual fund managers; and the financial news media. We now know the traditional ways to communicate with the news media, but what are the standard tactics for other members of the investment community? A warning before we proceed: As we discuss in Chapter 15, communications with the investment community are closely regulated by such organizations as the Securities and Exchange Commission and the major stock exchanges.

NEWSLETTERS AND MAGAZINES.   Some companies have periodic publications that they distribute to investors. Such publications can discuss company goals, changes in leadership, new product lines, or anything else that might affect the performance of the company's stock. The publications also can steer investors to the company's web site or its investor relations office for more current information.

LETTERS.   Databases allow companies to send personal letters to stockholders, addressing them by name and noting the number of shares they have as well as how much they're earning in dividends. These letters can be more intimate than comparatively

QuickBreak 9.2

BEATING THE ODDS: SUCCESSFUL NEWS RELEASES

Studies show that journalists have a favorite place for 92 to 98 percent of the news releases they receive: their wastebaskets, online or otherwise.

That's the bad news. The good news is that a tiny minority of well-written news releases do succeed. But what makes a good news release?

Journalism professor Linda Morton has conducted several national studies of what journalists seek in news releases, and she offers this advice:[5]

- Write in a simple style. Use short sentences and paragraphs and common words.
- Focus your news release on one of the four topics that succeed best with editors: consumer information, a coming event, interesting research, or a timely issue.
- Localize the news release. Practitioners often call such news releases "hometowners,"

because they clearly target an editor's specific audience.

- Above all else, serve the editor's audience. Research the information needs of each editor's audience, find a way in which your organization can address those needs, and then write an objective news story on that crucial link.

Morton's research shows that public relations practitioners who follow these basic guidelines place almost one-third of their news releases. That's about 700 percent better than the success rate of practitioners who ignore the needs of journalists and their audiences.

Page 1—or the wastebasket? You can make the difference.

impersonal newsletters and magazines. A company might use personal letters for sensitive situations, as in an effort to get minor shareholders either to buy more of the company's stock or to sell their few shares back to the company.

ANNUAL MEETINGS.   The Securities and Exchange Commission requires every United States–based company that sells stock to hold an annual meeting for its stockholders. Most stock exchanges also require annual meetings as a prerequisite for membership. Not only stockholders but investment analysts and members of the financial news media attend annual meetings. The **annual meeting** can be an excellent channel to investors; it allows a company to use controlled media tactics such as speeches, videos, and brochures.

Not every element of an annual meeting is controlled, however. Question-and-answer periods with investors can rattle even the toughest executives. Some investors, known as gadflies, buy a few shares of a company's stock just to earn the right to attend the annual meeting, where they ask confrontational questions. In the Canada to Costa Rica scenario, for example, you should prepare for the possibility that former employees or other residents of Toronto who own shares in your company may attend your next annual meeting and launch emotional attacks on your rationale for the move.

THE VIAGRA VNR

Distribution of video news releases can be high-tech (via satellites and web sites), mid-tech (on videocassettes), and *very* low-tech (by hand to journalists who bang on the door and beg for a copy). The door-banging route is how NBC acquired the VNR on Viagra, the hugely successful antiimpotence pill made by Pfizer, Inc.

On March 27, 1998, the U.S. Food and Drug Administration approved Viagra for distribution to the public. Within 24 hours, DS Simon Productions, distributor of the Viagra VNR, had made more than 300 telephone calls to journalists and faxed announcements to more than 850 TV stations. NBC couldn't wait for delivery; instead, an employee rushed to DS Simon to pick up the video footage that later would appear on NBC's *Today* show and *NBC Nightly News.*[6]

The Viagra VNR included footage from the production line, product shots, and interviews with medical experts. In less than a month, more than 430 TV stations had used parts of the VNR, reaching more than a hundred million viewers. Besides the NBC shows, parts of the VNR appeared on CBS, CNN, PBS, CNBC, MSNBC, and even the Comedy Channel.[7]

DS Simon Productions, which increased its staff to handle the avalanche of interest in the Viagra VNR, offers these tips on VNR distribution:

- Target your distribution to specific reporters that cover your industry on a regular basis. Don't send generic media advisories.

- Supply the media with local angles or stories that can be localized in as many markets as possible.

- Consider streaming the VNR to an accessible web site.[8]

ANNUAL REPORTS. Like annual meetings, annual reports are required by the Securities and Exchange Commission and by most stock exchanges. Anyone who owns even a single share of stock in a company receives its annual report, which often looks like a glossy magazine but can also exist in a second, complementary form such as a video, CD, or web site. By law, an **annual report** features recent financial information, a year-to-year comparison of financial figures, a description of the organization's upper-level management, and a letter from the company's leader that discusses the organization's health and direction.

Annual reports are also sent to investment analysts, mutual fund managers, the major financial news media, and any potential investor who requests a copy. Many organizations post their annual reports on their web sites.

WEB SITES. Web sites are an excellent way for companies to communicate with their investors. Stock prices can be updated continuously; e-mail links can be provided; special statements and news releases can be indexed; video tours can be offered; the text of recent speeches can be featured; and the annual report can be included, as can the quarterly updates filed with the SEC. A good, interactive web site can function as a daily newsletter for investors, investment analysts, and the financial news media.

TACTICS FOR INVESTMENT ANALYSTS, MUTUAL FUND MANAGERS, AND THE FINANCIAL NEWS MEDIA. Investment analysts, mutual fund managers, and financial journalists don't like to be surprised. They require current information on a company and immediate updates about any events that might affect the company's financial performance. Investor relations practitioners can ensure rapid, frequent communication through such tactics as meetings with company executives, factory or other facility tours, telephone conference calls, and letters. News releases and media advisories can be distributed to the financial news media, often through services such as PR Newswire and BusinessWire, which can electronically transfer these documents to news media throughout the world. Often, timely news releases are required by the SEC and the major stock markets (see Chapter 15).

Quick ✔ *Check*

1. How is a news release different from a media advisory? From a backgrounder? From a fact sheet? From a VNR?
2. What advice would you have for a friend who wants to hold a news conference?
3. What is an annual report? What publics does it target?

Community Groups

Community groups include churches, schools, professional organizations, clubs, chambers of commerce, and other local groups whose values somehow intersect with those of an organization. Relationship-building tactics for such groups can be high-tech; more often, however, community relations tactics fall into the roll-up-your-sleeves-and-get-involved category.

VOLUNTEERING. Many organizations encourage employees to volunteer at schools, churches, hospitals, senior centers, libraries, and other important local institutions. Some organizations allow time off for volunteer activities, and others make cash donations to community groups based on how many volunteer hours their employees donate. Volunteerism is a powerful, rewarding way to build positive relationships with community groups.

DONATIONS AND SPONSORSHIPS. After organizations have rolled up their sleeves and volunteered, they sometimes open their wallets and donate. Sometimes those donations take the form of sponsorships—for example, paying the bills for a local literacy program's fund-raising carnival. Such generosity can create goodwill for an organization, but letting someone else spend your money sometimes leads to unpleasant surprises. Be sure to specify in writing exactly what the donated money is for, and then monitor the situation to ensure that your donation was spent correctly.

Instead of money, some organizations donate goods or services or even the expertise of their employees. For example, a community bank might lend a tax expert to a local nonprofit organization to help it prepare its tax returns. Or a local manufacturing company might allow an executive to work half-time temporarily as the coordinator of the community's United Way campaign.

CAUSE MARKETING.   Organizations sometimes devote money, goods, services, and volunteerism to particular social needs, such as literacy or cancer research. In a sense, the organizations adopt a particular social need as their primary philanthropy. Such a community relations tactic is called **cause marketing.** Like special events, cause marketing often addresses more than one public. It certainly addresses people affected by the social need; most organizations that adopt a cause genuinely want to help. But the tactic also is designed to create goodwill among government officials, consumers, current and potential employees, and other important publics that can help the organization achieve its goals.

SPEECHES.   Professional and civic groups such as the Kiwanis Club, the Rotary Club, and the League of Women Voters often seek community leaders to speak on current issues at weekly or monthly meetings. If an organization has a stake in a local issue, a speech followed by a question-and-answer session can promote the organization's point of view and collect information about how other people feel.

OPEN HOUSES/TOURS.   Organizations that produce interesting goods or services can build goodwill in the community by sponsoring open houses and offering tours of company facilities. Open houses and tours often provide opportunities to use controlled media such as speeches, brochures, and videos. They also provide opportunities to distribute so-called specialty advertising products such as coffee mugs, Frisbees, ball caps, and other items that feature an organization's name and logo.

FACE-TO-FACE MEETINGS.   Community groups sometimes are activist groups. For example, an environmental group in Costa Rica may wonder how your company's new factory will dispose of toxic waste. At the first sign that such a group is studying your organization, it's vital that you open lines of communication with its members—ideally through face-to-face meetings. Many activist groups gather their research before they assume a firm public stance. If you can demonstrate your organization's good intentions before the activist group solidifies its position, you may defuse a crisis before it begins.

Unfortunately, activist groups, like all of us, sometimes act before they do their research. In 1996, for example, Greenpeace, an effective, highly respected environmental organization, had to apologize to Shell Oil for its very public opposition to Shell's plan to dump a huge oil container at sea. After doing its research—but following its successful protest—Greenpeace concluded that Shell's dump-at-sea plan made sense.[9]

In community relations, face-to-face meetings need not be limited to activist groups. An organization can conduct such meetings with a variety of neutral or friendly community groups in hopes of paving the way for alliances or partnerships on future problems or opportunities. Such a process is called **coalition building.**

Governments

Governmental action at any level—federal, state, county, or city—can profoundly affect an organization. Public relations practitioners thus use a portfolio of tactics to make their organizations' voices heard in the halls of government.

LOBBIES AND LOBBYISTS.   A **lobby** is a special-interest group that openly attempts to influence government actions, especially federal and state legislative processes. One of the most effective lobbies at the turn of this century, for example, has been the American Association of Retired Persons, which advances the interests of people age 55 and older. A *lobbyist* is someone who, acting on behalf of a special-interest group, tries to influence various forms of government regulation. Lobbies and lobbyists generally pass persuasive information along to government officials. They host special events for officials and their staffs, and they often respond to government officials' requests for information on particular issues.

At the federal level in the United States, lobbies and lobbyists are regulated by the Lobbying Disclosure Act, which mandates that people who are paid to lobby Congress or the executive branch of the federal government must register with the government. Paid lobbyists must specify whom they represent and how much they are being paid.

Students interested in careers as lobbyists should contact members of their state legislature to inquire about effective lobbying groups at the state level. You could also contact the Washington, D.C., offices of public relations agencies that openly market their lobbying services. Searching the web can lead you to agencies that specialize in lobbying and government relations, such as the Hoffman Group, online at www.hoffmangroup.com, and The Capital Edge, online at www.CapitalEdge.com.

GRASSROOTS LOBBYING.   Not all lobbyists must register with the federal government. If you write a letter to your congressional representatives asking them to increase funding for student loans, you're acting as a lobbyist for a special interest, but you need not register. Such informal, infrequent, "unprofessional" lobbying is often called **grassroots lobbying,** especially if you're acting with others to show legislators broad support for your opinion. Because grassroots lobbying is the "voice of the people," it can be highly influential with elected government officials.

POLITICAL ACTION COMMITTEES.   Political action committees, often called PACs, have one purpose: to donate money to candidates and political parties. Political action committees are sponsored by corporations, labor unions, special-interest groups, and other organizations. In 2000, 4,499 PACs were registered with the federal government; such registration is required for PACs that donate money to presidential or congressional candidates. State governments also have laws that govern PAC donations.

Corporations and labor unions aren't allowed to donate money directly to candidates for federal offices. But they can form PACs, which can accept voluntary—not mandatory—donations from employees, members, and others and route the money to candidates who support their views. Since 1974, when Congress created PACs in an attempt to clean up campaign financing, the number of PACs has soared from 608 to 4,499.[10]

SOFT MONEY. So-called **soft money** was money donated to political parties to be spent not on individual candidates but on noncandidate projects such as get-out-the-vote drives, voter education, and issues-oriented advertising. Critics of soft money contended that political parties often illegally used it to support candidates. In 2002, Congress passed legislation that stopped the flow of soft money to political parties. Proponents and opponents of soft money alike attacked the legislation. Proponents claimed it violated First Amendment guarantees of freedom of speech. Opponents of soft money claimed the legislation left open many loopholes, including hefty donations to national political conventions and to local branches of political parties. Proponents and opponents of soft money also agree that the legislation will change in the future. Public relations practitioners who specialize in government relations are well advised to monitor the legality of soft money.

DISCLOSURE DOCUMENTS. In the United States, companies that sell stock must, by law, communicate with the government. Often, investor relations practitioners help write and file a comprehensive annual report—called a 10-K—with the federal Securities and Exchange Commission. Other SEC forms that practitioners often help prepare or review are the 10-Q (quarterly financial report) and the 8-K (used to announce an event that might affect the price of the company's stock). Disclosure law is covered more fully in Chapter 15.

Customers

Customer relations is where public relations overlaps with marketing (see Chapter 13). Marketing, simply put, is the process of getting a customer to buy your product or service. Most marketing tactics lie outside the boundaries of traditional public relations; marketing tactics include advertising, direct-mail letters, coupons and other sales promotions, and face-to-face sales encounters. But public relations can add several tactics to what is called the marketing mix.

PRODUCT-ORIENTED NEWS RELEASES AND MEDIA KITS. We discussed news releases and media kits earlier in this chapter. When news releases or media kits focus on a newsworthy aspect of a product or service, they target customers and are part of the so-called marketing mix. The news media become an intervening public between an organization and the customers it's hoping to reach.

SPECIAL EVENTS. There's no telling who the next fictional hero for preschoolers will be. We've already seen a giant purple dinosaur and an aardvark named Arthur. One

QuickBreak 9.4

LOBBIES IN THE U.S.A.: WHO HAS THE CLOUT?

Of the hundreds of lobbies in Washington, D.C., which are the most powerful—and why? That's what *Fortune* magazine annually asks in a survey of members of Congress, congressional staffers, White House aides, lobbyists themselves, and other knowledgeable sources. The answers may surprise you.

Power doesn't come from a lobby's ability to funnel money to candidates through political action committees and other channels, *Fortune* has concluded. Instead, power comes from a lobby's ability to get out the vote. According to *Fortune,*[11] the most effective lobbying tactics include

- Delivering the straight facts to lawmakers.
- Having active allies in an elected official's district.
- Mobilizing grassroots action, such as phone calls and letters.

And who are the most powerful lobbies in Washington? According to *Fortune,* the Top Five in 2000[12] were

1. National Rifle Association
2. American Association of Retired Persons
3. National Federation of Independent Business
4. American Israel Public Affairs Committee
5. Association of Trial Lawyers of America

The true power of lobbies, *Fortune* has concluded, comes from "geographically dispersed and politically active members who focus their energies on a narrow range of issues."[13]

thing is certain: Whoever or whatever the next heroes are, costumed actors who portray them will visit our bookstores. Such a visit is a special event, which is any out-of-the-ordinary occurrence designed to attract customers.

OPEN HOUSES AND TOURS.   An organization with interesting products or services or unusual production technology can attract customers by inviting them to tour its facilities. During open houses and tours, customers often get to sample or test products or services. Wineries, for example, often offer tours and free samples to visitors of legal drinking age.

RESPONSES TO CUSTOMER CONTACTS.   Smart organizations respond quickly to phone calls, letters, and e-mail messages from customers and potential customers. Such two-way communication not only builds customer loyalty; it also helps an organization know what its customers are thinking.

BILL INSERTS.   Organizations that regularly mail bills or other financial statements to customers often include **bill inserts:** brochures or newsletters that focus on customer interests. Occasionally, short messages, such as *For more information, visit our web site at www.whatever,* are printed directly on a bill.

Congratulations!

YOU are the proud recipient of this limited edition official Callahan Creek Happy Fun Hat!

Don't be fooled by substandard paper headgear! Only the original Callahan Creek Happy Fun Hat is guaranteed to bring hours and hours of productive party enhancement.

Our exclusive "insert tab A into slot B" technology not only ensures a proper fit on all but the largest of heads, but also is designed to maximize your New Year's experience by tuning in a live broadcast of Dick Clark's New Year's Rockin' Eve*.

Only a select group of clients, employees, their families, past employees, their families, vendors, traveling salesmen, circus performers, carnival geeks, people in the meat processing industry, supermodels under 5'6", left-handed redheads, aluminum siding manufacturers and periodontal technicians have been chosen to receive this year's Callahan Creek Happy Fun Hat, so...

Consider yourself lucky and have a wonderful New Year!!!!

— From all your friends at Callahan Creek

Hat assembly instructions:
Insert tab A into slot B.

For assistance, call toll-free **1 800-CONEHEAD**. Operators are standing by to assist you.

Calls must be placed before Dec. 26, 1998.

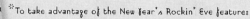

*To take advantage of the New Year's Rockin' Eve feature:
- simply assemble Happy Fun Hat
- situate your body in close proximity to a working television on New Year's Eve
- wait until twelve midnight
- tune television to local ABC affiliate

Callahan Creek

Party Hat and Flier Integrated marketing agency Callahan Creek crafted an innovative way to wish customers, potential customers, and friends a happy New Year. (Courtesy of Callahan Creek)

Brochure A popular brochure by H&R Block, a financial services company, builds relationships by addressing customers' often-insufficient knowledge of financial and tax terms. (Courtesy of H&R Block)

Constituents (Voters)

As we noted in Chapter 4, many organizations try to influence the legislative process by building relationships with eligible voters. But for public relations practitioners employed by democratically elected governments, voters are the most important public of all. We're already familiar with many of the tactics that government practitioners use to build productive relationships between elected or appointed officials and their constituents: letters and newsletters; news releases, media advisories, and news conferences; speeches; face-to-face meetings; and interactive web sites.

Although every organization should respond quickly to letters, phone calls, and e-mail messages from members of important publics, such responses are particularly significant in the relationship between elected or appointed government officials and voters. A quick, personalized reply, even if a more detailed follow-up response is necessary, is one of the most important tactics in constituent relations. These responses encourage constituents to feel connected to and valued by their representatives. Members of Congress, for example, have staff members who spend the majority of their working hours addressing constituent concerns. Contacts from constituents can also be an excellent source of research data regarding issues that concern potential voters.

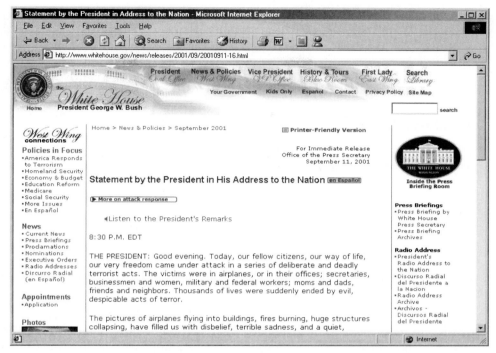

Speech Face-to-face communication is often the best tactic for important messages. On the day of the 2001 terrorist attacks on the World Trade Center and the Pentagon, President George W. Bush delivered this speech to millions of television viewers around the world. (Courtesy of the White House)

Businesses

Business-to-business communication is big business in the 21st century. If organizations are to reach their goals, they must use a variety of tactics to build relationships with other businesses such as suppliers and business customers. Just like tactics for individual customers, business-to-business tactics sometimes more closely resemble marketing than public relations. Such tactics include personal selling, price discounts, trade shows, and direct-mail advertising. But some business-to-business tactics are pure public relations.

STORIES IN TRADE MAGAZINES. Businesses can attract new customers as well as new suppliers by writing and submitting stories to trade, or professional, magazines. Often, such stories present a company official as an expert on a particular topic. Many magazines focus on trades or professions such as law, carpentry, and farming. Those magazines accept and publish well-written stories of interest to their readers. Such magazines also publish news releases, which generally are shorter than featured stories and do not include a byline.

EXTRANETS.   Extranets are controlled-access computer networks, similar to intranets. At a minimum, they usually include web sites and e-mail capabilities. Unlike intranets, extranets are for businesses outside the host business. For example, winemaker Robert Mondavi purchases NASA satellite photos of vineyards and posts them on its extranet so that its independent grape suppliers can spot problems before they become serious.[14]

Accomplishing the Tactics

Most of the research has been done. The plan has been written and approved. Now it's time to carry out the tactics. Though this section appears near the end of the chapter, it is, in reality, the center of gravity, the focus of this chapter. Simply selecting a tactic does not create communication. Rather, communication begins when the tactic is executed. High standards are essential at this point of the public relations process. No amount of research or planning can overcome sloppy communication efforts. Public relations practitioners, therefore, tend to stress six key factors as they execute a plan's tactics: delegation, deadlines, quality control, communication within the team, communication with clients or supervisors, and constant evaluation.

1. *Delegation.* Delegate the responsibility for a tactic's execution to a particular individual. With every tactic in a written plan, include the responsible individual's name. For example, in the Canada to Costa Rica scenario, your plan would charge one individual with the responsibility of creating a job-training and placement center. That individual wouldn't have to act alone—but he or she, ultimately, would bear the responsibility of creating the center. Naming names in this manner helps ensure successful results: No one wants to be the highly visible manager of a failed tactic.

2. *Deadlines.* In the written plan, establish a deadline for the completion of each tactic. For example, each local-interest news release necessary in the Canada to Costa Rica scenario would have a mailing or transmission deadline. The named manager of each tactic would be responsible for meeting that deadline.

3. *Quality control.* Conduct quality control. Have more than one editor and proofreader examine every document. Attend photo shoots to ensure that photographers are getting the picture you planned. Visit printing companies to ensure that the colors of your brochures and magazines are correct. (You may even get to shout, "Stop the press!") Look over a lot of shoulders as the tactics progress. In public relations for the move to Costa Rica, part of quality control would include double-checking the quality of Spanish-language news releases. And because the Spanish of Costa Rica is different from the Spanish of Spain, you would be wise to seek the assistance of native Costa Rican public relations professionals.

4. *Communication within the team.* Encourage communication among the practitioners who are executing the tactics. Frequent short meetings in which teammates update one another can be a good idea. For example, the manager of one of the news releases on the Costa Rica move may need to know that the job-training and placement center will indeed open on a particular date; it may be an important point in

her news release. Good communication within your team can ensure that the tactics of your plan complement one another as they are accomplished.

5. Communication with clients or supervisors. Communicate frequently with the clients and/or supervisors as the execution of the tactics progresses. Be sure to inform them of any problems, and try to present realistic solutions. In our scenario, perhaps a company executive phones you at the last moment, wanting to change some of the job-training and placement brochures from two colors to full color. You will need to communicate as quickly as possible with your supervisor, detailing the impact of the proposed change on budget and scheduling.

6. Constant evaluation. Evaluate the process as it progresses. Are news releases, videos, and web sites professional in every respect? Are deadlines being met? Do any sudden changes within your targeted publics or within the social or political environment require a change of tactics? Perhaps a video news release prepared for San José television stations, for example, doesn't run because, as you later discover, the stations wanted a longer Spanish-language question-and-answer session on the VNR's b-roll. If your plan calls for a second VNR, you can remedy that situation in hopes of improved media coverage.

Carrying out the tactics of a public relations plan is exciting. You've worked hard to create a realistic, effective plan, and now you're giving it your best shot. But even after the tactics are completed and you heave a heartfelt sigh of relief, the public relations process isn't over. Now it's time to evaluate the impact of the tactics. It's time to see whether your plan met its objectives and goals.

Quick ✓ Check

1. What is cause marketing?
2. What are the differences between a lobby and a political action committee?
3. What can you include in a written plan to help ensure that tactics are completed on schedule?

Summary

Accomplishing the tactics—often called communication—is the third phase of the public relations process, coming after research and planning. During this phase, practitioners complete well-defined actions to achieve a written plan's objectives. Each tactic targets a particular public and sends a message that does two things: appeals to the receiver's values and promotes the sender's objective. An effective tactic helps build a relationship that benefits a message's receiver as well as its sender.

A wide range of effective tactics can help organizations communicate with their traditional publics, including employees, the news media, investors, community groups, governments, customers, and constituents (voters). Ranging from low-tech face-to-face meetings to high-tech satellite media tours, such tactics strive to create win–win situations that benefit both an organization and the targeted public.

As public relations professionals execute the tactics of a plan, they are guided by the principles of delegation, deadlines, quality control, communication within the team, communication with clients or supervisors, and constant evaluation.

Public relations tactics, after all, are values in action. An organization's values lead to a mission statement. That mission statement leads to goals. Those goals lead to objectives. And those objectives lead to tactics. Tactics are actions that allow an organization to strive toward its highest values.

DISCUSSION QUESTIONS

1. In the Canada to Costa Rica scenario, what publics besides employees, stockholders, investment analysts, and the news media would you target with a public relations plan?
2. What message would you send to each public you identify in your answer to question 1? Can you create win–win messages?
3. What tactics could you use to send the messages that you described in your answer to question 2?
4. Why should tactics be evaluated as they're being implemented?

Memo
from the
Field

Shirley Barr, APR,
President, Shirleybarr
Public Relations,
Houston

Shirley Barr, APR, president of Shirleybarr Public Relations in Houston, is a consumer marketing specialist. She has won PRSA Excalibur Awards for services as diverse as the Women at Risk: Breast Implants program (an educational, informational, and practice-development campaign) and product introductions for Ben & Jerry's Ice Cream and Wolfgang Puck Frozen Pizzas. Other clients include American Express and the Smithsonian Institute.

Her clients have appeared on "Larry King Live," "The Today Show," and other national television programs, as well as in *Newsweek*, *USA Today*, the *New York Times*, and the *Wall Street Journal*.

Rather than looking beyond news releases, media kits, special events, media tours, and other tactics for "creative ideas," my technique for the past 30 years (time flies when you're having fun) has been to stay within those frameworks, making the very tactics fresh and inventive.

Not all of them have been as much fun as using a pizza box as our media kit for Wolfgang Puck Frozen Pizza with the accompanying Interview Opportunity sheet: "Here's an interview you can sink your teeth into." But a colorful chef like Puck deserved a flamboyant Texas launch for his new frozen pizza.

Not all of them have been as difficult to arrange (or as successful!) as bringing the Martini & Rossi 100 Years of the Martini exhibition of vintage posters and celebrity photos into Morton's of Chicago restaurants when it had previously been displayed only in galleries and museums. (Note to students: read/clip/save. I read about the Martini & Rossi exhibit when it was at the Art Institute of Houston two years before I presented the idea to Morton's for its two Dallas steakhouses.)

Not all of them have been a natural: Who wouldn't think of inviting journalists to test drive Chrysler-Plymouth's "America" car with a Drive Safe America rally? But fleshing out the idea took a team. My team worked with the Houston Police Department to design a route through the city and convert that into a map our media drivers would use. We worked with Rice University to secure the parking lot of the football field as the rally point for the new vehicles and expanded our Houston media list to include auto and lifestyle writers from as far away as Beaumont. We brought in car mechanics and AAA safety experts, which led to a cover story in the *Houston Chronicle* and five smaller Texas papers.

Essay contests have worked for selling American Express services and even diamonds! "What the Statue of Liberty Means to Me" essays by immigrants and third graders helped Amex showcase its support for the restoration of the venerable sculpture and of Ellis Island. They made for some nice coverage, but nothing spectacular. But one year the Houston winner of the annual Why My Mom Deserves a Diamond contest, sponsored by the Diamond Information Center, turned out to be a Chinese child prodigy pianist who had been taught by his concert violinist mother. The contest winner copped a front-page color photo with the headline "Jewel of an Essay Wins Mom a Diamond of a Deal" in many Texas daily newspapers plus TV news coverage on Mother's Day and the week after.

The venue and timing for announcing contest winners is also a critical element in media success. The Adam's Mark Hotel agreed to host the young essay finalists and their parents at its Mother's Day Buffet, where media were invited to photograph the winners and hear them read the essays.

Piggybacking a crowd also worked for the Baileys Dessert Heaven contest. Finalists (local chefs) were invited to bring dessert samples for media judges to taste at the opening party for the Nutcracker Market (a huge event at the convention center each December that benefits the Houston Ballet). All the media judges arrived with cameras to document the gorgeous desserts in the glitzy setting teeming with people. Baileys Original Irish Cream and its distributors drank a toast to the success of their contest and subsequent rise in sales.

Alliteration, gerundial leads, double entendres (e.g., "Jamba Juice Lemonade Stands for Charity"), and freshening old sayings with new twists all work well.

Staying close to universal values is the key. Sometimes, writing simply and tightly is the most creative aspect of all.

California Pizza Kitchen had been providing pizzas on Christmas Eve to Salvation Army Centers in its key markets for several years. When I was given the project in Florida, Georgia, and Texas, we added a few "creative toppings" that turned out the media: We bought Santa hats for the line cooks to wear while they prepared those hundreds of pizzas; we quoted Salvation Army majors saying, "Other people send turkey and dressing on Christmas Day, but CPK is the first company to remember the shelter on Christmas Eve." And we created the headline "Pizza on Earth, Good Will toward Men."

Case Study 9.1

The Great Canadian Cover-Up

Few organizations try to discourage business, especially among the highly desirable age 15–35 consumer group. But that's exactly what the Canadian Dermatology Association (CDA) is doing. Its doctors would like to see fewer young Canadians with skin cancer.

The CDA's goal of reducing cancer and reducing business is values-driven. Among the core values that unite the more than 500 dermatologists of the CDA is "a lifetime of healthier skin" for Canadians.[15]

The CDA reports that cases of a skin cancer called melanoma, one of the most common forms of cancer for Canadians 15 to 35 years old, have almost doubled since 1989. Excessive, unprotected exposure to sunlight, the association adds, is a leading cause of skin cancer.[16] Floppy hats and sunblock would do much to combat the problem—but try telling that to millions of teenagers seeking the perfect tan.

In describing the challenges that confronted the CDA's campaign to protect teens, the newsletter *PRNews* reported, "Teens are notorious for two things: their sun-worshipping ways and their deep-seated belief that they are Teflon-coated with respect to anything health threatening. Unfortunately, traditional PR tactics (i.e., news releases and primetime PSAs) have little impact on their behavior."[17]

GCI Group, the public relations agency hired by the CDA, also realized that standard public relations tactics wouldn't impress or even reach a teen audience. "Getting a bunch of articles in the paper is nice," said Nancy Croitoru, president of GCI Group's Canadian operations, "but teenagers don't read the papers; their parents do. And it's not like teens to listen to their parents."[18]

The CDA's budget presented another challenge. The association could provide $80,000 (in U.S. dollars) for the campaign: a sizable amount of money, but not enough for an expensive advertising campaign or enough to cover the expenses of a celebrity spokesperson.

When traditional public relations tactics seem inadequate, one alternative is the untraditional. That's the route GCI Group chose for an award-winning campaign it called "It's Cool to Cover Up." Tactics for the campaign included

- The "RayWatch" team, a group of well-toned, untanned teens who hit beaches, music festivals, sporting events, and other locations where young Canadians gathered in the sun. Attired in beachwear, the RayWatch teens clearly spoofed the popular "BayWatch" television show. Team members distributed containers of sunblock as well as fact sheets on skin protection. A professional dermatologist discreetly trailed the team to answer any technical questions. Before each Ray-Watch appearance, GCI Group notified local news media through media advisories that stressed photo opportunities.

    RayWatch gained additional publicity when two members of the team appeared in the *Toronto Sun* as "Sunshine Girl" and "Sunshine Boy." These two aspects of the newspaper generally feature nearly nude models who often praise a fun-in-the-sun way of life. The RayWatch teens put a safe-sun spin on that message.

- GCI Group also persuaded the MuchMusic channel, a Canadian version of MTV, to air a safe-sun commercial at reduced rates. The ad depicted a 16-year-old girl's smooth hand withering into a wrinkled, sun-scorched claw. MuchMusic's French-speaking sister station, Musique Plus in Quebec, also ran the ad. The ad's production and airing costs consumed nearly half the campaign's budget. Suzie McMeans, a GCI executive, said that MuchMusic was "the fastest way to reach the youth in Canada."[19]

- GCI Group sent "It's Cool to Cover Up" media kits to Canada's top youth-oriented radio stations. In addition to safe-sun facts, the kits included safe-sun packages containing RayWatch clothing, sunblock, and coupons for indoor activities such as movies. The radio stations used the kits to create their own "It's Cool to Cover Up" promotional giveaways.

By the end of the summer of 2000, GCI Group believed that the tactics were succeeding. "Young adults are traditionally the most difficult demographic to reach," Croitoru said. "This is especially true for a message about sun safety, which asks youth to give up their summer tans for their future health. Our team rose to the challenge by using humor and sex appeal to position sun safety as 'cool,' a life choice you can make without compromising your looks."[20]

GCI Group and the Canadian Dermatology Association are realistic about the likelihood of immediately changing teen behavior. "We don't expect teenagers to change their minds overnight," said CDA dermatologist Lynn From. "But we've reached an awful lot of people."[21]

PR practitioners noted the big impact of the moderately priced campaign. "Witty Campaign Puts PR Where the Sun Don't Shine" declared a headline in *PRNews*.[22]

Dermatologists also applauded the innovative campaign. In 2001, "It's Cool to Cover Up" won the Gold Triangle Award from the American Academy of Dermatology—the first time a Canadian campaign had won that award.[23]

The next step in evaluative research is to see whether teen behavior changes and cancer rates decline—but that's a long-term process. For now, GCI does know that its safe-sun message reached millions of teens. "We were extremely effective as a team," said GCI Group's McMeans. "And we had a lot of fun doing something fulfilling and for the greater good."[24]

DISCUSSION QUESTIONS

1. Imagine that GCI Group conducted an "It's Cool to Cover Up" campaign in the United States. What other tactics would you suggest to reach U.S. teens?
2. Although GCI Group emphasized public relations tactics, it also used advertising. What does GCI's choice of tactics say about the relative merits of public relations and advertising?
3. GCI's commercial on MuchMusic used an emotional appeal (*pathos*) to teens. In your opinion, was that an effective choice? How might *logos* and *ethos* have been used in a commercial?
4. To attract news media to RayWatch events, GCI used media advisories that emphasized excellent photo opportunities. If you were writing a photo opportunity sheet for the RayWatch events, what information would you include to attract photographers?

Case Study 9.2

The Dog That Didn't Bark: Abercrombie & Fitch and MADD

In "Silver Blaze," one of his most famous cases, Sherlock Holmes solves a mystery by noting what *didn't* happen: A dog that should have barked did not. The story doesn't mention public relations, but it contains a valuable lesson for today's practitioners: They should be ready to bark, figuratively speaking, at bad guys and bad ideas.

Like the dog in "Silver Blaze," the public relations team that serves Abercrombie & Fitch, a popular retailer of clothing for the college-age market, didn't bark when it should have. In summer 1998, A&F published almost 1 million copies of its 200-plus-page back-to-school catalog. Amid the attractive apparel and well-toned models was a section titled "Drinking 101." Containing recipes for alcoholic beverages with names such as Woo-Woo and Brain Hemorrhage, the two-page spread urged, "Rather than the standard beer binge, indulge in some creative drinking this semester."

A&F's hangover began July 16 when the national office of Mothers Against Drunk Driving launched a furious news release at the nation's news media. "This catalog is among the most blatantly irresponsible pieces of marketing we have ever seen," declared MADD President Karolyn Nunnallee. Noting that most college undergraduates are below the legal drinking age, Nunnallee added, "This catalog shows not only a total disrespect for the law, but a complete disregard for the well-being of [A&F's] customers." The MADD news release capped that quotation with statistics regarding the number of drinking-and-driving deaths for youths under age 21.[25]

Let's pause here to ask an important question. The notorious catalog was a *marketing* action, not a public relations tactic. Why, then, is it a failure of public relations?

As we stated in Chapter 8, the well-informed voice of the public relations team should be heard as an organization considers future courses of action. Ideally, no other area of the organization has a better understanding of the publics that influence and are affected by the organization's actions—including its marketing actions. As A&F's 1998 back-to-school catalog proves all too well, a marketing blunder can have severe consequences for public relations. It can damage relationships with activist groups, the news media, customers, and other publics whose actions spell success or failure for the organization.

The day after MADD's news release, NBC's *Today* show featured a live interview with Nunnallee, MADD's angry and articulate president. Host Matt Lauer read a lengthy statement from A&F that said, in part, "We condemn irresponsible and illegal drinking"—but Lauer closed the segment by saying, "We want to mention one more time that the folks at Abercrombie & Fitch denied our request for an interview on the subject."[26]

News anchor Tom Brokaw covered the story on *NBC Nightly News*, and Reuter's, an international news service, picked it up, as did the Associated Press. In the AP story, Nunnallee continued MADD's attack. "This catalog is an abomination," she said. "They have a responsibility, and that responsibility is not to promote unsafe behavior."[27] Nunnallee asked A&F to cease distribution of the catalog, send letters of apology to catalog recipients, and devote at least one page in the next four catalogs to the problems of underage drinking as well as drinking and driving.

A&F had stumbled a bit as it began to implement public relations tactics to minimize the damage. In its first response to MADD's fury, an A&F spokesman had said, "The catalog is out the door."[28]

However, A&F quickly issued its statement to NBC's *Today* show, and within six days of MADD's news release, A&F had added a page to its online version of the catalog. Under the heading Be Smart, a statement read, "We don't want to lose anybody to thoughtlessness and stupidity. For some, part of college life includes partying and drinking—be smart, and be responsible."[29]

Within nine days of MADD's news release, the Associated Press reported that A&F had agreed to attach stickers with the Be Smart message to catalogs in its stores and to send postcards bearing the same message to catalog subscribers.

"In retrospect, the company feels that it should have initially provided balance in that story," said a company spokesman.[30]

In other words, the dog should have barked before it was too late.

DISCUSSION QUESTIONS

1. Should Abercrombie & Fitch have sent a representative to appear on NBC's *Today* with MADD's president? Why or why not?
2. Suppose that, in a similar situation, a marketing department says, "We know our customers, and this won't offend them. Let's distribute the catalog." What should be the response of the public relations department?
3. What other groups besides MADD might have been offended by the "Drinking 101" spread? Can you name any publics that would approve of the spread?
4. Do you think Abercrombie & Fitch's public relations tactics did enough to defuse the situation? If not, what else would you have recommended?
5. Can you name marketing tactics by other companies that have created public relations problems?
6. Could the controversial A&F catalog actually have been a *good* public relations tactic? After all, it brought a great deal of media attention to the retailer and its catalog.

It's Your Turn

The Tuition Increase Revisited

In Chapter 4's It's Your Turn feature, we examined a scenario in which the top administrators of your college or university wanted your expertise in public relations because they were about to announce a 15 percent increase in tuition, scheduled to begin the next academic year. In that scenario, you identified the publics with whom the administrators would need to communicate to gain support for the tuition increase. Now imagine that the administrators are asking you for even more information.

As you'll recall, the plan is to use the tuition increase to fund four programs:

■ a small day-care center for the children of nontraditional students

■ an additional salary increase for professors (but not for other members of the staff)

■ 25 new annual scholarships for women athletes

■ 25 new annual scholarships for students from Latin America, a group that is underrepresented on campus

Earlier, you identified internal, external, and intervening publics; the values and opinion leaders/decision makers of each public; and the probable opinion of each public regarding the proposed tuition increase. Now the administrators are asking for more information:

1. What public relations objective or objectives (as discussed in Chapter 8) would you recommend for each public?
2. What tactics would you recommend to achieve those publics-focused objectives?

Ultimately, you would present your answers to the administrators as part of a well-written proposal. But imagine that you and your classmates schedule a preproposal brainstorming session. What objectives and what tactics would you recommend?

KEY TERMS

actualities, p. 277

annual meeting, p. 282

annual report, p. 283

association magazines, p. 281

backgrounder, p. 275

bill inserts, p. 288

b-roll, p. 277

cause marketing, p. 285

coalition building, p. 285

controlled media, p. 266

e-mail, p. 273

extranets, p. 292

fact sheet, p. 275

grassroots lobbying, p. 286

independent endorsement, p. 269

instant messaging, p. 273

intranet, p. 273

lobby, p. 286

media advisory, p. 277

media kit, p. 275

news conference, p. 277

news release, p. 274

photo opportunity sheet, p. 275

pitch letter, p. 277

political action committees (PACs), p. 286

pseudoevent, p. 266

public service announcements (PSAs),
    p. 279

satellite media tour (SMT), p. 281

soft money, p. 287

special event, p. 265

tactics, p. 263

third-party endorsement, p. 269

trade magazines, p. 281

uncontrolled media, p. 268

video news releases (VNRs), p. 277

NOTES

1. Marshall McLuhan, *Understanding Media: The Extensions of Man* (New York: McGraw-Hill, 1965), 7.
2. "Internet Election News Audience Seeks Convenience, Familiar Names," a report by the Pew Research Center for the People and the Press, 3 December 2000, online, www.press-people.org/online00rpt.htm. (Other information cited comes from this report.)
3. "The Lure of E-Mail May Be Deceiving," a news release issued by Watson Wyatt Worldwide, 26 July 1999, online, www.watsonwyatt.com/homepage/us/new/pres_rel/july99/comrpt99-tm.htm.
4. Jennifer McCullam, "Instant Enterprising," *Forbes,* 11 September 2000, 28.
5. Linda Morton, "Producing Publishable News Releases: A Research Perspective," *Public Relations Quarterly* 37, no. 4 (22 December 1992), online, Lexis-Nexis.
6. "Media Still Hot on Viagra News Trail," *Healthcare PR & Marketing News* 7, no. 1 (14 May 1998), online, Lexis-Nexis.
7. "Media Still Hot."
8. DS Simon Productions Inc. web site, www.dssimon.com.

9. Nick Nuttal, "Minister Attacks Greenpeace for Brent Spar Error," London *Times,* 6 September 1995, online, Lexis-Nexis.

10. "Summary of PAC Activity 1986–2000," a report by the Federal Election Commission, 31 May 2001, online, www.fec.gov.press/053101/pacfund/tables/pachis00.htm.

11. Jeffrey H. Birnbaum, "Washington's Power 25: Which Pressure Groups Are Best at Manipulating the Laws We Live By?" *Fortune,* 8 December 1997, online, Lexis-Nexis.

12. "Washington's Power 25 2000," *Fortune,* online, www.fortune.com.

13. Birnbaum.

14. Andy Reinhart, "Extranets: Log On, Link Up, Save Big," *Business Week,* 22 June 1998, online, Lexis-Nexis.

15. "RayWatch Team Spreads Sunscreen and Safe Sun Messages at Halifax Buskers' Festival," a news release issued via Canada NewsWire, 4 August 2000, online, Lexis-Nexis.

16. "Witty Campaign Puts PR Where the Sun Don't Shine," *PRNews,* 9 April 2001, online, Lexis-Nexis.

17. "Witty Campaign Puts PR Where the Sun Don't Shine."

18. "Witty Campaign Puts PR Where the Sun Don't Shine."

19. "Witty Campaign Puts PR Where the Sun Don't Shine."

20. "GCI Group Receives Prestigious Gold Triangle Award," a news release issued via PR Newswire, 29 March 2001, online, Lexis-Nexis.

21. "Witty Campaign Puts PR Where the Sun Don't Shine."

22. "Witty Campaign Puts PR Where the Sun Don't Shine."

23. "GCI Group Receives Prestigious Gold Triangle Award."

24. "Witty Campaign Puts PR Where the Sun Don't Shine."

25. "MADD Calls on Retailer to Pull Catalog Encouraging Underage Drinking," news release from Mothers Against Drunk Driving, 16 July 1998, online, www.madd.org/Wire/NewsList.asp?Object_ID=254328&SiteID=MADD.

26. NBC *Today* show, 17 July 1998, online, Lexis-Nexis.

27. *NBC Nightly News,* 16 July 1998, online, Lexis-Nexis; Reuters, 17 July 1998, online, www.yahoo.com; "Riding This Trend, Retailer Draws Fury," *Chicago Tribune,* 25 July 1998, online, Lexis-Nexis.

28. "Short Cuts," *Newsday,* 18 July 1998, online, Lexis-Nexis.

29. Abercrombie & Fitch web site, 22 July 1998, www.abercrombie.com/besmartright.html.

30. "Riding This Trend, Retailer Draws Fury."

10

Writing and Presentation Skills

objectives

After studying this chapter, you will be able to

■ describe and follow the different stages of the writing process

■ identify and use techniques that increase the effectiveness of spoken language

■ describe and follow the process of making a successful presentation

Publicizing Volunteer Clearinghouse

scenario

A college internship has led to your first job: You're now an assistant account executive with a public relations agency. As an intern, you impressed the agency's partners with your character, work ethic, team spirit, and writing abilities. At the end of your internship, the partners asked you to stay in touch, which you did, occasionally sending them class projects and successful assignments from other internships. One week before you graduated, the partners rewarded your talent and persistence with a job offer, which you accepted.

Your first task at the agency involves writing a news release for Volunteer Clear-inghouse, which coordinates volunteer recruitment for nonprofit social-service agencies in your county. Volunteer Clearinghouse is one of your agency's pro bono clients, meaning the agency doesn't charge for its services. Offering unpaid services to Volunteer Clearinghouse helps your agency honor one of its founding values: a commitment to building a better community through social responsibility.

The board of directors of Volunteer Clearinghouse has just named a new executive director. Her name is Elaine Anderson, and she succeeds Phil Connors, who accepted a similar position in another state. The board of directors would like your agency to write a news release announcing Anderson's hiring. The account executive who serves as a liaison to Volunteer Clearinghouse quickly agrees and turns to you.

It's 3:00 P.M., and the account executive would like the news release by 10:00 A.M. tomorrow.

It's the first assignment of your new job, and you want to do well. How and where do you start?

The Importance of Writing and Presentation Skills

"Writing is easy," said U.S. journalist and playwright Gene Fowler. "All you do is stare at a blank sheet of paper until drops of blood form on your forehead."[1]

We might update Fowler's description to include a computer screen, but his point remains: Good writing is hard work. In fact, more than one writer has compared the activity to spilling blood. Nobel Prize–winning novelist Ernest Hemingway declared, "Writing is easy. Just open a vein and bleed on paper."[2]

Whew! Tough business, this writing. Nothing could be more challenging, right? Wrong. How about making a presentation? By yourself. In front of a lot of people. With your reputation and a potential client at stake. According to *The Book of Lists*, public speaking ranks number one on the list of people's greatest fears, ahead of heights, sickness, and even death.[3]

This chapter focuses on spilling blood and tackling terrors worse than death. In other words, this chapter focuses on writing and presentation skills. Why? Because they're at the heart of the practice of public relations. Ninety percent of public relations employers list the ability to write well as one of their "top three sought-after skills." Also, between 80 and 90 percent of employers list experience, personality, and demeanor—key qualities for good presentations—as being among the top factors in hiring decisions.[4] And these qualities applied to all potential hires, not just entry-level applicants. Clearly, writing and presentation skills are prerequisites for success at every stage of a public relations career.

One objective of this chapter is to reduce the stress involved in writing and presenting by dividing those activities into small, achievable steps. Writing and presenting are processes. Rather than approaching them as jagged mountains to be scaled in one leap, we can learn to master writing and presenting by tackling them one step at a time—methodically climbing the mountain, so to speak, instead of trying to reach the top in one doomed jump.

However, this chapter doesn't pretend to tell you everything you need to know about writing and presenting. Those topics consume whole textbooks all by themselves. Instead, this chapter strives to cover the basics of writing and presenting, suggesting their fundamental importance to the profession of public relations. Let's begin with blood-spilling—that is, with writing.

A Context for Public Relations Writing

Journalists write to inform. Advertisers write to persuade. Informing and persuading are the respective contexts for the writing involved in those professions. What, then, is the context for public relations writing? In a sense, that question echoes one posed in Chapter 6: Are public relations practitioners objective communicators, like journalists, or are they persuasive advocates, like advertisers and lawyers? Our answer now—as it was then—is "none of the above." Public relations practitioners are neither journalists, nor lawyers, nor advertisers. They are relationship managers.

The context for public relations writing is relationship management. Sometimes the ethical management of relationships requires journalistic objectivity; other times, it may require persuasion. Often, it requires a little of both. As relationship-management tactics, public relations documents should address the values and interests of the writer's organization as well as the values and interests of the targeted public or publics. For example, a well-written news release certainly addresses the interests of the writer's organization: It communicates important information that the organization considers newsworthy. The same news release also addresses the interests of the news media, which rely on news releases to help them identify and communicate the news. Additionally, the news release addresses the interests of targeted publics within the news media's audiences—investors, perhaps, or local environmentalists. By addressing the individual interests of each of those parties, the news release maintains and even strengthens relationships that sustain the organization.

Think of our definition of public relations: *Public relations is the values-driven management of relationships between an organization and the publics that can affect its success.* Public relations writing supports that definition. Whatever the document may be—a speech, an annual report, or even an in-house memo—its aim is consistent: to be an effective tactic in the management of relationships vital to an organization's success.

The Writing Process

Writing a public relations document, whether it be a news release, a public service announcement, or something else altogether, can be intimidating. Writers respond to such anxiety in many ways. Sometimes they avoid the challenge by putting the

Good writing

"Good writing, like a good house, is an orderly arrangement of parts."

Mortimer Adler

Good writing is the core of effective corporate communication. Whether delivered in the form of a presentation, video, newsletter, annual report or other medium, most messages begin on a sheet of paper.

At Schaffner Communications we believe that good business communication belongs in the hands of skilled professional journalists, not of advertising copywriters who may sacrifice clarity for design, or aspiring novelists who could confuse the message with the medium.

Our clients agree. They recognize the need not only to master and tame the English language, but to conduct accompanying research, interviews and red pencil reviews that provide the framework for effective presentations. That's our style at Schaffner Communications.

Business communication, Schaffner-style, relies on pairing a client's message with the medium that's most appropriate for the audience and intent. Words are the heart of those messages, whether applied to printed, visual or audio materials.

Tools of the Trade

Good writing is at the core of effective communications programs, including all of the following:

Advertisements

Annual Reports

Books

Brochures

Columns

Correspondence

Documentation

Feature Stories

Flyers and Leaflets

Letters to the Editor

Magazine Articles

Manuals and Handbooks

Newsletters

Press Releases

Proposals

Public Service Announcements

Radio Copy

Scripts

Speeches and Presentations

Video News Releases

Brochure Chicago-based Schaffner Communications wins and keeps clients with its intense focus on good writing. (Courtesy of Schaffner Communications)

writing task off until the last moment. Or, conversely, perhaps they attack the challenge by flying to their computer keyboards and banging away. Both responses usually lead to frustration, however, not to good writing. Like public relations itself, writing is a process: It can't be started at the last moment, and it doesn't begin with your fingers flying over the keyboard. The **writing process** begins with values and ends with evaluation. Because writing is a process, its first step leads logically to a second step, which leads to a third, and so on.

The writing process, in fact, has something in common with **Maslow's Hierarchy of Needs,** presented in Chapter 5. As you'll recall, moving too high too fast in Maslow's hierarchy can be disastrous; the needs at each level of that pyramid must be fulfilled before you can move up to the next level. It's the same in the writing process: It's counterproductive to move to the fourth level, for example, when you haven't completed the first, second, and third levels. In fact, if you're stalled at a particular stage of a writing project, you should consider dropping down to the earlier levels. Perhaps a failure to complete one of them has led to your momentary dead end. At the very least, reviewing your progress may reveal a solution to your frustration.

Envisioning writing as a process can help you cope with the intimidation that sometimes accompanies important writing assignments. The writing process can help you avoid procrastination because it eases you into the actual writing; it helps you approach an assignment with confidence. And the writing process prevents you from wasting your time (and others' time) by jumping in too quickly and trying to write without adequate preparation. The writing process helps you tackle a writing assignment in a logical, productive fashion.

So what are the different stages of the writing process? As Figure 10.1 shows, the writing process for public relations consists of 10 stages. These stages, in order, are credibility, research, organization, writing, revision, macroediting, microediting, approval, distribution, and evaluation. Figure 10.1 also suggests that you should communicate with supervisors and/or clients—whoever is appropriate—as your writing assignment progresses. For a short newsletter story, communication with supervisors and/or clients might be brief: checking quotations, confirming deadlines, suggesting a new angle that your research has revealed, and submitting a draft before the deadline. But for a more extensive document, such as major sections of a corporation's annual report, communication might take the form of regularly scheduled meetings or a constant exchange of e-mail messages and rough drafts. Ask supervisors and clients how much communication they would like—and always inform them as new challenges and opportunities regarding an assignment arise.

Although our chapter focuses on the writing process within the context of public relations, the process applies to other situations, such as writing an advertisement, a short story, or even a love letter. However, some of the stages are more appropriate for public relations than for other writing situations; these stages include credibility, approval, and evaluation.

Let's now examine the individual stages of the writing process.

FIGURE 10.1   The Writing Process
Successful public relations writing begins with
credibility and ends with evaluating the success
of the written document. The 10 stages of the
writing process should be followed in order:
Research comes before organization, which
comes before writing, and so on. As the
document progresses, the writer should
discuss problems or new ideas with
supervisors and/or clients.

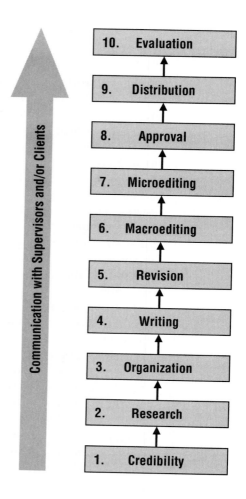

Credibility: Stage One of the Writing Process

This is *really* beginning at the beginning, but starting anywhere else would be misleading and counterproductive. As a communicator, you must have credibility, or there's no
point in trying to send a message. Clients and supervisors won't give an important writing assignment to an individual they don't trust. Receivers of a message may discount
it if they lack respect for the source. As we noted in Chapter 5, Aristotle praised the
strategies of appealing to an audience's intellect and to its emotions—but he said the
most powerful persuasive strategy of all is the character of the communicator.

So how can you establish character? Actually, as you know, you've been doing
that since you learned to think for yourself and to make your own decisions. But
character isn't static. It grows—or diminishes. As a public relations practitioner, you
can "grow" and establish your character by testing your actions and those of your

employer against your own values, the values of your employer, the values of the public relations profession (as stated in the ethics codes of organizations such as the Public Relations Society of America), and the values of the society in which you live.

In the scenario that opens this chapter, your character helped you move from being an intern to being a full-time employee. Your values-driven actions impressed the agency's partners so much that they paid you the ultimate compliment: They recruited and hired you.

QuickBreak 10.1

WRITING FOR DIVERSE PUBLICS: TIPS FOR INCLUSIVE LANGUAGE

Public relations writing builds relationships. The careless use of language, however, can inadvertently exclude valuable members of important publics. To create inclusive documents, consider the following guidelines:[5]

- In documents that cite individuals as sources, draw upon diverse individuals. In many organizations and publics, it's easy to rely on a steady stream of white Anglo-Saxon males in their 40s and 50s. Not all qualified sources are of that race, ethnicity, gender, or age.

- Balance personal pronouns. For unnamed, generic individuals such as a supervisor or senator, balance the use of *he* and *she*. Don't, however, include illogical shifts. A hypothetical supervisor shouldn't change gender within a paragraph. Another solution is to use plural nouns—*supervisors* and *senators*—that can be replaced by *they*.

- Avoid words that describe particular relationships: *your wife, your husband, your boyfriend, your girlfriend, your parents, your children.* Female readers generally are excluded by *your wife,* just as male readers generally are by *your husband.* Let your targeted public be your guide as to what is appropriate.

- Know the dates of major religious holidays. When is Rosh Hashanah? When is Ramadan?

- Don't describe individuals by race, ethnicity, religion, age, sexual orientation, or physical or mental disability unless the information is relevant to your document's purpose. If an individual must be so described, consider applying the same exactness of description to every other individual mentioned in your document.

- If you are responsible for a document's design, apply your quest for inclusiveness to photographs and other visual representations of individuals. Even if you're *not* in charge of the design, don't hesitate to point out lapses of diversity.

A Bureau of Labor Statistics survey of almost 60,000 households revealed the following preferences in racial and ethnic terminology:[6]

- Blacks prefer *black* (44.15 percent) to *African American* (28.07 percent) and *Afro-American* (12.12 percent).

- Hispanics prefer *Hispanic* (57.88 percent) to *of Spanish origin* (12.34 percent) and *Latino* (11.74 percent).

- American Indians prefer *American Indian* (49.76 percent) to *Native American* (37.35 percent).

- Multiracial individuals prefer *multiracial* (28.42 percent) to *mixed-race* (16.02 percent).

Words have power. They can include—or exclude. Use them wisely.

Establishing character can't be an occasional thing. The values that surround and help give meaning to your life should be with you every day. One of the many payoffs of values-driven public relations is that it helps make you a credible, trustworthy communicator.

Research: Stage Two of the Writing Process

Different public relations documents require different kinds of research: For example, a CEO's speech to a corporation's stockholders requires different research than an employee relations document on how to apply for a promotion. But regardless of what document they're preparing to write, public relations practitioners ask the following five questions.

1. WHAT IS MY PURPOSE IN WRITING?   In other words, what is the goal of this document? What does your organization hope this document will achieve? You should be able to answer this question with one clear, precise sentence. If that isn't possible, you don't understand the mission of the document, and you shouldn't proceed until you do.

For example, suppose that your supervisor asks you to write an employee newsletter story about your organization's new voluntary long-term disability insurance program. Great; but what's the goal? Should the story just inform employees about the new program? Or should it recruit them? Ideally, your supervisor can answer your questions—but if she can't, your story probably is on hold until you learn more about the story's precise purpose.

2. WHO IS MY TARGETED PUBLIC?   For most documents, this means *Who are my readers?* For the text of a speech or for a radio public service announcement, it means *Who are my listeners?* In all cases, it means *Who are the receivers of the message I intend to send?*

In Chapter 4 you encountered seven questions that public relations practitioners must answer to build successful relationships with important publics. These seven questions can help you answer *Who is my targeted public?*

- *How much can this targeted public influence my organization's ability to achieve its goals?* Because resources are limited, public relations practitioners must devote most of their attention and efforts to publics that can help their organization succeed.

- *Who are the opinion leaders and decision makers in my targeted public?* Can you appeal to those individuals without excluding other members of the targeted public?

- *What is the demographic profile of my targeted public?* What is the age range of its members? The education range? The male/female ratio? In other words, statistically speaking, who is your targeted public? What does **demographic information** say about your public's members?

- *What is the psychographic profile of my targeted public?* Are members of your targeted public politically conservative, liberal, or middle-of-the-road—or is the range too broad to generalize? Are they devoutly religious, assuredly secular, or scattered along the spectrum of religious intensity? **Psychographic information** includes data about what people believe, think, and feel.

- *What is my targeted public's opinion of my organization?* Are you approaching a friendly public, a neutral public, or a hostile public?
- *What is my targeted public's opinion of the subject I'm addressing?* How much do members of your targeted public already know about the subject you are preparing to address? Do levels of knowledge differ within your targeted public? You don't want to dwell on information they already know well; on the other hand, you don't want to make false assumptions about what you think they know. And beyond the targeted public's knowledge, what do its members *think* about your subject? Do its members agree, or do opinions vary?

These are six of the seven standard questions you can ask to help you answer, *Who is my targeted public?* The seventh question is so important that we reserve it for its own section, which follows: *What are the values and interests of my targeted public in this situation?*

3. WHAT ARE THE VALUES AND INTERESTS OF MY TARGETED PUBLIC IN THIS SITUATION?

One of the most important research functions in public relations writing is the identification of your targeted public's stake in your subject matter. Determining the targeted public's values and interests helps you do two things. First, you can quickly move to values and interests in your document, ensuring that your targeted public will pay attention (after all, its members have suddenly realized that you're addressing their concerns). Second, knowing your targeted public's values and interests can help you fulfill them, when possible. As you know, the best relationships in public relations are those in which both sides benefit: true win–win situations. You improve the odds of achieving a win–win relationship when you know your targeted public's stake in the relevant issue.

In Publicizing Volunteer Clearinghouse, our opening scenario, your consideration of your targeted public would provide extremely useful information for the news release you're about to write. You know that your targeted public is news media editors, and you know what they value: a newsworthy, objective, unbiased, local-interest story that they can deliver to their own audiences. You also know that they have a good opinion of Volunteer Clearinghouse and probably will use your news release—if you can meet their standards.

4. WHAT MESSAGE SHOULD I SEND?

You can answer this question by combining what you've learned from answering question 1 above *(What is my purpose in writing?)* and question 3 *(What are the values and interests of my targeted public in this situation?).* As you know from Chapter 8, a successful message combines the purpose of your document with the targeted public's values and interests.

Earlier, for example, we looked at a hypothetical situation in which you were asked to write an employee newsletter story on a new voluntary long-term disability insurance program. Your purpose, you learn, is to persuade employees to enroll in the program. But that's not your message; it doesn't yet have any appeal to the targeted public's values or interests. In researching your targeted public, you learn that your organization's employees have a powerful interest in the financial security of their families. *Now* you have a message: *Enroll in the new insurance program to provide additional financial security for your family.* You need not use those exact words, but that message needs to be the unmistakable theme of your newsletter story.

5. WHAT INFORMATION SUPPORTS MY MESSAGE?   What information does your organization want you to include in the document you're preparing to write? What information does your targeted public hope to learn from reading your document? Answers to those questions will guide you in your search for relevant information. In researching their stories, journalists seek specific information in six broad areas: *who, what, when, where, why,* and *how.* Those questions may not apply to every public relations writing situation, but asking them can help you anticipate the information requirements of your document.

With all this research gathered, you can turn with confidence to the next stage in the writing process: organization.

Quick ✔ Check

1. In what way is the writing process like Maslow's Hierarchy of Needs?
2. In the research stage of the writing process, what kinds of information should you gather about your targeted public?
3. In public relations, what qualities are essential in an effective message?

Organization: Stage Three of the Writing Process

The organization of a document should draw the targeted public's attention to the message and to the information that supports and develops it. Often, that means that the document moves gracefully but quickly to the message. Because the message directly targets the readers' or listeners' values and interests, the sooner we reach it, the sooner the targeted public knows why it should be reading, watching, or listening.

There are, however, exceptions to the general rule of moving quickly to the message. In bad-news situations, for example—in which you tell people something they don't want to hear—the message generally comes *after* a concise description of your reasons for the upcoming bad news. In other words, a quick explanation of *why* comes before you announce the bad news. If we simply announce the bad news first, our unhappy targeted public may tune out our explanation, and that could further damage our relationship. In rejecting employment applications, for example, many

What should make me suspect a piece of mail?

- It's unexpected or from someone you don't know.
- It's addressed to someone no longer at your address.
- It's handwritten and has no return address or bears one that you can't confirm is legitimate.
- It's lopsided or lumpy in appearance.
- It's sealed with excessive amounts of tape.
- It's marked with restrictive endorsements such as "Personal" or "Confidential."
- It has excessive postage.

What should I do with a suspicious piece of mail?

- Don't handle a letter or package that you suspect is contaminated.
- Don't shake it, bump it, or sniff it.
- Wash your hands thoroughly with soap and water.
- Notify local law enforcement authorities.

Flier When U.S. government and news media offices received mail contaminated with anthrax in 2001, the United States Postal Service created a well-organized, concise flier to address the concerns of customers throughout the nation. (Courtesy of the United States Postal Service)

organizations use business letters that place the *why* before the bad-news message: *Unfortunately, we have no positions open at this time. Therefore, we are unable to offer you a job.* The job applicant may not like the message, but at least he knows why his request cannot be satisfied.

Clearly, different documents are organized in different message-focused ways. But every document, no matter what its organization is, can benefit from an outline. Outlines needn't be the formal Roman-numeral lists that you learned to create in elementary school; a few scribbled notes for each paragraph may work just as well for you. And outlines aren't etched in stone: As you write a document, better ideas—and a better organization—may occur to you. But some form of outline, some written plan of how you're going to get from here to there, is essential. During spring break, for example, you wouldn't drive to some distant, sunny beach without a map. You *might* get there without one, but why waste time and risk failure? The same logic applies to writing. Use an outline.

In our Volunteer Clearinghouse scenario, the research you conducted in the previous stage of the writing process can now help you create an outline. You know that your targeted public consists of news editors, and you know that news editors want the news. Therefore, you decide to organize your news release in the **inverted pyramid** style of a traditional news story, with the most important information at the beginning and the least important at the end (see Figure 10.2). You review the most important

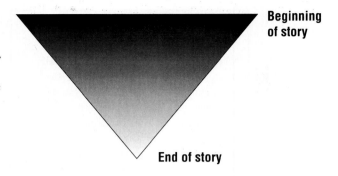

FIGURE 10.2   The Inverted Pyramid The inverted pyramid represents the traditional organization of a news story. Where the pyramid is widest, the information in the story is most important. The narrowing of the pyramid represents the decreasing importance of information as a news story progresses toward its ending. Thus, a traditional news story places the most important information at the beginning, which journalists call "the lead." In public relations, most news releases use the inverted pyramid organization.

Beginning of story

End of story

details in the areas of who, what, when, where, why, and how, and you organize the details in terms of importance. You decide that your first paragraph needs to announce the most important news: The board of directors has hired Elaine Anderson to be the new executive director of Volunteer Clearinghouse. You decide that it's also important to describe briefly who Anderson is and when she'll begin her new job.

In your research you got a quotation about Anderson's abilities from the chairman of the board, but you decide to place that near the end of the news release. Although it's a good quotation, you decide that it's just not as important as the announcement of Anderson's hiring and the details about her qualifications for this new job.

Your final outline might look something like this:

Paragraph 1:   Anderson hired for new exec director.

Brief note on who she is.

Brief note on what Volunteer Clearinghouse is.

Note when she starts.

Paragraph 2:   Anderson's biography.

Paragraph 3:   She succeeds Phil Connors. Note where he's gone.

Paragraph 4:   Quote from board chairman.

Paragraph 5:   Note that anyone interested in volunteering with community service agencies can call the Volunteer Clearinghouse. List phone number and address.

Now you're organized. You know how to get from here to there. It's time to write.

Writing: Stage Four of the Writing Process

Because you've completed the research and organization stages of the writing process, the question that now faces you isn't *What should I write?* Instead, it's *How should*

CowParade Holdings Corporation
Two Railroad Place | Westport | Connecticut 06880 | ph. 203-291-4538 | fax 203-291-4501
Corporate Center West | Suite 111 | 433 South Main Street | West Hartford | Connecticut 06110 | ph. 860-561-4710 | fax 860-561-5327

PLEASE RESPOND TO:

CONTACT: Sarah Nichols or Sheri Johnson, APR
Morningstar Communications Company
(913) 851-8700 x24 or x22
(816) 678-5083, after hours
sarah@morningstarcomm.com
www.cowparadekc.com

FOR IMMEDIATE RELEASE   **January 19, 2001**

The Plaza Sponsors a Herd in CowParade Kansas City 2001

(Kansas City, MO) – The Plaza is extending CowParade Kansas City 2001 to one of

Kansas City's most popular areas by sponsor

News Release The headline and first words of a news release should quickly satisfy a journalist's desire for specific details about a newsworthy story. (Courtesy of Morningstar Communications Company)

I write what's in my outline? That difference doesn't make writing easy—but it certainly makes it easier. Having an outline allows you to begin anywhere. If you're intimidated by the importance of the first paragraph, start with the second: Your outline tells you what information to include.

Another strategy for getting started is simply to start: Write the first paragraph, no matter how bad it seems. Then stop and evaluate it. If it really is bad, why? What specifically is wrong with it? Are the sentences too long? Does the paragraph fail to move toward the targeted public's values and interests in this situation? Does it not follow your outline? Identifying specific problems helps you fix them. This process is similar to carving a statue out of stone: At first, all we have is an awkward chunk

QuickBreak 10.2

TEN TIPS FOR WRITING BETTER SENTENCES[7]

1. *Challenge "to be" verbs.* Challenge *is, are, was, were, will be,* and every other form of the verb *to be.* Sometimes a *to be* verb best suits the needs of the sentence, but often you can find a stronger, more descriptive verb that might also shorten the sentence.

Original	Revision
He will be a good communicator.	He will communicate effectively.
We are inviting you. . .	We invite you. . .

2. *Use active voice.* In the **active voice,** the subject of the sentence does the action. In the **passive voice,** the subject receives the action.

Passive Voice	Active Voice
Our profits were affected by a sales slump.	A sales slump affected our profits.

Passive voice is grammatically correct, and it's the right choice when the action is more important than the action's doer. (Example: She

was fired.) But passive voice can seem timid, and it requires a *to be* verb. Active voice is confident and concise.

3. *Challenge modifiers.* **Modifiers** (adjectives and adverbs) can strengthen a sentence by sharpening your meaning. But sometimes they prop up weak words, especially nouns and verbs. A precise, well-chosen word needs no modification.

Original	Revision
We are very happy.	We are ecstatic.
She ran fast.	She sprinted.

4. *Challenge long words.* If a long word or phrase works best, use it. Otherwise, use a shorter option.

Original	Revision
utilize	use
revenue-enhancement measure	tax

5. *Challenge prepositional phrases.* Avoid strings of prepositional phrases:

---

of rock. But by chipping away, little by little, we gradually create something that approaches our high standards.

For example, let's imagine that you roll up your sleeves and, with a quick glance at your outline for the Volunteer Clearinghouse news release, you just start writing:

> *The board of directors of Volunteer Clearinghouse has announced that Elaine Anderson will be that organization's new executive director. Anderson is the former supervisor of the Coxwold County Red Cross. Volunteer Clearinghouse coordinates the recruitment and training of volunteers for the agencies of the Coxwold County Social Service League.*

Not bad. But you quickly identify the small points that you don't like:

1. It takes 10 words before we get to the real news: Elaine Anderson is the new executive director. Can't we move faster to what will interest our targeted public of news editors?

Original	Revision
We will meet on Thursday in Centerville at the Lancaster Hotel on McDaniel Street near the harbor.	We will meet Thursday at the Lancaster Hotel, 1423 McDaniel St., Centerville.

Some prepositional phrases can be tightened into adjectives:

Original	Revision
I will present the report in the meeting on Thursday.	I will present the report in Thursday's meeting.

6. *Challenge long sentences.* How long should a sentence be? Long enough to make its point effectively—and no longer. Challenge any sentence that exceeds 25 words. Eliminate *to be* verbs and tighten prepositional phrases when possible.

7. *Avoid overused expressions.* Clichés such as "It has come to my attention" and "I regret to inform you" lack original thought. They sound insincere. Overused figures of speech, such as "He's a fish out of water," don't create the engaging image they once did.

8. *Avoid placing important words or phrases in the middle of a sentence.* The beginning of a sentence breaks a silence and calls attention to itself. The last words of a sentence echo into a brief silence and gain emphasis. The middle of a sentence generally draws the least attention.

9. *Keep the focus on the reader.* Tell readers what they want and need to know—not just what you want them to know. Keep the focus on how they benefit from reading your document.

10. *Read your sentences aloud.* Or at least whisper them quietly to yourself. That's the surest way to check for effective sentence rhythms. Reading aloud can also be an effective editing technique.

2. The paragraph doesn't include Anderson's starting date.
3. The last sentence seems like an afterthought.

With the problems identified, you're ready to eliminate them. Your second draft might look like this:

> *Elaine Anderson, former supervisor of the Coxwold County Red Cross, will be the new executive director of Volunteer Clearinghouse, that organization's board of directors has announced. Anderson will begin her new job January 15. Volunteer Clearinghouse coordinates the recruitment and training of volunteers for the agencies of the Coxwold County Social Service League.*

That's better. There's room for improvement, but your first paragraph is now good enough to justify moving on to another section of your document. You'll get another chance to polish all sections of the document during the next stage of the writing process: revision.

Revision: Stage Five of the Writing Process

As writers consider revision, a seductive danger confronts them: the euphoria of creation. Good writers work hard to complete their first drafts, and when they're done, they're often relieved, excited, and justifiably pleased with themselves. *I've worked hard,* they think. *I've agonized over every sentence. I'm not going to change a thing, because this document is good!* That's the euphoria of creation: the feeling that your just-finished document is great and needs no revision. One of the few cures is to get away from the document for as long as possible. Put it aside, even if it's for only half an hour. Concentrate on something else. Let the euphoria of creation subside. Finally, reapproach your document with the faith that revision just might make it better.

That's the goal of revision: to make a good document even better. One way to improve a good document is to approach it with the reader's vision. In a book called *The Reader over Your Shoulder,* poet and novelist Robert Graves recommends imagining one of your intended readers leaning over your shoulder and saying, *But what does that mean? Can't this part be clearer? What's in this for me? What do I gain by reading this?*[8] Instead of banishing this annoying reader back to your imagination, do your best to satisfy his or her demands. Approach your document not as the writer but as a reader. Engage in a true *re-vision.*

A second method of revision is to test each sentence against the goal of the document. Your goal, probably, is to move your targeted public to an action or, at least, to an idea. As you reread your document, does *every* sentence work toward the goal? Could some sentences work toward the goal more effectively? Do some passages need to be longer and stronger? Are other passages needlessly repeating earlier points? One definition of poetry is "the best words in the best order." That's not a bad definition for a public relations document. Every word should contribute to the document's clear reason for existing.

Let's return again to our Volunteer Clearinghouse scenario. Having put your news release aside for about 45 minutes, you begin to reread it, imagining that the editor of a local newspaper is leaning over your shoulder. Because she's a journalist, she immediately tells you, *Give me specific details. No vagueness!* Your reader's vision leads you to reconsider your first sentence:

> *Elaine Anderson, former supervisor of the Coxwold County Red Cross, will be the new executive director of Volunteer Clearinghouse, that organization's board of directors has announced.*

You're specific about *who* and *what*—but exactly *when* was this announced? That's not clear. So to satisfy your reader's interest in getting the exact details, you revise the sentence:

> *Elaine Anderson, former supervisor of the Coxwold County Red Cross, will be the new executive director of Volunteer Clearinghouse, that organization's board of directors announced Monday.*

It's a small change, but it has a big impact: It helps to satisfy the needs of your readers. When you've worked through the entire document with a fresh perspective and tested each sentence against your goal, you're ready for the next stage of the writing process: macroediting.

Macroediting: Stage Six of the Writing Process

You've no doubt heard that a lawyer who represents himself or herself has a fool for a client. The same is partially true of editing: No writer should serve as the only editor of his or her writing. A qualified coworker should edit your document before you submit it to a supervisor or the client for approval. Does that mean that you as writer have no editing responsibilities? No: Your goal is to deliver a flawless document to the editor—and that means completing the first edit yourself. Your own edit should consist of two levels: the macroedit and the microedit.

Macroediting challenges the "big picture" of your document: the meaning, the organization, and the format. Among the important questions in a macroedit are

- Is the message of the document clear?
- Does the document answer a reporter's traditional questions: who? what? where? when? why? how?
- Is the document fair? (You don't have to present other points of view, but your document shouldn't distort reality, present half-truths, or ignore damaging information.)
- Does the document make any claims that seem unsubstantiated?
- Does the organization of the main points follow a logical order?
- Does one paragraph lead gracefully to the next?
- Is the format of the document correct? (For example, does the format of a news release identify a contact person?)
- Does the format assist the meaning? (For example, would internal headlines help?)

The macroediting stage is your last opportunity for significant rewriting before you deliver your document to others. If you are satisfied that the meaning, organization, and format are as good as they can be, it's time for the picky stage of the writing process: the microedit.

Microediting: Stage Seven of the Writing Process

Microediting means doing a sentence-by-sentence double-check of accuracy, spelling, grammar (including punctuation), and style. But by this point in the writing process, you've probably read your document at least a dozen times; you may even have parts of it memorized. This familiarity makes it hard for you to conduct an effective microedit: You may read what you *meant* to write instead of what you *accidentally* wrote. One way to increase your focus on the actual words in each sentence is to conduct the microedit backward, starting with the last full sentence. Moving through the document backward "defamiliarizes" it, helping you see what you've really written. When you're certain that the last sentence is flawless, move to the second-to-last sentence, and so on. As you might guess, proofreading backward isn't exciting, but it is effective.

To verify accuracy, double-check all names, titles, numbers—any fact that can be confirmed. Also double-check all spelling, punctuation, and common grammatical errors such as disagreements between verbs and their subjects. For style, verify that each sentence follows specific style guidelines preferred by its targeted public. In your Volunteer Clearinghouse news release, you probably would use Associated Press style, which many newspapers use. AP style, for example, asks you to abbreviate the words *street, avenue,* and *boulevard* when they're used with a specific street name and a specific address. Most news releases are written in newspaper style, which broadcast media rewrite to their specifications.

Imagine doing the microedit of your news release for Volunteer Clearinghouse. As you'll recall, you had revised your first sentence to this:

> *Elaine Anderson, former supervisor of the Coxwold County Red Cross, will be the new executive director of Volunteer Clearinghouse, that organization's board of directors announced Monday.*

This would be the last sentence to undergo a microedit, because you wisely began at the end of the document and moved backward one sentence at a time. Stifling a yawn, you double-check the spelling of Elaine Anderson's name against her résumé—and your yawn turns into a gasp: Her first name is spelled *Elayne*. As you type in the correction, you're grateful that you edited the document yourself before submitting it to another editor. Good microediting helped save your credibility as a writer.

When the editing process is through, the document is ready for an important test: the approval stage of the writing process.

Approval: Stage Eight of the Writing Process

Chances are that you've been to a party in the past few months. Remember what you did before leaving your residence? You examined yourself in the mirror. You may even have asked a friend, "How do I look?" You wondered how others would react to you, and you did everything possible to ensure a good impression.

It's not that different with documents—except that, oftentimes, many people want to review a document before it is distributed to its targeted public: your supervisor, your client, anyone who is quoted, anyone who supplied important information, key department heads . . . the list can seem endless. It's as if a dozen friends and family members suddenly arrived and wanted to approve your appearance before you left for the party. And many of these reviewers have the power to insist on changes. In the workplace, your supervisor can assist you in determining which of the requested changes should be made.

James Cash Penney
His Life and Legacy

Retail genius, philanthropist, "the man with a thousand partners," gentleman farmer, author, lecturer, world traveler, and the founder of the J.C. Penney Company: These are all words and phrases used to describe James Cash Penney.

The man whose name became synonymous with doing business according to the principles of the Golden Rule was born on September 16, 1875, on a small farm outside Hamilton, Mo. Penney's father was a poor farmer and unsalaried Baptist minister. His mother was a devout woman born of a genteel Southern family. Although raised in poverty, he would remain faithful to the rigorous teachings of his parents.

An abiding faith in God, the Christian ethic of the Golden Rule, self-reliance, self-discipline, and honor formed the foundation on which he built his entire life. Penney showed signs of becoming a merchant as early as age eight,

James Cash Penney, age 59.

Biography A corporate identity booklet, such as this biography of James Cash Penney, founder of the J.C. Penney Company, would be reviewed at many levels of an organization before publication. (Courtesy of J.C. Penney Company)

Who is in charge of the approval stage? That depends on the company or organization, but in many cases the writer is in charge of securing approvals. The approval process involves knowing who needs to review the document, how soon each reviewer must respond, and who has the final say over requested revisions. Along with the document, each reviewer should receive a memorandum that politely specifies a deadline for response. An important strategy for the approval stage of the writing process is to keep a chart for every document, noting to whom it was sent, when it was sent, when it was returned, what revisions were requested, and what revisions were made.

The approvals list for the Volunteer Clearinghouse news release, for example, probably would include your supervisor, a representative of the clearinghouse's board of directors, and perhaps Elayne Anderson herself. Some documents, such as corporate annual reports, have much longer approvals lists; for example, lawyers and accountants read every annual report to ensure that it meets all its legal and financial reporting requirements.

For most public relations documents, a second round of approvals generally is not necessary unless substantial revisions were requested and made. However, be sure your supervisor grants final approval before you proceed to the next stage of the writing process: distribution.

Distribution: Stage Nine of the Writing Process

Distribution differs from document to document. A news release can be hand delivered, mailed, e-mailed, faxed, posted on a web site, or routed through online distribution services such as PR Newswire. A policy and procedure document telling employees how a certain process works can be placed in employee mailboxes or on desktops, e-mailed, posted on an intranet, placed in a binder in the organization's library, or even tacked onto an old-fashioned wall-mounted bulletin board. The writer may be in charge of all or some of the distribution, or distribution may be delegated to others.

As more and more distribution occurs through e-mail and web sites, however, writers are assuming increasing responsibility for distribution. With improvements in technology, distribution through cyberspace can be triggered by the push of a button. But therein lies a new problem for public relations practitioners. Should that message be posted on the organization's public web site—or, perhaps, should it be only on the intranet or extranet site? If the document is to be e-mailed within an organization, should everyone receive it—or just top management? More than one communicator has been embarrassed by accidentally posting a private document to every electronic mailbox within an organization. The ease of online communication is accompanied, unfortunately, by the possibility of instantaneous errors in distribution.

Even when distribution is delegated to others, the writer may want to double-check that it did occur. A sad truth is that the best writer and the most polished document in the world can be defeated by faulty distribution. Many writers, therefore, carefully monitor the distribution stage of the writing process. Double-checking distribution can be as simple as checking a web site or as complicated as driving to different office buildings to ensure that posters are properly displayed.

Despite the countless ways of distributing a document, a few facts hold true for every method: Whenever possible, a document should be delivered in the manner and at the time and in the place preferred by the targeted public. Don't hesitate to ask members of the targeted public about their preferences. When we're satisfied that our distribution method meets these public-focused criteria, we're ready for the final stage of the writing process: evaluation.

Evaluation: Stage Ten of the Writing Process

In earlier chapters, when we discussed the four-stage public relations process of research, planning, communication, and evaluation, we noted that although evaluation is mentioned last, it actually occurs throughout the public relations process. It's the same in writing: Evalutation is ongoing throughout the process. Above all, however, we evaluate at the end of the writing process to see whether our document succeeded. Did it address the targeted public's values and interests well enough to be read and acted upon? For example, did journalists use the news release we wrote for Volunteer Clearinghouse? If so, which media used it, and how many of our main points did the coverage include? In short, how well did we succeed? If some journalists chose not to use the news release, why not? Without excessively troubling the journalists, can we determine why our news release didn't become news in certain media? In the writing process, evaluation helps us to identify and reinforce what we did well—and to identify and not repeat any errors we may have made.

And now we're at the end of the writing process. At this point, it's only human to ask whether it's really worth working through all these stages. What's the reward for such a meticulous approach to writing? Fortunately, the rewards are many. Adhering to the writing process can help prevent the nausea that comes from staring at a computer screen as a deadline approaches and not knowing what to say. Within the framework of the writing process, should such a moment happen, we can drop back to previous levels, strengthen them, and then move forward again with confidence. Using the writing process can mean job security and promotability. As we note at the beginning of the chapter, public relations relies on skillful, precise use of language. Using the writing process, finally, can earn you respect as a thoughtful, professional writer who knows how to strengthen relationships with the magic of words.

Quick ✔ Check

1. How formal does a writer's outline need to be?
2. What is "the euphoria of creation"? How can its influence be diminished?
3. What questions should a writer ask in the macroediting stage of the writing process?
4. Why and how does a writer move backward in the microediting stage of the writing process?

Writing for the Ear

We've seen how the writing process works for documents designed to be read, such as news releases. But the writing process works equally well for documents designed to be *heard,* such as speeches and radio public service announcements. Documents designed to be heard, however, require special writing techniques to ensure that targeted publics easily comprehend the speaker's meaning. After all, unlike readers, listeners can't simply reread a paragraph or pause to decipher a challenging passage. Professional speechwriters, broadcast news writers, and other professionals who write for the ear have developed several guidelines for effectively conveying meaning to their listeners:

- *Remember that the speaker has to breathe.* Use short sentences. Short sentences create frequent pauses, which allow the speaker to breathe. The pauses also give listeners a moment to consider the previous sentence. An average effective spoken sentence contains 9 to 10 words.

- *Limit each sentence to one idea.* Avoid linking clauses together with coordinating conjunctions such as *and* and *but* or with subordinating conjunctions such as *because* and *although.* By the time listeners receive the closing idea of a multiclause sentence, they may have forgotten the idea at the beginning.

- *Use concrete words and images, not abstractions.* Clear, explicit language helps your listeners stay focused. They won't pause to try to decipher the meaning of vague, abstract language. Charles Osgood of CBS-TV and CBS radio so believes in the power of concrete, evocative language that he ends his television broadcasts with these words: "*See* you on the radio."

- *Use precise nouns and verbs.* An imprecise verb needs an adverb to clarify its meaning. A vague noun needs an adjective to make it accurate. Choosing exactly the right word helps you create short, precise sentences. Avoid excessive use of *to be* verbs such as *am, is, was,* and *were.* Such verbs don't convey precise images to listeners.

- *Challenge every word in every sentence.* Is each word necessary? Can a more precise noun eliminate the need for an adjective? Can you replace a long word with a shorter word without losing meaning? Spoken language is not the place to impress an audience with your knowledge of sesquipedalian (long) words.

- *Spell out big numbers and give phonetic spellings for hard-to-pronounce words.* If the speaker stumbles, so do the listeners. Assist the speaker by providing pronunciation cues for big numbers and difficult names or words. For example, broadcast writers often write the number 5,200 as "52–hundred."

- *Use traditional syntax (word order).* In the English language, the simplest sentences begin with a subject, which is followed by a verb, which in turn is sometimes followed by a direct object and perhaps an indirect object. Traditional word order offers the fewest roadblocks to understanding.

- *Link sentences and paragraphs with clear transitions.* Often, you can create a clear **transition** by making the direct object of one sentence the subject of the following

GRAMMAR ON THE WEB

What's the difference between *who* and *whom*? How about *lay* and *lie*? Or *that* and *which*? Should an opening subordinate clause be set off by a comma—and what's an opening subordinate clause, anyway? Now imagine asking such questions in the middle of the night as you toil away at an important public relations document. Who can answer such questions when only you and the bakers in the local doughnut shop are awake?

Let the World Wide Web come to the rescue. The web abounds with sites sponsored by university writing centers, editing professors, and other cyberspace grammarians. Just go to your favorite search engine and type in the key word *grammar.*

Two of the best sites for college students have little in common except clarity and usefulness. The first is the first edition of the famous *Elements of Style* by William Strunk Jr., online at www.cc. columbia.edu:80/acis/bartleby/strunk/. Strunk clearly explains the blunt guidelines he offers, such as "Use the active voice" and "Omit needless words." The short, well-organized book closes with the sections "Words and Expressions Commonly Misused" and "Words Commonly Misspelled."

A second highly useful web site is *Guide to Grammar and Writing,* online at http://webster. commnet.edu/grammar/index.htm. This comprehensive, well-organized site can help answer your *who/whom, lay/lie,* and *that/which* questions. The site also includes quizzes, frequently asked questions, and links to other sites. Best of all, as a welcome relief, the entries are informal and reflect a sense of humor.

When questions of grammar arise, help may be only a few keystrokes away.

sentence. Note how objects become subjects in the following example: *In 1863 Abraham Lincoln wrote his greatest speech: the Gettysburg Address. The Gettysburg Address expresses principles that still guide us today. The most important of those principles is contained in the words "government of the people, by the people, and for the people."*

■ *Attribute direct quotations at the beginning of a sentence.* In written English, we often place the **attribution**—the *said Abraham Lincoln*—in the midst or at the end of a direct quotation. But listeners can't see quotation marks. Placing the attribution at the beginning of a quotation is the only way to signal clearly that the speaker is citing someone else's words.

■ *Introduce important points with general, descriptive sentences.* Let listeners know that an important point is coming. If a speaker simply says, *Sixty percent of our employees want better communication with top management,* listeners may not retain the percentage as they absorb the rest of the sentence. We can assist our listeners by writing, *A high percentage of our employees want better communication with top management. Sixty percent of our employees say that top management should communicate more often with people in our organization.*

■ *Gracefully repeat main points.* Know the main points that you hope to convey, and seek opportunities to state them more than once.

■ *Avoid closing with "In conclusion."* Readers can see the end of a document coming. But how do listeners identify an upcoming conclusion? A return to the broad theme of the document—a restatement of the main point—can signal that the end is near.

■ *Break any of the above guidelines when doing so will assist the listener.* These are only guidelines, not rigid laws. Usually, these guidelines help convey meaning to the listener. In cases where they interfere with meaning, discard them.

Writing the spoken word well is an art, as is all good writing. Writing the spoken word, in fact, leads logically to our next section. Public relations professionals sometimes stand and deliver the words they have written. Sometimes they make presentations.

Quick ✔ Check

1. How many words are in the average effective spoken sentence?
2. In general, do adjectives and adverbs add to or detract from the effectiveness of spoken language?
3. What are transitions?
4. In spoken language, why should an important point be introduced by a general, descriptive sentence?

Public Service Announcement
Radio public service announcements demonstrate how writing meant to be read aloud differs from ordinary print writing. Note the repeated phone number and the brevity of sentences in the 30-second PSA. (Courtesy of the National Diabetes Education Program)

Medicare Benefits and Controlling Your Diabetes

Radio Public Service Announcements

"Good News"

In this spot, a mature adult woman calls her friend with some good news about new Medicare benefits. The listeners are engaged because they both have diabetes.

Good News :30 seconds

Woman 1: (ringing phone) Hello?

Woman 2: Hi, Laura. I've got good news. Medicare will now help us pay...

Woman 1: (interrupts her) For our diabetes equipment and supplies... like glucose monitors, test strips and lancets.

Woman 2: That's right. I learned about it by calling 1-800-438-5383. How did you know?

Woman 1: The Internet – www.medicare.gov. What's that number again?

Woman 2: 1-800-438-5383. (admiring) The Internet? Laura, you're really something. (They laugh)

FADE OUT.

The Process of Successful Presentations

Comedian Jerry Seinfeld—someone who knows a thing or two about appearing before large groups—has no illusions about the difficulty of public speaking: At a funeral, he says, most of us would rather be the corpse than the person delivering the eulogy.[9] Cicero, the greatest of the Roman orators, wrote, "I turn pale at the outset of a speech and quake in every limb and in all my soul."[10] As we noted earlier, public speaking ranks number one among people's greatest fears.

Why the terror? Often, we fear making fools of ourselves—of being seen as impostors pretending to know something. Other times, we're afraid that the discomfort of being in front of a group will rattle us, making our voices tremble and our hands shake. People will see how nervous we are, and their awareness will intensify our nightmare. Make a presentation? No thanks. We'll schedule a root canal for that day (fear of dentists is not among people's top 14 fears).[11]

Public relations practitioners, however, cannot avoid presentations. Clients want proposals. The news media want statements. Community groups want speeches. The question is not *Will we make presentations?* We will. The question, rather, is *How can we make successful presentations?* Our answer should sound familiar: A successful presentation requires research, planning, communication, and evaluation—the four stages of the public relations process. By the time you actually deliver your presentation, it should be an old friend. It should fit you and your targeted public like a pair of comfortable shoes. With presentations, familiarity doesn't breed contempt. Instead, your familiarity with your presentation, your audience, and even the room in which you'll be speaking breeds confidence and success. And it all starts with research.

Researching Your Presentation

Presentation research begins with knowing your targeted public. Who are its members? What values and interests unite them? What do they want from you? How long do they expect you to speak? If the situation permits such a request, don't hesitate to ask members of your future audience what they hope to learn from you. To create an effective message, you should combine audience research with another area of research: research into what you want to tell the audience. As you know, an effective message combines your purpose with the values and interests of the targeted public. During your presentation, if you consistently address the concerns of your audience, you can expect to be rewarded with eye contact, nodding heads, and attentive listeners.

Another aspect of audience research is identifying the decision makers and opinion leaders within your audience. Of course, you should maintain eye contact with and speak to everyone in the room. But at important moments in your presentation, you may want to focus extra attention on the people who can most help you achieve your goals.

Researching a presentation also involves learning about the room in which you'll be speaking. Is there enough space to allow freedom of movement as you

Values Statement 10.1

speak? Are there windows that need to be shaded if you plan to project visuals onto a screen? Is there a screen? A projection system? A lectern? Answers to such questions not only improve the technical support of your presentation; they also increase your comfort level as you prepare for the presentation. You won't be walking into unknown territory.

Planning Your Presentation

Begin by planning to be yourself. Trying to be someone else during your presentation is stressful and distracting. You impress your targeted public more by addressing its values and interests than by maintaining icy composure at every moment. Have confidence in the message you create, and relax. Be yourself.

Planning includes message creation. Again, your message should combine your presentation's purpose with your audience's values and interests. Everything in your presentation should support the central, unifying theme of your message. But how long should "everything" be? Your research answers that question: Length is guided by what the audience wants. Ideally, a speech should take no more than 20 minutes and include no more than three main, message-related points. Presentation of a proposal to a client generally should take no more than one hour; anything longer might suggest a lack of respect for the client's time. During that hour, every point you make should be related to the central theme provided by your message. A brief statement to the news media may take only one minute. An educational presentation may take an entire day or two. Again, the ideal length for any presentation is established by the needs of the targeted public.

When you know the message and the length, you're ready to outline your presentation. Unless you're delivering a formal speech or a highly technical performance in which assistants trigger multimedia effects as you say specific words, experts suggest that you not have a word-for-word script. An outline allows you to maintain eye contact and helps you speak with—instead of read to—your audience. Many professionals recommend, however, that you memorize your introduction, your conclusion, and any important anecdotes. At those key moments, you want unflinching eye contact as you dazzle the audience with your sincere, articulate, and polished presentation.

Another aspect of planning for success is practice. And more practice. And even more practice. Practicing not only polishes your presentation; it also helps you become comfortable with it. And being comfortable with your presentation reduces the terror that freezes many of us at the mere thought of public speaking. Being comfortable with your presentation can actually make you eager to deliver it: You know it's good, you know you're ready, and (being human) you're eager for the praise you know you deserve. So practice. And then practice some more.

As you practice, try to duplicate the conditions and environment of the actual presentation. Practice in the room in which you'll make the real presentation. If that's not possible, practice in a similar room. Practice at the scheduled presentation time. If you intend to invite questions from your audience, have friends and coworkers observe your practice presentations and ask questions. Wear the comfortable clothing that you'll wear during the presentation—usually clothing at or just above the level of formality of your audience's attire. Use the technology and visual aids that you'll use in your actual presentation, and practice your solutions to sudden technological failures.

USING VISUAL AIDS.   Planned and used wisely, **visual aids** can enhance most presentations. Visual aids range from handouts to flip charts to overheads, slides, and computer projections. Recent studies show that well-designed visual aids can increase audience learning by 200 percent, increase audience retention of main points by 38 percent, and reduce explanation time by 40 percent.[12] Well-designed visuals are short and have headlines. Because you don't want your audience to read ahead of you, consider using a program such as PowerPoint, which allows you to use a computer projection system to build a visual one sentence or one image at a time. Although it's OK to look at your own visuals, don't turn your back and speak to them. Speak to your audience. If a gap occurs between one visual and the next, consider going to a blank screen—or covering your flip chart—so that an old visual doesn't become a distraction. And absolutely, positively avoid misspellings in your visuals.

Many audiences will be grateful for photocopies of visuals. Rather than interrupt your presentation to distribute them or make audience members wait until the presentation is over, have the attractively bound photocopies ready as the audience enters the room. Ideally, you have individualized both your visuals and the photocopies for this particular presentation. For example, if you're addressing your local chamber of commerce, the cover sheet of your bound photocopies should acknowledge that.

PLANNING FOR PROBLEMS.   You should also plan for trouble. If you're speaking from a script or an outline, you should have quick access to a second copy in case you misplace yours at the last moment. Ensure that extra lightbulbs are available for the projection system. If you're using a computer projection system, have overhead transparencies and access to an overhead projector in case your computer fails. If the journey to your presentation site involves airline travel, carry on—don't check—luggage

In the Beginning...

- Who(m) are you talking to?

- What are you trying to tell them?

- Why should they care?

_____

_____

_____

_____

_____

_____

Attribution Placement

- "The people at Union Medical Center are wonderful. Let me put it this way: I wouldn't be alive today without them," she said.

- "The people at Union Medical Center are wonderful," she said. "Let me put it this way: I wouldn't be alive today without them."

_____

_____

_____

_____

Eliminating "To Be" Verbs

- She is a good communicator.
  - She communicates well.
- The unit is staffed by registered nurses.
  - Registered nurses staff the unit.
- During November, the unit will be having meetings for each team.
  - During November, the unit will have a meeting for each team.

_____

_____

_____

_____

Presentation Handouts   Copies of presentation visuals can help audience members take notes and focus on a speaker's message. Most slide-creation programs have special print functions for handouts.

that includes presentation materials. Otherwise, as you arrive in Barcelona to make your presentation, your visual aids may be 40,000 feet above Honolulu. Consider shipping bulky handouts or technology to the presentation site several days early to ensure that they arrive.

Your final moment of trouble-shooting should occur approximately an hour before you start your presentation. Arrive early, and test the technology one last time.

Double-check the location of your backup technology, such as an overhead projector and transparencies or a flip chart. Ensure that you have access to two copies of your outline or script.

Preparing for trouble also means being flexible. Know your presentation so well that you can cut it short if your hosts decrease your time allotment. Watch for any changes in your subject matter that might alter the direction of your presentation. For example, a potential client company suddenly facing a lawsuit over one of its products may be more interested in crisis communications counseling than in your scheduled presentation on a CD media kit for the now-notorious product.

Finally, if someone will be introducing you, consider writing a short introduction for that individual to use. He or she may appreciate the assistance, and you won't be surprised by an inadequate or a too-lavish introduction. Be sure to send that introduction to your introducer at least a week before your presentation.

Making Your Presentation

It's the moment of truth. You've been introduced, and you're the center of attention. After thanking the person who introduces you, pause a moment before you begin. Smile. Look at the people in the room. Show them that you're confident, that you're quietly excited about the information you're about to share. Maintain eye contact, and begin your memorized introduction.

Should you begin with a joke? Most experts say no. It's not worth the risk of failing and beginning the presentation with an awkward silence or strained laughter. A more effective opening strategy can be an anecdote with which your audience can identify. Another effective strategy is to begin by targeting your audience's concerns: Tell audience members exactly what you hope they gain from your presentation. After that, you may want to establish the basic guidelines of the presentation, such as when you'll take questions.

As you speak, continue eye contact, looking at one person at a time, gracefully forcing that person to realize that you are acknowledging and valuing his or her presence. Again, single out decision makers and opinion leaders for extra eye contact. Unless you are giving a formal speech, try not to anchor yourself to a lectern or a technology table. A hand-held remote control can allow you to project visuals from any point in the room. If you move smoothly about the presentation area, the audience's eyes will follow you, helping everyone stay alert.

If your technology fails—and, eventually, in some presentation it will—don't try to hide the fact. You've prepared for this eventuality, and you're ready to handle it professionally. Acknowledge the failure; after all, everyone can see it. Toss off a quick joke, if appropriate, and move smoothly to your backup solution. Audience members probably are empathizing with you; it could just as easily be one of them suffering the failure. They'll be relieved and pleased to see you avoid panic. Your seamless move to an alternate plan will impress them, in part because it shows just how seriously you've taken this opportunity to speak with them. As we'll note in Chapter 12, sometimes a well-handled crisis creates a hero.

QuickBreak 10.4

CONQUERING THE PRESENTATION JITTERS

"We have nothing to fear but fear itself," said President Franklin Roosevelt. Of course, Roosevelt referred to fear created by a faltering economy, but his shrewd comment also applies to presentations. Frequently, the presentation itself is not what we fear; instead, we fear appearing nervous and uncertain in front of others. We're unnerved by the fear that our hands will shake and our voices will tremble.

Expert presenters offer this advice about fighting stage fright:

- Practice in front of others. Present to test audiences before you present to the ultimate audience.

- Deliver the goods. If you're conveying useful information to your audience, its members will think you're great.

- As you present, maintain eye contact. Don't think about yourself; think about your audience. Talk to people, not to the walls, floor, or ceiling.

- Channel your nervous energy into movement. If appropriate, walk around as you speak. Address different sections of the room. Use hand gestures that complement your words.

- Realize that you are your own worst critic. Few people in the audience are evaluating your performance. Instead, they're evaluating the quality of the information they're receiving—so, again, deliver the goods.

- After a presentation, reward yourself with a special purchase or some other treat. Be grateful to the presentation for giving you the excuse for a minor extravagance.

One last bit of advice. Attack your fear. Seek opportunities to do presentations. Franklin Roosevelt *didn't* say, "Practice makes perfect"—but, once again, the phrase applies to presentations.

When possible, close your presentation by calling for questions. A question-and-answer session can emphasize one last time your respect for your audience's particular concerns. Don't finish with an answer, however. Instead, after you answer the final question, deliver a summary statement, a strong, planned "cap" for your remarks. In presentations that are *not* formal speeches, consider this closing tactic: After your final statement, clap your hands once, bow slightly, straighten, and, looking your audience in the eyes, say, with a smile, "Thank you very much." Your own clap and your slight bow just might trigger applause.

Formal speeches generally do not include a question-and-answer session. Instead, if you're presenting such a speech, deliver a strong conclusion and close with a simple "Thank you." Applause automatically follows most speeches.

However you conclude your presentation, keep an eye (subtly) on the clock. No one appreciates a presentation that runs past its allotted time. An overlong presentation can show a serious lack of respect for the audience, undermining the powerful focus you've placed on addressing its values. Presentation coach Karen Susman recommends the following timing strategy: "Know your material and how long it takes to deliver. Follow the 75 percent rule. If you're scheduled to speak for one hour, plan 45 minutes of material. . . . Be so familiar with your presentation that you know where you can cut if you need to."[13]

After finishing your presentation, relax. That wasn't so bad, was it?

Evaluating Your Presentation

Don't bask in glory too long, though: Another presentation looms, and you can help make it great by applying what you've learned from your recent presentation and other past efforts. Wait 24 hours until the euphoria of finishing has passed, and then write yourself a memo, evaluating your recent presentation. What worked well? What didn't work as well as you had planned? How well did the technology perform? Did anything during the presentation surprise you? Was the audience responsive? If so, when? How do you know it was responsive? Did you finish on time? What questions and comments from the audience did you receive? When you've answered such questions, consider giving yourself a grade: *A* for excellent, *B* for good, and so on. Try to score a higher grade on your next similar presentation.

The ultimate evaluation, of course, comes from your targeted public. Did it receive and act on the message you delivered? If your presentation was a public relations tactic, did it help you achieve your objective? Ultimately, the success of your presentation must be judged by that standard.

Quick ✔ Check

1. Why is it important to be able to recognize the opinion leaders and decision makers in your audience?
2. Who determines the ideal length of a presentation?
3. Which parts of a presentation should be memorized?
4. What is the 75 percent rule for presentations?

Summary

The difficulty of writing and making presentations is matched by the importance of these two skills: They are core elements in the profession of public relations. Neither will ever be easy, but you can make them easier by following the process that each requires. Those processes are similar, moving through research, planning, implementation, and evaluation. Each stage must be completed before the practitioner can successfully grapple with the next stage. And after the last stage lies success.

As you gain more access to public relations professionals through guest lectures and internships, ask them when they last wrote a document or made a presentation. Their answers will underscore the importance of writing and presentation skills in the practice of public relations.

DISCUSSION QUESTIONS

1. Given what you know of writing for the ear, how would you rewrite the proposed first sentence of the Volunteer Clearinghouse news release to adapt it to a radio news story? Your final draft of the first sentence was *Elayne Anderson, former supervisor of the Coxwold County Red Cross, will be the new executive director of Volunteer Clearinghouse, that organization's board of directors announced Monday.*

2. Does the first sentence of the Volunteer Clearinghouse news release seem a little long? How might you shorten it? The text of the unrevised first paragraph of the news release appears on page 317.

3. Why do journalists prefer the inverted pyramid for news stories?

4. What is the difference between macroediting and microediting? Why aren't the two done simultaneously?

5. Have you ever approached a writing project without adequate preparation? How did you feel as you began writing? What were the results?

6. Can you quote memorable passages from famous speeches? How do those passages support or refute the guidelines for writing for the ear contained in this chapter?

7. Do you fear public speaking? If so, why? Be specific. Do you think the process for successful presentations outlined in this chapter could relieve some of your anxiety? Why or why not?

Memo *from the* Field

Regina Lynch-Hudson, President, The Write Publicist, Atlanta

Regina Lynch-Hudson is founder and president of The Write Publicist in Atlanta. Self-described as "the quintessential American mutt," Lynch-Hudson has a 15-year track record of conceptualizing print media campaigns for people, places, products, and performances.

The Write Publicist's handling of the 1996 National Black Arts Festival (the largest biennial festival of its kind in the world) earned Best PR Campaign of the Year Award from the Atlanta Association of Media Women. Today, she pens *Regina Roams,* featured in *Arrivals,* the inflight magazine of AirTran Airways.

Admittedly, when I was asked to contribute to this public relations textbook, I wondered what I would communicate to wide-eyed, idealistic students, when my own career path has not been conventional. But then "public relations" is such an ambiguous term.

I regard public relations as an art form, combining some theory and a great deal of impressionism. From the subliminal theatrics required to deliver memorable presentations to the gut spontaneity of merging words that evoke reaction—a wordsmith's success isn't tied to academia alone. My own college years were short-circuited, due to a family tragedy. NEWS FLASH: Kidney dialysis patient brutally murdered leaving hospital. *Victim's daughter turns to writing for solace.*

Ongoing courses in consumer behavior, body language, and psychology melded with world travel, and an oftentimes nontraditional mélange of seminars, workshops, and lectures enhanced my perspective. I relied on creative ripeness and ravenous "literary consumption" to whet my writing skills.

You should also develop a penchant to read anything you can get your hands on—newspapers, magazines, menus, billboards, and direct mail. You never know when you'll be writing about an automotive manufacturer; a software company; a humanitarian organization; or a corporation with international reach. Subconsciously we all plunder our past for material—and in the profoundest, most unexpected way up pops a tidbit of knowledge precisely when needed. Somewhere between writing's structure, public relations' principles, and imagination's abstractions, you'll discover a definite and confident style.

Be prepared to undergo years of clarifying and deepening your personal vision, of focusing your energies, of developing patience, just to objectively identify where *you* fit. Discovering one's strengths and weaknesses, maintaining one's commitment and capacity for learning, and perfecting one's craft are imperative in this business.

It's been said that life is a costume party and that we keep changing and changing and changing until we find the outfit that fits best. Some public relations practitioners blossom into world-class event coordinators. Many of us PR'ers are the "idea geniuses" who pen attention-grabbing news releases. Other PR-types possess a gift for gab and are better suited to "pitch" to editors or to deliver persuasive speeches. Tailor your career around a specialty that's a "fit," rather than with what the market seemingly needs. The market can be quite capricious. Embracing those skills that spur passion and inner solace, and daringly carving out a niche based on talents and interests, are not only necessary for productivity but are also necessary for longevity.

Poignancy sells. Regardless of the company or target audience, ability to elucidate a client, on paper, verbally, and even in your body language during oral presentations, requires varying degrees of ardor—delivered enthusiastically, succinctly, and with sincerity. Frankly, one must, to a certain extent, psychologically bond with the client's product or service to promote it. Genuineness is not easily feigned—unless you minor in drama and acting. And even then, audiences are not easily fooled over the long haul.

Originality rules. Oftentimes, originality implies being bold enough to go beyond accepted norms. It's how you pen (or peg) your clients as *distinct* that will brand them in the psyche of target audiences. Whether you are penning a proposal to reap sponsorship for an event, a speech to lure voters to a politician, or a script for a videotape to be used as a sales tool for a luxury resort, communicating what's "different" is fundamental. Knowing your clients enables you to gage how demonstrative you can be in your written, verbal, or pictorial personification of them. A bank or a life insurance company may require black-and-white doses of realism, whereas in promoting tourism, the arts, or food, you may add splashes of wit and whimsy.

Don't be afraid to stroke with a broad brush, to try new techniques, to make mistakes. Mistakes are the catalysts that germinate genius. There are no paint-by-number strategies for mastering public relations in the 21st century. The web and the 2000 Census reflect dramatic change in not only *how* we communicate but in the profile of who *we* are.

There's a big canvas out there, and, as Van Gogh illustrated, there is more than one way to paint a sunflower. Whether you work for a *Fortune* 500 giant or as a solo practitioner—it's how you distill millions of ideas and translate them into something cohesive that breathes life into the identity of your clients.

Case Study 10.1

"Letter from Birmingham Jail"

Although not traditionally thought of in a public relations context, one of the noblest examples of values-driven public relations of the 20th century began in a solitary-confinement jail cell in Birmingham, Alabama, in 1963. Dr. Martin Luther King Jr., who was to win the Nobel Peace Prize a year later for his civil rights efforts in the United States, had been jailed for leading an illegal nonviolent demonstration. In King's words, Birmingham was "probably the most thoroughly segregated city in the United States."[14]

King was arrested on April 12, when his newborn daughter, Bernice, was 16 days old. On April 13, as he read a smuggled-in copy of the *Birmingham News,* he saw this page 2 headline: "White Clergymen Urge Local Negroes to Withdraw from Demonstrations."[15] The article contained a statement from eight white Birmingham clergymen, including four bishops and one rabbi; the statement expressed their regret that the illegal demonstrations had inflamed racial tensions. The statement urged patience and a respect for the law. An ordained minister himself, King was deeply stung by the words of his peers who, instead of joining him, attacked his nonviolent methods in the dangerous quest for racial equality. Writing in the margins of the newspaper, he began a document that had to be hidden in his shirt and smuggled out of his cell. The collection of scribbled passages came to be known as the "Letter from Birmingham Jail."

As it slowly circulated, the letter seemed to have little impact. As a public relations tactic, it may initially have been a failure. None of the eight clergymen immediately recanted the statement attacking the demonstrations. Desegregation did not sweep across the United States. Decades later, however, the "Letter from Birmingham Jail" stands as an eloquent defense of the use of civil disobedience to fight injustice. Says King biographer David L. Lewis:

> Every nation has its stockpile of rhetorical memorabilia, addresses, and documents, which enshrine by their passionate sincerity and eloquence a moment of curtain call in the drama of its people's maturity. Washington's farewell address, the Webster-Hayne debates,

> Lincoln's *Gettysburg Address*, the inauguration speeches of Franklin Roosevelt and John Kennedy—these are milestones in the republic's growth. To this stockpile must be added Martin Luther King's *Letter from Birmingham Jail.* . . . [16]

Martin Luther King Jr. was assassinated April 4, 1968, but as a new century dawns, his "Letter from Birmingham Jail" continues to reach a public much wider than eight clergymen.

The power of King's letter comes partly from the nobility of its ideas. But others besides King had put forward compelling arguments for civil rights. Why has the "Letter from Birmingham Jail" become, in Lewis' words, "a milestone in the republic's growth"? One answer to that question is King's intense focus on each stage of the writing process. For example, with the very first words of his document, King establishes credibility by showing himself to be a part of the public he addresses: "My Dear Fellow Clergymen. . . ." With those words, King positions himself not as an outsider but rather as a colleague. He subtly implies that he and the recipients of his letter may have common values. Throughout the letter, he uses the pronouns *we* and *our* to link himself to the clergymen.

King uses his knowledge of his targeted public when he defends civil disobedience by citing the words of Saint Augustine and Saint Thomas Aquinas as well as Christian and Jewish prophets, theologians, and philosophers. Those individuals, in all likelihood, are "opinion leaders" for the eight clergymen. King tries to show the clergymen the justice of his cause by citing the words of the very leaders to whom the clergymen might turn for advice. His strategy, though not stated, is clear: If the leaders of your religion are with me, how can you stand against me?

King maintains his focus on the concerns of his targeted public as, one by one, he answers the questions the eight clergymen posed in their statement: Why did he feel the need to come to Birmingham? Why not negotiate instead of demonstrate? How can he justify breaking the law with an illegal march? Why not wait a little longer? The organization of the letter is built upon answering the exact questions asked by his targeted public.

In answering the question Why not wait?, King's letter soars to its greatest height. King could have answered by citing statistics about racial injustice. He could have enumerated federal laws outlawing discrimination. He could have answered with a generalization. Instead, in a sentence of 316 words, he shatters the question with a list of devastating images, forcing his readers to see and feel why black Americans could wait no longer for freedom:

> Perhaps it is easy for those who have never felt the stinging darts of segregation to say, "Wait." But when you have seen vicious mobs lynch your mothers and fathers at will and drown your sisters and brothers at whim; when you have seen hate-filled policemen curse, kick, and even kill your black brothers and sisters; when you see the vast majority of your twenty million Negro brothers smothering in an airtight cage of poverty in the midst of an affluent society; when you suddenly find your tongue twisted and your speech stammering as you seek to explain to your six-year-old daughter why she can't go to the public amusement park that has just been advertised on television, and see tears welling up in her eyes when she is told that Funtown is closed to colored children, and see ominous

clouds of inferiority beginning to form in her little mental sky, and see her beginning to distort her personality by developing an unconscious bitterness toward white people; when you have to concoct an answer for a five-year-old son who is asking, "Daddy, why do white people treat colored people so mean?"; when you take a cross-country drive and find it necessary to sleep night after night in the uncomfortable corners of your automobile because no motel will accept you; when you are humiliated day in and day out by nagging signs reading "white" and "colored"; when your first name becomes "nigger," your middle name becomes "boy" (however old you are) and your last name becomes "John," and your wife and mother are never given the respected title "Mrs."; when you are harried by day and haunted by night by the fact that you are a Negro, living constantly at tiptoe stance, never quite knowing what to expect next, and are plagued with inner fears and outer resentments; when you are forever fighting a degenerating sense of "nobodiness"— then you will understand why we find it difficult to wait.

King established his credibility. He researched his targeted public. He organized his document. He wrote with concrete language that directly addressed the issues raised by his readers. Did such a document need editing? Yes: In an author's note attached to the published version of the letter, King said of his first draft, "I have indulged in the author's prerogative of polishing it for publication."[17]

Martin Luther King Jr. spent nine days in the Birmingham jail. He emerged with a beard (no shaving in solitary confinement), an unquenched desire to continue the protests in Birmingham, and a document that, in the words of Pulitzer Prize–winning author Taylor Branch, became "a famous pronouncement of moral triumph."[18]

DISCUSSION QUESTIONS

1. Is it appropriate to see the "Letter from Birmingham Jail" as a public relations tactic?
2. What techniques does King use to build cohesiveness in his 316-word sentence?
3. Without reexamining the 316-word sentence, can you remember and describe some of the images it contains? If so, what made those images memorable?
4. Would national statistics on discrimination and segregation have been more effective than the 316-word sentence? Why or why not?
5. Should King have kept his letter private? After all, wasn't it addressed only to eight men?

Case Study 10.2

Online Outrage: Emulex and the Fake News Release

"In a moment of panic," said the lawyer, "this 23-year-old kid made a wrong decision that will affect him for the rest of his life. He is extremely remorseful for having been involved in these events. This was a response to a panic situation."[19]

That wrong decision cost investors millions of dollars and temporarily stole more than $2 billion in market value from an Internet communications company called

Emulex.[20] The problem began with an abuse of the writing process and ended in a flurry of communication. In the end, good writing swept aside the bad—but only after what *Newsweek* called "one of the web's biggest-ever stock manipulation frauds."[21]

Mark Jakob, 23, triggered the hemorrhage of money in August 2000 with a fake news release. Concerned by losses related to Emulex stock that he owned, he wrote a news release falsely reporting that Emulex' CEO had resigned amid rumors of incorrect financial statements and an impending investigation by the Securities and Exchange Commission. Jakob then sent the news release to Internet Wire, a news-release distribution company at which he had worked from April 1999 to August 2000. At Internet Wire, he had been a news release processor, and his knowledge of the proper tone and format of news releases helped him give the bogus document an authentic appearance.[22] United Press International even reported that Jakob knew enough to include certain attachments that persuaded his former colleagues that Emulex really had sent the news release to Internet Wire for distribution. On August 25, Internet Wire distributed the news release to the world's financial news media.

Journalists scooped up the information and quickly relayed it to investors. Within hours, the false story of Emulex' woes had been reported by leading financial news media such as Bloomberg News, Dow Jones News Service, CBSMarketwatch.com, and CNBC. Emulex stock prices plummeted 60 percent in 15 minutes, from $110 a share to $43 a share. "The hoax . . . made news across the country by dissolving shareholder millions in minutes," *Investor's Daily* reported.[23] As Emulex investors learned of the plunging price, many sold immediately to prevent more substantial losses. Others had standing orders with their investment advisors to sell automatically if Emulex fell to a certain price.[24] When prices suddenly rose again as investors learned the truth, losses to Emulex investors exceeded $100 million.

"Some shareholders lost money saved for their children's college education, and for others it was a loss of a comfortable retirement that they had worked years to achieve," said James DeSarno of the FBI.[25]

Jakob, however, made money—albeit temporarily. His illegal manipulation of Emulex stock netted him almost $250,000.[26]

Writing had been used to attack Emulex, and the company used writing to regain the initiative. Less than an hour after learning of the bogus news release, Emulex had fired off its own news release setting the record straight and had posted a similar statement on its web site. In part, the release said, "The negative statements in this fictitious press release are categorically false."[27]

Internet Wire fought back with a news release of its own, which stated, in part, "It appears the hoax was perpetrated by an individual (or individuals) who falsely represented himself or herself as a public relations agency representing Emulex."[28]

Emulex CEO Paul Folino directed the crisis communications against stiff odds. Switchboards were jammed with panicked investors, his public relations manager was stalled en route to the office with a flat tire, and his chief financial officer was sailing off California's coast, out of range of his cell phone. One public relations practitioner called Folino's response "masterful." Folino's own assessment of his performance was more subdued. "That's what they pay me for," he said bluntly.[29]

Six days after the hoax began, the FBI arrested Mark Jakob. Working with the Securities and Exchange Commission, the FBI had traced the bogus news release to a computer at El Camino Community College in Torrance, California, where Jakob was a student. Six months later, he arranged a plea bargain with prosecutors, confessing his guilt in return for a prison sentence of 37 to 46 months.[30]

Oddly, some financial analysts believe that the entire episode may have benefited Emulex—though none claim that it benefited investors. Folino's grace under pressure, the company's immediate launch of its own forceful news release, and its subsequent measures to increase security (including issuing satellite telephones to the chief financial officer and other top managers) impressed observers. "Emulex was off some people's radar scope," said financial analyst Glenn Hanus. "The hoax certainly got them on the nightly news."[31]

Other companies may need to learn from Folino's effective communication. "Disgruntled workers have found that the Internet makes it easy to take their frustration out by spreading false information in chat rooms or sending out fake news releases," reported the *New York Times* in 2001. In recent years, profits at Lucent Technologies slumped after a false news release, whereas another news release hoax boosted earnings at Pairgain, a manufacturer of Internet communications equipment. In both cases, federal authorities identified and filed charges against suspects.[32] (As your authors were writing this case study on October 19, 2001, a company called Extreme Networks suspended trading of its stock after a bogus news release appeared in a Yahoo! Finance chat room.[33])

"The speed with which . . . the FBI and SEC exposed Jakob's criminal activities demonstrates our joint commitment to solving these fast-moving Internet crimes," said Alejandro Mayorkas, U.S. attorney for the Central District of California. "Those who seek to manipulate the market as Mark Jakob did should take heed of the years in federal prison that he faces in light of his conduct."[34]

DISCUSSION QUESTIONS

1. How does the concept of credibility, stage one of the writing process, apply to the key players in this case study: Mark Jakob, Paul Folino, Emulex, Internet Wire, and the financial news media?
2. How might the Emulex hoax have been prevented?
3. Some financial analysts believe that the news release hoax actually benefited Emulex. Do you agree?
4. Emulex fought back mostly with written documents. What other tactics might it have used to counter the hoax?
5. The Emulex new release hoax may have damaged Internet Wire's relationships with important publics. If you were public relations director for Internet Wire, what relationships would you focus on, and what relationship-building tactics would you recommend?

It's Your Turn

Elayne Anderson's Speech

Elayne Anderson, the new executive director of Volunteer Clearinghouse, was very satisfied with the news release you wrote announcing her hiring. Now she'd like you to help her prepare a speech to be delivered to as many undergraduates as possible at your college or university. She knows her purpose: She wants undergraduates to volunteer at the nonprofit social-service agencies affiliated with Volunteer Clearinghouse. But that's all she knows. She has dozens of questions. When would be the best time to reach the students? Where should she speak? Why would any students attend? What's in it for them? Would any particular student groups be especially receptive to her message? Would visual aids be useful? If so, what kinds? How long should she talk? What should be the central message of her speech? She knows that there may be other questions she hasn't yet considered.

You can suggest additional public relations tactics, but be sure to give Elayne solid advice on her speech. She's your client, and she firmly believes that to do her job well, she must become a familiar figure on your campus.

Using your knowledge of your college or university, what answers and advice do you have for Elayne?

KEY TERMS

active voice, p. 316

attribution, p. 325

demographic information, p. 310

inverted pyramid, p. 313

macroediting, p. 319

Maslow's Hierarchy of Needs, p. 307

microediting, p. 319

modifiers, p. 316

passive voice, p. 316

psychographic information, p. 311

transition, p. 324

visual aids, p. 329

writing process, p. 307

NOTES

1. Writerly Things, online, www.ecentral.com/members/writers/quotes/writers.html.
2. Nexxus: A Place for Poetry, online, www.sage.net/~sgreene/nexxus.
3. David Wallechinsky, Irving Wallace, and Amy Wallace, *The Book of Lists* (New York: William Morrow, 1977), 469–470.
4. "Where the Jobs Are," *PRNews* (13 April 1998), online, Lexis-Nexis.
5. Adapted from Charles Marsh, *A Quick and (Not) Dirty Guide to Business Writing* (Englewood Cliffs, N.J.: Prentice-Hall, 1997).

6. Marsh, 8.

7. Adapted from Marsh.

8. Robert Graves and Alan Hodge, *The Reader over Your Shoulder,* 2nd ed. (New York: Vintage Books, 1979).

9. Rowena Crosbie, "Speak Your Way to Success," *Canadian Manager* 22, no. 4 (1997), online, Lexis-Nexis.

10. Cicero, "Of Oratory," in *The Rhetorical Tradition,* eds. Patricia Bizzell and Bruce Herzberg (Boston: Bedford Books, 1990), 217.

11. Wallechinsky et al., 469–470.

12. Crosbie.

13. Karen Susman, "Six Key Indicators Guaranteed to Reduce Audience Stress and Increase Your Applause," *Records Management Quarterly* 31, no. 3 (1997), online, Lexis-Nexis.

14. Martin Luther King Jr., "Letter from Birmingham Jail," cited in Edward P. J. Corbett, *Classical Rhetoric for the Modern Student,* 3rd ed. (New York: Oxford University Press, 1990), 344.

15. Taylor Branch, *Parting the Waters* (New York: Simon & Schuster, 1988), 737.

16. David L. Lewis, *King: A Critical Biography* (New York: Praeger, 1970), 187.

17. King, 342.

18. Branch, 744.

19. Martin Stone, "Emulex Scammer to See Slammer," *Newsbytes,* 2 January 2001, online, Lexis-Nexis.

20. Alex Berenson, "News Release Fakes Out Media, Upends Market," *New York Times,* 26 August 2000, online, Lexis-Nexis.

21. Stone.

22. Alex Berenson, "Guilty Plea Is Set in Internet Hoax Case Involving Emulex," *New York Times,* 29 December 2000, online, Lexis-Nexis.

23. Diane Lindquist, "Emulex Beat Hoax with Solid Product, Sales," *Investor's Daily,* 25 January 2001, online, Lexis-Nexis.

24. Berenson, "News Release Fakes Out Media, Upends Market."

25. "Jakob Pleads Guilty to Fraud Charges in $110 Million Emulex News Hoax," *White-Collar Crime Reporter* (February 2001), online, Lexis-Nexis.

26. "Jakob Pleads Guilty to Fraud Charges in $110 Million Emulex News Hoax."

27. Dick Kelsey, "Bogus News Release Sends Emulex Shares Plunging," *Newsbytes,* 25 August 2000, online, Lexis-Nexis.

28. Kelsey.

29. Karen Alexander, "Quick Response Stems Damage to Emulex," *Los Angeles Times,* 1 September 2000, online, Lexis-Nexis.

30. Berenson, "Guilty Plea Is Set in Internet Hoax Case Involving Emulex."

31. Lindquist.

32. Berenson, "News Release Fakes Out Media, Upends Market."

33. Julia Hood, "Extreme Victim of Fake News Release in Web Chatroom," *PR Week,* 19 October 2001, online, Lexis-Nexis.

34. Berenson, "Guilty Plea Is Set in Internet Hoax Case Involving Emulex."

chapter eleven

New Communications Technology

objectives

After studying this chapter, you will be able to

- describe the changes—as well as the implications of those changes—that are occurring in mass communications technology

- recognize the opportunities and challenges public relations practitioners face as a result of technological convergence

- identify the many new tools that practitioners now have for communicating with targeted publics

- appreciate that "new" doesn't always mean "better" and that in certain situations, traditional channels of communications are preferable to new high-tech channels

Differing Designs for the Future

scenario

Olds Young and Associates is one of the community's oldest architectural firms. One of the co-owners is Bud Olds, who founded the firm nearly three decades ago. The other owner is Betty Young, whose late father formed the original partnership with Olds.

In the five years since her father's death, Young has redirected the focus of the firm. Once known only as a local business, the firm has become nationally known for its designs of sports venues such as stadiums and arenas.

Because of increasing competition, your public relations agency has been asked to develop a public relations plan for Olds Young and Associates. As part of your initial research, you conducted separate interviews with the co-owners. It didn't take you long to discover a generation gap.

"We didn't use fancy public relations firms in the old days," said Olds. "If you wanted to generate new business, you went door-to-door and pressed the flesh. Who needs fancy PowerPoint presentations when a handshake and a smile will do the job? Don't let Betty talk you into proposing something as silly as a web site. Most people in this town have never even heard of the Internet."

"Bud Olds has been like a second father to me," said Young. "But we need to bring this firm into the 21st century. The days of Magic Markers and flip charts are gone forever. I want to see us on the Internet. We have potential customers all around the world that we need to reach."

"I think this firm is getting too big for its britches," said Olds.

"I have some big plans for our firm's future," said Young.

You have a problem. You have asked for a joint meeting with Olds and Young. What are you going to tell them?

New Technology in the Net Generation

If you are a traditional college student—one who is a recent high school graduate—then consider yourself to be one of the N-Gen.

Author Don Tapscott defines the Net Generation—also known as the N-Gen—as the 81.1 million children born between January 1977 and December 1997. Although this group has traditionally been called the Echo Generation, an echo of the baby boom that ran for nearly two decades following World War II, Tapscott believes his moniker is more appropriate.

"Just as the more limited medium of television influenced the values and culture of the baby boomers, a new force is helping shape the N-Gen wave," Tapscott wrote. "They are spending their formative years in a context and environment fundamentally different from their parents." Tapscott notes that the N-Gen coincides with the digital revolution. "Together, these two factors are producing a generation which is not just a demographic bulge but a wave of social transformation."[1]

Regardless of when you were born, the fact remains that technological growth is redefining who we are and the society in which we live. The PC on which you do your homework is more powerful than most of the computers used to send astronauts to the moon in 1969.

It is easy to be in awe of new technology. In many ways, technology can help us be more productive, healthy, happy, fulfilled, and self-confident. And technological advances have paralleled the tremendous growth of public relations. Practitioners have always been among the first to adapt technological advancements to their needs. Technology significantly contributes to every step of the public relations process: research, planning, communication, and evaluation. With a computer, a modem, and a telephone or cable line, today's practitioners have access to a world of information and opportunities.

The importance of new technology to the practice of public relations is reflected in the results of a joint PRSA-IABC survey. Respondents said technological advances have affected communication and public relations more than any other factor. Those surveyed cited the increased use of computer technology as the most significant development in recent years. One of every three practitioners questioned said he or she thinks technology offers the greatest opportunity for career advancement in the next five years.[2]

Is the Medium the Message?

New communications technology has made it possible for an instantaneous exchange of ideas and images with anyone in the world. At the dawn of the television age, Canadian philosopher Marshall McLuhan wrote that we are living in a **global village,** where everyone can share simultaneous experiences. He also believed that "the medium is the message." On one occasion McLuhan said: "In our time, we have devised ways of making the most trivial event affect everybody. One of the consequences of electronic environments is the total involvement of people in people."[3]

McLuhan's theories were developed long before anyone had ever heard of the Internet. And when you take into account the increasing interactivity of media, the Canadian theorist's words seem to hold even deeper meanings. The world is now wired to a degree that perhaps even McLuhan could not have imagined. For many, the selection of the medium has become an even more important decision than the content of the message to be delivered.

But this is where McLuhan's "the medium is the message" approach falls short. Although selecting an appropriate channel is critical in successful communication, developing the message is also critical. And while it is true that the medium can alter the perception of a message, the reverse also holds true. An appropriate message delivered

Digital Media Kit The ability to combine pictures, text, and sound digitally into a CD format allowed Becker Underwood Inc. to develop a comprehensive media kit. (Courtesy of Becker Underwood Inc.)

via an inappropriate medium is just as ineffective as an inappropriate message delivered via an appropriate medium. Message and medium must be equal considerations in communication. If not, true communication does not occur.

The Role of Values in Message and Medium Selection

More to the point, the selection of both message and medium is closely tied to the values of the communicator, as well as to those of the targeted public. Those values are not linked to changes in technology. Instead, they are expressions of who we are and who we want to be. The first book ever produced in mass quantities was the Bible. Since the days of Gutenberg, millions of copies of the Bible have been produced using an increasing variety of media, including audiocassettes, videotapes, CD-ROMs, DVDs, and web sites. Despite the many advances in communications technology, the values expressed in the Bible have not changed.

For an example of how values dictate the message and the medium, let's revisit the architectural firm of Olds Young and Associates mentioned in this chapter's opening scenario. At the heart of the dispute between Olds and Young are conflicting values. Olds sees the firm as one with strictly local clientele. Young has a different vision—that of a firm competing on a global scale. Before any decisions can be made on *how* to communicate, the two partners must first reach a consensus on *what* to communicate and to *whom*. Only when those issues are decided is it appropriate to discuss messages and media.

Part of your job with Olds Young is to help the partners reach that consensus. Fortunately, you are not confronted with the necessity of choosing one option over the other. It is commonplace for different divisions within the same company to target different publics. If the architectural firm is willing to commit the necessary resources, *both* partners can have their way. Bud Olds can focus on local customers, using more personalized communication channels. At the same time, Betty Young can use more technologically advanced methods to reach out to clients more accustomed to communicating at that level. This is one generation gap that the sound application of public relations practices can close.

The point of this chapter is to put technology in its proper perspective. Advanced technology is a useful tool in the practice of public relations. However, it is only a tool. Ultimately, the expression of our values determines how we use all the tools available to us.

The Digital Revolution

At the center of the explosion in communications technology is the *bit*, the basic element of transmission in digital communications. Nicholas Negroponte calls the bit "the smallest atomic element in the DNA of information."[4] Our increasing ability to transfer thoughts, images, and sounds into bits is changing the way we interact with our world.

The communications revolution of the late 20th century was a result of the ability to convert analog communication into digital formats. **Analog** communication relays all information present in the original message in the form of continuously varying signals. Those variations correspond to the changes in sound or light energy coming from the source.[5]

The conversion of analog communication into a **digital** format—into computer-readable bits—makes it possible to filter out unwanted information. Analog communication is like talking to a friend while seated in the stands of crowded Analog Stadium. You may have to strain to hear your friend above the cheering of the crowd, the noise of the game, and the whistling of the wind. At Digital Stadium, however, you would have no trouble hearing your friend. The crowd would grow silent, the game would cease, and the wind would stop blowing.

Digital communication also permits the simultaneous transfer of more information. Analog technology severely limited the number of calls a telephone company could transmit at any given moment. Essentially, telephone calls were handled one at a time along a vast copper wire network. With the introduction of digital communications and a fiberoptic network, the capacity of telephone communication systems dramatically multiplied.

Back at Analog Stadium, imagine what it would be like if thousands of people on one side of the field tried to communicate with a counterpart on the opposite side. It would be impossible to distinguish any one conversation in that din. However, it is a different story at Digital Stadium. Everyone on the east sideline would clearly hear their west sideline counterpart—and no one else!

We see this principle at work in television, through which it has become possible to transmit multiple programs on a cable TV or satellite channel that previously carried only one. Digital technology also makes it possible to store a remarkable amount of data in a relatively small space. An example is the typical compact disc, which has the capacity to store 5 billion bits of information. (A typical edition of the *Wall Street Journal* contains 10 billion bits.) Within a few years, that same CD or DVD will be able to store 50 billion bits.[6]

To take it one step further, digital communication also makes it possible for many to simultaneously share information from a single source. This capability is evolving into an on-demand delivery system, which allows consumers to choose what they want, whenever they want. Instead of waiting around all day for your favorite movie to be broadcast at a specific time, eventually you will be able to download it from a programming source just as the pizza arrives! It is as if everyone on the opposite side of Digital Stadium could, during the fourth quarter, filter out all other noise and focus on something you said before the game.

Convergence and Hypermedia

Perhaps the most important consequence of the digital revolution is a **convergence of media.** As different media adopt digital technology in their production and distribution, barriers that have traditionally stood between them are tumbling down. Practically every medium we interact with now is digital, from the telephone on which we speak, to the music CD we listen to, to the Internet we surf. The television signal you receive in your home is very likely digital. And before long, all television signals will be digital. The newspaper, seemingly an artifact of 18th-century technology, is currently produced—and may soon be delivered to your "electronic doorstep"—digitally.

A more dramatic development is the convergence of traditionally distinct media into one form. Integrated multimedia incorporating digital audio, visual, and text information are called **hypermedia.** To see hypermedia in action, one need only log on to the web site maintained by the Cable News Network (www.cnn.com), one of the web's most popular sites. CNN Interactive combines text from magazines such as *Time* and *Sports Illustrated* with video and audio supplied by CNN. The site also provides links to other sites where more information on subjects of personal interest can be sought.

The potential application of hypermedia goes beyond the Internet. Think of what the week before the start of each school year is like. You have to run to the bookstore to purchase the textbooks you need for the coming semester. Depending on how many classes you are taking, this errand can bring new meaning to the idea of "carrying a full load." In the future, however, it may not be necessary to leave home. You will be able to download the contents of all your texts into a single device, a digital book. These textbooks will be unlike any you have ever seen. You will be able to highlight a word and have its definition appear. Instead of footnotes, links will take you to vast quantities of background information. Video and audio will be inserted to complement the text. When you finish your assigned reading, you will be able to use the same electronic book to download the daily newspaper or one of the best-selling novels of the day. Just how distant is this brave new world? It may be closer than you think. One study has predicted that digital textbook sales will have grown to $1.3 billion and account for 14 percent of all textbook sales (including noncollege texts) by 2003.[7]

Convergence Issues

Although the convergence of technology opens up a world of possibilities for the 21st century, progress does not come without its price. Only now are we beginning to understand the social ramifications of this new digital world. Convergence has raised numerous issues for public policy makers and individuals to address. Among those are questions about media mergers, personal privacy, job security, and intellectual property rights.

MERGERS OF MEDIA COMPANIES.   The convergence of communications technology has brought about a convergence of media companies; that is, media companies have merged for competitive reasons. These new giant media conglomerates now own the means of production and distribution of a wide spectrum of media. The January 2001 merger of America Online and Time Warner is the prime example of this business convergence. According to its annual report, AOL-Time Warner's vast corporate umbrella includes Turner Broadcasting (including CNN, TBS Superstation, and the Atlanta Braves), Home Box Office, Time Inc. (including *Time, Sports Illustrated, People,* and *Fortune*), Warner Brothers, New Line Cinema, Time Warner Cable, and America Online (including Netscape, Moviefone, and CompuServe). This amounts to a global media empire that touches consumers more than 2.5 billion times each month.[8] Although a seemingly efficient arrangement, the concentration of numerous powerful channels of mass communication into the hands of a few corporations has caused some to worry. Some fear a loss of journalistic independence among the media outlets that have been consumed by these megamergers.

PRESERVATION OF PERSONAL PRIVACY.   The digital revolution has made it easier for people to gather, store, and transmit personal information. This is a matter of convenience for individuals as well as corporations. But there are risks. Even with sophisticated safeguards, digital information is not entirely secure. Privacy concerns extend to personal messages, whether sent via e-mail or wireless telephones. At a time when computer hackers are at least as knowledgeable as computer programmers, you never know who is accessing your private conversations. In the highly competitive economy of the 21st century, new technology opens the door to commercial espionage on an alarming scale.

JOB SECURITY.   The good news is that improved technology can make people more productive in the workplace. The bad news is that increased ability to do more with less lowers the demand for highly skilled workers. New communication technology is allowing many industries to outsource corporate functions. We have seen this in public relations, where many corporate public relations offices have been downsized. Much of the slack has been picked up on a per-job basis by independent consultants who do not receive any of the traditional corporate benefits (e.g., health coverage, retirement plans, or stock options). Then too, technological advances often disrupt successful companies, a phenomenon Clayton M. Christensen of the Harvard Business School has called "the innovator's dilemma" and about which he has written a book of the same name. The Digital Revolution has led to simpler, cheaper, and more user-friendly ways of doing things that can squeeze out the products of older companies. Although not a direct threat to public relations, these so-called disruptive technologies can threaten organizations in which it is practiced.[9]

PROTECTION OF INTELLECTUAL PROPERTY.   The fact that digital copies are both identical to original works and easy to alter poses a huge problem in the information age. A person's intellectual property has value. When others ignore copyright law (see Chapter 15) and use someone's intellectual property without permission or compensation, it is tantamount to theft. Today's digital technology makes it easier to copy and distribute the results of someone else's labors. This has always been a problem in the music industry, where the performances of top artists can be rapidly duplicated and shipped overseas for illegal sale in unregulated markets. And the problem is not limited to consumer goods. Specialized business software is also a prime target. In some instances, this piracy has national security implications.

Virtual Public Relations

Because public relations is an information-based profession, this brave new digital world is having a profound effect on public relations practitioners. The growth in communications technology allows practitioners to reach more people at less expense and in a manner that levels the playing field between the small one-person consultancy and the big multiemployee agency. Because of advancements in computer and telecommunications technology, one person can now do a job that once required several people. And if that one person has the energy, drive, and talent, it is often impossible for a client to tell the difference between the work of a one-person shop and an agency.

This development has led to the creation of what some have called **virtual public relations:** public relations work done by small, independent consultancies that, by all appearances, has the look and feel of work done by big-time agencies. This trend has been fed, in part, by the downsizing of corporate public relations offices. These independent consultancies have become increasingly important as more and more companies begin outsourcing their work. As already mentioned, outsourcing can reduce corporate operating costs, especially when it comes to paying employee benefits.

Quick ✔ Check

1. What are the differences between analog and digital communications?
2. What is meant by the phrase *media convergence,* and what are its implications?
3. What are hypermedia?

Computer Technology

No discussion of communications technology would be complete without a bow to one of the most important inventions of the 20th century, an invention second only to television in its social impact. The explosion of computer technology during the past quarter-century has launched the world into an era in which information itself has become a major commercial commodity.

The origin of computer technology goes back to 1822, when Charles Babbage, a mathematics professor at Cambridge University, created what he called a "difference engine," a mechanical calculator. His work did not progress very far because of a lack of manufacturing capabilities, a shortage of funds, and the British government's apathetic view of his efforts.[10] However, interest in the device would eventually be renewed. In 1890, for the first time, mechanical calculators were used in tabulating the U.S. Census. Military needs growing out of World War II spurred further development of computer technology, especially for uses in code breaking and missile guidance systems. By 1975 the first personal computer, the Altair, was introduced. Bill Gates, then a freshman at Harvard University, created a computer programming language for the Altair. That eventually led to founding the Microsoft Corporation, the world's largest personal computer software company.[11]

As computer technology advanced, it also became more accessible. Computers became smaller and more affordable. This accessibility has become especially evident in the workplace, where office typewriters have been replaced by desktop computers—and typing has been replaced by word processing. Skeptical employees soon discovered that these PCs were more than just fancy typewriters. In addition to word processing, these newfangled machines allowed them to analyze data, design publications, schedule meetings for many people at the same time, and communicate with others around the world. (However, supervisors soon discovered the dark side of this invention. These office PCs, equipped with game software and Internet connections, can distract employees. These distractions became such a concern that the governor of Virginia once ordered all the offending software to be removed from the office PCs of state employees!)

The ability to link, or network, computers has created its own revolution. It is now possible to perform tasks at home or on the road that once could be done only in the office. One useful development has been the creation of the **personal digital assistant** or **PDA** (also known as a personal data assistant), a pocket-sized information device that records handwritten scribbles and allows people on the move to stay in touch with various computer and telephone networks. Computer networks have also made it possible for many people, especially working or single parents, to earn a living without leaving their homes. Many companies allow some of their employees to telecommute, performing office tasks at home, but linked to the office by a computer and modem.

The impact of computer technology on the practice of public relations is undeniable. Public relations is about communicating, and computer technology has revolutionized communications. Computers have become critical in the preparation of messages delivered in the form of news releases, newsletters, and presentation slides. However, the role of computers in public relations extends far beyond message preparation. Computers also provide the delivery system for our messages, whether through e-mail, the Internet, or fax. Add to this the networking capabilities that make it easier for practitioners to operate outside the traditional office. Public relations practitioners have been quick to embrace each new technical achievement—because they, more than most, understand the value of exploring all methods of communication.

Values Statement 11.1

MOTOROLA, INC.

Motorola, headquartered in Schaumburg, Illinois, manufactures and sells communications and embedded electronic solutions, including wireless telephone and two-way radio systems and semiconductors.

Our Key Beliefs (How We Will Always Act)

People

To treat each employee with dignity, as an individual; to maintain an open atmosphere where direct communication with employees affords the opportunity to contribute to the maximum of their potential and fosters unity of purpose with Motorola; to provide personal opportunities for training and development to ensure the most capable and most effective workforce; to respect senior service; to compensate fairly by salary, benefits and, where possible, incentives; to promote on the basis of capability; and to practice the commonly accepted policies of equal opportunity and affirmative action.

Integrity and Ethics

To maintain the highest standards of honesty, integrity and ethics in all aspects of our business—with customers, suppliers, employees, governments and society at large—and to comply with the laws of each country and community in which we operate.

—"For Which We Stand,"
Motorola web site

The Internet

The omnipresent by-product of the computer age is the **Internet.** It has become a significant force in global communication. Public relations practitioners have been quick to embrace it—both as a new medium for reaching targeted publics and as a source of revenue.

In many ways, the Internet has helped to reduce the psychological distance that exists between an organization and the publics important to its success. Instead of being seen as a distant and obscure entity, the organization is now as close as the nearest computer screen. It is as if the Internet has become the organization's new front door and the **web site** the digital equivalent of the lobby, from which visitors are directed to various information sites within the organization. Interactive web sites allow visitors to communicate directly through e-mail links with key personnel within the organization. Through the integration of audio and video technology, visitors may be personally welcomed by the company CEO. For those looking for a particular nugget of information, many web sites are equipped with search engines that allow visitors to browse the entire site as well as company archives. It is even possible to take a virtual tour of an organization's facilities without leaving one's home. Add to this the role of corporate intranets and extranets (discussed in

Chapter 9). Because of these innovations, once seemingly distant companies are now only a mouse click away.

The Internet has valuable applications in the world of media relations. More and more practitioners are handling reporters' inquiries through e-mail. Many journalists receive the latest news releases via e-mail or by clicking onto organizations' web sites. More and more organizations are putting their media kits, containing detailed information about the organization and the issues confronting it, on the Internet. The web also provides a source of information reporters can access quickly regardless of the time of day. As is the case with conventional media relations, for online media information to be taken seriously by reporters, it must be accurate, nonpromotional, and of clear news value. Information placed on the Internet must also be regularly updated. Conversely, the Internet also offers public relations practitioners a fast and easy way to research media coverage of an issue or to locate a specific reporter's article.

Public relations agencies and consultants were among the first to use the Internet as a new front door. "We realized that we had to develop the skills needed to compete in today's market," said Carl Carter of Carter-Harwell Public Relations in Birmingham, Alabama. "Creating our own web site was a learning experience that provided the agency with a portfolio we could showcase."[12] Once practitioners developed their own skills, it became commonplace—and profitable—for them to assist other organizations in establishing their own Internet presence.

Marketing talents and services on the Internet is especially attractive to smaller agencies and consultancies. In many ways, it places them on the same level as their larger competitors. However, as always, the proof of the pudding is in the eating. Practitioners who fail to deliver on promises made on the web soon lose their most valuable commodity: credibility.

Practitioners have also found the web useful as a research and planning tool. Much in the manner of reporters, they can go online and find a wealth of information about a universe of subjects in relatively little time. By employing audio and video technology, practitioners now can interview individuals and conduct focus groups over great distances. Teleconferencing products such as electronic blackboards can help reduce travel and other business costs.

The History of the Internet

The roots of the Internet can be traced to 1957, when the United States created the Advanced Research Projects Agency in response to the Soviet Union's launch of the first artificial satellite, *Sputnik*. ARPA's mission was to establish the United States' lead in the military use of science and technology.[13] Recognizing the need to link computers at research centers across the country with one another, the agency created ARPANET, the forerunner of today's Internet. At the urging of the federal government, colleges and universities began using ARPANET for their own research

Sticker Thanks to the growth of the Internet, web-based companies such as Yahoo! have become household names. (Courtesy of Yahoo!)

purposes during the 1970s. And when all of the interconnected research networks adopted a common computer communications language in 1983, TCP/IP (Transmission Control Protocol/Internet Protocol), the Internet as we know it was born.[14]

At first the Internet remained the domain mostly of academics and researchers. Locating and accessing information from distant computers was both complicated and time consuming. The creation of the first network browsers at the University of Illinois simplified this. In 1990 researchers at CERN, the European Laboratory for Particle Physics, developed an Internet service that further simplified this process: the **World Wide Web.** Those outside the scientific and academic community immediately recognized the value of the web's global information access. Since that time, the growth in web use has been nothing short of astonishing. In June 1993, only 130 web sites existed. That number grew to more than 1 million in less than four years. By January 2000, the number of web sites had risen to almost 10 million and by the summer of 2001 had tripled to approximately 30 million.[15]

The Internet may have come of age on Friday, September 11, 1998. On that day the Judiciary Committee of the U.S. House of Representatives used the Internet to release a report of Independent Counsel Kenneth Starr's investigation into President Bill Clinton's relationship with a White House intern. It was on the basis of this report that, three months later, Clinton became only the second president impeached by the House of Representatives. An estimated 12 percent of U.S. adults, approximately 20

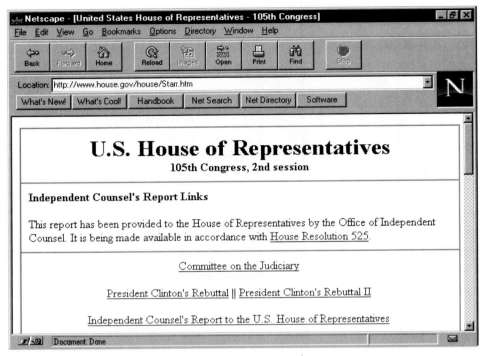

Starr Report Online The online release of Independent Counsel Kenneth Starr's report on his investigation of President Clinton became a major Internet event. (Courtesy of the United States House of Representatives and Netscape)

million, used the Internet to gain access to the Starr report. The Associated Press, which posted the 445-page document on its web site, said the report generated 20 times the site's normal traffic.[16] For the first time, the Internet had become an integral channel in an important national debate.

Today the Internet provides an interactive window to the world. Not only can you visit the web sites of organizations and individuals as fast as your modem allows, but the world can visit you. Most Internet providers permit you to create your own web site identity, some for free. At first, only those who understood the complicated programming language HTML (Hypertext Markup Language) were able to design their own homepages. But with the development of user-friendly design programs such as Netscape Composer and Microsoft Dreamweaver, the process of creating one's own presence on the Internet is easier than ever. Regardless of what program you use, however, you also need special FTP (file transfer protocol) software programs to download your web site to your Internet provider.

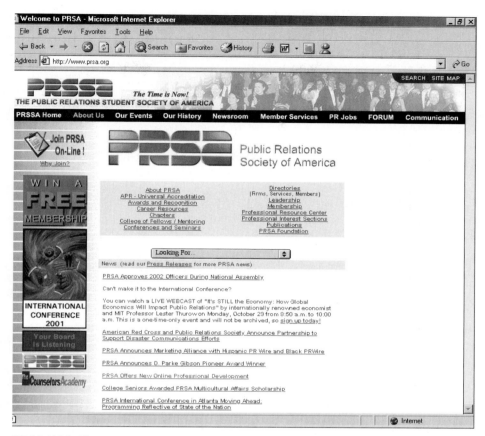

PRSA Web Site Many organizations, such as PRSA, use the Internet as a cost-effective channel for reaching important target publics. (Courtesy of the Public Relations Society of America and Microsoft Corporation)

Individuals as Gatekeepers

In Chapter 5 we discussed the evolution of communication theory. As you may remember, theorists once believed that mass media could control the public opinion process. They thought that editors at newspapers, magazines, and radio stations dictated what information people received and when they received it. However, the growth in communications technology has changed all that. The magic bullet theory evolved into uses and gratifications theory—the belief that each person has become his or her own information gatekeeper and picks and chooses from a wide variety of information sources.

QuickBreak 11.1

SPINNING THE WEB

OK, you have made the big decision—your organization is finally going on the web. Before relaxing to congratulate yourself for making such a momentous decision, stop and think. How you build your web site and the content you make available on it are much bigger issues than the mere fact of its existence.

Before doing anything else, you must decide whether you should be on the web at all. As with all other communication, the need is first to define the web site's audience and its purpose. These two concepts are intrinsically interwoven. Besides net surfers, whom do you want to visit your site? Are you trying to lure employees, stockholders, investment analysts, clients, reporters, or some other public to the site?

"Build a home page only if you have a strategic reason," said Steve Hoechster, vice president of Edelman Public Relations Worldwide, New York. "Avoid the process unless and until you can offer a rationale more sensible than: 'It's way cool.'"[17]

Organizations often integrate their web sites into their media relations. However, a study conducted by Dr. Jakob Nielsen, a leading expert on web usability, found that the press sections of corporate web sites often fail to meet journalists' basic needs. Reporters who were asked to search 10 sites for basic information, such as financial disclosure statements and public relations contacts, were successful only 60 percent of the time. "If these sites were being graded in a U.S. school, the average grade would be no higher than a D," Nielsen said.[18] Although Nielsen's study was limited in its scope, it points out the need for a clear understanding of each web site's purpose.

Christopher Ryan designed Media General Financial Services' web site (www.mgfs.com). "The strategy was to attract likely customers for MGFS," Ryan said. To encourage visitors to "look around the site and keep coming back," he added a Daily Market Barometer report to MGFS' homepage. Updated automatically, that report contains information especially useful to potential investors and investment analysts—the very audience MGFS is seeking to attract.

This evolution is significant for public relations. For example, **push technology** allows Internet users to decide what categories of information reach them at the exclusion of all other information. By signing up for various push services, individuals can request and customize information. They can choose, for example, news stories covering specific topics, sports scores, or the latest from the financial markets. If you represent a client that caters to people who travel extensively, creating a push service that provides the latest in travel news and tips would be a very attractive strategy for reaching this audience. It would provide value to the targeted consumers, who would welcome a steady stream of news that interests them, as well as to your client, who would have opened a regular channel of communications to an important public.

However, this also is an example of how communications innovations can mean both good news and bad news for public relations. Push technology may make it

"We figure that while they are on the site, they will go exploring," Ryan said. That's why the homepage also has links to information about various company services.[19]

Although content on a web site is critical, you shouldn't ignore technical issues. According to the authors of a popular web site design book, some of the most common web site complaints are difficulty of locating the site, poor graphic design and layout, gratuitous use of bells and whistles, designer-centeredness, inappropriate tone, endlessly ongoing construction, and lack of attention to detail.[20]

According to Hoechster, your homepage also needs what realtors call curb appeal. "If the place doesn't look good from the street, why bother going in? The same holds true with a home page."[21]

Several other concerns are important. You want to ensure that your web site is compatible with the most popular browsers, the navigational software that guides users around the web. You want to secure an easy-to-remember URL, your Internet address. And you want to keep your web site fresh by constantly updating it with new and interesting information.

No consensus has been reached on the important question of who within the organization should control the web site. Robert W. Grupp, director of corporate communications at Eli Lilly and Company, wrote that public relations practitioners should control web sites: "We in public relations have a stewardship role for the content of information on the Internet that is otherwise an unfiltered commodity."[22] William G. Margaritas, corporate vice president of Worldwide Communications and Investor Relations at FedEx Corporation, countered, "For a business transaction–oriented web site, a 'one-for-all and all-for-one' collaborative approach is the most optimal."[23]

If you have decided that you want your own site on a World Wide Web of dreams, remember this: Build it right, and they will come.

harder to get the attention of certain individuals. In the mass media, editors serve as information gatekeepers. But with push technology, individuals can become their own editors. That can make targeting publics more difficult. Opportunities for exposing your message may lessen. That, in turn, means making the best of the chances that remain.

Individuals as Publishers

Not only have individuals become information gatekeepers; they have also become self-publishers. Digital communications technology has made it possible for people to communicate more effectively and efficiently than ever. In the past, if your campus organization wanted to typeset and print a meeting notice for posting around campus, it was necessary to employ the services of a designer and the local photocopy shop. Today, those tasks can be accomplished by just one person using a laptop computer and a printer. In the past, if your organization wanted to contact a large number of people off campus, the job might require the use of direct mail, advertising, or telephone solicitations—expensive and time-consuming procedures. Today, e-mail and faxes can do the job cheaper and quicker, though they would reach smaller, more targeted publics. In the past, only media moguls had the resources necessary to reach a worldwide audience. Today, all you need is your own web site.

Again, there is a downside. The fact that everyone can become his or her own publisher doesn't necessarily mean that he or she should. It will take you only a few minutes of surfing the World Wide Web to realize that there are a lot of people on the Internet with nothing to say. In many respects, these people have taken McLuhan too literally: They believe the medium is the message and don't want to be bogged down with "content issues." As a result, it is getting harder and harder to cut through the clutter. Substantial information of vital public importance is being drowned in a sea of babble. This is particularly disconcerting to companies that have spent a lot of money developing a substantial presence on the Internet, only to have the whole web devalued by pretenders and wannabes.

Perhaps an even bigger problem is that much of what is self-published, electronically or otherwise, does not go through the scrutiny that an editor applies to more traditional publications. Many self-published materials are inaccurate, incomplete, or biased—not to mention poorly written. Because of this, the need for constant monitoring of the Internet is growing. Organizations, especially publicly held companies, have a lot to lose from inaccurate information being flashed globally. The ease of self-publishing also brings into focus the need for rapid response plans to counter false or negative information on the Internet.

In his 1997 book *What Will Be*, Michael Dertouzos wrote that new communications technology will dramatically affect human behavior within organizations. With an increased ability to monitor all aspects of the organization, executives, Dertouzos said, will be able to hold their employees more accountable for their actions. He said this "will improve a firm's efficiency, even though its employees may be unhappy to have their individual work so open to inspection and critique."[24] Dertouzos also said the new technology will shift responsibility further down the corporate ladder, thus creating a greater need for employees to understand and embrace their organization's goals and values:

> For an organization to extract this increased decision power from its people, it will have to provide them with more knowledge about why some things are done and who does them, and why certain decisions are made and who makes them.[25]

With this growing reliance on employee communications, public relations will remain an important management responsibility in the 21st century.

Quick ✔ Check

1. What are some of the ways public relations practitioners can take advantage of new communications technology?
2. What are some of the potential disadvantages resulting from the introduction of new communications technology?
3. What are the implications of new communications technology for employee relations?

Other Internet Issues

For all the possibilities the Internet has created, it is still not the answer to all the problems that public relations practitioners face. Let's look briefly at a variety of Internet-related issues a practitioner should consider.

THE ONLINE GENERATION GAP.   The rapid expansion of the web has indeed opened new avenues for reaching certain targeted publics. Contrary to the popular assumption that online traffic is dominated by teenage computer hackers, a 1997 survey found that 73 percent of those whom researchers considered "connected" were between 30 and 54 years old. This digital generation gap is fading as computer prices fall and baby boomers grow older.[26] Online statistics seem to support this idea. According to Nielsen//NetRatings, U.S. at-home Internet penetration rose to 58 percent in July 2001. That was up from 39 percent only two years earlier.[27] In time, as more people go online, Internet demographics are likely to become more inclusive. But for the time being, the Internet is not the best channel if reaching everybody is your goal.

THE DIGITAL DIVIDE.   Age is not the only factor in Internet use. Where people live and their socioeconomic status also dictate their ability to reach the web. This uneven Internet access is known as the **digital divide,** and it has great social and economic ramifications for the future. Only 1 in 20 people worldwide is online. Although North America accounts for only 5 percent of the world's population, it is home to 60 percent of all Internet users.[28] Even in countries with high Internet use, a disparity exists between rich and poor. For example, one study found that, in the United States, only 35 percent of those in the lower-socioeconomic classification had Internet access. That compared with 53 percent in the lower-middle bracket, 79 percent in the upper-middle bracket, and 83 percent in the top bracket.[29] Once again, this reminds us that the web is not necessarily a good channel for reaching all audiences.

INTERNET RESEARCH PROBLEMS.   As a research tool, the Internet is, in many ways, a mile wide and an inch deep. For all the information readily available online, the total represents only a small fraction of what can be gathered through more traditional

QuickBreak 11.2

THE MILLENNIUM BUG

To some people, Peter De Jager ranks right up there with Chicken Little, the boy who cried wolf, and the hyperbolic spin doctors of public relations.

De Jager was among the first to warn about the dangers of the Y2K computer problem. Writing in *Computerworld* in 1993, De Jager predicted that widespread disruptions would occur at midnight on New Year's Day 2000 because of outdated computers unequipped to deal with passage into the new millennium.[30] To give a simplistic explanation of the problem: The clocks on these antiquated computers would see the calendar click over to the year 2000, believe it was the year 1900, and shut everything down. Worse, others thought it would be—literally—the end of the world.

Lift your eyes from this page and look around. Still here? Of course you are. And that has led many to wonder whether De Jager, government officials, and the public relations in-

dustry didn't unnecessarily alarm the public. They also question whether the $500-billion price tag for inoculating the world—at an estimated $360 for every person in the United States—was too heavy a burden to pay for fixing the millennium bug.[31]

Needless to say, De Jager, the government, and the public relations industry disagree.

Although the world did not end, there were some glitches. In the United States, problems included a 30-minute power outage in Carson City, Nevada; a one-day delay in $50 million of Medicare payments; a brief breakdown of the 911 emergency telephone system in Charlotte, North Carolina; a three-hour cash-register-systems failure at the Godiva Chocolates store in New York; and the shutdown of 800 slot machines in Delaware. Problems elsewhere in the world included telephone outages in southern Australia, police department fax and telex system problems in Botswana, prison door sys-

forms of research. For example, many libraries do not have the necessary resources to digitize everything in their archives; a lot of vital information exists in print and on the shelves, but not online. Also, more can be learned through a personal examination of historical artifacts than by looking at digitized pictures of them. There is also the aforementioned problem of accuracy of Internet information. Any information gathered from an unfamiliar source should be verified.

THE INTERNET AS AN EQUALIZER.   Although the Internet can make it easier for an organization to communicate its values and goals, it can do the same for others who do not share that vision. In a sense, the Internet is an equalizer, providing a public forum for social activists who once felt they were voiceless in public debate. It has also made it easier for groups with common interests to join forces, exerting greater public pressure than they might be able to do by acting alone. "Prior to the Internet, activists relied upon media advocacy (publicity efforts) to forge links to other stakeholders," wrote W. Timothy Coombs of Illinois State University. Now, however, "the activists can state their message directly to other stakeholders in the network."[32] Because of the Inter-

tems failures in Canada, and the failure of eight traffic lights in Jamaica.[33]

"The premise is that there was no problem, that the only reason we spent this money is because people like myself convinced you to do it," De Jager said. "But the reality is they didn't spend money because we said there was a problem. They spent the money because they looked at their systems and went 'Oh my God, we have a problem.'"[34]

A congressional committee that monitored U.S. government efforts to prepare for Y2K agreed. "It is the Committee's judgment that the level of effort was justified," it said in its final report. "The risks and consequences of inaction were too dire to justify a lesser effort."[35]

Little did anyone know that the calamity they feared—and the need to use their Y2K plans—would come less than two years later. When terrorists attacked New York and Washington in September 2001, much of the world's normal operating systems were disrupted. But the *Wall Street Journal* reported two days after the attack, "For the most part, companies maneuvered safely through their respective shoals." Although the catastrophe forced companies to use what the newspaper called "a mixture of improvisation and managerial sleight of hand," most were able to maintain their operations. A spokesperson for SunTrust Banks Inc. of Atlanta noted that "Y2K gave us a great deal of experience and helped us polish our contingency procedures."[36]

As for the Chicken Little atmosphere that doomsayers thought would accompany the start of the new millennium, many credit public relations for keeping a lid on things. Although a few people hoarded food and locked themselves in bomb shelters, most people went about their lives on New Year's Day 2000 without a hint of concern.

net's leveling of the playing field, public policy debate is taking on a whole new dimension. The good news is that the Internet has increased public participation in democratic societies. However, when viewed from the perspective of an organization against which this new wave of cyber-activism is aligned, this can also be bad news.

PASSIVE COMMUNICATION.   It is important to remember that the Internet is a passive way for an organization to communicate. People have to go to a web site; it does not automatically come to them. Although push technology allows organizations to send information via the Internet to subscribers, users must first sign up for the service.

MARKETING USES.   The Internet still has a way to go before it become widely accepted as a marketing tool. Senior managers and marketing executives worldwide say that the web needs more speed, availability, and security before it can become a significant commercial conduit. Although e-commerce is growing, it is still a tiny part of the economy. The U.S. Census Bureau reported that online sales by retail establishments totaled $5.3 billion, or just 0.64 percent of all retail sales, during the fourth quarter of 1999.[37] However, those concerns may evaporate, as the technology improves, more companies come online, and encryption technology to protect data becomes more sophisticated.[38] In addition, some Internet marketing tactics can be counterproductive. Anyone who has been "spammed"—who has received unsolicited e-mail that advertises a product or service—knows that this kind of communication often is unwelcome and unreliable.

CAREER IMPLICATIONS.   The rapid growth of the Internet has created a demand for college graduates capable of serving as webmasters. However, before you are tempted to skip all your other studies to focus on developing web site programming skills, let us sound a cautionary note. One of the consequences of the advancement of technology is that, with the passage of time, it becomes more user-friendly. It may not be too long before anyone can create his or her own web site, thus pulling the rug out from under those who have only technical skills. Those who are more well-rounded will be able to cope with this change and thrive. They are the folks who will give web sites their substance. The bottom line, therefore, is that you should not give up on your studies quite yet.

Wireless Communications Technology

Another area in which technological advancements have had a tremendous impact upon the practice of public relations is wireless technology. Our ability to communicate with others over great distances is no longer restricted by the length of a wire. The ability to communicate from anywhere using a variety of communication devices—telephones, computer modems, radios, video, facsimile (fax) machines, and satellites—has made us more mobile, responsive, and cost effective. Through the use of miniature transmitters and global positioning satellites, it is possible to locate the exact position of anyone and anything on the planet—particularly important in both commerce and travel. And what may have been the most important social, economic, and technological development of the 20th century, wireless communications technology, such as television, makes it possible for peoples in all corners of the world to share simultaneously in a common experience—in much the way the world watched in horror as terrorists attacked the World Trade Center and the Pentagon on September 11, 2001.

Look at what has happened in just the past few years. Because of the growth of the Internet, advancements in digital communications, and the availability of less expensive and more compact portable telephones, the demand for telephone service has exploded. It has been estimated that one in four of the world's 1.2 billion telephone subscribers has a mobile telephone.[39] Palm-sized computers, which serve as both portable telephones and fax machines, have become standard equipment for executives on the move.

The prevalence of cellular telephones became painfully obvious during the aforementioned terrorist attacks on New York and Washington. Passengers on the four hijacked jets and workers trapped in the World Trade Center used their telephones to deliver heart-wrenching farewells to loved ones. Evidence exists that passengers on one of the planes were prompted to confront their hijackers because of information received through wireless telephone communication. That plane crashed in western Pennsylvania, short of the terrorists' intended targets in Washington, D.C.

Just as important, the growth in cheaper, more accessible wireless communication is making the world a smaller place. Globally, there are currently telephone lines for only one person out of every eight. Most of these lines are located in the developed nations of the Western world. In fact, 80 percent of the world's people share only 30 percent of its telephone lines. However, access to phones will change dramatically over the next quarter-century as developing nations embrace wireless communications technology. Frances Cairncross, senior editor of *The Economist,* has written that this change will have significant geopolitical consequences. In her book *The Death of Distance,* Cairncross argues that the expansion of wireless technology will remove one of the Western world's key competitive edges, the vast superiority of its communications system. The worldwide economic impact of this shift in competitive equilibrium, she believes, will rival that of the collapse of communism.[40]

Quick ✔ Check

1. What are some ways public relations practitioners are using the Internet?
2. Despite its many advantages, why are some people reluctant to use the Internet?
3. What has been the impact of the growth of wireless communications?

Satellite Communications

On a summer afternoon in 1962, a wondrous event flickered across television screens in the United States and Europe. For the first time, viewers could see live television images from both sides of the Atlantic. The successful launch of Telstar, the first communications satellite, literally opened up a world of communications possibilities.

Today the earth is covered by a global geosynchronous satellite network that transmits our favorite television programs, telephone calls from overseas, computer data links, directions on how to get from one city to another, and even elevator music.

From the viewpoint of public relations practitioners, satellite technology provides the means for reaching a large audience when time is of the essence. It has played key roles in ending crises that threatened the financial stability of major U.S. corporations. Two famous examples are discussed in a case study at the end of Chapter 12. Executives at both Johnson & Johnson and Pepsi used satellite technology to communicate with key constituencies during product-tampering crises. Both companies avoided financial disasters because of the speed at which they delivered their messages to key publics.

SATELLITE MEDIA TOURS

In his movie role as Superman, the popular actor Christopher Reeve could fly to any point on the globe in the wink of an eye. Despite a tragic horse-riding accident that left him quadriplegic, Reeve was still capable of traveling at "superspeed" to Barnes & Noble bookstores in different corners of the country to promote his book *Still Me*. And he did it without ever leaving a local TV studio.[41]

Satellite media tours, SMTs, have become a powerful tool of public relations. SMTs allow book authors, politicians, celebrities, and various experts to engage in one-to-one conversations with journalists. Instead of embarking on exhausting and time-consuming travel, a newsmaker can give "exclusive" interviews to reporters in dozens of cities in a single afternoon.

"SMTs save time and money by placing the interviews in a dozen or more markets in a matter of hours," said Nick Peters, vice president of the satellite distribution company Medialink. "Clients like it because it's cost-effective and exciting."[42]

As local television stations have expanded the amount of time devoted to local news program-

Satellite media tours make it possible for a newsmaker to meet individually with reporters all over the world at a fraction of the time and cost involved in a conventional media tour. (Courtesy of Medialink)

ming, SMTs have played an increasingly larger role. One survey discovered that of SMTs and

As noted in Chapter 9, one of the recent innovations in the use of satellite technology has been the **satellite media tour (SMT)**. Let's say that your client is the publisher of a new book. Your goal is to generate publicity about the book that will, in turn, generate sales. It used to be that you and the book's author would have to pack your bags and go on the road for weeks, visiting bookstores and radio interviewers and journalists in city after city. Today, there is no need to travel any farther than a local television studio. From there, the author's words and image are beamed via satellite to waiting reporters in various locations across the nation. By prearrangement, each reporter is given a block of time to talk with the author. This gives the reporters what they want, an exclusive interview with the author. And it gives you what you want, simultaneous publicity in numerous cities, without requiring you to spend a lot of time or money for travel.

video news releases that make the airwaves, 44 percent show up on locally produced morning news shows, compared with 37 percent shown during evening news shows, 29 percent during noontime newscasts, and 14 percent during late night.[43]

SMTs often serve a dual purpose, both giving practitioners access to a television audience and giving local stations access to big-name personalities they might not otherwise get. "Interviewing a hard-to-reach celebrity gives the station some clout," said one local television news producer in Decatur, Illinois. A satellite feed coordinator at a Miami, Florida, television station said, "If the SMT story is an 'evergreen' (a story with no time constraints on its use), it gives the station an option of using an interview on the weekends when we have a smaller staff on hand."[44]

When organizations face crises, every second counts. More and more, SMTs are becoming a preferred way for communicating when the heat is on. "Satellite media tours are about hard news," said Susan Silk, president of Media Strategy in Chicago. "There's no other way when things hit the fan but to have your guy's face on camera."[45]

No longer a novelty, SMTs are becoming more sophisticated. And they have to, considering the intense competition for valuable air time in this media-savvy world. Today, for example, the SMTs with extra impact are those that leave the studio and offer an exotic location as a backdrop. Former automobile executive Robert Eaton once did an SMT with U.S. television stations from the floor of the Tokyo Auto Show to highlight his company's entry into the Japanese car market. "When a story is making news from abroad, it certainly adds some panache to the SMT," said Sally Jewett, whose company produced the Eaton video. "It makes it irresistible."[46]

"The acceptance for SMTs is much higher than for VNRs in the larger markets," said Mark Denbo of West Glen Communications. "The real selling point is the ability to reach the top markets in a very short period of time with a concentrated message."[47]

SMTs have been used to publicize Super Bowl television commercials, attract viewers to the annual Jerry Lewis Labor Day muscular dystrophy telethon, promote new movies, and get voters to support candidates for the presidency of the United States. Although nothing is better than personal one-to-one contact, SMTs often provide an acceptable, cost-effective alternative.

Satellite technology has other valuable applications in the practice of public relations. Through satellite teleconferencing, organizations with widely dispersed operations can be linked for various purposes, including conducting sales meetings, training employees, and announcing important news. Satellites are used to transmit computer data between headquarters and regional offices. Companies in the information business, such as private weather services or financial market analysts, use satellites for getting their "product" to consumers. For more traditional manufacturers,

QuickBreak 11.4

HIGH-TECH TOOLS

With technology in a constant state of change, it is difficult for anyone—including the authors of this book—to keep up with all the latest developments. That is one reason why this chapter focuses more on the trends and implications of technological development than on the technology itself. Nevertheless, this discussion of communications technology would not be complete without a tip of the hat to some high-tech tools that have made public relations practitioners more productive.

Electronic mail (aka e-mail): The Internet makes it just as easy to send a message to someone overseas as it is to send a note down the hall. The downside is e-mail's convenience can be a curse. It is way too easy to write something in haste and regret it later. At the receiving end, the person (or the many people) reading your ill-considered words may print them out on paper, thus immortalizing your momentary lapse of good sense.

CD-ROMs: Because an incredible amount of digital information can be stored on the small **CD-ROM** (compact disc read-only memory) format, it has become an effective tool in generating publicity. CDs are being used to distribute multimedia presentations containing video,

audio, text, and data. Manufacturing companies are using CDs to supplement or replace the old paper catalog.

DVDs: A close cousin to CD-ROMs, the **DVD** (digital video disc or digital versatile disc) is rapidly becoming a popular substitute for videotapes. As the cost of DVD players and burners steadily decline, this medium could become a popular educational and marketing tool for public relations practitioners.

PDAs (aka personal digital assistants): These palm-sized devices have become popular among those with hectic schedules. They allow the user to schedule, access addresses, take notes, track expenses, and even play games. Some PDAs also provide wireless communication and Internet access.

Facsimile (aka fax) machines: A popular and sometimes overused tool, fax machines transmit duplicates of documents over telephone lines. Broadcast faxes permit the sender to send a single document to multiple locations with the push of one button. Fax-on-demand allows a caller with the proper password to receive, via his or her own fax machine, selected documents stored elsewhere in a computer's memory.

global positioning satellites can track the product's progress from the factory to the warehouse to the store shelf. With the ability to react to changing global conditions becoming increasingly important, satellite technology has made it easier for organizations to keep an eye on world events. Satellite signals are used to activate pagers—even when you don't want to be found. And, yes, satellites are used for distributing that often annoying background music you hear when shopping at the mall.

Intranets: An intranet—an organization's computer network—looks a lot like the Internet, except that it may be used only by those authorized to access it. In addition to processing e-mail, intranets have the advantage of allowing people working in different locations to share the same documents and data. Intranets can serve as useful internal communications channels for public relations practitioners.

Extranets: These computer networks are similar to intranets with one important difference. These are controlled-access sites for selected external publics, such as vendors or distributors.

Voice mail: Tired of playing "phone tag" and writing down long messages for other people? Voice mail eliminates much of the need for doing those tasks. Voice mail also makes it possible for management to deliver detailed messages—such as news of bad-weather closings or computer system problems—to everyone in the organization.

Pagers (aka beepers) and cellular telephones: In this day of high-speed communications, a rapid response from everyone in the organization is essential. Pagers and cellular telephones allow organizations to contact employees who are out of the office—even when they would rather not be found. Cell phones are especially important during times of crises, when the regular telephone system may be jammed, inoperative or unavailable. Cell phones also enable public relations practitioners to be available 24 hours a day to members of important publics such as the news media.

Nonlinear video editors: Linear editors, which edit videotape, are like typewriters—unforgiving to those who make mistakes or change their minds. Nonlinear editors are like word processors in the sense that making changes is not a problem. Digitized video makes it possible to change the order of scenes without having to start from scratch.

Databases: Want to look up an old newspaper article? What is a company's financial history? What media are located in a particular city? Who are your customers, and how often do they buy your products? These are just a few examples of the wide variety of information that is stored in **databases.** Through a system of computer time-sharing, many people can have access to the same information simultaneously. Many commercial databases are available to subscribers either online or on CD-ROMs. Many organizations maintain private databases for their own purposes.

Quick ✔ Check

1. In what ways can the Internet cause problems for an organization?
2. What are some ways public relations practitioners have used satellite technology?
3. What are SMTs?

Why New Isn't Always Better

The introduction of new communications technology does not automatically spell doom for the old. Let's go back to Gutenberg's invention of the movable-type printing press in 1455. Many at the time predicted that it would mean the end of handwritten text. However, it had just the opposite effect. As vast quantities of inexpensive reading materials became more accessible, literacy rates grew; and, in turn, so did the calligraphic arts. Similarly, materials online and on CD-ROMs have not destroyed book sales. To the contrary, book sales to adults rose from 776 million in 1991 to more than 1 billion in 1995.[48]

The reason older technologies are able to survive the onslaught of newer technologies is that they are able to develop a niche in the new world order. Despite their use of 18th-century technology, newspapers continue to flourish in the 21st century. Why? Because they deliver something of value that consumers can't get elsewhere—in this case inexpensive and comprehensive coverage of local, regional, national, and global news. (We may, however, soon see the electronic delivery of newspapers.) Similarly, although many people thought radio would fade into oblivion after commercial television was introduced to the United States in 1947, it didn't; instead, radio evolved from a national source of entertainment programming into a local source of music and information. And the beat goes on.

In a public relations context, the introduction of new communications technology has created new ways of reaching and being reached by targeted publics. It is hard to imagine what life for the public relations practitioner was like without fax machines, cellular telephones, e-mail, and satellite media tours. But even in this age of technological wonders, it is equally difficult to envision the practice of public relations without some of the old standbys, such as brochures, media kits, news releases, and good old-fashioned face-to-face communication. Dertouzos wrote, "The Information Marketplace must be supported with all the traditional methods for building human bonds, including face-to-face, real-life experiences, if it is to serve organizations as more than a high-tech postal system."[49] The real challenge for the future is to stay up to date on what is new without forgetting what has worked well in the past.

As with all communication, the choice of communications technology ultimately comes down to recognizing one's audience and purpose. Public relations practitioners must understand their audience: What are its needs, what is its level of knowledge, and what are the best ways to reach it? Practitioners must also be clear about their purpose—especially because some media are better suited for some purposes than for others. The choice of which technology to adopt rests more on whether the technology works than on whether it is new.

Summary

The rapid advance of communications technology has profoundly affected the practice of public relations. Digitizing has improved the speed and quality of communication. It has also caused a technological convergence of media, meaning that a communication used in one medium can be easily adapted for use in another. Among the media in which this convergence is occurring is the Internet, where words, sound, graphics, and video come together on a single web site. Other important advances have been made in computer technology, wireless communication, and satellite communication.

The growth in communications technology has improved our personal and professional lives in many ways, but it has also raised many serious questions for the future. Powerful channels of mass communication are being concentrated in the hands of relatively few corporations. Issues of privacy, job security, and protection of intellectual property have also been raised. And although it is important to keep up with technological advances, it is also important to remember that new doesn't always mean better. In some circumstances, more traditional forms of communication may be more effective than new approaches. Regardless of advances in technology, the decision of which message to deliver and which medium to use depends on the communicator's targeted public and purpose.

DISCUSSION QUESTIONS

1. Marshall McLuhan argued that "the medium is the message." What did he mean by that, and do you agree with him?
2. In what ways has the introduction of digital communications technology influenced the practice of public relations?
3. What are some considerations public relations practitioners face when deciding whether to adopt new communications technology over more traditional channels of communication?
4. What are some of the ways public relations practitioners can use the Internet? Are there situations where the Internet may not be the best choice?

Memo *from the* Field

Craig Settles,
President,
Successful.com,
Oakland, California

Craig Settles is one of the pioneers in Internet marketing, working to set new standards for creativity in this field. As president of Successful. com, he has led a team spearheading projects to help AT&T, Microsoft, Tektronix, Symantec, Lotus, and others leverage the Internet as an effective business communications tool. He has published several books and articles on the subject, and he is a regular speaker at business and high-tech industry conferences in the United States and internationally.

In 1994, I took my client on a press tour to show off a new version of his company's OnTime group-scheduling program. To demonstrate one of the product features, we had scheduled wireless alerts for each meeting sent to us on alphanumeric pagers.

Besides keeping us on schedule, this wireless capability allowed us to have a senior tech person available in case an editor needed some detailed information but without the expense of bringing him along or keeping him tied up waiting by the phone. It also was a convenient way for the office to send us updates and answers to questions while we were on the road.

It's likely that the journalists you work with will be a little slower at adapting wireless technology, but wireless will still play an important role in those operational issues that affect your PR efforts. My client and I didn't consider ourselves wireless pioneers in '94. We weren't even aware of the net. However, when someone showed us the technology, we seized the opportunity to make the press tour run a little more smoothly.

Even with some of their rough edges and limitations, I'm more convinced than ever that those who seize the moment to use cell phones and PDAs with Internet access will help their clients and agencies prosper. In fact it appears PR people are grasping the potential of wireless more than they understand how to use the web, and it's been with us for several years.

Both agency and in-house PR people have demanding bosses, senior executives who are constantly in motion around the office and around the world, and a press audience that feels more besieged as economic and business dynamics change. Meetings, travel, and more meetings are the staple of business life. In this crazed environment, wireless mobile devices give PR staff the ability to better manage the people who meet the press.

Client (and executive) management, particularly in times of crises or important breaking news, is much easier when you have everyone linked wirelessly. The Web has opened the world to instant communication, which exposes your organization to new and often significant opportunities and potential pitfalls. The line between opportunity and pitfall is a wireless one, and one that PR people should have well in hand.

Good technology poorly applied is a recipe for bad news. It's not enough to give your PR people and top executives mobile devices. You must also have a plan. PR executives are drawing up scenarios for using wireless communication for investor relations and crisis management, and backing these up with rehearsals. You have to be certain how you will communicate, strategize, and respond to the press with a unified consistent message when executives are in different locations all over the map.

Close monitoring of news and Internet sources that deliver information to you wirelessly will keep you ahead of the curve so that you do less dodging of the pitfalls and more exploiting of the opportunities. With the exception of natural and man-made disasters, you can avoid a lot of bad press by having early warning systems in which your PR staff uncovers issues before they become problems then channels them to the right executives for quick resolution.

This type of implementation also positions you to discover fresh opportunities to stay in front of editors with news they can use. Keep your wireless fingers on the pulse of competitor announcements, changing industry trends and new business practices. Again, planning is the key, along with an aggressive willingness to use the technology at hand.

Of course, PR professionals have an equal obligation to the press community. It's true that PR people are often in the middle of a tug of war between their company's or clients' needs and journalists' demands. This often uncomfortable position can be converted to a position of strength by using wireless technology to make sure journalists get the information they want in a timely fashion and by staying ahead of their needs.

If you spend the time to walk a mile in the shoes of your journalist contacts, you will know what's important to them. When you are monitoring news sources, you can spot items of interest, send them to clients wirelessly for comments, assemble other important materials and deliver them to journalists ASAP.

This is valuable even if the delivery channel isn't wireless. Journalists don't like to get scooped, so once they see what you're doing, they'll be faster to adopt the technology, which plays in your favor because you will already have mastered this wireless beast.

Case Study 11.1

The Mount Everest Tragedy

NBC's web site Everest Assault '96 promised visitors "all of the excitement, but none of the risks" that go with attempts to scale the world's largest mountain.[50] Tragically, that promise was fully kept.

On May 10, 1996, nine people from four expeditions died when they were caught in a violent blizzard near the summit of Mount Everest. Those who survived to tell the story of Everest's most deadly day are physically and/or emotionally scarred for life. And most of them say the same thing: It didn't have to happen. NBC's web site made Internet history by providing the first accounts of the horrible events unfolding in the Himalayas—but the chilling reality is that many cite the presence of the web site as a factor contributing to the disaster.

No place on Earth is more remote or unforgiving than Mount Everest. That is the lure of the mountain. For adventure seekers, it is the ultimate challenge. At 29,028 feet above sea level—nearly five and one-half miles—the summit is accessible to only the most skilled and courageous climbers. Everest has treacherous, icy slopes where one misstep can result in sudden death. At the top of the world the air is so thin that humans cannot survive for long without bottled oxygen. Add to that sudden blinding blizzards, hurricane-force winds, and temperatures that dip lower than 100 degrees below zero. Everest is certainly not a place for poor decision making. However, by most accounts, that's exactly what happened in 1996.

The disaster has been well documented by newspaper stories, magazine articles, television documentaries, best-selling books, and at least two movies. All tell a story of unfulfilled expectations, lapses in judgment, and just plain bad luck. They also speak of incredible courage and the resilience of the human spirit. In this context, however, we will focus on just the events surrounding NBC's web site and NBC's correspondent on the mountain, Sandy Hill Pittman.

Depending on the commentator's point of view, Pittman has been described as a millionaire, a socialite, or a social climber. However, one fact was indisputable: Pittman was not a newcomer to mountain climbing. By the time of her ill-fated assault on Everest, she had successfully scaled six of the highest mountains in the world. She wanted Mount Everest to be her seventh, especially after two prior failures to reach its summit.

Reaching the place where heaven meets Earth requires a team effort. For every person who achieves the summit, dozens more are left behind in base camps down the mountain to hand-carry the tons of food and supplies required for an Everest assault. Added to this tonnage was Pittman's 40-pound satellite telephone—her link to the world. At the other end of that link was the NBC web site, which served as a resource for educators, journalists, and novices following Pittman's progress up the mountain.

Forty pounds may not sound like much. However, in an environment where every ounce results in the consumption of precious energy and oxygen, it represented a substantial burden. Sherpa Lopsang, who carried the equipment up the mountain for Pittman, was exhausted when he reached Base Camp Three, 24,000 feet above sea level. Although he initially refused to carry the heavy device any farther, he later changed his mind after discussing the situation with expedition leader Scott Fischer. Ironically, the satellite telephone failed to work when it arrived at Base Camp Four, the final staging area for the assault on the summit.

Pittman herself had difficulty during her climb to Base Camp Three, still nearly a mile below the summit. Several accounts confirm that Pittman had to be "short-roped," a technique in which a weak climber is tied to a stronger climber. In fairness, Pittman has said she didn't ask to be short-roped. Before his death in an unrelated climbing accident more than a year later, Lopsang, who helped Pittman up the mountain, gave several conflicting accounts of his decision to short-rope her.

One thing that is not in dispute is that Pittman was singled out for special treatment. The reason was the publicity she would bring to Fischer and his commercial climbing enterprise, Mountain Madness Guided Expeditions. Fischer, who was to die on the mountain, reportedly said, "If I can get Sandy to the summit, I'll bet she will be on TV talk shows. Do you think she will include me in her fame and fanfare?"[51]

The disaster of May 10 cannot be traced to a single incident. It was, quite literally, a tragedy of errors. Key preparations for the final push to reach the summit were left undone. The climbers left Base Camp Four behind schedule. Because of the number of expeditions to Everest, the progress of climbers was hindered by what some have called a traffic jam at the top of the world. The leaders of various expeditions, concerned about publicity and client satisfaction, violated their own safety rules.

Climbers lingered at the summit three hours past an agreed-upon 2:00 P.M. deadline for turning around and returning to camp. And as day was turning into night, a killing blizzard engulfed Everest. Nineteen people were stranded on the mountain without shelter or bottled oxygen. Only 10 of them would return.

Since the accident, much of the blame has focused on Pittman and the drive for publicity her technology-enhanced presence fueled. As one publication noted, "Otherwise-sophisticated Manhattanites blame Pittman for killing 'all those people on Everest.'"[52] This is not entirely fair. Although even she might admit to making some mistakes on the mountain, others made far more catastrophic decisions. However, her silence upon returning to the United States did not help her cause.

No one person is responsible for the tragedy on Mount Everest. At the core of this disaster was a clash of values. No one suspected that this clash would become a life-or-death struggle. At several critical junctures, a reckless desire to succeed overshadowed what was supposed to be the real purpose of the journey: to climb safely to the top of Mount Everest and live to tell about it.

DISCUSSION QUESTIONS

1. Discuss the pros and cons of Sandy Hill Pittman's presence on the ill-fated Mount Everest expedition. What, if anything, might you have done differently?
2. What lessons can public relations practitioners learn from this disaster?
3. Do you agree with the authors that this tragedy was caused "by a clash of values"? What values does this phrase refer to? Explain your reasoning.
4. Can you think of any other circumstances in which the desire for publicity comes into conflict with other values?
5. If you had been in Sandy Hill Pittman's shoes, how would you have handled the criticism she received upon returning to the United States?

Case Study 11.2

Caught in the Eye of Hurricane Chad

Rather than listen to election-night returns from the 2000 presidential election, Craig Waters opted to watch *Gladiator* on pay-per-view television. In just a few short hours, he plunged into a public contest almost as ferocious as the one faced by the Russell Crowe character in the movie.

Waters, the director of public information for the Supreme Court of Florida, woke up the next morning with the rest of the nation to find that the presidential contest between George W. Bush and Al Gore was a virtual tie. Everything hinged on the Florida count. Bush led Gore by a razor-thin margin, and the numbers were in dispute. It was then that Waters—who had both journalism and legal training—knew that the attention of the world would soon fall upon a courtroom in Tallahassee and the seven justices he served.

Florida Supreme Court spokesman Craig Waters *(center)* found himself to be the focus of world-wide attention during the disputed 2000 presidential election. His announcements of court rulings from the steps of the courthouse often marked major moments in the 36-day drama. (Courtesy of the Supreme Court of Florida)

"The court had been through election disputes before," Waters said. "But knowing full well that the presidency of the United States could hang on this one, I had some inkling at that point that this was going to be different."[53]

Was it ever. Journalists around the world called the Florida election dispute "Hurricane Chad"—named after the tiny, perforated pieces of paper supposed to form the holes in punch ballots. The degree to which a ballot was—or wasn't—punched became a national obsession. Terms such as *dimpled chad, pregnant chad,* and *hanging chad* were at the center of the debate over who would become the next president of the United States.

Fortunately for everyone involved, the Florida Supreme Court had aggressively pursued what became known as its Access Initiative in 1996. A survey at that time showed widespread public misunderstanding of the role of the court. Led by then–Chief Justice Gerald Kogan, the court realized that it had to do a better job of educating the media and the public. The court's response to this challenge led to the creation of two communication channels that served it well during the postelection drama of 2000.

The first channel was the World Wide Web. Waters said that his was the first court in the world to have its own web site. A media page on the web site was introduced two years later. This helped change the relationship between the court and reporters from one that had been reactive and negative to one that is generally proactive and positive.

During the 36-day dispute, the court placed the nearly 100 filings in the presidential election case on the web for immediate access by both the media and the public. This attracted millions of hits from Internet users around the globe. Careful planning anticipated the tidal wave of web surfers, and the site ran without interruption. The presidential election cases site remains intact today for historians and others curious about the events of that memorable period.

The second channel was television. Working with Florida State University, the court secured a $300,000 legislative grant in 1996 to permit live broadcasts of its proceedings. Four remote-control television cameras were installed in the courtroom. A transmission line was run from the courthouse to the nearby FSU Communications Center. From there, the pictures and sound were distributed worldwide on a state-owned satellite transponder.

During the days leading up to *George W. Bush, et al., Petitioners v. Albert Gore, Jr. et al.*, the court clarified and reinforced its channels of internal communications. Waters worked closely with the clerk of the court and the webmaster. He also worked out a system in which the seven justices reviewed and edited his public statements. Because the Code of Judicial Conduct governing behavior by judges forbade the justices from discussing pending cases, the task of speaking to the media fell on Waters' shoulders. Even then, his job was to announce judicial decisions—not to interpret them.

Despite the effectiveness of these communication channels, Waters and the court staff had to improvise. Up to 850 reporters and six dozen television satellite transmission trucks had descended upon a four-block area of central Tallahassee. In four downtown locations, officials established drop boxes that allowed reporters to plug into courtroom video and audio. They set up a temporary news conference area on the front steps of the courthouse. They positioned the television network camera pool in front of the building. An assembly line for distributing documents took over the courthouse lobby. Media were credentialed. Security measures were taken. Since the number of seats in the courtroom was limited, a media lottery for guaranteed seating was held. Waters also created an early warning system to give the television networks a 30-minute notice of upcoming court announcements.

And then came the day when the court's photocopier—in Waters' words—"crashed and burned." Because of the court's pioneering efforts in Internet use, Waters admits he underestimated the demand for paper copies. He hadn't counted on the hundreds of reporters coming into town without any Internet access. "They all wanted paper," Waters said.

When the photocopier broke down under the strain of the presidential dispute, drastic measures were taken. "We had to conscript secretaries and everyone we could to go to every copy machine available to use in the building," Waters said. He estimated that his team printed 800,000 photocopy pages during the five-week period.

Ironically, the so-called photocopier disaster had an upside. On the day of the meltdown, reporters using the web received court documents 90 minutes before those waiting on paper copies. As a result, the out-of-town reporters scrambled to get web connections, and the demand for paper copies eased.

Other challenges arose. During the election dispute, Waters received 15,000 emails—many of which were unfriendly. More than 700 incoming calls were charged to his cell phone account. Because of the flood of calls to his office from private citizens who had seen Waters on television, the court established a special telephone line for media use.

But even this outpouring of public comment had a positive aspect. "It provided me feedback that I wouldn't have had any other way," Waters said. "It gave me an insight into some of the misconceptions that were created in the public eye by whatever happened. . . . It allowed me to either go out and address the misconceptions the best I could or change the way I was presenting information so that the misconceptions were not created."

Because of the world's intense interest in the outcome of the presidential election, Waters became what one newspaper called "something of a cult figure." An Ohio tourist who was taking in the activity outside the courthouse said, "I want to see Craig Waters. I've seen him on television so much, I feel like he's my neighbor."[54]

Waters did not realize how closely the world was watching his every move until Thanksgiving week, when he commiserated with reporters concerned with the prospect of having to wait outside the courthouse through the holiday weekend. In an effort to reassure the media contingent, Waters said that he, too, would like to avoid missing Thanksgiving dinner with his Aunt Ethel in Alabama. By the time he returned to his office, Waters had received e-mails about his aunt. The BBC wanted to send a crew to Alabama to cover the family reunion. The *Miami Herald* published Aunt Ethel's Thanksgiving menu. She was also mentioned in the pages of the *New York Times* and by Diane Sawyer on *Good Morning America*.

In the end, the Florida Supreme Court received high marks for its handling of Hurricane Chad. "Florida has become the butt of many jokes because of a flawed election process," one newspaper columnist wrote. "But our open government laws, which make our officials operate in public and produce public records, have been widely praised by the national news media."[55]

"Every one of the 36 days I came to the office realizing that there were a thousand ways to fail," Waters said. "The fact that we were able to do what we did here speaks very loudly about the success of our overall policy of openness."

For the record, Craig Waters enjoyed *Christmas* dinner with Aunt Ethel.

DISCUSSION QUESTIONS

1. What values came into play that assisted the Florida Supreme Court in dealing with the intense pressure of world attention?
2. What role did technology play in this case? What were its limitations?

3. What publics did Craig Waters try to reach with his communications tactics? Why were those publics important to the Florida Supreme Court?
4. What lessons can others learn from the Florida Supreme Court's experience?

It's Your Turn

Hale & Hardy All-Natural Granola Bars

Hale & Hardy Foods Inc. is a manufacturer of nutritious foods for health-conscious consumers. Your research has identified these consumers as being 25 to 40 years old and well educated; many are professionals in the higher income brackets. To cultivate the company's image among this target audience, company cofounders Pat Hale and Robin Hardy have actively supported various environmental causes.

The company's best-known product is the Hale & Hardy All-Natural Granola Bar, marketed as a wholesome snack with no artificial ingredients for the man or woman on the go. The product generates a major portion of the company's profits. In an effort to keep up with consumer demand, Hale and Hardy have decided to build a new manufacturing facility on the banks of a scenic river in an economically depressed region that needs the jobs the plant will bring.

However, not everyone is happy about the new plant. A local environmental group fears the plant will pollute the river and destroy the natural beauty of the surrounding area. The group is hoping to generate enough opposition both locally and nationally to force the company to build its plant elsewhere.

Just as the company begins to grapple with this controversy, another equally serious problem emerges from an unexpected source. The company learns that its most important product, the Hale & Hardy All-Natural Granola Bar, has been a hot topic of discussion in Internet chat rooms. Company critics are falsely asserting that the Granola Bar, promoted as "all-natural," actually contains artificial ingredients. For the first time in two years, the product's monthly sales figures show a slight decrease.

Your public relations agency has been asked to develop strategies to address this two-pronged problem. Among the issues you must address:

1. What is the best way to deal with the environmental group?
2. If you can't reach an accommodation with the environmental group, toward whom should you target the company's public relations efforts?
3. What are key messages you need to deliver to those publics, and what channels of communication should you use?
4. What is the best way to address the false rumors being spread on the Internet?
5. What are some long-term strategies the company can pursue to avoid these kinds of problems in the future?

KEY TERMS

analog, p. 348

CD-ROM, p. 368

convergence of media, p. 348

databases, p. 369

digital, p. 348

digital divide, p. 361

DVD, p. 368

global village, p. 345

hypermedia, p. 349

Internet, p. 353

personal digital assistant (PDA), p. 352

push technology, p. 358

satellite media tour (SMT), p. 366

virtual public relations, p. 351

web site, p. 353

World Wide Web, p. 355

NOTES

1. Don Tapscott, *Growing Up Digital: The Rise of the Net Generation* (New York: McGraw Hill, 1998), 1–33.

2. "Profile 2000—A Survey of the Profession," *Communication World* (June–July 2000): A3 and A18–A19.

3. Gerald E. Stearn, *McLuhan Hot & Cool* (New York: Dial, 1967), cited online, www.beaulieuhome.com/mcluhan/stearn.html.

4. Nicholas Negroponte, *Being Digital* (New York: Knopf, 1995), 14.

5. Joseph Straubhaar and Robert LaRose, *Communications Media in the Information Society* (Belmont, Calif.: Wadsworth, 1996), 16.

6. Negroponte, 68.

7. Goldie Blumenstyk, "Publishers Promote E-Textbooks, but Many Students and Professors Are Skeptical," *Chronicle of Higher Education,* 18 May 2001, A36.

8. *AOL Time Warner 2000 Annual Report,* 1.

9. Paul T. Hill, a review of *The Innovator's Dilemma, Education Week on the Web,* 14 June 2000, online, www.edweek.org/ew/ewstory.cfm?slug=40hill.h19.

10. Straubhaar and LaRose, 288.

11. Straubhaar and LaRose, 292–293.

12. Charles Pizzo Jr., "The Wild, Wild Web," *Public Relations Tactics* (March 1996): 1.

13. Robert H. Zakon, "Hobbes' Internet Timeline," online, www.zakon.org/robert/internet/timeline.

14. Mary Ann Pike, *Using the Internet with Windows 95* (Indianapolis: Que Corporation, 1998), 9–10.

15. Zakon.

16. "20 Million Americans See Starr's Report on Internet," online, CNN Interactive, 13 September 1998, www.cnn.com.

17. Steve Hoechster, "Building a Home Page on the World Wide Web," *Public Relations Tactics* (June 1995): 13.

18. Jakob Nielsen, "Corporate Websites Get a 'D' in PR," *Jakob Nielsen's Alertbox,* 1 April 2001, online, www.useit.com/alertbox/20010401.html.

19. Christopher Ryan, interview, 13 October 1998.

20. Louis Rosenfeld and Peter Morville, *Information Architecture for the World Wide Web*, (Sebastopol, Calif.: O'Reilly and Associates), 4–6.

21. Hoechster.

22. Robert Grupp, "Public Relations Must Control the Web Site," *Public Relations Strategist* (Winter 2000): 34.

23. William G. Margaritas, "Web Site Demands Collaborative Control," *Public Relations Strategist* (Winter 2000): 33.

24. Michael Dertouzos, *What Will Be: How the New World of Information Will Change Our Lives* (New York: HarperCollins, 1997), 210–211.

25. Dertouzos, 211–212.

26. Cheryl Russell, "The Haves and the Want-Nots," *American Demographics* (April 1998): 10–12.

27. "U.S. Internet Audience Up 16 Percent in Past Year," CyberAtlas, 13 August 2001, online, http://cyberatlas.internet.com/big_picture/geographics/print/0,,5911_864541,00.html.

28. "What Is the Digital Divide?" Reuters, 22 July 2000, online, www.abcnews.com.

29. Jim Wolf, "Digital Divide Still Looms," Reuters, 2 October 2000, online, www.abcnews.com.

30. Dominique Deckmyn, "De Jager Defends Y2K Hype," online, CNN Interactive, 4 January 2000, www.cnn.com/2000/TECH/computing/01/04/dejager.y2k.idg/index.html.

31. "Y2K Billions May Pay Dividends in the Long Run," online, CNN Interactive, 3 January 2000, www.cnn.com/2000/TECH/computing/01/03/y2k.long.term/:7Findex.html.

32. W. Timothy Coombs, "The Internet as Potential Equalizer: New Leverage for Confronting Social Irresponsibility," *Public Relations Review* 24, no. 3 (Fall 1999): 299.

33. *Y2K Aftermath—Crisis Averted, Final Committee Report*, The United States Senate Special Committee on the Year 2000 Technology Problem, 29 February 2000, 37–49.

34. Deckmyn.

35. *Y2K Aftermath—Crisis Averted, Final Committee Report*.

36. Daniel Machalaba and Carrick Mollenkamp, "Companies Struggle to Cope with Chaos, Breakdowns and Trauma," *Wall Street Journal*, 13 September 2001, B1.

37. *Digital Economy 2000*, U.S. Department of Commerce, online, http//:www.commerce.gov.

38. Chuck Paustian, "Internet Marketing: How the Business World Views the World Wide Web," *Advertising Age* (27 May 1996): M7.

39. Gregory C. Staple, ed., *TeleGeography 1996–97: Global Telecommunications Traffic Statistics and Commentary: TeleGeography* (Washington, D.C., 1997), xiii.

40. Frances Cairncross, *The Death of Distance: How the Communications Revolution Will Change Our Lives* (Boston: Harvard Business School Press, 1997), 28.

41. Sally Jewett, "What's 'In Store' for SMTs," *Public Relations Tactics* (July 1998): 20.

42. "Survey Finds Increasing Interest in Satellite Media Tours," Medialink news release transmitted on PR Newswire, 14 January 1992.

43. Nick Galifianakis, "Did You Know . . . Air Supply" (graphic), *Public Relations Tactics* (July 1998): 1.

44. "Survey Finds Increasing Interest in Satellite Media Tours."

45. Jodi B. Katzman, "Interactive Video Gets Bigger Play," *Public Relations Journal* (May 1995): 6.

46. Adam Shell, "Satellite Shorts," *Public Relations Tactics* (August 1996): 25.

47. Shell.

48. Rebecca Piirto Heath, "In So Many Words: How Technology Reshapes the Reading Habit," *American Demographics* (March 1997): 39.

49. Dertouzos, 205.

50. Pam Snook, "Web Site Breaks News of Mount Everest Tragedy," *Public Relations Tactics* (August 1996): 6.

51. Jon Krakauer, *Into Thin Air* (New York: Villard, 1997), 170.

52. Deborah Mitchell, "Pitons Are Served," *Salon,* June 1997, online, www.salonmagazine.com/june97/media/media970611.html.

53. Craig Waters, telephone interview by author, 20 August 2001.

54. Amy Driscoll, "Capitol an Offbeat Attraction," *Miami Herald,* 12 December 2000, online, www.simulsite.com/miami_herald.html.

55. Lucy Morgan, "As Glare Hits Court, Aide Shares the Light," *St. Petersburg Times Online,* 25 November 2000, online, www.sptimes.com/News/112500/Election2000.

Crisis Communications

After studying this chapter, you will be able to

■ understand what crises are and how they develop

■ recognize that crisis situations often create opportunities

■ appreciate the importance of anticipating crises and planning for them before they happen

■ explain the elements of an effective crisis communications plan

The Rumor

scenario   *You are the head of corporate communications for a company that produces one of the nation's most popular snack foods. The company prides itself on making products that are both delicious and nutritionally sound. In your advertising you brag of using only natural ingredients with no artificial flavorings or other additives.*

Recently a rumor cropped up on the Internet asserting that a leak from a nearby nuclear power plant has made most of your company's snack foods radioactive.

Officials at the nuclear power plant say there has been no such leak. Despite this re-assurance, the company has noticed a small decline in sales. To make matters worse, a producer from a nationally syndicated tabloid television show has called and wants to know whether it is true that the company's snack food products glow in the dark.

What are you going to do?

A New "Day of Infamy"

During the 20th century, U.S. citizens remembered December 7, 1941, the day Pearl Harbor was attacked, as a day of infamy. At the start of the 21st century, September 11, 2001, became a new day of infamy.

Approximately 3,000 people died and 8,700 were injured in the terrorist attacks on the World Trade Center, at the Pentagon, and on four hijacked aircraft. A bright late-summer Tuesday morning was transformed into a time of unspeakable horror, remarkable bravery, tragic sorrow, and determined resolve. Although these attacks

Firefighters placed a U.S. flag on the remains of the broadcast tower that once stood atop the North Tower of the World Trade Center. (Courtesy of the Federal Emergency Management Agency)

occurred in the United States, they were really an attack on the civilized world as people of more than 80 nationalities perished.

The shock wave from the events of those two chaotic hours were felt globally within minutes. Major financial markets closed. The Federal Aviation Administration ordered all planes in U.S. airspace to land immediately. The United States sealed its borders. Government agencies in Washington, D.C., abruptly shut down. The White House and the U.S. Capitol were evacuated. News sites on the Internet received a record number of visitors. Regular television programming gave way to nonstop news. Business meetings were cancelled. Major League Baseball postponed its entire schedule—followed soon thereafter by other professional and amateur sports. Stores sold out of their inventories of U.S. flags. Churches overflowed with mourners. People waited in long lines to donate blood to the American Red Cross.

But that's just the big picture. Dramas played out on a smaller scale in board rooms and at water coolers everywhere. Once the initial shock and sadness of the tragic deaths in New York, Washington, and western Pennsylvania subsided, the flood of questions began: Are any of our people in New York? Where are our employees who were traveling at the time of the attacks? How will this affect business or fund-raising? What would we do if our operations were disrupted or our facilities were destroyed? What would we have done if key officials of our organization were killed or incapacitated? What do we tell our employees? The questions just kept coming.

As we look back on the events of September 11, 2001, perhaps most memorable are *the things that did not go wrong.* More than 25,000 people in the WTC complex were saved by emergency personnel, many of whom lost their own lives. Most companies and organizations—even those located in the WTC and the Pentagon—resumed operations. The financial markets returned, as did baseball, football, and Broadway. The nation and much of the world united in a new determination to end terrorism and its causes.

We also remember the heroes—those who died and those who were left to rebuild. The personification of these heroes was New York City Mayor Rudolph Giuliani. Prior to the attack, he was seen by some as abrupt, abrasive, and callous—everything New York. However, his inspired leadership in the days and weeks following the catastrophe caused many critics to reevaluate the man they now called "Rudy." He was viewed as tough, resilient, and courageous—everything New York.

Other heroes emerged from everyday life, many of whom were public relations practitioners (see Case Study 16.2). In a time of chaos and fear, they kept their cool. They assessed the dangers and responded appropriately—just as they had planned. Although few could anticipate the toll of human suffering and physical devastation thrust upon them, many were prepared to act. They had emergency plans in place. As noted in Chapter 11, many dusted off their Y2K business recovery plans. Their employees had been trained. They knew what to do. And because these farsighted organizations had crisis communications plans, their stakeholders remained informed and—most important—remained calm.

Putting Crisis Plans in Action

The first job for those at ground zero in New York was to assess the human toll. More than 50,000 people regularly worked in the Twin Towers and other buildings in the WTC complex. In the confusion that followed the attacks, companies worked frantically to get a headcount of employees. Because the first plane struck 1 World Trade Center at 8:45 A.M., just as people were arriving for work, there was no way to know how many people were at their desks.

It was the same story for many companies, as managers stayed up all night trying to reach employees by phone. Susan Zimmerman, human resources vice president at MassMutual Financial Group, said, "We would not rest until we knew everyone was safe."[1]

Even as managers sought to locate missing employees, the focus turned to letting important stakeholders know what was happening and how their companies were responding. During this crisis, public relations was not a luxury. The World Trade Center had been at the heart of the nation's—and arguably the world's—financial system. The list of tenants at the WTC complex read like a Who's Who of international commerce. The rapid dissemination of information was essential to avoiding a global economic panic.

The Internet and e-mail proved to be valuable tools in addressing investor concerns. Morgan Stanley, a brokerage and investment-banking firm, had 3,500 employees occupying 19 floors of 2 World Trade Center. Within hours of the attack, Chairman and Chief Executive Officer Philip Purcell, in a message posted on the Morgan Stanley web site, expressed his sympathy for the victims of the tragedy. He then said, "We want our clients to know today that in spite of this tragedy, all of our businesses are functioning and will continue to function."[2]

Communication played a critical role in both the grieving and recovery process. Cantor Fitzgerald, a bond trading company that lost 700 of its 1,000 employees in the disaster, established a family services center at the Pierre Hotel in Manhattan. It was there that Chairman Howard Lutnick, who had lost his own brother in the collapse of the towers, met with grieving relatives and surviving employees. "At the same time, his surviving lieutenants worked around the clock at backup offices in New Jersey and London to save Cantor's computer systems," the *Wall Street Journal* reported. "By Thursday morning, despite gaping holes in the staff, they had reopened Cantor's electronic bond-trading network."[3]

If getting back to business just two days after this horrendous tragedy sounds cold to you, please remember this: Cantor Fitzgerald was a leading player in world bond markets, brokering trades on 75 percent of long-term U.S. Treasury notes. Although the surviving Cantor employees wanted to get back to work as a tribute to their fallen comrades, much of the world's economy *needed* them back at work. It is a hard reality we all must face at some time or another: crises occur—and difficult as it may be, life goes on.

Crises Can Happen to Anyone

The world changed on that day of infamy. However, the unforgiving truth is that bad things do happen to good people. When we hear of misfortune happening to others, we may easily rationalize that "it couldn't happen here." However, recent history suggests otherwise:

- An act of revenge by two social outcasts left 15 people dead at a Denver-area high school.
- An act of domestic terrorism claimed 168 lives in Oklahoma City.
- Protests over the effects of globalization turned downtown Seattle into a war zone.
- Air France and British Airways grounded their fleet of supersonic jet airliners after 113 people died in a Concorde crash near Paris.
- Officials in four European countries briefly restricted or banned the sale of Coca Cola after hundreds complained of getting sick after consuming the world's most popular soft drink.
- A previously obscure California congressman became the subject of national scrutiny and derision after an intern with whom he had had an affair suddenly disappeared.
- A derailment and fire in a downtown Baltimore railroad tunnel slowed nation-wide Internet traffic, forced evacuation of the city's commercial district, and postponed several Major League Baseball games.

If anything, these and other incidents testify to this reality: Anything can happen. However unexpected, the sad truth is that most crises are not wholly unpredictable. Perhaps even sadder is the fact that many, if not most, are avoidable. By identifying and analyzing potential risks, we can eliminate many crises before they ever happen.

Quick ✔ Check

1. What steps did companies take in the hours following the September 2001 attack on the World Trade Center? What were the highest priorities of managers?
2. Why was it important for corporate executives to focus on business recovery so quickly after an incident that killed or injured thousands?
3. Are most crises unpredictable and therefore unavoidable?

The Anatomy of a Crisis

"If economics is the dismal science," disaster recovery consultant Kenneth Myers writes, "then contingency planning is the abysmal science. No one likes to look into the abyss."[4] But like it or not, crisis planning has become an imperative in the 21st

QuickBreak 12.1

THE LESSONS OF DALLAS

Anyone over the age of 45 can tell you exactly what he or she was doing around 12:30 P.M. EST on Friday, November 22, 1963. News of the assassination of President John F. Kennedy spread like wildfire across the country. A University of Chicago study concluded that within 30 minutes of the shooting, 68 percent of all adults in the United States knew of the assassination. By the end of the afternoon, 99.8 percent had learned the horrible news.[5]

The weekend following the assassination is pretty much a blur for all those who lived it. However, few images stand out more than events in the basement of the Dallas Police De-

With John F. Kennedy's widow at his side aboard Air Force One on November 22, 1963, Lyndon B. Johnson is sworn in as the 36th president of the United States. (LBJ Library photo by Cecil Stoughton)

partment on Sunday, November 24. Lee Harvey Oswald, an ex-Marine who had briefly defected to the Soviet Union, was charged with the murders of Kennedy and a Dallas police officer. Then, less than 48 hours after his arrest, Oswald himself was murdered in front of a nationwide television audience by Dallas nightclub owner Jack Ruby. That singular event elevated the Kennedy assassination to the greatest murder mystery of the 20th century, spawned dozens of conspiracy theories, and created an atmosphere of mistrust for "official" explanations.

Although much has been written and speculated about the events of that weekend in Texas, there is one undeniable fact: The death of Lee Harvey Oswald left many unanswered questions. Had the Dallas Police Department properly exercised its public relations responsibilities, perhaps the nation might have been spared much of this controversy.

It is not reasonable to blame Dallas police for the death of President Kennedy. Others, notably the FBI and the Secret Service, had the primary responsibility for the president's security. In fact, Oswald's arrest only 90 minutes after the assassination is an example of excellent police work. It was during that brief but intense manhunt that Dallas Police Officer J. D. Tippet was gunned down in the line of duty by Oswald.

For Oswald's death, however, the Dallas police must be held responsible. Regardless of the various conspiracy theories floating about, it is clear that the DPD did a poor job of handling the tidal wave of reporters that washed across police headquarters. One writer describing the scene said it was as if the "animals" had overcome their "keepers." A Se-

cret Service agent said he was left with "the sober impression that the press had taken over police headquarters."[6] Amid this confusion, little wonder that Ruby, a local character with many police acquaintances, managed at least twice to slip into the building with a loaded handgun in his pocket.

Dallas police that weekend were so concerned with trying to keep reporters happy that they lost track of their most important mission: ensuring public safety. That included protecting their prisoner so that he could be brought to trial to answer for his alleged crimes. Although the DPD did have some vague regulations covering media relations, those rules did not anticipate a situation in which hundreds of reporters would invade headquarters demanding immediate answers. On one occasion the DPD served up Oswald to reporters for an impromptu news conference without Oswald's consent, without his legal counsel present, and with a gun-toting Ruby in attendance. Even if Oswald had survived the weekend, his handling by the DPD might have made a fair trial—a cornerstone of this nation's democracy—impossible.

What was needed was a crisis communications plan. Although no one could reasonably have expected a presidential assassination, the police should have been prepared to deal with the large contingents of reporters that cover events common in any major city, such as major fires, civil disturbances, or industrial accidents. Instead, accommodations were made to the media on an ad hoc basis—and with tragic results.

Think how different history might have been.

century for big and small organizations alike. "Any small business owner who doesn't have a crisis management plan is derelict in his duties," says Martin Cooper of Cooper Communications in Encino, California.[7] As researchers Donald Chisholm and Martin Landau have pointedly noted, "When people believe that because nothing has gone wrong, nothing will go wrong, they court disaster. There is noise in every system and in every design. If this fact is ignored, nature soon reminds us of our folly."[8]

Despite countless examples of crises and their consequences, many organizations are not prepared. *Public Relations Journal* reported in 1984 that only 53 percent of companies surveyed by Western Union had an operational crisis communications plan. There was little change three years later, when only 57 percent of the respondents said they had an operational crisis plan.[9] A 1992 University of Kansas study achieved similar results. Only 56.9 percent of those surveyed had written crisis plans. Worse than that, only one in three (36.3 percent) had plans that were both written *and* practiced. In a related finding, the Kansas study reported that the more crises an organization had experienced, the closer the public relations function now was to the organization's top management. Another way of looking at it: Too many organizations had learned the hard way—after the fact.[10]

What Is a Crisis?

The word *crisis*, just like the term *public relations*, is often misused by those who do not know it has a specific meaning. Everyone instinctively understands that flash floods, hurricanes, and earthquakes can usually be classified as crises. But what about a flat tire, missed homework, or being stood up on a date? Are these crises, too?

The difference between a **problem** and a **crisis** is a matter of scope. Problems are commonplace occurrences and fairly predictable. They usually can be addressed in a limited time frame, often without arousing public attention or without draining an organization's resources. On the other hand, crises tend to be less predictable. They require a considerable investment of time and resources to resolve and often bring unwanted public attention. And more than problems, crises can challenge an organization's core values.

Researchers Thierry C. Pauchant and Ian I. Mitroff have written that a crisis is "a disruption that physically affects a system as a whole and threatens its basic assumptions, its subjective sense of self, its existential core."[11] According to Pauchant and Mitroff, crises can threaten the legitimacy of an industry, reverse the strategic mission of an organization, and disturb the way people see the world and themselves.[12]

Steven Fink, a noted crisis consultant, has characterized crises as being prodromal situations (situations often marked by forewarning) that run the risk of

- escalating in intensity;
- falling under close media or government scrutiny;
- interfering with the normal operations of business;

- jeopardizing the positive public image enjoyed by a company and its officers; and
- damaging a company's bottom line.[13]

Laurence Barton refines the terminology even further, describing a crisis as a major event that "has potentially negative results. The event and its aftermath may significantly damage an organization and its employees, products, services, financial condition, and reputation."[14]

Crisis Dynamics and the Lessons of *Challenger*

As you might imagine, crises can come in many shapes and sizes. They can also influence public perceptions of organizations in vastly different ways. Some crises cast organizations in the role of *victim*. In other crises, organizations may be seen as the *villain*. And in a few cases, well-prepared organizations have emerged from crises in the role of *hero*.

Most people would rather be seen as a hero than as either a victim or a villain. At the same time, many people operate under a false assumption that crises and their consequences are unavoidable. However, public relations practitioners can do much to influence events before they happen and, in some instances, to avert crises altogether. That role of public relations is a focus of this chapter.

But before trying to change the course of events, we should understand the dynamics of a crisis. It is a mistake to believe that crises operate as randomly as next week's lottery. In fact, they follow predictable patterns. Although various researchers have adopted different terminology to describe these patterns, there is general agreement that crises tend to develop in four stages (Figure 12.1).

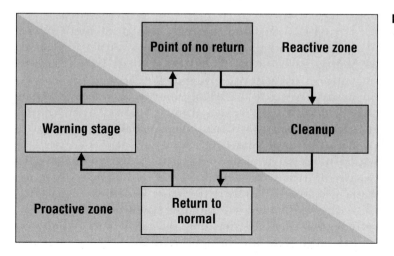

FIGURE 12.1   Crisis Dynamics

It may be useful to place crisis dynamics in the context of a national tragedy that scientists later demonstrated should never have happened. The events surrounding the January 1986 explosion of the space shuttle *Challenger* clearly exemplify the four different stages of a crisis—and why it is important that we understand and recognize them.

First, some background: *Challenger* exploded 71 seconds after lift-off from the Kennedy Space Center. After several moments of confusion, the voice of Mission Control announced, "Obviously, we have a major malfunction." A few seconds later, after confirming that the orbiter had exploded, NASA fell silent. It was hours before space agency officials met with reporters to discuss the disaster. Even then, they were not willing to acknowledge what had become painfully obvious to millions of television viewers who had watched repeated replays of the explosion: that the seven-member crew, including much-publicized "teacher in space" Christa McAuliffe, had died.

Subsequent investigations of the explosion revealed that the launch had been preceded by an internal debate over whether to attempt it in such cold weather. Some engineers at Morton Thiokol, the maker of the shuttle's solid rocket boosters, were concerned about O-rings leaking in cold weather. These O-rings sealed the joints between sections of the shuttle's side-mounted rockets. However, investigators blamed Morton Thiokol and NASA for abandoning their often-stated value of safety first in order to meet an ambitious launch schedule that was already lagging behind.

The failure of NASA management was also mirrored on that day by the dismal performance of the agency's Public Affairs Office (PAO). Despite a crisis plan that required an announcement of an in-flight death or injury within 20 minutes, NASA was silent about the fate of the crew for five hours. The agency either forgot or ignored its 10-year-old crisis communications plan. Many of the people present at the time of the plan's creation had left NASA. Officials never found the time to train employees in the use of the plan.

That takes us to the first stage of a crisis, the **warning stage.** In reality, most crises don't "just happen." Usually, there are advance signs of trouble. At this stage trouble may still be averted, but the clock is ticking. In the warning stage we have an ability to be proactive and control events *before* they happen. This is one of the greatest challenges in crisis communications: to recognize the potential for danger and then to act accordingly.

The warning stage for the *Challenger* disaster began when Morton Thiokol and NASA engineers first discovered problems with the O-rings that sealed sections of the shuttle's solid rocket boosters. This discovery occurred almost six months before the explosion. Engineers already knew that the problem was especially acute in cold weather—a matter of agonized debate in the hours leading up to the January launch. Although it would be unfair to say the space agency ignored the warnings, NASA certainly minimized them. By launching the space shuttle in adverse weather conditions, NASA failed to defuse the impending crisis during the warning stage.

The second stage of a crisis is the **point of no return.** At this moment the crisis has become unavoidable and we are forced to be reactive. Some damage will be done. How much damage remains to be seen and depends, to a large degree, on the organization's response. This is often the time when most publics critical to the success of the organization first become aware of the crisis. From this point on, they are watching very closely.

Usually it is easy to pinpoint the point of no return. In the *Challenger* disaster, it occurred 71 seconds after launch: the instant the orbiter exploded. At that moment, NASA could do nothing to save the shuttle crew—or to spare itself from intense public scrutiny.

Even when the point of no return has been reached and the public spotlight shines on the organization in crisis, an opportunity to minimize damage still exists. That comes in the third crisis stage, the **cleanup phase.** During this phase, we continue to be in a reactive mode, trying to deal with the crisis and its aftermath. How long this period lasts depends largely on how well prepared the organization is to deal with the crisis. The cleanup phase is also a period of recovery and investigation, both internal and external.

Fink says this is often the point at which the "carcass gets picked clean." In the case of the ill-prepared NASA, that is exactly what happened. The space agency's failure to

NASA's failure to adhere to basic core values was one of the factors that led to the death of teacher-in-space Christa McAuliffe and six other astronauts in the January 1986 explosion of the space shuttle *Challenger.* (Courtesy of NASA)

heed its own "safety first" policy, combined with its inability to communicate effectively after the explosion, led to a lengthy shutdown of space shuttle flights. NASA's performance also resulted in the premature end of many promising careers. Although NASA would again enjoy success in space, it had lost its untarnished reputation.

The final stage of a crisis is when **things return to normal.** However, this handle is a bit deceptive. If *normal* is defined as "the way things were before the crisis," then things will probably never be "normal" again. Following a crisis, normal operations may be radically different than before. New management may also be in place. In addition to these changes, some valuable lessons probably were learned. A vigorous evaluation of the organization's performance in dealing with the crisis can result in plans for dealing with—or, better, averting—the next crisis.

This brings us to an important point: The crisis dynamics model implies that we automatically move from one crisis to another through a cyclical process. However, that doesn't have to be the case. Management can take steps to minimize or eliminate crises in two ways. One is by identifying the warning signs of a looming crisis and taking forceful action before the point of no return is reached. The other opportunity comes after the crisis: When things return to normal, management should take time to evaluate its performance and apply the lessons it has learned. If no such evaluation is done, management runs the risk of making the same mistakes again and creating a new crisis. After all, history does have a tendency to repeat itself.

QuickBreak 12.2

FIRE IN THE HOLE

Thanks to good crisis planning and training, the people of Charm City lived a charmed life during the summer of 2001.

Baltimore, Maryland, one of the oldest cities in the United States, is affectionately known to its residents as Charm City. Its resources and courage were tested on July 18, 2001, when a 60-car CSX freight train derailed in the 1.7-mile Howard Street Tunnel under Baltimore's downtown district. In addition to a cargo of paper, wood pulp, soy, oil, and bricks, the train carried toxic chemicals. Within minutes, thick, black smoke poured out of both ends of the tunnel. A few blocks from the south end of the tunnel, thousands of baseball fans, unaware of the drama unfolding nearby, watched the first game of a day-night doubleheader between the Baltimore Orioles and the Texas Rangers.

Within minutes, civil defense sirens blared, downtown was evacuated, the second game of the doubleheader was canceled, and rush hour was reduced to gridlock.

Aside from the danger of toxic fumes spreading over the city, other problems arose. Roadblocks shut down major highways leading into and out of the city. A water main that traversed the tunnel broke, flooding several downtown buildings with a torrent of 60 million gallons. Major telecommunications lines serving most of the eastern United States snapped, disrupting e-mail service around the world. And although the cancellation of two Orioles home games may seem like a minor inconvenience, it resulted in millions of dollars of lost revenue by both the team and neighborhood merchants.[15]

That is the greatest irony of the *Challenger* catastrophe: History had repeated itself at NASA—not once, but twice. In January 1967 three astronauts died in a launch pad fire while practicing for the first Apollo mission. NASA was criticized for shoddy engineering, putting its schedule ahead of safety, and poor public communications—the same complaints that would surface two decades later. Acting with conviction and purpose, the agency worked to correct its problems. The next time it faced a major crisis, during the aborted moon mission of *Apollo 13*, NASA did everything right. As a character in the Ron Howard film about the flight said, even though *Apollo 13* failed to reach its objective, its safe return was NASA's "finest hour."

Crises Can Bring Opportunity

The *Apollo 13* experience also serves as an example of another important aspect of crisis communications: Crises can bring opportunity. Notice that none of the crisis definitions previously discussed say that damage to individuals, property, or reputations is a certainty. At most, they indicate that potential for such damage exists.

Gerald C. Meyers, a former automobile industry executive who has written and lectured extensively on the subject of crisis communications, says a "window of opportunity" opens during the warning and point-of-no-return stages of crises.[16] During these stages key stakeholders tend to sit back and withhold their judgment while

Firefighters and emergency management officials worked for more than four days to bring the fire under control and safely remove the derailed cars. And although it would take months to determine the cause of the accident, the verdict on the city's emergency response was swift and positive.

"(I was) proud to witness the deft and professional handling of a PR crisis situation by our city's leadership," local public relations counselor David Warschawski said. "Thankfully, Baltimore's real-life made-for-TV movie had a happy ending."[17]

A local newspaper editorial also praised officials for exercising caution. "City, state, and federal authorities were right to err on the side of caution in closing roads, waterways, baseball, business, and normal life until public safety was secured."[18]

Even before the fire was out, the city began to evaluate its emergency response. Not everything had gone as planned. However, one thing was clear: The city had benefited from an aggressive training program. Although no drills had been conducted that specifically involved the Howard Street Tunnel, the city's public safety agencies had performed a mock rescue of commuter train passengers stranded by a hypothetical fire in another railroad tunnel only six weeks earlier. Three years earlier, the city had conducted a drill in which firefighters responded to a simulated collision between a train and a truck carrying toxic chemicals.[19]

placing the organization in crisis under close scrutiny. How long the window of opportunity remains open depends on the organization's reputation. NASA's window of opportunity was open much longer before the *Challenger* accident than after.

Meyers says seven potential benefits can be reaped from a crisis:[20]

1. *Heroes are born.* Crises can make people the focus of public attention. Those who respond well to that scrutiny are often seen as heroes.

2. *Change is accelerated.* People and organizations resist change. When change is suggested, you often hear, "But we have always done it this way." Crises often finally compel organizations and individuals that have lagged behind various social and technological trends to change the way they do things.

3. *Latent problems are faced.* When things are going well, it is easy to ignore some problems. This fact is reflected by the "if it ain't broke, don't fix it" mentality. During crises, however, organizations often have no choice other than to tackle these problems head-on.

4. *People can be changed.* This item has a double meaning. On the one hand, it means that the attitudes and behavior of people can be changed, as has been dramatically demonstrated by society's loss of patience with sexual harassment in the workplace. However, "changing people" can have a pragmatic meaning: Sometimes it is necessary to replace some people with others who have a fresh perspective and new ideas.

5. *New strategies evolve.* Important lessons can be learned from crises. We often discover a better way of doing things or perceive new paths to opportunity.

6. *Early warning systems develop.* Experience is a wonderful teacher. If we know what the warning signs are, we can recognize a crisis on its way. As a child, you may have been told never to touch a pan on the stove without first checking to see whether the stove was hot. The same principle applies here.

7. *New competitive edges appear.* It has been said that nothing is more exhilarating than having someone shoot a gun at you and miss. Organizations and individuals often feel like this after surviving a crisis. The sense of teamwork and accomplishment that comes with a job well done often carries over to the next challenge. Because of the various changes that occur during the crisis cleanup, organizations are often better equipped to compete in the new environment.

Quick ✔ Check

1. What is the difference between a problem and a crisis?

2. Do crises follow a predictable pattern?

3. Do crises always result in negative outcomes? If not, what are some positive outcomes that can emerge from crises?

Crisis Communications Planning

Public relations, which by definition is a management function, plays a critical role during times of crisis. In an ideal setting, practitioners should be in a position to advise management before, during, and after each incident. Mayer Nudel and Norman Antokol, veterans of the U.S. Foreign Service, have written that communications specialists should be involved in every aspect of crisis communications.[21] Robert F. Littlejohn, who has experience in both academic and emergency management communities, favors the inclusion of a good communicator on a crisis management team, saying that strong communication skills are an essential quality of the team leader.[22]

Nobody likes to think about the consequences of disasters. However, the stark reality is that no one is immune to their effects. As the events of recent years have shown, crises can strike at any time and place. Public relations practitioners owe it to themselves, to their employers, and to all their many stakeholder publics to confront these unpleasant issues head-on and map out a course of action for dealing with crises that is consistent with their organization's values. In the final analysis, planning for a hurricane while it is still out at sea is a lot easier than when you are in the eye of the storm.

Effective crisis communications, like the public relations process as a whole, involves four steps: *risk assessment, crisis communications planning, response,* and *recovery.* Let's look more closely at each of these phases in turn.

Step One: Risk Assessment

At the heart of proactive crisis communications is **risk assessment:** the identification of the various threats under which an organization operates. Some potential crises are common to most organizations. These include problems created by bad weather, fires, financial difficulties, and on-the-job accidents. Other crises are more closely related to the specific nature of the product or service a given organization provides. These can include dangers inherent in the product/service itself (e.g., accidents involving public transportation or contamination of a food product) and toxic by-products from manufacturing processes (e.g., radiation from a nuclear power plant). Compared with private companies, publicly owned companies operate in an environment in which their crises are often more visible. The same holds true for well-known as opposed to lesser-known organizations. Sometimes crises have to do less with *what* business you are in than with *where* you are doing business. For example, the location of an office within a floodplain or in a country with an unstable political environment entails risks not faced elsewhere.

But the goal of risk assessment is not just the identification of potential hazards. Once a threat is identified, steps should be taken to eliminate or lessen it. The wisdom of this can be seen in the experiences of Nokia Corporation of Finland and Telefon AB L.M. Ericsson of neighboring Sweden. Both were leaders in the sale of mobile telephone handsets. Both relied on the same New Mexico semiconductor plant to supply them with computer chips. A March 17, 2000, lightning strike caused a fire that dramatically reduced the plant's ability to produce the critical components. Without the chips, neither company would be able to make its products. Because of more aggressive monitoring and better internal communication, Nokia officials recognized the crisis first. They immediately began working with the supplier on developing alternative sources of the computer chips. Ericsson officials were slower to react to the news out of New Mexico. By the time they realized the problem, it was too late. Nokia had effectively cornered the supply of the critical component and became the market leader. Ericsson's sales plunged. Remember: The best crises are those that are averted.

Many organizations can avert crises by clearly articulating and actively implementing their core values. By doing so, they can make all aware of the legal and ethical limits under which they choose to operate. This is much easier to do during a period of relative calm than it is during the heat of a crisis. Decisions made during a crisis without consideration of organization values can have long-term ramifications that can eventually trigger new crises.

A federal judge cited such a failure of values in a court ruling against A.H. Robins. In 1971 Robins introduced an intrauterine birth control device called the Dalkon Shield. Within three years the shield was being used by approximately 4 million women in the United States. However, doctors and consumers raised concerns about the device. Almost immediately complaints arose concerning infections, septic abortions, and infertility associated with the Dalkon Shield. Despite documented evidence that the product was potentially unsafe, the company took a hard-line approach and challenged every medical finding. In some cases the company even attacked the character of its accusers. In 1984, Federal District Judge Miles Lord summoned three company executives to his Minneapolis courtroom and told them, "You have taken the bottom line as your guiding beacon and low road your route." When Robins was acquired by American Home Products in December 1989, it agreed with the bankruptcy court to set aside $2.35 billion in a trust fund to settle the more than 6,500 claims.[23]

When undertaking a program of risk assessment, organizations can choose either to hire outside consultants or to perform an in-house evaluation. Some organizations, in fact, choose to do both. Often, outside consultants assume a training role after the planning is complete. These consultants can be expensive, costing from $5,000 to $15,000.[24]

For those who decide to do in-house planning and training, the development of a broad-based **crisis planning team** (**CPT**) is a logical step. The makeup of these teams varies. According to a National Association of Manufacturers study, the chief legal counsel is the company official most often assigned to the CPT, followed by the director of public affairs, the director of security, and the chief operating officer.

It is not enough for the management to dictate a crisis response to the rank and file. The plan will be more successful if employees have some ownership of it. For this reason, employees at all levels of the organization should take part in the risk assessment

THE CRISIS PLOTTING GRID

Steven Fink is a public relations and management consultant who has firsthand knowledge of crises. During the Three Mile Island nuclear power plant crisis in 1979, Fink provided valuable advice to Governor Richard Thornburgh of Pennsylvania that, in the long run, helped prevent public panic. In his 1986 book *Crisis Management: Planning for the Inevitable*, Fink developed a useful tool for risk assessment: the **crisis plotting grid** (Figure 12.2). By placing every potential crisis on the grid, an organization can easily identify the areas where its crisis planning is most needed.

The vertical axis of the grid, which runs from 0 to 10, represents the **crisis impact value (CIV).** Fink says you should respond to the following five questions for each potential crisis on a scale of 0 to 10, with 0 being the lowest

level of impact on your organization and 10 being the highest:

1. If the crisis runs the risk of escalating in intensity, how intense can it get and how quickly can it escalate?

2. To what extent will the crisis fall under the watchful eye of key stakeholders, including the media, regulators, shareholders, and so on?

3. To what extent will the crisis interfere with the organization's normal operations?

4. To what degree is the organization the culprit?

5. To what extent can the organization's bottom line be damaged?

Add up the total from the five questions (maximum 50 points) and divide by 5. The resulting figure is the CIV for that potential crisis.

The horizontal axis represents the **crisis probability factor (CPF).** Determine the CPF for the crisis in question by estimating the probability of the crisis on a scale of 0 percent (absolutely no likelihood that the crisis will occur) to 100 percent (the crisis is an absolute certainty).

The CIV and CPF axes intersect at their midpoints (5 and 50 percent). Fink says the grid now becomes a barometer for crises facing an organization. Potential crises whose scores place them in the red zone are ones that present an organization with the greatest danger and require immediate attention.  The next priority is to address crises that fall in the amber and gray zones. Potential crises located in the green zone shouldn't be ignored altogether but require less of your attention.

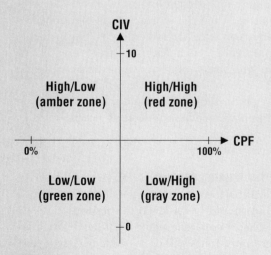

FIGURE 12.2   The Crisis Plotting Grid

process. This brings different and valuable perspectives to the process. If two heads are better than one, think how much better the risk assessment can be if many heads contribute to the final product.

Quick ✔ Check

1. What are the four steps of the crisis communications process? Do these remind you of any other process you have seen?
2. What is risk assessment?
3. What role do values play in crisis communications?

Step Two: Developing the Plan

Crisis communications planning means developing communications strategies for identified risks—making as many decisions and taking as many steps as you possibly can *before* a crisis occurs. The best decisions are usually made when you have time to think through their ramifications.

Because crises vary in their scope and nature, it is best to have a flexible crisis plan that is not event specific. The contents of such a plan include crisis definitions, a list of crisis managers, stakeholder communication strategies, planned coordination and information sites, and an employee training program.

CRISIS DEFINITIONS. Different people conjure up different images when they hear the phrase *public relations,* and the same is true when the word *crisis* is mentioned. A good crisis plan eliminates the guesswork as to whether something is "an incident" or "a crisis." One pharmaceutical manufacturer has a "decision tree" on the first page of its crisis communications plan in which a series of questions helps gauge the nature and intensity of each situation. Developing a common language is also critical for interactions with those outside an organization. Electric utilities with nuclear generators are required to ensure that public agencies, as well as people residing within 10 miles of these facilities, are familiar with terminology that relates to various emergencies and the possible responses to those emergencies.

A LIST OF INDIVIDUALS WHO WILL MANAGE THE CRISIS RESPONSE. When possible, crises should not be allowed to keep an organization from conducting its daily operations. A special **crisis management team (CMT)** should be assigned the responsibility for monitoring and responding to any crisis. These people should be identified by their job titles, not by name—who knows whether Frank Jones will be working here two years from now? Backup persons should also be identified. Ideally, this team should consist of the following members:

■ *The CEO or a designated crisis manager.* Deciding whether the CEO should head the CMT depends on the nature of the crisis. Sometimes no one else will do. In other instances, however, someone who has the CEO's confidence can head the team. If the presence of the CEO inhibits frank discussion among the CMT members, it is better to appoint a **crisis manager,** someone who represents the interests of the CEO and to whom is delegated decision-making authority.

What is not as clear is *when* the executive should publicly leap into the fray. A misjudgment can be very damaging. When Exxon Chairman of the Board Lawrence Rawl waited one week to comment on the *Exxon Valdez* oil spill in Alaska, he believed that public opinion issues should take a back seat to more important issues relating to the cleanup. "We thought the first task should be to assist our operating people to get the incident under control," Exxon President Lee Raymond told reporters. Based on public reaction, that was a mistake.

"When a major crisis occurs, the CEO must step out immediately into the glare of TV lights and tell the public what is being done to fix the problem," said Andy Bowen of Atlanta-based Fletcher Martin Ewing Public Relations. "The CEO can't wait until all of the information is in."[25]

■ *Legal counsel.* Lawyers often present business communicators with their most difficult challenges during crises. Gerald Meyers, a veteran of many skirmishes with attorneys while he was head of American Motors, believes that the best advice is often to "cage your lawyers." He wrote, "Smart executives are not intimidated by lawyers who do not have to run the business once the legal skirmishing is over."[26]

This does not suggest that legal counsel should be excluded from CMTs. Even their critics, including Meyers, say lawyers have an important role in crisis discussions and can provide valuable legal advice. But it is important to remember that the organization must answer to more than just a court of law. It also answers to the court of public opinion, where the judgment can be more devastating. That is why the legal and public relations counsels must have a good working relationship.

■ *Public relations counsel.* Public relations is a management function. In this capacity, the practitioner advises how best to communicate with important stakeholders and, when necessary, represents these stakeholders' views to the CMT. The public relations counsel also advises the CMT on public opinion and potential reactions to the proposed crisis responses. The public relations practitioner is also responsible for serving as the organization's conscience, making certain the organization's actions square with its stated values.

■ *Financial counsel.* Many crises have the potential for severely damaging the company's bottom line. Someone with hands-on knowledge of organization finances can be a valuable asset to the CMT.

■ *Appropriate technical experts.* These people may vary from crisis to crisis. After identifying the various threats to the organization, the crisis communications plan should then identify experts who can assist in the resolution of each type of crisis.

■ *Support personnel.* The CMT may require any of a variety of support services, including people with secretarial skills, people with computer skills, and artist–illustrators.

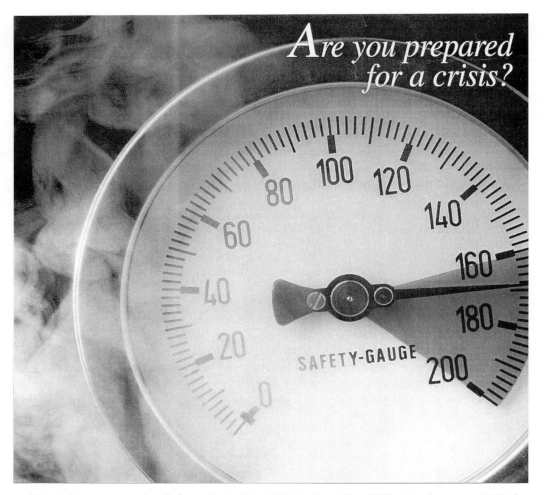

Sooner or later, your organization will face a situation that could damage its reputation. CrisisTRAK, a unique program developed by Barkley Evergreen & Partners, identifies the crises most likely to occur and develops plans to react quickly and appropriately. Twenty-four hours a day, seven days a week, a toll-free call to the CrisisTRAK Hotline will put an experienced crisis management team to work solving any communications problems that arise. Call BE&P Public Relations today, and let us show you how we can deliver under pressure.   CrisisTRAK℠

BARKLEY EVERGREEN & **PARTNERS**, Inc.
Managing Reputations Every Day
1-888-444-0088
423 West 8th Street • Suite 700 • Kansas City, MO 64105-1408
PARTNER
PREX

Advertisement Crisis communications consulting is one of the fastest-growing areas of public relations. (Courtesy of Barkley Evergreen & Partners)

STAKEHOLDER COMMUNICATION STRATEGIES.   The plan should identify the various stakeholders who must be contacted and should provide appropriate telephone numbers, fax numbers, and e-mail addresses. Given adequate warning of a potential problem, some organizations prepare news releases and other stakeholder communications in advance.

The importance of communicating with key stakeholders was demonstrated in June 1999, when more than a thousand people in Western Europe complained of nausea after drinking Coca-Cola products. Investigators linked the problem to production at an Antwerp bottling plant. However, it wasn't until two weeks after the first reports of the illnesses—and after four countries banned or restricted Coca-Cola products—that the company apologized to consumers, who were angered by the silence. In full-page ads placed in Belgian newspapers, Coca-Cola Chairman M. Douglas Ivester wrote, "I should have spoken with you earlier."[27]

Key stakeholders with whom organizations need to communicate during crises include

■ *Employees.* This may be the most important group. Too often, employees are overlooked. Long after the reporters have left, these people remain. The plan needs to outline how employees will be notified of an emergency on short notice. It should also include plans for providing employees with updated information on a regular basis.

■ *The media.* It is critically important that an organization speak with one voice during a crisis. The plan should designate an official spokesperson. A procedure should be established for the timely release of information through news releases or regularly scheduled briefings. The plan should also include provisions for monitoring media reports. The establishment of a media information center (MIC) is discussed below.

■ *Other key stakeholders.* The plan should designate the individual or individuals responsible for serving as liaisons with people who require "special" attention. These key stakeholders include members of the board of directors, major stockholders, financial analysts, regulators/public officials, unions, and community leaders.

■ *The curious public.* Some crises attract a lot of public attention. In those cases, it is a good idea to have a rumor control center where people can telephone and have their questions promptly answered. This is a very useful mechanism for tracking down the source of erroneous information and squelching false rumors before they spread.

WHERE THE RESPONSE IS COORDINATED.   The CMT meets in what is called the **emergency operations center (EOC)**. The EOC is the command post for the organization's crisis response; therefore, it should be in a secure location. That doesn't mean that the meetings should be held in Fort Knox. However, CMT members should be free to do their work without interruption and without the peering eyes of reporters, curious employees, and other rubberneckers. The meeting place should have adequate communications capabilities, including televisions and radios for monitoring the media (see Figure 12.3). It should also be close to the place where the media are briefed.

WHERE REPORTERS CAN GO TO GET INFORMATION.   The place set aside for meeting with reporters covering your crisis is the **media information center (MIC).** The most important goal in its operation is to make the MIC the only place journalists can go for information during a crisis. When it comes to interagency and multiorganizational communication with the media, this is the place where all responding organizations ensure they are "singing off the same sheet of music." The MIC has to be close enough to the action to satisfy reporters, but far enough away to prevent journalists from getting in the way. A procedure for verifying the identity of working reporters, known as **credentialing,** should be established. Reporters and officials should have separate entrances into the building. Furnishings for the MIC should include a lectern or table capable of handling many microphones, adequate lighting and background for photography, tables and chairs for writing, access to telecommunications, and a place for distributing and posting news releases (Figure 12.4). The MIC should also

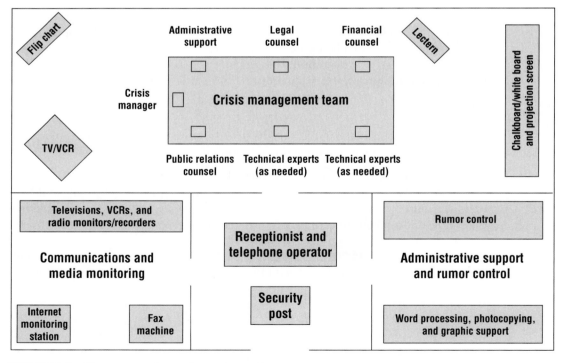

FIGURE 12.3   Emergency Operations Center Layout

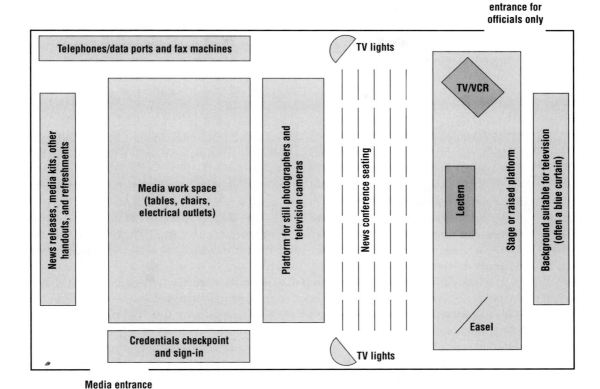

FIGURE 12.4   Media Information Center Layout

be staffed at all times with a media center coordinator who can assist reporters in getting their questions answered.

THE ROLE OF THE INTERNET.   Organizations in crisis are increasingly turning to the Internet as a means of outreach. A web site can serve several audiences, including news media, employees, and others affected by a crisis. Swissair received high praise for its use of the Internet when one of its planes crashed off the Nova Scotia coast in September 1998, killing 228 people. Within an hour of receiving the news, the company used its web site to provide the latest information on the crash. E-mail messages began to pour in from frantic relatives and friends who thought they had loved ones aboard the downed New York-to-Geneva flight. An effort was made to respond to each message within three minutes. For any e-mail that included a telephone number, a Swissair official followed up with a telephone call. Once confirmed, the passenger list was posted on the web site. Swissair also posted all its news releases and public statements. "The web did help a lot," said Swissair spokesman Hans Klaus.[28]

EMPLOYEE TRAINING. Crisis communications training should occur as a normal part of employee orientation. Periodic reminders of each person's responsibilities also are in order—even if those responsibilities consist of nothing more than referring a matter to someone else. Mid- to upper-level managers should have more rigorous training, including tabletop exercises and role-playing scenarios. Part of this training should also focus on the language used and the information gathered when managers report a potential crisis. Inaccurate language and incomplete information can lead to misunderstandings that could cause an organization either to over- or underreact.

Every employee needs to know what to do when disaster strikes. Since Hurricane Andrew, one Miami law firm has issued a disaster-preparedness manual to all its employees. The manual includes emergency contacts, evacuation procedures, and instructions on what to do in the event of a variety of calamities. The firm has also set up an emergency telephone contact system so it can keep track of employees and their needs during crises.[29]

Everyone needs to know whom they should call at the first sign of a crisis. The most important person in a crisis is often the first person to recognize it as such. That person's actions (or inactions) go a long way toward dictating the nature and quality of an organization's response. Employees should feel comfortable reporting trouble if even the slightest thing seems amiss. If the culture of the organization discourages such feedback, the organization may end up missing early warning signs that, if acted upon, could have averted trouble.

Quick ✔ Check

1. What are the advantages of designating a crisis management team? Who should be in charge of it?
2. Why must a good working relationship exist between an organization's lawyer and its public relations counsel?
3. What are some things one should do in anticipation of possible crises?

Step Three: Response

Crisis **response** is the execution of crisis communications strategies. If all the necessary steps have been taken, this is where the organization is rewarded for its hard work. Critical decisions on whom to call and how to respond have already been made. In some cases, actions may have already been taken to avert or minimize the crisis.

At the risk of being repetitive, the response phase is where employee training provides its greatest dividends. Employees who have been trained in how to respond—even if the preferred response is to defer to someone else—are less likely to make critical errors that compound the crisis. That is why it is important that every employee know what he or she should do.

However, just as with any public relations plan, a crisis communications plan must be flexible. Every crisis is unique. And although most crises are predictable, some are not. A crisis communications plan should guide, not dictate, the organization's response. It may be that because of some unanticipated factors, the organization's planned response may be inappropriate. The crisis in question could involve a group of stakeholders with whom the organization has little or no experience. And in some circumstances, such as the case of a catastrophic explosion, some of the response mechanisms anticipated in the plan may no longer be available.

Does this mean that a crisis communications plan is useless? Of course not. Think of a crisis communications plan in the same way a coach sees his or her game plan. Like a good game plan, a good crisis communications plan lays the foundation for success. All the training has been geared toward successful execution of the plan. However, both coaches and crisis managers can be faced with circumstances that force them to change their plans. In sports, a key player may get hurt. In crisis management, some key decision makers may be unavailable. That may force some changes in the original plan, but the changes will be based on options and resources provided for in the plan. Even when one is forced to improvise, good planning can mean success.

Step Four: Recovery

When the immediate threat of a crisis ends, the natural instinct is to relax and to move on to a normal routine. However, it is important to resist that temptation. There is an important final step: **recovery**, in which the organization should evaluate the quality of its response and take appropriate actions on the basis of lessons learned. The questions asked at the end of one crisis may make the difference in averting or minimizing the next crisis. Some questions that need to be asked are

- Were our actions during and after the crisis consistent with our organization's values?
- What aspects of the crisis did our plan anticipate? How can we build upon these successes?
- What aspects of the crisis did our plan fail to anticipate? What changes do we need to make?
- How well did our employees perform? Were they adequately trained?
- What are the lingering effects of the crisis? Are there follow-up actions we should take?

QuickBreak 12.4

THINGS TO DO *BEFORE* A CRISIS BREAKS

With an overwhelming consensus on the importance of a rapid response during a developing emergency, many actions can be taken before a crisis occurs. These include compiling organization data, training personnel, planning crisis center logistics, putting backups in place, developing internal communications channels, and providing psychological support for key publics affected by the crisis.

In advance of a crisis, key information about the organization needs to be at the public relations practitioner's fingertips. This ready-to-use data bank should include information on how many people an organization employs; a record of organization philanthropy and volunteer activity; a master list of all facilities (including names of plant managers, number of employees at each site, value of each plant for insurance purposes, and whether each facility is owned by a subsidiary or in a joint venture with another organization); profiles of products and services of the

organization; and a historical overview of the organization.[30]

Additional information needs to include the home and office telephone numbers of key employees and a list of media contacts, including after-hours telephone numbers. Martin Cooper of Cooper Communications in Encino, California, recommends carrying in a wallet a list of names and home telephone numbers of lawyers, finance managers, and other members of the crisis team.[31]

Organizations that rely heavily on computers and data in their daily operations have an added burden of protecting their technological assets. Five steps recommended by *Nation's Business* are maintaining regular backups of computer data, disaster-proofing the office by putting computer equipment in less vulnerable areas, buying a generator to provide a backup source of electrical power, designing a mobile office plan that allows the business to pick up and move to an alternate location, and negoti-

- How have our stakeholders' views of the organization changed since the onset of the crisis?
- What actions can either take advantage of new opportunities created by the crisis or repair damage created by it?

Not every crisis response is successful. Some organizations are better prepared for crises than others. Some events are more unexpected than others. However, there is little sympathy or tolerance for those who fail to learn the lessons of the past. That is why a period of honest evaluation is absolutely essential. This point is reminiscent of the old saying "Fool me once, shame on you. Fool me twice, shame on me."

Crisis Planning Ethics

At a time when "big government" and "big business" are under increasing attack for being out of touch with the people, proactive crisis communications planning can be critical to an organization's continued success. Through this approach, many crises

ating ahead of time to rent temporary office space should a disaster strike.[32]

More and more organizations are recognizing the value of providing support systems designed to help employees cope with the trauma that often accompanies crises. These are often easier to develop before problems occur. This support can take many forms. Simply providing food, clothing, or money to meet basic needs can go a long way toward restoring normalcy. In the wake of Hurricane Andrew, many Miami-area businesses came to the aid of their employees. One company estimated it spent more than $100,000 in labor and materials to help the families of 35 employees whose homes had been either severely damaged or destroyed by the storm.[33]

There are times, however, when food, clothing, and money are not enough to address the psychological trauma employees face. "Try to understand that there are bona fide stages of a disaster that people go through," said Pamela L. Deroian, a clinical psychologist at the University of Miami. According to Deroian, reactions to disasters include a sense that life is out of balance, disbelief, sadness, anger, and survivor's guilt.[34]

Firms such as Crisis Management International Inc. of Atlanta have a worldwide network of mental health professionals on contract and able to travel to the site of a disaster within hours. "Getting to people right away is the key," CMI President Bruce Blythe said. "You must make them feel safe and secure. You must let them know that someone cares." Among CMI's clients have been United Airlines, which hired the firm to counsel the survivors of a DC-10 crash in Sioux City, Iowa, and Standard Gravure Corporation, where a disgruntled former employee walked into its Louisville, Kentucky, plant and shot and killed 7 employees, wounding 14 others.[35]

that confront organizations can be averted or, at least, minimized. However, many organizations' lack of planning for crises is a cause for great concern. Crises, as well as inappropriate responses to them, pose societal threats on a variety of levels. There are tangible losses associated with them, such as damage to property and financial setbacks. There are also intangible losses, as evidenced by the psychological damage to crisis victims and a loss of public confidence in organizations. Even more, who can determine a value and assess the cost when the outcome of a crisis is the loss of human lives?

Is crisis communications planning an ethical imperative? In the minds of researchers Pauchant and Mitroff, the answer is a resounding yes. Although they have a certain degree of "empathy" for those caught in the vortex of a crisis, they also express "moral outrage" when crises and their subsequent fallouts are preventable.[36] Although PRSA's *Member Code of Ethics 2000* does not specifically mention crisis communications planning, one of the professional values it identifies is honesty. "We adhere to the highest standards of accuracy and truth in advancing the interests of those we represent and in communicating with the public," the code states.[37] That

Values Statement 12.1

PEPSICO

Tracing its origins to a popular soda pop first developed in 1898, PepsiCo emerged in 1965 as a corporation that specializes in soft drinks and snack foods. Its headquarters are in Purchase, New York.

PepsiCo's overall mission is to increase the value of our shareholders' investment. We do this through sales growth, cost controls and wise investment of resources. We believe our commercial success depends upon offering quality and value to our consumers and customers; providing products that are safe, wholesome, economically efficient and environmentally sound; and providing a fair return to our investors while adhering to the highest standards of integrity.

—"Mission Statement,"
PepsiCo web site

wording prompts the question "Can one claim to have acted in such a manner when one has failed to take reasonable precautions against predictable crises?"

It is not enough to develop technical contingencies to meet the logistical needs of an organization in crisis. Developing plans for communicating during times of stress is critical to the success, if not the very survival, of organizations. As one postmortem of Exxon's Alaskan oil spill noted,

The Exxon Valdez spill clearly shows the penalty for perceived unreadiness in the face of an environmental disaster. But it also shows the importance of having insurance for when things go wrong. It would be unthinkable to go without liability insurance against claims for loss or negligence. Why then do some companies fail to take out strong public relations "insurance" for claims against image?[38]

Although ethical arguments might move some of the unconcerned and unprepared to action, tangible evidence of the consequences of such failures may prove more convincing.

Summary

Crises don't just happen. Usually warning signs indicate that trouble is on the way. Too often, however, people fail to recognize these signs. When this failure occurs, a considerable amount of an organization's time and resources must be spent dealing with a crisis.

Crises tend to develop in four stages: a warning stage, a point of no return, a cleanup, and a return to normalcy—although crises can alter what normalcy means for an affected organization.

Crises don't have to have exclusively negative outcomes. Good things can come out of a crisis—if an organization is prepared. But the sad truth is that most organizations are not. Many do not even have a written crisis communications plan. Among those that do, many have not properly trained their employees in its use.

Crisis communications planning is one of the most proactive things a public relations practitioner can do. However, it is not something he or she does alone. A good crisis plan is one that has been developed in collaboration with people throughout the organization *and* has the wholehearted support of top management. A good crisis plan also reflects an organization's values—and there is usually no more important time for communicating those values than during a crisis.

Good crisis communications planning begins with an honest assessment of the potential risks an organization may face. It follows with a plan that identifies the members of the crisis management team, key stakeholders, and the logistics necessary for a swift and appropriate response. The training of all employees is the key to a good response. Although the organization should be guided by its crisis communications plan, its response should not be dictated by it. As is the case with all plans, it should be flexible enough to address unanticipated circumstances. As the crisis ends and the organization moves into the recovery phase, it is important to evaluate what happened and why. This is the first step in preparing for—and possibly preventing—future crises.

DISCUSSION QUESTIONS

1. Can you name a crisis and identify how it proceeded through its four stages?
2. What are some lessons to be learned from the September 2001 terrorist attacks on New York and Washington, D.C.?
3. What do you think are some excuses organizations may proffer for not having adequate crisis communications plans? How would you counter those arguments?
4. Identify some crises that officials at your college or university might face. Where would you place each on Steven Fink's crisis plotting grid?
5. What role do organizational values play in crisis planning?

Memo from the Field

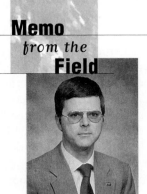

Tom Ditt, Public Information Officer, North Carolina Division of Emergency Management, Raleigh, North Carolina

Tom Ditt is a public information officer with the North Carolina Division of Emergency Management. He is also the State Emergency Alert System coordinator. For more than a decade, he has been involved in the preparedness, response, and recovery phases for every natural disaster or statewide emergency in North Carolina. These have included hurricanes, tornadoes, and floods.

"What do you guys do? Is there anything else I need to know that I haven't asked?" These opening and closing questions announce to public information professionals that the reporters they are facing are probably not prepared for the story they have been sent to do.

They have been given an assignment by "the desk" (an assigning editor). It may be a breaking story or an ongoing one. They may be asked to "localize" a story from an event occurring elsewhere. Reporters are at the desk's mercy. Public information people understand well this element of the news media.

Far too many reporters are not prepared for their assignments. It's hard, too, when they are expected to become instant experts with an end-product "package" of a 30-second VOT (voice on tape), a 20-second talking head, and a 30-second stand-up. It gets scary when a reporter says, "I'm not interested in the facts, just the story."

Yes, the second question—"Is there anything else I need to know that I haven't asked?"—is a reporter's tool. It is like casting a large net. More than likely the answer will be "No." The public information people I know really enjoy working with knowledgeable reporters. They shouldn't have to teach journalism.

The goal of public information is to get the message out.

My background is anchored in print, radio, and television. Because of this, I am better able to provide the information reporters want and still get my message out. Reporters appreciate my having been in "their business." To stay knowledgeable, I read as much as I can both in hard copy and on the Internet. Writing well is a mandatory skill in this work. Computer and photographic skills are also a must. After all, we are talking about communicating.

Public information in an adrenaline-pumping crisis situation such as a hurricane or tornado is a challenge. I know the larger the disaster, the larger the amount of interest there will be in it. News is a worldwide commodity. You can be talking with a reporter for a morning talk show in New York when someone hands you a note saying the BBC from London, where it is nearly midday news time, is holding. Then your next call may be from SkyNews–Australia, where they are preparing for tomorrow night's late news. You have to remember the time zone changes as you do the interview. I enjoy these times.

The information you provide during an emergency, especially on radio and television, must be given in a concise, clear, and easily understood manner. Lives may depend on the correct protective actions you are advising people to take. You do not speculate with reporters. You have to be knowledgeable about the threat or emergency. Your delivery and mannerisms are crucial in getting the correct message out. If you can convey all that is needed in the 20- to 30-second sound bites reporters want, then you have done your job. You have to do this with the knowledge that the reporter interviewing you may have just arrived in this market from somewhere where hurricanes do not occur. This is not the time to try to educate him on the dynamics of a hurricane when your goal is getting people to safety!

On the night of September 22, 1989, Dr. Neil Frank, the former director of the National Hurricane Center, was interviewed on the *CBS Evening News* after Hurricane Hugo raked North Carolina. "Were you surprised that the loss of life, so far as we now know, was so low?" asked Dan Rather.

"People did respond to the advice to get out. And I think that speaks well for the education programs that we have along our coastline today, and that is particularly true there in North Carolina," responded Dr. Frank. Having developed and coordinated our hurricane awareness program, I found his words very sweet.

Case Study 12.1

SSGN Kursk and USS Greeneville

Russian officials learned a hard lesson about the need for candor when one of their submarines sank. That lesson was lost upon the U.S. Navy just six months later.

The armed forces of the Russian Federation have declined sharply since the demise of the Soviet Union in 1991. A lack of money has led to lower morale among soldiers and sailors as well as to a steady deterioration of military equipment.

Despite this trend, the *SSGN Kursk* was a relatively new Oscar-class cruise missile submarine. The nuclear-powered submarine, commissioned in 1995, carried a crew of 118. It was designed to carry 24 cruise missiles, 36 torpedoes, and nuclear warheads. Oscar-class submarines are smaller and faster than other Russian submarines, allowing them to enter the waters of foreign nations.[39]

The *Kursk* was conducting naval exercises in the Barents Sea on August 12, 2000, when two explosions caused it to sink 350 feet below the surface. Russian officials speculated that the blasts were caused either by a collision with another submarine (presumably British or U.S.) or by a malfunction in a torpedo tube. At one point, they even suggested that the submarine had fallen victim to terrorists from Chechnya, a province that had been engaged in a savage war for independence against the Russian Federation.

The following outcry of angry public opinion startled Russian President Vladimir Putin. Relatives of the victims thought that the government was slow to respond to the crisis, slow to release information, and slow to tell the truth about what happened. It took the government nine days to confirm that everyone on board had died. Putin didn't help his image when he refused to cancel his vacation during the first five days of the *Kursk* crisis. "I think I did the right thing," he told reporters. "The presence of high-placed officials in the disaster area would not help and more often would hamper work."[40]

The public became even more outraged when a woman who had lost a son on the *Kursk* was forcibly sedated during a meeting with Russian officials. She had been berating Russian Deputy Prime Minister Ilya Klebanov about the government's slow response to the crisis. A nationwide television audience saw a female medic sneak up behind the woman and inject her with a sedative. At the time, the incident evoked dark memories of atrocities committed by the former communist regime. It wasn't until later that the public learned that family members had asked that the woman be sedated.

The public's outrage became more intense when some of the bodies were recovered. Lieutenant Captain Dmitry Kolenikov left a note written in total darkness indicating that he and at least 22 others had survived the two blasts. "Here is a list of the crew who are in the ninth compartment and will try to get out," Kolenikov wrote. "Greetings to everyone, don't lose hope."[41]

"It shows that they have really very little understanding of the media and the nature of criticism in contemporary Russia," said Roy Allison of the London-based Royal Institute of International Affairs.[42] Mike Willard of the Kiev-based Willard Group wrote, "Paraphrasing military parlance, Putin was absent without conscience."[43]

In February 2001, the U.S. Navy faced its own submarine disaster. Although circumstances differed from the Russian tragedy, many of the same public relations blunders occurred.

Ironically, the *USS Greeneville,* a nuclear-powered Los Angeles–class attack submarine, was engaged in a public relations exercise when disaster struck. It left its base in Pearl Harbor, Hawaii, with 16 civilians on board as part of the Navy's Distinguished Visitors program. Civilians, including politicians and civic leaders, are routinely taken on trips to familiarize them with Navy submarines. Often, these civilians take a turn at the controls under the supervision of trained personnel.[44]

The accident occurred during a demonstration of what submariners call an emergency main ballast blow, a rapid surfacing of the ship. In its quick rise to the surface, the *Greeneville* had failed to detect the presence of a Japanese fishing training ship, the *Ehime Maru.* The submarine struck the training ship from below, sinking it and killing nine Japanese citizens. The U.S. Coast Guard rescued the remaining 26 persons from the training ship. No one on the *Greeneville* was injured, and it safely returned to port with moderate damage.

Although the U.S. government moved quickly to apologize for the accident and to launch an investigation, the Navy was not forthcoming with all the facts. It did not initially acknowledge that civilians were on board. Navy officials also refused to identify the passengers and were slow to acknowledge that two of them were sitting at controls during the incident.

Commander Scott D. Waddle, the commanding officer of the *Greeneville,* was also tight-lipped. Early in the investigation, Waddle would not comment on the incident. This drew criticism in Japan, where Waddle was expected to provide nothing short of a full apology.

After three weeks, Waddle opened what one public relations commentator called "an aggressive PR initiative to save his own scalp."[45] Waddle sent a letter to apology to the families of the victims. He gave television and magazine interviews. In doing so, Waddle gave a human face to the *Greeneville's* side of the tragedy.

Still, contradictions continued. Waddle told *Time* magazine, "I didn't cause the accident. I gave orders that resulted in the accident. And I take full responsibility."[46] Although some called that candor, others said it was the equivalent of trying to have one's cake and eat it, too. Waddle did publicly express remorse for the loss of life, but his attorney also said he hoped his client could get a movie or book deal as a reward for what had been "an incredibly difficult time."[47]

In the end, Waddle was removed from his command, reprimanded, and allowed to retire with full benefits. At that time, some practitioners wrote that the relatively light disciplinary action was a public relations triumph for Waddle. Considering that it ended an otherwise unblemished naval career, Waddle's victory was, at best, hollow.

DISCUSSION QUESTIONS

1. In what ways were the crisis responses of the Russian and U.S. navies similar? In what ways were they different?
2. How might risk assessment have affected the U.S. Navy's *Greeneville* crisis?
3. Do you agree with public relations observers who suggest that Commander Scott Waddle avoided harsher punishment because of an effective public relations strategy? Please explain your reasoning.
4. What steps could Russian and U.S. naval officials have taken to better address the concerns of victims' families?

Case Study 12.2

Classic Crises: Tylenol and Pepsi

When the discussion turns to crisis communications, two cases invariably come to mind: Tylenol and Pepsi. And why not? The two companies involved, Johnson & Johnson and PepsiCo, showed the world how it is possible to save both one's reputation and the bottom line.

The Tylenol scare resulted in seven deaths; the Pepsi incident resulted in none. Despite this major difference, however, tremendous similarities exist between the two cases. Both involved potential tampering with popular products important to the financial health of each company. On two occasions, in 1982 and again in 1986, deaths were linked to cyanide-laced Tylenol capsules. For Pepsi, the crisis during the summer of 1993 was reports of medical syringe needles being found in cans of Diet Pepsi. Although the needle "discoveries" would later be shown to be hoaxes, they raised fear among consumers at a time of heightened awareness of infectious diseases such as AIDS.

Because the Tylenol and Diet Pepsi scares both involved threats to the health and safety of consumers, there was significant potential for a major financial impact on both companies. Within two weeks of the first Tylenol tampering incident, the value of Johnson & Johnson stock dropped $657 million. It was also estimated that the company had received as much as $300 million worth of negative publicity.[48] Reports of needles in Diet Pepsi cans could not have come at a worse time: Summer is the peak season for soft-drink purchases. Immediately, Pepsi saw sales dip 3 percent. They would rise 7 percent after the hoaxes were exposed.

Both companies had the potential to be perceived as villains. However, the two companies enjoyed good reputations, and the public was willing to adopt a wait-and-see attitude toward both. Both companies moved quickly to establish credibility: Johnson & Johnson recalled the Tylenol capsules and Pepsi distributed a video news release demonstrating how difficult it would be to tamper with the canning process.

In both cases, the Food and Drug Administration advised against a massive product recall out of the fear that such a move could spawn copycat crimes. Pepsi heeded the government's advice. However, no one had died from drinking Diet Pepsi. With seven people dead in two separate tampering incidents, Johnson & Johnson officials felt they had no choice but to demonstrate their concern for consumer safety by recalling their product. To calm an uneasy public, Johnson & Johnson placed Tylenol capsules in triple-sealed safety packaging after the first incident. After the second, the company replaced the capsules with tamperproof caplets.

The makers of Tylenol took another important step to maintain their credibility. In early statements the company had indicated that no cyanide was present in its manufacturing plants. However, that statement was wrong. To correct that unintentional error and to avoid having an enterprising reporter discover this potentially damaging fact, Johnson & Johnson immediately issued an update. The news release may have said, "We made a mistake." But what it really said, between the lines, was, "You can trust us to tell you the truth."

Another important similarity is the high-profile role executives in both companies played in the resolution of each crisis. Both James E. Burke of Johnson & Johnson and Craig Weatherup of Pepsi-Cola North America effectively reassured consumers through numerous media interviews. Both also reached important stakeholders through alternative channels: Burke via a video teleconference beamed to locations around the nation and Weatherup through appearances in a series of video news releases.

The stakeholders in the crises facing both companies were similar: consumers, employees, shareholders, distributors, merchants, government regulators, and the media. Both companies did an excellent job of keeping these groups updated on the latest developments. In the case of Pepsi, these stakeholder communications had an added bonus. Through the channels the company developed with the merchants that sell Diet Pepsi, Pepsi officials became aware of a store surveillance-camera video that caught a woman placing a needle in her just-purchased can of soda. This video was immediately beamed worldwide in a video news release and effectively took the air out of the hoax.

Not as apparent, but critical to success, was the fact that both companies were well prepared to deal with crises. Both had crisis communications plans in place. Both left the response to each crisis up to their crisis management teams. Employees in both organizations were well trained in their responsibilities. As a result, the two companies emerged from crises seen not as villains but as heroes.

DISCUSSION QUESTIONS

1. Should corporate profits be a concern when a company responds to a crisis? How did Johnson & Johnson and PepsiCo address this issue in their crises?

2. How does a company's reputation affect its ability to respond to crises? What influence did the reputations of Johnson & Johnson and PepsiCo have in their respective crises?

3. In the two Tylenol tampering incidents, seven people died. No one died in the Diet Pepsi hoax. How might this fact have affected the two companies' crisis communications?

4. Tylenol was pulled from store shelves after each tampering incident. Cans of Diet Pepsi were not. How do these actions reflect on each company's values? Could each company have faced competing or conflicting values? (Johnson & Johnson's values statement is on p. 269. PepsiCo's mission statement is on p. 410.)

It's Your Turn

Death of a Salesman

Although no time is a good time for a crisis, right now is a particularly bad time for one to strike your company. After many long months of planning, the company goes public tomorrow: Shares of its stock will start being sold on the New York Stock Exchange. This is a big moment for your growing company, one that will soon make possible the company's ambitious plans for expansion into new markets.

A special ceremony on the floor of the stock exchange is planned for tomorrow morning. After the ceremony, the CEO is scheduled to conduct a series of meetings with investment analysts at several major brokerage houses.

You (the director of public relations) and the CEO are about to leave for the airport to catch a plane to New York. It is at this moment that your assistant walks in, ashen faced, to tell you bad news: A car driven by one of your salesmen has been involved in a head-on crash with a full school bus. Information about the accident is sketchy, but police have confirmed that the salesman, an original employee of your company, has been killed. The police also say that there are at least two dozen injuries on the school bus. However, the extent of these injuries is not known.

Several questions race through your mind:

1. Should the boss go to New York?
2. Should you go to New York with the boss or stay on the scene to coordinate the public relations response?
3. Whom, if anyone, should you contact?
4. Should the New York event go forward as scheduled?
5. Should you plan a news conference?
6. What should you do if it turns out that the accident was the dead salesman's fault?

You have only 15 minutes before you must leave for the airport. What will you do?

KEY TERMS

cleanup phase, p. 393
credentialing, p. 404
crisis, p. 390
crisis communications planning, p. 400
crisis impact value (CIV), p. 399
crisis management team (CMT), p. 400
crisis manager, p. 401
crisis planning team (CPT), p. 398
crisis plotting grid, p. 399
crisis probability factor (CPF), p. 399

emergency operations center (EOC),
    p. 403
media information center (MIC), p. 404
point of no return, p. 393
problem, p. 390
recovery, p. 407
response, p. 406
risk assessment, p. 397
things return to normal, p. 394
warning stage, p. 392

NOTES

1. Matt Murray and Rick Schmitt, "For Bosses and Workers Alike, Getting Back to Work Takes Patience and Determination," *Wall Street Journal,* 12 September 2001, B1.
2. "Message from Morgan Stanley Chairman Philip Purcell," Morgan Stanley web site, 11 September 2001, www.morganstanley.com.
3. Carol Hymowitz, "In a Crisis, Leaders Put People First, But Also Get Back to Business," *Wall Street Journal,* 18 September 2001, B1.
4. Kenneth N. Myers, *Total Contingency Planning for Disasters* (New York: Wiley, 1993), 2.
5. William Manchester, *The Death of a President* (New York: Arbor House, 1967), 189.
6. Jim Bishop, *The Day President Kennedy Was Shot* (Toronto: HarperCollins, 1968), 582–583.
7. Jane Applegate, "Why Crisis Management Plans Are Essential," *Los Angeles Times,* 29 December 1989, D3.
8. Donald Chisholm and Martin Landau, "Set Aside That Optimism If We Want to Avoid Disaster," *Los Angeles Times,* 18 April 1989, sec. II, p. 7.
9. "Many Still Aren't Prepared," *Public Relations Journal* (September 1989): 16.
10. David W. Guth, "Organizational Crisis Experience and Public Relations Roles," *Public Relations Review* (summer 1995): 123–136.
11. Thierry C. Pauchant and Ian I. Mitroff, *Transforming the Crisis-Prone Organization* (San Francisco: Jossey-Bass, 1992), 12.
12. Pauchant and Mitroff, 15–16.
13. Steven Fink, *Crisis Management: Planning for the Inevitable* (New York: AMACOM, 1986), 15–16.
14. Laurence Barton, *Crisis in Organizations: Managing and Communicating in the Heat of Chaos* (Cincinnati: South-Western Publishing, 1993), 2.
15. Dan Fesperman, "Chronology: With a Rumble, Chaos," *Baltimore Sun,* 21 July 2001, online, www.sunspot.net.

16. Gerald C. Meyers with John Holusha, *When It Hits the Fan: Managing the Nine Crises of Business* (Boston: Houghton Mifflin, 1986), 9–10.

17. "PR Case History: Putting Out a Fire," *O'Dwyer's PR Daily,* 6 August 2001, online, www.odwyerpr.com/0806case.htm.

18. "There When You Need Them," *Baltimore Sun,* 20 July 2001, online, www.sunspot.net.

19. Heather Dewar, "Officials to Improve City Emergency Plan," *Baltimore Sun,* 27 July 2001, online, www.sunspot.net.

20. Meyers, 28.

21. Mayer Nudel and Norman Antokol, *The Handbook for Effective Emergency and Crisis Management* (Lexington, Mass.: D.C. Heath, 1988), 36.

22. Robert F. Littlejohn, *Crisis Management: A Team Approach* (New York: American Management Association, 1983), 18–32.

23. Barton, 48–50.

24. Applegate.

25. Andy Bowen, "Crisis Procedures That Stand the Test of Time," *Public Relations Tactics* (August 2001): 16.

26. Meyers, 232–236.

27. Raf Casert, "Coca-Cola Apologizes to Belgians," Associated Press, online, Yahoo! Finance, 22 June 1999, http://biz.yahoo.com.

28. Sharon Machlis, "Web Aids Swissair Response," online, CNN Interactive, 15 September 1998, www.cnn.com.

29. Sharon Nelton, "Prepare for the Worst," *Nation's Business* (September 1993): 22.

30. Barton, 175.

31. Applegate.

32. Rosalind Resnick, "Protecting Computers and Data," *Nation's Business* (September 1993): 25.

33. Nelton, 25.

34. Nelton, 23.

35. Keith Thomas, "Atlanta Firm Helps Workers Cope with Tragedy," *Atlanta Journal and Constitution,* 17 September 1989, A12.

36. Pauchant and Mitroff, 5–6.

37. *Public Relations Society of America Member Code of Ethics 2000,* online, www.prsa.org.

38. E. Bruce Harrison with Tom Prugh, "Assessing the Damage: Practitioner Perspectives on the Valdez," *Public Relations Journal* (October 1989): 42.

39. Carissa Almeida and Owen Wood, "Backgrounder: Russian Submarines," CBC News Online, August 2000, http://cbc.ca/news/indepth/facts/russian_subs.html.

40. Charles Digges, "What Will Putin Learn from Media Circus?" *St. Petersburg Times,* 25 August 2000, 1.

41. "Private Farewell for Kursk Letter Writer," online, CNN Interactive, 2 November 2000, www.cnn.com/2000/WORLD/europe/11/02/russia.kursk/index.html.

42. Dick Durham, "Shock after Kursk Mother Is Forcibly Sedated," online, CNN Interactive, 24 August 2000, www.cnn.com/2000/WORLD/europe/08/24/russia.needle/index.html.

43. "Embracing the Bear: U.S. PR Pro Calls Russia Home," *Public Relations Tactics* (October 2000): 34.

44. Sally Apgar, "Navy Withholding Identity of Civilians Aboard Sub," *Honolulu Advertiser*, 14 February 2001, online, http://the.honoluluadvertiser.com/2001/Feb/14/214localnews18.html.

45. Fraser P. Seitel, "Aggressive PR Saves Waddle," *O'Dwyer's PR Daily*, 23 April 2001, online, www.odwyerpr.com.

46. Seitel.

47. "Waddle's Attorney Says Client Deserves Reward," *The Honolulu Advertiser*, 29 April 2001, online, http:/the.honoluluadvertiser.com/article/2001/Apr/29/In/In01a.html.

48. "Tylenol Tries for a Comeback," *Newsweek,* 1 November 1982, 78.

13

Public Relations and Marketing

objectives

After studying this chapter, you will be able to

- describe recent changes in marketing

- define integrated marketing communications

- explain the differences between public relations, advertising, and marketing

- describe marketing public relations

- summarize the process of integrated marketing communications

Face the Music

scenario

What a dream job. You've just been appointed marketing director for a new chain of music stores that feature hard-to-find alternative rock CDs. Your company has opened stores in 12 major college cities around the United States. Unfortunately, you've been hired only two months before the stores open. Now your associates are asking you for a marketing plan that will bring students flocking into the stores. Some associates want advertising; others prefer public relations. But, fortunately, you soon determine that everyone is flexible and is eager to be innovative in the company's marketing efforts.

You have an adequate marketing budget but not enough money to advertise on national television or in magazines such as Spin.

What do you do?

Public Relations and Marketing

Let's begin by addressing a question you may be asking right now: *Why am I reading about marketing in a public relations textbook?*

Good question. Here are some answers:

1. Marketing focuses on consumers, as does consumer relations, or customer relations, which is part of public relations. Traditional consumer relations tactics, such as product-oriented news releases, can work hand in hand with marketing tactics such as direct mail and in-store displays.

2. Other areas of public relations, such as government relations and employee relations, can affect the success of marketing programs—and vice versa. Some of the biggest headaches in public relations, in fact, come from mishandled marketing programs that damage important relationships. For example, McDonald's Corporation faced immediate problems with employee, government, media, investor, and customer publics in 2001 when news broke that one of its suppliers had illegally rigged some of the restaurant chain's in-store games.

3. Marketing in the 21st century is undergoing dramatic changes. Far from just persuading consumers to buy products *now,* new marketing strategies seek to build long-term, productive relationships with consumers. That should sound a lot like public relations to you. These new relationship-oriented marketing theories signal a profound shift from the mass-marketing programs of the past.

The Decline of Mass Marketing

Life seemed easier when professionals in public relations and advertising believed they could rely on the awesome power of the mass media. When Company X wanted to sell its new and improved gizmo to millions of eager customers, it simply bought ads on the right TV and radio shows and did the same with a few newspapers and magazines that delivered huge audiences. Company X often tried to place news releases in the same media. With the boom of network television in the mid–20th century, such a marketing plan really seemed to work . . . for a while.

However, we're now witnessing the weakening of the mass media. In a world with hundreds of cable and satellite channels, the traditional television networks (ABC, CBS, NBC, and perhaps CNN, Fox, and WB) can no longer automatically deliver a mass audience. In addition, thousands of specialized e-mail or fax-delivered newsletters, web sites, and other new media have helped plow over the few broad paths that once reached millions of consumers. No longer can public relations and advertising professionals reach a mass audience of consumers simply by placing news releases and ads in a few national print media and on the television networks your parents watched.

"It's time that public relations, advertising, sales promotion, and marketing pause for a reality check," says E.W. Brody, a respected public relations professor and practitioner.[1]

And what does our reality check reveal? These facts, says Brody:

1. Mass media continue to proliferate (which leads to the next point).
2. Audiences continue to fragment.
3. New media, often beyond practitioners' reach, are supplanting the old.
4. Media that reach individuals one at a time with personalized messages are growing in efficiency and effectiveness.

The Growth of Consumer-Focused Marketing

In this new reality, many organizations are decreasing their reliance on mass marketing. Instead, they are embracing what we will call consumer-focused marketing. Consumer-focused marketing uses a variety of media to build relationships with individual consumers. In the past decade, one of the most popular forms of consumer-focused marketing has been **integrated marketing communications** (IMC). As early as 1993, marketing executives identified IMC as the top consideration in creating marketing strategies for the 21st century.[2]

IMC is distinctly different from mass marketing:

1. IMC practitioners focus on individual consumers. Products are developed to fill consumers' specific needs, and sales messages are created to target specific consumers' self-interests. (Because IMC targets consumers, not all of public relations is part of IMC. Public relations, of course, targets other publics as well: employees, government officials, and stockholders, to name just a few.)
2. IMC practitioners use **databases** to target individual consumers rather than mass audiences. These databases contain a wealth of information on individual consumers' wants, needs, and preferences.
3. IMC practitioners send a well-focused message to each consumer through a variety of approaches: advertising, public relations, direct mail, and all other forms of marketing communications, including packaging and pricing.
4. IMC practitioners use consumer-preferred media to send their marketing messages.
5. IMC practitioners favor interactive media, constantly seeking information from consumers. Thus, new media such as interactive web sites can be ideal for IMC.

Just as public relations has evolved over the decades, consumer-focused marketing is growing and changing. Although IMC is the best-known form of consumer-focused marketing, other forms exist, and they are helping to shape the future of marketing. IMC was preceded by database marketing, which helped turn marketing away from mass audiences and toward individuals. Other approaches that can be grouped under the broad umbrella of consumer-focused marketing include relationship marketing, customer relationship management (CRM), and integrated brand communication (IBC). QuickBreak 13.1 discusses similarities and differences among these new consumer-focused marketing approaches.

Public Relations, Advertising, and Marketing: Working Together

The three main pillars of IMC, as we said in Chapter 1, are public relations, advertising, and marketing. Although these three disciplines have much in common, much also differentiates them (Figure 13.1). Let's quickly review the definitions we established previously for each discipline:

> **Advertising** is the use of controlled media (media in which one pays for the privilege of dictating message content, placement, and frequency) in an attempt to influence the actions of targeted publics.

> **Marketing** is the process of researching, creating, refining, and promoting a product or service and distributing that product or service to targeted consumers. Marketing promotion disciplines include sales promotions (such as coupons), personal selling, direct marketing—and, often, aspects of advertising and public relations.

> **Public relations** is the values-driven management of relationships between an organization and the publics that can affect its success.

Advertising, marketing, and public relations follow the same process: research, planning, communication, evaluation. But unlike marketing, public relations focuses on

FIGURE 13.1   The Relationship among Advertising, Marketing, and Public Relations
Advertising, marketing, and public relations are three distinct professions with important areas of convergence. But not all advertising is marketing; nor is all public relations marketing.

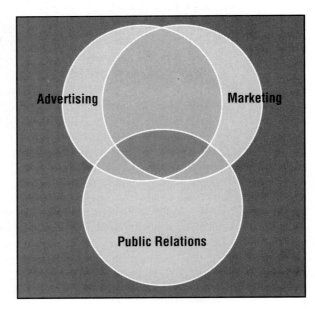

many publics, not just on consumers. And unlike advertising, public relations doesn't control its messages by purchasing specific placements for them.

The Impact of Consumer-Focused Marketing on Public Relations

Consumer-focused marketing makes so much sense that some practitioners say, "We've been doing this for years. There's nothing new here." And, to some degree, they're right. Although certain aspects of IMC, for example, are relatively new, including the extensive use of databases and the use of new and innovative communications technologies, IMC is still based on a traditional commonsense approach familiar to most practitioners of good public relations: focusing on the values of a particular public and responding with a clear message.

But consumer-focused marketing *is* changing some aspects of public relations. The growing number of mergers of advertising and public relations agencies is evidence of this change. A generation ago, public relations constituted only a small portion of the activities of advertising agencies—almost an afterthought. But in recent years ad agencies have widened their range of services to serve clients better and to counter a decline in advertising's share of marketing budgets. Some agencies are expanding through mergers. Others are forming strategic partnerships with public relations agencies. Still others are building public relations departments from scratch. In some agencies, advertising and public relations divisions act as separate profit centers, partnering only when circumstances dictate the need for an IMC approach.

Consumer-focused marketing also is changing **marketing public relations,** the part of our profession that exists to promote organizations' products. More practitioners are learning—or at least learning about—disciplines such as direct mail, product packaging, and other forms of advertising and marketing. IMC, for example, is increasing the communications options of marketing public relations practitioners.

The Impact of Public Relations on Consumer-Focused Marketing

But the influence flows both ways: Public relations has also had a profound influence on consumer-focused marketing. Public relations professionals have always believed in breaking down publics into their smallest units, just as consumer-focused marketing does. And good public relations has always been two-way; the best practitioners have always listened—not just talked—to their publics. Two-way symmetrical public relations by definition seeks to identify and honor the values and interests of important publics. Critics of traditional marketing communications charge—perhaps not altogether fairly—that consumer values and interests were left out of the traditional marketing process. Those critics say that companies designed products and sent marketing messages with very little analysis of what individual consumers really wanted. Whether or not that's true, it is undeniable that consumer-focused marketing is increasing the power of the consumer in the marketing process.

QuickBreak 13.1

IMC AND MORE

Databases and new methods of communication have revolutionized marketing. In the 1990s those two developments came together in integrated marketing communications (IMC), probably today's best-known consumer-focused marketing philosophy. But consumer-focused marketing includes other, closely related philosophies that you should know: database marketing, relationship marketing, customer relationship management (CRM), and integrated brand communication (IBC).

Database marketing.   The new consumer-focused marketing philosophies began with database marketing. A computerized database can store vast amounts of information about individual consumers: what they buy, when they buy, how often they buy, how much they spend, how and how often your organization contacts them, and much more. "Database marketing," says management consultant Mindi McKenna "involves the collection, storage, analysis, and use of information regarding customers and the past purchase behaviors to guide future marketing decisions."[3]

Relationship marketing.   John Dalla Costa, president of the Center for Ethical Orientation, says that the true value of modern organizations "involves a return on relationship. . . . The worth of companies depends more and more on the worth of [their] varied relationships."[4] Relationship marketing looks beyond profits to individual relationships with specific consumers, all in the belief that if the relationships are good, profits automatically follow.

Customer relationship management.   The Conference Board, a U.S.-based business-research association, defines CRM as "the business processes an organization performs to identify, select, acquire, develop, retain, and better serve customers. These processes encompass an organization's . . . engagement with its customers and prospects over the lifetime of its relationship with them."[5] CRM combines the technology of database marketing with the philosophy of relationship marketing to develop lifelong relationships with individual customers.

Integrated brand communication.   According to marketing professors Don Schultz and Beth Barnes, integrated brand communication goes beyond IMC, which focuses on sales. It goes beyond CRM, which focuses on relationships between organizations and customers. Instead, IBC focuses on relationships between consumers and brands. Schultz and Barnes define brand as "the bond between the buyer and the seller."[6] In IBC, a brand is an individual consumer's perception of his or her relationship with a product or an organization. The goal of IBC is to discover each consumer's view of the brand and to align it with the organization's view. To do so, the organization must identify and integrate all forms of communication, sending one, clear message—just as in IMC.

These consumer-focused marketing strategies, including IMC, are closely related to one another. And with their increasing focus on building two-way, win–win relationships with important publics, they are closely related to public relations.

Public relations practitioners seek communication with publics through media that those publics prefer; consumer-focused marketers do the same. Two-way symmetrical public relations involves the notion that sometimes an organization has to

Values Statement 13.1

THE J.M. SMUCKER COMPANY

The J.M. Smucker Company manufactures jams, jellies, preserves, ice cream toppings, and natural peanut butter. The company was founded in 1897 and is based in Orrville, Ohio.

Quality applies to our products, our manufacturing methods, our marketing efforts, our people, and our relationships with each other. We will only produce and sell products that enhance the quality of life and well-being. These will be the highest quality products offered in our respective markets because the Company's growth and business success have been built on quality. We will continuously look for ways to achieve daily improvements which will, over time, result in consistently superior products and performance.

At the J.M. Smucker Company, quality comes first. Sales growth and earnings will follow.

—Excerpt from "Our Basic Beliefs,"
J.M. Smucker web site

change to meet the needs of the publics, just as consumer-focused marketing involves realizing that a product may need to change. In fact, modern marketing's basic philosophy of respecting and listening to consumers may well be a contribution from the practice of successful public relations.

Differences between Public Relations and Consumer-Focused Marketing

A problem with some interpretations of consumer-focused marketing is the mistaken belief that all public relations is part of marketing communications. Knocking down that idea is easy. Marketing focuses on a very important public: consumers. But that's only one public. Public relations must focus on developing healthy long-term relationships with employees, stockholders, news media, and any other public essential to an organization's success. Certainly the two professions need to work together. But as Figure 13.1 indicates, public relations and marketing are distinct, complementary professions.

In *Excellence in Public Relations and Communication Management*, a landmark study on how award-winning public relations works, Professor James Grunig of the University of Maryland declares, "The public relations function of excellent organizations exists separately from the marketing function, and excellent public relations departments are not subsumed into the marketing function."[7] In 1991, with the increasing importance of public relations tactics in marketing campaigns, a panel of marketing and public relations experts assembled to study the relationship between the two professions. The panel concluded that marketing and public relations were "separate and equal, but related functions" that should exist in separate departments. "The major difference is in the outcomes they seek to achieve," the panel reported, noting that while marketing focuses on consumers and financial goals, public relations focuses on building relationships with many other groups that can help an organization achieve its broader mission.[8]

Public relations isn't marketing. Marketing isn't public relations. But public relations and consumer-focused marketing certainly share important values. Both focus on the needs and interests of a public or publics. Both try to listen as much as they speak. And both act to strengthen an organization.

Quick ✔ Check

1. How does consumer-focused marketing differ from mass marketing?
2. How and why does consumer-focused marketing use databases?
3. What are the differences among public relations, advertising, and marketing?

A Closer Look at Marketing

Before beginning this chapter, you probably had a basic understanding of marketing. After all, you encounter it every day. And earlier in this chapter, we defined marketing. But as you might suspect, we're about to tell you even more. Understanding how marketing works can make you a better public relations practitioner.

At its core, marketing means making the consumer want to buy your product. The so-called **marketing mix** consists of everything from product research and design to packaging, pricing, and product demonstrations. It even includes selecting the product's name. Years ago, marketing professors Jerome McCarthy and Philip Kotler defined the marketing mix with what they called the four P's of marketing:

1. *Product* (including name, design, and packaging)
2. *Price*
3. *Place* (where, exactly, can the customer buy it?)
4. *Promotion*

To these four P's, Kotler recently added a fifth:

5. *Public relations*[9]

Public relations, according to Kotler, is becoming increasingly important in sending consumers the kinds of messages that lead to purchases and to product loyalty.

One of IMC's greatest contributions to marketing is the belief that every bit of the marketing mix communicates to consumers. A product's name sends a message to the consumer, as do design, packaging, price, the place consumers purchase the product, and the promotions that publicize the product. Humor columnist Dave Barry accurately reported that North Dakota was considering a name change because the word *North* suggests cold, snow-swept plains to potential tourists. Barry then stretched the truth—but illustrated the communicative power of names—by adding, "In contrast, SOUTH Dakota is universally believed to be a tropical paradise with palm trees swaying on surf-kissed beaches."[10] Like names, price and place also can send consumers a message. A lavishly packaged product that sells for an eye-poppingly high price at the most exclusive store in town has a different image in consumers' minds than a product sold for 25¢ at the town's grungiest gas station.

One problem with traditional marketing, some critics say, is that these various forms of communication may be sending different messages about the same product. And if consumers don't have a clear vision of the product, they won't buy it. For example, consumers may easily be confused by a product whose advertising suggests exclusivity and luxury—yet whose price suggests availability and cheapness.

"Most marketers send out a communications hodgepodge to the consumer, a mass message saying one thing, a price promo creating a different signal, a product label creating still another message, sales literature having an entirely different vocabulary, a sales force pitching nothing but 'price,' 'price,' 'price' to the retailer," say the authors of *Integrated Marketing Communications*, an excellent book on IMC. "Mixed-up, mass-directed, incompatible communication stems from the manufacturer's wishes rather than from customer needs."[11]

IMC tries to end that hodgepodge of messages by ensuring that every aspect of the marketing mix sends the same clear message to highly targeted consumers.

Marketing Public Relations

Before we take a closer look at how IMC in particular works, let's look at marketing public relations, which is the part of public relations that fits into marketing. Marketing public relations focuses on building relationships with consumers, with the intent, of course, of persuading them to buy a product.

Professional wrestler "Macho Man" Randy Savage helped Slim Jim meat snacks gain international exposure through an innovative marketing public relations appearance on ESPN's X-Games. (Courtesy of GoodMark Foods and Richard French & Associates)

GoodMark Foods, maker of Slim Jim products, uses marketing public relations, together with other IMC tactics, to dominate the multimillion-dollar meat snacks market. For example, knowing that sports broadcasters covering live events constantly need new and newsworthy information, GoodMark sent professional wrestler "Macho Man" Randy Savage, one of its celebrity endorsers, to ESPN's X-Games. Savage is news wherever he goes, and an ESPN broadcaster quickly grabbed the wrestler, who just happened to steer the on-air interview toward Slim Jim products.

How much did GoodMark Foods pay ESPN for that international exposure? Zero. Zip. Nada.

The Macho Man's appearance was a form of media relations—of providing material that sports media want and need. And because Savage's appearance was product related, it became marketing public relations. GoodMark Vice President of Marketing Jeff Slater credits the company's public relations agency, Richard French & Associates, with helping to create such innovative marketing public relations tactics.[12]

Other tactics in marketing public relations include

- product- or service-oriented news releases and media kits;
- video news releases (VNRs) featuring newsworthy products or services;
- news conferences to announce significant new products or services;
- satellite media tours (SMTs), in which a spokesperson for a newsworthy product or service gives individual interviews to local television stations via satellite;
- displays at trade shows, where industry analysts and interested consumers gather to examine new products and services;
- special events designed to attract media attention to a particular product; and
- spokesperson appearances in the media (including Internet chat rooms) and at special events.

Marketing public relations can work alone or, better, as part of a marketing campaign. The public it targets is the consumer—sometimes through intervening publics such as the news media, where marketing public relations can win an independent, third-party endorsement for a product or service. Other parts of public relations certainly don't ignore the consumer; but, as we noted earlier, they generally work apart from marketing, targeting publics such as employees, the government, investors, and so on.

A Closer Look at IMC

Enough background. Let's jump into a deeper definition of integrated marketing communications. IMC, say the authors of the book *Integrated Marketing Communications,* is "planned, developed, executed, and evaluated with affecting one specific consumer behavior in mind, the process of making purchases now or in the future."[13]

Focusing on Individual Consumers

In IMC, individual consumers are the focus of thematically consistent messages sent through a variety of media. In fact, marketing professor Robert Lauterborn suggests that the traditional four P's of marketing have become the four C's:[14]

1. *Product* has become *consumer wants and needs:* These shape every aspect of the marketing process.
2. *Price* has become *consumer's cost:* For example, a price of $500 is a higher cost to a college student than it is to a movie star.
3. *Place* has become *convenience to buy.*
4. *Promotion* has become *communication:* This is two-way communication that actively seeks consumer input.

Sending thematically consistent messages through a variety of media may sound familiar. In Chapter 1, we discussed how an organization must identify its values and then ensure that all its actions, including its communications, are consistent with those values.

As we said earlier, IMC recognizes the ineffectiveness of trying to use only the old mass media to affect masses of people. Instead, IMC uses a variety of media to communicate with small groups and, ideally, individuals. For example, Kimberly-Clark recently introduced its new Kleenex Cottonelle toilet paper to consumers through a $30-million television advertising campaign. However, it balanced that mass-media tactic with a more individualized approach: It hung 10 million free samples on doorknobs in the eastern United States.[15]

Free-sample tactics often include rebate offers or other special-value promotions that gather information for databases. Databases are an indispensable element in IMC campaigns. As we've noted, computerized databases do more than record names, locations, phone numbers, and e-mail addresses; they can record when, where, and how a product was purchased. Databases also can record when and how consumers were contacted, when and how they responded, and what the organization and the consumer said. Every contact with a consumer becomes a chance to refine the database.

Sending One Clear Message

If the database lies at the heart of successful integrated marketing communications, so does the philosophy of sending one clear message—or, at least, thematically consistent messages—to consumers. Generally, marketing public relations helps send that one consistent message. However, with its expertise in supplying newsworthy stories to the news media, on some occasions marketing public relations may send a slightly different message than do the other tactics in an IMC campaign.

For example, First Alert, Inc., maker of First Alert smoke detectors and carbon monoxide detectors, discovered a problem when it first prepared to market its carbon monoxide detectors. The marketing message of the First Alert carbon monoxide detector was simple: This product can save your life. So what was the problem?

QuickBreak 13.2

DIRECT MAIL: ALSO KNOWN AS JUNK MAIL

These days, you probably don't get many letters addressed to "Resident" or "Occupant." Instead, letters bearing invitations to purchase a product are addressed to you by name, not just on the envelope but in the letter as well.

Chances are the product being offered is something that at least moderately interests you: a magazine subscription or a credit card application, for example.

You can thank databases for those personal touches.

Direct mail—also sometimes known as junk mail—belongs to the bigger family of direct marketing, which is the opposite of mass marketing. Whereas mass marketing uses a popular medium such as network television to appeal to the masses, direct marketing targets potential customers one at a time, using as much personal information as possible. No wonder it's also called database marketing .

Direct marketers can purchase from list brokers lists of names of members of particular publics—for example, environmentalists between ages 18 and 45. *The Direct Marketing List Source,* published by Standard Rate and Data Service (SRDS), groups many of the available lists by category.

Direct marketing also exists in cyberspace, where its laziest manifestation is called **spamming.** Spamming usually involves collecting e-mail addresses from members of online interest groups, also known as **usenet groups** or **newsgroups.** Group members then receive the same promotional e-mail letter—spam—pitching the sender's products. Needless to say, spamming is poor netiquette. It ranks just above a system crash in cyberspace's Hall of Shame.

By using databases to focus on individuals, direct marketing can be an inexpensive and highly effective, though sometimes annoying, partner in an effective consumer-focused marketing campaign.

Wheatley Blair Inc., the public relations agency assisting in the launch of First Alert's new detector, discovered through research that the U.S. public didn't understand how dangerous carbon monoxide gas is.

"Most people didn't realize that every appliance in their home that runs on combustible fuel produces carbon monoxide every time it operates," said Bob Wheatley, a partner in Wheatley Blair. "They didn't understand that if appliances such as gas stoves, driers, fireplaces, furnaces, and water heaters aren't functioning properly, they can release into the home a gas that is odorless, colorless, and highly toxic."[16]

The bottom line of Wheatley Blair's research was this: Consumers might not respond to a marketing message stressing safety—because they didn't know that they were in danger.

Wheatley Blair and other members of the First Alert marketing team consequently crafted the following timetable and strategy. First, a public relations campaign targeting the news media would roll out. Mention of the First Alert carbon monoxide detector would be secondary; the campaign's primary goal would be to

Media Kit Materials Before safety-oriented advertisements for First Alert carbon monoxide detectors could work, consumers needed to learn of the dangers of the odorless, colorless, lethal gas. First Alert used media kits containing news releases, brochures, charts, and other material to inform news media about the dangers of carbon monoxide poisoning. (Courtesy of Wheatley Blair, Inc.)

emphasize the threat of carbon monoxide poisoning. The detector itself then would be shipped to ensure availability. Finally, the advertising campaign would roll out in October, the beginning of the home heating season.

"For the ads to really work well, you needed to have a basic knowledge of what carbon monoxide is, where it comes from, and why it's bad for you," said Wheatley. "Otherwise, you're not going to get it. What we did was to generate newspaper and TV stories all over the country on carbon monoxide poisoning. A lot of the headlines were 'Silent, deadly killer is invading your home.'"

Radio and TV placements were also key to the public relations campaign. Wheatley Blair helped generate stories on CBS, NBC, and CNN network news.

Wheatley Blair's campaign included personal calls to science and home products editors, a comprehensive media kit, video news releases, sponsorship of interviews with scientists and medical personnel, and a toll-free information number.

Wheatley Blair's news-media strategy succeeded in raising public awareness of the dangers of carbon monoxide from 2 percent of consumers to 75 percent, and the entire First Alert IMC campaign was a success. Representatives of Wal-Mart told the makers of First Alert that the new carbon monoxide detector was the most successful new product introduction, up to that time, in the history of Wal-Mart's hardware/home products department. For its role in the First Alert campaign, Wheatley Blair won a Silver Anvil, the highest award bestowed by the Public Relations Society of America.

"What we did, in essence," said Wheatley, "was use public relations to approach media vehicles that were highly credible. And that created an environment in which the advertising could work harder and be more effective than it might have been."

In most IMC campaigns, public relations sends the same message that other elements of the marketing process send. But, as the First Alert example shows, marketing public relations is flexible. By sending a slightly different preliminary message, public relations can help create receptivity for a subsequent IMC campaign.

Quick ✔ Check

1. What do public relations and IMC have in common? Is all of public relations part of IMC?
2. What are the five P's of marketing? What are the four C's of IMC?
3. What are some of the traditional tactics of marketing public relations?

How IMC Works

Professor Tom Duncan of the IMC graduate program at the University of Colorado at Boulder recommends starting an IMC campaign with an **IMC audit**. An IMC audit is similar in intent to the ethics audit (Chapter 6) and the communication audit (Chapter 7) we examined earlier in this book. As with all audits, the goal is to determine where an organization stands right now—and, perhaps, to make recommendations for future actions. Again and again, it's worth noting that the public relations process begins with good research.

Duncan recommends an IMC audit that consists of five steps:[17]

1. Analysis of the communications network used to develop marketing communications programs
2. Identification and prioritization of key stakeholder groups
3. Evaluation of the organization's customer databases
4. Content analysis of all messages (ads, public relations releases, packaging, video news releases, signage, sales promotion pieces, direct response mailings, etc.) used within the past year
5. Assessment of knowledge of, and attitudes toward, IMC on the part of marketing managers, top management, and key agency managers

With the information a marketing team gathers from an IMC audit, it forms a good idea of the environment from which it intends to launch an IMC campaign. If that environment is favorable to an IMC campaign, great! Full speed ahead. But if the audit shows that an organization has no customer database and a hodgepodge of contradictory marketing messages, then it must make some technological and philosophical changes before it can launch a successful IMC campaign. Perhaps the organization must even reexamine its core values in light of the proposed IMC campaign.

Creating an IMC Campaign

With an IMC audit completed, we now know where we are. But how do we get to where we want to be? Using our knowledge of current resources and attitudes, how do we build a successful IMC campaign? The following seven strategies are among several recommended by Matthew P. Gonring, vice president of corporate communications for Baxter International:[18]

1. *"Create shared performance measures. Develop systems to evaluate communications activities,"* Gonring advises. Recall Chapter 8 on planning: We need to have a goal and measurable objectives to prove to others the effectiveness of our program. Setting precise sales goals may be too ambitious—but we can certainly specify the number and nature of relationships that we intend to create.

2. *"Use database development and issues management to understand your stakeholders."* Here's another expert telling us that a database is essential to a successful IMC campaign. A database details the individual consumer wants and needs that have been identified through interactive communication with consumers. Issues management, as we noted in Chapter 7, is a process of identifying and managing emerging issues that can affect your organization and the publics important to your organization.

3. *"Identify all contact points for the company and its products."* Some experts recommend an even broader look at contact points, or **contacts.** *"Contacts* will likely be a new term for many advertising and promotion people, particularly the way it is used in IMC,"* say the authors of the book *Integrated Marketing Communications.*

Marketing Materials Bow-Dry, known as BowDry in some markets, is a ground-drying machine popular with managers of golf courses and other athletic fields. Its marketing team communicates one clear message—"Clears Standing Water Fast"—through a variety of marketing and public relations tactics, including these trade show materials. (Courtesy of Bowcom)

"We define a contact as any information-bearing experience that a customer or a prospect has with the brand, product category, or the market that relates to the marketer's product or service."[19]

4. *"Create business and communication plans for each local market."* As your IMC program improves, you may want to strive for the goal of developing a plan for every individual customer within your database. Ideally, all those messages to slightly different publics must be consistent with one another.

5. *"Create compatible themes, tones, and quality across all communications media."* Remember: All elements of the marketing process need to send consistent messages about your product.

6. *"Hire only team players."* Jealousy and insecurity can destroy an IMC campaign. Public relations practitioners can't always insist on using public relations tactics, nor can advertisers always insist on using advertising. Members of the IMC team must agree to use the messages and the media that consumers prefer.

7. *"Link IMC with management processes."* Robert Dilenschneider, the former head of Hill & Knowlton, one of the world's largest public relations agencies, offers solid advice: "Think in terms of what the manager wants to achieve, and tie everything you suggest to a financial or business result."[20]

If clearly identified consumer values, wants, and needs are shaping each step of your marketing process, from product design to follow-up after a purchase, the odds are good that you have a successful IMC campaign.

Applying IMC

Let's return to our record-store scenario for a moment. What sorts of strategies and tactics might an IMC campaign include? After doing an IMC audit and learning that your organization will support an integrated marketing approach, you gain agreement on a consistent message to be sent to potential customers: "Hard-to-find music at hard-to-beat prices." A quick scientific survey of potential customers shows that this is an effective message. Your mission now is to deliver that message effectively and to bring buyers into your stores. Among the tactics you might consider are

- developing a web site and including its address in all your communications. A web site can be a highly interactive medium, and interactive media can generate information for the database you decide to build.
- placing ads in student newspapers. The ads include your web address and a coupon. Consumers who answer the few questions on the coupon get a 10 percent discount. The coupons provide more information for your database.
- sponsoring alternative rock concerts and passing out flyers with coupons.
- offering your store managers to local media as experts on little-known but high-quality bands. You particularly try to place the managers on call-in radio shows, where direct interaction with potential customers is possible.

QuickBreak 13.3

UNSAFE HARBOR

With its many divisions such as IMC, CRM, and IBC, consumer-focused marketing can certainly seem complicated. But we can console ourselves by remembering that one constant is the database, right?

Well . . .

Worldwide database marketing sustained a serious blow in 1998 when the European Union, a league of 15 European nations, began implementing its Directive on Data Protection. Multinational companies based in the United States read its provisions with a chorus of groans and gnashing teeth. The directive established these rules for organizations using database marketing in the European Union:

- Organizations cannot gather and record information in databases without the permission of each consumer to be included in the database.

- Organizations must have a single, well-defined purpose for collecting consumer information and must explain that purpose to each included consumer.

- Organizations must publicize how included consumers can review and correct information in the database.

- Organizations can use the database only for the original purpose. A proposed new use of the database's information requires each included consumer's permission and the launch of a new, separate database.

- Organizations cannot transfer database information to nations outside the European Union that do not have equally stringent database laws. (This would prohibit database information from flowing to the United States.)[21]

Organizations that do not meet these legal requirements cannot use any form of database marketing in European Union nations.

Urged on by U.S.-based multinational companies, officials of the U.S. Department of Commerce negotiated a so-called safe harbor agreement with officials of the European Commission, the administrative branch of the European Union. The agreement allows U.S.-based companies to import information from its European databases if they provide consumers a chance to "opt out" of the new database. High-tech giants with worldwide customers, such as Microsoft, Intel, and Hewlett-Packard, immediately sailed into the safe harbor. Unfortunately, the waters there have been anything but calm.

"The European Commission and the United States are again at loggerheads over the free flow of data from Europe to U.S. companies, only eight months after the two sides reached an agreement on 'safe harbor' provisions," reported *DM News,* a direct marketing publication, in April 2001.[22] Disagreements about U.S. organizations not in the safe harbor sparked the new debate.

And the choppy waters of the safe harbor agreement apply only to European database information flowing to the United States—not to U.S. companies' databases maintained in Europe for European consumers. The American Marketing Association has concluded, "Marketers at home should prepare to adjust their direct mail and database marketing practices to conform to European privacy standards—even if it means having to operate separate customer service and customer relationship management systems."

Meanwhile, New Zealand has adopted database laws similar to those of the European Union, and other countries are considering such restrictions.[23]

IMC, CRM, and IBC may not travel well beyond the U.S.A.

- mailing a brief newsletter to all the names in your database. In the newsletter, you offer to e-mail the newsletter instead of mailing it. Consumers can request that service by visiting your web site. You could simply spam everyone in your database, but you wisely decide not to do so.

- launching a direct e-mail campaign that lets customers know when one of their favorite bands has released a new CD. You know each customer's favorite bands because that information is in your database. You use e-mail because students move so often that street addresses are unreliable and because e-mail is more permanent than a phone call. And, of course, you send such messages only to students who agree, in advance, that they want them. In those messages you ask students to let you know whether they're interested in other bands as well.

For each of the above tactics, you also would establish some measures of evaluation. Evaluation of your tactics would help you determine which are most successful in helping your company achieve its marketing goals.

You can probably think of more and better ideas, but note what the above tactics have in common: They deliver approximately the same consumer-focused message, they tend to target individuals rather than mass audiences, they're not limited to traditional public relations and advertising tactics, they're interactive, and they seek information for an increasingly detailed database.

Hey, give yourself a raise.

Problems with 21st-Century Marketing

We hope you're excited about IMC, CRM, and the other approaches to consumer-focused marketing. However, we also hope that you're realistic. These relatively new approaches to marketing still face problems that can limit their effectiveness.

We've already hinted at one: jealousy, or so-called turf battles, with every member of the marketing team promoting only his or her own area of expertise. Two of the tactics described earlier in this chapter—conducting an IMC audit and hiring only team players—can help eliminate this problem.

A second problem in consumer-focused marketing involves technology. As databases become more sophisticated, their costs often rise and their complexity increases, causing some organizations to approach modern marketing with lower-level, insufficient technology. One study in Great Britain predicted that 70 percent of customer relationship management programs will fail to meet their goals, partly because of inadequate technology and training.[24]

A third problem in consumer-focused marketing is privacy. As noted in Quick-Break 13.3, the United States and the European Union have different standards regarding consumers' rights to privacy. And within the United States, concern for individual privacy increases as marketers seek more and more information on individuals. A 1999 survey of marketing professionals in the midwestern United States found that 74 percent favored government intervention to ensure additional privacy

clears
standing water fast!

Golf Course Owners & Superintendents

Casual water has many costs:

Lost Revenue!
Hundreds of dollars per hour in greens fees can be lost for just a 1/2 hour delay. The quicker you remove the water, the quicker you open the course.

Increased Maintenance Time!
Capable of removing (not pushing!) water at nearly 15 gallons per minute, Bow-Dry can do the job of 6 squeegees. Superintendents spend less time on water removal, more time on course care!

Disappointing Tournaments!
Water may not stop an important tournament, but it can still ruin it! Bow-Dry was present (and used!) at the 2000 Solheim Cup and Cisco World Cup Match Play in Europe!

Reputation!
Customers remember casual water on greens and fairways. They also remember what your club does to take care of it. Using Bow-Dry lets them know you're doing the most for them AND your course!

Damaged Turf!
The longer water stays on ANY turf...fairways, greens, tee boxes ....the greater the chance for costly damage. Remove it fast with Bow-Dry!

Magazine Advertisement   Marketing tactics for Bow-Dry include a magazine advertisement that, like other tactics in the Bow-Dry campaign, delivers the key message—this time in the headline. (Courtesy of Bowcom)

for consumers; only 7 percent strongly opposed government intervention. The authors of the study concluded, "The respondents . . . want legislation to protect privacy even though it might encroach upon their professional activities, partially to suppress their culpability and also because they desire such protections in their own lives."[25]

Finally, the very nature of consumer-focused marketing can be a problem. Excessive focus on consumers' desires could pull a company away from its core values. An organization that lives only to satisfy the whims of consumers may well lack the deeply felt, enduring values that characterize successful organizations. Consumer-focused marketing will succeed best when it operates on a solid foundation of organizational values. "The integrity of the corporation that stands behind the brand is even more important than the marketing or promoting of the brand itself," says Frank Vogl, president of Vogl Communications in Washington, D.C. "So many people involved in the integrated marketing and communications of corporate brands have not paid adequate attention to the values that should be seen at the core of the brand itself."[26]

No one can deny that consumer-focused marketing faces serious challenges. However, at the beginning of the 21st century, the new, database-driven approaches to marketing offer significant opportunities for public relations practitioners.

Quick ✔ Check

1. What is an IMC audit? What steps does it involve?
2. In marketing, what is a contact or contact point?
3. Why are team players essential to a successful IMC campaign?

Summary

Consumer-focused marketing is not a passing fad. It's a growing reality for organizations that want their products to have clear, consistent, appealing images in the marketplace. It's also a growing expectation on the part of consumers, who seek more and more individual attention from organizations as new technologies make such communication possible. Unlike mass marketing, consumer-focused marketing begins not with a public but with an individual. Products are designed to accommodate, as much as possible, individual needs and desires. Sales messages focus on those same individual self-interests, which are discovered through two-way communication and are recorded in databases.

Integrated marketing communications unites a variety of communications tactics to address individual self-interests: advertising, public relations, marketing promotions, packaging, pricing, direct mail, and any other approach that can send an effective message to a potential customer. Despite the wide array of available tactics, the messages in an IMC campaign are integrated: Consumers should receive a consistent message about an organization's product or service. The message of an advertisement, for example, should be consistent with the message of the price and of a product-oriented news release.

Not all of public relations is part of consumer-focused marketing, of course. Marketing addresses one very important public: consumers. Public relations builds relationships with any public that can affect an organization's success, including employees, stockholders, and government regulators. But one of the most exciting areas in the future of public relations is its role in consumer-focused marketing. In the 21st century, marketing means building relationships with individual consumers, and that's good news for public relations.

DISCUSSION QUESTIONS

1. How are the philosophies of public relations and consumer-focused marketing similar? How are they different?
2. What is "integrated" about integrated marketing communications?
3. What are the benefits of using consumer-focused marketing instead of mass marketing?
4. Does IMC, as it is currently practiced, have any problems or potential problems?
5. How is an IMC audit similar to an ethics audit and a communication audit?

Memo
from the
Field

Vin Cipolla, Chairman and CEO, HNW Inc., New York and Boston

Vin Cipolla is chairman and CEO of HNW Inc., a New York– and Boston-based marketing company that provides research, strategies, and tactics to help clients build lasting relationships with high-net-worth consumers. Its clients include UBS PaineWebber, Merrill Lynch, and Citigroup Private Bank.

Before joining HNW, Cipolla was founder and president of Pamet Inc., an integrated marketing communications company. Cipolla is director emeritus of the Electronic Frontier Foundation and has served as vice chairman of that organization. His community service includes leadership positions with the National Trust for Historic Preservation and the American Repertory Theater.

Cipolla is a Phi Beta Kappa graduate of Clark University.

There's a very good reason why integrated marketing has become so popular lately. Basically, without it, we marketers are doomed. In fact, when a company doesn't present a consistent marketing message to the public, it not only wastes a lot of money, it also risks its own reputation.

But that's not all. These days it's not enough for marketing functions like advertising, PR, and direct mail to work together. Now, marketing needs to be integrated throughout the entire company—with departments like customer service, sales, distribution, and manufacturing all working together on corporate objectives. The goal today is to make certain that everyone in the company is conveying the same message. Not just the marketing department.

Not convinced? Think about it. Imagine watching a heartwarming television advertisement promoting a particular airline's commitment to friendly service. Now, the next time you fly, you certainly expect that airline's in-flight personnel to be extra friendly, right? You certainly expect that airline to have spent as much effort maintaining high customer service standards as it did creating that expensive television advertisement.

The fact is, we expect more now as consumers than we did a few years ago. Interactive technology, web sites, and sophisticated database marketing have all raised the standard of customer service by facilitating dynamic two-way communication between business and consumers. Today it's not enough simply to sell products; companies must also build relationships with customers if they want to compete.

For example, consumers like to feel remembered and appreciated. That's one reason why some mail-order companies have started to track customer orders more effectively. Perhaps the next time you call, they may thank you for your repeat order and ask if you'd like the same size as before. It's that type of personal attention that is becoming the new norm.

That level of integration isn't easy to achieve. It requires a centralized database in which every customer contact position (e.g., billing, marketing, and service) is integrated so that valuable customer data is captured, analyzed, and maximized fully. That's a challenge. Maybe that centralized customer data isn't available yet. Or maybe it is, but the company doesn't know how to interpret it so the data provides valuable insight.

Another problem may be the company's own staff. Internal power struggles are responsible for the failure of many integrated marketing programs. Unfortunately, many employees aren't trained to work in cross-departmental partnerships. Finance managers speak a different language than marketing managers. Customer service has different priorities than sales. And rarely is there a company incentive for these disparate employees to work together in teams on company goals.

That's why the most successful companies have strong leadership at the top. Only the CEO or president has the authority to cross so many departmental borders. Without that senior-level support, a truly effective integrated marketing program will remain a distant dream.

So what does all this mean for you? It means your job just became a lot more difficult. Now you don't just need to work well with other marketing divisions. You also need to work well with customer service, billing, and distribution too.

The more you understand how the entire company functions, the better you'll perform your own job. The more you understand what these various managers consider important, the easier a time you'll have working with them on the corporate goals. And, finally, the more you understand how emerging technology is impacting marketing, the more successfully you'll play by today's new marketing rules.

As you take on the challenge, I wish you all the luck in the world.

Case Study 13.1

Revolvolution

In the 1990 movie *Crazy People,* comedian Dudley Moore plays an advertising executive who disavows exaggeration and pledges that his advertisements will feature only the truth. His new slogan for Volvo automobiles? "Boxy—but good."

Audiences laughed, but Volvo executives groaned.

They groaned again in 1998 when Robert Sevier, author of *Integrated Marketing for Colleges,* said, "If you want safety in cars, it's Volvo."[27]

Ask any baby boomer about Volvo's image, and you'll probably get an answer like this: "Well built, very safe—but they look like a shoebox on wheels."

Volvo executives have nothing against safety; their cars are renowned throughout the world for engineering that protects drivers and passengers. But they wanted a broader image. They wanted a new generation of consumers to think of Volvos as—stylish.

Enter a "revolvolution," Volvo's term for the expansion of its image. In 2001, Volvo launched a high-tech integrated marketing communications campaign "to redefine the way the Volvo brand is viewed by consumers."[28]

Volvo tied the campaign to one of the biggest media events of the year: college basketball's March Madness national tournament. One lucky basketball fan would win a Volvo S60 sports sedan, the car designed to prove that Volvos could be both safe and stylish. On March 15, Volvo launched an integrated series of tactics that featured a consistent message and that strove to lead consumers to a Revolvolution web site. Once at the web site, consumers could fill out a simple survey and enter other contests with prizes such as tickets to the tournament's championship game. Information from that survey would, of course, go into Volvo's consumer database.

Public relations kicked off the campaign. Through PR Newswire, a news release distribution service, Volvo sent online news releases describing the campaign and the contests to automotive and technology journalists throughout the United States.

Next came television commercials. Volvo ran the ads throughout the basketball tournament, promoting the S60 and directing viewers to the Revolvolution web site, where they could enter the contests. The company also announced the national winner of the S60 during a live webcast on its Revolvolution site.

Volvo placed web ads on CBS's Sportsline.com, a web site operated by the television network that broadcast the tournament. Like the television ads, the web ads directed consumers to the Revolvolution web site.

WebTV viewers were able to use their interactive televisions to click through Volvo ads and enter the S60 contest. Similar technology allowed users of wireless personal digital assistants and telephones to enter Volvo's contest. When sports fans used those devices to check game scores, they received brief invitations to enter the contest. Consumers who submitted entries without visiting the Revolvolution web site received e-mails informing them of the site and of the opportunities to complete a survey and enter additional contests.

Despite this diversity, the tactics had much in common. Most targeted individuals, not mass audiences; most were interactive and sought additional information from consumers; and, in the best spirit of integrated marketing, all delivered a consistent message: The S60 was safe and stylish.

"The language and the graphics and so forth were very branded to Volvo," said Arthur Ceria, interactive creative director of Fuel North America, one of the agencies that assisted Volvo with the campaign.[29]

Volvo also tried to ensure that neither the campaign nor the requests for information annoyed consumers. "This integrated campaign was all about not being intrusive," Ceria said. "We weren't pushing the users to go through a long experience. It was up to them to decide what information they wanted to give."[30]

Volvo's IMC campaign seems to be working. Beginning in April 2001, when the March Madness promotion ended, Volvo reeled off five straight months of improved sales, culminating in record sales for August 2001. And among the sales leaders was the S60. "Business was very impressive across most of our car lines," said Vic Doolan, CEO of Volvo Cars of North America. "However, the V70 Cross Country and the S60 are really distinguishing themselves."[31]

Volvo's image problems may have become famous in a movie called *Crazy People*, but thanks to an integrated marketing campaign that emphasized one clear message, that largely targeted individual consumers, that built and used a database, and that integrated a variety of interactive tactics, the only crazy people around may be the ones who still think Volvos are boxy and boring.

DISCUSSION QUESTIONS

1. Has Volvo's revolvolution succeeded? What is your image of Volvo cars?
2. What qualities made Volvo's revolvolution marketing campaign an IMC campaign?
3. Why do you think the revolvolution campaign began with public relations tactics?
4. In your opinion, was Volvo gambling by avoiding conventional media in favor of high-tech new media?
5. Can you name other products that have sought to change or expand their images? Did they succeed?

Case Study 13.2
_____

Reebok and the Incubus

On February 18, 1997, Peter Jennings closed ABC's *World News Tonight* with this story:

> Finally this evening, the great shoe mess and how the giant maker of sports shoes, Reebok, stepped right into it. When we heard today from our affiliate in Phoenix, Arizona, about what Reebok had called one of its running shoes for women—well, even Reebok agreed it was a mess. ABC's Judy Muller on the strange case of the Incubus.[32]

Why a strange case? And what's an incubus? The answers to those questions describe a marketing campaign gone awry.

Reebok makes athletic shoes and athletic apparel. Like all organizations, it also sometimes makes mistakes. And sometimes it makes a doozy.

In the mid-1990s Reebok launched a new running shoe for women: the Incubus. In 1996 it shipped more than 50,000 pairs at a retail price of $57.99.

So what does *incubus* mean? London's *Financial Times* reported that Reebok chose the word because it sounded like *incubate,* a name that the company's marketers hoped would conjure up images of comfort and rebirth.[33]

Sounds reasonable. But what does *incubus* mean? Before using it, Reebok did ensure that the name wasn't trademarked.

That was prudent. But, really, what does *incubus* mean? Fortunately, although the name was on the shoe box and in marketing materials, it wasn't on the shoe itself.

Enough stalling: What does *incubus* mean? Turns out that no one at headquarters had consulted a dictionary. Had Reebok marketers done so, they might have encountered this definition, from *The American Heritage Dictionary* (3rd edition): "Incubus: An evil spirit believed to descend upon and have sexual intercourse with women as they sleep."

On *World News Tonight,* Judy Muller shared a similar definition with America.

"I'm horrified, and the company is horrified," a Reebok representative immediately told the Associated Press. "How the name got on the shoe and went forward, I do not know. We are a company that has built its business on women's footwear, so to do anything that's denigrating to women is not what we're about."

The day after the fateful ABC broadcast, a Reuter's story quoted another Reebok representative as saying, "We apologize. Certainly it is very inappropriate. . . . Obviously, it became very apparent to us yesterday why nobody else [had trademarked] the name."

Reebok's marketers sought to convey a consistent image of warmth and nurturing for the new shoe. Instead, the name undercut that message with suggestions of evil and terror.

As all young romantics know, Shakespeare's Juliet innocently said, "What's in a name? that which we call a rose / By any other name would smell as sweet." Marketers, however, are supposed to know better. When Juliet ignored the power of names and what they stand for, she helped bring about her own death. Reebok's tragedy wasn't exactly of Shakespearean proportions, but it's a safe bet that every marketer in the company now has a dictionary within easy reach.

DISCUSSION QUESTIONS

1. How is a product's name part of an IMC campaign?
2. What do you think of Reebok's response to the disaster?
3. If you had been a Reebok official at the time, what actions, if any, would you have suggested that the company take to end the problem and repair the damage?
4. What stories have you heard about other badly named products?

It's Your Turn

Making the Pitch

The Women's National Professional Softball Association is a new sports league that will launch in 18 communities throughout the United States at the beginning of the next baseball season. One of the franchises will play in a new stadium just a few miles from your college or university. The owners wisely have hired you as the team's marketing director, and they are requesting an integrated marketing campaign.

Your team is named The Sluggers, and although it has no household-name stars, it features several superb athletes and has realistic hopes of winning the league's first championship.

The new league has conducted extensive marketing research, which shows that women's professional softball appeals to the following groups:

- female "tweens," girls between ages 9 and 14;
- families with children ages 6 to 12;
- female athletes of all ages;
- college-age females and their dates;
- single males in their early to mid-20s; and
- members of women's organizations, such as the National Organization for Women.

Ticket prices are a bargain—the most expensive seats are $10—and the league office has lined up dozens of corporate sponsors who, at different games, will give away softballs, ball caps, T-shirts, and other sports-related merchandise. Your team hopes to draw fans from everywhere within 60 miles of the ballpark, and you have a small but adequate marketing budget.

The owners of your team have several questions for you. Using your knowledge of the region surrounding your college or university, please answer these questions:

1. What specific groups would you target as potential fans?
2. What message would you send to each group?

3. In sending those messages, what specific advertising tactics and media would you use? What specific public relations tactics? What marketing or promotional tactics? What direct-mail tactics, if any? (Sometimes the distinctions between these categories may be blurred.)

4. How could you establish interactive communications to gather information for your database? What kind of information would you want in your database?

5. Near the end of the regular season, how might you use the database you've built to help sell tickets to the play-offs?

You'll do extensive research in the coming months, of course; but what are your first answers to these questions? The owners are waiting. . . .

KEY TERMS

advertising, p. 424

contacts, p. 435

customer relationship management (CRM), p. 426

database marketing, p. 426

databases, p. 423

direct mail, p. 432

IMC audit, p. 434

integrated brand communication, p. 426

integrated marketing communications (IMC), p. 423

marketing, p. 424

marketing mix, p. 428

marketing public relations, p. 425

newsgroups, p. 432

public relations, p. 424

relationship marketing, p. 426

spamming, p. 432

usenet groups, p. 432

NOTES

1. E.W. Brody, "PR Is to Experience What Marketing Is to Expectations," *Public Relations Quarterly* 39, no. 2 (1994), online, Lexis-Nexis.

2. Scot Hume, "Integrated Marketing: Who's in Charge Here?" *Advertising Age*, 22 March 1992, online, Lexis-Nexis.

3. "Will Database Marketing Work in Health Care?" *Marketing Health Services* (fall 2001), online, Lexis-Nexis.

4. John Dalla Costa, *The Ethical Imperative* (Reading, Mass.: Addison-Wesley, 1998), 178.

5. "Customer Relationship Management Programs: New Hot Business Issue," a news release issued by PR Newswire, 28 August 2001, online, Lexis-Nexis.

6. Don E. Schultz and Beth E. Barnes, *Strategic Brand Communication Campaigns* (Lincolnwood, Ill.: NTC Business Books, 1999), 44.

7. William P. Ehling, Jon White, and James E. Grunig, "Public Relations and Marketing Practices," in *Excellence in Public Relations and Communication Management*, ed. James E. Grunig (Hillsdale, N.J.: Lawrence Erlbaum, 1992), 390.

8. Glen M. Broom, Martha M. Lauzen, and Kerry Tucker, "Public Relations and Marketing: Dividing the Conceptual Domain and Operational Turf," *Public Relations Review* (fall 1991): 224, 223.

9. Ehling, White, and Grunig, 378; Schultz and Barnes, 5.

10. Dave Barry, "North Dakota Name Change Lacks Direction," *Lawrence Journal-World,* 12 August 2001, 9B.

11. Don E. Schultz, Stanley I. Tannenbaum, and Robert F. Lauterborn, *Integrated Marketing Communications* (Chicago: NTC Business Books, 1993), 22.

12. Betsy Spethmann, "Jerky Match," *Promo* (February 2000), online, Lexis-Nexis.

13. Schultz, Tannenbaum, and Lauterborn, 107.

14. Schultz, Tannenbaum, and Lauterborn, 12–13.

15. Tara Parker Pope, "The Tricky Business of Rolling Out a New Toilet Paper," *Wall Street Journal,* 12 January 1998, B1.

16. Bob Wheatley, telephone interview by author, 24 March 1994.

17. Tom Duncan, "Is Your Marketing Communications Integrated?" *Advertising Age* (24 January 1994), online, Lexis-Nexis.

18. Matthew P. Gonring, "Putting Integrated Marketing Communications to Work Today," *Public Relations Quarterly* 39, no. 3 (1994), online, Lexis-Nexis.

19. Schultz, Tannenbaum, and Lauterborn, 51.

20. Cliff McGoon, "Secrets of Building Influence," *Communication World* (March 1995): 18.

21. Eve M. Caudill and Patrick E. Murphy, "Consumer Online Privacy: Legal and Ethical Issues," *Marketing and Public Policy* (spring 2000), online, Lexis-Nexis; Ross D. Petty, "Marketing without Consent: Consumer Choice and Costs, Privacy, and Public Policy" (spring 2000), online, Lexis-Nexis; Bodo Schegelmilch, *Marketing Ethics: An International Perspective* (London: International Thomson Business Press, 1998), 100.

22. Thomas Weyr, "U.S., E.C. Bicker over Free Data Flow," *DM News,* 9 April 2001, online, Lexis-Nexis.

23. Schlegelmilch, 101–102.

24. "Seven Out of 10 CRM Projects Will Fail," a news release issued by Global News Wire, 17 August 2001, online, Lexis-Nexis.

25. Stuart L. Esrock and John P. Ferré, "A Dichotomy of Privacy: Personal and Professional Attitudes of Marketers," *Business and Society Review* (spring 1999): 113, 121, 123.

26. "Enviro Activists Use Ethics to Drive Powerful PR Strategies," *PR News,* 12 March 2001, online, Lexis-Nexis.

27. Jamie Smith, "Put Out the Word: University Sets Branding Example," *Marketing News TM,* 7 May 2001, online, Lexis-Nexis.

28. "Volvo Cars of North America Pioneers World's First Fully Integrated Interactive Television Advertising Promotion," a news release issued by Volvo Cars of North America, 16 March 2001, online, Lexis-Nexis.

29. Sandy Hunter, "Interactive: Some of Those Clever Folks Bent on Dragging Advertising into the 21st Century Speak Out," *Boards,* 1 May 2001, online, Lexis-Nexis.

30. Hunter.

31. "Volvo Continues to Post Record Sales," a news release issued by Volvo Cars of North America, 4 September 2001, online, Lexis-Nexis.

32. Judy Muller and Peter Jennings, *ABC World News Tonight,* 18 February 1997, online, Lexis-Nexis.

33. "Foot in Mouth," *Financial Times,* 24 February 1997, online, Lexis-Nexis.

chapter fourteen

Cross-Cultural Communication

objectives

After studying this chapter, you will be able to

- describe broad areas that historically have distinguished one culture from another

- explain the differences between a culture and a public

- discuss traditional obstacles to successful cross-cultural communication

- describe a nine-step process organizations and individuals can use to achieve effective cross-cultural communication

East Meets West

You are the new senior communications specialist for a multinational producer of breakfast cereals. Your company is based in the United States, and your are eager to begin traveling internationally. You've been to Mexico and Canada but have never been overseas. The director of corporate communications has just asked you to launch a magazine for employees in the three countries in which your company operates: the United States, Spain, and Japan.

You quickly learn the names of the company's senior communications officials in Spain and Japan and, with the director's permission, invite them to the United States to help plan the magazine. You know that a lot rides on the success of these meetings. You're new with the company, and you want to impress your employers. Your guests from Spain and Japan report to you, and you don't want them to entertain doubts about their new boss. And you know that the director of corporate communications wants a great magazine that will impress the company's chief executive officer.

As the three-day meeting approaches, you're excited as you review the preparations. You've scheduled a comfortable meeting room, reserved tables in your city's best restaurants, and arranged entertainment for two evenings. You're startled, however, when a colleague asks about cultural differences.

Cultural differences? You will be dealing with individuals from highly developed economies who, in addition to their native languages, speak fluent English. Could there really be important cultural differences? And could those differences affect the success of your magazine project?

That's a risk you must avoid, but what can you do? How do you cope with the challenges of cross-cultural communication?

Cultures: Realities and Definitions

The job seemed easy for the U.S.-based poultry company: It wanted to translate its English-language slogan—"It takes a tough man to make a tender chicken"—into Spanish. But the Spanish rendition may have startled Hispanic consumers: "It takes a sexually aroused man to make a chick affectionate."[1]

Affection was in short supply when insurance giant Aetna acquired U.S. Healthcare, creating what should have been an $8.3-billion corporate juggernaut. However, Aetna's stock prices plunged as employees and customers alike reeled from the jagged collision of two wholly different corporate cultures. Almost two years after the acquisition, the *Hartford Courant*, Aetna's hometown newspaper, reported, "Some Aetna employees are still suffering culture shock from the corporate marriage. . . . Some Aetna employees complain that U.S. Healthcare . . . put Aetna values on the back burner."[2]

Promoters of a Seattle-area rave—a huge, uninhibited dance party—unintentionally offended Muslims in 2001 when they lifted Arabic passages from the Koran, the holy book of Islam, to decorate a brochure. Devout Muslims honor the Koran so much that they wash their hands and mouths three times before touching and reading from the book.

"This is a disgrace to Islam," said a spokesman for a Seattle mosque. "The activities in raves are totally immoral."

The brochure's designer apologized and confessed that he found the passages in a school textbook. "We had no idea what any of it meant," he said. "It looked good on [the brochure]. It is a beautiful language. And we had a desert and a camel in there. It was a theme."[3]

The theme of these three anecdotes is cross-cultural communication. Each of these damaging mishaps occurred when different cultures intentionally or unintentionally met. In each case, important values were at issue. Those values grew, in part, out of **demographics** (nonattitudinal characteristics), **psychographics** (attitudinal characteristics), and **geographics** (behavioral patterns based on where a person or group lives). But the values grew from more than these three "-graphics." The values shaped and were shaped by unique cultures.

The term **culture,** in the sense of a group of people unified by shared characteristics, defies precise definition. "It seems obvious from the use of the word in our everyday language that it is impregnated with multiple meanings," says Anindita Niyogi Balslev of the Center for Cultural Research in the Netherlands.[4] In fact, as early as 1952 scholars had identified more than 150 definitions of *culture.*[5] The *Dictionary of Anthropology* defines a culture as "a social group that is smaller than a civilization but larger than an industry,"[6] with *industry* being an anthropological term for a small community. A culture, therefore, is usually larger than a public. In fact, a culture may consist of countless different publics, all of which are influenced by the traits of that culture.

Communication errors such as those of the poultry company, Aetna, and the Seattle rave occur because, in the words of Stephen Banks, author of *Multicultural Public Relations,* "scant attention is paid in research or practice to the predicaments of culturally diverse populations and the necessity for learning to communicate effectively across cultural differences."[7] In 2001, a representative of the National Association of Corporate Directors recommended that, to negotiate successfully with diverse cultures throughout the world, each U.S. business should create an Office of Foreign Affairs to study trends, politics, moods, and opinions in regions where the business wishes to operate.[8] The authors of this book respectfully suggest that such an office should already exist: the organization's public relations department.

International Public Relations

Not all cross-cultural communication involves relationships between two nations. For example, Aetna's acquisition of U.S. Healthcare involved the awkward merger of two business cultures. And the wealth of ethnic groups within the United States, Canada, and other nations can make cross-cultural communication an everyday experience. In the current global economy, however, when public relations practitioners study unfamiliar cultures, they often are studying consumers and business partners in other nations. "Cultural diversity and identity," says the author of *Multicultural Public Relations,* "tend strongly to conform to national borders."[9] For example, a recent survey of European tourists found that 25 percent of visitors to Italy went there hoping for a love affair with an Italian male. Only Italy's natural beauty scored higher; the lovers outscored museums and other attractions. Right or wrong, a large percentage of European tourists believe that romance and passion are cultural characteristics of Italian males.[10]

Musician Randy Newman has a satirical song that envisions the world becoming "just another American town"—a humorously offbeat premise for a song but a disastrous notion for international public relations. If the world were a town, it would be stunningly diverse—not at all a representation of a culture familiar to most readers of this book. In 2001, *Fast Company* magazine reported that if the world were a village of 100 people, current worldwide demographic and psychographic ratios would make the village look like this:[11]

- 80 residents would be non-white.
- 67 would be non-Christian.
- 60 would be Asians.
- 50 would be female.
- 25 would live in substandard housing.
- 20 would earn 89 percent of the village's wealth.
- 13 would suffer from malnutrition.
- 12 would be Europeans.
- 9 would be Latin Americans.
- 5 would be North Americans.
- 4 would own a computer.
- 2 would have a college education.

Successful international public relations recognizes such diversity and attempts to create harmonious, productive relationships through well-researched cross-cultural communication.

Cultural Attributes

Without a research strategy, studying a different culture can seem impossible. Where do we start? What information should we gather? Fortunately, social scientists and business experts have created systems for categorizing important cultural attributes. One of the best-known systems was created by marketing professional Marlene Rossman.[12] Rossman's system distinguishes among cultures by analyzing attitudes regarding eight characteristics. Let's examine each to see how it can differ from culture to culture.

Attitudes about Time

Different cultures have different attitudes about time. In some Latin American nations, a dinner party scheduled for 8:00 P.M. may not really begin until near midnight.

In other cultures, arriving later than 8:00 P.M. would insult your hosts. In some cultures, a designated time is a flexible guideline; in others, it is a specific target. On a working vacation in Zurich, Switzerland, one of your authors was warned by Swiss colleagues to avoid the center of the city on a particular Thursday afternoon; college students would be holding a spontaneous demonstration at that time, he was told. A scheduled spontaneous demonstration: something to be expected from a nation famed for making clocks and other timepieces.

In a study of national attitudes toward time, *American Demographics* magazine reported that, of 31 nations studied, Switzerland ranked first in terms of a rapid, time-oriented pace of life. The United States ranked in the middle at number 16, and Mexico ranked last. In general, Japan and Western European countries had the fastest pace of life. Developing nations in Africa, Asia, the Middle East, and Latin America had the slowest, most flexible pace.[13]

In our East Meets West scenario, differing attitudes toward time could affect the success of your meetings. Like North Americans, Japanese tend to be punctual about business meetings. If a meeting is scheduled for 9:00 A.M., businesspeople in Japan and the United States generally are ready to sit at the table and begin at that hour. In Spain, however, businesspeople are more casual about specified starting times. Roger Axtell, author of *Do's and Taboos around the World*, says that in Spain "the only time punctuality is taken seriously is when attending a bullfight."[14] Is that wrong? No: It's just different.

And how about early-afternoon meetings? No problem for your Japanese guest, but will your Spanish guest expect a traditional siesta at that time? In Spain and several other nations in Europe and Latin America, businesses often close from lunch until late afternoon.

Attitudes about Formality

Should you address a new business associate from another nation by his or her first name? Should you hug? Bow? Shake hands? The answers depend, of course, on cultural preferences. As a rule, however, formality is safer than informality in new business relationships.

Syrians often embrace new acquaintances. Pakistanis shake hands, though never a man with a woman. Zambians shake hands with the left hand supporting the right. Norwegians rarely use first names until relationships are well established. Japanese almost never use first names in business settings.

What do cross-cultural experts say about the visitors you're expecting for your magazine-planning meeting? A warm handshake and even an accompanying pat on the back would be acceptable as you greet your Spanish visitor. The Spanish make no distinction about shaking hands with men or women. With your Japanese guest, however, be prepared to bow, even though he or she may offer to shake hands. You can flatter your Japanese guest by bowing first. In Japan, the person who initiates a bow is acknowledging the high social status of the other person. If you exchange business cards with your Japanese visitor, bow slightly and extend yours with both hands. You should accept your visitor's card in the same manner and should look at it respectfully after receiving it.[15]

Attitudes about Individualism

People in the United States pride themselves on the rugged individualism that turned a diverse group of immigrants into a powerful nation of highly mobile individuals. It's comparatively rare in our society to live one's life in the town of one's birth surrounded by family. Other cultures, however, especially those of Asian and Hispanic origin, often place more emphasis on preserving extended families. Chinese names, for example, place the family name before the individual name.

Japanese businesspeople in particular see themselves as part of a team; in fact, only 8 percent of Japanese adults say they respect entrepreneurs.[16] An individual may speak on behalf of an organization, but not until he or she has painstakingly built consensus on the issue under discussion. The Japanese call the consensus-building process

Business Card The exchange of business cards with colleagues from Asian nations can be more formal than the casual exchanges that characterize business in the United States.

nemawashi; it precedes virtually all important organizational decisions. "As a result," says Sanae Kobayashi, an executive with LBS Company in Tokyo, "decision making in Japanese organizations usually takes more time than it does in the West. However, as compensation, in Japan the execution is made with more speed and completeness."[17]

Because of the importance of *nemawashi* throughout their culture, the Japanese are reluctant to say no. In your magazine-planning meeting, for example, it would be unusual for your Japanese guest to veto a particular proposal. Instead, he or she might meet the idea with thoughtful silence and a polite "If only . . ."

Attitudes about Rank and Hierarchy

In cultural terms, rank and hierarchy extend beyond organizations: They exist within society itself. India, for example, still struggles to overthrow a traditional caste system of Brahmans—often Hindu priests—at the top and so-called untouchables at the bottom. Knowing the social status of a business associate and understanding the consequent signs of respect he or she expects can be essential to successful cross-cultural communications. For example, your Spanish guest would be honored to be seated at your right during meals—a sign of respect in Spain. And when you initiate a bowing sequence with your Japanese guest, you courteously suggest that he or she outranks you.[18]

Attitudes about Religion

Knowing the religious conventions and traditions of a culture can help prevent unintended errors that can hamper cross-cultural communication. For example, Muslims fast from dawn to sunset during the holy month of Ramadan. Inviting an Islamic business associate to a working lunch during that time could inadvertently suggest a lack of respect for his or her religious beliefs. The Jewish Sabbath extends from Friday evening to Saturday evening and, in Judaism, is a day of rest. Scheduling a Friday evening business dinner in Israel, where Judaism is the dominant religion, could be a serious cultural faux pas.

In October 1998, the frantic pace of round-the-clock U.S.-sponsored negotiations between the Palestine Liberation Organization and Israel was due in part to the desire to sign a pact before sundown on a Friday. The delegations had met for nine days, and negotiators feared that a 24-hour delay for the Sabbath might stall the mo-

THE MELTING-POT MYTH

Much of this chapter focuses on cultures beyond the borders of the United States. Can we assume, then, that the United States is a uniform hot-dogs-and-apple-pie culture? Hardly.

"Population shifts during the 1990s show continued geographic concentrations of minority groups in specific regions and a handful of metro areas," says demographer William H. Frey of the Population Studies Center at the University of Michigan. Frey's research shows that in the entire United States, only 21 counties can truly be called racially diverse. Those 21 counties have populations in which white residents are slightly below the national average and in which at least two minority groups are present in numbers slightly higher than their national averages.[19]

But can culture and race really be linked? Studies show that race can indeed be an indicator of a unique culture. A recent survey of racial and ethnic groups within the United States, for example, concluded that blacks, Asians, Hispanics, and non-Hispanic whites (a U.S. Census Bureau designation) spend their time in different ways. Asians spend more time each week on education than do blacks, Hispanics, or whites. Blacks devote more time to religion each week than do the other racial and ethnic groups. Hispanics spend more time caring for their children than do the other groups. Whites spend more time at work than Asians, blacks, or Hispanics.[20]

"The trend in every aspect of American life is toward greater cultural, ethnic, and linguistic diversity," says marketing expert Marlene Rossman. "Not only are minority groups increasing in size, they are also not assimilating the way many minority and ethnic (especially immigrant) groups did in the past. . . . Our cultural model is becoming the mosaic, not the melting pot."[21]

mentum. An earlier cross-cultural mistake, in fact, had made the U.S. negotiators very aware of the Jewish Sabbath: A week earlier, the Israeli prime minister and his entire delegation had declined to attend a Friday evening dinner meeting hosted by the U.S. secretary of state.[22]

Attitudes about Taste and Diet

For many public relations practitioners, cuisine is the reward for mastering the subtleties of cross-cultural communication. Perhaps it's arroz con pollo (chicken with rice) in Costa Rica or couscous in Algeria or bratwurst in Germany or grits in the southern United States. The culinary diversity of the world's cultures is dazzling and gratifying—but also rife with opportunities for serious blunders. Religion and other cultural influences often prohibit the consumption of certain foods. Hindus don't eat beef; cattle are exalted in that religion, which encompasses the belief that souls return to Earth again and again as different life forms. Strict Judaism forbids the consumption of pork products and shellfish, which are considered unclean.

Attitudes about Colors, Numbers, and Symbols

What's the unlucky number in mainstream U.S. culture? Thirteen, of course. How about in Japanese culture? It's four. One of your authors learned that the hard way when he titled an article for a multinational corporate magazine "Four from Japan." Every culture develops an unofficial language of colors, numbers, and symbols that often speaks louder than words. For example, the logo of the HSBC Group, one of the world's largest financial institutions, is a red hexagon. HSBC began in Hong Kong and Shanghai, where red is considered a lucky color. But when HSBC expanded to the Middle East, it learned that red was a symbol of conflict. In that region of the world, HSBC chose to use its secondary colors, black and gray.[23]

Symbols can be just as fraught with meaning as colors and numbers. For example, most of us interpret the thumbs-up symbol used for case studies in this book as a sign of approval. In Australia and Nigeria, however, the symbol and the gesture mean anything but approval. In those societies, the upward thumb is an obscene sign of disrespect.[24]

Attitudes about Assimilation and Acculturation

How quickly can members of one culture adjust to the traditions of another? How accepting are people of new ideas and nontraditional thinking? Such flexibility can help characterize a culture. The more a culture resists outside influences, the more powerful its own traditions can become. The French Academy, for example, which is the legal watchdog of the French language as it's spoken in France, has officially banned English terms such as *hot dog* and *drugstore*. In 2001, Russian President Vladimir Putin began a similar anti-English campaign, instituting fines and even imprisonment for Russians who used English derivatives such as *biznismeni* for *businessmen*.[25] More tolerant is the attitude of former South African President Nelson Mandela, who drew cheers from young adults attending an R.E.M. concert in London by declaring, "I am now almost 100 years old, but I am so proud because my roots are in South Africa but my gaze reaches beyond the horizon to places like Britain where we are tied together by unbreakable bonds."[26]

Sometimes assimilation and acculturation occur so gradually that the process escapes our notice. More than one observer, for example, has noted that U.S. dominance of the technology and content of the Internet is subtly piping U.S. influences into offices and homes around the world. Says Jerry W. Thomas of Decision Analyst Inc.:

> One of the most significant and pervasive implications of the Internet will be the diffusion of Western (and specifically the United States') culture and influence around the globe. A majority of the programming content of the Internet originates in the United States. The Internet largely runs on U.S. software, is accessed by U.S. software, and is controlled by U.S. software. United States' products, services, information, and entertainment dominate the Internet. The English language, already established as the first language of international commerce, will spread more rapidly and become even more dominant as the lan-

guage of international commerce and conversation. The Internet, like the movies, music and television before it, will be a marketing agent for American culture.[27]

No doubt true. But any public relations practitioner who assumes that the world has become one big U.S.-based culture runs the risk of studying a different phenomenon: the culture of the unemployment line.

To Rossman's list of eight characteristics, we might add one more: attitudes about business communication. For example, although executives in the United States and Canada frequently use voice mail and e-mail, executives in European nations generally prefer "real-time," simultaneous communications; thus the use of cell phones in Europe exceeds usage in United States and Canada. Executives in France and Germany, however, prefer paper-based communications to other forms; their use of postal services and fax machines exceeds usage rates in other nations.[28] Part of successful cross-cultural communication involves learning how members of other cultures prefer to receive their business messages.

Quick ✔ Check

1. What is the purpose of the analytical system created by Marlene Rossman?
2. Would it be fair to say that the United States is all one culture? Why or why not?
3. What is the difference between a culture and a public?

Cross-Cultural Communication: Definitions and Dangers

Clearly, this chapter uses the term *cross-cultural communication* to refer to exchanges of messages among the members of different cultures. But it's worth stopping to ask what, exactly, is meant by **cross-cultural**. Many sociologists and communication specialists use the term *intercultural* to denote exchanges of various kinds between cultures. Your authors, like many public relations practitioners, prefer the term *cross-cultural* because it prompts an image of crossing a border, of going into partially unknown territory. *Cross-cultural* urges caution and encourages you to stay constantly aware of the obstacles to successful communication between members of different cultures.

And what do we mean by **communication**? We mean more than words can say. In Chapter 13, for example, we noted that every aspect of a product sends a message to consumers. Besides the verbal messages of news releases and advertisements, a product's price, packaging, and distribution all send nonverbal messages to potential purchasers. Consumers in West African communities were horrified when one U.S. company tried to sell its popular brand of baby food in their stores. The labels featured a smiling baby—very popular in the United States, but intensely disturbing in a culture that relies on pictures to identify the contents of jars and cans.[29] Briefly, by *communication,* we mean any exchange of information—verbal and/or nonverbal—between the sender and the receiver of a message.

Encoding and Decoding

In Chapter 5 we examined a basic **communication model,** which, as you'll recall, looks like this:

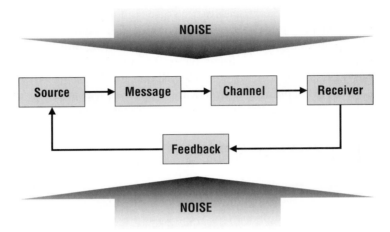

More complex versions of this basic model include two elements that become particularly important in communication between cultures: encoding and decoding. **Encoding** involves the sender's selection of words, images, and other forms of communication that create the message. **Decoding** involves the receiver's attempt to produce meaning from the sender's message. With those additional elements, the communication model looks like this:

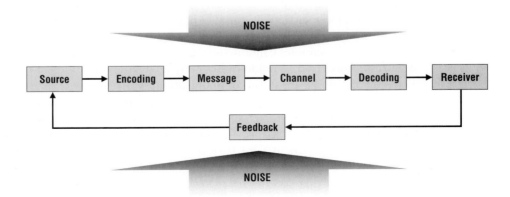

In successful cross-cultural communication, senders must understand how a message will be decoded before they can effectively encode it. The perils of encoding errors are illustrated by yet another U.S. company's adventures abroad. When the Coca-Cola Company translated its name into Chinese, the phonetic version—KeKou Kela—instructed Chinese consumers to "Bite the wax tadpole."[30] It's hard to guess who was most surprised by that particular cross-cultural encoding–decoding glitch.

Even though an organization's message may need different encodings for different cultures, the message should ideally remain shaped by the values that unite the organization. A successful organization cannot embrace one set of values with the elderly in South Africa, a different set of values with women in China, a third set of values with Russian immigrants in Australia, and so on. Such duplicity would be more than dishonest; maintaining so many different personalities would be exhausting. In successful organizations, all messages emanate from a set of clearly understood core values, as well as from the business goals that grow out of those values. Says Jean-Louis Tronc, director of human resources and corporate communications for DuPont de Nemours of France, "There are a certain number of global values within a company which must remain the same everywhere."[31] As we note many times throughout this book, successful public relations is a values-driven process.

Gestures and Clothing

Our broad definition of communication also applies to interpersonal communication. Our gestures, clothing, and expressions can be every bit as communicative as our words. In Taiwan, blinking at someone is considered an insult. In the Islamic faith, shoes are absolutely forbidden on the grounds of mosques. In many Asian cultures, shoes are removed and left at the front doors of residences. The A–OK expression made by forming a circle of the thumb and forefinger and raising the other three fingers is, like thumbs-up, a sign of approval in the United States. But in Japan it's a symbol for money. In Australia and some Latin American nations, it's an obscene gesture. During a 1950s visit to a Latin American country, Vice President Richard Nixon grandly made the A–OK gesture—and was stunned by an immediate chorus of boos.[32]

Because people from almost every culture use their hands when they speak, gestures—more so than clothing or expressions—can send unintended messages during cross-cultural communication. Speaking to a group of journalists in the Central Asian nation of Kyrgyzstan, one of your authors illustrated a point by bringing one fist down on top of the other two or three times. Halting in midsentence, his shocked interpreter leaned over and hissed in his ear that he was signaling, in the crudest possible way, that he wanted to make love to his audience. Fortunately, your author's stricken expression led his audience to forgive him with friendly laughter. That story has two morals: Cross-cultural mistakes can be very embarrassing—and people can be very forgiving if they sense your good will.

Stereotyping

Another sure ticket to failure in cross-cultural communication is **stereotyping:** the assumption that all members of a particular culture act, think, feel, and believe in the same way. Are all Hispanics family-oriented? Are all Swiss punctual? Are all Japanese polite? Are all U.S. citizens blunt? Do all teenagers like loud music? Do all baby boomers like the Beatles? Cultures *do* exist, but they consist of individuals, none of whom are exactly alike. "After all," says Harvard Professor H. L. Gates Jr., "culture is always a conversation among different voices."[33]

Finally, public relations practitioners should be prepared for the distinct possibility that their colleagues from different cultures *also* are studying cross-cultural communication. Your Japanese guest, for example, may insist on shaking hands rather than bowing. Your Spanish guest may ask for an early-afternoon meeting to show his or her willingness to adapt to your culture. So who prevails in such complicated situations? Often, it's easiest to follow the culture of the host, but the host still should seek opportunities to honor the cultures of his or her guests. An abundance of courtesy is a good beginning for cross-cultural communication.

Cross-cultural communication has become an unavoidable challenge for the public relations profession. One recent study shows that two-thirds of international business mergers fail because "cultures and people are often incompatible, national differences emerging."[34] Says Elizabeth Howard, principal partner of an international consulting firm, "Today it is difficult, probably impossible, to find a business that has not been affected in one way or another by the new global economy." Indeed, it's not unusual for farmers from the midwestern United States to find themselves part of trade delegations in Asia or Latin America, seeking new markets for U.S. agricultural products. And those farmers, like others engaged in cross-cultural business discussions, constantly confront the question posed by sociologist and anthropologist David Howes: "What happens when the culture of production and the culture of consumption are not the same?"[35]

These cultural gulfs must be bridged if the producers and the consumers are to achieve their goals. In the next section we offer a nine-step process that can help organizations and individuals achieve successful cross-cultural communication.

Quick ✔ Check

1. What do *encoding* and *decoding* mean?
2. Should an organization's core values change as it communicates with different cultures?
3. What does *stereotyping* mean? How can it threaten successful cross-cultural communication?

LOST IN TRANSLATION: PART ONE

Computerized translation programs would seem to hold promise for cross-cultural communication, automatically translating e-mail messages, web site text, and other electronically transferred messages from the language of the sender into the language of the receiver. Unfortunately, computerized translation sometimes becomes computerized frustration.

Here's what one popular translation program rendered when the first sentences of Ivy Lee's famous "Declaration of Principles" (see Chapter 3) were translated into other languages and then back into English:

Original: This is not a secret press bureau. All our work is done in the open. We aim to supply news. This is not an advertising agency; if you think any of our matter ought properly to go to your business office, do not use it.

English—German—English: This is not a secret press agency. Our whole work is completed in the opened. We direct off to indicate messages. This is not an advertising agency; if you think, any of our material to your business premises, uses it is to go correctly not.

English—Spanish—English: This is not a secret press office. All our work becomes in the open one. We aimed to provide the news. This is not a publicity agency; if you think anyone of our matter ought to go correctly to your office of business, she does not use it.

English—Portuguese—English: This is not a private department of the press. All our work is made in the opened one. We point to supply the notice. This is not an agency announcing; if you to think some of our substance ought correctly to go its office of business, do not use it.

English—French—English: It is not a secret Press Office. All our work is carried out in the open one. Us minks to be ensured of the news. It is not an advertising agency; if you think any of our matter must correctly go to your commercial room, does not use it.

Before trusting computerized translation programs for cross-cultural communications, remember Ivy Lee and those French minks who want to be ensured of the news.

Achieving Successful Cross-Cultural Public Relations: A Process

At this point in our chapter, two facts are clear: Cross-cultural communication can be difficult—and it is inevitable. Painstaking encoding and decoding of cross-cultural messages have become everyday challenges. Given that reality, how can public relations practitioners in the 21st century become effective cross-cultural communicators? We recommend a process consisting of nine stages: awareness, commitment, research, local partnership, diversity, testing, evaluation, advocacy, and continuing education. We begin with awareness. If public relations practitioners aren't sensitive to the presence or potential difficulties of a cross-cultural encounter, they have little hope of communicating effectively.

Stage One: Awareness

You can start enhancing your awareness of cross-cultural situations right now—by studying a foreign language and enrolling in liberal arts courses that allow you to explore the traits and traditions of other cultures. If your college or university has an international students association, consider joining it. If it has a study abroad program, plan to spend a semester in another country. Higher education offers you rare opportunities to discover that the rest of the world doesn't think, act, dress, eat, and communicate as you do.

Achieving fluency in a foreign language can keep you from being the butt of an old joke that remains all too current. As the joke goes, someone who speaks three languages is trilingual; someone who speaks two languages is bilingual; someone who speaks one language is a U.S. citizen. English indeed has become the language of international commerce, but learning to speak the language of a foreign business acquaintance—even if you master only a few key phrases—may heighten your sensitivity to cross-cultural issues. More important, perhaps, learning a second language can improve the success of your cross-cultural communication by creating good will. On business in Paris, one of your authors was able to persuade a new acquaintance to work late by using his shaky knowledge of French, gained in college. When the Parisian apologized, in English, for missing a deadline, your author was able to respond *C'est la même chose pour tout le monde, n'est-ce pas?*—roughly, "It happens everywhere, doesn't it?" The Parisian was surprised that an American could speak even bad French. The conversation sputtered along in French until the amused Parisian switched back to English and agreed to stay late to finish the project.

Organizations throughout the United States are imitating the college experience by sponsoring courses in multiculturalism and cross-cultural communication. Burson-Marsteller and Hill & Knowlton, two of the largest public relations agencies in the world, routinely organize multiday courses to sensitize executives to cross-cultural realities and possibilities. Such sessions include problem-solving exercises, case studies, role playing, and other techniques that immerse participants in cross-cultural communication situations.[36]

Another powerful way to increase sensitivity is to diversify the workplace, bringing multiculturalism and cross-cultural communication into the everyday business of the office. This strategy will be discussed in greater detail below.

Stage Two: Commitment

Reporters have a technique called "parachute journalism"—dropping into a locality the reporter doesn't know well to write a quick story about that same little-known locality. Journalists aren't proud of parachute journalism. Nor should public relations practitioners be proud of using a similar strategy in their profession: parachuting, so to speak, into a little-known culture to do some hit-and-run relationship building. Successful cross-cultural communication requires personal commitment, as well as commitment from an organization's highest levels, to doing the arduous background

McDonald's *NOTICIAS*

McDonald's Corporation • One McDonald's Plaza • Oak Brook, Illinois 60523

PARA DISTRIBUCIÓN INMEDIATA

Para más información:
Mario Flores, McDonald's
630/623-6731
mario.flores@mcd.com

Maritza Baca, VPE Public Relations
626/ 793-9335
maritza@vpepr.com

ELVIS CRESPO SE UNE A McDONALD'S® PARA ANUNCIAR LA CELEBRACIÓN NACIONAL DE *LO McXIMO DE LA MÚSICA LATINA*

La Celebración Incluye un Sorteo para Asistir al Concierto Privado el 13 de Octubre en los Estudios Disney-MGM del Walt Disney World Resort y la Transmisión Web en Vivo en el sitio Terra.com

LOS ANGELES, CA (10 de agosto de 2001) – El artista latino Elvis Crespo, ganador del

Premio Grammy, se unió recientemente a McDonald's para anunciar *Lo Mcximo de la*

Música Latina, una celebración nacional a la herencia hispana que lleva el espíritu de la

News Release The growing power of Hispanic markets in the United States has led progressive companies such as McDonald's Corporation to issue news releases in Spanish. For an English-language version of this news release, see page 121. (Courtesy of Valencia, Pérez & Echeveste Public Relations)

work that allows the effective encoding and decoding of messages to and from another culture.

Stage Three: Research

Commitment implies a willingness to do the research demanded by successful cross-cultural communication. Standard reference sources for this research include magazines such as *Communication World* and *American Demographics;* books such as Roger Axtell's *Do's and Taboos around the World* and *Gestures: The Do's and Taboos of Body Language around the World;* and online resources such as the web site sponsored by the International Trade Administration, a division of the U.S. Department of Commerce. The ITA web site includes information on business etiquette in almost

QuickBreak 14.3

LOST IN TRANSLATION: PART TWO

Throughout this chapter, we've noted some disastrous, though funny, attempts by U.S. companies to communicate with people from different, unfamiliar cultures. Embarrassment can be a two-way street, however. The attempts of foreign companies to communicate with consumers in the United States occasionally have equally disastrous, and equally humorous, results.

Electrolux vacuum cleaners, for example, made by a Swedish-based company, are known worldwide for quality and dependability. So how could a new advertising campaign create distrust and laughter among consumers in the United States and England? Perhaps it was the slogan: "Nothing sucks like an Electrolux."[37]

Foreign automobiles are a common sight on U.S. roads. We see Toyotas and Hondas from Japan, BMWs and VWs from Germany, and Jaguars from England. Why don't we see Cit-roens from France—fine cars, by all accounts? Perhaps because *Citroen* evokes *citron,* the French word for "lemon," U.S. slang for a lousy car. A prized memento among car collectors in the United States is a particular hood ornament from a 1920s Citroen: a flying lemon.

A favorite pastime among some U.S. public relations and marketing practitioners who travel to other countries is to collect product names that might encounter difficulties in U.S. markets. Two current favorites are Mexico's Bimbo bread and an Iranian dishwashing detergent with an unfortunate name printed boldly on its English-language labels: Barf.

Perhaps the humorous missteps of foreign marketers can make practitioners in the United States even more sensitive to the challenges of cross-cultural communication.

every nation around the world. Hosting a meeting for colleagues from Botswana? Confirm your meeting 24 hours ahead of time, and don't be offended if your guests arrive late. Don't call them by their first names until they initiate that practice, and don't schedule the meeting for September 30: That's Botswana Day. Need more information? See the ITA web site at www.ita.doc.gov/ita_home/itacnreg.html.

Believe it or not, the Central Intelligence Agency also makes available some of its highly detailed data on different nations around the world. Check out the CIA's World Factbook at www.odci.gov/cia/publications/factbook.

A good reference librarian can steer you to other current sources. Such research might help you remember to take off your shoes when you enter the hotel room of your Japanese guest in our East Meets West scenario.

Stage Four: Local Partnership

No matter how much research you conduct, you'll never know as much about a foreign culture as does someone reared in it. When an organization begins a long-term cross-cultural relationship, it should consider bringing a member of that culture onto its communications team. "You must have representation on the ground in different

QuickBreak 14.4

DOUBLE-WHAMMY CULTURE CLASH

Merging two company cultures into one new business can be tough. But when those two companies come from different nations, the merger faces a cultural double-whammy. That's what happened when German car manufacturer Daimler-Benz bought U.S.-based Chrysler Corporation in 1998.

"These two cultures . . . were bound to collide," said a former U.S. auto executive.[38]

"Problems are caused when an acquirer's corporate culture fails to mesh with that of its new subsidiary," wrote a British business analyst. "That's the biggest single risk in all cross-border acquisitions."[39]

Still, optimism abounded when the two companies joined forces. "The merger of Daimler and Chrysler was hailed as a marriage made in heaven," reported a British financial analyst. "But the honeymoon was shortlived."[40] Within three years, the new DaimlerChrysler was worth only half its initial value, key Chrysler executives had resigned, and the new company was preparing to close six Chrysler factories.[41] Ob-

servers inside and outside the company knew what to blame: clashing cultures.

"[Germans] can't understand this cultural mentality that is forever focusing on the bottom line and quarterly results," said an industry consultant.[42]

"German workforces expect to be consulted at all stages of any strategic deal, while at Chrysler the unions aim to beat down the management and vice versa," said another.[43]

"In the case of DaimlerChrysler, there was a total clash of cultures," said a British business professor.[44]

All sides should have listened to an investment banker who had worked with both companies before the merger. "It could take them at least a year to learn each other's true character and identity," the banker warned. "That's why these transatlantic mergers are always trickier than they look on paper."[45]

parts of the world, but you should be extremely cautious about hiring a major global PR agency," says Robert Wakefield, former chairman of the International Section of the Public Relations Society of America. "Instead, tap into the worldwide network of small local agencies or talented native PR consultants who can guide you through the maze of PR issues in their own country."[46]

Stage Five: Diversity

Not all different cultures are beyond the borders of the United States. As QuickBreak 14.1 notes, the United States is hardly a melting pot; instead, it's a mosaic of different cultures. Diversity within an organization's public relations team can help ensure successful cross-cultural communication at home. Furthermore, it can increase an organization's awareness of cultural differences, which benefits communication both at home and abroad. Pitney Bowes, a multinational company examined in Case Study 14.1, believes that a diverse workforce boosts company profits.

Stage Six: Testing

As every actor knows, it's better to bomb in rehearsal than on opening night. When possible, test your relationship-building tactics on trusted members of the culture you plan to address. For example, in this chapter's East Meets West scenario, you could show a detailed itinerary of your business and entertainment plans to natives of Japan and Spain. You just might learn, for example, that Spanish business dinners don't begin until late evening—often past 9:00 P.M.—and that Japanese business dinners can go on for hours and often end in nightclubs.[47]

Stage Seven: Evaluation

A constant goal in public relations is to learn from our successes as well as from our mistakes. As soon as possible, public relations professionals should evaluate the effectiveness of completed cross-cultural communication efforts, seeking ways to reinforce the good and revise the bad. In the East Meets West scenario, for example, did your Japanese guest wince when you offered her a gift as you met her at the airport? Your consequent research might show that although the Japanese enjoy receiving gifts, they often are embarrassed if they cannot reciprocate immediately.[48] The gift may have been a blunder, but it was a valuable misstep: It taught you to be sensitive to the intricacies of offering a gift to a member of another culture.

Stage Eight: Advocacy

Cross-cultural communication works best when an entire organization commits to it. Commitment requires a persistent focus, and a persistent focus requires an advocate. Perhaps that advocate can be you. Says international communication consultant Mary Jo Jacobi:

> No matter where a multinational company operates, it must remain conscious of the fact that it has audiences in many other parts of the world and that whatever its executives do and say locally could have far-reaching ramifications and business implications. As a result, we must seek to ensure that we communicate a consistent message worldwide, particularly on sensitive matters. Getting this clearly in the minds of colleagues is one of the most important roles that we, as professional communicators, must undertake.[49]

Stage Nine: Continuing Education

The cross-cultural seminars at Burson-Marsteller and Hill & Knowlton are examples of continuing education, as are exchanges of executives between local branches of multinational companies. Other forms of continuing education can be as simple as reading international publications, watching international television programming, attending lectures, or—gasp!—returning to a university for an occasional night course on a foreign language or an unfamiliar culture. Fortunately, learning doesn't stop at graduation. It's a big, exciting world out there, burgeoning with opportunities for anyone who can cross its boundaries with knowledge, diplomacy, and confidence.

ТОРГОВЛЯ С АМЕРИКОЙ

СПРАВОЧНИК ПО ПРОГРАММАМ ПРАВИТЕЛЬСТВА США

Публикация BISNIS -
Службы деловой информации о странах Содружества независимых государств
Министерства торговли США

Business Guide An indication of the increasing importance of cross-cultural communication
is this U.S. Department of Commerce Russian-language publication, *Doing Business in America.*

Quick ✔ Check

1. In the nine-step process for successful cross-cultural public relations, what does local partnership mean? Why is it necessary?
2. What sources could you consult for information on the cultures of other countries?
3. Specifically, how does cross-cultural communication mean more than international communication?

Summary

As we noted in Chapter 11, a generation ago Canadian philosopher Marshall McLuhan argued that the world was becoming a "global village." In many ways, he was right. Modern technology can make communication between Kenya and China faster and easier than the task faced by a 19th-century Toronto resident who simply wanted to deliver a message across town. Yet the global village is hardly a community in the traditional sense. Every street has its own customs, biases, traditions, fears, religion, diet, and language. Every street, in other words, has its own culture.

If the global village is to thrive, those streets need to learn to communicate with one another. The conversations won't be easy. We need only to read a daily newspaper to see that the conversations often fail. We can increase the chances of success, however, by learning a process for effective cross-cultural communication—a nine-step process that begins with awareness and includes commitment, research, local partnership, diversity, testing, evaluation, advocacy, and continuing education. That process needs well-educated, talented, versatile communicators. In fact, the process of cross-cultural public relations needs you.

Cross-cultural communication is so essential to the present and future of public relations that we're not yet ready to put the subject aside. We will return to it in Chapter 16, in which we'll examine predictions for the increasing diversity of publics around the world.

DISCUSSION QUESTIONS

1. Besides the gaffes mentioned in this chapter, what cross-cultural communication errors have you heard of? Have any happened to you?
2. What is a culture? What other definitions besides those offered in this chapter can you find? How do *you* define a culture?
3. How might you respond to a colleague who makes the following statement: "You're wasting your time with that cross-cultural stuff. We're all humans, and we're a lot more alike than we are different."
4. In the East Meets West scenario, would it be smarter to meet separately with your international visitors from Japan and Spain? Why or why not?
5. What cross-cultural educational opportunities exist at your college or university? Are you taking advantage of them?

Memo *from the* **Field**

Bill Imada, President, Imada Wong Communications Group, Los Angeles

Bill Imada is the president and founder of Imada Wong Communications Group, a Los Angeles–based advertising and public relations agency specializing in the Asian American market. The agency represents a variety of major corporations and governmental agencies, including AT&T, Northwest Airlines, Merrill Lynch, Washington Mutual, Chevron Corporation, and the American Legacy Foundation.

Values play a critical role in the way people think, react, relate, communicate, and make decisions. As a student of public relations, take a moment to think about the values that shape your own personality and the way you make decisions in life. As the authors of this book clearly note, there are a host of common values that people around the world share. When you walk into a room filled with nationals from Japan, Spain, or any other country in the world, consider all of the values you might share first. You will be pleasantly surprised by the number of values you have in common with your colleagues from another country or even another neighborhood or community. Your efforts to communicate will be made easier and more enjoyable when you find the values that bring you together. Afterwards, take time to discover the things that make you different and unique. Celebrate what you have learned from one another, and share what you have learned with others.

As you move forward with your studies in public relations and communications, take a moment to think about some of the values you may take for granted. In this chapter, the authors talk about the concept of time. Many people from Western countries often talk about the lack of time we have to accomplish things. Americans, for instance, often say "time flies." On the contrary, many Latin American and Asian cultures may say "time walks." From a cultural point of view, which phrase is right? Both are right. How might this concept of time influence the way you interact and negotiate with your counterparts from Japan and Spain?

Now think of some other values that shape your views on life and ask yourself and your classmates to evaluate how these values might influence the way you think, react, relate, communicate, and make decisions. What thoughts come to mind when you think of these values:

- Independence
- Family
- Sales
- Equality

Now ask people from other cultures to talk with you about their views on these values. I think you will find their answers enlightening and thought-provoking.

The authors also talk about the significance of gestures in other cultures. It is important to note that gestures are an important method of communicating in many cultures around the world. In Japan, public relations professionals often say that the Japanese can say "no" 40 different ways without even uttering the word. Facial expressions, hand movements, and body positions can signal a variety of different messages. As public relations practitioners, it is essential for you to learn how gestures can and will play a role in cross-cultural communication.

Lastly, think about what you have learned in the past about getting from one point in life to another. What did your teachers, professors, and parents tell you about getting from point A to point B? You and your classmates may say that the best way to get from point A to point B is a straight line. Why? Because it is considered the most efficient, cost-effective, and timely way to reach your desired destination. As you move forward in your public relations career, remember that there can many different and unique ways to get from one point to another—and not necessarily by taking the direct approach. The most effective public relations practitioners will recognize early on that there are a myriad of different ways to reach where you'd like to go. Take time to explore each route. You'll be pleased that you did.

Case Study 14.1

Pitney Bowes Sends a Message

Sixty years ago, the sales team of a U.S.-based multinational company attended an awards ceremony at a prestigious hotel. Nothing unusual about that. One member of the team was black, and the hotel refused to admit him. Unfortunately, nothing unusual about that either. "Whites Only" policies characterized some U.S. businesses until the 1960s. What happened next, however, *was* unusual. Led by the company chairman, the entire sales team walked out of the hotel and refused to attend the ceremony.[50]

What kind of company would risk offending clients, industry partners, and social leaders to stand up for equal rights and the value of diversity? A company named Pitney Bowes.

In terms of equal rights and the value of diversity, much has changed in 60 years. Pitney Bowes' values haven't. The company remains a worldwide leader in creating a diverse workforce.

"For over 50 years, a key component of our successful business model has been an employee population that reflects the global marketplace," says Pitney Bowes Chairman and CEO Michael Critelli. "We believe that the diversity of thought and life experience in our employee population helps us produce superior products and services."[51]

Pitney Bowes is a $5-billion-a-year developer and supplier of message- and document-management systems. Its customers include more than 2 million businesses in more than 130 countries around the world. To cope with such a diverse customer base, Pitney Bowes aggressively seeks a diverse workforce. Minority employees constitute more than 40 percent of the company's personnel. More than 20 percent of the management staff consists of minority employees.[52] "Our executive leadership team is over 50 percent people of color and/or non–U.S. born," Critelli says.[53]

To maintain and strengthen productive relationships among its diverse workforce, Pitney Bowes follows a process familiar to students of public relations: research, planning, communication, and evaluation.

The company's diversity-related research began in 1987 with the goal of identifying barriers that prohibited the advancement of women and minority-group employees. In that year, Pitney Bowes created the Women's Resource Group and the Minority Resource Group to spearhead research efforts. To study the business value of diversity, Pitney Bowes launched a research project with the University of Pennsylvania in 1996.

As its research began to highlight areas for improvement, Pitney Bowes initiated the planning phase. It created a Diversity Task Force to develop specific objectives for promoting diversity at all levels of the company. One element of the plan recommended that Pitney Bowes' top managers present annual diversity-promotion plans with measurable objectives.

As one of the world's top message-management companies, Pitney Bowes didn't lack ideas for communicating its diversity objectives to employees. Internal newsletters routinely cover diversity issues; every training session for new managers includes a Managing Diversity segment; and the company crafted a short, memorable diversity policy featured in a variety of media, including its web site: "Diversity is essential to innovation and growth. Pitney Bowes encourages and maintains diversity in every aspect of its operations, from our own workforce to the customers, business partners, and communities with whom we work." Pitney Bowes' main "Statement of Value," which it features on its web site, in its annual reports, and in other media, also bluntly states, "We value diversity."[54]

Finally, Pitney Bowes evaluates the success of its research, planning, and communication. Every year, each business unit within the company submits a report showing the degree to which it achieved its specific diversity objectives. Top managers also review the impact of the company's overall diversity policies on profits, employee advancement, diversity of business partners, and other areas.[55]

As a result of its dedication to diversity, the company routinely wins praise from its own employees, magazines such as *Business Week*, books such as *The 100 Best Companies to Work For in America*, and organizations such as the National Urban League. That praise soared in 1998 and 1999 when five different magazines, including *Hispanic* and *Working Woman*, named Pitney Bowes a top company for minority-group employees.

Michel Critelli emphasizes that his company's successful quest for diversity is fueled by more than morality. Pitney Bowes also firmly believes that diversity strengthens important relationships with customers and business partners. "We clearly recognize the growth opportunities that diversity creates," he says, "not only in expanding our market access but in widening our base of mutually beneficial relationships, especially with minority- and women-owned companies."[56]

Critelli also believes that a diverse management team increases Pitney Bowes' international competitiveness. When he announced the promotion of Keith Williamson, a high-ranking black manager, to the position of president of the company's Capital Services division, he praised Williamson's "extensive legal and tax knowledge and sound business judgment." But he added, "His appointment underscores Pitney Bowes' belief that leveraging the diversity of our employees helps us sustain our competitive leadership."[57]

As he surveys the global economy in which his company operates, Williamson—recently named one of the "top 50 blacks in corporate America" by *Black Enterprise* magazine—also stresses the business value of diversity. "We live in a world that's getting faster every day, and it's harder for companies to do everything on their own," he says. "Knowing how to make connections with others to maneuver into new areas will be critical to the success of my company—and my career."[58]

DISCUSSION QUESTIONS

1. The Pitney Bowes sales team risked social condemnation when it walked out of that 1940s awards ceremony. What did it gain?
2. Pitney Bowes believes that diversity makes good business sense. What is its logic?
3. Women are not a minority group. Why does Pitney Bowes include them in its diversity programs?
4. In your opinion, do Pitney Bowes' actions live up to the company's diversity policy "Statement of Value"?
5. How does the specificity of Pitney Bowes' diversity plans help the evaluation process?

Case Study 14.2

Border Wars for Wal-Mart

"Fool me once," says the cliché, "and shame on you. Fool me twice, and shame on me." To their credit, officials at Wal-Mart, the most successful retailer in the United States, shouldered the blame in 1994 when their company tripped twice over cross-cultural language problems.

In January 1994 Wal-Mart moved aggressively into Canada, purchasing 122 stores from the Woolco retail organization. Always cost conscious, Wal-Mart gathered fliers printed for U.S. stores and distributed them throughout Quebec—French-speaking Quebec, where laws zealously protect the prevalence of the French language. As potential customers were bristling at the unintended insult, Wal-Mart dropped another English bomb on a Canadian public—this time its own employees. A letter from Wal-Mart's Canadian headquarters asking Quebec employees to work longer hours was written in English.

The reaction of the Quebecois did little to further international relations. "Vultures of savage capitalism," thundered the leader of Quebec's Confederation of National Trade Unions.[59] A columnist for *Le Journal de Montreal* shuddered at Wal-Mart's very name, declaring, "Even uttering the word is disgusting, like chewing on an old Kleenex that was forgotten in the pocket of a winter coat."[60]

Other Canadians were more restrained in their assessments of Wal-Mart's cross-cultural blunders. "They came so quickly to take advantage of the Woolco opportunity that they didn't have time to do their homework," said a retail analyst.[61]

Wal-Mart sent letters of apology to its employees in Quebec and vowed to do better. "It never should have happened," said a Wal-Mart representative.[62] But it happened again the same year. This time, the setting was Mexico.

In March 1994 the Mexican government announced a strict new product-labeling law requiring Spanish-language labels for all imported products. As merchandise logjammed at the U.S. border, Mexican trade officials quickly instituted a 90-day grace period, stating that they would clarify the new regulations.

In September of the previous year, Wal-Mart had opened a 240,000-square-foot supercenter in Mexico City, selling mostly clothing with product tags in English. As the 90-day grace period came to an end, officials of the Mexican government gave the store an additional 30 days to comply with the labeling law. But after only 6 days, the officials returned and closed the store.

"It came out of the blue," said a Wal-Mart representative.[63]

The store remained closed for less than 24 hours as the company rented a warehouse in Laredo, Texas, and in the summer heat hastily assembled a team to affix new labels to the products. "It wasn't fun," said one exhausted worker. Retail experts estimate that the Mexico City store lost $330,000 during the brief shutdown.[64]

The entire episode, said company officials, was "unfortunate"—doubly so, perhaps, because *unfortunate* was the very word Wal-Mart had used earlier that year to describe the cross-cultural confusion in Canada.[65]

DISCUSSION QUESTIONS

1. Confusion did exist over the details of Mexico's label law, yet Wal-Mart didn't publicly complain. In your opinion, why not? Should the company have publicly complained?
2. Was Wal-Mart really "fooled twice"? Is it fair to compare the two situations? Why should an event in Canada affect the company's actions in Mexico?
3. Would you shop at a discount apparel store in the United States that had products with labels only in Spanish or French? What nonverbal messages might such labels send?
4. Some Canadians reacted angrily to Wal-Mart's cultural errors; others reacted with understanding. What are the advantages and disadvantages of each position?
5. Can you name other examples of language interfering with successful cross-cultural communication?

It's Your Turn

Cultures Close to Home

As you know, multinational organizations often hire representatives of particular cultures to assist with cross-cultural communication. Imagine that an Argentinean producer of a lemon-flavored soft drink hires you to help provide a cultural profile of students at your college or university. What information will your report include? Do different cultures exist at your college or university? What distinguishes each one? In identifying the different cultures, do you encounter potentially uncomfortable stereotypes? Where might you seek research that could support or refute those stereotypes?

Is there a dominant culture at your college or university? If so, what are its attitudes and traditions regarding time; formality; individualism; rank and hierarchy; religion; taste and diet; colors, numbers, and symbols; and assimilation and acculturation? In addition, is it possible to create a demographic profile of the dominant culture?

Finally, are you a member of the dominant culture? With what culture or cultures do you identify?

KEY TERMS

communication, p. 459
communication model, p. 460
cross-cultural, p. 459
culture, p. 452
decoding, p. 460

demographic information, p. 452
encoding, p. 460
geographics, p. 452
psychographic information, p. 452
stereotyping, p. 462

NOTES

1. Marlene Rossman, *Multicultural Marketing* (New York: Amacom, 1994), 6.
2. Diane Levick, "Taking Its Medicine: Recovering from a Painful Merger, Aetna Learns Important Lessons," *Hartford Courant,* 2 March 1998, online, Lexis-Nexis.
3. Mike Lindblom, "Muslims Protest Koran Use in Rave Ad," *Seattle Times,* 10 February 2001, online, Lexis-Nexis.
4. Anindita Niyogi Balslev, ed., *Cross-Cultural Conversation* (Atlanta: Scholars Press, 1996), 10.
5. Stephen P. Banks, *Multicultural Public Relations*, 2nd ed. (Ames, Iowa: Iowa State University Press, 2000), 9.
6. Charles Winick, *Dictionary of Anthropology* (Totowa, N.J.: Littlefield, Adams, 1972), 144.
7. Banks, ix.
8. John Budd Jr., "Opinion . . . Foreign Policy Acumen Needed by Global CEOs," *Public Relations Review* (summer 2001): 132.

9. Banks, 105.
10. "Italian Stallions," *Times* (of London), 1 May 2001, 17.
11. "Go Ahead, Forward This E-Mail," *Fast Company* (May 2001), online, www. fastcompany.com/invent/invent_feature/email2.html.
12. Rossman.
13. Robert Levine, "The Pace of Life in 31 Countries," *American Demographics* (November 1997): 20.
14. Roger Axtell, *Do's and Taboos around the World*, 3rd ed. (New York: Wiley, 1993), 68.
15. Much of the information in this section comes from two excellent books by Roger Axtell: *Do's and Taboos around the World* (note 14 above) and *Gestures: The Do's and Taboos of Body Language around the World* (New York: Wiley, 1991).
16. Budd, 131.
17. Sanae Kobayashi, "Characteristics of Japanese Communication," *Communication World* (December/January 1996–97): 15.
18. Axtell, *Gestures*, 150.
19. William H. Frey, "The Diversity Myth," *American Demographics* (June 1998): 39, 41.
20. John Robinson, Bart Landry, and Ronica Rooks, "Time and the Melting Pot," *American Demographics* (June 1998): 20.
21. Rossman, 6, 12.
22. "Wye River Agreement Signed as Sabbath Approaches," Agence Presse France, 24 October 1998, online, Lexis-Nexis.
23. Mary Jo Jacobi, "Communications without Borders: Thinking Globally While Acting Locally" (speech delivered to the 1998 annual meeting of the International Public Relations Association, London, 17 July 1998).
24. Axtell, *Gestures*, 50.
25. Alice Lagnado, "Putin to Purge Russian Tongue of Foreign Elements," *Times*, 1 May 2001, 16.
26. Adam Sherwin, "Mandela Steals Show in Trafalgar Square," *Times*, 30 April 2001, 8.
27. Jerry W. Thomas, "Brave New World," *Communication World* (March 1998): 38.
28. "Pitney Bowes Messaging Study Reveals Hidden Cultural Pitfalls for Communicating with Colleagues and Customers outside the United States," a news release issued by Pitney Bowes, 31 July 2000, online, www.PitneyBowes.com.
29. David Howes, ed., *Cross-Cultural Consumption* (London: Routledge, 1996), 1.
30. Naseem Javed, "Naming for Global Power," *Communication World* (October/November 1997): 33.
31. Maud Tixier, "How Cultural Factors Affect Internal and External Communication," *Communication World* (February/March 1997): 25.
32. Information in this paragraph comes from Axtell's *Do's and Taboos* and *Gestures* (notes 14 and 15 above).
33. Henry Louis Gates Jr., "Whose Culture Is It, Anyway?" *Cast a Cold Eye* (New York: Four Walls Eight Windows, 1991), 263.
34. Budd, 126.
35. Howes, 2.
36. Susan Fry Bovet, "Firms Send Promising Internationalists to 'College,'" *Public Relations Journal* (August/September 1994): 28.

37. Ilana DeBare, "But Some Entry-Level Workers Still Face Difficulties," *San Francisco Chronicle,* 7 April 1997, online, Lexis-Nexis.

38. Peter Jennings, Bob Jamieson, and Bob Woodruff, *ABC World News Tonight,* 25 January 2001, online, Lexis-Nexis.

39. Peter Martin, "Shoals across the Pond," *Financial Times,* 2 June 2001, online, Lexis-Nexis.

40. Widget Finn, "Mind the Culture Gap," *Daily Telegraph,* 14 June 2001, online, Lexis-Nexis.

41. Jennings, Jamieson, and Woodruff; William Drozdiak, "Alacatel Aims to Purchase Lucent," *Washington Post,* 29 May 2001, online, Lexis-Nexis; "When Business Pops the Question," *Engineer,* 18 May 2001, online, Lexis-Nexis.

42. Jennings, Jamieson, and Woodruff.

43. Finn.

44. Andrew Leach, "DaimlerChrysler Just the Latest Example of a Merger Most Foul," *Daily Mail,* 21 January 2001, online, Lexis-Nexis.

45. Drozdiak.

46. Cynthia Kemper, "Challenges Facing Public Relations Efforts Are Intensified Abroad," *Denver Post,* 1 March 1998, online, Lexis-Nexis.

47. Axtell, *Do's and Taboos,* 68, 89.

48. Ibid., 90.

49. Jacobi.

50. "Diversity Initiatives," Pitney Bowes web site, www.pitneybowes.com.

51. "Pitney Bowes Celebrates Diversity around the World," a news release issued by Pitney Bowes, 29 February 2000, online, www.pitneybowes.com.

52. "Pitney Bowes Names Keith Williamson President of Capital Services Division," a news release issued by Business Wire, 31 March 1999, online, Lexis-Nexis.

53. "Pitney Bowes Celebrates Diversity around the World."

54. Pitney Bowes web site, www.pitneybowes.com.

55. Pitney Bowes web site, www.pitneybowes.com.

56. Pitney Bowes web site, www.pitneybowes.com.

57. "Pitney Bowes Names Keith Williamson President of Capital Services."

58. Marjorie Whigham-Desir and Robyn D. Clarke, "The Top 50 Blacks in Corporate America," *Black Enterprise* (February 2000), online, Lexis-Nexis.

59. Anne Swardson, "Top U.S. Retailer Heads North," *Washington Post,* 17 June 1994, online, Lexis-Nexis.

60. Swardson.

61. Darren Schuettler, "Wal-Mart Predicts Dramatic Growth in Canada," *The Reuter Business Report,* 2 May 1994, online, Lexis-Nexis.

62. Schuettler.

63. *HFD: The Weekly Home Furnishings Newspaper,* 4 July 1994, online, Lexis-Nexis.

64. Joanna Ramey and Jim Ostroff, "Wal-Mart Mexico City Unit Reopens after Shutdown," *Women's Wear Daily,* 24 June 1994, online, Lexis-Nexis; John Freivalds, "Managing Languages in the 21st Century," *Communication World* (October/November 1997): 36.

65. *HFD;* Schuettler.

Public Relations and the Law

objectives

After studying this chapter, you will be able to

- understand the differences between and the regulation of political and commercial speech

- appreciate how privacy and copyright laws affect the practice of public relations

- identify the higher burden of proof public officials and public figures have in libel cases

- recognize the increasing role public relations has in the judicial system

The Annual Report

scenario

You are vice president of investor relations for a publicly owned corporation. The company's annual report is the most visible product to come out of your office. For that reason, you always take extra care to make certain everything is absolutely perfect. The deadline is rapidly approaching, and you still have several decisions to make.

This year, for example, you want to tell shareholders about the company's new commercial spokesman, Billy Joe Touchdown. Touchdown was voted Most Valuable Player as he led his team to the championship. There's a great picture of Billy Joe holding up the championship trophy in a national sports magazine. You wonder whether you can use it in your annual report.

Then there is the financial information that the government wants included in the annual report. You mutter to yourself, "Who is going to read all of this gobbledygook? Is it really necessary?"

But before you can deal with either of these issues, the chief executive officer tells you that, because the company has lost money during the year (having lost several major contracts), the CEO plans to consolidate corporate offices and to move the headquarters to a new city. This raises several questions in your mind: Should we announce these moves right away? Can they wait until I am finished working on the annual report? What does all this mean for my job? Should I call my stockbroker and sell my shares of company stock before we announce the headquarters move and negative publicity results?

Time is wasting, and you have to make a number of important decisions. What are you going to do?

Public Relations, the Law, and You

There are daily reminders that litigation has become an integral part of U.S. culture. Look at today's newspaper. It is a sure bet that it won't be very long before you come across a story in which someone is accused of breaking a law, a business is accused of harming its customers, or some company's policies are challenged for any of a thousand reasons. According to the Administrative Office of the U.S. Courts, lawsuit-related filings in federal district courts alone totaled 322,262 in 2000. More than 80 percent of that number, 259,517, were civil cases (noncriminal actions initiated against individuals or corporations).[1] And these figures do not even take into account lawsuits filed in state and municipal courts. Like it or not, this is the reality of today's society.

This fact should not be lost upon public relations practitioners. They are often thrust into the limelight when their employer's actions face legal challenges. Practitioners also require an intimate knowledge of the laws governing what they may or must say or do in a variety of situations. For example, a certain degree of exaggeration is perfectly acceptable at times. However, other times it is not. Depending on whom the practitioner is representing, some information can be considered public for all to see or very private.

The challenge for public relations practitioners is to understand the many laws and regulations that govern or, at least, influence their practice. If you are the practitioner in the scenario at the beginning of this chapter, it is obvious that you need to know a lot. First, on the question of whether you can use someone else's picture of Billy Joe Touchdown, you need to understand copyright law. As to the question of what information is required in an annual report, you need to be familiar with the regulations of the Securities and Exchange Commission and the stock markets. Those same regulations will give you answers to the questions about the timing of the release of information and the decision to sell your stock. (We touch on all these issues later in the chapter.)

Unfortunately, at least one study suggests that many practitioners do not have a good understanding of the laws and regulations governing the public relations profession. More than half the practitioners questioned in one survey indicated they had no familiarity with SEC regulations. In the same survey, more than 48 percent said they were not familiar with laws relating to professional malpractice, 45 percent were not familiar with laws governing financial public relations, and 40 percent were not familiar with laws pertaining to commercial speech. These responses led the author of the study to this conclusion:

> The finding that most practitioners are only somewhat or not at all familiar with important legal issues, combined with the finding that most of their work is either not reviewed or subject to limited review by legal counsel, suggests that many public relations practitioners may be placing both themselves and their clients at risk of legal liability.[2]

Attorney Morton J. Simon said that public relations practitioners "can and have cost companies millions of dollars. While the incidence of legal implications [to the practice of public relations] may vary, their importance when they exist cannot be minimized."[3]

Public Relations and the First Amendment

As noted in Chapter 3, the most important event in the development of public relations in the United States was the adoption of the **First Amendment** to the Constitution. The freedoms guaranteed by the First Amendment provide the framework for the nation's social, political, and commercial discourse:

> Congress shall make no law respecting an establishment of religion, or prohibiting the free exercise thereof; or abridging the freedom of speech, or of the press, or of the right of the people peaceably to assemble, and to petition the Government for a redress of grievances.[4]

In the more than two centuries since its adoption, a great deal of thought and debate has surrounded what the First Amendment does and does not guarantee. There have been many instances in which free expression has come in conflict with other social interests. Does a person's First Amendment right to freedom of speech supersede someone else's Sixth Amendment right to a trial by "an impartial jury"? Does freedom of expression allow one to yell "fire" in a crowded theater? Clearly, the freedoms embodied in the First Amendment are not absolute. It has been left up to the courts, and, ultimately, the Supreme Court, to decide upon the amendment's limits.

It would be nice if the rules governing free expression were clearly defined for everyone to understand. However, we are members of an increasingly complex community in a constantly evolving world. Not only are the channels of communication rapidly changing—witness the growth of the Internet during the 1990s—but so are concepts of personal freedom. With these changes come inevitable clashes and efforts to redefine the rules. And public relations, itself an act of free expression, is on the cutting edge of that change.

Political versus Commercial Speech

Although public relations enjoys certain protections under the First Amendment to the U.S. Constitution, these rights are not without some limitations. The practice of public relations often falls into a gray area between what the law characterizes as political speech and commercial speech. **Political speech** is defined as expression associated with the normal conduct of a democracy—such as news articles, public debates, and individuals' expressions of their opinions about the events of the day. In general, the U.S. Supreme Court has been reluctant to limit political speech. Justice William Brennan wrote in 1964 that there is a "profound national commitment to the principle that debate on public issues should be uninhibited, robust, and wide-open, and that it may well include vehement, caustic, and sometimes unpleasantly sharp attacks on government and public officials."[5]

Commercial speech, which is defined as expression "intended to generate marketplace transactions," is more restricted.[6] In fact, for much of the nation's history, commercial speech has been treated by courts as if it were unprotected by the First Amendment. In 1976, however, the Supreme Court ruled that a Virginia law prohibiting pharmacists from advertising prescription drug prices was unconstitutional. In doing so, the court recognized limited First Amendment protection for "pure commercial speech":

> Generalizing, society also may have a strong interest in the free flow of commercial information. Even an individual advertisement, though entirely "commercial," may be of general public interest. . . . And if it is indispensable to the proper allocation of resources in a free enterprise system, it is also indispensable to the formation of intelligent opinions as to how that system ought to be regulated or altered. Therefore, even if the First Amendment were thought to be primarily an instrument to enlighten public decision making in a democracy, we could not say that the free flow of information does not serve that goal.[7]

Supreme Court Justice Harry Blackmun also wrote in *Virginia State Board of Pharmacy v. Virginia Citizens Consumer Council Inc.,* "In concluding that commercial speech, like other varieties, is protected, we of course do not hold that it can never be regulated in any way. Some forms of commercial speech regulation are surely permissible."[8] Two years later, in *First National Bank of Boston v. Bellotti,* the Court also affirmed that corporations do enjoy some rights of political speech.

The Supreme Court further defined the limits of commercial speech in the 1980 case *Central Hudson Gas & Electric Corp. v. Public Service Commission of New York*. In that case, Central Hudson Gas & Electric successfully challenged a state ban on promotional advertising by electric utilities. The Court said that there are times when restrictions on commercial speech are justified because they serve certain social interests. In *Central Hudson,* however, the justices felt that the regulation in question was "more extensive than necessary to serve that interest." The Court sided with the utility, saying that the government interest could have been accomplished with less restrictive regulation.[9] The Court clarified what it meant by "not more extensive than necessary" in 1989, when it ruled that the government can "reasonably" restrict commercial speech, even when other means can achieve the "substantial governmental interest" involved.[10]

In recent years, state and federal courts have given commercial speech greater legal protection. The Supreme Court ruled in June 2000 that state governments may not place greater restrictions on tobacco advertising than those required by federal law. California's top appeals court ruled that same year that a Nike advertising campaign in which the company denied using sweatshop labor has First Amendment protection. The U.S. Court of Appeals in New York in 1998 overturned a state liquor authority ban of certain Bad Frog Beer labels—ones that featured a frog making what many people consider an obscene gesture.[11]

Is public relations considered political speech, or is it considered commercial speech? The answer largely depends on the public being targeted, the purpose of the message, and the court's interpretation. Despite this somewhat murky answer, two things are very clear. First, there are limits to both political and commercial speech. And second, public relations practitioners need to know what those limits are.

Quick ✔ Check

1. What does the research cited in this section say about practitioners' knowledge of the laws and regulations governing public relations?
2. What is the difference between the ways the U.S. Supreme Court has treated cases involving political speech and those involving commercial speech?
3. Is public relations considered political speech, or is it considered commercial speech?

The Key: Know Your Own Business

It is not suggested here that every public relations practitioner should be ready to take the state bar exam. However, you don't have to be a lawyer to have a good working knowledge of the law. And that understanding should begin in the workplace. All public relations professionals need to know the laws and regulations that govern their organization.

Many of these laws and regulations relate to the handling of private information. For example, hospital public information officers need to know the rules pertaining to the confidentiality of patient records. Most of the information found in a patient's file is considered private. An improper release of that information could open the practitioner and the hospital to civil or criminal litigation. If you work in a financial institution, there are dozens of regulations regarding the release and content of financial information. And at your college, there are limits on how much of your personal record—including your grades—can be made public.

The actions of practitioners can also be controlled by the legal status of the organizations they represent. Government practitioners must learn that all their records are open to public inspection, except records specifically exempted by law. The best-known federal law guaranteeing access to government information is the **Freedom of Information Act (FOIA)**. Although this law is often associated with journalists, anyone can use it to gain access to information kept or generated by the federal government.

The FOIA applies to all federal agencies and departments except the president and his advisers, Congress and its subsidiary committees and agencies, and the federal judicial system.[12] Although there are specific exemptions to the FOIA, a vast majority of federal government records are available for anyone to inspect. Similar laws covering records held by state and local governments have been enacted nationwide. State and federal "sunshine" laws also require that meetings of government agencies at which official decisions are made must be open to the public. However, as is the case with open records laws, specific exemptions permit some government business to be conducted in private. Typically, these exemptions involve meetings with attorneys, land purchase negotiations, security issues, and discussions of personnel matters.

Practitioners employed by nongovernmental organizations enjoy a much greater degree of privacy than do their government counterparts. However, even they may be governed by state and federal requirements relating to disclosure (a concept that we discuss later in greater depth), taxation, and ethical conduct. For example, people hired for the purpose of influencing the actions of state and federal officials must register as lobbyists. Practitioners representing the interests of governments or organizations based outside the United States must also register as foreign agents. Both lobbyists and foreign agents must file periodic reports on their activities with designated agencies.

Federal Agencies That Regulate Speech

The federal government does not license public relations practitioners. Several federal agencies, however, do have a major impact on the practice of public relations. These agencies create and enforce regulations designed to protect the public's best interests. These rules often cover company or organization communications, especially in areas considered to involve commercial speech. Four of the most prominent of these agencies are the Federal Trade Commission, the Securities and Exchange Commission, the Federal Communications Commission, and the Food and Drug Administration.

The Federal Trade Commission

When public relations practitioners promote a particular product or service, their actions may fall under the watchful gaze of the **Federal Trade Commission (FTC)**. The FTC was established in 1914 "to ensure that the nation's markets function competitively . . . are vigorous . . . and free of undue restrictions."[13] The commission is the source of most federal regulation of advertising. However, it also has jurisdiction over product-related publicity generated by public relations practitioners.

The Federal Trade Commission Act empowers the FTC to "prevent unfair methods of competition, and unfair or deceptive acts or practices in or affecting commerce."[14] This includes advertisements and publicity that may be considered false or misleading, including claims that are unsubstantiated, ambiguous, or exaggerated. The FTC is especially sensitive when the product or service being promoted may adversely affect personal health or when it requires a considerable investment of money before the consumer can determine its effectiveness.

If the FTC believes a violation of the law has occurred, it may obtain voluntary compliance through what is known as a **consent order.** However, if such an agreement cannot be reached, the commission can take a complaint before an **administrative law judge.** This person hears testimony and reviews evidence, much like the judge and jury in a civil or criminal case. An administrative law judge can issue a **cease and desist**

QuickBreak 15.1

THE FREEDOM OF INFORMATION ACT

Under the federal Freedom of Information Act, a U.S. government agency has 10 days to respond to a request for information. There are nine specific circumstances under which FOIA does not apply:

1. Information properly classified as secret to protect national security, intelligence operations, and/or military plans
2. Internal practices and personnel rules of an agency
3. Records specifically exempted by statute
4. Proprietary business information such as trade secrets
5. Inter- or intra-agency memoranda and excerpts of working documents not normally made part of the public record
6. Private personnel and medical files
7. Investigatory records compiled for law enforcement purposes, except records that can be disclosed without interfering in an ongoing investigation, identifying confidential sources, invading privacy, endangering lives, or preventing a fair trial
8. Records pertaining to the operation and conditions of financial institutions
9. Private geological and geophysical information pertaining to gas and oil wells

If an FOIA request is denied, the law prescribes a process for appeal that ultimately can lead to the court system.

order. This decision can be appealed to the full commission, then to the U.S. Court of Appeals, and ultimately to the U.S. Supreme Court. If the FTC's ruling is upheld, it can then seek **injunctions, consumer redress,** and **civil penalties** through the federal court system. In the case of ongoing consumer fraud, the FTC can go directly to federal court in an effort to protect consumers.[15]

The Securities and Exchange Commission

Remember the opening scenario of this chapter? Our practitioner complained about the financial "gobbledygook" in the annual report and asked, "Is it really necessary?" The answer, in a word, is a resounding yes. And if the required information is not in the report, the company—and the practitioner—will soon hear from the government agency that oversees the nation's financial markets, the **Securities and Exchange Commission (SEC).**

As a result of the 1929 stock market crash that triggered the Great Depression, the federal government closely monitors the financial affairs of publicly traded companies. Congress created the Securities and Exchange Commission in 1934 to "administer federal securities laws and issue rules and regulations to provide protection for investors and ensure that the securities markets are fair and honest."[16] In other words, the SEC's job is to see to it that everyone is operating on a level playing field. It does so by ensuring that investors can base their decisions on timely and accurate information.

The concept of **disclosure** is the foundation of SEC regulation. Under the Securities Act of 1933, publicly held companies—companies that issue financial securities, such as stocks and bonds, for public sale—have an obligation to disclose frankly, comprehensively, and immediately any information that is considered important to an investor's decision to buy, sell, or even hold the organization's securities.

Return for a moment to the scenario at the beginning of this chapter. The SEC has very explicit guidelines for the release of information important in the decision to buy or sell stock. The fact that a company is losing money and is being forced to streamline its operations is clearly of interest to investors. Under these circumstances, the company is expected to make timely disclosure of these facts. This disclosure should take several forms, including filing a Form 8-K directly with the SEC and distributing news releases to financial news media.

A real-life example of the need to disclose timely and accurate information was the Year 2000 or Y2K computer problem. As the new millennium approached, a great deal of concern was expressed about the fact that many computer programs used only two digits to identify a year in the date field. The fear was that these computers would read the year 00 as 1900, thus creating a data-processing nightmare. Aware of these concerns, the SEC issued a bulletin in October 1997 to "remind public operating companies, investment advisers, and investment companies to consider their disclosure obligations relating to anticipated costs, problems, and uncertainties associated with the

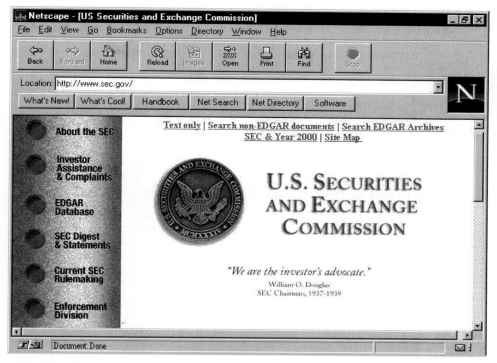

Web Site The Securities and Exchange Commission operates a web site that provides instant access to a variety of public records and federal regulations. (Courtesy of the U.S. Securities and Exchange Commission and Netscape)

Year 2000 issue."[17] Fortunately, as discussed in Chapter 11, the world entered the new millennium without any major computer-related failures.

Although companies are required to file a large variety of reports with the SEC and other federal agencies, the most recognizable channels of disclosure are Form 10-K to the SEC and the annual report to shareholders. Publicly held corporations annually file a **Form 10-K** with the SEC. In it, a company is required to disclose specific information about its financial health and direction. This includes annual and multiyear reports on net sales, gross profit, income, total assets, and long-term financial obligations. The 10-K report also includes a management discussion and analysis of the company's financial condition.

Form 10-K usually provides the basis for the more familiar corporate **annual report,** which has to be in the hands of shareholders no less than 15 days before the corporate annual meeting. Typically, these annual reports are written and designed to make the investor feel good about his or her decision to own stock in the company. But serious investors and analysts look beyond the color pictures printed on glossy

Annual Report Publicly held businesses such as the Sonic restaurant chain are required by law to inform shareholders about the company's financial health and other issues that could affect the value of the shareholders' investments. (Courtesy of Sonic, America's Drive-In)

paper. They focus on Form 10-K, which is often inserted at the back of the annual report and printed on plain paper. All the small print may seem like gobbledygook to the practitioner in this chapter's opening scenario, but it *is* necessary; and the information required in Form 10-K also has to be included in the annual report. Among the SEC requirements for an annual report are

- audited financial statements
- supplementary financial information, such as net sales, gross profits, and per-share data based on income or loss
- management discussion and analysis of the company's financial condition and any unusual events, transactions, or economic changes
- a brief description of the company's business (products and/or services)
- the identities of company directors and executive officers
- a description of any significant litigation in which the company or its directors or officers are involved

UNITED STATES
SECURITIES AND EXCHANGE COMMISSION
Washington, D.C. 20549

FORM 10-K

[X}   **ANNUAL REPORT PURSUANT TO SECTION 13 OR 15(d) OF THE SECURITIES EXCHANGE ACT OF 1934 FOR THE FISCAL YEAR ENDED JUNE 30, 2000**

[_]   **TRANSITION REPORT PURSUANT TO SECTION 13 OR 15(d) OF THE SECURITIES EXCHANGE ACT OF 1934 FOR THE TRANSITION PERIOD FROM _____ TO _____**

Commission File Number 0-14278

MICROSOFT CORPORATION

Washington   **91-1144442**
(State of incorporation)   **(I.R.S. ID)**

One Microsoft Way, Redmond, Washington 98052-6399

(425) 882-8080

Securities registered pursuant to Section 12(b) of the Act:

None

Securities registered pursuant to Section 12(g) of the Act:

Common Stock

Form 10-K Disclosure statements filed by publicly held companies, such as this 10-K filing by Microsoft, are a matter of public record and are available, online and otherwise, from the Securities and Exchange Commission.

QuickBreak 15.2

SEC RULE 10b-5

Any practitioner engaged in financial public relations must study SEC Rule 10b-5, which prohibits fraudulent or misleading corporate communications in matters that could affect investment decisions. Rule 10b-5 states that it is illegal "to make any untrue statements of a material fact or to omit to state a material fact necessary in order to make the statements made, in light of the circumstances under which they were made, not misleading." The rule also prohibits "any act, practice, or course of business which operates or would operate as a fraud or deceit upon any person, in connection with the purchase or sale of any security."[18]

One area in which this rule has a major impact on the practice of public relations is insider trading. That was the issue in 1985, when the SEC filed charges against Anthony M. Franco, the owner of a Detroit public rela-

tions firm and national president-elect of the Public Relations Society of America. The SEC complaint stemmed from a news release Franco had prepared in which his client, Crowley, Milner and Company, announced its intentions to buy another firm, Oakland Holding Company.

The SEC suit claimed that Franco purchased 3,000 shares of Oakland Holding Company stock in anticipation of making a sizable profit upon the public announcement of the proposed buyout. When the unusual transaction caught the attention of American Stock Exchange officials, Franco rescinded the trade. He claimed that his stockbroker had acted without his authorization. The SEC suit was resolved when Franco signed a consent decree, in which he did not acknowledge any wrongdoing but promised to obey the law in the future. When the affair became public knowledge in

---

This is only a thumbnail sketch of SEC annual report reporting requirements.[19] It is a good idea to check with the SEC each year to keep up with changes in disclosure requirements.

The SEC came into great prominence in the 1980s when many investors, including a president of the Public Relations Society of America, were accused of what is known as **insider trading.** A person is considered in violation of insider trading rules if he or she buys or sells securities on the basis of inside information not available to other investors. People who provide insider information may also be considered in violation of the law—even if they did not buy or sell stocks on their own. In the chapter opening scenario, you would risk criminal prosecution by selling your stock before giving appropriate public disclosure of your company's bad news.

If the public is to have confidence in the nation's financial institutions, everyone has to play by the same rules. As the SEC states on its web site, "Because insider trading undermines investor confidence in the fairness and integrity of the securities markets, the [SEC] has treated the detection and prosecution of insider trading violations as one of its enforcement priorities."[20]

1986, *after* he had assumed the PRSA presidency, Franco was forced to resign that post. Threatened with action by the PRSA Board of Ethics, he also resigned his membership in October 1986.[21]

Rule 10b-5 is also important in the area of timely and accurate disclosure. This was a central issue in a 1968 landmark case involving the Texas Gulf Sulfur Company. TGS geologists discovered a major deposit of valuable minerals in eastern Canada in November 1963. During the five months between the discovery and its public announcement, a handful of TGS executives—the few people who knew the secret—bought more than 20,000 shares of company stock. To squelch rumors of a major ore strike, TGS issued a news release on April 12, 1964, that said, in part, "The drilling done to date has not been conclusive."[22] Four days later, a second news release announced a major ore strike. An appeals court eventually ruled that the April 12 news release was misleading and a violation of Rule 10b-5. Many of the TGS executives involved in the incident were fined and ordered to repay profits made as a result of the inside information.

PRSA's *Member Code of Ethics 2000* addresses these issues under the section dealing with the disclosure of information. It lists among its guidelines that members shall "be honest and accurate in all communications" and "investigate the truthfulness and accuracy of information released on behalf of those represented." The code cites as an example of improper conduct "Lying by omission: A practitioner for a corporation knowingly fails to release financial information, giving a misleading impression of the corporation's performance."[23]

The Federal Communications Commission

Public relations practitioners who work for political candidates or whose clients may be subject to public criticism should be familiar with the federal agency that has regulated the nation's broadcast media since 1934, the **Federal Communications Commission (FCC).** Originally created as the Federal Radio Commission in 1927, the FCC has the primary responsibility for ensuring the orderly use of the nation's airwaves in the public interest. Because a finite number of radio wave frequencies are available for public use, radio and television stations operate under licenses granted by the federal government. In contrast, print media face relatively little government oversight because of historic precedents and First Amendment protections. Since the Telecommunications Act of 1996, broadcast licenses are granted for a period of eight years and may be renewed after a review of the licensee's performance.

Public relations practitioners representing political candidates should also be aware of section 315 of the 1934 Communications Act, better known as the **equal opportunity provision.** Whenever a legally qualified candidate for public office appears in a radio or television broadcast, all other candidates for that office must be afforded

Values Statement 15.1

AGENCY FOR TOXIC SUBSTANCES AND DISEASE REGISTRY

In 1980 Congress created the Agency for Toxic Substances and Disease Registry (ATSDR) to implement the health-related sections of laws that protect the public from hazardous wastes and environmental spills of hazardous substances. Based in Atlanta, ATSDR is a division of the federal Department of Health and Human Services.

ATSDR's highest priority is protection of the public health. In meeting that priority, the Agency and its employees commit to the following values:

Act at all times in the best interest of the public health.

Treat the public respectfully and courteously and respond promptly to requests with accurate, up-to-date information.

Treat each other courteously and respectfully.

Meet high performance standards, produce quality work, and seek innovative means of accomplishing our work.

Base hiring and promotions on job-related qualifications; the Agency is committed to equal employment opportunity.

Promote employees' career development through education, training, and quality work experiences.

Follow the Department of Health and Human Services' Standards of Conduct for all employees.

—ATSDR web site

equal opportunities for access. It means that if a candidate appears in a broadcast at no cost, all other qualified candidates for that office must be offered the same opportunity. Under another provision of the law, legally qualified candidates must be allowed to purchase commercials at the station's lowest advertising rate.

Section 315 is usually applied to political advertising but can also be triggered by the appearance of a qualified candidate in a product commercial, a public service announcement, or entertainment programming. For example, television stations stopped airing old Ronald Reagan films in 1976 after Reagan announced his candidacy for the Republican presidential nomination. However, there are exemptions to the rule. The equal time provision does not apply when a candidate appears in a bona fide newscast, news interview, news documentary, or on-the-spot coverage of a bona fide news event. In these days of tabloid TV, however, it can be difficult to distinguish between what is and is not bona fide news programming.

The FCC used to have a rule known as the "fairness doctrine." It required broadcasters to "devote a reasonable amount of their programming to controversial issues of public importance, and provide contrasting viewpoints on those issues."[24] However, unlike the equal opportunity provision, no rigid formula was devised for compliance. Under the pressure of legal challenges, the FCC abandoned the fairness doctrine in 1987.

Remnants of the fairness doctrine remain, however. One such remnant is the **personal attack rule,** which requires stations to provide free air time to persons subjected to a character attack during a broadcast presentation on a public issue. Unlike section 315, the personal attack rule does not necessarily require equal air time. In other words, if the character attack occurred during a prime-time television show, the station does not have to offer the exact same time slot. The station is obliged only to offer a "reasonable" opportunity for response. If the rule sounds vague on what is "reasonable," that is because it is. It is also an area of the law under constant review.

One other significant point must be made about the FCC. Confusing though this may seem, most FCC regulations do not apply to nonbroadcast media outlets on cable television, such as MTV, ESPN, and CNN. In general, the Supreme Court has ruled that when it comes to matters of program content, cable television should be treated in much the same fashion as print media. This is because cable television does not use the public airwaves to distribute its signals.[25]

The Food and Drug Administration

As public relations ventures deeper into the integrated marketing of products and services, practitioners are having to familiarize themselves with the regulations of yet another federal agency, the **Food and Drug Administration (FDA)**. The FDA was created to "protect, promote, and enhance the health of the American people." The agency has responsibility for ensuring that "foods are safe, wholesome, and sanitary; human and veterinary drugs, biological products, and medical devices are safe and effective; cosmetics are safe; and electronic products that emit radiation are safe."[26]

The area in which public relations practitioners are most likely to encounter this agency is in the promotion of products or services that are regulated by the FDA. The FDA enforces laws and regulations designed to ensure that regulated products are "honestly, accurately, and informatively represented."[27] FDA rules include restrictions on the labeling and promotion of prescription drugs. Both advertising and public relations professionals working in the health-care field must be aware of these limitations.

In recent years the FDA has played an important role in helping the media, consumer groups, and health professionals provide the public with current and accurate information about regulated products. During the 1990s, for example, former FDA Commissioner David Kessler was an outspoken critic of what he said were the tobacco industry's attempts at marketing cigarettes to children. Occasionally the agency has also proved itself to be an ally of business. For example, Kessler helped PepsiCo convince a concerned public in 1993 that reports of medical syringes in cans of Diet Pepsi were hoaxes.

Quick Check

1. Why is it important for public relations practitioners to understand the laws and regulations that govern their organizations?
2. Which federal agency serves as a watchdog against false and misleading advertising claims?
3. What does *disclosure* mean, and why are disclosure rules so vigorously enforced?

Libel

Another area in which public relations practitioners may be restricted in their use of free expression involves **libel**, which is loosely defined as "a false communication that wrongfully injures the reputation of others."[28] To put it another way, when you bad-mouth someone, you had better have your facts!

There are two major reasons why public relations practitioners need to have a good understanding of libel law. First, they need to know that there are limits to free speech, especially when it involves another person's or company's reputation. They also need to understand that the courts have—under certain circumstances—given people great latitude in expressing their opinions on matters of public concern.

Libel law is very complex. The authors of this book want to familiarize you with this very important topic, but we do not present an exhaustive discussion. In an attempt to bring clarity to the subject, we use broad generalizations in some instances. If you are seeking an interpretation of a specific event, this book is probably not your best source for legal advice. You would be better served by seeking out a lawyer schooled in libel and mass communications law. By the way, the legal term for what you just read is *disclaimer*.

The Burden of Proof in Libel

Before 1964, people seeking damages under a claim that they had been libeled needed to prove five things: defamation, publication, identification, damage, and fault. These five things are known as the **burden of proof.**

DEFAMATION.   **Defamation** is any communication that unfairly injures a person's reputation and/or ability to maintain social contacts. Untruthful allegations that someone is a Nazi or has AIDS are examples of defamatory statements. It is also possible to defame a company, product, or service. In determining whether defamation has occurred, the court takes into account the context in which the statement was made, asking questions such as whether a reasonable person would understand the comment to be a parody or a joke. A truthful statement cannot be considered defamatory. Also, under the law you cannot defame a dead person.

PUBLICATION.   **Publication** is the communication of a defamatory statement to a third party. Don't let the term *publication* fool you. This burden of proof is not restricted to print media; it is met regardless of the communication channel used. Another important concept closely related to this is the *republication rule*. If you repeat a defamatory statement made by someone else, *you* can be subject to a separate libel claim, even if you accurately quoted the original source. However, there are exceptions to the republication rule. For example, you may accurately repeat a defamatory statement contained in an official court document or during a meeting of an official governmental body such as Congress.

IDENTIFICATION.   Identification is the requirement that the person or organization alleging libel has to be identified in such a way that a reasonable person could infer that the defamatory statements applied to the plaintiff. This is easy to prove when names are used. However, this requirement can also be satisfied when no names are mentioned, if the defamatory statement provides information that can lead a reasonable person to believe it describes a particular individual or organization. It is even possible to defame members of a group. An allegation that someone at your college is a crook probably does not satisfy this burden. However, an allegation that someone in your family is a crook probably does.

DAMAGE.   There has to be evidence that the person or organization suffered injury or **damage** as a result of the defamation. This is not limited to financial injury, such as the loss of a job. Damage can also consist of loss of social esteem, such as losing all of your friends. Although this kind of damage may be intangible, juries have been known to give out some very high monetary awards as compensation for loss of social esteem.

FAULT.   A plaintiff can demonstrate **fault** by proving that the defamatory statement is untrue. (Remember, a truthful statement is not defamatory.) Before 1964, the burden was on the defendant to show that the statement was true. Even if the statement was made as a result of unintentional error, the fact that an error was made was all that really mattered. However, it is on this burden of proof—fault, or falseness—that in 1964 the Supreme Court made what many have argued was one of its most significant rulings involving freedom of expression. In that ruling the Court articulated the doctrine of *actual malice,* to which we now turn.

Actual Malice

In the case of **The New York Times v. Sullivan,** the Court set a higher burden of proof in libel cases involving public officials. It also shifted the burden of proving the falsity of a statement to the plaintiffs. In essence, the justices said public officials had to show not only that the statements made about them were not true but that the source of those statements knew—or should have known—they were not true. This higher burden of proof is known as **actual malice,** which the Court defined as knowing falsehood or reckless disregard for the truth.

Why did the Supreme Court make it harder for public officials to sue for libel? The case came out of the civil rights struggle of the 1960s. A civil rights group had run a full-page advertisement titled "Heed Their Rising Voices" in the *New York Times.* In the ad the group accused Montgomery, Alabama, officials of illegally suppressing lawful dissent. The basic thrust of the advertisement was accurate. However, some of the statements made in it were not—such as the number of times Martin Luther King Jr. had been arrested (four, not seven as stated in the advertisement). Because of the republication rule, Montgomery Police Commissioner L. B. Sullivan decided to sue the newspaper for libel. The purpose of this tactic was clearly understood by all: to make the nation's news media think twice before accepting the word of civil rights advocates. A jury awarded Sullivan $500,000 in damages, and the Alabama Supreme Court upheld the ruling. The U.S. Supreme Court, however, overturned the decision in a 5–4 vote.

In writing for the Court, Justice William Brennan said this higher burden of proof was necessary to guarantee healthy public debate:

> A rule compelling the critic of official conduct to guarantee the truth of all his factual assertions—and to do so on pain of libel judgments virtually unlimited in amount—leads to . . . "self-censorship." Allowance of the defense of truth, with the burden of proving it on the defendant, does not mean that only false speech will be deterred. . . . Under such a rule, would-be critics of official conduct may be deterred from voicing their criticism, even though it is believed to be true and even though it is in fact true, because of doubt whether it can be proved in court or fear of expense of having to do so. . . . The rule thus dampens the vigor and limits the variety of public debate. It is inconsistent with the First and Fourteenth Amendments.[29]

Subsequent court decisions have defined a **public official** as a person elected to public office (and potentially criticized in that role) or anyone who has significant public responsibility and is engaged in policy making. In another decision, *Gertz v. Robert Welch, Inc.,* the Supreme Court extended the actual malice burden to libel cases involving **public figures**—people who have widespread notoriety or have injected themselves into a public controversy in an attempt to influence its outcome. The Reverend Jesse Jackson may not be a public official, but when it comes to civil rights, he is considered a public figure.

This takes us back to something we stated earlier: People are often given great latitude in expressing their opinions on matters of public concern. As hard a pill as it may be to swallow, there is often little that public relations practitioners can do when they or their bosses are harshly criticized in the media. If a boss qualifies as either a public official or a public figure, then he or she is part of the public discourse and must meet a higher burden of proof, actual malice, to sue successfully for libel. Although a few public officials and public figures have won libel cases, most have not.

Common Law Libel

In the mid-1980s the courts handled two libel cases under common law rules. Common law consists of legal rules and principles that originate from judicial decisions, as opposed to those that are enacted by legislators or regulatory agencies.[30] The nature of these **common law libel** cases raises a red flag for business communicators because both cases involve everyday business practices in which human nature can lead to "mistakes." Several elements of these cases are of particular note. First is the lack of constitutional protection. Communication of "a private matter" is not protected by First Amendment; in these cases, therefore, the plaintiff needed to show only negligence to win punitive damages. Second, in one of the cases the plaintiff won damages on defamatory but true information that exceeded the company's privilege to share such information.

QuickBreak 15.3

"FREE SPEECH ROCKS!"

"It has just stopped me cold from eating another burger," said TV talk show host Oprah Winfrey.[31] Those words, spoken during an April 16, 1996, show on the safety of the U.S. food supply, soon became the focal point of a Texas-sized showdown over free speech.

Vegetarian activist Howard Lyman had just accused the cattle industry in the United States of using the same practices suspected in the spread of the so-called mad cow disease in Britain. At the time of Lyman's remarks, 23 people had died from the disease and British beef had been pulled off the market in much of the world. When Winfrey asked, "You said this disease could make AIDS look like the common cold?" Lyman said, "Absolutely."[32]

Within hours of the broadcast, U.S. beef prices fell in what cattle industry executives called "the Oprah crash." Prices fell almost $7 per hundredweight right after the broadcast and continued to fall over a two-week period. Cattle executives responded with an $11 million lawsuit, claiming that the talk show host had "carefully and maliciously edited statements that were designed to hype the ratings at the expense of the American cattle industry."[33]

Winfrey was sued under a Texas state law that forbids food disparagement. **Food disparagement laws**—known informally as "veggie libel laws"—were an outgrowth of a 1989 controversy over the use of the pesticide Alar on apple orchards. When the TV newsmagazine *60 Minutes* ran a report linking Alar to cancer in children, apple sales fell and growers sued. Although the growers eventually lost, the incident spawned the adoption of food disparagement laws in more than a dozen states.[34]

Constitutional law expert Richard Epstein of the University of Chicago said veggie libel laws reside in a gray area between fact and opinion. "There is a large body of law which says that, if you utter matters of opinion, these are absolutely protected," Epstein said. "But if you make false statements about a fact about a given product or a given person, these can be libelous."[35]

After five weeks of testimony and two days of jury deliberations, an Amarillo, Texas, jury ruled in favor of Winfrey. Her case was aided by a judge's ruling that the case could not go forward under the veggie libel law because the plaintiffs had not proved that cattle are a "perishable food" or that "knowingly false" statements were made. U.S. District Court Judge Mary Lou Robinson's ruling meant that the case had to meet a higher burden of proof—a burden similar to the actual malice standard in traditional libel cases. Judge Robinson said the plaintiffs had to show that Winfrey had deliberately or recklessly hurt the beef business by making false statements.[36]

"Obviously, we're disappointed," said Paul Engler, one of the cattle industry executives who had brought the action. "At the same time, we do believe that we made one very strong point—that U.S. beef is safe."

"Free speech not only lives, it rocks," Winfrey told reporters after the decision. She added, "I'm still off hamburgers."[37]

The first case involved the credit reporting firm Dun & Bradstreet, which had issued an erroneous credit report on Greenmoss Builders, a building contractor. The Supreme Court ruled that this was a "private matter" not involving "matters of public concern" and permitted Greenmoss to recover $50,000 in presumed damages and

$300,000 in punitive damages.[38] Although a complicated decision, the ruling appears to exclude nonmedia defendants from constitutional protection.

The second case involved a DuPont company memo following the firing of an employee for sexual harassment. The memo referred to the recent firing and then restated company policies and procedures regarding the issue. Eventually word of the firing, including the identity of the former employee, spread through the community. The former employee sued DuPont for common law libel and won. The court ruled that the company had gone too far in identifying the ex-employee to those who did not need to know his name. The ruling came despite the fact that the information about the employee was true, and despite the company's recognized privilege to pass that information around on a need-to-know basis. Thus, in this common law libel case, truth was *not* a defense. True information that exceeds privilege, in this case someone's legitimate need to know, can cost your company in libel damages.

Privacy

Libel is not the only area of the law to distinguish between truly private individuals and persons in the limelight. This distinction is also evident in privacy law. The legal debate over an individual's right to privacy is very complicated and, in many instances, unresolved. It often surprises people to discover that the U.S. Constitution does not specifically mention an individual's right to privacy. However, such a right has developed over the years through the passage of laws and through judicial decisions. As a general rule, private individuals have an easier time suing for invasion of privacy than do public figures.

The Four Torts of Privacy

Although the word *privacy* has one meaning in common everyday usage, it carries a different meaning when used in a legal context. *Black's Law Dictionary* has defined **privacy** as "the right to be left alone; the right of a person to be free from unwarranted publicity."[39] The law recognizes four torts, or wrongful acts, that constitute an invasion of privacy: intrusion, false light, publication of private facts, and appropriation.

INTRUSION.   Intrusion is defined as an improper and intentional invasion of a person's physical seclusion or private affairs. This area of privacy law hinges on whether a person has a reasonable expectation of privacy. Examples of intrusion involve trespassing on private property and illegally bugging telephone conversations. But if a television crew positioned on a public sidewalk photographed you inside your home through an open window, that would not, in a legal sense, be considered intrusion.

FALSE LIGHT.   You can be sued if you present someone in a **false light,** even if the communication in question isn't defamatory. For example, a picture of a man holding a mug of water in his hand is not, in and of itself, defamatory. But if the man is a member of a religion that prohibits its followers from drinking alcohol, and if the picture's caption implies that he is enjoying a beer, that could result in a claim of false light invasion of privacy. Categories of false light are distortion (the unintentional distortion of reality), fabrication (knowing falsehood perpetrated through alteration or embellishment of the facts), and fictionalization (publication of something, usually a book or movie, that is presented as fiction but closely mirrors real life).

PUBLICATION OF PRIVATE FACTS.   **Publication of private facts** involves the public disclosure of true personal information that is embarrassing and potentially offensive. The courts have ruled, in essence, that we are entitled to keep some secrets about ourselves. However, to make a successful claim under this tort, a plaintiff must show that the information is neither newsworthy nor from a public record. If an ordinary person drinks too much in the privacy of his or her home and doesn't break any laws, it is likely that the courts will consider this private information. However, if this same person is an elected official and gets picked up for drunken driving, his or her drinking problem becomes a public matter.

APPROPRIATION.   **Appropriation** is defined as the commercial use of someone's name, voice, likeness, or other defining characteristics without consent. For example, entertainer Bette Midler was once forced to tone down her stage act because she too closely mimicked the voice and mannerisms of legendary actress Mae West. "The Divine Miss M" herself later successfully used this aspect of privacy law to prevent a Midler sound-alike from appearing in an advertisement. The commercial use of a person's likeness without consent is often referred to either as *misappropriation* or as infringement of an individual's *right of publicity*. This right does not necessarily end with a person's death. In several states, California among them, the deceased's heirs retain the "right of publicity." However, the courts have said that in some circumstances a claim of misappropriation is not valid. For example, news content is not considered a commercial use. Nor is it considered a commercial use when a media outlet uses a likeness in promoting itself. Written consent is the best protection from a claim of misappropriation.

Privacy Issues in Public Relations

Privacy issues can arise in countless aspects of the practice of public relations. Practitioners routinely prepare news releases, publicity photos, videos, newsletters, annual reports, brochures, posters, and web sites for public dissemination. An invasion of privacy suit can originate from any of these communications. For example, let's return to the scenario at the beginning of this chapter. If you were to use the image, voice, or name of Billy Joe Touchdown without his permission, your company could be sued for misappropriation. And you could be looking for a new job. Always get permission—in writing.

One area in which the practitioner has to be especially sensitive to privacy rights is employee relations. "It should not be assumed that a person's status as an employee waives his/her right to privacy," writes Frank Walsh, an expert in public relations law. "However, there are circumstances in which the employment relationship may provide an implied consent or waiver sufficient to invalidate an invasion of privacy suit." As an example Walsh cites information about an employee that is published within an internal company newsletter. In that context, the item may be considered newsworthy by the newsletter's audience and, therefore, not subject to a claim of invasion of privacy. However, Walsh says, the same item published without consent in an external publication may not enjoy the same legal protection.[40] Frankly, as a matter of common courtesy, it would be best to ask the employee anyway.

Privacy concerns also come into play when reporters make inquiries about employees. There are restrictions on the kinds of employee information that can be made public. The laws vary by location and profession. Typically, practitioners are limited to confirming a person's employment, job title, job description, date hired, and, in some cases, date terminated. A good guideline to follow: Check first with the personnel or human resources department about what is considered public or private employee information.

The growth of the Internet has raised many workplace questions. For example, the degree to which an employer may monitor an employee's e-mail may depend on whether a reasonable expectation of privacy exists. In some corporations employees are told that their e-mail will be monitored. Other companies, in search of time-wasting and inappropriate behavior, regularly review printouts of the web sites their employees visit while on the job. Because the widespread use of the Internet is a recent phenomenon, there are not many legal precedents to serve as guides.

Copyright

Although privacy protections are not specifically mentioned in the U.S. Constitution, **copyright** protections are. Copyrights protect original works from unauthorized use. Central to any discussion of copyright protections is the concept of **intellectual property,** which federal law defines as "original works of authorship that are fixed in a tangible form of expression." Copyrights cover seven forms of expression: literary works; musical works; dramatic works; pantomimes and choreographic works; pictorial, graphic, and sculptural works; motion pictures and other audiovisual works; and sound recordings.[41] Because the development of digital technology has made it nearly impossible to tell a copy from an original, the protection of intellectual property is a legal area of vital importance.

Copyright concerns about protecting one's own property and respecting the rights of others are a common issue for public relations practitioners. Copyright law confronts us all in many different ways every day. Is it all right to take a funny editorial cartoon published in the morning newspaper and reprint it in the company newsletter? Can someone use one company's products to promote another's without permission? Is it legal to take an image off a web site and use it in another medium? Are you allowed to photocopy this book?

Copyright Guidelines

As is true with other aspects of public relations law, the best place to get answers to these and other questions about copyrights are people who have expertise in this area—in this case, copyright lawyers and the U.S. Copyright Office. That said, some general rules of copyright are worth remembering:

- Copyright protection exists from the moment a work is created in a fixed, tangible form. In other words, the law presumes that a work becomes the intellectual property of the author at the moment of its creation.

- Copyrights do not protect works that have not been fixed in a tangible form of expression. Although it is possible to copyright an author's written description of a particular location, that does not prohibit someone else from offering a different description of the same setting.

- If a work is prepared by someone within the scope of his or her employment, it is considered **work for hire** and becomes the intellectual property of the employer. The work belongs to the employer if it was produced while the employee was "on the clock." Even after hours, the employer retains the rights if company resources (such as computers, copiers) were used.

- It is possible for the copyright owner, such as a photographer or writer or artist, to grant limited use of the work while retaining copyright ownership.

- Copyrights do not protect ideas, methods, systems, processes, concepts, principles, and discoveries. They do, however, protect the manner in which these are expressed.

- Government documents and other publicly owned works may not be copyrighted.

The Digital Millennium Copyright Act

The ability to make exact copies of digital files without any measurable decline in quality is one of the great blessings of the Digital Age. However, in the view of copyright holders, it is also one of the great curses.

As noted in Chapter 11, digital technology has made it easier to copy and distribute the fruits of someone else's labors. This is of particular concern to the entertainment and computer software industries, which have seen their intellectual property rights eroded by the manufacturing and distribution of illegal copies.

These industries use special technology designed to foil piracy. For example, when a Hollywood movie studio distributes its latest movie on DVD, it encrypts the data on the disk to prevent unauthorized copying. That should be enough.

QuickBreak 15.4

R.I.P. LARRY BUD MELMAN?

There are no monuments to Larry Bud Melman. He isn't dead. And because he is a fictional character, he isn't really alive, either. He is actually in legal limbo—missing in action as a result of the late-night TV talk show wars.

Melman, played by New York character actor Calvert DeForest, had become a fixture on the long-running NBC series *Late Night with David Letterman*. To put it kindly, Melman was ragged, rumpled, and remarkably ordinary—the antithesis of what many consider a typical television performer. He would show up anywhere and do almost anything for a laugh. In the show's "Ask Mr. Melman" segment, DeForest would "dispense advice to audience members on matters emotional, sexual, financial and legal, and in other areas in which he had absolutely no expertise."[42]

Letterman left NBC in 1993 after a prolonged controversy over whether he or Jay Leno would succeed the retiring Johnny Carson as host of the *Tonight Show*. When Leno got the

Although Calvert DeForest had to drop his moniker "Larry Bud Melman," he and David Letterman got the last laugh on NBC. (Courtesy of Big Look Management)

However, in a world in which the frontiers of computer knowledge are breached every day, it is not. To use an analogy, locksmiths would face the same problem if every time they built a better lock, someone came along behind them and built an even better key.

In an effort to address this problem, the U.S. Congress passed the **Digital Millennium Copyright Act** in 1998. The DMCA established new rules for downloading, sharing, and viewing copyrighted material on the Internet. It made it a crime to circumvent antipiracy measures built into most commercial software, videos, and DVDs. It also outlawed code-cracking devices used to copy software illegally. Violators can be fined up to $2,500 for each violation.

The law is controversial. Academics, computer researchers, and librarians have argued that DMCA limits their right to copy and share a limited amount of material for educational and noncommercial purposes. However, it also provides these same groups certain exemptions, including limited liability for most colleges and universities concerned about copyright infringement committed by faculty or students. Still,

nod, Letterman bolted to CBS to launch his own late-night offering, *The Late Show with David Letterman*.

For Letterman and NBC, it was a bitter divorce. And when Letterman announced his intention to take the Melman character and other elements of the old show with him to his new network, NBC executives protested. They claimed that all the comedy material produced for *Late Night* was the intellectual property of NBC, the owner of the show. This included rights to Melman, Letterman's famous "Top Ten" lists, "Stupid Pet Tricks," and "The World's Most Dangerous Band," the moniker used by bandleader Paul Shaffer and his musicians. NBC's message was clear: If the new show looks like the old show, we will sue!

Letterman and CBS took the threat very seriously. They hired copyright attorneys as a precaution. DeForest dropped the Melman name. "The World's Most Dangerous Band"

became the "CBS Orchestra." The old opening monologue, consisting of only three jokes on *Late Night*, was lengthened for *The Late Show*. But Letterman clung to his "Top Ten" lists and "Stupid Pet Tricks." The *real* trick was to retain as much of the old as possible while making the new show distinctive. Letterman and CBS waited. NBC chose not to carry out its threat.

For the August 30, 1993, premiere of *The Late Show*, the comedian coaxed an old friend, *NBC Nightly News* anchor Tom Brokaw, to walk on stage in the middle of the monologue, snatch up some cue cards, claim that they were the intellectual property of NBC, and walk off the stage in a huff. And as for DeForest, his was the first face viewers saw, popping out of the network's "eye" logo bellowing, "This is CBS!"[43]

As might be expected, Letterman got the last laugh.

service providers are expected to remove material that violates copyrights from user web sites.

Fair Use

The courts have said it is all right to use copyrighted works without their owners' permission in some circumstances. These instances fall under the concept known as **fair use,** which the law has said is the use of copyrighted material "for purposes such as criticism, comments, news reporting, and teaching."[44] Again, fair use is a very complex area of the law. However, it is usually considered fair use if the copyrighted work is used for an educational as opposed to a commercial purpose.

The degree to which the copyrighted material is copied and the effect upon its potential market value also affect whether a claim of fair use is valid. It is probably safe for professors to photocopy a paragraph from a book and distribute the copies to their classes. Copy shops have stopped reproducing book chapters for professors using course packets, however, because the courts have ruled that this practice harms the book's potential market value.

In a ruling that further defined fair use rights, the U.S. Supreme Court strengthened the rights of freelance writers in 2001. The court ruled by a 7–2 margin that major publishing companies may not reproduce the work of freelancers in electronic form without their consent. The effect of the ruling was to give the writers a voice in whether their work, originally published in one form, could be electronically published in an online database. As a practical matter, the Court's ruling largely affects only that material produced in the pre–Internet era—before freelance contracts specified whether the material could be used online.

Public relations practitioners often claim fair use when taking a quotation from a copyrighted publication for use in a news release, brochure, report, or speech. (For example, we have engaged in this practice in writing this book.) However, a claim of fair use cannot be made without appropriate attribution of the copyrighted material to its owner. As your writing and editing teachers will remind you, this is just one more reason why it is necessary to use quotation marks and to properly cite sources of information.

Protecting Your Intellectual Property Rights

To assert a right of copyright protection, the work in question should bear a copyright notice that cites the year of the copyright and the name of its owner. An example: Copyright © 1999 John Q. Public. An even more complete way of securing copyright protection is to register a work within three months of its creation with the U.S. Copyright Office, Library of Congress, Washington, D.C. 20559. There is a $20 nonrefundable filing fee. Although registration is not required to claim ownership, it is required to bring an infringement of copyright lawsuit. Copyright protection lasts for the life of the author plus 50 years. Works copyrighted by businesses or organizations are protected for 75 years.

So what about the picture of Billy Joe Touchdown in the opening scenario? Can you use it? The key to answering that question is identifying the owner of the rights to the picture. Does the national sports publication own them, or are they owned by someone else and published with the owner's permission? Once ownership is determined, the procedure is simple: You secure written permission to publish from the owner. You may have to pay for the privilege. If the picture is considered a public document, you may not have to pay anything at all. But always check first. In this case, you would want to check first with the publisher of the magazine in question.

Similar to copyrights are trademarks and service marks. Both protect intellectual property rights. **Trademarks** (™) protect names, designs, slogans, and symbols that are associated with specific products. When you see the symbol ®, that indicates that the trademark is registered with the U.S. Office of Patents and Trademarks. For example, pick up a 12-ounce can of Coca-Cola®. Both the name Coca-Cola® and its derivative, Coke®, are registered trademarks. So is the design of the can and style of the lettering.

When organizations want to protect names, designs, slogans, and designs associated with a particular service, they apply for a **service mark,** indicated by the symbol ^{SM}.

Quick ✓ Check

1. What is the higher burden of proof that public officials and public figures must meet to make a claim of libel?
2. In terms of privacy law, what is appropriation?
3. What steps have been taken to protect intellectual property rights on the Internet?

Litigation Public Relations

Up to this point, our look at the relationship between public relations and the law has focused of freedom of expression and how it is may be restricted. However, with the *New York Times* proclaiming this "the era of the lawyer as press agent," another aspect of the relationship merits attention—the growing practice of **litigation public relations (LPR).**[45]

Litigation public relations is the use of mass communication techniques to influence events surrounding legal cases. Although it often focuses on lawyers' dealings with reporters, including preparation of news releases, coaching for interviews, and monitoring media, LPR can also involve the use of other public relations practices. These include focus groups and surveys as well as courtroom exhibit preparation.

Public Relations as a Legal Strategy

A rash of high-profile cases—most notably the double-murder trial of O. J. Simpson—has brought the ethics of LPR practitioners into question. It is an ethical controversy rooted in the Constitution. The First Amendment guarantees freedom of speech and of the press. The Sixth Amendment guarantees fair and open trials. In this age of pervasive media, these two social interests often come into conflict.

While serving as chairman of the Criminal Justice Standards Committee of the American Bar Association (ABA), William Jeffress Jr. said, "A lot of us think defense attorneys and prosecutors shouldn't be playing to the press and becoming public relations agents for their clients."[46] One New York judge complained, "Lawyers now feel it is the essence of their function to try the case in the public media."[47]

Not surprisingly, some lawyers vigorously defend the use of public relations in connection with their practices. The late William M. Kunstler, who served as defense counsel in some of the most controversial trials of the past generation, believed that the use of pretrial publicity was necessary to balance scales of justice he thought were tipped unfairly toward the prosecution. "Whenever and wherever practicable, fire must be met with fire," Kunstler wrote.[48]

And just how far should this jockeying for public opinion go? Noted defense attorney Eric Naiburg once told a room full of journalism educators that he had no problem misleading the news media to advance the position of a client. If the news media publish something untrue, Naiburg said, "it is not my problem." A reporter on the same panel as Naiburg called this "manipulation" and questioned whether the use of public relations in high-profile cases was for the benefit of the client or "a marketing tool for attorneys."[49]

Because few states have laws that limit what prosecutors and defense attorneys can say before trial, it is generally left to state bar associations to regulate pretrial comment.[50] Most of these regulations mirror Rule 3.6 of the ABA's Model Rules of Professional Conduct. The rule states that "a lawyer shall not make an extrajudicial statement that a reasonable person would expect to be disseminated by means of public communication if the lawyer knows or reasonably should know that it will have a substantial likelihood of materially prejudicing an adjudicative proceeding."[51] However, this rule is rarely enforced. "It's hard to prove that some out-of-court statement has an impact on a trial," said New York University law professor Stephen Gillers. "So, essentially, there's a rule but there really isn't any rule."[52]

The waters were muddied even further by the U.S. Supreme Court in June 1991, when the Court reversed sanctions against a Nevada attorney who had conducted a news conference to counter negative publicity about his client. In *Dominic P. Gentile v. State Bar of Nevada*, the Court said the rule, as interpreted by the Nevada state bar, was too vague. In his opinion for the majority, Justice Anthony M. Kennedy wrote, "In some circumstances press comment is necessary to protect the rights of the client and prevent abuse of the courts."[53]

The Use of LPR Tactics

One survey of trial lawyers suggests that although most do not, as a rule, use mass communication techniques in their practices, a majority approve of their use. Nine out of 10 litigators surveyed said that in certain circumstances it is appropriate to speak to the media on behalf of a client. And by a more than 2-to-1 ratio, those who were surveyed and expressed an opinion said they thought the media had been fair in reporting cases in which they had personally been involved. Still, most lawyers appear to be uneasy about being under the glare of the media. Nearly three out of every five lawyers questioned in that same survey disagreed with the notion that the people of the United States have a better understanding of the courts through extended television coverage, and four out of five disagreed with the notion that the O. J. Simpson trial coverage advanced public understanding of the courts.[54]

When public relations practitioners are engaged in LPR, they usually work for the lawyer, not the client. LPR practitioners often aid in pretrial research by using public opinion polls and focus groups to determine the mood of the jury pool. Lawyers sometimes use this information to test specific approaches that may be employed in court. Practitioners often coach both lawyers and clients on how to deal with the media, how to be interviewed, and how to be proactive in defending their reputation. A practitioner's roles also may include preparation of courtroom exhibits; service as a contact point for the media; and, in the most controversial aspect of LPR, assistance in efforts to influence the jury pool before a trial ever takes place.

Even when the practitioner works independently of a lawyer, it is often the lawyer who has the closest access to the client. The reason for this is simple: The lawyer, not the practitioner, has legal immunity. One very public example of this surfaced in 1998, when then–presidential spokesman Mike McCurry told reporters that he had not asked President Clinton about his relationship with a White House intern. McCurry said he did not want to be subpoenaed by the special prosecutor investigating the allegations surrounding Clinton:

> On matters like this that are going to be under investigation, I think it could conceivably jeopardize the legal representation the president is entitled to, so I choose not to ask him directly about these things and rely on what counsel tells me. And then we work with the president to figure how we're going to respond to questions.[55]

For any practitioner, the reality of this lawyer–client **privilege** issue can be difficult to swallow—especially when it runs counter to the professional need to have direct access to management. It was especially frustrating for McCurry, who told reporters at one White House briefing, "I think you all know the constraints that I'm laboring under here, and I don't want to belabor the pain and anguish I feel."[56]

Is LPR in Society's Best Interests?

Is LPR a good thing for our society? No pun intended, but the jury is still out. On the one hand, people and companies should have every right to defend their reputations in the court of public opinion. However, many are bothered by attempts to use extrajudicial statements (statements made outside a court) to influence proceedings inside the court.

Some argue that the U.S. judicial system often favors the rich. If the 1991 Los Angeles police beating of Rodney King had not been videotaped, would King, a black man with a history of run-ins with the law, have had the same level of legal representation? As William Kunstler noted, prosecutors have the government public information apparatus at their command. One LPR expert has suggested that it might not be a bad idea to provide less well off defendants with court-appointed public relations counsel (just as court-appointed public defenders are provided). Richard Stack of American University said this form of legal aid would "balance the scales of justice."

Our understanding of the courts has been blurred by the images we see on television. For many years, television lawyers such as Perry Mason and Ben Matlock gave many people an unrealistic view of how the courts operate. Now, because of the fairly recent introduction of cameras and microphones into the courtroom, we are seeing courts as they really are: usually boring and sometimes messy. Some of the public disillusionment with our criminal justice system may have to do with getting

Media Analysis Report A media analysis report can help litigation public relations practitioners show clients the effectiveness of media relations strategies and tactics. (Courtesy of Levick Strategic Communications)

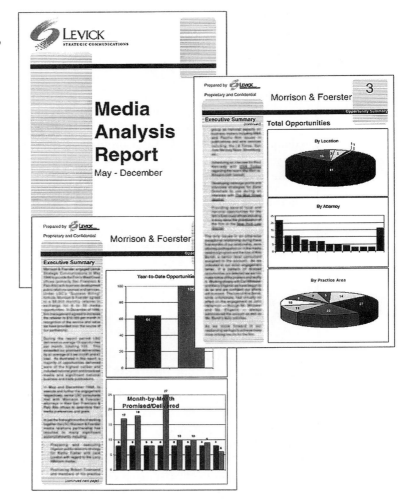

this cold dose of reality. Certainly, a public revulsion against excess litigation has something to do with it, as well.

It all comes down to the difficult balancing act left us by the framers of the Constitution. A built-in conflict exists between the First and Sixth Amendments. Judges, lawyers, and public relations practitioners must carefully navigate these uncharted waters. We must also remember that, as public relations practitioners, we have our own codes of ethics to uphold. The PRSA *Member Code of Ethics 2000* says that practitioners must "serve the public interest by acting as responsible advocates for those we represent." The code also says that "a member shall preserve the integrity of the process of communication." Though not explicit statements on LPR, they do, nevertheless, provide meaningful guidance.

In these muddy and uncharted waters, professional and personal values are the best guide as to what is best for our clients and for society.

Quick ✔ Check

1. What is litigation public relations?
2. Why must litigation public relations practitioners sometimes deal only with lawyers instead of the lawyers' clients?
3. What are the arguments for and against the use of litigation public relations?

Summary

In today's litigious society, it is not enough for a public relations practitioner to understand how to communicate. Practitioners need to know the laws that govern communication. Many practitioners appear to be woefully ignorant of the rules and regulations governing many aspects of their jobs, but, as anyone who has had driver's education can tell you, ignorance of the law is no excuse.

First Amendment protection for the practice of public relations lies in the gray area between political and commercial speech. The underlying purpose of each communication determines the degree of constitutional protection it enjoys. In addition to constitutional issues, laws govern various aspects of specific businesses. Among the most notable of these are disclosure laws pertaining to publicly held companies. Practitioners also are often confronted by a need to understand libel, privacy, and copyright laws. In the case of libel and privacy laws, they also need to understand the different burdens of proof for public and private individuals. The growth of the Internet and digital technologies have triggered legal issues undreamt of a generation ago.

Public relations is having a growing—and not necessarily positive—effect on our civil and criminal justice systems. The practice of litigation public relations is expanding dramatically—thanks in part to the built-in conflict that exists between our constitutional freedom of expression and our constitutional right to a fair and open trial. Here, as in other areas of public relations, we should be guided by our values.

DISCUSSION QUESTIONS

1. Devise a response to this statement from a fellow public relations practitioner: "This is the United States. I have freedom of speech. I can say whatever I want on behalf of my clients."
2. How do federal agencies regulate commercial speech?
3. What is the burden of proof for libel? Are all persons treated the same under libel law?
4. How do privacy rights affect the practice of public relations?
5. What are some tasks undertaken by a practitioner of litigation public relations? Under what constraints do LPR practitioners operate?

Memo *from the* Field

Richard S. Levick, President, Levick Strategic Communications, Washington, D.C.

Richard S. Levick, Esq., is the president of Levick Strategic Communications, a worldwide leader in law firm media relations, crisis media intervention, and editorial coverage. Founded in February 1998, the company has been featured by *Small Business Computing* magazine as one of the "Ten Most Technology-Savvy Small Businesses in the United States." For more than seven years Levick was the director of publicity for Jaffe Associates, where he developed the award-winning Legal News Service.

Levick has provided business-development communications consultation to more than 100 law firms and directed public relations for many of the major law firm mergers over the past decade. He is the former director of American University's School of Public Affairs Leadership Program, where he is a frequent guest lecturer. He holds a bachelor of arts in Urban Studies from the University of Maryland, a master of science in Environmental Advocacy (Communications) from the University of Michigan, and a juris doctor degree from American University's Washington College of Law.

It's 3:30 Saturday afternoon during Labor Day weekend when you return home to the telephone ringing. The managing partner of a major national law firm is on the other end. The death penalty case a senior partner has represented pro bono has turned ugly after the execution, with the governor going on television accusing the law firm of criminal activity. The accusations are false, but the television cameras are waiting outside the lawyer's hotel room. He needs to read a statement to the news media in 15 minutes. Can you call him and fax him his statement?

A disgruntled customer goes on the Internet and sets up a web site highly critical (and only modestly accurate) about your company's business practices. Soon he has six others who feel the same way and files a class-action lawsuit, claiming hundreds of millions of dollars in damages. Your company will likely win the case, but the damage to market share, reputation, and company morale may be significant. What media strategies do you recommend?

The debate over litigation public relations spends all of its time on the edges of the issue: the attempts by practitioners to use the media to influence jury pools or identify class plaintiffs. The truth is, most litigation public relations is about law firms and their clients working with the media to preserve market share, reputation, and morale. To this extent, there is no debate. Companies and individuals have a nearly unmitigated right to speak out about their interests.

As to law firms, the U.S. Supreme Court ruled in 1977, in *Bates v. Arizona*, that while state bar associations could place minor restrictions on what law firms could say, they could not prohibit outright law firms from exercising their First Amendment rights. Canada and the United Kingdom followed suit a decade later. In the international marketplace, with more law firms expanding globally, this is the future.

The National Law Journal reported in 1998 that consumer products and services companies were increasingly choosing to settle weak and even frivolous claims because settling is now perceived as less expensive than the potential for devastating public relations—and its subsequent potential damaging impact on market share and reputations—involved in legal proceedings. With the growth of television magazines and other media and with their indefatigable thirst for controversy, even the most benign disagreement can take on the air of a pitched battle when conciliatory facts are left on the cutting-room floor.

Clients, particularly defense clients, come to law firms with business problems, not legal ones. Lawyers must recognize that there are times, particularly when a client has a strong position in the courts and a message they want to get out to their publics, that economic concerns rule legal issues. Lawyers unaware of this potential cannot even counsel their clients to consider these economic issues. The worst-case scenario for a lawyer insensitive to the power of public perception is that the lawyer wins the case while the client loses market share.

Lawyers are among the most difficult clients to work for, with their intellectual acumen, demand for excellence, considerable ethical requirements, and scales of perfection. Litigation public relations must work synergistically with the legal effort. This means that public relations always defers to legal and ethical issues. It also means that public relations counsel must be familiar with legal, business, political, and public relations issues and how they work together. Individual practitioners or teams of public relations specialists must have the capability to sort this matrix of competing demands and counsel a proper approach.

For the student interested in entering litigation public relations, the three most important things you can do are:

1. Read newspapers, particularly the *Wall Street Journal* with its careful and clever headlines, as a critical consumer, getting a gut instinct for "news."
2. Search the web for the leading legal web sites, and subscribe to free legal news services such as Law News Network at www.lawnewsnetwork.com and the Legal News Network at www.legalnewsnet.com. This will keep you apprised of the day's legal news and give you a chance to "reverse engineer" where legal news comes from.
3. Read *The 22 Immutable Laws of Marketing* by Al Ries and Jack Trout, an excellent and succinct book about communicating with your target audience.

And when you do start, begin with noncrisis "business development" public relations activities for the legal profession. This will allow you to learn how the legal community works before you face a crisis—when there is no time for contemplation, only action.

Case Study 15.1

The Court of Public Opinion

An estimated audience of 150 million people stopped what they were doing on Tuesday, October 3, 1995, to witness the end of what had become television's most riveting daytime drama: *The State of California v. O. J. Simpson*. Simpson had been accused of murdering his ex-wife, Nicole Brown Simpson, and her friend Ron Goldman. Although the criminal phase of the Simpson story ended that day with the defendant's acquittal, the fallout from the trial continues.

A lot of issues were played out during the Simpson trial. Many people wondered whether the rich and famous get the same level of justice as the poor and anonymous. Many people raised questions about the treatment of minority defendants by the U.S. criminal justice system. Others focused on the domestic violence aspects of the case. Still others questioned the feasibility of conducting a fair and open trial in a hyperintensive media environment.

And then there was the question of the role of public relations. Both the prosecution and the defense made extensive use of public relations tactics. Each side attempted to try the case in the court of public opinion long before it came before Judge Lance Ito.

"The Simpson case validates the practice of litigation PR," said Fred Garcia, a communications ethics teacher at New York University. "For the media, covering the legal process is nearly as important as covering the outcome of the case. That makes litigation PR a hot growth area."[57]

One skirmish, very early in the proceedings, typified the jockeying for position in the battle for public opinion. During a pretrial hearing, Simpson attorney Robert Shapiro asked prosecutor Marcia Clark to produce a "bloody ski mask," the existence of which had been erroneously reported in the media. Shapiro forced Clark to admit in open court what both sides already knew, that there was no ski mask. The absence of the ski mask was destined to be the lead story on the network newscasts—that is, until Los Angeles District Attorney Gil Garcetti did Shapiro one better. Later that same day, Garcetti's office released an October 1993 recording of a 911 call by Simpson's ex-wife, in which an enraged O. J. Simpson could be clearly heard in the background. That tape was what led the evening newscasts.

Trying to sway the opinion of jurors is nothing new—that is what a trial is all about. But trying to sway the passions of jurors *before* they are even selected or have heard testimony is a relatively new—and disturbing—trend. Lawyers are hired to represent the interests of their clients, but they are also officers of the court and sworn to protect the integrity of the judicial system. A growing number of lawyers are now conducting focus groups, holding news conferences, and developing multimedia presentations that are designed to do just one thing—influence potential jurors. There is even evidence to suggest that extrajudicial publicity can influence presiding judges.

One such case involved a 12-year-old Florida boy, who became nationally known as the child who wanted to divorce his parents. His legal team included a public relations practitioner who was instrumental in having the young man, Gregory Kingsley, interviewed for the ABC-TV newsmagazine *20/20*. The interview was broadcast during the closing stages of the trial. The judge, who was supposed to make his decision based solely on evidence presented during the trial, cited comments made in that TV interview in granting the boy's request.[58]

Some argue that litigation public relations helps to balance the scales of justice in a system in which the prosecution has a built-in advantage. An example is the case of an Orlando orthopedic surgeon. William Zink, who was also on the faculty of a medical school, had taken nude medical photographs of an injury suffered by a young male patient. He had done so to document an injury for teaching purposes. The child's parents objected, claiming the pictures were pornographic. When the local prosecutor first declined to press charges, the child's family raised an uproar in the local media that ultimately resulted in an indictment.

At this point Zink's attorney hired a public relations consultant, Marti Mackenzie, who helped to soften the doctor's tarnished image. Although Zink was later acquitted, Mackenzie argued that effective publicity could have countered the family's efforts to inflame public opinion. Because the doctor lacked an adequate defense in the court of public opinion, Mackenzie said, the district attorney was forced to take the most politically expedient action: turning the question over to an emotionally charged grand jury.[59]

Although the controversy over the proper use of litigation public relations is likely to continue in the coming years, this much is known: The foundation of the U.S. judicial system is the belief that a jury of ordinary citizens, acting on evidence presented in a court of law, can decide without prejudice the innocence or guilt of a defendant. In the media frenzy that is often fueled by public relations tactics, it is often forgotten that a court trial is not a competition but a search for truth and justice.

DISCUSSION QUESTIONS

1. Can you cite other famous court cases in which litigation public relations was extensively involved? What were some of the tactics used by the opposing sides?
2. In your opinion, is it appropriate to serve on the defense team of a client who you believe is guilty?
3. Some believe litigation public relations helps to balance the scales of justice, although others feel it focuses too much on winning at any cost. What do you think?

Case Study 15.2

The Lion Roars

When the North Carolina–based Food Lion grocery-store chain was accused by a network news show of selling spoiled meat to its customers, the company fought back, using a unique—and controversial—legal strategy.

The story began when Food Lion unknowingly hired a reporter armed with a hidden television camera to work in the meat departments of two of its stores. During her brief 11 days on the job, reporter Lynne Neufer Litt collected more than 50 hours of videotape. That footage was the foundation of a 1992 *Prime Time Live* investigative report that purportedly showed Food Lion workers engaged in unsanitary meat-handling practices.

Food Lion officials felt that the report was false and that it was inspired by the program's quest for higher ratings. The subsequent release of hidden camera footage not broadcast also suggested that selective editing may have presented a distorted picture of reality. In addition, the company noted that the source of most of the allegations had been the United Food and Commercial Workers Union, which had for a decade unsuccessfully sought to unionize Food Lion stores. The union had coached Litt on how to pose as an experienced meat cutter and had arranged a phony letter of reference to help her gain employment with Food Lion.

Immediately after the program was broadcast, Food Lion President and CEO Tom Smith went on television in North Carolina and called the *Prime Time Live* segment "video magic." He said, "This stuff belongs in the tabloids, along with Elvis and UFO sightings."[60] Despite Smith's reassurances, the value of Food Lion stock dropped 10 percent the very next day. In the weeks and months following the broadcast, company revenues were also down.

Instead of suing the network for libel, the supermarket chain filed a $30 million lawsuit alleging that ABC had violated federal racketeering laws by using fraudulent means to gain employment for a reporter. A libel action would have required Food Lion to prove that ABC was guilty of actual malice, which is defined as knowing falsehood and reckless disregard for the truth. Fraud—in this case the manner in which the reporter obtained employment with Food Lion—would be much easier to prove. However, the downside of this tactic was that the company chose to challenge ABC on the manner in which it gathered its information but not on the veracity of it.

"In many ways this case is highly unusual if not absolutely unique," said Hugh Stevens, counsel for the North Carolina Press Association and a local counsel for ABC. "It certainly punishes the news media for what is a truthful report about a matter of public interest because of the way it was gathered."[61]

William S. Weiss, a New Jersey–based public relations consultant, had a different perspective on the case. Writing in *Public Relations Tactics,* Weiss said, "Obviously jurors were more disgusted by the fraudulent and illegal ways *Prime Time Live* obtained its evidence, and by the network's refusal to use video showing employees behaving responsibly."[62]

Initially, the unusual legal strategy appeared to have paid off for Food Lion. A North Carolina jury sided with the supermarket chain and awarded Food Lion $5.5 million in damages. However, a federal appeals judge later reduced the award by more than 90 percent to $315,000, saying that the initial award was too high and "constitutionally unsustainable."[63]

In the end, both sides claimed victory. In October 1999, the U.S. Court of Appeals for the Fourth Circuit reduced the damage award to $2—$1 for the employee's breach of loyalty and $1 for trespass. Ironically, the court threw out the fraud claim—and the remainder of the compensatory and punitive damages—because Food Lion had failed to assert a claim of libel. However, the court also rejected the network's claim that its hidden-camera news-gathering technique had First Amendment protection. In essence, the court said that ABC could have done its job without using questionable tactics.[64]

First Amendment experts and the media criticized the initial decision, claiming that it would have a chilling effect on investigative journalism. Washington-based attorney Bruce Sanford said, "It's punishing the messenger plain and simple."[65] However, the jurors did not see it that way. "The media has the right to bring the news, but they have guidelines too," said jury foreman Gregory Mack. "When you look at a football game, you see boundaries all around. You go out of bounds, you go out of bounds."[66]

DISCUSSION QUESTIONS

1. Should Food Lion have challenged *Prime Time Live* on the truthfulness of its reporting, or was the company right to adopt this unusual legal strategy?
2. How would you have handled a similar situation, in which a television reporter used a hidden camera to present an unflattering—and possibly inaccurate—picture of your company?
3. Suppose you work for a company and discover that a hidden television camera has caught your employees doing something illegal. The program is scheduled to air in a few days. How will you handle this situation?

It's Your Turn

SuperGas

You are the owner of a public relations agency. One of your agency's major clients is the XYZ Petroleum and Gas Company, a publicly held corporation listed on the New York Stock Exchange. XYZ has hired your agency to prepare media kits and promotional materials in advance of a major announcement.

The company is planning to announce that it has developed SuperGas: a new gasoline that increases car mileage, reduces automobile exhaust emissions, and costs a fraction of the price of conventional gasoline. XYZ officials predict that SuperGas will quadruple the value of company stock within one year. The announcement has been delayed while all the necessary patents were being registered. You have just been told that that process is complete and the news conference will be tomorrow.

As your staff prepares for the big announcement, you are faced with several sticky questions:

1. You want to use the XYZ company logo on the promotional materials you are developing. However, the logo was created by another public relations agency that used to represent XYZ. Can you use it?

2. Someone on your staff has suggested this marketing slogan: "SuperGas—the Rolls-Royce of Gasolines." You like it. But can you use it?

3. A reporter asks the XYZ officials about rumors of a major announcement that will shake up Wall Street. Some company officials want to say "No comment." Others want to deny the rumor and provide misleading information to the reporter. What advice will you give?

4. You know that you can't purchase any XYZ stock until after the public announcement of SuperGas. That would be considered insider trading. But as long as you did not make any money on the deal, would it be all right to pass along a stock tip to your best friend *before* the announcement? How about *after* the announcement?

KEY TERMS

actual malice, p. 495
administrative law judge, p. 485
annual report, p. 487
appropriation, p. 499
burden of proof, p. 494
cease and desist order, p. 485
civil penalties, p. 486
commercial speech, p. 482
common law libel, p. 496
consent order, p. 485
consumer redress, p. 486
copyright, p. 500
damage, p. 495
defamation, p. 494
Digital Millennium Copyright Act, p. 502
disclosure, p. 486
equal opportunity provision, p. 491
fair use, p. 503
false light, p. 498
fault, p. 495
Federal Communications Commission (FCC), p. 491

Federal Trade Commission (FTC), p. 485
First Amendment, p. 481
Food and Drug Administration (FDA), p. 493
food disparagement laws, p. 497
Form 10-K, p. 487
Freedom of Information Act (FOIA), p. 484
identification, p. 495
injunctions, p. 486
insider trading, p. 490
intellectual property, p. 500
intrusion, p. 498
libel, p. 494
litigation public relations (LPR), p. 505
The New York Times v. Sullivan, p. 495
personal attack rule, p. 492
political speech, p. 482
privacy, p. 498

privilege, p. 507
publication, p. 494
publication of private facts, p. 499
public figures, p. 496
public official, p. 496

Securities and Exchange Commission
 (SEC), p. 486
service mark, p. 505
trademarks, p. 504
work for hire, p. 501

NOTES

1. "Caseload Remains High in Federal Courts in Fiscal Year 2000," news release, Administrative Office of the U.S. Courts, 14 March 2001, online, www.uscourts.gov/Press_Releases/fy00case.pdf.

2. Kathy R. Fitzpatrick, "Public Relations and the Law: A Survey of Practitioners," *Public Relations Review* (spring 1996): 1–8.

3. Morton J. Simon, *Public Relations Law* (New York: Meredith, 1969), 4.

4. *The Constitution of the United States and The Declaration of Independence* (Commission on the Bicentennial of the United States Constitution, 1992).

5. *New York Times Co. v. Sullivan,* 376 US 255, 270 (1964).

6. *Virginia State Board of Pharmacy v. Virginia Citizens Consumer Council, Inc.,* 425 US 764, 765 (1976).

7. *Virginia State Board of Pharmacy v. Virginia Citizens Consumer Council, Inc.,* 425 US 764, 765 (1976).

8. *Virginia State Board of Pharmacy v. Virginia Citizens Consumer Council, Inc.,* 425 US 770 (1976).

9. *Central Hudson Gas and Electric Corp. v. Public Service Commission of New York,* 447 US 557, 100 S. Ct. 2343 (1980).

10. John D. Zelezny, *Communications Law: Liberties, Restraints, and the Modern Media* (Belmont, Calif.: Wadsworth, 1997), 361; Based on *Board of Trustees v. Fox,* 492 US 469, 480 (1989).

11. Robert S. Greenberger, "More Courts Are Granting Advertisements First Amendment Protection," *Wall Street Journal,* 3 July 2001, B1.

12. David W. Guth and Paul Wenske, *Media Guide for Attorneys* (Kansas Bar Association, 1995), 28.

13. Federal Trade Commission web site, www.ftc.gov.

14. FTC web site.

15. FTC web site.

16. Securities and Exchange Commission web site, www.sec.gov.

17. Securities and Exchange Commission, Staff Legal Bulletin No. 5 (CF/IM) (12 January 1998).

18. Zelezny, 331; 17 C.F.R. § 240.10b-5 (1992).

19. Robert W. Taft, "Discretionary Disclosure," *Public Relations Journal* (April 1983): 34–35.

20. SEC web site.

21. Dennis L. Wilcox, Phillip H. Ault, and Warren K. Agee, *Public Relations Strategies and Tactics,* 3rd ed. (New York: HarperCollins, 1992), 142–143.

22. *Securities and Exchange Commission v. Texas Gulf Sulfur,* 446 F. 2nd 1301 (2nd Cir 1966).

23. Public Relations Society of America, *Member Code of Ethics 2000,* online, www.prsa.org/codeofethics.html.

24. Zelezny, 424.

25. Zelezny, 430.

26. Food and Drug Administration web site, www.fda.gov.

27. FDA web site.

28. Zelezny, 519.

29. *New York Times Co. v. Sullivan,* 376 US 254, 279 (1964).

30. This information on common law libel has been graciously supplied by Associate Professor Thomas W. Volek of the University of Kansas.

31. *Texas Beef Group et al. v. Oprah Winfrey et al.,* complaint filed December 30, 1997, in U.S. District Court, Northern District of Texas, Amarillo Division, p. 4.

32. *Texas Beef Group et al. v. Oprah Winfrey et al.*

33. *Texas Beef Group et al. v. Oprah Winfrey et al.,* 2.

34. Adam Cohen, "Trial of the Savory," *Time,* 2 February 1998, 77.

35. Richard Epstein, transcript, online, CNN Interactive, 26 February 1998, www.cnn.com.

36. Associated Press, "Texas Jury Has No Beef with Oprah," in *Lawrence (Kansas) Journal World,* 27 February 1998, 3A.

37. "Oprah: 'Free Speech Rocks,' " online, CNN Interactive, 27 February 1998, www.cnn.com.

38. *Dun & Bradstreet v. Greenmoss Builders,* 472 US 749 (1985).

39. *Black's Law Dictionary,* 5th ed. (St. Paul: West, 1979), 1075.

40. Frank Walsh, *Public Relations & the Law* (New York: Foundation for Public Relations Education and Research, 1988), 15.

41. I. Fred Koenigsberg, *How to Handle Basic Copyright and Trademark Problems, 1991* (New York: Practising Law Institute, 1991), 31.

42. Calvert DeForest (Himself, or "The Artist Formerly Known as 'Larry Bud Melman'"), *Late Show with David Letterman* web site, http://marketing.cbs.com/lateshow.

43. Bill Carter, *The Late Shift* (New York: Hyperion, 1994), 416–432.

44. Walsh, 61.

45. Jan Hoffman, "May It Please the Public: Lawyers Exploit Media Attention as a Defense Tactic," *New York Times,* 22 April 1994, B1.

46. B. Drummond Ayres, "Simpson Case Has California Debating Muzzles for Lawyers," *New York Times,* 21 August 1994, sec. 1, p. 40.

47. Hoffman.

48. William M. Kunstler, "The Lawyer: 'A Chill Wind Blows,' " *Media Studies Journal* (winter 1992): 79.

49. M.L. Stein, "Lawyer Says It's OK to Lie to the Media," *Editor & Publisher,* 28 August 1993, 9–10.

50. Ayres.

51. Rule 3.6 (subsection a), *American Bar Association Rules of Professional Conduct,* 1983.

52. Ayres.

53. *Dominic P. Gentile, Petitioner v. State Bar of Nevada, U.S. Supreme Court Reports,* 115 L Ed 2nd, 888–912.

54. David W. Guth, "The Acceptance and Use of Public Relations Practices among Kansas Litigators," *Public Relations Review* (winter 1996): 341–354.

55. White House press briefing, 23 January 1998, 1:35 P.M.

56. Karen Tumulty, "Caught in the Town's Most Thankless Job," *Time,* 9 March 1998, 68.

57. Fraser P. Seitel, "Lawyers and Leaks: The O.J. Simpson Saga," *Public Relations Tactics* (August 1994): 1.

58. Guth and Wenske, 4.

59. Guth and Wenske, 4

60. Statement by Tom E. Smith, President and CEO of Food Lion, in Response to ABC's *Prime Time Live* Food Lion Segment, PR Newswire, 5 November 1992.

61. April Jones, "No Special Privileges," *The UNC Journalist* (spring 1997): 9–12.

62. William S. Weiss, "Food Lion Jury Roars at 'Primetime Live,'" *Public Relations Tactics* (April 1997): 5.

63. Paul Nowell, "Food Lion Wants More Time," Associated Press report, online, ABC News web site, www.abcnews.com.

64. Barbara Wartelle Wall, "Food Lion vs. ABC: A Good News/Bad News Decision," Gannett News Watch, online, www.gannett.com/go/newswatch/99/October/new1029.htm.

65. "Experts: Public Is Loser in Food Lion Verdict," online, CNN Interactive, 23 January 1997, www.cnn.com.

66. "Experts: Public Is Loser in Food Lion Verdict."

chapter sixteen

Your Future in Public Relations

objectives

After studying this chapter, you will be able to

- understand better the forces that are shaping the future of society

- recognize the trends that are changing the practice of public relations

- recognize the leadership role women and minority practitioners are playing and will play in public relations

- pinpoint steps you can take today to secure a successful future in public relations

The Government Contract

scenario

The excitement of your agency's winning a big contract from a new client has begun to wear off. The reality of this opportunity is settling in—and you re-alize you need to hire four more people to handle the increased workload.

Besides you, the agency that you head has 10 people: three white females, two Hispanic females, three white males, one black female, and one black male. Your new client, a government agency, requires that its contractors have diverse workplaces that mirror the gender and racial makeup of society at large.

After advertising the positions in local and professional publications, you have determined that only four of the applicants meet your highly technical minimum education and experience requirements. However, all four finalists are white males.

You are committed to cultural diversity in the workplace; you were particularly hoping to hire an Asian American practitioner. Both your client and various community groups are closely watching your hiring practices and insist on diversity. However, you have conducted what you considered an open and fair recruitment process. You also have four qualified applicants ready to go to work and a bunch of work piling up. What are you going to do?

A New Century with New Challenges

So where do we go from here?

This is the question confronting the profession of public relations at the start of the 21st century. When the Publicity Bureau opened its doors in Boston in 1900, the modern profession was in its infancy. It didn't even have a name. In the century that has passed, however, public relations has made a name for itself. "The social justification for public relations in a free society is to ethically and effectively plead the cause of a client or organization in the free-wheeling forum of public debate," wrote the late public relations educator and historian Scott Cutlip. "It is a basic democratic right that every idea, individual, and institution shall have a full and fair hearing in the public forum—that their merit ultimately must be determined by their ability to be accepted in the marketplace."[1]

Public Relations' Mixed Legacy

As we look ahead to modern public relations' second century, it is useful to look back on both the positive and the negative effects public relations has had on society. Cutlip compiled what he called a list of the profession's "pluses and minuses":

Pluses
1. By stressing to executives the need for public approval, practitioners improve the public conduct of the organizations they serve.
2. Practitioners serve the public interest by making all points of view heard in the public forum.
3. Practitioners serve our segmented, scattered society by using their talents of communication and mediation to replace misinformation with information, discord with concord.

Minuses
1. Public relations has cluttered our already choked channels of communication with the debris of pseudoevents and phony sound bites that confuse rather than clarify. This is especially true of today's damaged political process.
2. Public relations has corroded our channels of communication on which the public must depend with cynicism and "credibility gaps."[2]

If practitioners are willing to take it to heart, Cutlip's critique can serve as a starting point for the profession's second century. Any steps practitioners can take to reinforce the positives and eliminate the negatives will go a long way toward securing the future of public relations in a rapidly changing world.

Social Forces and Public Relations

Public relations—now and in the future—cannot operate in a vacuum. Just as its practitioners seek to exert influence on various aspects of society, social forces are at work that influence the profession. Understanding those forces is a key to unlocking the mysteries about the future of public relations.

QuickBreak 16.1

PUBLIC RELATIONS IN THE NEW RUSSIA

Since the collapse of the Soviet Union in 1991, the Russian Federation has traveled a rocky road toward democracy. For many, the transition from a tightly controlled economy to free-market capitalism has been difficult. The old safety nets that used to exist under Communist rule—such as guaranteed jobs and fixed prices—disappeared overnight. Although a few individuals—the so-called New Russians—got rich quick under the new economic structure, most people suffered a decline in their quality of life.

It is in this fluid environment that two-way public relations is beginning to take shape in Russia.[3] Although making valid cross-cultural comparisons is always problematic, there are similarities between the Russia of today and the United States at the dawn of the 20th century. Public relations in the United States was born during a period in which democracy and its institutions were maturing. With the growth of the middle class, the relationships among government, business, and the voting public changed. Public opinion became more important. Modern public relations developed as a means of coping with this change. Similar forces are at work today in Russia.

However, differences do exist. Public relations in the United States emerged from the private sector in a society that had long-standing democratic traditions. That is clearly not the case in Russia. At the birth of democratic Russia, the government public relations apparatus is far more established than public relations practices in the commercial sector. And, depending on whom you talk to, Russian government public relations is either a positive force in democratization or a vestige of the old authoritarian regime.

Commercial public relations in Russia, both corporate and agency, lags behind government public relations in development. The growth in the private sector is being led by foreign-based corporations and agencies that import their public relations practices and values. "It has been hard to convince Russian companies that they need public relations," said Andrei Barannikov of Gronat, a public relations and advertising agency in St. Petersburg.[4]

Olga Chernishova, a public relations manager with Coca-Cola–St. Petersburg, said much of her job focuses on internal affairs. "It is an

The Global Spread of Democracy

One powerful social force is the global spread of democracy. Much of the history of the 20th century centered on the worldwide struggle against forces of tyranny and oppression. Most of that century's wars and great social movements grew out of a desire either to gain or to protect individual freedoms. With the end of the Cold War between democracy and communism, many nations embraced democratic institutions and ideas for the first time.

The changeover from an authoritarian to a democratic society is not easy. Democracy is more than just a set of rules. It is a way of life. Imagine what it would be like to live in a society where the government watched over every aspect of your life. For as long as you can remember, someone was always telling you what you could do,

American company, trying to uphold company policies, while trying to make employees loyal to the company," Chernishova said.

Another important aspect of her job is building and maintaining relations with an intrusive government bureaucracy that hasn't fully embraced the concept of a free-market economy. Although public relations tactics can sometimes smooth over differences with Russian officials, bribery is commonplace.

"My job is to convince inspectors that the activities of Coca-Cola are not dangerous for customers," Chernishova said. "Coca-Cola can't decide for itself if it has the right to exist. The government structure has to be involved."[5]

Interest in public relations among Russians is high. Evidence of this can be seen in the growing number of public relations programs that have sprung up at various colleges and universities. U.S. universities, private foundations, and government agencies such as the United States Information Service have been helping Russian schools establish public relations curricula.

Perhaps the best sign of progress is that Russian practitioners voice many of the same complaints as their Western counterparts. "When there is good news, the boss wants to be on the television screen," said Vsevolod Morozov, press secretary for the Leningrad Oblast Committee for Medical Promotion. "When there is bad news, he wants to hide behind his press secretary."[6]

A sign of the growing importance of public relations in the Russian Federation is this public relations educators conference at a St. Petersburg university. (Courtesy of David Guth)

think, or say. Now imagine what it would be like to have all those restrictions suddenly lifted. After the euphoria of liberation had dissipated, you would confront the cold reality of your new way of life. Before, someone else made your decisions for you. Now, you have to make your own choices and live with the consequences of those choices.

To ease this transition, many public and private agencies have engaged in aggressive programs of education and technical support in the newly emerging democracies. At the forefront of these efforts have been journalists, marketers, and public relations practitioners teaching the virtues of free expression. By the thousands, these professionals have crisscrossed the globe in an effort to instill democratic values and traditions in places where historically there have been none. The challenge is to do so in a culturally sensitive manner. The fact that something works well in the United States does not necessarily mean it will work somewhere else. The most successful efforts at spreading democracy have been those mindful of local traditions and values.

Quick ✔ Check

1. What are some positive and some negative effects that public relations has had on society?
2. How has the end of the Cold War influenced the global growth of public relations?
3. What are some challenges facing the development of public relations in the former Soviet Union?

Globalization

Another major social force influencing the future of public relations is **globalization.** The United Nations Development Program defines globalization as "the growing interdependence of the world's people through shrinking space, shrinking time, and disappearing borders."[7] With each passing day, the peoples of the earth are being drawn closer together by a vast array of forces. We live in a world where the economies of different nations are inexorably linked. Advances in communications technology have made it possible for us to know what is happening on the opposite side of the world instantaneously. Improvements in transportation have made it possible for you to travel in mere hours distances that took your grandparents weeks and months to cover.

Working in combination, these forces have given us a sense of **interconnectedness** and created a world of opportunities for public relations practitioners. Marshall McLuhan's global village (which we discussed in Chapters 11 and 14) has, in many ways, become a reality. Targeting certain audiences and effectively reaching them are, in many ways, easier than ever. But as we already have discussed in Chapter 11, these advances have also forced practitioners to face serious challenges and make some difficult choices. Thanks to the global reach of digital telecommunications, crises can now spread at the speed of light. And in a world in which the Internet makes it possible for anyone with a "cause" to become a self-publisher, it is becoming more difficult for organizations to identify potential threats.

Although some see globalization as an opportunity, others see it as a threat. Still others see it as both. Antiglobalization forces are concerned that the world's richest nations exploit the poorest in the name of economic development. They are concerned about the relocation of manufacturing jobs to poorer countries where laborers receive only a fraction of pay and have fewer human rights protections than their counterparts in industrialized nations. The exploitation of natural resources and the resulting damage to the environment are also a concern. In addition, technology and knowledge gaps are widening between rich and poor nations.

Although it is difficult to gauge the strength of antiglobalization forces, they have made their voices heard. Massive protests in cities hosting international trade meetings have become commonplace in recent years. A July 2001 meeting of world leaders in Genoa, Italy, was marred by a series of violent clashes between antiglobalization protesters and Italian police. One protester was shot dead, 200 were injured, and 300 arrested.

The Changing Face of the United States

Interconnectedness means more than international relations, however. One need only look at the changing face of the United States. During the Industrial Revolution in the late 1800s, most of the immigration into this country came from Europe. The predominance of new arrivals from Europe remained fairly consistent for decades. But by the 1980s there had been a shift. Of the nearly 20 million foreign-born residents counted by the U.S. Census in 1990, 44 percent were added in the 1980s. Of the new arrivals, almost half came from Latin America and nearly one-third from Asia. According to the 1990 census, three out of every four persons living in the United States were of white European ancestry. By the middle of the 21st century, that group is expected to shrink to just over half the U.S. population.[8]

The 2000 census provides a snapshot of the changes in U.S. society. The nation's population on April 1, 2000, was 281,421,906, a 13.2 percent increase over the 1990 census. Although the "white" population continued to constitute the largest racial group, its percentage of the total population had slipped from 80.2 percent in 1990 to 75.1 percent in 2000. For the first time in the nation's history, people of "Hispanic or Latino" origin were counted as the nation's largest minority group, totaling 35,305,818 or 12.5 percent of the U.S. population. They edged past the "black or African American" population, which totaled 34,658,190 or 12.3 percent of the population.[9]

In an ideal world, public relations should mirror the societies it serves. However, several studies have all come to the same conclusion: People of color are underrepresented in the profession. This issue confronts you as the head of the fictional agency in the opening scenario of this chapter: You are being torn by competing values. On the one hand, you believe in the value of a multicultural workplace and know that the client and community expect it. On the other hand, you question the fairness to the four individuals who followed the rules you established and emerged as finalists. And not to be forgotten is the competing value of getting the job done. This is a very real-life scenario; it has no easy answers. The choices are difficult:

1. You could turn down the contract and avoid the hassles. But this could have a devastating effect on employee morale and could damage your agency's ability to compete for major contracts in the future.
2. You could hire the four white males and defend the decision on the basis of sticking by the rules you established at the outset. However, you would do so at the risk of alienating the community and, possibly, losing the contract.
3. You could reopen the search from scratch and expand the geographical area in which you advertise the positions. This might bring in more qualified candidates who are women or persons of color. But it might not, and you would run the risk of losing the candidates you have already identified.
4. You could hire one or two of the finalists and expand the search for the remaining positions. This might ease the immediate situation; but, for reasons already mentioned, there is no guarantee that this course will lead to a long-term solution.

There is no one correct answer. It all comes down to which value you hold highest. The first option seems the least viable: You wouldn't have sought the contract if you didn't value entrepreneurship and the business it would bring to your agency. The second option indicates that the integrity of the process you established is your highest value. The third option places multiculturalism at the top of your list of values. Many would choose the fourth option because it has the appeal of addressing all three values: entrepreneurship, fairness, and multiculturalism. Of course, it is a compromise without any permanent guarantees. But it still has the advantage of leaving your options open.

The Growth in World Population

Another factor with significant implications, both for the practice of public relations and for society as a whole, is the rapid growth of the world's population. That there will be a lot more of us in the 21st century is a sobering fact in and of itself. But it is the nature and the consequences of the growth that bring the greatest challenges.

World population growth is especially rapid in non-Western nations. The numbers tell the story. According to the U.S. Census Bureau, the population of the United States in late 2001 was approximately 285 million. By the year 2050, that number is expected to climb to just under 404 million, an increase of more than 41 percent. Compare that with the rate of growth of the world population, estimated at nearly 6.2 billion in late 2001 and projected to be 9.1 billion in 2050, a 47 percent increase.[10]

There is another way to look at this. See Table 16.1 for a list of the 10 most populated nations on Earth in the year 2000. Now compare those rankings with the projections for the year 2050 in Table 16.2. You may be thinking to yourself, "That's interesting. But what does it have to do with me?" In a word: Plenty.

TABLE 16.1	The Ten Most Populated Nations on Earth in the Year 2000	
RANK	COUNTRY	POPULATION
1	China	1,261,832,482
2	India	1,014,003,817
3	United States	275,562,673
4	Indonesia	224,784,210
5	Brazil	172,860,370
6	Russia	146,001,176
7	Pakistan	141,553,775
8	Bangladesh	129,194,224
9	Japan	126,549,976
10	Nigeria	123,337,822

(*Source:* U.S. Census Bureau)

TABLE 16.2	The Ten Most Populated Nations on Earth in the Year 2050	
RANK	COUNTRY	POPULATION
1	India	1,619,582,271
2	China	1,470,468,924
3	United States	403,943,147
4	Indonesia	337,807,011
5	Nigeria	303,986,770
6	Pakistan	267,813,495
7	Brazil	206,751,477
8	Bangladesh	205,093,861
9	Ethiopia	187,892,174
10	Congo (Kinshasa)	181,922,656

(*Source:* U.S. Census Bureau)

With the world's population growing rapidly—especially in nations outside the industrialized West—the competition for Earth's limited resources is becoming more vigorous. In the best of all possible scenarios, this means increased economic trade and international cooperation—activities that the practice of public relations can help foster. However, in the worse of all possible scenarios, the intense competition for Earth's dwindling resources could lead to wars, terrorism, and other forms of social

THE GROWING HISPANIC MARKET

Not only is the face of the United States changing, so is the U.S. marketplace. The Selig Center for Economic Growth at the University of Georgia estimated Hispanic purchasing power in 2001 at $452.4 billion—an increase of 118 percent over 1990.[11] For public relations practitioners, this market presents a major opportunity. However, it also presents its own challenges.

For many years the potential of the Hispanic market in the United States was largely underrated. According to Luis M. Salces, an executive at a Chicago firm specializing in Hispanic communications, corporate decision makers tended to see the Hispanic market as one where little money could be made. However, the recent growth in advertising revenues in Spanish-language media has caused many to take a second look.[12]

Before jumping into the Hispanic marketplace, you need to remember that there's more to it than just translating everything into Spanish. There are significant cultural differences that go far deeper than language.

Isabel Valdes, president of Los Angeles-based Hispanic Market Connections Inc., has written that practitioners should "develop strategies that are compatible with Latino points of view, and know the fundamental differences that distinguish U.S. Hispanic consumers from mainstream American consumers." Valdes also wrote that it is important to be aware of regional differences among Hispanic groups, such as differences between people of Cuban ancestry and people from Mexico.[13]

The list of successes in reaching this increasingly important public is growing. For example, by making all of its customer services bilingual, Bank of America saw an increase of more than 5,000 Hispanic households monthly.[14] And, as might be expected, the presence of Hispanic-owned public relations firms is growing in the profession. Several major corporations, including AT&T, MCI WorldCom, McDonald's, Kraft, General Foods, Anheuser-Busch, and Coca-Cola, have hired Latino-owned firms or retained Hispanic communicators to build relationships with Hispanic publics.[15]

Because of aggressive marketing and public relations, Hispanic consumers spend an estimated $2 billion a year at Sears, Roebuck & Company. To reach this important market, Sears relies heavily on broadcast advertising—using generic Spanish-language commercials and others that specifically target Cubans or Puerto Ricans. The company also has a Spanish-language web site. Gilbert Davila, vice president of multicultural and relationship marketing at Sears, said that the chain's outlets in Hispanic areas are "among our best performing stores."[16]

Although targeting the Hispanic market is more than just translating from one language to another, being able to speak Spanish fluently is a real plus for today's college graduates. Multilingual practitioners will be in great demand in our increasingly multilingual society.

unrest. The constructive application of public relations in its role as a catalyst for consensus is critical in helping human populations avoid these dire outcomes.

The growth in world population also foreshadows future environmental problems. The air we breathe, the water we drink, and the land on which we depend for

Booklet and Brochures With the assistance of Valencia, Pérez & Echeveste Public Relations, the California Department of Health Services prepared these recipes and good nutrition tips for Hispanic consumers. (Courtesy of Valencia, Pérez & Echeveste Public Relations)

IT'S NOT EASY BEING GREEN

When is green *really* green? And when it comes to the environment, is public relations part of the problem, part of the solution, or both?

Modern public relations and the environmental movement both evolved during the early 20th century. Theodore Roosevelt, if he were alive today, would probably be considered an environmental activist. But he also had considerable public relations savvy (see Chapter 3). Roosevelt effectively marshaled public opinion in May 1908 when, for the first time, he brought all the states' governors together at the same place to discuss the preservation of the nation's natural resources. According to public relations historian Scott Cutlip, it may well have been the White House Conference of Governors on Conservation that "embedded the word *conservation* into the nation's vocabulary."[17]

And since the 1960s, the environmental movement has played a significant role in the nation's social and economic development. Businesses and industries are no longer judged on their profitability alone. They are now held accountable for how environmentally friendly they are. This change has contributed to what many have called **green public relations.**

The 3M Company was among the first of the major corporations to reap the benefits of going green. Its 3P program, which stands for "Pollution Prevention Pays," was launched in 1975. Developed by two environmental engineers and an environmental communications specialist, 3P projects saved 3M more than half a billion dollars during the program's first 15 years—and have earned the company praise from environmental groups and the media. In 1990 3M launched a new environmental effort, 3P Plus, by investing $150 million to reduce hazardous air emissions at its manufacturing facilities.[18]

McDonald's, once a target of environmentalists, is now praised for its aggressive waste reduction efforts. "McDonald's believes it has a special responsibility to protect our environment for future generations," proclaims a statement on the company web site. "This responsibility is derived from our unique relationship with millions of consumers worldwide—whose quality of life tomorrow will be affected by our stewardship of the environment today."[19]

One of the company's most praised environmental efforts has been its partnership with Conservation International and Clemson University to protect 2.7 million acres of rain forest along the Costa Rican–Panamanian border. Through the Amistad Conservation and Development Initiative, McDonald's has encouraged local farmers to maintain sound environmental practices while achieving economic prosperity. The company also will not purchase beef raised in rain forests or on recently deforested rain forest land.[20]

Many in the environmental movement do not share the same enthusiasm for green public relations. In fact, they have another term for it— **greenwash.** San Francisco–based CorpWatch, which opposes what it calls "corporate-led globalization," gives out bimonthly Greenwash Awards to companies its says "put more money, time, and energy into slick PR campaigns aimed at promoting their eco-friendly images than they do to actually protecting the environment." Some of its "winners" include the Nuclear Energy Institute, the American Chemistry Council, and British Petroleum.

The Ford Motor Company received the organization's wrath for its April 2000 sponsorship of the Heroes for the Planet concert in San Francisco. In handing out its Greenwash Award, CorpWatch noted that the Union of Concerned Scientists had cited Ford as the second-worst polluter among automakers and asked, "From where does Ford derive the moral authority to associate itself with environmental heroes?"[21]

The irony is that CorpWatch and its allies have chosen to use public relations strategies to counter the public relations efforts of others. But that is just how values-driven public relations is supposed to work.

our food are all threatened by an encroaching human population. One of the most immediate concerns is the loss of tropical rain forests, which are being clear-cut and burned to make way for people, animals, and crops. By destroying these rain forests, humanity is losing an irreplaceable source of numerous species of health-giving herbs and flowers, not to mention oxygen. Many of the people who clear-cut and burn the rain forests are not evil. They are just poor and looking for a way to improve their lives. Many companies, such as McDonald's, have developed partnerships that promote alternatives to the destruction of the environment. These and other public relations activities can serve as models for future environmental cooperation.

In addition to these global trends, major changes are taking place within the United States that will have a dramatic impact on future public relations practitioners in this country: the aging of the U.S. population. The **baby boom generation,** born between 1945 and 1964, will place a tremendous strain on the generations that have followed. Baby boomers will start reaching retirement age in 2010. Between 2001 and 2030, the percentage of people 65 years of age and older will grow from just under 13 percent to more than 20 percent. The number of people living in the United States over the age of 100 will grow from 72,000 to 381,000 during the same period.[22] From a political and social standpoint, this means that issues important to older citizens—issues such as Social Security, health care, and the stability of personal investments—will take on increasing importance.

However, the graying of America will have an even deeper impact on today's college students. The percentage of **breadwinners,** people between the ages of 18 and 65 who typically make up the nation's labor pool, is declining. During 2001, breadwinners made up almost 69 percent of the U.S. population. By 2030, the U.S. Census Bureau estimates that the percentage of breadwinners will dip below 63 percent.[23] In other words, a smaller percentage of breadwinners will carry most of the tax burden for the rest of the nation. That trend, in turn, has a variety of implications for the future—including the likelihood that cost-effective public relations will become increasingly important.

Quick ✔ Check

1. Why is an increasing marketing focus being placed on the Hispanic community in the United States?
2. What are the implications of the higher population growth rate in non-Western nations?
3. What effect will the aging of the baby boom generation have on society?

Feminization of the Workplace

Today's students often take for granted something that was relatively new just a generation earlier: the presence of women in the workplace. It is estimated that women

SEXUAL HARASSMENT

According to the U.S. Equal Employment Opportunity Commission (EEOC), sexual harassment is a form of sex discrimination that violates Title VII of the Civil Rights Act of 1964. The EEOC defines workplace **sexual harassment** as "unwelcome sexual advances, requests for sexual favors, and other verbal or physical conduct of a sexual nature . . . when submission to or rejection of this conduct explicitly or implicitly affects an individual's employment, unreasonably interferes with an individual's work performance or creates an intimidating, hostile or offensive work environment."[24]

The U.S. government reports that 15,836 sexual harassment cases were filed with federal and state agencies during fiscal year (FY) 2000, a 50 percent increase over FY 1992. However, these numbers are somewhat deceptive. An examination of FY 2000 statistics shows a finding of "no reasonable cause" in 44.1 percent of the cases. Another 18 percent involved settlements or withdrawals with benefits. Nevertheless, sexual harassment is expensive. More than $54 million was awarded to victims of sexual harassment in FY 2000—and that figure does not count any monetary awards obtained through litigation.[25] According to a 1995 random sampling of Public Relations Society of America members, 22 percent of women and 19 percent of men said they thought sexual harassment existed in their organizations. In the same survey, 39 percent of women and 37 percent of men said they thought the problem existed throughout the public relations industry.[26]

Although there are legal remedies for dealing with blatant sexual harassment, many victims are reluctant to report it because of a fear of damaging their careers. Then there is a more covert form of harassment, dubbed by some as **lookism,** which is defined as a tendency to focus more on a woman's appearance than on her job performance. In one focus group a female practitioner complained that she had to fight the perception of some of her older male colleagues that a woman traveling by herself or out alone after dark is "available."[27]

Sexual harassment in the workplace threatens more than just employees. Companies that do not take steps to enforce sexual harassment policies face increasing risk of stiff financial penalties. In an effort to force companies to take this problem more seriously, Congress amended the Civil Rights Act in 1991. The amendment made it possible for successful plaintiffs to collect not only lost wages but also up to $300,000 in punitive damages against offending companies.[28] The U.S. Supreme Court has also weighed in on this issue. The court said an employer is responsible for sexual harassment committed by a supervisor even if the employer was unaware of the supervisor's behavior. The Court also ruled that workers can still file sexual harassment charges against supervisors even in the absence of adverse job consequences.[29]

It should be noted that sexual harassment is not just about men acting inappropriately toward women. According to the EEOC, men filed 13.6 percent of sexual harassment claims in FY 2000.[30] The U.S. Supreme Court has also recognized that illegal harassment can occur between people of the same sex.[31]

Public relations practitioners will play a critical role in eliminating this offensive behavior from the work environment—both inside and outside their profession. As the EEOC has noted, employers "should clearly communicate that sexual harassment will not be tolerated."[32] That's one of the jobs of public relations.

Public relations professionals—both men and women—appear to be up to the challenge. In the previously mentioned poll of PRSA members, both men and women appeared willing to take the actions necessary to create a harassment-free environment. As the study's authors noted, "That men and women are not only aware of but also willing to address sexual harassment issues is a healthy sign."[33]

will constitute 47.5 percent of the nation's labor force in 2008, compared with 41.7 percent in 1978.[34] This movement—what some have called **feminization** of the workplace—has dramatically changed our social and political landscapes.

Women constitute approximately 51 percent of the nation's population. And in recent years they have begun to use their numerical advantage to shape public policy. More women are being elected to public office. Certain concerns traditionally thought of as "women's issues," such as home leave and breast cancer research, have moved to the top of society's agenda. It is increasingly commonplace to see women in top managerial roles. Even political pundits are more frequently identifying women among the field of potential candidates for president of the United States. In many ways, the 21st century may become known as a "women's century," much as the 20th century has been referred to as "the American century." However, before that happens, significant shifts in areas such as workplace sexual harassment and **salary equity**—equal pay for equal work—must occur.

Many of you reading this book are aware of the social aspects of this feminization of the working world. Although some women choose to dedicate their energies to home, children, and community, more and more are postponing family life for a chance to launch a professional career. This trend is evident in the statistics for first-time marriages in the United States. People are waiting longer than ever to get married. In 1992, 38.6 percent of men and 25.6 percent of women between the ages of 25 and 36 had never been married. Those percentages are projected to rise to 50.3 percent of men and 33.1 percent of women by 2010.[35]

However, if you are concerned about your prospects for a lasting relationship, there is room for hope. "The trend toward delayed marriage can't keep up at this pace," one population expert said. "If it does, virtually no young adults will get married in 2010. We expect that love will continue to triumph, and that young people will still get married."[36]

Few fields have shown a more dramatic increase in the presence of women in the workplace than has public relations. Seven out of 10 public relations practitioners are women, a complete reversal from just 30 years ago. Collegiate women public relations students outnumber their male counterparts by more than a 2-to-1 margin. Thirty-seven of the nation's top 100 public relations firms (ranked by 1999 income) are headed by women.[37]

This trend may have a downside. Findings in a 1986 study commissioned by the International Association of Business Communicators suggested that the field was becoming a **velvet ghetto**—an employment area in which women hold the numerous lower-paying technical positions and men predominate in the few high-paying managerial positions.[38] As one researcher noted:

> This "feminization" of the field has been heralded by some. Women, they argue, are uniquely suited for public relations because of their natural orientation toward "relationships" and their facility with verbal tasks. More often, though, women's entrance into public relations has been viewed with concern. People worry that so many women in the field will lower salaries and frustrate public relations' efforts to be taken seriously as a management function. These fears are bolstered by extensive research that shows women

lag behind their male peers in salary and advancement. And this gender gap cannot be explained by age, level of education, or years of experience.[39]

The gender debate took new life during 2000, when Harold Burson, founder and chair of Burson-Marsteller, suggested that a public relations industry dominated by women may not be a good thing. "Unless more men are attracted to public relations, it runs the risk of being regarded as a 'woman's job,'" Burson said. Although some women agreed with Burson, others strongly disagreed. "That's not even a point for discussion," said Sabrina Horn, head of a San Franciso–based agency.[40]

Even with women holding a numerical advantage in the practice of public relations, their male counterparts are still getting better pay for the same work. Although gender pay equity is an issue throughout society, it is especially acute among practitioners. Weekly earnings among U.S. women rose from 66.7 percent of their male counterparts' salaries in 1983 to 76.5 percent in 1999. That's a modest rise—one that leaves plenty of room for improvement. However, compare those numbers to weekly earnings among female marketing, advertising, and public relations managers: 60.1 percent in 1983 and 64.5 percent in 1999. The U.S. Labor Department has identified the marketing, advertising, and public relations industries has having one of the lowest women's-to-men's salary ratios among all the occupations it has classified.[41]

Even those who agree that gender discrimination exists often disagree on how to rectify the situation. Some argue that women should seek out more professional expertise—that improving their strategic and professional skills will allow them to compete at the same level as men. Others argue that women should push for **empowerment**—not only ensuring that they have the tools for success, but also demanding to be included in decision making.[42] Although sincere people may argue about which is the best path to take, none disagree on the common goal: equity.

A hopeful sign can be found in a recent gender study on job satisfaction among public relations practitioners. Although men and women viewed job satisfaction from decidedly different perspectives, evidence supported a growing respect for each other. "Both groups appear to be willing to respect the other, and, perhaps more importantly, to engage in dialogue on the issues in ways that will result in collaboration and benefits for both," the study said. "The willingness on both sides to work toward just solutions is especially critical at this point in the evolution of a workplace where people can be satisfied."[43]

Quick ✔ Check

1. What is the meaning of the phrase *velvet ghetto*?
2. What are the differing views on how to level the playing field for men and women in public relations?
3. What is workplace sexual harassment?

Values Statement 16.1

LEAGUE OF WOMEN VOTERS OF THE UNITED STATES

The League of Women Voters encourages informed and active participation of citizens in government and influences public policy through education and advocacy.

The goal of the League of Women Voters of the United States is to empower citizens to shape better communities worldwide. We are a nonpartisan political organization.

We:

- act after study and member agreement to achieve solutions in the public interest on key community issues at all government levels.

- build citizen participation in the democratic process.

- engage communities in promoting positive solutions to public policy issues through education and advocacy.

We believe in:

- respect for individuals.

- the value of diversity.

- the empowerment of the grassroots, both within the League and its communities.

- the power of collective decision making for the common good.

We will:

- act with trust, integrity and professionalism.

- operate in an open and effective manner to meet the needs of those we serve, both members and the public.

- take the initiative in seeking diversity in membership.

- acknowledge our heritage as we seek our path to the future.

—"Vision, Beliefs and Intentions,"
LWV web site

Where Public Relations Is Headed

As modern public relations moves into its second century, the signs are generally positive. As it did during its first century, the profession of public relations has to adapt to a changing social environment. However, not everything will change. There will be a continuing need for the profession to address some of the same old questions, including those relating to its ethical standards and its social value. Let's survey briefly some of the key trends for the future of public relations.

GROWTH.   Both the number of practitioners and the influence of the profession are growing steadily. According to the Bureau of Labor Statistics, employment of public relations specialists and managers is expected to grow "faster than the average" of other professions through 2008. To put it another way, the government expects public relations employment to increase 21 to 25 percent during this decade. "The need for good public relations in an increasingly competitive business environment should spur demand for public relations specialists in organizations of all sizes," the bureau concludes in its *Occupational Outlook Handbook, 2000–01 Edition*.[44] At the same time that the profession's numbers are growing, so is its presence in the boardroom. Although many still think of practitioners as technicians, an increasing number of organizations recognize the profession's role in enhancing and maintaining relationships with key stakeholders.

THE STRUGGLE FOR CREDIBILITY.   After 100 years, the modern profession still isn't sure what it wants to call itself. Because people who do not understand the profession have used *public relations* as a pejorative term since the time of Edward Bernays, many organizations have shied away from that phrase. Others have said the term is too broad or too narrow, depending on the context. By one accounting, "corporate communications" and "communications departments" outnumbered "public relations departments" at Fortune 500 companies by a 2-to-1 margin.[45] Concerns about the profession's credibility may be at the heart of this issue. The Public Relations Society of America Foundation created the National Credibility Index to track the way U.S. citizens perceive information sources. The good news: Many public relations tactics received a high index rating. The bad news: Public relations practitioners were rated near the bottom—below student activists, candidates for public office, and famous athletes.[46] This ambivalence can also be seen in the results of a 1998 survey of New York–area PRSA members. Although most were positive about their profession, a majority also said they felt that public relations does not have a good public image. "There is a wide disparity between how public relations people view their chosen profession and how they think others see it," said New York PRSA Chapter President Christopher L. Guidette. "Closing this perception gap obviously would benefit public relations professionals, the people we work for, and those who will follow."[47]

GREATER INTEGRATION.   Public relations activities are being more closely aligned with those of marketing and advertising. As we discussed in Chapter 13, the concept of integrated marketing communications (IMC) is the current rage. But as we also discussed, differences of opinion exist regarding just where public relations fits in the mix. Some see public relations as an element under a broad marketing umbrella. Others (your authors among them) see public relations practitioners as using a separate management discipline whose values often coincide with those of marketers. Regardless of one's point of view, one fact is undeniable: Today's clients are demanding more than just the persuasive messages of advertising and marketing. They also want the credibility that comes through third-party endorsement. For that, they need public relations. This is especially true when it comes to cause-related marketing, something for which public relations is well suited. According to New Jersey public relations executive John Rosica, "Cause-related marketing can increase brand equity, create a more positive image for corporations and establish a preferred brand name with customers and potential customers."[48]

GREATER ACCOUNTABILITY.   The profession of public relations is under greater scrutiny than ever before. "There's an increased emphasis on accountability, measuring success in every way we can," said Pat Stocker, director of executive programs at the College of Business and Management at the University of Maryland.[49] Katy Paine of Delahaye Medialink, a public relations measurement and analysis firm, said, "I don't think that there's a program proposed any more that doesn't have a measurement element."[50] However, accountability now extends beyond an organization's bottom line. Ever since Ralph Nader's assault on General Motors in the mid-1960s, the public has expected organizations to reflect social values. Corporations are expected to value public interest as well as profitability. Public relations practitioners' role is well suited for monitoring the conduct of organizations. At the same time, however, practitioners must hold themselves to those same high standards. Failure to do so has often given the profession a bad name. Accountability in public relations also requires that practitioners enthusiastically embrace equal opportunity without regard to gender, race, religion, national origin, or sexual orientation. That aspect of accountability will require aggressive recruitment of a more inclusive workforce, one that mirrors the diversity of society.

TARGETING.   As a result of social and technological changes, we are living in a world of increasingly fragmented values and desires. Public opinion and public policies are being ruled by ever shifting and constantly self-defining coalitions of interests. At the same time, the explosion in the number of communication channels has dispersed the audience. The challenge for public relations practitioners is clear: Reaching key publics in the future will require more targeted approaches. Designing those approaches, in turn, requires a greater precision in research methodologies and planning strategies.

RAPID RESPONSE.   In the race to influence public opinion, time is an enemy. President Abraham Lincoln concerned himself with stories that appeared in the daily newspaper. President Franklin Roosevelt had to respond to stories on hourly radio newscasts. Today the president is confronted with minute-by-minute developments in stories on 24-hour news channels and the Internet. The window of opportunity for getting across one's point of view is narrowing. By implication, this means that public relations practitioners must plan even further ahead. They must do a better job of anticipating events that could shape the public view of their organization. For that reason, issues management skills will in all likelihood become increasingly important.

A NONTRADITIONAL WORKPLACE.   "Anyone can tell you that this is not our parents' economy," wrote U.S. Labor Secretary Elaine L. Chao. "Around 10 million people work away from their corporate office at least three days a month."[51] Other estimates place the number of at-home workers in the United States at 30 million. And according to the American Home Business Association, as many as 8,000 more people join the home-working movement every day.[52] It should come as no surprise that public relations practitioners are at the forefront of this movement. As discussed in Chapter 11, advances in communications technology have been the catalyst for the growth of virtual public relations agencies—but things are changing even in the traditional

VIRTUAL PUBLIC RELATIONS

A standard piece of advice given to public relations practitioners who embark upon the perilous but exciting world of private consulting has been to stick the phrase "and Associates" behind their names. For example, Mary Jones would call her one-person agency "Mary Jones and Associates." The idea is to imply a support network that puts the consultancy on the same footing as established agencies.

The advancement of communications technology, combined with formalized strategic alliances between consultants, has made it easier for these single-person agencies to stand up, be noticed, and become serious players in the industry. And now the work done by these entities has a new name: **virtual public relations.**

When Jerry Brown left his job as director of media relations for U.S. West Communications in 1996, he announced that he was going to establish his own virtual public relations agency. Because of corporate downsizing and the increasing amount of work being outsourced to independent practitioners, Brown said his move was "the wave of the future."

"More and more highly qualified professionals are doing what I'm doing—going out on their own and linking up with other top talent on a project-by-project basis to serve the needs of clients," Brown said. "Becoming independent used to mean going it alone. Not anymore."[53]

Here is how a virtual public relations agency works: Consultant A is a specialist in public opinion polling. Consultant B's expertise is in the area of political communications. Consultant C is experienced in the use of video news releases and satellite media tours. In a virtual agency, A, B, and C come together to work on behalf of, say, a candidate for public office. When the campaign is over, they go their separate ways. Although it is possible that they will work together again, it is likely that they will temporarily link to other consultants working for other clients facing other challenges.

Virtual public relations agencies can operate out of an office; from the home; or even, as in the case of Dick Grove, from the seat of a motorcycle. Grove is the CEO of Ink Inc., an international media relations firm headquartered in Westport, Missouri. But don't look for Grove in the office. It isn't unusual for him to place stories, check e-mail, or fax clients from the back of his Harley-Davidson while inspecting his 27-acre Kansas farm.

"Reporters don't care whether a story idea is pitched from a cabin in Montana or a high-rise office complex," Grove says. "They are only interested in whether it is a good story."[54]

The term *virtual public relations* is borrowed from "virtual reality" technology, which allows users to share certain experiences without the cost and, in some cases, the inherent risk of doing what is being simulated. With that in mind, it can be argued that "virtual public relations" is an appropriate moniker, especially when one considers how intertwined consultants and new technologies have become.

However, labeling this activity "virtual public relations" can also be misleading. The term might seem to suggest that what these professionals do is somehow unreal, only "close to lifelike." Actually, it is real-life public relations in every sense, just performed with a smaller overhead.

office setting. Intranets allow organizations with widely dispersed offices to operate more smoothly. Telecommunications technology has made offices portable, an asset in a global marketplace. Many workers are engaged in time shifting (working condensed schedules or during nontraditional hours) and job sharing (in which two part-time workers share the same job). In addition, as already noted, the labor pool is becoming more diverse in its gender and racial composition. By the time your children graduate from college, the workplace will have a very different look and feel.

VISION.   The demands of a rapid-paced society tend to focus on the problems of the moment and to ignore the potential challenges of the future. The charge of short-term thinking is often leveled against business and industry in the United States. Public relations practitioners share the responsibility for this state of affairs. With public relations practitioners being held more accountable for a company's bottom line, many move from one planning cycle to another without having a real sense of direction. What organizations—and practitioners—need is a sense of vision. They need to have a sense of where they want to be 5, 10, and 20 years down the road. Here is where values, research, and strategic planning pay dividends. A longer-term outlook also requires practitioners to demonstrate that they have what is commonly referred to as "backbone"—the courage to stand by their vision. Backbones do have flexibility, however; visions can change.

Quick ✓ Check

1. What trends are influencing the future of public relations?
2. In what ways will public relations practitioners be held more accountable in the future?
3. What is meant by the need for "vision"?

Your Future in Public Relations

By now it should be obvious that modern public relations is a profession that continues to evolve as it moves into its second century. That is what makes it both challenging and exciting. Every day in public relations brings with it a new adventure. Are you ready for it? The short answer is no—at this stage of your academic and professional life, you probably are not quite ready. But the good news is that if you continue doing the right things, you will be.

Your decision to earn a college degree was the first big step in the right direction. Although exceptions to the rule exist, a college diploma is usually necessary if you are going to make the first cut in the employment process. As to what kind of degree you obtain, that is probably less important than what you studied in earning the degree. Not everyone in the profession has received a degree in public relations. And although the study of public relations is traditionally centered in either journalism or communications studies programs, degrees from other departments can also lead to successful public relations careers.

So what constitutes a good educational foundation for the practice of public relations? Educators and practitioners at a 1998 conference on public relations education said a student seeking a public relations career should earn a degree that "reflects an integration of a broad education with a liberal arts orientation." According to the conferees, that "broad education" should include a theoretical understanding of the processes of communication, the liberal arts, the social sciences, sociopolitical trends, general business practices, and "the principles and skills specific to the profession of public relations."[55]

Perhaps the best news from that conference, "Dialogue on Public Relations Education," was the release of survey results showing practitioners and educators in general agreement about the preparation students need for a career in public relations. The survey identified the three most highly desired qualifications for entry-level employees: having news release writing skills, being a "self-starter," and having critical thinking and problem-solving skills. Unfortunately, that same survey suggested that educators and practitioners were not wholly satisfied with the skills graduating students possessed in those three areas.[56] Significantly, each of these skills involves knowledge above and beyond that taught in public relations classes. A well-rounded college education is the basis for success. The implication for today's college students is clear: Treat all your course work as if it were relevant to your major. It is!

Internships—supervised workplace experiences—also figure prominently in public relations career preparation, especially in light of corporate downsizing and the growth of virtual public relations. More than ever, internships give students the opportunity to get hands-on experience in a wide range of public relations activities. Think of internships as an extension of a college education—with one major difference: The "classroom" is the real world. If you are not certain what kind of public relations you want to practice—agency, government, nonprofit, or corporate—having several different internships during college can give you a taste of the different aspects of the field.

Internship experience can be crucial in getting that first job. "Keen competition will likely continue for entry-level public relations jobs as the number of qualified applicants is expected to exceed the number of job openings," a federal study concludes. "Public relations work experience as an intern is an asset in competing for entry-level jobs. Applicants without the appropriate educational background or work experience will face the toughest obstacles."[57]

Membership in student public relations organizations also provides a good foundation for a public relations career. Some schools have **Public Relations Student Society of America (PRSSA)** chapters, which are affiliated with PRSA. IABC also sponsors student organizations. Other student groups operate independently. Whatever route one chooses, these student organizations can provide valuable job/internship information, networking opportunities, and professional experience that can be listed on a résumé. Some professional organizations give students who were active in their school's public relations organization a membership discount upon graduation. These student groups also offer opportunities for getting together with people who share common career interests. However, as with other student organizations, what you get out of any such group largely depends on what you put into it.

The Future of Values-Driven Public Relations

Some view the future with hope. Others fear the future. Either way, like it or not, the future is coming.

What kind of future lies ahead? At best, we can only make educated guesses. In the final analysis, however, who on Earth really knows what is just beyond the horizon? Perhaps our time is better spent on the present and on the things we can do today to prepare ourselves for tomorrow.

Each of us perceives the future in different ways. That's because we are unique individuals who view the world through different prisms. For that reason, the best preparation for the future is getting to know the one individual who will exert the most influence over the future as you will know it. In other words, the person you most need to get in touch with is yourself.

At the risk of being too philosophical, what is life but a series of choices? Some choices, such as what to have for lunch or what color socks to wear, are not particularly challenging. Other times we are confronted with choices that can quite literally mean the difference between life and death. The funny thing about choices, however, is you can't always know the ultimate outcome of what may seem at the time to be the most trivial of decisions. Those are the decisions that steer us to unexpected paths in our lives. The best we can hope for is developing the habit of making good decisions.

That is why values are important. Values are the road map by which we, both as professionals and as individuals, chart a course into the future. Having values alone is not a guarantee of taking a smooth road. In fact, sticking to values can lead to a more treacherous road than traveling down the path of least resistance. But at least when we stick to our values we *know* we may be headed down a bumpy road. Often the path of least resistance does not turn out to be as smooth as it looks.

After a century of modern public relations, it is somewhat disheartening to know that practitioners are still compelled to demonstrate their worth to employers, clients, coworkers—and even to themselves. In the words of a Public Relations Society of America report on the stature of the profession,

> Public relations has evolved from a fringe function to a basic element of society in a comparatively short period of time, despite a number of handicaps. One of the greatest of these is the field's failure to act according to its own precepts. It has allowed prejudices against it to persist, misconceptions to entrench themselves and weaknesses within the field to be perceived as endemic. Public relations, like most elements of society, is now confronted with critical questioning. Its practitioners are questioning its stature and role as pointedly as outsiders. Like other elements of society, it must respond to its challengers or lose even its present stature and role. That role must be clarified; its goals must be set; its practitioners must earn optimal stature; means to achieve the goals must be established.[58]

In its own way, this report, prepared by PRSA's College of Fellows, is a plea for the very same concept advocated throughout this book: *values-driven public relations*. It is a recognition—and a warning—that until practitioners fully embrace the relationship-building values on which this profession was supposedly built, our period of self-doubt will continue.

Granted, that's a heavy load to place on the shoulders of someone still in college. However, real change can occur if we remember that 21st-century public relations will be built one person at a time.

As you ponder the many choices that await you, here are some guidelines to help you steer down the uncertain paths of the future:

- *Be true to your values.* If you can't be true to yourself, then to whom can you be true? If something doesn't pass the "Can you look at yourself in the mirror?" test, don't do it.

- *Pay your dues.* No one is going to hand you the keys to the executive washroom—at least not yet. Hard work and personal commitment are your investments in the future. Your time will come.

- *Make your own luck.* A wise person once said that luck is where opportunity meets preparation. Circumstances may place you in the right place at the right time. But it will be your talent and professionalism that will keep you there.

- *Learn from your mistakes.* Mistakes are often more instructive than successes. If you are willing to look objectively at a situation and, when necessary, shoulder the blame, it is unlikely that you will make the same mistake again.

- *Celebrate victories.* Just as it is important to learn from mistakes, it is important to accept credit when credit is due. You want to encourage success, not ignore it. Life is too short not to enjoy the good times. Don't take them for granted.

- *Keep learning.* Your education is just beginning. The world is rapidly changing, and you need to keep up with it. Don't pass up opportunities to learn something new; you never know when this knowledge will come in handy. Knowledge is power.

- *Command new technology—and don't let it command you.* Technological advances offer new and exciting ways to reach out to targeted publics. However, having the ability to use a new technology doesn't mean we should. Values, audience, and purpose should govern our decisions on which channels we choose.

- *Pass it on!* It is very likely that you will owe some aspect of your career advancement to mentoring from a more experienced practitioner who took you under his or her wing. The best way you can honor that special person is to become a mentor yourself and show someone else the ropes.

- *Maintain perspective.* Former University of North Carolina basketball coach Dean Smith retired with the most victories in the history of major college basketball. But he lost quite a few games as well. That's why he once told a reporter that he didn't treat every game as if it were a life-or-death situation. "If you do," Smith said, "you will be dead a lot."

- *Exercise your rights as a citizen—especially your First Amendment rights.* Freedom can't be taken for granted. It must always be defended and used responsibly. That's why it is important that you vote and speak out on important issues. That is also why you should resist anyone who tries to curb someone else's freedoms. How do you know that your freedoms won't be next on someone's hit list?

One practitioner at a time. That is how values-driven public relations will be established during the modern profession's second century.

Summary

As modern public relations moves into its second century, it has the potential to do both good and harm in society. Its good rests in the profession's ability to bring people together to reach consensus. However, some applications of public relations have been used to block consensus.

Major social forces are shaping the future. Among them are the global spread of democracy, the economic and cultural effects of globalization, the growth in world population, and the increasing feminization of the workplace. The growing presence of women has had and will have a dramatic effect on the field of public relations. Although women in public relations continue to face the same challenges as women everywhere, there appears to be a consensus for addressing salary equity and sexual harassment issues in the industry.

The growth of public relations is expected to continue in the forseeable future. Public relations will continue to work closely with other marketing disciplines—all of which will be held more accountable. Many of the old problems of the past, such as the search for respect, credibility, and ethics, will continue. Although the workplace in which public relations is practiced may change, the profession's need to adhere to enduring values remains constant.

DISCUSSION QUESTIONS

1. What social, political, or demographic trend will have the most significant impact on the practice of public relations in the 21st century? Please explain your reasoning.
2. How will world and national population trends affect public relations?
3. What steps do you think are necessary to make the profession of public relations more inclusive and representative of the population as a whole?
4. What steps are you taking to prepare for a career in public relations?
5. Public relations scholar Scott Cutlip said that public relations has had both positive and negative effects on society. As a whole, do you think the profession's overall influence has been more positive or negative? Please explain your answer.

Memo *from the* **Field**

Dirk Munson, 2001–2002 PRSSA National President, University of Northern Iowa

Dirk Munson was the 2001–2002 national president of the Public Relations Student Society of America (PRSSA). He graduated from the University of Northern Iowa in May 2002 with a degree in communications/public relations, and minors in journalism and marketing. With over 6,500 members at 227 chapters nationwide, PRSSA is the preeminent preprofessional organization for students of public relations.

Public relations is a dynamic field that has much to offer to those who actively pursue a career. In a field that continues to grow and diversify in its practice, it is becoming increasingly important for those who are entering the field to have obtained a vast amount of knowledge and experience. You can make your journey into the field of public relations a smooth one by taking steps to build your portfolio and to gain experience. Here are a few pointers that should help you along the way:

- *Get your foot in the door.* Join the Public Relations Student Society of America (PRSSA) or another preprofessional organization that will help you to gain experience in PR and establish a network of contacts. Building a large network of professionals can help you in many situations. It helps to know someone who might be able to help you down the line. Attend a conference, volunteer on campus, make a name for yourself by being a warm and receptive person.

- *Read everything you can.* Good public relations practitioners can be described as jacks of all trades. They need to know a little bit about everything. Start by reading a newspaper every day; this will help you to stay informed of the environment that surrounds you as well as the people and organizations you encounter. There are also a number of trade publications, such as *Public Relations Tactics*, a monthly publication for members of PRSSA and PRSA. Textbooks, although they may seem monotonous at times, can also help you to build your foundation of public relations knowledge, as can magazines, journals, and other publications.

- *Find a mentor.* Tapping into the wealth of knowledge of someone who has been in the field for a few years is one of the greatest ways to ready yourself for a career. Running your ideas, thoughts, and ambitions by someone who has already been through it is a great way to enhance and improve your own capabilities. Befriend someone who is willing to provide you with constructive criticism, and meet with that person from time to time.

- *Get some experience.* Take an internship, no matter how big or small. Any experience you can gain in public relations or related areas will help to build a foundation of knowledge you will use for your entire career. Writing for your school newspaper or volunteering for a local nonprofit organization is a way to get yourself started.

- *Have a broad base of knowledge.* In addition to your classes in public relations, you may want to broaden your horizons by taking some additional classes or a minor in a related field. For instance, a minor in journalism or graphic design will help you immensely and can give you the edge you'll need to land that first job.

These are the pointers I have seen to be effective. Discover for yourself what a good blend of career preparation is; things usually work best when you customize them to your own talents and desires. With a strong sense of enthusiasm and hard work, you can accomplish anything you set out to do. Best of luck for a successful and rewarding career in this great field!

Case Study 16.1

The Nestlé Boycott

If the purpose of values-driven public relations is to build mutually beneficial relationships, then the manner in which the Nestlé Company has handled the controversy over its marketing of powdered infant formula in developing nations is a miserable failure.

With the exception of four years in the mid-1980s, the Swiss-based company has been the target of a worldwide boycott since 1977. To put that into perspective, the boycott is older than many of the people reading this book. And as the second edition of this book goes to press, no end is in sight.

In and of itself, nothing is wrong with powdered baby formula. However, even the makers of the formula agree that nothing is better for a baby than natural mother's milk that comes from breast feeding. Still, the formula provides an alternative when breast feeding is either impractical or impossible. Commercially, breast milk substitutes generate approximately $6 billion in worldwide sales annually.[59]

But starting in the 1970s, the marketing of powdered baby formula in poor, developing nations earned the ire of health-care professionals and religious organizations. The powdered formula must be mixed with water. In developing countries, that can involve unsanitary conditions, which can make infants seriously ill. Another concern is the cost of the powdered formula, which, in developing countries, usually represents a substantial percentage of a consumer's meager income. The temptation is to make the powder last longer by watering down each serving. With less nutrition reaching infants, they can slowly starve to death.

However, one practice angered industry critics more than others. It had become common to use "milk nurses," or "mother craft workers," wearing white uniforms, to travel to villages to sell the product. Although these salespeople were usually trained nurses, critics complained that the uniforms falsely lent an air of authority to the sales pitch. With these salespeople being paid on commission, critics raised concerns about a built-in conflict of interest: These "milk nurses" had an economic incentive to recommend the powdered formula over the preferred breast feeding.[60]

As public awareness of the controversy grew, several major multinational organizations took up the fight, including the Interfaith Center on Corporate Responsibility (ICCR). One of the tactics ICCR used was to purchase stocks in the publicly held companies that manufactured the powdered formula. This gave critics legal access to shareholder meetings and allowed them to vote on company practices at annual shareholder meetings.

"A massive sales campaign presently encourages poor mothers to abandon breast feeding for this more expensive, mechanically complex and less healthful method," wrote the ICCR's Leah Margulies. "There could be no more dramatic illustration of manufacturing a need that wasn't there."[61]

Other organizations, including the United Nations and the World Health Organization, took up the cause. The WHO/UNICEF International Code of Marketing of Breastmilk Substitutes, adopted by the World Health Assembly (WHA) in 1981, supported a ban of all promotion of bottle feeding and set out requirements for labeling and information on infant feeding.

Nestlé chose confrontation rather than compliance. It vigorously challenged a series of shareholder fights designed to spotlight its questionable marketing practices. Unwilling to compromise, Nestlé challenged critics on every point. This led to an international boycott of Nestlé products, which ran from 1977 until 1984. It ended when the company said it would follow the terms of the WHA code. Company critics claim the boycott cost Nestlé "several billion dollars in lost sales and additional expenses."[62]

Unfortunately, the story does not end here. The boycott against Nestlé was reinstated in 1988 when critics claimed the company violated its promises by supplying free samples of baby formula to developing nations' hospitals. Although the company acknowledged providing some supplies to hospitals, a company spokesman called the boycott "stupid" and said the company wouldn't change its marketing practices.

"For [our critics] to say that we're dumping supplies in hospitals just simply isn't true," Nestlé spokesman Thad Jackson said. "We're supplying the materials that the hospitals ask for."[63]

The company has tried to address the latest boycott with no success. It reportedly rejected one public relations firm's proposals because they were too confrontational.[64] In 1991, the company launched an advertising and health clinic poster campaign promoting breast feeding. Although the campaign received some praise, cynics noted that it targeted women who got free infant formula from the government. That formula is supplied by Nestlé's competitors. In part due to the ongoing controversy, Nestlé does not have any government contracts.[65]

In fairness, Nestlé promotes breastfeeding on its web site, verybestbaby.com. "Experts agree breastmilk is best for babies," web visitors are told. "Not only is it the most nutritionally complete food your newborn will ever eat, but it also benefits your baby in other ways—some that will last a lifetime."[66] Nestlé's Corporate Governance Principles proclaim that the company has also always "respected the social, political, and cultural tradition of all countries in which it operates."[67]

However, these statements have not silenced the critics. In its report *Breaking the Rules, Stretching the Rules 2001*, the Infant Baby Food Action Network said Nestlé is "responsible for more violations than any other company and takes the lead in attempting to undermine implementation of the Code and Resolutions by governments and other bodies."[68]

A generation after this issue was first raised, the baby formula controversy remains unresolved. "Nestlé could go to 20 PR agencies and 19 of them would give the same advice: stop marketing this stuff," one crisis management expert said. "The trouble is, that is not what management wants to hear."[69]

DISCUSSION QUESTIONS

1. Despite a generation of protests against its marketing of infant formula, Nestlé remains a very profitable company. In what ways, if any, do you think the company has been hurt by this issue?
2. This case study mentions that Nestlé rejected one public relations agency's proposals because they were too confrontational. One of those proposals was for Nestlé to try to infiltrate opposition groups. What do you think of this tactic?
3. Do infant formula manufacturers bear any moral responsibility if consumers misuse and are hurt by misuse of their safe product? Can you think of any other products that may fall into this category?
4. Has the boycott against Nestlé been a success or a failure? What do you think of the practice of using an economic boycott as a tactic to influence a company's actions?

Case Study 16.2

PR in the Face of Terror

The first challenge was to survive. Many did not.

For the survivors of September 11, 2001, the second challenge was to move beyond the terror and pick up the pieces of a world suddenly gone mad. Many did just that. Public relations played an important role in the recovery.

Much has been (and will be) written about the heroes of that infamous day. Terrorists hijacked four passenger jets and turned them into weapons of mass destruction. Within a span of two horrific and chaotic hours, New York's World Trade Center was

Just hours after a terrorist attack on the Pentagon left almost 200 people dead, U.S. Secretary of Defense Donald Rumsfeld briefs news media in another part of the building. (Courtesy of the U.S. Department of Defense)

destroyed, the Pentagon in Washington was severely damaged, an airliner crashed in western Pennsylvania, and thousands of innocent people—people who were guilty of nothing more than being in the wrong place at the wrong time—were dead.

And the world was a much different place.

Cantor Fitzgerald, one of the nation's largest bond dealers, employed 1,000 people on the top four floors of the WTC's North Tower. Rescue officials believe that none of the more than 700 Cantor employees in the office on September 11 escaped the building before its collapse. Edelman Public Relations Worldwide helped the shattered company coordinate its initial response to the tragedy. Approximately 50 Edelman employees volunteered at bereavement centers established at nearby hotels for the families of the dead and missing. Edelman also coordinated television interviews for Chief Executive Officer Howard Lutnick, who arrived at the WTC just as the first plane struck.[70]

"We've got to make our company be able to take care of my 700 families," Lutnick said. One of those families belonged to his younger brother Gary, a Cantor employee trapped in the North Tower.

Two days after the attack, the bond market reopened. So did Cantor Fitzgerald.

Morgan Stanley, a major financial brokerage, was the largest tenant of the WTC, with 3,500 employees. Most of its employees survived, thanks to fortunate timing and geography. Its offices were located in the South Tower, the second building hit. Unlike those of Cantor Fitzgerald, Morgan Stanley's offices were below the impact point. Those two factors gave Morgan Stanley employees enough time to scramble to safety.

The job for Morgan Stanley's corporate communicators was twofold: They needed to address the human tragedy that had befallen their company and they had to reassured frightened customers that their investments were safe.

"We have all been saddened and outraged by the attack on America, and extend our deepest sympathies and prayers to all of the people affected," Morgan Stanley Chairman Philip Purcell said in a statement posted that afternoon on the company's web site. "All our clients should rest assured that their assets are safe and our Financial Advisors will soon be in contact with our individual investors to answer questions and address their concerns."[71]

Shortly after the attack on the World Trade Center, a hijacked jet slammed into the Pentagon. The White House, the Capitol, and dozens of other government buildings were evacuated. However, the United States government continued to function. Spokespersons for the Federal Aviation Administration announced an unprecedented grounding of all commercial air traffic in the United States. U.S. Securities and Exchange Commission Chairman Harvey L. Pitt issued a statement assuring a nervous nation that the disruption of the financial markets was "a temporary phenomenon."[72]

Even while fire and rescue crews searched a collapsed and burning section of the Pentagon for their fallen comrades, Defense Department and military officials conducted media briefings in another part of the building. "It's an indication that the United States government is functioning in the face of this terrible act against our country," Defense Secretary Donald H. Rumsfeld said. "The Pentagon is functioning. It will be in business tomorrow."[73]

The need to communicate with stakeholders was especially acute for officials at Chicago-based United Airlines and Fort Worth–based American Airlines. Their crews and passengers had been victims, and their aircraft had been the instruments of the terrorists' deadly plot. The two companies had to communicate immediately to a wide range of stakeholders, including relatives of the victims, employees, news media, and federal investigators. They also had a number of key messages to deliver, including sympathy and support for the victims' families and cooperation with federal authorities. Both airlines mobilized their employees in response to the tragedies. Some went to the departure and destination airports of the four flights. Others staffed emergency hotline telephones. The airlines also dispatched technical teams to crash sites to assist federal investigators.

"I know that I speak for every employee at American Airlines when I extend our deepest sympathy to those who lost a loved one, family member, or friend on American Airlines Flight 11, American Airlines Flight 77, United Airlines Flight 93, United Airlines Flight 175, or at the sites of these tragic accidents," said CEO Donald J. Carty in a statement posted on the company's web site.[74]

On his company's web site, United CEO James E. Goodwin expressed similar sentiments. And like his counterpart at American, Goodwin pledged full support for victims' families. He added, "We are also making every resource available at our company to assist all of the relevant authorities—including the FBI—with the ultimate goal of bringing to justice the individuals or organizations responsible for these horrific criminal acts."[75]

The ripple effects of the terrorist attack were felt in many places. An example is the National Association of Insurance Commissioners, an information clearinghouse for state insurance regulatory agencies, headquartered in Kansas City, Missouri. NAIC's Securities Valuation Office was in 7 World Trade Center, a building that caught fire and eventually collapsed following the attack. All the company's New York employees survived. By following a crisis plan initially developed as a defense against the millennium bug (see Chapter 11), NAIC was able to recover critical computer records before the building lost electrical power.

"We developed our Business Recovery Plan with the idea that it would ready us for any emergency situation that would cause loss of a critical service, loss of access to a facility, or loss of a facility itself," said NAIC's Executive Vice President and CEO Catherine J. Weatherford. "The concept we developed went beyond the scope of just responding to Y2K. . . . However, none of us could have anticipated the type of tragedy that would afflict our nation on September 11."[76]

Following the attack, public relations practitioners played a role in the nation's recovery. In the New York area, the Public Relations Society of America organized volunteers to help companies needing communications. The International Association of Business Communicators offered crisis resources to its members at no charge. Several New York public relations agencies helped find office space for practitioners displaced from lower Manhattan. On The Scene Productions and Medialink made their satellite uplink facilities available to those affected by the WTC disaster "at substantial discounts."[77] When it really mattered, the public relations community had no competitors, just colleagues.

The role of public relations in a time of national distress was captured by PRSA Chair and CEO Kathleen L. Lewton in a message to members just two weeks after the attack:

> As always in time of tragedy, PR professionals have been in the midst of the maelstrom, in many capacities. Serving as spokespersons for hospitals, airlines, and governments; handling media inquiries and releasing statements for companies directly impacted; managing efforts to reach employees at remote locations; providing agency support for clients in crisis—as the tragedy unfolded, even those of us who were watching from afar were well aware that behind the scenes, there were thousands of public relations people hard at work, trying to cope.
>
> Our profession is such that in times of crisis, we are essential. We can never step back or step aside, we can never demur, we rarely even have the chance to ask for a moment to reflect and grieve. Our companies and organizations and communities rely on our skills most in times of disruption and peril, and I know that I speak for the entire public relations profession when I offer our admiration and our commendations to the colleagues who labored so tirelessly and so heroically in the first days of the crisis, and to all those who today are working to help our nation recover.[78]

Among those killed on United Flight 93 was public relations practitioner Mark Bingham. Although his actions did not involve the practice of public relations, his role in the events of September 11 may have been more significant than any other practitioner.

We may never know exactly what happened on Flight 93. Based on information gleaned from cellular telephone conversations between passengers and family, Bingham was among a group of passengers who said they would try to overpower the hijackers. The plane crashed approximately 80 miles southeast of Pittsburgh, Pennsylvania, killing all on board. Authorities believe that the hijackers were foiled in their attempt to attack the White House or the U.S. Capitol.

September 11, 2001, was the nation's bloodiest day since the Civil War. Ironically, Flight 93 crashed in the state that was home to that conflict's most celebrated battle. In giving what Abraham Lincoln described in the Gettysburg Address as "the last full measure of devotion," Mark Bingham embodied the practitioner's commitment to serving the public interest.

DISCUSSION QUESTIONS

1. What lessons can public relations practitioners learn from the events of September 11, 2001? How do you think practitioners performed?
2. Why do you think American Airlines and United Airlines used their web sites to deliver messages to stakeholders? What other tactics/media could have been used?
3. At a time of great calamity, such as the terrorist attacks on New York City and Washington, D.C., what role does public relations play?
4. Is a practitioner's advocacy on behalf of a client's interests inconsistent with broader public interests during national emergencies? Where does the commitment to the client end and the commitment to the broader public interest begin? How do one's personal interests figure into the equation?

It's Your Turn

Battling Bambi

How would you like it if someone came up to you and started screaming that you are a "Bambi killer"? Because the community you work for is about to embark upon a controversial "deer management" program, you are facing this unwelcome prospect.

With urban sprawl encroaching deeper into once rural areas, the deer problem has long been a confrontation waiting to happen. Deer thrive in suburbia because it is an area that is typically off-limits to hunters.

The overpopulation of deer causes more than $1 billion in property damage in the United States every year. Nationwide in 1996, more than 100 people died in deer–automobile collisions. Deer are carriers of Lyme disease, an increasing problem in certain parts of the United States. Deer herds have also been known to virtually strip some areas of vegetation. Business leaders and homeowners in many communities have complained about the deer.

You are the public information officer for your local city government, and you have learned that the city manager is considering a proposal for a supervised hunt to "thin" the local deer herd. The city manager has concluded that more humane relocation and sterilization programs are too costly and would require a substantial increase in local taxes.

There are several active environmental groups in the community. You anticipate a loud and long protest if such a policy is pursued.

The city manager asks you how to gain public acceptance of the proposal. What advice will you give?

KEY TERMS

baby boom generation, p. 531
breadwinners, p. 531
empowerment, p. 534
feminization, p. 533
globalization, p. 524
green public relations, p. 530
greenwash, p. 530
interconnectedness, p. 524

internships, p. 540
lookism, p. 532
Public Relations Student Society of America (PRSSA), p. 540
salary equity, p. 533
sexual harassment, p. 532
velvet ghetto, p. 533
virtual public relations, p. 538

NOTES

1. Scott M. Cutlip, *The Unseen Power: Public Relations, a History* (Hillsdale, N.J.: Lawrence Erlbaum, 1994), xii.
2. Cutlip, xiii.
3. Information in this QuickBreak comes from personal interviews conducted by David W. Guth in St. Petersburg, Russia, in June 1998. Some of these interviews have previously appeared in David W. Guth, "Public Relations in the New Russia," *The Public Relations Strategist* 4, no. 3: 51–54.
4. Guth.
5. Guth.
6. Guth.
7. *Human Development Report 1999*, United Nations Development Program, online, www.undp.org/hdro.

8. Alejandro Portes, ed., *The New Second Generation* (New York: Russell Sage Foundation, 1996), 54–81.

9. Data from the 1990 census and 2000 census, U.S. Census Bureau, online, www.census.gov.

10. U.S. Census Bureau, online, www.census.gov.

11. Hispanic Association on Corporate Responsibility web site, www.hacr.org/demographics/purchasing.html.

12. "Marketers Underrate Hispanic Potential," *Public Relations Journal* (February 1991): 30.

13. Isabel Valdes, "Seven Secrets to Tapping into the Growing Hispanic Market," *Public Relations Tactics* (October 1995): 4.

14. Valdes.

15. Octavio Emillio Nuiry, "Latino PR Melting Pot 'Boiling Over,'" *O'Dwyer's PR Services Report* (May 1994): 51.

16. Jim Forkan, "Media See Latino Market as 'Caliente,'" *Multichannel News*, 11 June 2001, online, www.findarticles.com/cf_0/m3535/24_22/75620699/print.jhtml.

17. Cutlip, 31 (italics in original).

18. Lowell F. Ludford, "3P Program Pays Off in Cost Savings of $500 Million for 3M," *Public Relations Journal* (April 1991): 20–21.

19. McDonald's Corporation web site, www.mcdonalds.com.

20. McDonald's web site.

21. CorpWatch web site, www.corpwatch.org.

22. U.S. Census Bureau, online, www.census.gov.

23. U.S. Census Bureau, online, www.census.gov.

24. "Facts about Sexual Harassment," U.S. Equal Employment Opportunity Commission web site, www.eeoc.gov/facts/fs-sex.html.

25. "Sexual Harassment Charges, EEOC & FEPAs Combined: FY 1992–FY 2000," U.S. Equal Employment Opportunity Commission, online, www.eeoc.gov/stats/harass.html.

26. Shirley A. Serini et al., "Power, Gender, and Public Relations: Sexual Harassment as a Threat to the Practice," *Journal of Public Relations Research* 10, no. 3 (1998): 193–218.

27. Hon, 54.

28. Roberts and Mann.

29. The applicable cases are *Faragher v. City of Boca Raton*, 118 S. Ct. 2275 (1998) and *Burlington Industries Inc. v. Ellerth*, 118 S. Ct. 2257 (1998).

30. "Sexual Harassment Charges, EEOC & FEPAs Combined: FY 1992–FY 2000."

31. The applicable case is *Oncale v. Sundowner Offshore Services, Inc.*, 118 S. Ct. 998 (1998).

32. "Facts about Sexual Harassment."

33. Serini et al.

34. U.S. Bureau of Labor Statistics, online, http://stats.bls.gov.

35. Diane Crispell, "Marital Bust," *American Demographics* (June 1994): 59.

36. Crispell.

37. Rick Hampson, "Women Dominate PR . . . Is That Good?" *USA Today*, 31 May 2001, online, www.usatoday.com/money/advertising/2001-04-25-prwomen.htm.

38. L. L. Cline et al., *The Velvet Ghetto: The Impact of the Increasing Percentage of Women in Public Relations and Organizational Communications* (San Francisco: IABC Research Foundation, 1986).

39. Linda Hon, "Feminism and Public Relations," *The Public Relations Strategist* 1, no. 2 (summer 1995): 20.

40. Hampson.

41. U.S. Department of Labor statistics, online, www.dol.gov.

42. Linda Childers Hon, "Toward a Feminist Theory of Public Relations," *Journal of Public Relations Research* 7, no. 1 (1995): 33–34.

43. Shirley A. Serini et al., "Watch for Falling Glass . . . Women, Men and Job Satisfaction in Public Relations: A Preliminary Analysis," *Journal of Public Relations Research* 9, no. 2 (1997): 116–117.

44. *Occupational Outlook Handbook, 2000–01,* U.S. Department of Labor Bureau of Labor Statistics, online, www.stats.bls.gov/oco/ocos086.htm.

45. Cynthia Fritsch, researcher, "'Communications' Tops 'PR' by 2–1 Margin at Fortune 500," *O'Dwyer's PR Services Report* (February 1996): 1.

46. National Credibility Index, Public Relations Society of America web site, www/prsa.org/nci/nci.html.

47. "NY Area Public Relations Professionals Positive about Profession but Believe Self-Image Is Not Shared by Others," news release, New York chapter, Public Relations Society of America, 2 December 1998.

48. "Targeting, Relationship-Building Define Marketing Today," *PRNews* 52, no. 13, 25 March 1996, online, Lexis-Nexis.

49. "Targeting, Relationship-Building Define Marketing Today."

50. "Measurement Driving More PR Programs," *PRNews* 52, no. 12, 18 March 1996, online, Lexis-Nexis.

51. *Report on the American Workforce, 2001,* U.S. Department of Labor Bureau of Labor Statistics, online, http://stats.bls.gov/opub/rtaw/message.htm.

52. Kati S. Allen and Gloria Flynn Moorman, "Leaving Home: The Emigration of Home-Office Workers," *American Demographics* (October 1995): 57.

53. "Veteran Denver Journalist Leaves U.S. West to Create Virtual PR Agency," PR Newswire, 2 June 1996.

54. Kim Newton Gronniger, "Grove Generates Good News His Own Way," *Kansas Alumni* 5 (1998): 41.

55. "Outcomes Task Team Report," report of National Communication Association 1998 Summer Conference: Dialogue on Public Relations Education, Arlington, Virginia.

56. Don W. Stacks et al., "Perceptions of Public Relations Education: A Survey of Public Relations Curriculum, Outcomes, Assessment, and Pedagogy," released at the National Communication Association 1998 Summer Conference: Dialogue on Public Relations Education, Arlington, Virginia, 10 July 1998.

57. *Occupational Outlook Handbook, 2000–01.*

58. "Excerpt from Report on Stature of PR: Factors Inhibiting Stature and Role of PR," *O'Dwyer's PR Services Report* (March 1992): 31.

59. Rosalind Rachid, "Switzerland's Nestlé Nurses Its Sullied Baby Food Image," *Journal of Commerce,* 7 August 1989, 1A.

60. Allen H. Center and Frank E. Walsh, *Public Relations Practices: Managerial Case Studies and Problems,* 3rd ed. (Englewood Cliffs, N.J.: Prentice-Hall, 1985), 366.

61. Leah Margulies, "Baby Formula Abroad: Exporting Infant Malnutrition," *Christianity and Crisis,* 10 November 1975, 264–67.

62. Laurie Duncan, "Group Calls for Resumption of Nestlé Boycott; Says It Broke Promise Not to Promote Baby Formula in Third World," *Los Angeles Times,* 5 October 1988, 4-1.

63. Duncan, 4-1.

64. "Plan Is Nestlé's Best PR," *Journal of Commerce,* 7 August 1989, 5A.

65. Bradley Johnson, "Nestlé Ads Pitch Breast-Feeding," *Advertising Age,* 2 December 1991, 40.

66. Nestlé web site, www.verybestbaby.com.

67. Corporate Governance Principles, Nestlé Corporate web site, www/nestle.com/investor_relations.

68. *Breaking the Rules, Stretching the Rules 2001,* Infant Baby Food Action Network, on-line, www.ibfan.org/english/codewatch/btr01/INDEX-en.HTM.

69. "Plan Is Nestlé's Best PR."

70. "Cantor Fitzgerald Turns to Edelman," *O'Dwyer's PR Daily,* 21 September 2001, on-line, www.odwyerpr.com/0921cantor.htm.

71. "Message from Morgan Stanley Chairman Phillip Purcell," Morgan Stanley web site, 11 September 2001, www.morganstanley.com.

72. Statement by SEC Chairman Harvey L. Pitt (2001–90), U.S. Securities and Exchange Commission, 11 September 2001, online, www.sec.gov.

73. Transcript of Department of Defense News Briefing on Pentagon Attack, U.S. Department of Defense, 11 September 2001, (6:42 P.M. EDT), online, www.defenselink.mil.

74. "A Message from American Airlines Chief Executive Officer Don Carty," American Airlines web site, 11 September 2001, www/aa.com.

75. "A Message from United Airlines CEO James E. Goodwin," United Airlines web site, 11 September 2001, www.ual.com.

76. Catherine J. Weatherford, interview by authors, 28 September 2001.

77. "PR Community Pitches In," *O'Dwyer's PR Services,* 13 September 2001, online, www.odwyerpr.com/0913pr_community.htm.

78. E-mail message of Kathleen Larey Lewton, APR, Fellow PRSA Chair and CEO, Public Relations Society of America, 26 September 2001.

Appendix

Member Code of Ethics 2000

Approved by the PRSA Assembly, October 2000

Preamble

Public Relations Society of America Member Code of Ethics 2000

> Professional Values
> Principles of Conduct
> Commitment and Compliance

This Code applies to PRSA members. The Code is designed to be a useful guide for PRSA members as they carry out their ethical responsibilities. This document is designed to anticipate and accommodate, by precedent, ethical challenges that may arise. The scenarios outlined in the Code provision are actual examples of misconduct. More will be added as experience with the Code occurs.

The Public Relations Society of America (PRSA) is committed to ethical practices. The level of public trust PRSA members seek, as we serve the public good, means we have taken on a special obligation to operate ethically.

The value of member reputation depends upon the ethical conduct of everyone affiliated with the Public Relations Society of America. Each of us sets an example for each other—as well as other professionals—by our pursuit of excellence with powerful standards of performance, professionalism, and ethical conduct.

Emphasis on enforcement of the Code has been eliminated. But, the PRSA Board of Directors retains the right to bar from membership or expel from the Society any individual who has been or is sanctioned by a government agency or convicted in a court of law of an action that is in violation of this Code.

Ethical practice is the most important obligation of a PRSA member. We view the Member Code of Ethics as a model for other professions, organizations, and professionals.

PRSA Member Statement of Professional Values

This statement presents the core values of PRSA members and, more broadly, of the public relations profession. These values provide the foundation for the Member

Code of Ethics and set the industry standard for the professional practice of public relations. These values are the fundamental beliefs that guide our behaviors and decision-making process. We believe our professional values are vital to the integrity of the profession as a whole.

ADVOCACY

We serve the public interest by acting as responsible advocates for those we represent.

We provide a voice in the marketplace of ideas, facts, and viewpoints to aid informed public debate.

HONESTY

We adhere to the highest standards of accuracy and truth in advancing the interests of those we represent and in communicating with the public.

EXPERTISE

We acquire and responsibly use specialized knowledge and experience.

We advance the profession through continued professional development, research, and education.

We build mutual understanding, credibility, and relationships among a wide array of institutions and audiences.

INDEPENDENCE

We provide objective counsel to those we represent.

We are accountable for our actions.

LOYALTY

We are faithful to those we represent, while honoring our obligation to serve the public interest.

FAIRNESS

We deal fairly with clients, employers, competitors, peers, vendors, the media, and the general public.

We respect all opinions and support the right of free expression.

PRSA Code Provisions

Free Flow of Information

CORE PRINCIPLE

Protecting and advancing the free flow of accurate and truthful information is essential to serving the public interest and contributing to informed decision making in a democratic society.

Courtesy of the Public Relations Society of America

INTENT

To maintain the integrity of relationships with the media, government officials, and the public.

To aid informed decision-making.

GUIDELINES

A member shall:

> Preserve the integrity of the process of communication.
>
> Be honest and accurate in all communications.
>
> Act promptly to correct erroneous communications for which the practitioner is responsible.
>
> Preserve the free flow of unprejudiced information when giving or receiving gifts by ensuring that gifts are nominal, legal, and infrequent.

EXAMPLES OF IMPROPER CONDUCT UNDER THIS PROVISION:

A member representing a ski manufacturer gives a pair of expensive racing skis to a sports magazine columnist, to influence the columnist to write favorable articles about the product.

A member entertains a government official beyond legal limits and/or in violation of government reporting requirements.

Competition

CORE PRINCIPLE

Promoting healthy and fair competition among professionals preserves an ethical climate while fostering a robust business environment.

INTENT

To promote respect and fair competition among public relations professionals.

To serve the public interest by providing the widest choice of practitioner options.

GUIDELINES

A member shall:

> Follow ethical hiring practices designed to respect free and open competition without deliberately undermining a competitor.
>
> Preserve intellectual property rights in the marketplace.

EXAMPLES OF IMPROPER CONDUCT UNDER THIS PROVISION:

A member employed by a "client organization" shares helpful information with a counseling firm that is competing with others for the organization's business.

A member spreads malicious and unfounded rumors about a competitor in order to alienate the competitor's clients and employees in a ploy to recruit people and business.

Disclosure of Information

CORE PRINCIPLE

Open communication fosters informed decision making in a democratic society.

INTENT

To build trust with the public by revealing all information needed for responsible decision making.

GUIDELINES

A member shall:

Be honest and accurate in all communications.

Act promptly to correct erroneous communications for which the member is responsible.

Investigate the truthfulness and accuracy of information released on behalf of those represented.

Reveal the sponsors for causes and interests represented.

Disclose financial interest (such as stock ownership) in a client's organization.

Avoid deceptive practices.

EXAMPLES OF IMPROPER CONDUCT UNDER THIS PROVISION:

Front groups: A member implements "grass roots" campaigns or letter-writing campaigns to legislators on behalf of undisclosed interest groups.

Lying by omission: A practitioner for a corporation knowingly fails to release financial information, giving a misleading impression of the corporation's performance.

A member discovers inaccurate information disseminated via a web site or media kit and does not correct the information.

A member deceives the public by employing people to pose as volunteers to speak at public hearings and participate in "grass roots" campaigns.

Safeguarding Confidences

CORE PRINCIPLE

Client trust requires appropriate protection of confidential and private information.

INTENT

To protect the privacy rights of clients, organizations, and individuals by safeguarding confidential information.

GUIDELINES

A member shall:

Safeguard the confidences and privacy rights of present, former, and prospective clients and employees.

Protect privileged, confidential, or insider information gained from a client or organization.

Immediately advise an appropriate authority if a member discovers that confidential information is being divulged by an employee of a client company or organization.

EXAMPLES OF IMPROPER CONDUCT UNDER THIS PROVISION:

A member changes jobs, takes confidential information, and uses that information in the new position to the detriment of the former employer.

A member intentionally leaks proprietary information to the detriment of some other party.

Conflicts of Interest

CORE PRINCIPLE

Avoiding real, potential, or perceived conflicts of interest builds the trust of clients, employers, and the publics.

INTENT

To earn trust and mutual respect with clients or employers.

To build trust with the public by avoiding or ending situations that put one's personal or professional interests in conflict with society's interests.

GUIDELINES

A member shall:

Act in the best interests of the client or employer, even subordinating the member's personal interests.

Avoid actions and circumstances that may appear to compromise good business judgment or create a conflict between personal and professional interests.

Disclose promptly any existing or potential conflict of interest to affected clients or organizations.

Encourage clients and customers to determine if a conflict exists after notifying all affected parties.

EXAMPLES OF IMPROPER CONDUCT UNDER THIS PROVISION:

The member fails to disclose that he or she has a strong financial interest in a client's chief competitor.

The member represents a "competitor company" or a "conflicting interest" without informing a prospective client.

Enhancing the Profession

CORE PRINCIPLE

Public relations professionals work constantly to strengthen the public's trust in the profession.

INTENT

To build respect and credibility with the public for the profession of public relations.

To improve, adapt, and expand professional practices.

GUIDELINES

A member shall:

Acknowledge that there is an obligation to protect and enhance the profession.

Keep informed and educated about practices in the profession to ensure ethical conduct.

Actively pursue personal professional development.

Decline representation of clients or organizations that urge or require actions contrary to this Code.

Accurately define what public relations activities can accomplish.

Counsel subordinates in proper ethical decision making.

Require that subordinates adhere to the ethical requirements of the Code.

Report ethical violations, whether committed by PRSA members or not, to the appropriate authority.

EXAMPLES OF IMPROPER CONDUCT UNDER THIS PROVISION:

A PRSA member declares publicly that a product the client sells is safe, without disclosing evidence to the contrary.

A member initially assigns some questionable client work to a non-member practitioner to avoid the ethical obligation of PRSA membership.

Resources

RULES AND GUIDELINES

The following PRSA documents, available online at www.prsa.org, provide detailed rules and guidelines to help guide your professional behavior. If, after reviewing them, you still have a question or issue, contact PRSA headquarters as noted below.

PRSA Bylaws

PRSA Administrative Rules

Member Code of Ethics

QUESTIONS

The PRSA is here to help. If you have a serious concern or simply need clarification, please contact Kim Baldwin at (212) 460-1404.

PRSA Member Code of Ethics Pledge

I pledge:

To conduct myself professionally, with truth, accuracy, fairness, and responsibility to the public; To improve my individual competence and advance the knowledge and proficiency of the profession through continuing research and education; And to adhere to the articles of the Member Code of Ethics 2000 for the practice of public relations as adopted by the governing Assembly of the Public Relations Society of America.

I understand and accept that there is a consequence for misconduct, up to and including membership revocation.

And, I understand that those who have been or are sanctioned by a government agency or convicted in a court of law of an action that is in violation of this Code may be barred from membership or expelled from the Society.

_____

Signature

_____

Date

Glossary

Terms in the Glossary match those of the Key Terms section in each chapter and reflect the usage in the text. Thus, some entries in the Glossary are singular and others are plural.

account executive The individual at a public relations agency with the responsibility for managing a client's account and the people working on that account.

Accredited Business Communicator (ABC) Designation given to accredited members of the International Association of Business Communicators.

Accredited in Public Relations (APR) Designation given to accredited members of the Public Relations Society of America.

action When used in the context of Monroe's Motivated Sequence, the process of explicitly telling an audience the action one wishes it to take.

active public A group whose members understand that they are united by a common interest, value, or values in a particular situation and are actively working to promote their interest or values.

active public opinion Expressed behavioral inclination exhibited when people act—formally and informally—to influence the opinions and actions of others.

active voice A grammatical term designating that, within a sentence, the subject does the action denoted by the verb (see *passive voice*). In most grammatical situations, writers prefer active voice to passive voice.

actualities Recorded quotable quotes or sound bites supplied to radio stations on cassette tape or via a dial-in phone system or a web site.

actual malice The higher burden of proof that public officials and public figures must satisfy in libel cases: In addition to showing that a defamatory statement is false, a public figure must also show knowing falsehood or reckless disregard for the truth.

ad hoc plan A plan created for a single, short-term purpose; from the Latin phrase meaning "for this purpose only."

administrative law judge The presiding officer in hearings about alleged violations of government regulations. This person hears testimony and reviews evidence, much like the judge and jury in a civil or criminal case. If federal regulations are at issue, this judge's decision can ultimately be appealed to the federal court system.

advertising The process of creating and sending a persuasive message through controlled media, which allow the sender, for a price, to dictate message, placement, and frequency.

agenda-setting hypothesis The idea that the mass media tell us not what to think, but what to think about. This hypothesis is the most widely accepted view of how mass media interact with society.

analog Transmitted in the form of continuously varying signals. Those variations correspond to changes in sound and light energy coming from the source.

annual meeting A once-a-year informational conference that a publicly held company must, by law, hold for its stockholders.

annual report A once-a-year informational statement that a publicly held company must, by law, send to its stockholders.

appropriation A tort in libel law. In this context, it is the commercial use of someone's name, voice, likeness, or other defining characteristic without the person's consent.

association magazines Magazines for members of associations, such as the American Library Association.

attention When used in the context of Monroe's Motivated Sequence, the process of gaining the interest of listeners by telling them why the topic is relevant.

attitude A behavioral inclination.

attributes Characteristics or qualities that describe an object or individual, such as gender, age, weight, height, political affiliation, and religious affiliation.

attribution The part of a sentence that identifies the speaker of a direct quotation. In the sentence *"Public relations is a values-driven profession," she said,* the words *she said* are the attribution.

aware public A group whose members understand that they are united by a common interest, value, or values in a particular situation but who have not yet formed plans or acted on their interest or values.

aware public opinion Expressed behavioral inclination that occurs when people grow aware of an emerging interest.

baby boom generation People born between 1945 and 1964. The name comes from the record post–World War II surge in population. As the baby boomers reach retirement age early in the 21st century, they are expected to place a tremendous strain on services geared toward the elderly.

backgrounder A document that supplies information to supplement a news release. Written as publishable stories, backgrounders are often included in media kits.

Barnum, Phineas Taylor (P.T.) Nineteenth-century showman whose efforts to gain publicity through wild and exaggerated claims made him the "father of press-agentry"—and a symbol that modern public relations practitioners have sought to shed.

belief A commitment to a particular idea or concept based on either personal experience or some credible external authority.

Bernays, Edward L. The man often acknowledged as the "father of public relations"—a notion he openly promoted. In his landmark 1923 book *Crystallizing Public Opinion,* Bernays coined the phrase "public relations counsel" and first articulated the concept of two-way public relations. Bernays was a nephew of noted psychoanalyst Sigmund Freud.

bill inserts Leaflets or other marketing documents that can be included with the bills that a company sends to its customers.

bivariate analysis Analysis of research data that examines two variables.

boundary role The function of representing a public's values to an organization and, conversely, representing the values of the organization to that public.

brainstorming A collaborative and speculative process in which options for possible courses of action are explored.

breadwinners People between the ages of 18 and 65 who typically constitute the labor force. As the so-called baby boom generation reaches retirement age, the percentage of breadwinners relative to the total U.S. population will decline.

b-roll Unedited video footage that follows a video news release. Rather than use the VNR as provided, some television stations prefer using b-roll footage to create their own news stories.

burden of proof The legal standard a plaintiff must meet to establish a defendant's guilt. For example, to prove a case of libel, the plaintiff must show defamation, identification, publication, damage, and fault or actual malice.

categorical imperative A concept created by Immanuel Kant; the idea that individuals ought to make ethical decisions by imagining what would happen if a given course of action were to become a universal maxim, a clear principle designed to apply to everyone.

cause marketing A concerted effort on the part of an organization to address a social need through special events and, perhaps, other marketing tactics.

CD-ROM The acronym for "compact disc–read-only memory," a medium for storage of digital data. It is a popular format for storage of music, computer software, and databases. CD-ROMs are increasingly popular among public relations practitioners for the distribution of multimedia and interactive communications.

cease and desist order An order issued by an FTC administrative law judge upon a ruling that a company or individual has violated fed-eral laws governing marketplace transactions, including advertising.

census Survey of every member of a sampling frame.

channel The medium used to transmit a message.

civil penalties Penalties imposed under civil law for the violation of government regulations. These penalties usually involve the levy of a fine or placement of certain restrictions against the individual or organization found to be in violation.

cleanup phase The third stage of a crisis. During this stage, an organization deals with a crisis and its aftermath. How long this period lasts is influenced by the degree to which the organization is prepared to handle crises.

client research The gathering of information about the client, company, or organization on whose behalf the practitioner is working. Typically, this information includes the organization's size, products or services, history, staffing requirements, markets and customers, budget, legal environment, reputation, and mission.

closed-ended questions Questions for which the response set is specifically defined; answers must be selected from a predetermined menu of options.

cluster sampling A sampling technique used to compensate for an unrepresentative sampling frame. It involves breaking the population into homogeneous clusters and then selecting a sample from each cluster.

coalition building Efforts to promote consensus among influential publics on important issues through tactics such as face-to-face meetings.

cognitive dissonance The mental discomfort people can experience when they encounter information or opinions that oppose their opinions.

commercial speech   Expression intended to generate marketplace transactions. The U.S. Supreme Court has recognized a government interest in its regulation.

commitment   The extent to which each party in a relationship thinks that the relationship is worth the time, cost, and effort.

Committee for Public Information (CPI)   Committee created by President Woodrow Wilson to rally public opinion in support of U.S. efforts during World War I. Often referred to as the Creel Committee, it was headed by former journalist George Creel and served as a training ground for many early public relations practitioners.

common law libel   Libel defined by judicial rulings rather than by legislators or regulators; can occur in private communications, such as internal business memoranda.

communal relationship   A relationship characterized by the provision of benefits to both members of the relationship out of concern and without expectation of anything in return.

communication   The exchange of information, verbal and nonverbal, between individuals. Also the third step in the four-step public relations process. Because the process is dynamic, however, communication can occur at any time.

communication audits   Research procedures used to determine whether an organization's public statements and publications are consistent with its values-driven mission and goals.

communication model   A diagram that depicts the elements of the process of communication.

communications grid   A tool used during communication audits to illustrate the distribution patterns of an organization's communi-

cations. The various media used are listed on one axis, stakeholders important to the organization on the other.

communications specialist   Job title given to some public relations practitioners, whose jobs usually entail the preparation of communications.

community relations   The maintenance of mutually beneficial contacts between an organization and key publics within communities important to its success.

compliance-gaining tactic   An action designed to influence the behavior of a person or public. Ideally, the action is consistent both with an organization's goals and values and with the person's or public's self-interests and values.

components of relationships   As defined by researchers Linda Childers Hon and James E. Grunig, the six key components that should be used in measuring the strength of a relationship: control mutuality, trust, satisfaction, commitment, exchange relationship, and communal relationship.

confidence levels   The statistical degree to which one can reasonably assume that a survey outcome is an accurate reflection of the entire population.

consent order   Ruling issued by the FTC when a company or individual voluntarily agrees to end a potentially unlawful practice without making an admission of guilt.

consumer redress   Compensation for consumers harmed by misleading or illegal marketplace practices. Under federal law, consumer redress can be sought by the Securities and Exchange Commission.

consumer relations   The maintenance of mutually beneficial communication between an organization and the people who use or are potential users of its products and/or services.

contacts In marketing, all informative encounters, direct or indirect, that a customer or potential customer has with an organization's product or with the organization itself.

contingency plan A plan created for use when a certain set of circumstances arises. Crisis communications plans are examples of contingency plans.

contingency questions Questions that are asked on the basis of questionnaire respondents' answers to earlier questions.

controlled media Communication channels, such as newsletters, in which the sender of the message controls the message as well as its timing and frequency.

control mutuality The degree to which parties in a relationship agree on and willingly accept which party has the power to influence the actions of the other.

convenience sampling The administration of a survey based on the availability of subjects without regard to representativeness.

convergence of media A blending of media made possible by digitization. As different media adopt digital technology in their production and distribution processes, the differences among them become less apparent, and various media begin to incorporate one another's characteristics.

Cooke, Jay Organizer of the United States' first fund-raising campaign, which sold bonds to support the Union cause during the Civil War.

coorientation A process in which practitioners seek similarities and differences between their organization's opinions regarding a public and that public's opinion of the practitioners' organizations.

copyright A legal designation that protects original works from unauthorized use. The notation ©, meaning copyright, indicates ownership of intellectual property.

credentialing A process for establishing the identity of people working in an otherwise restricted area. Usually used in connection with reporters, credentialing involves issuing passes or badges that give access to an area such as a media information center.

crisis An event that if allowed to escalate can disrupt an organization's normal operations, jeopardize its reputation, and damage its bottom line.

crisis communications planning The second step in effective crisis communications. In this step practitioners use the information gathered during risk assessment to develop strategies for communicating with key publics during crises; they also train employees in what they are supposed to do in a crisis.

crisis impact value (CIV) The vertical axis on Steven Fink's crisis plotting grid. Specific questions are used to measure the impact a given crisis would have on an organization's operations.

crisis management team (CMT) An internal task force established to manage an organization's response to a crisis while allowing other operations to continue.

crisis manager The person designated as the leader of a crisis management team. When this person is not the chief executive of an organization, he or she is usually someone appointed by the chief executive.

crisis planning team (CPT) A broad-based internal task force that develops an organization's crisis communications plan.

crisis plotting grid A risk assessment tool developed by crisis planning expert Steven Fink for prioritizing crisis communications planning needs.

crisis probability factor (CPF)   The horizontal axis on Steven Fink's crisis plotting grid. It is an estimate of the probability that a given crisis will occur.

cross-cultural   Occurring between members of different cultures.

Crystallizing Public Opinion   Book authored by Edward L. Bernays in 1923, in which the term "public relations counsel" first appeared. In the book Bernays also became the first to articulate the concept of two-way public relations.

culture   A collection of distinct publics bound together by shared characteristics such as language, nationality, attitudes, tastes, and religious beliefs.

customer relationship management (CRM)   The use of individual consumer information, stored in a database, to identify, select, and retain customers.

damage   A burden of proof in libel. In that context, to prove damage is to demonstrate that the person or organization claiming libel suffered injury as a result of defamation.

database marketing   The use of individual consumer information, stored in a database, to help plan marketing decisions.

databases   Structured data storage and retrieval systems. In certain situations, such as with commercial online databases, these systems can be accessed by multiple computer users simultaneously.

decision makers   Any persons or group of people who make decisions for publics.

Declaration of Principles   Ivy Ledbetter Lee's 1906 articulation of an ethical foundation for the yet-to-be-named profession of public relations. In his declaration Lee committed his publicity agency to a standard of openness, truth, and accuracy—one that was not, unfortunately, always met.

decoding   The process of deriving meaning from a message.

defamation   A burden of proof in libel. In that context, defamation is any communication that unfairly injures a person's reputation and ability to maintain social contacts.

demographic information   Data on nonattitudinal characteristics of a person or group, such as race, gender, age, and income.

dichotomous questions   In a questionnaire, either/or questions such as yes/no and true/false items.

diffusion theory   A belief that the power of the mass media rests in their ability to provide information; individuals who act upon that information then influence the actions of others in their peer group or society.

digital   Transmitted in a computer-readable format. Digital information is easy to use in a variety of media.

digital divide   The term used to describe the uneven distribution of Internet access along geographical and socioeconomic lines.

Digital Millennium Copyright Act   A federal law enacted in 1998 that established rules for downloading, sharing, or viewing copyrighted material on the Internet. It also makes it a crime to circumvent antipiracy and code-cracking measures.

digital video disk (DVD)   A computer disk that stores video in a digital format.

direct mail   The delivery of individualized advertising to consumers one at a time, as opposed to mass advertising.

disclosure   The full and timely communication of any information relevant to investors' decisions to buy or sell stocks and bonds; a legal obligation of publicly held companies.

domestic publics   Groups that are united by a common interest, value, or values in a particular situation and that exist primarily within an organization's home country.

downsizing   Reduction in an organization's workforce. Because of economic globalization and technological advances during the last quarter of the 20th century, organizations were forced to do more with fewer employees to remain competitive.

e-mail   A process by which a written message is sent electronically via computer to a receiver or receivers.

emergency operations center (EOC)   The place where a crisis management team meets to develop its response to a crisis. It is in a secure location, one where the CMT can work free from interruptions.

employee relations   The maintenance of mutually beneficial relations between an organization and its employees.

empowerment   The process through which an individual or a public gains power and influence over personal and/or organizational actions.

encoding   Selecting words, images, and other forms of communication to create a message.

equal opportunity provision   The requirement that legally qualified candidates for public office be afforded equal access to broadcast media. This provision does not apply if a candidate's appearance is in the context of news coverage.

ethics   Beliefs about right and wrong that guide the way we think and act.

ethics audit   A process through which an organization evaluates its own ethical conduct and makes recommendations to improve it.

ethos   An Aristotelian term denoting persuasive appeal based on a speaker's character and reputation.

evaluation   The fourth step of the public relations process. However, because public relations involves a dynamic process, evaluation can occur at any time.

evaluation research   Fact-gathering designed to help a practitioner determine whether a public relations plan met its goal(s) and objectives.

exchange relationship   A relationship characterized by the giving of benefits to one party in the relationship in return for past benefits received or for the expectation of future benefits.

executive summary   A description, usually one page in length, covering the essentials of a public relations proposal.

external publics   Groups that are united by a common interest, value, or values in a particular situation and that are not part of a public relations practitioner's organization.

extranets   Controlled-access extensions of organizations' intranets to selected external publics such as suppliers.

fact sheet   A who–what–when–where–why–how breakdown of a news release. Unlike a news release, a fact sheet is not meant for publication; instead, it gives just the facts of the story contained in the news release. Fact sheets are often included in media kits.

fair use   A legal principle stating that portions of copyrighted works can be used without the owner's permission under certain conditions. Commonly, fair use includes noncommercial news reporting and certain educational purposes.

false light   A tort in privacy law. A person can be sued for invasion of privacy if he or she presents someone in a false and offensive light, even if the communication in question isn't defamatory.

fault A burden of proof in libel cases involving private individuals. In that context, to prove fault (falseness) is to show that a defamatory statement is untrue.

Federal Communications Commission (FCC) A federal agency established to ensure the orderly use of the nation's broadcast airwaves in the public interest.

Federalist letters Letters written to New York newspapers by John Hamilton, James Madison, and John Jay under the nom de plume "Publius" in support of ratification of the U.S. Constitution. The letters have been called "the finest public relations effort in history."

Federal Trade Commission (FTC) A federal agency established to ensure a competitive marketplace. The FTC is the source of most federal regulation governing advertising.

feedback The receiver's reaction to a message.

feedback research The examination of evidence—often unsolicited—of various publics' responses to an organization's actions. This evidence can take many forms, such as letters and telephone calls.

feminization The process through which the increasing influence of women is felt upon social, political, and economic issues.

First Amendment The constitutional guarantee of freedom of expression, freedom of the press, and freedom of religion. Its ratification in 1789 is considered the most significant event in the development of public relations in the United States.

focus groups An informal research method in which interviewers meet with groups of selected individuals to determine their opinions, predispositions, concerns, and attitudes.

Food and Drug Administration (FDA) A federal agency established to protect, promote, and enhance the health of the people of the United States. The FDA regulates the promotion of food, drug, and cosmetic products and services.

food disparagement laws Laws adopted in several states to protect products and services from defamatory statements that damage their market value; also known as veggie libel laws.

formal research Research that uses scientific methods to create an accurate representation of reality.

Form 10-K A comprehensive financial disclosure form that publicly held companies are required to file annually with the SEC.

Four-Minute Men A speakers' bureau utilized by the Committee for Public Information (Creel Committee) during World War I. Its members would make short presentations in support of the U.S. war effort during the four-minute intermissions between reels at movie theaters.

framing theory Communicating an idea in such a manner that an audience, either intentionally or unintentionally, is influenced by the way it is imparted.

Freedom of Information Act (FOIA) A federal law requiring all government documents, except those covered by specific exemptions, to be open for public inspection.

gatekeepers Members of the news media, such as editors, who determine which stories a given medium will include.

geographics A marketing term for the examination of behavioral patterns based upon where people live.

globalization The growing economic interdependence of the world's people as a result of technological advances and increasing world trade.

global village Concept first articulated by Canadian communications theorist Marshall McLuhan, suggesting that because of advances in telecommunications technology, we live in a world in which everyone can share simultaneous experiences.

goal The outcome a public relations plan is designed to achieve.

golden mean A concept created by Aristotle and Confucius. In Aristotelian ethics, the golden mean is the point of ideal ethical balance between deficiency and excess of a quality—for example, between deficient honesty and excessive honesty.

government relations The maintenance of mutually beneficial relations between an organization and the local, state, and federal government agencies important to its success.

grassroots lobbying Organized efforts by ordinary citizens to influence legislative and regulatory governmental processes.

green public relations Public relations activities geared toward demonstrating an organization's commitment to the environment. Increased environmental commitment is sometimes referred to as "going green."

greenwash A term environmentalists use to describe disinformation disseminated by an organization in an effort to present an environmentally responsible image.

hypermedia Integrated multimedia incorporating audio, visual, and text information in a single delivery system.

identification A burden of proof in libel. To prove identification is to show that a reasonable person would infer that a defamatory statement applies to the plaintiff.

IMC audit An organization's examination and analysis of its own marketing communi-

cations: procedures, databases, personnel, messages, and so on.

independent endorsement Verification by a disinterested outside party, which can lend credibility to a message, as when the media decide to air or publish a news story based on an organization's news release.

independent public relations consultant An individual practitioner who is, in essence, a one-person public relations agency providing services for others on a per-job basis, contract, or retainer.

Industrial Revolution The period in the 19th and early 20th centuries during which the United States and other Western nations moved from an agricultural to a manufacturing economy.

informal research Research that describes some aspect of reality but does not necessarily create an accurate representation of the larger reality.

injunctions Court orders that prohibit the enjoined person from taking a specified action.

insider trading The purchase or sale of stocks or bonds on the basis of inside information that is not available to other investors. It is a violation of federal law and professional codes of ethics.

instant messaging An electronic process that allows two or more people to conduct a real-time, written conversation via computer.

institutional investors Large companies or organizations that purchase stocks and other securities on behalf of their members, usually in enormous quantities.

integrated brand communication The coordination of an organization's marketing communications to clarify and strengthen individual consumers' beliefs about a particular brand.

integrated marketing communications (IMC)
The coordinated use of public relations, advertising, and marketing strategies and tactics to send well-defined, interactive messages to individual consumers.

intellectual property   Original works of authorship that are fixed in a tangible form of expression.

interconnectedness   The effect of a variety of forces that tend to draw the people of the world closer together. These forces include technological advances, world population growth, and multiculturalism.

internal publics   Groups that are united by a common interest, value, or values in a particular situation and that are part of a public relations practitioner's organization.

International Association of Business Communicators (IABC)   The world's second-largest public relations professional association, with approximately 12,500 members. It was founded in 1970 and is headquartered in San Francisco.

international publics   Groups that are united by a common interest, value, or values in a particular situation and that exist primarily beyond the boundaries of an organization's home country.

Internet   A global network, originally created for military and scientific research, that links computer networks to allow the sharing of information in a digital format.

internships   Temporary, supervised workplace experiences that employers offer students. Some interns work for academic credit. Others receive a nominal wage for their services. Internships are considered a valuable precursor to a public relations career.

intervening public   Any group that helps send a public relations message to another group. The news media are often considered to be an intervening public.

intranet   A controlled-access internal computer network available only to the employees of an organization.

intrusion   A tort in privacy law. In that context intrusion is defined as an improper and intentional invasion of a person's physical seclusion or private affairs.

inverted pyramid   A symbol that represents the traditional organization of a news story. In a traditional news story, the most important information occurs within the first few sentences; as the story progresses, the information becomes less important.

investor relations   The maintenance of mutually beneficial relations between publicly owned companies and shareholders, potential shareholders, and those who influence investment decisions.

issues management   A form of problem–opportunity research in which an organization identifies and analyzes emerging trends and issues for the purpose of preparing a timely and appropriate response.

Kendall, Amos   The first presidential press secretary, appointed by President Andrew Jackson to serve in his "kitchen cabinet."

latent public   A group whose members do not yet realize that they share a common interest, value, or values in a particular situation.

latent public opinion   A behavioral inclination that exists when people have interest in a topic or issue but are unaware of the similar interests of others.

Lee, Ivy Ledbetter   Author of the "Declaration of Principles" in 1906. Lee became the first practitioner to articulate a vision of open, honest, and ethical communication for the profession—

but became known by his critics as "Poison Ivy" for not living up to those standards.

libel A false communication that wrongfully injures the reputation of another. To make a successful claim of libel, a plaintiff must meet the requirements of a five-point burden of proof.

litigation public relations (LPR) The use of public relations research, strategies, and tactics to influence events surrounding legal cases.

lobby In a public relations context, an organization that exists solely to influence governmental legislative and regulatory processes on behalf of a client. The word *lobby* may also be used as a verb to denote the act of lobbying.

logos An Aristotelian term denoting persuasive appeal to the intellect.

lookism A covert form of sexual harassment: attention that focuses more on a woman's appearance than on her job performance.

macroediting A stage in the writing process in which the writer examines the "big picture" of a document, including format, organization, and completeness of information.

magic bullet theory The belief that the mass media wield such great power that by delivering just the right message, the so-called magic bullet, the media can persuade people to do anything.

manipulation In a public relations context, an attempt to influence a person's actions without regard to his or her self-interests.

marketing The process of researching, creating, refining, and promoting a product or service and distributing that product or service to targeted consumers.

marketing mix The four traditional aspects of marketing: product, price, place (distribution), and promotion.

marketing public relations The use of the public relations process to promote an organization's goods or services.

Maslow's Hierarchy of Needs Developed by psychologist Abraham Maslow, a multitiered list of ranked factors that determine a person's self-interests and motivations. Under Maslow's theory, people must meet their most basic needs before acting upon those less pressing.

media advisory A fact sheet that is faxed or e-mailed to news media to alert them of a breaking news story or an event they may wish to cover.

media information center (MIC) A place where a large number of reporters can gather to collect information on a crisis. It should be close to, but separate from, the emergency operations center established for the crisis.

media kit A package of documents and other items offering extensive coverage of a news story to the news media. A media kit contains at least one news release as well as other materials, such as backgrounders, fact sheets, photo opportunity sheets, and product samples.

media relations The maintenance of mutually beneficial relations between an organization and the journalists and other media people who report on its activities.

message The content of a communication that a sender attempts to deliver to a targeted receiver.

microediting A stage in the writing process in which the writer examines each sentence of a document for factual accuracy as well as correct grammar, spelling, punctuation, and style.

mission statement A concise written account of why an organization exists; an explanation of the purpose of an organization's many actions.

modifiers Words or phrases that develop the meaning of another word, such as an adjective that modifies a noun or an adverb that modifies a verb.

monitoring In the context of issues management, the sustained scrutiny and evaluation of an issue that could affect an organization.

Monroe's Motivated Sequence Created in the mid-1920s by Purdue University Professor Alan H. Monroe, a five-step process (attention, need, satisfaction, visualization, and action) that organizes persuasive messages.

multivariate analysis Analysis of research data that examines three or more variables.

mutual fund managers Individuals responsible for purchasing stocks and other securities on behalf of a mutual fund's investors; the investors participate by purchasing shares in the fund.

need When used in the context of Monroe's Motivated Sequence, the process of describing to an audience a relevant problem that requires attention.

news conference A structured meeting between an organization's representative(s) and the news media for the purpose of providing information for news stories.

newsgroup An online special-interest group in which members exchange messages.

news release A client-related news story that a public relations practitioner writes and distributes to the news media.

The New York Times v. Sullivan Landmark 1964 U.S. Supreme Court ruling that established a higher burden of proof in libel cases brought by public officials.

noise In the context of the communication model, distractions that envelop communication and often inhibit it. Noise can be both physical and intangible. It is sometimes referred to as static.

nonprobability sampling The process of selecting a research sample without regard to

whether everyone in the public has an equal chance of being selected.

nontraditional publics Groups that are united by a common interest, value, or values in a particular situation but that are unfamiliar to an organization, but with which the organization now has a relationship.

n-step theory A theory of mass communications suggesting that the mass media influence opinion leaders, who change from issue to issue, and that these opinion leaders, in turn, wield influence over the public.

objectives Specific milestones that measure progress toward achievement of a goal. Written objectives begin with an infinitive, are measurable, and state a specific deadline.

Office of War Information (OWI) An agency created by President Franklin Roosevelt to disseminate government information during World War II. Headed by former journalist Elmer Davis, it was a training ground for future public relations practitioners. It evolved after the war into the United States Information Agency.

open-ended questions Questionnaire items for which the number of possible answers is undefined and unrestricted.

opinion An expressed behavior inclination.

opinion leaders Individuals to whom members of a public turn for advice.

outcomes The actions of a targeted public generated as a result of a tactic or program.

outputs Measures of activity associated with implementation of a particular tactic or program.

Paine, Thomas Colonial era writer whose *Common Sense* and *The American Crisis* promoted independence of the American colonies from Great Britain.

passive voice A grammatical term designating that, within a sentence, the subject does not do the action denoted by the verb (see *active voice*). Instead, the subject is affected by the action denoted by the verb, as in *She was hired.* In most grammatical situations, writers prefer active voice to passive voice.

pathos   An Aristotlelian term denoting persuasive appeal to the emotions.

personal attack rule   An FCC requirement that broadcast stations provide free air time to persons subjected to a character attack during a presentation on a public issue.

personal digital assistant (PDA)   A hand-held wireless communication device that incorporates the functions of a conventional notebook into a small computer.

persuasion   In a public relations context, an attempt to influence a person's actions through an appeal to his or her self-interest.

photo opportunity sheet   A document that promotes the visual interest of an upcoming event. Photo opportunity sheets are sent to photojournalists and television stations. When appropriate, photo opportunity sheets are included in media kits.

pitch letter   A letter sent by a public relations practitioner to a journalist, often on an exclusive basis, describing a newsworthy human-interest story whose publication would generate helpful publicity for an organization.

planning   The second step in the four-step public relations process. Because the process is dynamic, however, planning can actually occur at any time.

point of no return   The second stage of a crisis. Once this moment is reached, a crisis becomes unavoidable.

political action committees (PACs)   Organizations representing particular special interests that collect money and contribute it to political candidates.

political speech   Expression associated with the normal conduct of a democratic society. The U.S. Supreme Court historically has been reluctant to regulate it.

Potter Box   A tool designed by Harvard Professor Ralph Potter for ethical decision making. Using the Potter Box involves defining an ethical issue and then identifying competing values, principles, and loyalties.

press agentry/publicity model   A form of public relations that focuses on getting favorable coverage from the media. In this model, accuracy and truth are not seen as essential.

press secretary   The individual given the responsibility to speak for and handle media inquiries on behalf of a political or government official.

primary public   Any group that is united by a common interest, value, or values in a particular situation and that can directly affect an organization's pursuit of its goals.

primary research   Original research not derived from the results of any earlier researcher's efforts.

privacy   A person's right to be left alone and be free from unwarranted publicity.

privilege   Exemption of certain communications from court-ordered disclosure. For example, communication between a client and his or her attorney is considered privileged. However, communication between that same client and a public relations practitioner may not be privileged, and the practitioner could be required to testify.

probability sampling   The process of selecting a research sample that is representative of the population or public from which it is selected.

problem   A commonplace occurrence of limited scope. People often confuse problems with crises.

problem–opportunity research The gathering of information to answer two critical questions at the outset of any public relations effort: What is at issue, and what stake, if any, does our organization have in this issue?

Progressive Era Running from the early 1890s until the start of World War I, a period in which a series of political and social reforms, primarily in the United States, occurred in reaction to the growth of business and industry during the Industrial Revolution.

propaganda A systematic effort to disseminate information, some of which may be inaccurate or incomplete, in an attempt to influence public opinion. A propagandist advocates a particular idea or perspective to the exclusion of all others.

proposal A formal document that details specific, goal-oriented public relations tactics recommended for a client.

pseudoevent A special event, often of questionable news value, created for the purpose of attracting the attention of the news media.

psychographic information Data on attitudinal characteristics of a person or group, such as political philosophy and religious beliefs.

public In a public relations context, any group of people who share a common interest, value, or values in a particular situation.

public affairs officer The person responsible for maintaining mutually beneficial relations between a government agency or official and important publics. The term *public affairs* is also used by some nongovernment organizations as a synonym for government relations or community relations.

publication A burden of proof in libel. In that context, publication is the communication of a defamatory statement to a third party.

publication of private facts A tort in libel law. In that context, publication of private facts involves the public disclosure of personal information that is embarrassing and potentially offensive.

public figures For the purposes of libel law, individuals who have widespread notoriety or who inject themselves into a public controversy for the purpose of influencing its outcome.

public information model A form of public relations that focuses on the dissemination of objective and accurate information.

public information officer The individual given the responsibility to speak for and handle media inquiries on behalf of a government agency.

Publicity Bureau The first public relations agency, founded by George V. S. Michaelis and two partners in Boston in 1900.

public official For the purposes of libel law, any individual elected to public office and/or with substantial public decision-making or policy-making authority.

public opinion The average expressed behavioral inclination.

public relations The management of relationships between an organization and the publics that can affect its success. The term to describe the emerging profession was first used in 1923 by Edward L. Bernays in *Crystallizing Public Opinion*.

public relations agency A company that provides public relations services for other organizations on a per-job basis, by contract, or on retainer.

public relations managers Practitioners whose job responsibilities are more strategic than tactical in nature. These practioners solve problems, advise others, make policy decisions, and take responsibility for the outcome of a public relations program.

Public Relations Society of America (PRSA) The world's largest public relations professional association, with approximately 20,000 members. Founded in 1947, it is headquartered in New York.

Public Relations Student Society of America (PRSSA) An organization for public relations students. It is affiliated with the Public Relations Society of America.

public relations technicians Practitioners whose job responsibilities are more tactical than strategic in nature. Their primary role is to prepare communications that help execute the public relations policies of others.

public service announcements (PSAs) Broadcast announcements made on behalf of nonprofit organizations or social causes. Because of legal requirements to serve the public interest, the broadcast media do not charge for PSAs, as they do for commercial announcements. This term is also used to describe free advertising space granted by print media; however, the print media are under no legal requirement to provide the space.

push technology Computer software that permits users to customize information received automatically from the Internet.

rating scale questions Questionnaire items designed to measure the range, degree, or intensity of respondents' attitudes on the topic being studied.

receiver The person or persons for whom a message is intended.

recovery The fourth and final step in effective crisis communications. In this step practitioners evaluate the quality of the organization's response to a crisis and take appropriate actions as a result of the lessons learned.

relationship management The use of public relations strategies and tactics to foster and enhance the shared interests and values of an organization and the publics important to its success.

relationship marketing Placing relationships with individual consumers above profits, in the belief that good relationships lead to increased profits.

representative sample Population sample selected by procedures that ensure that all members of the population or public being studied have an equal chance of being chosen for the sample. A representative sample must also be sufficiently large to allow researchers to draw conclusions about the population as a whole.

research The first step of the public relations process. However, because the public relations process is dynamic, research can occur at any time.

research strategy A plan that defines what the researcher wants to know and how he or she will gather that information.

resource dependency theory The premise that organizations form relationships with publics to acquire the resources they need to fulfill their values.

response The third step in effective crisis communications. In this step practitioners utilize their crisis communications plan.

rhetoric The use of communication for the purpose of persuasion. In some of its applications, the practice of public relations is a rhetorical activity.

Rhetoric Aristotle's treatise on the art and science of persuasion.

risk assessment The first step in effective crisis communications. In this step practitioners identify potential hazards their organization may face.

Roosevelt, Theodore The 26th president of the United States. Considered the first modern president, he used the "bully pulpit" of the

White House to influence public opinion in support of his legislative agenda.

salary equity   Equal pay for equal work.

sample   In a research context, the segment of a population or public being studied to enable researchers to draw conclusions about the public as a whole.

sampling frame   The actual list from which a research sample, or some stage of the sample, is drawn.

satellite media tour (SMT)   A series of interviews with reporters in different cities, conducted by means of satellite technology; the newsmaker stays in one location, eliminating expensive and time-consuming travel.

satisfaction   When used in the context of Monroe's Motivated Sequence, the process of presenting an audience with a solution to a problem that has already been identified. When used in the context of measuring the strength of relationships, a reference to the degree to which the benefits of the relationship outweigh its costs. When used in the context of Mick Jagger, something of which he "can't get no."

scanning   In the context of issues management, the process of identifying future issues that could affect an organization.

secondary publics   Groups that are united by a common interest, value, or values in a particular situation and that have a relationship with a public relations practitioner's organization, but which have little power to affect that organization's pursuit of its goals.

secondary research   Research utilizing information generated by someone else, sometimes for purposes entirely different from your own; also known as *library research*.

Securities and Exchange Commission (SEC) A federal agency that administers federal securities laws to ensure that the nation's securities markets are fair and honest.

Seedbed Years   A term coined by public relations historian Scott Cutlip that refers to the period during the late 19th and early 20th centuries in which the modern practice of public relations emerged.

service marks   A legal designation indicated by the symbol ^{SM} to protect names, designs, slogans, and symbols associated with a particular service.

sexual harassment   Unwelcome sexual advances. Workplace sexual harassment is harassment that may affect an individual's employment, unreasonably interfere with an individual's work performance, or create an intimidating, hostile, or offensive work environment.

simple random sampling   A basic and often impractical form of probability sampling that involves assigning a number to every person within the sampling frame, followed by random selection of numbers.

situation analysis   In a written public relations proposal, a statement that accurately and objectively describes an opportunity or threat for which public relations actions are recommended.

soft money   Money donated to national political parties for general expenses. Legislation passed in 2002 restricted such donations but allowed contributions to local political parties and national political conventions.

source   The originator of a message.

spamming   The mass distribution of an advertising-oriented e-mail message.

special event   A planned happening that serves as a public relations tactic.

stakeholder   A public that has an interest in an organization or in an issue potentially involving that organization.

stakeholder research   Research that focuses on identifying and describing specific publics important to the success of an organization.

standing plan   A plan that remains in effect over an extended period of time. Its tactics are routinely reenacted to sustain fulfillment of the plan's goal(s) and objectives.

statement of purpose   In a written public relations proposal, a declaration that the proposal presents a plan to address a given situation.

stereotyping   The assumption that all members of a particular group or culture are the same and act in the same manner.

survey research   Formal research conducted through the use of carefully selected population samples and specifically worded questionnaires.

systematic sampling   A probability sampling technique that uses a standardized selection process to create a sample that is both representative and easy to develop. At its most basic level, systematic sampling involves the selection of every Kth member of a sampling frame.

tactics   Specific recommended actions designed to help an organization achieve the objectives stated in a public relations plan.

things return to normal   The fourth and final stage of a crisis. During this stage the immediate threat created by the crisis is over, but its lingering effects are still felt. Although things may have returned to "normal," normality now may be much different from what it was before the crisis.

third-party endorsement   Verification of a story's newsworthiness that the news media provide when they publish or broadcast the story. Appearance in an uncontrolled news medium lends credibility to a story, because the media are neither the sender nor the receiver but an independent third party.

trade magazines   Magazines for members of particular trades or professions, such as carpenters or lawyers.

trademarks   A legal designation indicated by the symbol ® that protects names, designs, slogans, and symbols associated with specific products.

traditional publics   Groups that are united by a common interest, value, or values in a particular situation and with which an organization has an ongoing, long-term relationship.

transition   A device that clarifies the introduction of a new topic within a document. One traditional transition device is a sentence that shows the relationship of the previous topic to the new topic. Such a sentence follows the previous topic and precedes the new topic.

trust   The willingness of one party in a relationship to open itself to the other.

two-step theory   A theory of mass communication suggesting that the mass media influence society's opinion leaders, who, in turn, influence society.

two-way asymmetrical model   A form of public relations in which research is used in an effort to persuade important publics to adopt a particular point of view.

two-way symmetrical model   A form of public relations that focuses on two-way communication as a means of conflict resolution and for the promotion of mutual understanding between an organization and its important publics.

uncontrolled media   Communication channels, such as newspaper stories, in which a public relations practitioner cannot control the message, its timing, or its frequency.

units of analysis   What or whom a researcher is studying in order to create a summary description of all such units.

univariate analysis   Analysis of research data that examines just one variable.

usenet group   An online special-interest group in which members exchange messages.

uses and gratifications theory   The belief that people have the power to pick and choose the mass media channels that, in turn, influence their actions.

utilitarianism   A philosophy developed by Jeremy Bentham and John Stuart Mill that holds that all actions should be directed at producing the greatest good for the greatest number of people.

values-driven public relations   The values-driven management of relationships between an organization and the publics that can affect its success.

values statement   A written declaration of the principles that an organization will strive to follow in all its actions.

variables   The logical grouping of qualities that describe a particular attribute. Variables must be exhaustive (incorporating all possible qualities) and mutually exclusive.

veil of ignorance   A term and concept created by philosopher John Rawls. The veil of ignorance strategy asks decision makers to examine a situation objectively from all points of view, especially from those of the affected publics.

velvet ghetto   Situation that exists when women predominate in lower-paying technical or middle management jobs, with men dominating upper-level managerial positions.

video news releases (VNRs)   Videotaped news stories that an organization produces and distributes to the news media. VNRs often include b-roll footage.

virtual public relations   A term used to describe the work of many small public relations consultancies; as a result of advances in communications technology, these consultancies can have the look, feel, and service capabilities of much larger public relations agencies.

visual aids   Displays presented to an audience to enhance the meaning of a speaker's words. Visual aids can include computer projections, slides, flip charts, handouts, and overhead-projector transparencies.

visualization   When used in the context of Monroe's Motivated Sequence, the process of explicitly telling an audience the consequences of its choices.

vox populi   Latin for "voice of the people." The phrase refers to the importance of public opinion.

warning stage   The first stage of a crisis. If warning signs are recognized and appropriate action is taken quickly, the negative effects of a crisis can be averted or minimized.

web site   A series of computer files maintained by an organization or individual that can be accessed via the Internet. Web sites are created to project an organization's image and to share information with various publics. They are also useful for marketing goods, services, or ideas and for generating feedback.

work for hire   Anything prepared by someone within the scope of employment and, therefore, considered the property of the employer.

World Wide Web   A graphics-oriented computer network developed in 1991 that made the Internet more accessible and attractive and helped spur its rapid development.

writing process   An organized system for producing effective public relations documents. The writing process begins with the credibility of the writer and moves through 10 separate steps: credibility, research, organization, writing, revision, macroediting, microediting, approval, distribution, and evaluation.

Index

ABC, 422, 446
Abercrombie & Fitch, 298–300
Abortion, 60
Account executive, 39, 563
Accountability, 536–537
Accredited Business
    Communicator (ABC),
    12, 563
Accredited in Public Relations
    (APR), 12, 563
Accuracy, 319
Active voice, 316, 563
Actualities, 277, 563
Actual malice, 495–496, 563
    (see also Libel)
Ad Council, 280
Administration on Aging, U.S.,
    97
Administrative law judge, 485,
    563
Adolph Coors Company, 19,
    24
Advanced Research Projects
    Agency, 354–355
Advertising
    and controlled media, 265,
        266–270
    definition, 10, 424, 563
    and integrated marketing
        communications,
        424–425, 572
    and the World Wide Web,
        280
Advertising Standards
    Authority, United
    Kingdom, 227
Aetna, 451, 452
African Americans (see Black
    Americans)

Agency for Toxic Substances
    and Disease Registry,
    492
Agenda-setting hypothesis,
    143–146, 564
A.H. Robins, 398
AIDS, 200
Air France, 387
AirTran Airways, 334
Alar, 497
Alfred P. Murrah Federal
    Building, 81–84
Allergy and Asthma Network/
    Mothers of Asthmatics
    Inc., 192
Allison, Roy, 414
All Things Considered, 280
Almanac of American Politics,
    110, 122
Altair, The, 352
Amazon.com, 117
American Academy of
    Dermatology, 298
American Airlines, 549
American Association of
    Industrial Editors, 74
American Association of
    Retired Persons, 286,
    288
American Bar Association, 505,
    506
American Chemistry Council,
    530
American Council on Public
    Relations, 74, 75
American Crisis, The, 62
American Demographics
    magazine, 116, 118,
    465

American Home Business
    Association, 537
American Home Products, 398
American Indians (see Native
    Americans)
American Israel Public Affairs
    Committee, 288
American Library Association,
    37
American Marketing
    Association, 438
American Medical Association,
    38
American Motors, 401
American Newspaper Publishers
    Association, 64
American Red Cross, 385
American Society of
    Composers, Authors
    and Publishers, 52
American Society of Newspaper
    Editors, 107, 108
American Stock Exchange, 490
American Telephone &
    Telegraph (see AT&T)
American Tobacco Company,
    71, 84
America West Airlines, 52
Amistad Conservation and
    Development Initiative,
    530
Analog communications, 348,
    564
Anheuser-Busch, 528
Annual meetings, 282, 564
Annual reports, 115, 283, 488,
    564
Anthracite Coal Operators, 67
Anthrax, 313

Anti-Defamation League, 24
Antokol, Norman, 397
AOL-Time Warner, 349–350
Apollo 13, 395
Appalachian Regional
    Commission, 209
Approvals process, 320–322
Aquinas, Saint Thomas, 337
Argentina, 106
Aristotle, 152, 174, 183, 191,
    308
ARPANET, 353–354
Asian Americans, 116, 122,
    455, 457, 461 (*see also*
    Diversity)
    population, 120
Associated Press, 192–193, 213,
    299, 320, 356
Association of Trial Lawyers of
    America, 288
AT&T, 64, 75, 528
Athens, 57
Atlanta Braves, 350
Atomic bomb, 140
Attitude, 153, 564
Attribution, 325
Augustine, Saint, 337
Australia, 458, 461
Axtell, Roger, 454, 465

Babbage, Charles, 351
Baby boomers, 77, 105, 344,
    531, 564
Baby formula, 545–547
Backgrounders, 275, 564
Bacon's Clipping Bureau,
    207
Bad Frog Beer, 483
Bailys Original Irish Cream,
    295
Balslev, Anindita Niyogi, 452
Baltimore, Maryland, 387,
    394–395
Baltimore Orioles, 394
Bangladesh, 527
Bank of America, 528
Banks, Stephen, 452
Banners, 280
Barannikov, Andrei, 522
Barf, 466

Barkley Evergreen & Partners,
    48–49, 402
Barner, Robert, 102
Barnes, Beth, 426
Barnum, Phineas T., 63, 257, 564
Baromètre, 158
Barr, Shirley, 294–296
Barron's, 127
Barry, Dave, 428
Barton, Laurence, 391
Bates v. Arizona, 510
Baxter, Leone, 72
Baxter International, 435
Beatles, The, 148
Becker Underwood Inc., 346
Belief, 153, 564
Ben & Jerry's Homemade, Inc.,
    32
Bentham, Jeremy, 185
Bernays, Edward L., 69–73,
    536, 564
    and Fleischman, Doris, 72
    and Lee, Ivy, 73
    and licensing, 12
    and tobacco clients, 84–85
Betty Crocker, 67
Bible, 57, 347
Bill inserts, 288, 564
Bill of Rights, 61
Bimbo bread, 466
Binge drinking, 229–230
Bingham, Mark, 551
Biotechnology, 226–228
Birmingham, Alabama,
    336–338
Bit, 347–348
Black Americans, 116, 122, 457
    (*see also* Diversity)
    ethnic terminology, 309
    population, 120, 525
Black Enterprise magazine, 474
Blackmun, Harry, 482
Bloomberg News, 339
Blythe, Bruce, 409
Boeing, William, 255
Boeing Company, 242, 255–257
Bond, James, 111
Book of Lists, The, 304
Boorstin, Daniel, 60
Boston Tea Party, 60, 61

Botswana, 362, 466
Boundary role, 44, 564–565
Bow-Dry, 436, 440
Bowen, Andy, 401
Bowling Green State University,
    8–9, 230
Brainstorming, 243–244, 565
Branch, Taylor, 338
Brands, 426, 536
Brazil, 77, 527
Breadwinners, 531
*Breaking the Rules, Stretching
    the Rules 2001,* 547
Breast cancer, 178, 533
Brennan, William, 496
Bridgestone-Firestone, 17, 26–27
British Airways, 387
British Petroleum, 530
Brochures, 275, 290, 436
Brody, E. W., 423
Brokaw, Tom, 213, 299, 503
B-roll, 277, 565
Broom, Glen, 251
Brosnan, Pierce, 111
Brown, Jerry, 538
Brown University, 191
Browning, Lewis, 40
Bruno, Harry, 66
Bryan, William Jennings, 63
Budgets, 249, 252
Buffett, Jimmy, 109
*Built to Last: Successful Habits
    of Visionary
    Companies,* 38
Bulletin boards, 272
Bull Run, 147
Bureau of the Census, U.S., 97,
    118, 226
Bureau of Labor Statistics, U.S.,
    97, 104, 116, 204, 226
Burke, James, 416
Burns, Ken, 147
Burson, Harold, 534
Burson-Marsteller, 39, 464,
    468, 534
Bush, George, 77, 151, 162
Bush, George W., 2, 77, 83,
    120, 144–145, 146,
    213, 239, 278, 291,
    375–379

Business cards, 454–455
Business Ethics magazine, 18, 19, 24
Business relations
 business publics, 36, 94, 122–123
 tactics, 291–292
Business-to-business communications (*see* Business relations)
Business Week magazine, 112, 123, 473
BusinessWire, 267, 274, 284
Byoir, Carl, 75

Cable News Network (*see* CNN)
Cairncross, Frances, 365
California Department of Health Services, 529
California Pizza Kitchen, 296
California Public Employees Retirement System, 112, 281
Callahan Creek, 289
Camargue, 123
Cameron, Glen, 44
Canada, 45, 296–298, 363, 459, 511
 employee publics, 102, 104, 106
 investor publics in, 113
 and Wal-Mart, 474–475
Canadian Dermatology Association, 296–298
Cantor Fitzgerald, 386, 548
Cantril, Hadley, 155
Capital Edge, The, 286
Carnegie, Andrew, 59
Carson, Johnny, 502
Carson City, Nevada, 362
Carter, Carl, 354
Carter-Harwell Public Relations, 354
Carty, Donald, 549
Caruso, Enrico, 72
Carville, James, 77
Catan, Wayne, 50–51
Categorical imperative, 179, 565
Cause marketing, 285, 536, 565

Caux Principles of Business, 168–169
Caux Round Table, 168
CBS, 283, 422, 434, 503
CBS Evening News, 412
CBSMarketwatch, 339
CBS Radio, 71
CBS SportsLine.com, 445
CD-ROMs, 277, 283, 346, 368, 565
Cease and desist order, 485–486, 565
Cellular telephones, 364–365, 369, 372, 459
Census, U.S., 77, 206, 219
Center for Cultural Research, 452
Center for Ethical Orientation, 426
Central Hudson Gas & Electric Corp. v. Public Service Commission of New York, 483
Central Intelligence Agency, 34, 466
Central Power and Light Company, 254
Ceria, Arthur, 445
CERN, 355
Challenger, 392–395
Channel, 139, 264, 460, 565
Chao, Elaine, 537
Charles, Prince of Wales, 161
Charlotte, North Carolina, 362
Chernishova, Olga, 522–523
Chernobyl, 144
Chicago Tribune, 109
Childs, Harwood, 75
China, 455, 461
 employee publics in, 106
 investor publics in, 113
 and land mines, 161
 population, 527
Chisholm, Donald, 390
Chlorofluorocarbons, 192–193
Christianity, 57, 68
Christenson, Clayton, 350
Chronicle of Philanthropy, The, 118

Chrysler Corporation, 294, 295, 467
CIA (*see* Central Intelligence Agency)
Cicero, 327
Cipolla, Vin, 442–444
Citizen Lazlo!: The Lazlo Letters, Volume 2, 117
Citizens for a Free Kuwait, 162–164
Citroen, 466
Civil penalties, 486, 565
Civil Rights acts, 532 (*see also* Civil rights movement)
Civil rights movement, 60, 74, 77, 156, 336–338, 495–496
Clark, Marcia, 512
Clemson University, 530
Clichés, 317
Clinton, Bill, 77, 83, 144, 145, 151, 355, 507
Clutter (*see* Noise)
CNBC, 283, 339
CNN, 283, 349, 350, 422, 434, 493
CNN.com, 267
Coalition building, 285, 565
Coast Guard, U.S., 414
Coca-Cola Company, 17, 387, 403, 461, 523, 528
Cognitive dissonance, 155, 565–566
Cold War, 74, 77, 151, 523
Collins, James, 38
Colson, Charles, 154
Columbine High School, 4, 387
Comedy Channel, 283
Commentaries, 280
Commercial speech, 482–483, 566
Commission on Public Relations Measurement and Evaluation, 225
Commitment, 203, 566
Committee for Public Information, 68–69, 74, 566
Committee to Protect MDIs, 192–193

Common law libel, 496–498, 566 (*see also* Libel)
Common Sense, 62
Communal relationship, 203, 566
Communication, 135–166, 566
  cross-cultural communication, 450–476
  ethics in, 180–181
  and the public relations process, 14–15
  sympathetic, 255
  and tactics, 262–301
  and technology, 343–382
Communication audit, 206–209, 566
  communication grid, 207
Communication model, 138–141, 460, 566
  and tactics, 264–269
  and values, 461
Communications Act of 1934, 491
Communications specialist, 38, 566
Communication World magazine, 104, 465
Community relations, 34, 566
  community publics, 94, 118–120
  tactics, 284–285
Compliance gaining tactics, 152, 566
Components of relationships, 203, 566
CompuServe, 350
Computers, 46, 345, 351–352
Concorde, 387
Concrete language, 324
Condit, Gary, 387
Condit, Philip, 257
Confederation of National Trade Unions, 474
Conference Board, The, 426
Conference calls, 284
Confucius, 174
Congo (Kinshasa), 527

Congregatio de Propaganda Fide, 57, 68
Congressional Human Rights Caucus, 162–164
Conjunctions, 324
Consent order, 485, 566
Conservation International, 530
Constituent relations, 38–39
  constituent publics, 120–122
  tactics, 290
Constitution of the United States, 61, 481, 498 (*see also* First Amendment; Sixth Amendment)
Consumer redress, 486, 566
Consumer relations, 34, 421–448, 566
  consumer publics, 94, 114–118
  tactics, 287–289
Contacts, 435–437, 567
Controlled media, 265, 266–270, 567
Control mutuality, 203, 567
Convergence of media, 108, 348–351, 567
Cooke, Jay, 63, 567
Coombs, W. Timothy, 362
Cooper, Martin, 390, 408
Cooper Communications, 390, 408
Coorientation, 101, 138, 567
Coors Brewing Company, 19, 24–26
Coors, Peter, 19
Copyright law, 500–505, 567
  Digital Millennium Copyright Act, 501–503, 568
  fair use, 503–504, 569
  work for hire, 501, 580
Copyright Office, U.S., 501, 504
Cornell University, 229
CorpWatch, 530
Costa Rica, 530
Court of Appeals, U.S., 483, 486, 515
Crazy People, 444
Credibility gap, 77

Creel, George, 68, 69–70
Creel Committee (*see* Committee for Public Information)
Crigger, Gary, 27
Crisis communications, 383–418, 567
  crisis dynamics, 391–395
    cleanup phase, 393–394, 565
    point of no return, 393, 575
    things return to normal, 394–395, 579
    warning stage, 392, 580
  and ethics, 408–410
  experience and, 9, 390
  planning, 397–408, 567
    credentialing, 404, 567
    crisis management team, 400–402, 567
    crisis planning team, 398, 567
    crisis plotting grid, 399, 567
    emergency operations center, 403–404, 569
    media information center, 404–405, 573
    recovery, 407–408, 577
    response, 406–407, 577
    risk assessment, 397–400, 577
Crisis Management International Inc., 409
Crisis Management: Planning for the Inevitable, 399
CrisisTRAK, 402
Critelli, Michael, 472–474
Critical-thinking skills, 540
Croitoru, Nancy, 296, 297
Cross-cultural communication, 450–476
  definition, 452, 568
  international public relations, 452–452
  process of, 463–470
  and values, 452
Crowe, Russell, 375

Crowley, Milner and Company, 490
Crystallizing Public Opinion, 70, 71, 568
CSX, 394
Cultural relativism, 176–177
Cultures, 452, 568
Customer relations (*see* Consumer relations)
Customer relationship management, 424, 426, 568
Cutlip, Scott, 63, 72, 521, 530

Daimler-Benz, 467
DaimlerChrysler, 467
Dalkon Shield, 398
Dalla Costa, John, 426
Dallas Police Department, 388–389
Dartmouth College, 230
Darwin, Charles, 154
Database marketing, 426, 568
Databases, 369, 423, 426, 431, 435, 438, 439, 568
Davila, Gilbert, 528
Davis, Elmer, 73
DAY, 75
Day trading, 114
Death of Distance, The, 365
Decision Analyst Inc., 458
Decision makers, 99, 310, 568
"Declaration of Principles," 66, 73, 463, 568
Decoding, 460, 568
Defamation (*see* Libel)
DeForest, Calvert, 502–503
De Jager, Peter, 362
Delahaye Medialink, 537
Demographics, 310, 453
    changing in United States, 77, 525–526
    definition, 100, 452, 568
    of Internet users, 267, 361
Denbo, Mark, 367
Denmark, 106
Denny's, 118–119
Department of Agriculture, U.S., 227

Department of Commerce, U.S., 116, 438, 465, 469
Department of Education, U.S., 230
Department of Energy, U.S., 64
Department of Health and Human Services, U.S., 492
Department of Justice, U.S., 85
Department of Labor, U.S., 105, 534
Department of Public Assisted Housing, District of Columbia, 52
Deroian, Pamela, 409
Dertouzos, Michael, 360, 370
DeSarno, James, 339
Devlin, Michael, 79–81
Dewey, Thomas E., 213
"Dialogue on Public Relations Education," 540
Diana, Princess of Wales, 161–162
Difference engine, 351
Diffusion theory, 143, 568
Digital communication, 346, 348, 501–503, 524, 568
Digital divide, 361
Digital Millennium Copyright Act, 501–503, 568
Dilenschneider, Robert, 437
Directive on Data Protection, European Union, 438
Direct mail, 432, 568
Direct Marketing List Source, The, 432
Disclosure law, 287, 486, 568
Disney California Adventure, 3
Disney's America, 147
Distribution, 322–323
Ditt, Tom, 411–413
Diversity, 450–476
    ethnic terminology, 309
    inclusive language, 309
    of U.S. government workers, 110–112
    of U.S. investors, 114
    of U.S. journalists, 108
    of U.S. population, 116, 117, 118–120, 525

of U.S. voters, 122
of U.S. workforce, 105
Doctrine of the mean, 174
Doing Business in America, 469
Dominic P. Gentile v. State Bar of Nevada, 506
Donaldson, Thomas, 176
Donations, 284–285
Donovan, Jeanne, 25
Doolan, Vic, 445
Do's and Taboos around the World, 454, 465
Dow Jones News Service, 206, 339
Downsizing, 76, 569
Dozier, David, 42, 251
Dreamweaver, 356
DS Simon Productions, 283
Dudley, Pendleton, 75
Dun & Bradstreet, 497
Duncan, Tom, 434–435
Dungeons & Dragons, 250
Dunlap, Albert, 126
DuPont, 461, 498
DVDs, 368, 568

Eaton, Dorman, 71
Eaton, Robert, 367
Ebay, 117
Echo Generation, 344
E-commerce, 117, 363–364
Edelman Public Relations Worldwide, 39, 358, 548
Edison, Thomas, 63
Editing
    macroediting, 319, 573
    microediting, 319–320, 573
Editorial board, 280
Editorials, 280
Ehime Maru, 414
8-K, 287, 486
Electrolux, 466
Elements of Style, The, 325
Eli Lilly and Company, 359
Ellis Island, 58
E-mail, 273, 283, 322, 352, 368, 386, 459, 569
    and consumers, 288
    and intranets, 273, 572
    spam, 364, 432, 578

Employee relations, 33, 403, 467, 569
    employee publics, 36, 94, 102–107, 531–534
    and ethics, 172
    tactics, 271–274
Empowerment, 534, 569
Emulex, 338–340
Encoding, 460, 569
Engler, Paul, 497
Entman, Robert, 144
Environmentalism, 60, 74 (*see also* Green public relations)
Epstein, Richard, 497
Equal Employment Opportunity Commission, U.S., 532
Equal opportunity provision, 491, 569
ESPN, 429, 430, 493
Ethical imperialism, 176–177
Ethics, 167–194, 569
    and crisis communications, 408–410
    ethics audits, 179, 180, 569
    etymology, 168
Ethiopia, 527
Ethos, 152, 168, 569
European Laboratory for Particle Physics (*see* CERN)
European Union, 438
Evaluation, 197–232, 569
    ethics in, 180–181
    evaluation research, 204–205, 238, 569
    measuring relationships, 203
    and presentations, 333
    and the public relations process, 14, 15
    of tactics, 293
    and the writing process, 323, 580
"Everest Assault '96," 373–375
Evolution, 154
Excellence in Public Relations and Communication Management, 146, 254, 427

Exchange relationship, 203, 569
Extranets, 292, 353–354, 369, 569
Extreme Networks, 340
Exxon Corporation, 401, 410
Exxon Valdez, 401, 410
Eye contact, 331, 332

Face-to-face meetings, 104, 271–272, 285, 290
Facsimile machines, 352, 368
Fact sheets, 275, 277, 569
Fairness doctrine, 492
Fair Trade coffee beans, 191
Fair use, 503–504, 569
Families and Work Institute of New York, 46
Fast Company magazine, 453
Fax machines (*see* Facsimile machines)
FBI, 339, 550
Federal Aviation Administration, U.S., 385
Federal Bureau of Prisons, U.S., 97
Federal Communications Commission, U.S., 491–493, 570
Federal Express, 359
Federal government, U.S., 110
Federalist letters, 61, 570
Federal Radio Commission, U.S., 491
Federal Trade Commission, U.S., 485–486, 570
FedStats, 97, 110, 206
Feedback, 139, 460, 570
Feminization, 531–534, 570 (*see also* Public relations, gender issues)
Feuerstein, Aaron, 170, 171
Fiber optics, 348
File transfer protocol (*see* FTP)
Financial public relations, 281–284
Fineman Associates Public Relations, 52–53

Fink, Steven, 390, 393, 399
Firestone, 17, 26–27
First Alert, Inc., 431–434
First Amendment, 12, 61–62, 107–108, 481–483, 496, 505, 508, 511, 515, 543, 570
First National Bank of Boston v. Bellotti, 482
Fischer, Scott, 374–375
Fleischman, Doris E., 72
Fleishman-Hillard, 27, 39
Fletcher Martin Ewing Public Relations, 401
Fliers, 313
Florida, role in 2000 presidential election, 144–145, 213, 375–379
Florida Dental Association, 200
Focus groups, 209–211, 570
Folino, Paul, 339–340
Food and Drug Administration, U.S., 85, 192, 283, 416, 493, 570
Food disparagement laws, 497, 570
Food Lion, 513–515
Ford Motor Company, 17, 26–27, 530
Foreign Service, U.S., 397
Form 8-K (*see* 8-K)
Form 10-K (*see* 10-K)
Form 10-Q (*see* 10-Q)
Fortune magazine, 24, 119, 288, 350
Four-Minute Men, 69, 570
Fowler, Gene, 304
Fox network, 422
Framing theory, 144–145, 570
France, 459
    investor publics in, 113
Francis of Assisi, 57
Franco, Anthony M., 490
Frank, Neil, 412–413
Freedom of Information Act, 484, 485, 570
French, Blaire Atherton, 65
French Academy, 458
Freud, Sigmund, 69
Frey, William H., 457

Friends of the Earth, 228
From, Lynn, 297
FTP, 356
Fuel North America, 445
Fundamental Principles of the Metaphysic of Morals, 179

Gadflies, 282
Gale Directory of Publications and Broadcast Media, 107
Gamba, Jeanette, 81
Garcetti, Gil, 512
Garcia, Fred, 512
Garry, Joan, 96
Gatekeepers, 107, 146, 274, 275, 357–359, 570
Gates, Bill, 352
Gates, H. L., 462
Gay and Lesbian Alliance Against Defamation, 96
Gay publics, 74, 95, 96
GCI Group, 296–298
Gender issues (*see* Public relations, gender issues)
General Foods, 528
General Motors, 72, 74, 537
Generation X, 105
Generation Y, 105
Genetically modified food, 226–228
Geographics, 452, 570
George W. Bush, et al., Petitioners v. Albert Gore, Jr. et al., 377
German Dye Trust, 68
Germany, 76, 459, 467
Gertz v. Robert Welch, Inc., 496
Gestures, 461–462
Gestures: The Do's and Taboos of Body Language around the World, 465
Gettysburg Address, 551
Gibbon, Edward, 169
Gillers, Stephen, 506
Gillett amendment, 39
Ginn, John, 168
Giuliani, Rudolph, 385

Gladiator, 375
GlaxoSmithKline, 193
Glaxo Wellcome, 192–193
Globalization, 387, 461, 524–525, 570
Global village, 345, 470, 524, 571
Glodow Nead Communications, 250
Goals, 202, 245, 246, 571
Godiva Chocolates, 362
Goebbels, Joseph, 68
Goldberg, Jan, 40
Golden mean, 174, 183, 571
Goldman, Ron, 512
Gold Medal Flour, 67
Gold Triangle Award, 298
Gonring, Matthew, 435–437
Good Fulton & Farrell, 103
GoodMark Foods, 430
Goodwill Industries of Orange County, 183
Goodwin, James, 549
Gore, Al, 2, 77, 120, 144–145, 207, 213, 375–379
Got milk? campaign, 17
Governing magazine, 110, 122
Government relations, 33, 571
  government publics, 94, 109–111
  tactics, 286–287
Grammar, 319–320, 325
Granger, Kay, 95
Grassroots lobbying, 286, 571
Graves, Robert, 318
Great Britain, 8 (*see also* United Kingdom)
  investor publics in, 113
Great Depression, 74, 486
Greeneville, USS, 413–415
Greenmoss Builders, 497
Greenpeace, 151, 228, 285
Green public relations, 530, 571
Greenwash, 530, 571
Greenwich, 530
Grefe, Edward, 75
Gronat, 522
Grove, Dick, 538

Grunig, James E., 5, 9, 203, 427
Grupp, Robert, 359
Guide to Grammar and Writing, 325
"Guidelines for Measuring Relationships in Public Relations," 203
Guidette, Christopher L., 536
Gulf States Utilities, 254
Gutenberg, Johannes, 57, 347, 370

Hackers, 350
Hallmark Cards, 20
Hamilton, Alexander, 61
H&R Block, 290
Hanus, Glenn, 340
Harley-Davidson Motor Company, 199, 201
Harlow, Rex, 5, 75
Harper, Charles, 52
Harry Potter and the Goblet of Fire, 2
Heinrichs, E. H., 75
Hemingway, Ernest, 304
Henderson, Julie K., 2
Henderson, Teresa, 257
Hendrix, Jerry, 118
Herman Miller Inc., 115
Hewlett-Packard, 438
Hill, George W., 84
Hill, John W., 75, 85
Hill & Knowlton, 39, 75, 85, 162–164, 175, 437, 464, 468
Himmler, Heinrich, 136
Hindus, 457
Hiroshima, 140
Hispanic Americans, 116, 122, 455, 457 (*see also* Diversity)
  ethnic terminology, 309
  and marketing, 465, 528
  population, 120, 525
Hispanic Magazine, 473
Hispanic Market Connections Inc., 528
Hitler, Adolf, 68, 136
HIV, 200

HNW Inc., 442
Hobart and Williams College, 229
Hoechster, Steve, 358
Hoffman Group, 286
Holmes, Sherlock, 298
Holocaust, 136
Holyfield, Evander, 50
Home Box Office, 350
Hometowners, 282
Hon, Linda Childers, 203
Hong Kong, 458
Horn, Sabrina, 534
Hostess Twinkies, 40
House of Representatives, U.S., 355
Howard, Elizabeth, 462
Howard, Ron, 395
Howes, David, 462
HSBC Group, 458
HTML, 356
Hughes, Karen, 239
Humana, 32
Hungary, 106
Hunt, Todd, 5, 9
Hunt-Grunig models of public relations, 9
Hurricane Andrew, 406, 409
Hurricane Hugo, 412–413
Hypermedia, 349, 571
Hypertext markup language (*see* HTML)

IABC (*see* International Association of Business Communicators)
IBM, 38
I.G. Farben, 68
Imada, Bill, 471–472
Imada Wong Communications Group, 471
IMC (*see* Integrated marketing communications)
Immigration, 58, 59–60, 77, 119–120, 525
Immigration and Naturalization Service, U.S., 118
Impeachment, 355
Inclusive language, 309

Incubus, 446–447
Independent endorsement, 107, 536, 571
India, 456, 527
Indonesia, 527
Industrial Revolution, 58, 59, 68, 74, 525, 571
Infant Baby Food Action Network, 547
Information Age, 78
Injunctions, 486, 571
Ink Inc., 538
Insider, The, 176
Insider trading, 490, 571
Instant messaging, 273, 571
Institute of Public Relations, 203, 225, 247
Institutional investors, 112, 281, 571
Integrated brand communication, 424, 426, 571
Integrated marketing communications (IMC), 423–448, 493, 536, 572
and contacts, 435–437, 567
and databases, 423, 431, 435, 438, 439
decline of mass marketing, 423–424
definition, 423
and the four C's, 431
IMC audit, 434–435, 571
and marketing public relations, 425, 430, 573
problems with IMC, 439–441
relationship with public relations, 10, 424–425, 427
and values, 441
Integrated Marketing Communications, 429, 430, 435–437
Integrated Marketing for Colleges, 444
Intel, 438
Intellectual property, 350–351, 500, 572

Interconnectedness, 524, 572
Interfaith Center on Corporate Responsibility, 546
International Association of Business Communicators, 540, 572
Accredited Business Communicator program, 12
Code of Ethics for Professional Communicators, 169, 170
Ethics Committee, 170
history of, 74
Research Foundation, 146, 242, 254
and September 11, 2001, 550
International Campaign to Ban Land Mines, 160–162
International Council of Industrial Editors, 74
International Federation of Stock Exchanges, 112, 113
International Fund for Animal Welfare, 111
International Guild of Professional Butlers, 36
International public relations, 452–453
International Trade Administration, 465
Internet, 59, 78, 161, 267, 352, 353–364, 388, 405–406, 524, 572
and career options, 364
demographics of users, 344–345, 361
and the economy, 114, 117
and gatekeepers, 357–359
as a news medium, 267, 354, 375–376, 385, 386, 537
problems related to, 361–363, 524
and push technology, 358–359, 577
and research, 361–362, 372

United States' influence on, 458–459
Internet Wire, 339–340
Internships, 41, 540, 545, 572
Interstate Brands Corporation, 40
Interviews, 280–281
Intranets, 273, 353–354, 369, 572
Inverted pyramid, 313–314, 572
Investment analysts, 112, 281, 283, 284
Investor relations, 36, 572
  investor publics, 94, 112–114
  tactics, 281–284
Iran, 175
Iraq, 162–164
Islam, 170, 451–452, 456, 461
Israel, 456
Issues, 154
Issues management, 200, 572
  monitoring, 200, 237, 574
  scanning, 200, 237, 578
Italy, 452–453
Ito, Lance, 512
Ivers, Kevin, 95
Ivester, M. Douglas, 403

Jack O'Dwyer's Newsletter, 170
Jackson, Andrew, 63
Jackson, Jesse, 496
Jackson, Thad, 546
Jacobi, Mary Jo, 468
Japan, 76, 414
  cultural characteristics, 454, 455–456, 461
  population, 527
  worker satisfaction, 105, 106
  and World War II, 140
Jakob, Mark, 338–340
Jamaica, 363
Jay, John, 61
J.C. Penney Company, 13, 20, 125, 171, 321
Jefferson, Thomas, 71
Jeffress, William, Jr., 505
Jennings, Peter, 446
Jewett, Sally, 367

J.M. Smucker Company, 427
Job application letters, 41
Job interviews, 41
Jobs (see Public relations, jobs in)
Job sharing, 538
Johnson, Hiram, 164
Johnson, Lyndon, 77, 388
Johnson & Johnson, 38
  Credo, 20, 269
  Tylenol crisis, 176, 365, 415–417
Jokes, 331
Jordan Associates, 81
Journal of the American Medical Association, 38
Judaism, 456–457

Kansas City Chiefs, 275
Kansas State Board of Education, 154
Kant, Immanuel, 179
Kellogg Company, 328
Kendall, Amos, 63, 572
Kennedy, Anthony M., 506
Kennedy, Jacqueline, 388
Kennedy, John F., 388
Kerner Commission, 108
Kessler, David, 493
Ketchum Public Relations Worldwide, 202, 209, 225
Killeen Communications, 22
Killeen, Joann E., 22–24
Kimberly-Clark, 431
King, Martin Luther, Jr., 336–338, 495
King, Rodney, 507
Kingsley, Gregory, 513
Kinkead, Robert W., 76
Klaus, Hans, 406
Klebanov, Ilya, 413
Kleenex Cottonelle, 431
Knowlton, Don, 75
Kobayashi, Sanae, 456
Kogan, Gerald 376
Kolenikov, Dmitry, 414
Koran, The, 170, 451–452
Kotler, Philip, 428

Kraft Foods, 528
Kunstler, William, 505–597
Kursk, SSGN, 413–414
Kuwait, 162–164
Kyrgyzstan, 461

Laconia, 71
Ladies' Home Journal, The, 59
Landau, Martin, 390
Land mines, 160–162
Landon, Alf, 213
Lariscy, Ruth Ann Weaver, 44
Late Night with David Letterman, 502–503
Late Show with David Letterman, The, 502–503
Latina Style, 24
Latinos (see Hispanic Americans)
Lauer, Matt, 299
Lauterborn, Robert, 431
Law News Network, 511
Laws affecting public relations, 479–517
Lawsuits, 480
Lawyers, 401, 505–509
LBS Company, 456
League of Nations, 70
League of Women Voters, The, 121, 122, 535
Leatherdale, Douglas, 19
Lee, Ivy Ledbetter, 66–68, 73, 463, 572–573
  and Bernays, Edward, 73
  and Rockefeller, John D., 67
Lee Apparel Company, 178
Lee National Denim Day, 178
Legal News Network, 511
Legal News Service, 510
Leningrad Oblast Committee for Medical Promotion, 523
Leno, Jay, 502
Lesbian publics, 95, 96
"Letter from Birmingham Jail," 336–338
Letterman, David, 145, 502–503

Letters, 281–282, 288, 290
Letters to the editor, 280
Levick, Richard S., 510–511
Levick Strategic
    Communications, 508,
    510
Lewis, David L., 336
Lewis, Jerry, 367
Lewton, Kathleen, 550
Lexis-Nexis, 206
Libel, 494–498, 514, 573
    actual malice, 495–496, 563
    burden of proof, 494, 565
    common law libel, 496–498,
        566
    damage, 495, 568
    defamation, 494, 568
    fault, 495, 570
    food disparagement laws,
        497, 570
    identification, 495, 571
    publication, 494, 576
    public figure, 496, 576
    republication, 494
Life magazine, 73
Lincoln, Abraham, 537, 551
Lindbergh, Charles, 66
Lindenmann, Walter K., 202,
    225–226
Lindsey, Gordon, 125
Linsky, Martin, 75
Litchfield, Andrew, 123
Literary Digest, 213
Litigation public relations,
    505–509, 510–511, 573
Litt, Lynne Neufer, 514
Littlejohn, Robert, 397
Lobbies, 110, 286, 573
    grassroots lobbying, 286,
        571
Lobbying Disclosure Act, 286
Local governments, U.S.,
    110–111
Log Cabin Republicans, 95
Logos, 152, 573
Lookism, 532, 573
Lopsang, Sherpa, 374
Lord, Miles, 398
Louisiana State University, 229

Lucent Technologies, 340
Lucky Strike cigarettes, 84
Lugosi, Bela, 236
Luminary, 35
Lusitania, 70
Lutnick, Howard, 386, 548
Lyman, Howard, 497
Lynch-Hudson, Regina,
    334–336

McAuliffe, Christa, 392–395
McCain, John, 109
McCarthy, Jerome, 428
McCurry, Mike, 507
McDonald's Corporation, 117,
    121, 422, 465, 528,
    530, 531
Mack, Gregory, 515
Mackenzie, Marti, 513
McKenna, Mindi, 426
McKinley, William, 63, 65
McLuhan, Marshall, 264, 345,
    360, 470, 524
McVeigh, Timothy, 82–84
Mad cow disease, 497
MADD (*see* Mothers Against
    Drunk Driving)
Madison, James, 61
Magazines
    association magazines, 281,
        564
    and employees, 272
    and investors, 281
    numbers of, 107
    trade magazines, 281, 291,
        579
Magic bullet theory, 141, 357,
    573
Major League Baseball, 385,
    387
Major League Soccer, 33
Malden Mills Industries, 170,
    171
Management by objectives
    (MBO), 248
Management by walking
    around (MBWA),
    272
Managing Public Relations, 5

Manassas National Battlefield,
    147
Mandela, Nelson, 458
*Man in the Gray Flannel Suit,
    The*, 2
Manipulation, 156–157, 573
Margaritas, William, 359
Margulies, Leah, 546
Marketing, 421–448, 536, 573
    (*see also* Integrated
        marketing
        communications)
    four P's, 428
    definition, 10, 424
    marketing mix, 287, 573
    marketing public relations,
        425, 573
    problems with marketing,
        439–441
    and values, 441
Marketing communications, 34
    (*see also* Consumer
        relations; Integrated
        marketing
        communications)
*Marketing Ethics: An
    International
    Perspective*, 177
Martini & Rossi, 295
Maslow, Abraham, 148
Maslow's Hierarchy of Needs,
    148–151, 307, 573
Mason, Perry, 507
Mass Mutual Financial Group,
    386
Matlock, Ben, 507
Mayorkas, Alejandro, 340
Media
    controlled, 265, 266–270,
        567
    news media (*see* News
        media)
    uncontrolled, 265, 268–270,
        579
Media advisories, 277, 284,
    290, 573
Media analysis report, 508
Media General Financial
    Services, 358

Media kits
and backgrounders, 275, 564
and CD-ROMs, 277, 346
and consumer relations, 287
definition, 275, 573
digital, 346
examples, 276, 346, 433
and fact sheets, 275, 277,
569
and marketing public
relations, 430, 573
and photo opportunity
sheets, 275, 575
and web sites, 354
Medialink, 366, 550
Media relations, 33, 258–259,
403, 573
and independent
endorsement, 107, 269,
571
and media information
centers, 404–405, 573
publics, 33, 94, 97, 107–109,
118, 283, 354
and push technology,
357–359, 363, 577
tactics, 274–281
and third-party endorsement,
107, 536, 579
and web sites, 354
Media Strategy, 367
Medicare, 362
Melanoma, 296
Melman, Larry Bud, 502–503
Mercer, Ken, 256
Mergers
of advertising and public
relations agencies, 425
of corporations, 462, 467
of media companies,
349–350
Message, 139, 264, 311–312,
345–347, 460, 573
Mexico, 71, 98, 106, 111, 454,
475
Meyers, Gerald, 395–396, 401
Michaelis, George V. S., 75
Michigan State University, 229,
230

Microsoft Corporation, 329,
352, 356, 438, 489
Midler, Bette, 499
Milk nurses, 546
Mill, John Stuart, 183, 185
Millennium Dome, 258–259
Miller Genuine Draft Beer, 199,
201
Miss America pageant, 60
Mission statements, 21, 573
Mitroff, Ian, 390, 409
Mitsubishi Corporation, 111
Modifiers, 316, 573–574
Moet & Chandon Champagne,
189
Mokusatsu, 316
Monroe, Alan, 150
Monroe's Motivated Sequence,
150, 574
Monsanto, 226–228
Montgomery, Alabama, 496–497
Monthly Labor Review, 104
Moore, Dudley, 444
Morgan, J. P., 59
Morgan Stanley, 358, 548–549
Morningstar Communications
Company, 35
Morozov, Vsevolod, 523
Morton, Linda, 282
Morton Thiokol, 392–395
Mother craft workers, 546
Mothers Against Drunk
Driving, 17, 298–299
Motorola, Inc., 38, 353
Mountain Madness Guided
Expeditions, 373–375
Mount Everest, 373–375
Moviefone, 350
MSN, 267
MSNBC, 283
MSNBC.com, 267
MTV, 297, 493
MuchMusic, 297
Muckraking journalism, 65
Muller, Judy, 446
Muller, Robert, 161
Multiculturalism, 309
Multicultural Public Relations,
452

Muncy, Chris, 128–129
Munson, Dirk, 544–545
Musique Plus, 297
Muslims, 170, 451–452, 456
Mutual fund managers, 112,
281, 283, 284, 574
Mutual Life Insurance
Company, 63
Myers, Kenneth, 387

Nader, Ralph, 74, 118, 120,
537
Nagasaki, 140
Naiburg, Eric, 506
Namibia, 96
NASA (*see* National
Aeronautics and Space
Administration)
NASDAQ, 113
Nasser, Jacques, 26
National Aeronautics and Space
Administration, 292,
392–395
and *Apollo 13*, 395
and *Challenger*, 392–395
National Agricultural Statistics
Service, U.S., 97
National Association for the
Advancement of
Colored People, 24
National Association of
Corporate Directors,
452
National Association of
Insurance
Commissioners, 550
National Association of Local
Government Officers,
U.K., 58
National Association of
Manufacturers, 398
National Association of Public
Relations
Counsel, 74
National Association of
Women Business
Owners, 24
National Audit Office, U.K.,
259

National Business Ethics Survey, 178
National Credibility Index, 536
National Federation of Independent Business, 288
National Football League, 275
National Highway Traffic Safety Administration, 17, 26
National Public Radio, 280
National Rifle Association, 288
National Science Teachers Association, 154
Native Americans (*see also* Diversity)
  ethic terminology, 309
  as a nontraditional public, 92
  population, 120
Navy, U.S., 413–415
Nayirah, 162–164
Nazi Germany, 68
NBC, 283, 373, 422
NBC Nightly News, 283, 299, 434
Negroponte, Nicholas, 347
Nemawashi, 456
Ness, Donald, 104
Nestlé, 545–547
Net Generation, 344–345
Netscape, 350, 356
New Corporate Activism, The, 75
New Federalism, 76
New Line Cinema, 350
Newman, Randy, 453
News conferences, 65–66, 277–279, 290, 430, 574
newsgroups, 432, 574
Newsletters
  and constituents, 290
  and employees, 272
  examples, 35
  and investors, 281
News media
  news media publics, 33, 94, 97, 107–109, 118, 281, 283, 354

relationship-building tactics, 274–281
Newspapers
  diversity of workforce, 108
  numbers of, 107
  and technology, 370
News releases
  and constituent relations, 290
  and consumer relations, 287
  and cross-cultural communication, 465
  definition, 274, 574
  and distribution, 275
  and e-mail, 275
  examples, 34, 315, 465
  and inverted pyramid, 314, 572
  and investor relations, 283, 284, 572
  and marketing public relations, 430, 573
  style, 274, 282
  and web sites, 275
New York Stock Exchange, 112, 113
New York Telephone, 201
New York Times v. Sullivan, The, 495–496, 574
New Zealand, 438
Nielsen, Jakob, 357
Nielsen//Netratings, 361
Nigeria, 458, 527
Nike, 483
Nixon, Richard, 77, 140, 461
Noise, 137, 138, 460, 574
Nokia Corporation, 397–398
Nonlinear video editors, 369
Norick, Ron, 81
North Carolina Emergency Management, 411–413
North Carolina Press Association, 514
North Dakota, 428
Norway
  cultural characteristics, 454
  investor publics in, 113
Novello, Don, 117

N-step theory, 142, 574
Nuclear Energy Institute, 530
Nudel, Mayer, 397
Nunnallee, Karolyn, 299

Oakland Holding Company, 490
Objectives, 245, 246–248, 251, 574
Occupational Outlook Handbook, 2000–2001, 11, 535
Office of Patents and Trademarks, U.S., 504
Office of War Information, 73–74, 574
Ogilvy & Mather, 75
Oklahoma City bombing, 81–84, 387
Oklahoma City National Memorial, 81–84, 389
O'Leary, Hazel, 64
100 Best Companies to Work for in America, The, 473
Online shopping (*see* E-commerce)
Online trading, 114
On the Scene Productions, 550
Open houses, 265, 285, 288
Opinion, 153, 574
Opinion leaders, 99, 142, 310, 574
Organization, 312–314
  and the inverted pyramid, 314, 572
  and outlines, 313–314
Oswald, Lee Harvey, 389
Outcomes, 203, 574
Outputs, 203, 574

Pacific Islander Americans (*see also* Diversity)
  population, 120
Page, Arthur W., 75
Pagers, 369
Paine, Katy, 537
Paine, Thomas, 62, 574
Pairgain, 340

Pakistan, 454, 527
Palestine Liberation
    Organization, 456
Panama, 530
Parachute journalism, 464
Paramount Pictures Television
    Group, 96
Parker, George, 66
Parker and Lee agency, 64
Parrott, Virginia, 128–129
Passive voice, 316, 574–575
Pathos, 152, 575
Patino, Hugo, 25
Pauchant, Thierry, 390, 409
PBS, 283
Pearl Harbor, 384
Pelletier, René, 158–160
Penney, James Cash, 321
Pennsylvania Railroad, 67
Pennsylvania State University,
    229
Pentagon, U.S., 113, 291, 364,
    384–387, 547–551 (*see
    also* September 11,
    2001)
People magazine, 350
People for the Ethical Treatment
    of Animals, 17
PepsiCo
    mission statement, 410
    and product tampering, 365,
        415–417, 493
Pericles, 57
Perkins, Wesley, 329
Pershing's Crusaders, 69
Persian Gulf War, 153, 155,
    162–164
Personal attack rule, 492, 575
Personal digital assistant, 352,
    368, 372, 575
Persuasion, 151–157, 575
    and ethics, 152
    and manipulation, 156–157,
        573
    and public opinion, 151–157
    and public relations, 8
Peters, Nick, 366
Pets.com, 50, 51
Pet Sitters International, 50–51

Pew Research Center, 107, 267
Pfizer, Inc., 283
Pharmaceutical Business News,
    193
Photographs, 275
Photo opportunity sheets, 275,
    575
Piedmont Environmental
    Council, 147
Pitch letters, 277, 575
Pitney Bowes, 93, 467,
    472–474
Pitt, Harvey, 549
Pittman, Sandy Hill, 374–375
Plan 9 from Outer Space, 236
Planning, 234–260, 575
    ad hoc plans, 237, 563
    and behavioral changes,
        241–242
    brainstorming, 243–244, 565
    budgets, 249, 252
    and consensus building, 241,
        243
    contingency plans, 238–239,
        567
    ethics in, 180–181
    examples, 250
    goals, 245, 246, 571
    management by objectives
        (MBO), 248
    measurability, 251
    objectives, 245, 246–248,
        251, 574
    planning for the
        organization, 239
    and presentations, 328–331
    and proposals, 251–252, 576
    PRSA planning grid,
        246–247
        PIPP, 246–247
        POST, 246–247
        TASC, 246–247
    and the public relations
        process, 14, 15
    qualities of good plans,
        252–253
    and research, 236
    standing plans, 237–238,
        579

tactics, 245, 248–249,
    262–301
and values, 236–237, 239
Planning grid (*see* Planning,
    PRSA planning grid)
Plentiful Harvest, A, 188
Political action committees
    (PACs), 286–287, 575
Political speech, 482, 575
Population, world, 526–531
Population Studies Center, 457
Porras, Jerry, 38
Potsdam Declaration, 140
Potter, Ralph, 181
Potter Box, 179, 180–186, 575
PowerPoint, 329
Poynter Institute for Media
    Studies, 107
Prepositional phrases, 316
Presentations, 327–334
Presidential election 2000, 2,
    120, 144–145, 151,
    213, 267, 375–379
Press agentry/publicity model of
    public relations, 9, 575
Press box, 33
Press kits (*see* Media kits)
Press releases (*see* News
    releases)
Press secretary, 38, 575
Prime Time Live, 514–515
Prison Fellowship Ministries,
    154
Privacy, 350, 439–441,
    498–500, 575
    appropriation, 499, 564
        misappropriation, 499
        right of publicity, 499
    false light, 498–499,
        569–570
    intrusion, 498, 572
    publication of private facts,
        499, 576
Privilege, 507, 575
PR Newswire, 267, 274, 284,
    322, 444
Problem-solving skills, 540
Procter & Gamble, 38, 71
Progressive era, 59, 576

Project on Corporate
    Responsibility, 74
Proofreading, 319–320
Propaganda, 57, 68–73, 141,
    576
Proposals, 251–252, 576
    executive summary, 251, 569
    situation analysis, 252, 578
    statement of purpose, 252,
        579
Provincial Emergency Program,
    156
PRSA (see Public Relations
    Society of America)
PRWeek, 50, 51
Pseudoevent, 60, 266, 576
Psychographics, 100, 310–311,
    452, 453, 576
Public affairs, 33
Public affairs officer, 38, 576
Public Citizen, 17
Public figure, 496, 576
Public information model of
    public relations, 9, 576
Public information officer, 38,
    576
Publicity Bureau, 64, 75, 521,
    576
Public official, 496, 576
Public opinion, 135–194, 576
    definition, 153, 576
    active, 153, 563
    aware, 153, 564
    checklist, 155
    evolution of, 153–156
    latent, 153, 572
Public relations
    access to top management,
        46, 173, 536
    accountability, 536–537
    accreditation, 46
    billing, 42, 44
    communication (see
        Communication)
    and crisis communications,
        383–418
    and cross-cultural
        communication,
        450–476
    definitions, 4–8, 10, 424, 576

common elements of
    definitions, 7
and democracy, 62, 522–524
and education, 12, 23, 46,
    71, 539–540
and ethics, 167–194
evaluation (see Evaluation)
and the First Amendment,
    12, 61–62, 107–108,
    481–483, 496, 505,
    508, 511, 515, 543, 570
and the future, 520–552
and gender issues, 43, 45,
    46, 531–534
and globalization, 524–525,
    570
green public relations, 530,
    571
history of, 56–87
Hunt-Grunig models of, 9
    press agentry/publicity
        model, 9, 575
    public information model,
        9, 576
    two-way asymmetrical
        model, 9, 254, 579
    two-way symmetrical
        model, 9, 93, 146–147,
        242, 254–255,
        425–427, 579
and integrated marketing
    communications, 10,
    423–448, 572
international, 452–453
and interconnectedness, 524,
    572
and the Internet, 353–364
job satisfaction, 46–47
jobs in, 11–12, 31–54, 535
    corporations, 11, 32–36,
        45
    duties and tasks, 42–44
    governments, 11, 32, 38–39
    independent public
        relations consultants,
        12, 32, 39–40, 45
    nonprofit organizations,
        12, 32, 39–40, 45
    organizational structures,
        11–13

public relations agencies,
    11, 32, 39, 45, 576
    trade associations, 12
job stress, 10
and the law, 479–517
licensing debate, 12
litigation public relations,
    505–509, 573
and marketing, 421–448,
    536
measuring relationships, 203
number of practitioners, 11
planning (see Planning)
process, 198, 199, 327–333
    dynamic model, 15
    ethics in, 180–181
    RACE, 14
    ROPE, 14
    traditional four-step
        model, 14–15, 180
    and values, 180–181
professional standards, 6,
    556–562
profession/trade debate, 12
and public opinion,
    135–194, 576
publics, 90–130
research (see Research)
in Russia, 522–523
salaries, 45, 534
and technology, 46, 345
and values, 16, 17–20, 152,
    347
values-driven public
    relations, 17–20, 152,
    580
virtual public relations, 177,
    351, 538, 580
and women (see Gender
    issues)
and World War I, 68–71, 141
and World War II, 70,
    73–74, 140
Public relations managers,
    42–44, 576
Public Relations Society of
    America, 13, 490, 577
    Accreditation Board, 246
    Accredited in Public
        Relations program, 12

Code of Professional Standards, 163, 192–193
College of Fellows, 22, 542
history of, 74
Member Code of Ethics 2000, 169, 170, 409, 491, 508, 556–562
National Credibility Index, 536
New York chapter, 536
Official Statement on Public Relations, 6
planning grid, 246–247
PIPP, 246–247
POST, 246–247
TASC, 246–247
and September 11, 2001, 550
Silver Anvil awards, 250, 434
Statement of Professional Values, 37
web site, 357
Public Relations Student Society of America, 540–541, 544–545, 577
Public relations technicians, 43–44, 577
Publics, 90–130, 576
active, 96–97, 563
aware, 96, 564
businesses, 94, 122–123, 291–292
community groups, 94, 118–120, 284–285
constituents, 120–122, 290
consumers, 94, 114–118
decision makers, 99, 310, 568
definition, 7, 91, 576
domestic, 98, 569
employees, 94, 102–107, 271–274
external, 98, 569
governments, 94, 109–111, 286–287
internal, 98, 281–284, 572
international, 98, 572
intervening, 97, 274, 572

investors, 94, 112–114, 281–284
latent, 96, 572
news media, 94, 107–109, 274–281
nontraditional, 95–96, 574
opinion leaders, 99, 142, 310, 574
primary, 97–98, 575
secondary, 97–98, 578
traditional, 94–95, 579
and values, 311
Public service advertisements, 280
Public service announcements (PSAs), 279–280, 326, 577
Public service messages, 280
Publius, 61
Purcell, Philip, 386, 549
Push technology, 358–359, 577
Putin, Vladimir, 413, 458

Quebec, 474
Questionnaires (*see* Research, survey instruments)

RACE (research, action, communication, evaluation), 14
Radio, 59, 141
diversity of workforce, 108
number of stations, 107
Radio Margaritaville, 109
Rain forests, 77
Ramadan, 456
Rand McNally, 128–129
Rand McNally Road Atlas, 128–129
Rather, Dan, 213, 412
Rawl, Lawrence G., 401
Rawls, John, 183, 186
Raymond, Lee, 410
RayWatch, 265, 297–298
Reader over Your Shoulder, The, 318
Reader's Digest, The, 85
Reagan, Ronald, 76, 137, 492
Real People Working in Communications, 40

Receiver, 139, 460, 577
Reebok, 446–447
Reeve, Christopher, 366
Relationship management, 7–8, 577
Relationship marketing, 423, 426, 577 (*see also* Integrated marketing communication)
Religion, 456–457
R.E.M., 458
Rentner, Terry, 230
Repper, Fred, 254–255
Research, 12, 197–232, 577
client research, 202, 565
communication audit, 206–209, 566
communications grid, 208, 566
and cross-cultural communication, 465–466
ethics in, 180–181
evaluation research, 204–205
feedback research, 206, 570
focus groups, 209–211, 570
formal research, 205, 570
informal research, 205, 571
and the Internet, 361–362
lack of in public relations, 202
measuring relationships, 203
and presentations, 333–334
primary research, 206, 575
problem-opportunity research, 204, 576
and the public-relations process, 14, 15
sample, 212, 214, 578
sampling, 217–219
census, 217–219, 565
cluster sampling, 217, 218, 565
confidence levels, 214, 566
convenience sampling, 215, 567
definition, 212, 214, 578
nonprobability sampling, 215–216, 574

Research *continued*
  sampling *continued*
    probability sampling,
      214–215, 216–219, 575
    representative sample,
      212, 577
    sampling frame, 214, 578
    simple random sampling,
      216, 578
    systematic sampling,
      216–217, 579
    units of analysis, 214, 579
  secondary (library) research,
    205–206, 578
  stakeholder research,
    99–101, 202–204, 579
  strategy, 202–212, 577
  survey instruments, 219–221
    closed-ended questions,
      220, 565
    contingency questions,
      220, 567
    dichotomous questions,
      220, 568
    open-ended questions,
      220, 574
    rating scale questions,
      220, 577
  survey research, 158–160,
    212–223, 579
    attributes, 222, 564
    bivariate analysis, 222,
      564
    confidence levels, 214, 566
    multivariate analysis, 222,
      574
    univariate analysis, 222,
      580
  uses of, 201
  variables, 222, 580
  and the World Wide Web,
    354, 361–362
  and the writing process,
    310–312
Resource dependency theory,
  92–93, 577
Résumés, 41
Revision, 318–319
Rhetoric, 57, 577

Rhetoric (Aristotle), 152, 577
RHI Management Resources,
  104
Richard French & Associates,
  430
Ries, Al, 511
Rissler, Jane, 228
R.J. Reynolds, 52
Robert Half International, 41
Robert Mondavi, 292
Rock and Roll Hall of Fame
  and Museum, 79–81
Rockefeller, John D., 59, 67
Roman republic, 57
Roosevelt, Franklin, 213, 332,
  537
Roosevelt, Theodore, 65–66,
  530, 577–578
ROPE (research, objective,
  planning, evaluation), 14
Rosh Hashanah, 309
Rosica, John, 536
Rossman, Marlene, 453, 457
Royal Institute of International
  Affairs, 414
Ruby, Jack, 389
Rule 10b5, 490–491
Rumsfeld, Donald, 548, 549
Rummell, Peter, 147
Russia
  investor publics in, 113
  news media in, 95–96
  population, 527
  public relations in, 413–414,
    469
Ryan, Christopher, 358
Ryan, George, 257

Sabbath, 456–457
Sabol Sports, 51
*Sabotage in the American
  Workplace*, 106
Sacramento Police Department,
  108
Safe harbor agreement, 438
St. Paul Companies, 18
St. Vincent's Hospital, 190
Salaries (*see* Public relations,
  salaries)

Salary equity, 534, 578
Salces, Luis M., 528
Sallot, Lynne, 44
Salvation Army, The, 296
Sampling (*see* Research,
  sampling)
San Diego Padres, 96
Sanford, Bruce, 515
Satellite communications,
  365–369
Satellite media tours (SMTs),
  281, 366–367, 430, 578
Satisfaction, 203, 578
Saturn, 96
Savage, Randy, 429, 430
Schaffner Communications, 306
Schlegelmilch, Bodo, 177
Schlessinger, Laura, 96
Schmertz, Herb, 8
Schramm, Wilbur, 142
Schultz, Don, 426
Schwarzenegger, Arnold, 226
Securities Act of 1933, 486
Securities and Exchange
  Commission, U.S., 112,
  126, 206, 281, 282,
  283, 287, 339, 481,
  486–491, 549, 578
  EDGAR search engine, 206
Seedbed Years, The, 63, 578
Seinfeld, Jerry, 327
Selig Center for Economic
  Growth, 528
Sentence length, 317, 324
September 11, 2001, 113,
  189–192, 291, 363,
  364–365, 384–387,
  547–551 (*see also*
  Pentagon and World
  Trade Center)
Serageldin, Ismael, 327
Service marks, 505, 578
Settles, Craig, 371–373
75 percent rule, 333
Sevier, Robert, 444
Sexual harassment, 532, 578
Shaffer, Paul, 503
Shapiro, Robert (attorney), 512
Shapiro, Robert (CEO), 228

Shaw, Bernard, 213
Shell Oil, 285
Shirleybarr Public Relations, 294–296
Silk, Susan, 367
"Silver Blaze," 298
Simon, Morton, 481
Simpson, Nicole Brown, 512
Simpson, O. J., 505, 506, 512
Sixth Amendment, 481, 505, 508
60 Minutes, 176, 497
Skruggs, Jan, 83
Slater, Jeff, 430
Slim Jim, 429, 430
Smigel, Robert, 51
Smith, Dean, 542
Smith, Liz, 16
Smith, Orin, 190
Smith, Tom, 514
Smith, William Wolf, 64
SmithKline Beecham, 193
Smokey Bear, 280
Social Security, 114, 151, 531
Soft money, 287, 578
Sonic, 488
Sosa, Sammy, 50
Source, 138, 460, 578
Southern Baptist Convention, 96
Soviet Union, 77, 522
Spain, 454, 456
Special events, 265–266, 430, 578
    and consumers, 287–288
    and employees, 273–274
Special Olympics, 456
Speeches (*see also* Presentations)
    and community groups, 285
    and constituents, 290, 291
    and employees, 273
Spelling, 319–320, 324
Spokespersons, 430
Sponsorships, 265, 284–285
Sports Illustrated, 349, 350
Sprint Corporation, 184
Sputnik, 354
Square Deal, 65
SRDS, 432

Stack, Richard, 507
Stakeholders (*see also* Publics)
    definition, 7, 91–92, 578
    research of, 99–101
Standard Gravure Corporation, 409
Standard Rate and Data Service
    (*see* SRDS)
Starbucks Coffee Company, 189–192
Starr, Kenneth, 355–356
State governments, U.S., 110–111
State of California v. O. J. Simpson, 512
Static, 138
Stephanopoulos, George, 77
Stereotyping, 462, 579
Stevens, Hugh, 514
Still Me, 366
Stocker, Pat, 537
Structural Dynamics Research Corporation, 52
Strunk, William, Jr., 325
Successful.com, 371
Sullivan, L. B., 495
Sunbeam Corporation, 126–127
Sunshine laws, 484
SunTrust Banks, 363
Supreme Court, U.S., 62, 145, 213, 481, 482, 486, 493, 495, 496, 497–498, 504, 506, 532
Supreme Court of Alabama, 496
Supreme Court of Florida, 375–379
Surgeon General, U.S., 85
Survey instruments (*see* Research, survey instruments)
Surveys (*see* Research, survey research)
Susman, Karen, 332
Suzuki, Kantaro, 140
Swenson, Mike, 48–49
Swissair, 19, 405–406

Sympathetic communication, 255
Syntax, 324
Syria, 454

Tactics, 245, 248–249, 262–301, 579
    accomplishment of, 292–293
    as messages and channels, 264–269
    qualities of, 270
Taiwan, 461
Tapscott, Don, 344
Taylor, Dora, 118–119
TBS Superstation, 350
TCI/IP, 355
Technology, 331, 343–382, 439
Telecommunications Act of 1996, 491
Telecommuting, 537
Telefon AB L.M. Ericsson, 397–398
Telephones
    cellular, 364–365, 369, 372, 459
    and voice mail, 369, 459
    wireless, 350, 364–365
Television, 59
    broadcast, 107
    cable, 107
    diversity of workforce, 108
Telstar, 365
Temporary workers, 104
10b5 (*see* Rule 10b5)
Ten Commandments, 169
10-K, 287, 487, 489, 570
10-Q, 287
Terminator, 226–228
Terrie Williams Agency, The, 188
Texas Gulf Sulfur Company, 491
Texas Rangers, 394
Theory of Justice, A, 186
Third-party endorsement, 107, 536, 579
Thomas, Jerry, 458–459
Thornburgh, Richard, 399
3Com Company, 105, 530

Three Mile Island, 144, 399
Time Inc., 350
Time magazine, 349, 350
Times (of London), 258, 259
Time sheets, 42, 44
Time shifting, 538
Time Warner, 349, 350
Tippet, J. D., 389
Tobacco Institute Research
     Committee, 85
Tobacco Society for Voice
     Culture, 84
To be verbs, 316
Today, 283, 299
Tonight Show, 502
Toronto Sun, 297
Toth, Lazlo, 117
Tours, 285, 288
Trademarks, 504, 579
Trade shows, 430, 436
Transitions, 324, 579
Translation programs, 463
Transparency, 228
Tronc, Jean-Louis, 461
Trout, Jack, 511
Truman, Harry, 140, 179, 213
Trust, 203, 579
Tumbler Ridge, 4
Turner Broadcasting, 350
20/20, 513
*22 Immutable Laws of
     Marketing, The*, 511
Twinkies (*see* Hostess Twinkies)
Two-step theory, 142, 579
2000, 258–259
Two-way asymmetrical model
     of public relations, 9,
     254, 579
Two-way symmetrical model of
     public relations, 9, 93,
     146–147, 242,
     254–255, 425–427,
     579
Tylenol, 176, 415–417

Ukraine, 106
Uncontrolled media, 265,
     268–270, 579
Under Four Flags, 69

Union of Concerned Scientists,
     228
Union of Soviet Socialist
     Republics (*see* Russia;
     Soviet Union)
United Airlines, 96, 409, 549,
     551
United Food and Commercial
     Workers Union, 514
United Kingdom, 58, 258, 511
United Nations, 163, 546
United States (*see also*
     Demographics;
     Diversity)
  and land mines, 161
  population, 120, 525, 526,
     527
  worker satisfaction, 105–107
United States Campaign to Band
     Land Mines, 161
United States Chamber of
     Commerce, 123
United States Information
     Agency, 73
United States Information
     Service, 523
United States Postal Service, 313
University of Arizona, 230
University of Delaware, 230
University of Florida, 203
University of Kansas, 9
University of Illinois, 229
University of Michigan, 59
Unsafe at Any Speed, 74
Usenet groups, 432, 580
Uses and gratifications theory,
     146, 357, 580
U.S. Healthcare, 451, 452
*Using Research in Public
     Relations*, 251
U.S. West Communications, 538
Utilitarianism, 183, 185, 580
Utilitarianism, 185

Vail, Theodore, 75
Valdes, Isabel, 528
Valencia, Pérez & Echeveste
     Public Relations, 529
Value Line, 112

Values
  and the communication
     model, 461
  and cross-cultural
     communication, 461
  and marketing, 441
  and organizations, 38
  and planning, 180, 181
  and public relations, 16,
     17–20, 152, 347
  and the public relations
     process, 16, 180–181
  and publics, 311
  values statements, 20
Values-driven public relations,
     17–20, 93, 152, 541
  definition, 17, 580
  and ethics codes, 168–171
  and the future, 541–543
Values statements, 20–21, 580
  examples, 13, 37, 61, 108,
     156, 183, 204, 242,
     269, 328, 353, 410,
     427, 456, 492, 535
Veggie libel laws (*see* Food
     disparagement laws)
Veil of ignorance, 183, 186,
     580
Velvet ghetto, 533, 580
Vendors, 36
Verlander, Neil, 228
Versailles Peace Conference, 69
Verus Group, 4
Viagra, 276, 283
Video news releases (VNRs), 277
  and b-roll, 277
  definition, 277, 580
  and Diet Pepsi, 416
  and marketing public
     relations, 430, 573
  and Viagra, 283
Videos (*see also* Video news
     releases)
  and employees, 272
  and nonlinear editing, 369
Vietnam, 77
Vietnam Veterans Memorial, 83
Vietnam Veterans of America
     Foundation, 161

Virginia State Board of Pharmacy v. Virginia Citizens Consumer Council Inc., 482
Virtual public relations, 177, 351, 538, 580
Visual aids, 329, 580
Vogl, Frank, 441
Vogl Communications, 441
Voice mail, 369, 459
Volunteering, 284
Volvo, 444–445
VOT, 412
Voter News Service, 213
Voter relations (*see* Constituent relations)
Voting rights, 59
Vox populi, 57, 580

Waddle, Scott, 414–415
Wag the Dog, 156
Wakefield, Robert, 467
Wall Street Journal, 41, 112, 348, 511
Wall Street Week, 112
Wal-Mart, 434, 474–475
Walsh, Frank, 500
Walt Disney Company, 3, 4, 38, 96, 147
Wareham, Mary, 161
Warner Brothers, 350
Warschawski, David, 395
Washington, George, 62
Watergate scandal, 77
Waters, Craig, 375–379
Watkins, Kari, 81–84
WB network, 422
Weatherford, Catherine, 550
Weatherup, Craig, 416
Web sites, 117, 283, 290, 291, 322, 353, 373, 375–376, 405–406, 423, 444–445, 465–466, 487, 580
construction, 358–359

features of, 358–359
and media relations, 275
WebTV, 445
Weiss, William, 514
West, Mae, 499
West Glen Communications, 367
Westinghouse, 75
Westinghouse, George, 63
What Will Be, 360
Wheaties, 67
Wheatley, Bob, 432–434
Wheatley Blair Inc., 432–434
Whitaker, Clem, 75
White House Conference of Governors on Conservation, 530
WHO/UNICEF International Code of Marketing of Breastmilk Substitutes, 546
Wigand, Jeffrey, 176
Willard, Mike, 414
Willard Group, 414
Williams, Jody, 161
Williams, Terrie, 188–189
Williamson, Keith, 474
Wilson, Woodrow, 68, 69, 70
Winfrey, Oprah, 497
Winokur, Dena, 76
Wireless communications technology, 364–369
Wirthlin Group, 162
Wittgenstein, Ludwig, 168
Wizards of the Coast, 250
Wolfgang Puck Frozen Pizzas, 294, 295
Women's rights, 60, 74 (*see also* Public relations, and gender issues)
Women (*see* Public relations, and women)
Woolco, 474
Working Woman magazine, 473
Work for hire, 501, 580

World Bank, 227
World Health Assembly, 546
World Health Organization, 546
World Trade Center, 113, 189–192, 291, 364–365, 384–387, 547–551 (*see also* September 11, 2001)
World Trade Organization, 18
World University Games, 201
World War I (*see* Public relations, World War I)
World War II, 352 (*see also* Public relations, World War II)
World Wide Web, 117, 267, 325, 355, 358–359, 361, 376–377, 580
World Wrestling Federation, 32
WPYX-FM, 52–53
Wright, Hamilton, 75
Write Publicist, The, 334
Writing process, the, 305–323, 580
Writing skills, 303–341
importance of, 23, 304
and values, 305
writing for the ear, 324–326
and the writing process, 305–323, 580

Yahoo! Inc., 123, 267, 355
Year 2000 problem (*see* Y2K problem)
Yellow journalism, 60
Y2K problem, 362, 385, 486, 550

Zambia, 454
Zedillo, Ernesto, 111
Zimmerman, Arthur, 71
Zimmerman, Susan, 388
Zimmerman telegram, 70
Zink, William, 513

Text Credits